So Ya' Wanna' Be A Teacher!

So Ya' Wanna' Be A Teacher!

**By
Jay Dubya**

www.bookstandpublishing.com

Published by
Bookstand Publishing
Pasadena, CA 91101
1777_23

Copyright © 2021 by Jay Dubya
All rights reserved. No part of this publication may be reproduced or transmitted in any form or by any means, electronic or mechanical, including photocopy, recording, or any information storage and retrieval system, without permission in writing from the copyright owner.

ISBN 978-1-931921-70-1

Other Books by Jay Dubya

Pieces of Eight
Pieces of Eight, Part II
Pieces of Eight, Part III
Pieces of Eight, Part IV
Nine New Novellas
Nine New Novellas, Part II
Nine New Novellas, Part III
Nine New Novellas, Part IV
Black Leather and Blue Denim, A '50s Novel
The Great Teen Fruit War, A 1960 Novel
Frat' Brats, A '60s Novel
Ron Coyote, Man of La Mangia
The Wholly Book of Genesis
The Wholly Book of Exodus
The Wholly Book of Doo-Doo-Rot-on-Me
Mauled Maimed Mangled Mutilated Mythology
Fractured Frazzled Folk Fables and Fairy Farces
Fractured Frazzled Folk Fables and Fairy Farces, Part II
Thirteen Sick Tasteless Classics
Thirteen Sick Tasteless Classics, Part II
Thirteen Sick Tasteless Classics, Part III
Thirteen Sick Tasteless Classics, Part IV
Thirteen Sick Tasteless Classics, Part V
RAM: Random Articles and Manuscripts
One Baker's Dozen
Two Baker's Dozen
UFO: Utterly Fantastic Occurrences
Shakespeare: Slammed, Smeared, Savaged and Slaughtered
Shakespeare: S, S, S, and S, Part II
Snake Eyes and Boxcars
Snake Eyes and Boxcars, Part II
Suite 16
O. Henry: Obscenely and Outrageously Obliterated
Twain: Tattered, Trounced, Tortured and Traumatized
Poe: Pelted, Pounded, Pummeled and Pulverized
London: Lashed, Lacerated, Lampooned and Lambasted
Hawthorne: Hazed Hooked Hammered and Hijacked
Hawthorne Hacked, Shakespeare Sacked & Thurber Thwacked
Time Travel Tales
PLOTS

THEMES
The Psychic Dimension
The Psychic Dimension, Part II
Prime-Time Crime Time
First Person Stories
Modern Mythology
The FBI Inspector
The Arcane Arcade
Thirteen Tantalizing Tales

Young Adult Fantasy Novels

Enchanta
Space Bugs, Earth Invasion
Pot of Gold
The Eighteen Story Gingerbread House

Contents

Chapter 1	"Generally Speaking"	1
Chapter 2	"The Teacher as a Vital Non-Entity"	7
Chapter 3	"Role Reinforcement"	17
Chapter 4	"The Concept of Office"	25
Chapter 5	"Little Things Add' Up"	33
Chapter 6	"A Teacher Mentor"	43
Chapter 7	"The College Academic Experience"	49
Chapter 8	"College Cheating"	61
Chapter 9	"Becoming a Teacher"	69
Chapter 10	"The Copernicus Play"	77
Chapter 11	"Other Members of the Class"	85
Chapter 12	"Bureaucracy, Teachers and Parents"	97
Chapter 13	"A Mistake in Judgment"	105
Chapter 14	"Summer Employment"	111
Chapter 15	"High School Permanent Sub"	125
Chapter 16	"Bill and I Get It Done"	135
Chapter 17	"Educational Socialism "	141
Chapter 18	"The High School Faculty"	151
Chapter 19	"The MEATs"	165
Chapter 20	"A Nightmare Vacation Trip"	177
Chapter 21	"The Need for Competition"	185
Chapter 22	"The Problem Child"	197
Chapter 23	"The Parent Conference"	203
Chapter 24	"My Way"	215
Chapter 25	"Joe Dodge Graduates"	223
Chapter 26	"Homogeneous Grouping"	229
Chapter 27	"The Problem Class"	239
Chapter 28	"Group Un-therapy"	253
Chapter 29	"The Teacher's Lowly Legacy"	267
Chapter 30	"The Teacher and the Community"	275
Chapter 31	"Proud Parents"	283
Chapter 32	"Why Jimmy Brown Doesn't Write"	289

Chapter 33	"School Assemblies"	299
Chapter 34	"The Educational Aristocracy"	309
Chapter 35	"Minor Duties"	321
Chapter 36	"Degrading Grading"	333
Chapter 37	"The Williamsburg Field Trips"	343
Chapter 38	"The Guidance Game"	357
Chapter 39	"The Overprotective Parent"	367
Chapter 40	"Democracy and Education"	381
Chapter 41	"Crazy Things Happen"	389
Chapter 42	"The Board of Education"	399
Chapter 43	"A Tale of Four Professionals"	407
Chapter 44	"Contract Negotiations"	419
Chapter 45	"School Board Proposals"	425
Chapter 46	"Problem Students, Problem Parents"	431
Chapter 47	"Inefficient Schools"	443
Chapter 48	"Fighting in Schools"	451
Chapter 49	"Teachers and Administrators"	463
Chapter 50	"Multicultural Education"	475
Chapter 51	"The End of a Career"	487
Addendum:	"Darwin, Einstein and John Dewey"	501

Chapter 1
"Generally Speaking"

In 1974, I had published a book titled *Teacher Serfdom in America*, which chronicled the myriad difficulties public school educators face in their daily attempt to seek professional status while endeavoring to transmit American culture and academic skills to *students*. This literary endeavor *(So Ya' Wanna' Be A Teacher!)* will further identify and elaborate upon the factors that prevent teachers from reaching the designation "professionals".

Whenever I watch television miniseries or documentaries about American public schools, I can't help but think that the scripts of those dramatizations and programs are skewed, distorted and incompatible with actual classroom and school building situations. *Hollywood* and *Madison Avenue* have collaborated to glorify teaching as being a rewarding and leisurely pursuit, and *students* are painted as ambitious, receptive conscientious *children* thirsting for knowledge. This book should help bridge the great chasm between the imaginary TV studio classroom and the very real and daunting classroom environment.

Many misconceptions abound about teachers, and perhaps the most popular ones are that "teachers have a cake job" and that "teaching is easy". Inane generalizations exist' such as: "If you can't do anything else, then become a teacher," and "if you can't teach, become a school administrator"! I hope to dispel the former part of the second stereotype in this work while there might be a degree of credence in the latter speculation.

Much of my thinking about American education is based on thirty-four years of very real classroom experience. Over that time span, I have observed many inconsistencies that eventually became interwoven into a distinguishable design. I gradually became aware of the inadequacies of American public-school education, and for a while, like thousands of my colleagues across the United States, I was tricked into believing that the great faults of our educational institutions were a result of teacher ineffectiveness.

In time, a revolutionary thought occurred to me. 'Public schools are *not* academic institutions,' I theorized. 'They are really *sociological institutions* reflecting the appearance of being academic places.' And so, public schools should not be academically judged and criticized until they actually and truly become *academic* institutions.

1

In today's public schools, it is more important that *children* learn to get along with one another than for them to develop skills in grammar or in mathematics. Teachers are relegated to "babysitters" trying to impart academic knowledge upon *students* that have other things on their minds besides learning about verbs, ancient history, the *Civil War*, O. Henry, Alaska, right triangles and kinetic energy.

And as my teaching career finally meandered onward toward retirement, I very rationally realized how irate parents, nasty *students,* pie-in-the-sky State Commissioners of Education, ethereal college professors and local school hierarchies all contribute to the fantastic blundering that the press and the media almost exclusively blame teachers for causing.

I am fully aware that much of this text is purely subjective and is predicated on my own personal teaching experiences. I am aware that policies and formats vary from school district to school district, and that much that is presented in this work (although it happened to be true to me) might be non-reality elsewhere. Not only do teachers, *students*, administrators and boards of education vary from place to place, but also so do philosophies and practices. Despite the dissimilarities, I am quite confident that many veteran teachers reading this volume will find elements of truth that relate to their own teaching careers. Hopefully, this work will also be read and studied by idealistic college *students* planning to become the future educators of America.

After graduating from a prestigious teachers' college, like most teaching novices, I soon became disappointed in discovering that the function of the public-school teacher was far remote from what I had originally envisioned it. Teachers have very little authority in the school power structure but are conferred with great responsibility to which *we* are held accountable. I found that upon graduating from that prestigious teachers' college, I was very well-prepared with the subject matter taught in the areas of *Junior High School Language Arts and Social Studies*. But I was vastly unprepared to confront the very aggravating "social conditions" of belligerent *students*, public-relations-oriented administrators, defensive/protective parents and image-conscious board of education members.

I don't intend for this work to be sulking or cynical, even though much of it will amply demonstrate how education is often a *self-satire.* The author's principal intent is the uplifting of the teaching profession above its present *educational serfdom* status. On the other side of the coin, if I had not found much satisfaction as a teacher, then I (like many of my disenchanted and disillusioned colleagues) would have ascended into school administration or into school guidance many moons ago.

But despite the many annoyances, I loved to teach English and endured that noble pursuit to the end of my career. It had always been the extremely abominable but very real non-instructional (unprofessional/nonprofessional/non-classroom) aspects of teaching coupled with the detrimental shielding of delinquent and obnoxious *students* by the wretched monsters known as "educational psychology" and "democracy in education" that together have made me gravitate towards burn-out pessimism.

Eighty percent of the *children* I have taught have been genuine *students,* and I have always treasured my professional relationships with them. The good kids kept me going and motivated. But the remaining twenty percent of the school population has the potential to send middle and high school teachers into early retirement or directly into early graves.

In all of the world's educational systems, only in America are teenaged recalcitrant scalawags allowed to perpetually batter their teachers with their clownish antics and semantics. Many examples will be provided in this work that substantiate the truth that harassed instructors are manacled by "professional ethics", "the law", "modern educational philosophy" and "educational psychology". Administrators tell teachers that *they* must adjust to *student* misbehavior and handle most annoying disciplinary incidents themselves. And if a teacher sends too many "Discipline Referral Cards" down to the Main Office, then the teacher is indicting himself or herself for not being able to use ineffective "educational psychology" to keep the lid on inside the classroom.

Even though a defiant abrasive *student* might be twice a teacher's size, "educational psychology" still refers to him as "the child" and "educational democracy" attaches to the chronic offender the misleading misnomer of "student". Getting uncooperative and disruptive *students* out of the academic/sociological learning environment is perhaps the greatest challenge confronting contemporary American education today. It seems that few educators have the much-needed courage to address the problem of *student* dereliction of classroom and homework responsibility and *student* insolence to adult authority.

For seven years, I had served on my teachers' association negotiating team, and that activity greatly contributed to my ability to pinpoint what I consider additional faults of American education. I soon became aware that many school board members have a low regard for teachers and for *their* chosen "profession". School board members almost always side with school administrators, forming a potent cartel united against the advancement of the teaching profession. The members of the powerful cartel (the Educational Aristocracy) are generally very interested in safeguarding the taxpayers' dollars and in promoting *their* own political ambitions and personal influences in local, county and state governments. The school board seat often serves as a springboard to other greater political aspirations on town council, for county freeholder seats or for lucrative positions in state and federal government.

After thirty-four years of exposure to administrative, school board, *student* and parental negative attitudes, I have become inspired to develop the central themes that verify the reality of teacher exploitation existing in American public schools. "Child-centered curriculums", teacher non-professional duties (I call them *Howdy Duties),* modern educational philosophy and psychology, educational democracy along with poor community attitudes towards teachers all combine to generate what I had formerly described as *Teacher Serfdom in America.*

Teacher Serfdom is reinforced by the mandates of school adminis*trivia*, the "concept of office", *Walter Mitty* college professors and by the subordination of public-school instructors to daily administrative whim and folly. When all of the aforementioned forces combine into "the Educational Aristocracy" (administrators, superintendents, school board members), the plaintiffs (irate parents and bellicose *students*) and the recipient serfs (teachers), the advancement of the teaching profession is ultimately and most definitely stifled and deterred.

The greatest polluting factor in the vast American educational wasteland is the undeniable truth that the power in public school education is *not* in the hands of teachers. But regardless of *that* obvious fact, teachers are held responsible and accountable for ongoing failure in an educational system that is both designed and doomed for failure.

Local education is governed by the wacky bureaucracy of amateur school board members, *Mother Goosed* college professors and wishy-washy, malleable school administrators. Included in this author's presentation is the hidden half of the educational puzzle that has skillfully been camouflaged from public evaluation by the crafty "Educational Aristocracy". And as was true in medieval times, the serfs (the encumbered teachers) keep the fiefs (school systems) going for the privileged Aristocracy.

I don't intend for this book to arraign the school district that had employed me for thirty-four years. In fact, my former school system is generally regarded as a model district devoid of the serious problems that plague urban and suburban schools. If I had spent the last three and a half decades teaching in a school teeming with racial strife and fraught with widespread academic disorganization, then this work (*So Ya' Wanna' Be A Teacher!)* would have been three times its current length.

I have hypothesized from my own personal educational adventures the drastic need for reform in the important areas of teacher rights, public attitudes of parents and taxpayers towards teachers, and in the final analysis, the need for the teaching *profession* to be emancipated from the caprices and fancies of the *Educational Aristocracy*.

Throughout this living satire, I introduce suggestions intended to alleviate the grotesque flaws intertwined with the daily functions, activities, duties and responsibilities of classroom teachers. I aim to prove that teachers are expected to support a power structure that yields mediocre academic performance while practicing tolerance of recalcitrant *student* misbehavior in addition to pursuing the futile engineering of adolescent sociological adjustment as dictated by wacky college and university professors.

For far too long, American teachers have been the domesticated cattle of the educational farm. Being one of the more aggressive bulls in the extensive pasture having a voracious appetite to both learn and communicate, I know that certain people will take umbrage with the overall content of this controversial book. These individuals probably have a vested interest in public school education (administrators, teacher college professors, school board members, teacher union representatives), and those individuals might be *grazed* by the revolutionary ideas advanced by this *undomesticated* whistle-blowing teacher/author.

Chapter 2
"The Teacher as a Vital Non-Entity"

One axiom is paramount in understanding the functioning of any standard American school system. The teachers are the glue that holds the system together. Credit is often diverted to school administrators, supervisors, superintendents and boards of education, but the lowest common denominator of any successful school district is the vital interaction of its teachers with its *students*.

By sheer numbers, a middle school might have fifty-seventy-five teachers with four to eight people in management positions. A high school may have eighty to two hundred instructors and eight to twenty bureaucrats supervising the *educational process* (notice I intentionally neglected using the reference *academic process*, because the designation "educational process" is three-quarters sociological and around one fourth academic). In the United States, *academic* happens in private academies, and *education* is what transpires in public schools. The two terms are not interchangeable.

The two principal elements of any viable school are *students* and teachers, in that order. If everyone in school management stays home on any given day, the school could easily still function in their absence. If the teaching staff is not there on any given day, then chaos and disorganization will ensue, and for practical purposes, that school would have to be closed in a short time frame. Take the teachers out of the educational equation and then the true faults of American public schools would be very evident with administrators, superintendents, supervisors, guidance counselors, the Child Study Team and curriculum coordinators (along with a bevy of substitute teachers) left to educate the *children*.

Instead of rewarding good teachers for their competency, the rule of thumb employed by school management is to inundate them with a myriad of clubs, activities and duties sufficient enough to eventually stifle enthusiasm and motivation. The dominant message is quite clear. Administration equals power. Teaching equals obedience and subservience to arbitrary, bureaucratic authority. Administrators are stratified on the higher echelon as the employers. Teachers are *employees* and *not* really "professional" personnel.

Clunkers constitute five percent of the members of any given "profession" whether the practitioners are lawyers, doctors or accountants. That's the nature of the beast. This social truism also holds true for teachers, and in the public's eye, good, dedicated instructors are often measured and evaluated in the court of public opinion by the egregious misdeeds of their faculty colleagues.

If a teacher's strong suit is discipline, his or her compensation is to annually be assigned daily cafeteria duty where two-to-three-hundred screaming rascals are raucously testing *their* larynxes' limits. In my teaching career, which spanned thirty-four years, I had pulled the horrid "cafeteria duty" twenty-eight times. In my three and a half-decade tenure, I had the displeasure of breaking-up over two hundred and fifty *student* fights, and I can attest that at least half of those scuffles have been while serving on *cafeteria duty*.

I have long been an advocate of police presence in public schools. I believe that the police should patrol the school cafeteria, the corridors before and during the change of classes, and the main doors before and after the school day. I do not believe that the police should be in classrooms and should only enter if a *student* is causing a major disturbance. A patrolman's presence in the classroom should only be warranted when a besieged teacher summons one to quickly remove a defiant *child*.

Teachers in most states are not allowed to lay a finger on *students* because of the existence of strict corporal punishment laws. "Educational psychology" does not work when two *students* are pummeling each other, and the teacher is expected to effectively quell the violence. In many schools, *student* violence and *assault* result in three days suspension, but if *the law* were involved in the resolution of a *student* conflict, the consequences would be much more serious, and then the "*student* risk-reward" equation would be drastically altered. But under present scenarios, a typical *student* concludes that a meager school *fight* rendered to defend his or her pride and honor in front of peers (and peer pressure) is definitely worth only three days of suspension as a trade-off.

Administrators, superintendents and supervisors want to always stay *above the fray*. Teachers are designated the ones (by assignment to trouble areas like the cafeteria) to intervene in *student* altercations. Principals and vice-principals want to judge what has happened and ostensibly, and conversely, don't want any part of what is happening or what has happened.

The teacher first breaks-up the fight, escorts the violators to the Main Office and then must fill-out *Discipline Referral Cards* that describe and report in detail the altercation to the administrator. On several occasions, *students* have balked that I had used too much physical force in breaking-up wild fights, so the school principal had asked me more than once, "Now, Mr. Wiessner. I want to hear *your* version of the story."

"If you really want to know, there is no 'my version of the story'," I indignantly answered. "I broke-up a wicked fight in the cafeteria. The battlers wouldn't stop, so after they continued pounding each other for a third time, I had to use brute strength to separate them."

"But a *student* and a parent complained you had injured *him* when you knocked him through the cafeteria doors!" the "don't-rock-the-boat" school official retorted.

"Look, the next time a serious fight breaks-out in the cafeteria," I angrily answered, "I'll just casually stroll to the intercom and request that *you* get off your fanny, exit your comfortable office and come down and personally intervene in the melee. I don't come to this place every morning to referee boxing or wrestling matches," I emphasized. "Whether you realize it, or not, I come here every day to try and teach kids!" I yelled back.

"Regardless," my boss authoritatively stated. "You still must write a detailed letter to the superintendent describing the incident in case this sensitive matter comes before the board of education."

Here's exactly how school management works. The order of organization dictates that weaker teachers' who cannot handle the rigors of cafeteria patrol are spared of that *duty* where his or her lack of Prussian discipline might be evident. The reward for these meeker instructors is often a small study hall *duty* with few *students*. Such an assignment is better tailored to his or her "school rules enforcement level" than a conceivable mismatch with young thugs masquerading as *students* in the cafeteria. The essential point is that no teacher should ever have to have an *unprofessional* assignment like cafeteria duty and be compelled to role-play being a policeman.

But if two policemen along with three aides were in charge of the cafeteria, teachers could then be placed in more "professional situations" like teaching an additional class or correcting papers, compositions and tests, or tutoring a *student* during that very perplexing forty-five-minute daily *student* lunch session. Schools would operate more efficiently with police officers in charge of the cafeteria, and teachers would be efficiently utilized performing "professional" responsibilities and not engaged in an unprofessional non-teaching *duty*. In many cases, teachers get fully involved in conflictive cafeteria situations with erratic *students* that *they* don't even teach or don't even know; that is, until *Discipline Referral Cards* are filled-out in the Main Office.

Cynics might criticize that the cost of cafeteria aides and other aides replacing all teacher-assigned duties would be prohibitive. But if teacher college preparation were to be extended from a four-year to a five-year program, then each prospective instructor could serve a full year working in a public school as an unpaid aide, and a "free work pool" would automatically be created. Then school administrators could evaluate "on-the-job" performance of dedicated candidates aspiring to become classroom instructors.

Getting back to the present reality, a critic might advance the argument that administrators are discreet in placing the stronger discipline teachers in the cafeteria because they can more adequately handle the challenges associated with *that* particular mission. But what does thirty consecutive years of that brutal exposure do to the spirit and attitude of the veteran teacher? He or she feels victimized and exploited. He or she knows that some teachers never pull the degrading duty simply because certain *students* don't listen to or obey *their* commands in mass situations.

I have known several teachers that have deliberately done a lackluster job while on the indignity known as cafeteria duty. Instead of being reprimanded, those teachers were rewarded for their mediocre "non-professional effort" and removed from the cafeteria Bastille and given an alternate placement much more to his or her liking. So, by demonstrating lackadaisical school enforcement skills and by exhibiting "burn-out apathy", those more-moderate tenure teachers were finally released from the cafeteria tinderbox by lethargically exercising lazy commitment to administrative "non-professional" expectations.

After six or seven years of wear and tear on their fragile nervous systems, and after flirting with cardiac arrest, many teachers begin questioning their role of prominence in the highly-structured school hierarchy. Soon, the hardcore reality of the bewildered teachers' quandary materializes. 'I am basically impotent and powerless within the school anatomy!' becomes the logical conclusion. 'I am answerable to administrators, to the state, to the taxpayers, to supervisors, to parents, to *students*, to guidance counselors and to the omnipotent board of education! I have tremendous responsibility but can exercise little authority. The authority that I project to *students* is only feigned and assumed. Any *student* could fabricate a gaudy lie and get me suspended tomorrow simply on the basis of an imaginative allegation!'

Some teachers honestly admit that their tolerance for brazen obnoxious *students* has reached the dangerous "burn-out level".

Other teachers might substitute their lack of prestige in the system with the aspiration, 'I want to advance myself in education by studying school administration,' or 'I want to work one-on-one with *students* and become a guidance counselor. Who needs teaching a hundred and thirty kids every day plus the daily trauma of the cafeteria?' they conclude.

Let's be pragmatic about the hard reality of teaching in American public middle and high schools. Who needs the constant bombardment of *student* insults and abuses? Who needs the endless administrative paperwork, the parent conferences, the writing of weekly lesson plans, along with the issuance of warning letters and progress reports? Who needs the drafting of report cards, the correction of papers and tests, the submission of grade distribution sheets and the added scourge of serving Office Detention? Who needs hostile parent conferences, the mania of the school cafeteria, the performance of before and after school bus duty, lavatory patrol, hall duty between changing classes, in addition to the arsenal of other accumulative pressures and tasks that accompany being the lowest echelon on the academic totem pole? Who actually needs this plethora of daily, weekly and monthly emotional devastation?

The reasonable alternative soon becomes increasingly crystal-clear to the classroom teacher. The flavor of the truth is sometimes sour to the mind's taste. It is often disguised in the notion that a teacher could "improve himself or herself" by utilizing the college circuit again as an essential escape mechanism from the unappreciated instructional classroom doldrums. The second educational circuit on the university plane is as a prospective school administrator.

School administrators earn about three times the diminutive salary of a non-tenure teacher, and they command respect by issuing directives within the stratified school superstructure. All of this mental burlesque is done under the guise of *professional growth and self-improvement*. But most candidates for school administration are desperately attempting to escape the tremendous vexations associated with classroom *responsibility* and with "busy work" school *duties*. Unfortunately, responsibilities and *duties* are perceived in the community by parents and taxpayers as being one and the same thing.

Generally, school administrators are nothing more than teachers' who have endured the rigors of the college factory for thirty-six or so more credits than classroom teachers have. A school administrator is merely a glorified teacher that no longer teaches or wants to teach.

Teaching suddenly becomes *below* him or her. I don't mean to be facetious in claiming this fact.

As former classroom teachers, most school administrators have spent nearly three-fourths of their formal college education learning to become teachers and only one-fourth of their professional graduate school preparation mastering the intricate mechanics of school administration. Because of this obvious disparity, many school officials are inadequately prepared to address the enormous responsibilities and accountabilities that high-salaried business executives get paid big bucks to perform.

Some unique qualities that made for an excellent teacher might now interfere with an administrator's talent for making executive decisions. For example, superintendents and principals delegate responsibility to the instructional staff. In this way, *they* absolve themselves from personal accountability, and the teachers then become responsible and answerable, as in the case of the cafeteria fight where a parent (who did not witness the cafeteria brawl) protested that the teacher had used excessive force in breaking-up the fracas. By delegating full accountability to the teacher, the administrator could then be the objective "judge and jury" in the matter without ever getting personally involved in controversy. Administrative culpability for any wrongdoing could be adroitly evaded by school executives by assigning teachers to be responsible for everything and anything. Then the administrator just sits in his or her office and waits for something to develop so that *he or she* could then role-play being *Supreme Court Justice*.

Most school principals sadly lack the business acumen that corporate executives possess. True, schools are run like factories where teachers are "employees" and the *students* are the products of a twelve-year manufacturing process, but the school administrator is basically safe because he or she operates a factory where no accountability for "profit" has to be made. Hence, his or her factory could be as unproductive (and his or her product could be as mediocre) as the next school district's process and factory, but it really doesn't matter.

Schools are not *in the business* of making money or producing quality merchandise in a free enterprise system. They are simply *in the business*, and that's that. The administrator must make the school look like it is functioning smoothly, so appearance often becomes more important than results, and illusion often becomes more vital than daily educational truth.

But despite their shortcomings most school administrators manage to hoodwink gullible boards of education with impressive and nifty cliches that somehow justify and reinforce *their* roles of importance. Even if an administrator has poor writing skills, he quickly learns how to "verbalize the game".

Once back in the early '70s, a teacher friend that was an administrative candidate approached me and asked if I would critique and then correct his thesis for grammatical mistakes. I (along with another English teacher) wound-up rewriting and editing the entire thesis from stem to stern, making it sound logical in addition to amending an excess of spelling, punctuation, transition, coherence and grammar errors. This person went on to receive his master's degree in school administration even though his language writing skills were on a middle school achievement level. But in time, that administrator learned how to "talk a good game" to the board of education and also to his dedicated staff.

I have worked for several dozen school administrators over my three and a half decade career. Most of them have been sincere; many of them have been very supportive, and a few administrators I have regarded as being charlatans and quite detrimental to the advancement of education.

I have mentioned where administrators prefer to delegate responsibility to faculty members under the false guise of "teacher authority". In several disciplinary situations, I have gotten the school sultans out of their walnut-paneled offices and have made "my problem" into "their problem".

Once back in the early '70s, it happened to be the last day of school. I had heard that several students might cause some trouble after dismissal and notified the administration of that concern. The principal and vice-principal came out of their caves (offices) and stepped outside the building to observe the *students* merrily departing the property on their all-too-familiar yellow buses. A bold *student* pointed a super jet-power water gun out of a window and effectively drenched several administrators and teachers standing on bus duty.

The school executives did not think that the act of insolence was too wonderful. Instead of "delegating" and sending teachers onto the school bus, *they* physically removed the *student* along with his squirting apparatus (the evidence), and when the bus pulled-away, the audacious *student* felt compelled to defend his ego in front of his departing peers by resisting the administrators' grasps. The school officials wrestled the dastardly violator to the ground amidst the swirl of exhaust fumes from exiting school buses in addition to the loud taunts and shrieks of delighted high school *student* passengers aboard the yellow vehicles.

On another occasion, I swiftly stepped into the principal's office and said to the school chieftain, "I notice that Felix X. has skipped *your* after-school Office Detention."

"Was he in school today?" the principal perceptively asked as he checked the daily absentee list.

"Yes, he was, and he's standing right down there on the asphalt below your office!" I alertly reported as I pointed out the closed window in the air-conditioned room.

The flustered principal opened his side window and yelled, "Felix; you're supposed to be in Office Detention. Get back into the building right away!"

"Fuck you!" The perturbed kid defiantly yelled-up to the astonished principal.

"What did you say?" the administrator incredulously demanded after being publicly humiliated in front of two-dozen laughing *students* standing outside.

"I said, 'Fuck you, asshole'!" the obnoxious *student* boisterously and emphatically returned.

The principal looked at me with an alarmed expression upon his countenance with his mouth agape, as if *that* instance were the first time that he had ever heard such language originating from the mouth of a human being let alone an insubordinate *student*.

"I don't think the *student* used the terminology *asshole* the first time!" I reminded the principal as I stared into his appalled face. "He definitely didn't call you an 'asshole' the first time!"

"That remark will give *him* three more days of Office Detention!" the principal promised as he closed the office window to keep the room air-conditioned.

"Great!" I responded. "Thanks a lot. I'll now have to be in that assigned detention room with *him* for most of next week!" And so, when a teacher is too conscientious in reporting a student deviation, he or she often winds-up inadvertently punishing himself or herself.

Back in the '70s, I became quite unhappy with a particular *student* that would constantly interrupt my sacred English class with such inane questions as: "Mr. Wiessner, how often do you have sex?" "I gotta' take a shit!" "My balls itch!" along with other similar unfortunate unsolicited commentaries.

It got to a point where I would have an "Office Discipline Referral Card" made-out in advance for the indiscreet *student* every day before he entered my revered sanctuary. The principal and vice-principal became so tired of seeing the transgressor in their offices that *they* referred the *child* to the superintendent, who immediately saw the opportunity as a surefire way of rehabilitating a confused *student* that had temporarily gone astray from mainstream society.

The well-intentioned superintendent and the *student* soon got into a mild argument over differences in educational philosophies and separate roles within the school. The *student* disrespectfully picked-up a chair and threatened to hammer the superintendent with the raised object. The alert-but-very-frightened superintendent quickly summoned the tough-guy vice-principal, who immediately and obediently rushed into the top brass's plush office.

Another argument ensued when the stubborn *student* refused to leave the superintendent's office upon the vice-principal's insistence. The rebellious kid suddenly felt threatened and then neurotically dashed out of the *super's* office, sprinted down the corridor and out of the building with the dedicated vice-principal following *his* path in hot pursuit.

As I glanced out the window while lecturing a class on the singular writing style of Edgar Allan Poe, I observed the fleeing *student* streaking past while being chased across the lawn by the vice-principal, which to me automatically looked like the *Roadrunner* being pursued by *Wile E. Coyote.*

Suddenly, the fatigued kid stopped to catch his breath, and the exhausted, burly vice-principal also simultaneously halted fifty-feet-behind. The *child* then yelled out at the top of his lungs, "Fuck you!" and then the frantic chase resumed. Ten minutes later, the two again stopped outside my classroom window when I was reading *Annabel Lee* to the class, but this time the marathon participants had been rushing past the high school's windows in the opposite direction. The *student* again stopped and hollered to the highly agitated vice-principal "Fuck you, asshole!" And then, much to my class's enjoyment, the bizarre chase was re-initiated.

When parents and townspeople drive by public-schools, they probably think that 'wonderful things are happening inside'. And for the most part, *they* are right. Many terrific things do happen inside the building. But many crazy, chaotic things also happen inside, and those absurd events often escape public scrutiny or knowledge.

Sensitive administrators don't want to get the local police department involved because a report would have to be filed and then the local newspapers would have access to the incident's occurrence. Negative publicity would reflect badly on the school, so

15

public-relations-minded administrators attempt to "keep the lid on" at all times. Consequently, teachers must live with the everyday reality, and it is a very ugly part of *their* daily serfdom ordeal.

It will not be until all perspectives of the *educational* environment are presented to boards of education and to the public that the real problems inherent in American education will be finally addressed. Teacher input and teacher viewpoints are often discouraged and regarded as "unprofessional" to reveal to parents, to boards of education, or to local newspapers. Many teachers fear loss of job security or being punished by being given bad classes and undesirable duties, so *they* remain mum and go along with the administration's "don't rock the boat" and "keep the lid on" games that dominate schools today.

But educational disorganization is becoming much more rampant, and what will happen when the patients (*students*) gain control of the asylum, and when the inmates (*students*) take charge of the cellblocks? As long as administrators withhold essential information from the public, and as long as administrative opinion is valued as the sole basis for school policy, without teacher consultation, then partial ignorance will be captaining the vast majority of ships navigating in the great educational harbor.

American public-school teachers today are Vital Non-Entities; and conversely, administrators, superintendents and supervisors are Non-Vital Entities. The school moguls reckon that in terms of prestige and financial compensation, it is better to be a high-salaried Non-Vital Entity than being a lower-salaried Vital Non-Entity having *assumed* authority and carrying the burden of great responsibility.

Chapter 3
"Role Reinforcement"

Role reinforcement is one way that administrators and supervisors establish who *they* are in the pecking order and who teachers are in the pecking order *beneath* them. School management (administrivia) immediately takes priority over classroom activity (education). Most school administrators refuse to teach one course a day to keep at least one foot embedded in educational reality. The art of teaching is undoubtedly a *subordinate* pursuit that is *beneath* them, and so teachers teach and administrators manage inside the static and stratified neo-factory educational environment.

I recollect that once at an annual end of the year teacher retirement dinner a school superintendent said to me, "*John,* rank has its privileges." No sooner had he said those descriptive words that his loyal secretary brought *him* a mixed drink upon a tray.

Teachers quickly get the message that when an administrator calls him or her by his or her first name, everything is all right and normal. But when an administrator says something formal like "*Mr. Wiessner,* I'd like to talk to you in my office," then some offended supervisor, disgruntled parent or upset *student* has registered an official complaint against you. And now *you* (as the recipient) on the spur of the moment must transform into your own defense attorney without any specific background as to what the impromptu conference might be about.

Teachers quickly learn that prestige is achieved by advancing to the coveted administrative shelf, and the teacher who is fortunate enough to ascend to that lofty plateau often carries with him or her teeming idealism and naivete. Those stellar characteristics might have made him or her an excellent teacher, but that accompanying baggage might also make him or her an impractical financial wizard or program coordinator.

"Well," a pundit might argue, "the school executives deserve higher remuneration because they have more overall accountability than the ordinary classroom teacher does." Exactly who develops curriculum? Who handles all of the extra-curricular activities? Who schedules and chaperones field trips? Who are the purveyors of knowledge? Who are the class advisers? Who has to tackle tough stints like cafeteria duty and massive study halls? Who must monitor class migrations between periods? Who negotiates the school's teacher contract and salary schedules with the board of education?

The answer in each particular instance is rather vivid and distinct: the faculty members do.

Perhaps the most formidable daily challenge that confronts administrators is the perplexity of decision-making and how to avoid it by delegating specific tasks to teachers. Evasive tactics and "power ping-pong" are integral parts of the mystical administrative persona. A smart administrator firmly believes that *he* won't fall out of the boat if he sits in the middle. But the more perceptive veteran teachers understand that when the boat rocks, the captains up on the bridge deck feel the intense swaying the most.

Smart administrators realize that it is educational heresy to endorse policies that commit *them* to a definite course of action. Never render allegiance to any aspect of a multi-faceted topic that might entail controversy. If fate determines that a program is unfeasible, then the administrator can absolve himself' or herself and ascribe blame and failure to the teacher that had been assigned the activity.

The *Pontius Pilate Syndrome* is alive and kicking in most American public-school systems. This phenomenon is a peculiar psychological disease that almost exclusively infects school administrators. The theory is to wash *your* hands of touchy gray-area judgment responsibilities and quickly abdicate from them if possible. The administrator is then exonerated from direct involvement in any glaring school failure.

By delegating responsibility to the teachers, administrators can share programs' successes and shrewdly enter the setting via a hidden door and pilfer most of the praise that rightfully belonged to the teacher assigned the obligation. If the program becomes a dismal deficiency, the administrator has the luxury of reprimanding the teacher for failure and then cleverly escapes all association with the embarrassing school boomerang.

The entire fiasco soon becomes a cat and mouse fantasy game where the teachers are always either the exploited, victimized rodents. It is a lot safer to become an administrator, a utopian college professor or a guidance counselor going one-on-one with a *student* than to daily do combat with a hundred and thirty hormone-driven kids. Many of the acne-faced adolescents don't want to be anywhere in *your* magical presence while you're futilely attempting to organize constructive activities or studies.

College professors fully know that it is easier to fascinate a captive audience of self-motivated post high-school *students* than to motivate fourteen-to-eighteen-year-olds in a standard public-school environment. Yes, tell prospective schoolteachers that *they* must motivate juvenile middle and high school paragons and proclaim the edict from the safety of ivory-tower university classrooms. This amounts to hypocrisy at its grandest level since the worst teaching (lecture method) exists on the college level and probably the best instruction occurs from kindergarten to grade six where children only have ten-to-thirty-minute attention spans and short learning time intervals to grasp basic language and math' concepts.

So, when that enthusiastic pie-in-the-sky college professor insists that prospective teachers must stimulate *students* to participate in activities so that the *children* can perform enviable creativity, the sagacious advice constitutes little more than worthless hogwash. The professor is lecturing to his entranced college *students*, and they are ravenously taking notes on his or her purported gospel truth. But the professor violates every tenet of good teaching because he or she is employing the *lecture method* of instruction. I recall one professor throwing a wild temper tantrum because an admiring college *student* had the audacity to bring a tape recorder to class and dare obtain the good doctor's lecture content without *his* expressed permission.

And when young teachers go into public-school classrooms and imitate the suspect instructional *lecture method* that had been employed by their esteemed college professors, their initiatives are doomed to failure and will certainly be sabotaged by a plentitude of *student* discipline problems.

On the other hand, public school *students* like to get out of their desks and move around the room. This practice is encouraged by the new "cooperative learning" activity method. But any sane teacher realizes that the more activity there is in the classroom, the more noise naturally results. Administrators generally don't like noise emanating from room to room and into the corridors, and the stressed-out teacher in the room next to yours might register a strong complaint. A teaching career espousing the philosophy of continuous *student* mobility in the classroom will more than likely be short-lived because of general fatigue, neuron collapse, or hospitalization due to detrimental mental or physical breakdown.

In the waning years of my career, I found it increasingly difficult to teach English the way it had been taught in the past. Kids would be used to moving around in various classrooms from computer to desk to computer, or anxiously moving from learning station to learning station. My eighth graders couldn't sit still for forty-five minutes and delve into grammar exercises on the various kinds of phrases, or identifying and correcting run-on sentences. They were restless and wanted to move around like they were doing in their "cooperative learning" classes. Their entire existence was predicated upon "instant gratification", and when they were denied it by having to exhibit "self-discipline" in an academic lesson, they became turned-off and some even became rebellious. And so, the sound-byte learning trend has migrated from *MTV* and TV commercials into the American classroom. Kids don't like concentrating for more than fifteen minutes at a time because extensive thinking represents "hard work", which in today's world engenders unhappiness.

Over my career, I have witnessed scores of young teachers (many of whom were former *students*) come fresh out of college ablaze with enthusiasm, bright-eyed and bushy-tailed. In September, their *messiah complexes* radiate the glorious message of "meeting the *children's* needs" and/or "treating the avid learners with love, understanding and freedom".

Come November, statements of doubt become intertwined amidst the newcomers sputtering epistles of educational romanticism. Come March tears dampen the new instructors' altruistic vision. Fierce seismic waves slam the young teachers' hearts, meandering between philosophical illusion and classroom reality. "What is wrong?" many of them ask. "I've done everything my professors had taught me, but the kids are not responding! Many of them are taking advantage of me and my kindness!"

Come June, the new teacher is hanging on to survival in sheer desperation. Despair and frustration dominate his or her psyche. Fantasies taught in teacher colleges such as "humanizing" your course of study and giving the *students democracy* to ensure individual responsibility have proven to be palpable chicanery.

The young teacher that continues to endorse the chimeras of his or her college professors finds himself or herself on a collision course with hostile educational reality. Middle and high school age *students* are interested in sex, partying, alcohol, drugs, the opposite gender, designer clothes, fast cars, rock and roll and rap music, the *Internet* and video games. If your curriculum cannot relate to those egocentric dynamics, then forget what's inside your subject's textbook and file away what those ethereal college professors predicted would work for you.

To effectively implement the "child-centered curriculum", a teacher must be highly skilled and experienced. Until the novice teacher masters the art of accurately gauging *student* potential, and until he or she perfects the elusive science of making sound classroom judgments, all of the zest and idealism in the world is inconsequential. The whole abstract matter is analogous to trying to water-ski while wearing ice skates.

Confused and dangerous liberal hypocrites dominate most schools of higher education. Prospective teachers are counseled by professors that *they* must learn as much as possible about each of their *students*. Prospective teachers are told that *they* must investigate thoroughly into the home life of their *students*, assess past teachers' comments inside confidential records, and study the case histories of "problem *children*" that happen to be six-foot-four and weigh two-hundred and fifty-pounds. But when the beleaguered instructor has six teaching classes with a hundred and thirty to a hundred and fifty diverse *students*, the administrative expectations far exceed the ability to effectively execute the game plan.

I have had college professors that *lecture* their classes to utilize the psychological tool of praise when instructing *children*. As a result, kids expect to always be praised, even after completing very mediocre tasks. A definite phoniness pervades most public schools where every *student* expects to be praised daily for doing very average or less than average work. All of this flattery leads to a false atmosphere, and when praising mediocre performance becomes the hallmark of a school, academic excellence is sacrificed in deference to continuous sociological complimenting. The outside world does not function on artificial and cursory praise for doing average work. An adult in the real world is *praised* for doing *superior* work.

Then I have seen those same college professors harass *students* that don't conform to *their* lofty personal standards. The college professor does not practice what he or she preaches. Few get to know any of their apprentices on an interpersonal basis, and most professors could care less about personal problems their *students* might be having. It is much less troublesome lecturing to vulnerable idealistic college *students* than to waste valuable time fooling around with disrespectful and often-offensive high school *students*. Hopefully, soon the entire university educational system will come to its senses and realize that there is an inadequate supply of elephants available to furnish the raw material needed to construct all of the hallowed, college campus *ivory* towers.

Now compare the instructional load of a school administrator, a college professor and a regular high school teacher. The school administrator prefers to teach no classes. The whole central idea of school administration is to become a superintendent and not see or teach any kids at all. And yet principals, vice-principals and superintendents still insist on being called *educators* despite the fact they no longer teach anyone and really don't desire (even once a day) to perform that function that is now acknowledged being *beneath* them. Their motto is: "Stay above the fray and remain remote from any school problem until it is time to judge how a teacher failed to execute properly in a particular duty or responsibility."

Now let's analyze and compare the instructional load of a college professor and a high school teacher. The former may teach a maximum of twelve hours a week. The poor high school mentor will have a comparable workload capsulated into less than a half week. Of course, the college professor is into his "publish or perish mode", and he or she would prefer to do armchair research and not teach any graduate course. The high school teacher is lucky if he or she has time to read an article in a professional journal let alone engage in writing an article in one.

The college professor has no real anxiety-oriented functions such as cafeteria duty, office detention, bus duty, hall duty, lavatory duty or chaperone duty. Those bothersome functions are all part of the high school teacher's daily life in addition to being assigned a club or activity to advise.

The college professor has classes of select docile and cooperative *students* that want to learn and desire to advance in life. The jinxed high school instructor is in charge of a potpourri of heterogeneous pupils, some of them with severe sociological and psychological problems, and others that don't give one iota about the teacher, or about the subject, about learning, about their classmates or even about themselves.

About twenty percent of high school *students* want out of the building no matter how hard the system tries to accommodate them. They see no purpose in being there, see no connection between school and their future, and don't even care about their future because they have no realistic goals. They might want to be a *Hollywood* movie star, a New York model or a professional basketball or football player, but those dreams are mere artificial aspirations and not genuine attainable objectives.

The college professor works with a selective breed of self-motivated *students*, and the school administrator doesn't want to work with or instruct any *students*, while the classroom teacher must evolve into a masochist trying to cope with as many as a hundred and fifty isolated personalities daily.

The college prof' has few or no discipline problems, but his high school teaching counterpart is deluged with as many as ten or more major and minor infractions a day. It doesn't require *PhD* credentials to determine that anyone can tell others to *motivate*, but only a gifted few can consistently accomplish the challenge on a daily basis.

In keeping with *their* lowly status in the educational pecking order, teachers are quite aware of the limited wiggle space they have functioning inside the overall system. Instructors must role-play being subservient to college professors and school administrators. Meanwhile, enter now some other players onto the scene; the local board of education.

Board members role-play that their main function is to safeguard the taxpayers' dollars and to deal directly with and monitor the administration. The school board members concern themselves with teachers mostly when *they* are being reprimanded, having *their* pay increments withheld, being suspended with or without pay, or when some irate parent files a vehement complaint about something controversial or questionable that had happened inside her or his *child's* classroom.

The board of education members preach to the community's taxpayers that they desire "quality education" at the most moderate expense. Teachers get caught in the treacherous and ambivalent "quality versus quantity" shuffle. They must teach and evaluate one hundred and fifty *students* (quantity) and somehow provide a *quality* education to each one.

How could the overtaxed teacher get to know each of his or her scholars as his or her quixotic college professors had advocated? How can he or she grade papers (especially six-paragraph compositions that resemble decompositions) and discuss the merits of each *student's* writing prowess when twenty to thirty of those same *students* are absent from school each day? Where else but in the classroom can you find a versatile *professional* person harnessed to a hundred and fifty autonomous receptors of knowledge? The teacher is quite a splendid and marvelous workhorse indeed, and very economical, too!

The public buys into the misconception that teaching is "an easy job" because the administrators sugarcoat everything in the local newspapers to look especially wonderful. The public then believes that teaching is an occupation similar to babysitting. Nasty relegations of this kind are painful to sustain, specifically when encumbered teachers are subjected to needless harassment and degradation at the *students'* family supper tables. And the public's erroneous rationalization that the art of teaching is comparable to common babysitting is legitimized because the taxpayers provide the teachers' salaries.

The presumptuous taxpayers in the community fail to acknowledge that teachers are taxpayers too and thus contribute toward *their* own salaries. Teachers also buy many of the products that taxpayers' employers manufacture, and they also utilize the services of community accountants, doctors, dentists, pharmacists, phone and utility companies, barbers, insurance agents and lawyers.

But if an element of the public maintains that the art and science of teaching is indeed *babysitting*, then teachers ought to be reimbursed as babysitters are compensated. My oldest son pays a teenager three dollars an hour to watch his two children. Using that standard to establish an index, if a teacher has a hundred and fifty *students* a day and puts in thirty-five hours of instruction time per week, then the average teacher should receive a very generous stipend. Let's figure it out. It amounts to $2,200.00 a week if paid at babysitting wages (21 students an hour x $3.00 per hour' X 7 hours a day X 5 days a week). And that's just basic compensation for an elementary school, self-contained classroom job performance (at many dollars an hour below minimum wage).

Now to extend this arithmetical reasoning even further, the teacher might be responsible for managing two hundred boisterous high school *students* for forty-five minutes during cafeteria duty. Using the babysitting pay model, a teacher on duty could amass nearly five hundred dollars a day for his or her cafeteria expertise at a nominal $3.00 per hour babysitting wages.

So, whenever a member of the public says that teaching is babysitting, I gladly reply by stating, "Teachers ought to be paid like babysitters!" But unfortunately, the taxpayers and the local educational powers that be are not so generous with their bestowments. They prefer naming what the townspeople call *babysitting* "the teaching profession", and then overburden the *professionals* with a host of debilitating duties to complement an exhaustive daily schedule reimbursed at below babysitting standards.

And the teacher is constantly reminded of his or her role in the stratified pecking order from perpetual reinforcement given by school administrators, by college professors, by curriculum coordinators, by supervisors, by superintendents, by boards of education and by the critical-but-uninformed general public.

Chapter 4
"The Concept of Office"

Almost every school day a *student* would enter into my room between the change of classes and say, "Mr. Wiessner, the office wants to see me!"

"Who is the office?" I always instinctively questioned. "I know no one by the name of Mr. or Mrs. Office! You make it sound as if the office is an actual person having a distinct personality! Would you care to rephrase your statement?"

"A secretary called me down over the intercom," the neurotic *student* would usually clarify. "I heard my name read along with six or seven others."

"Do you have a note or hall pass?" I habitually would ask.

"No; I *told* you that a secretary from the office read my name between the change of classes," the shocked *student* would normally reply, wondering why I showed such a lack of respect or awe for the people working in the office or for the mighty office's supreme power (and its propensity to daily generate adminis*trivia*).

"Well, since you have no note or permission to leave my classroom," I would elaborate, "just have a seat inside your desk and wait. If it's really that important, they'll call you again!"

Students believe that "the office" (and everyone working in it) is the ultimate authority in the school. Whenever a *student* is summoned to the main office without notice, the kid automatically thinks that he or she is in trouble. That's the way a teenager's mind operates. The office represents power; a power that transcends teacher authority, or for that matter, anything else that goes on in the whole building.

Teachers are also called to the office over the intercom during their lunch periods or between the changing of classes. Usually, the reason is an important message from their husbands or wives, or an instructor had inadvertently left his or her roll book in a classroom, or a textbook salesman wants to see him or her, or usually something trivial like that. But invariably, after I had been called to the office a *student* will ask me in the hall, "What did you do wrong Mr. Wiessner? *The office* wants to see you?"

Kids think that teachers get in trouble with the principal the same way *they* do, and most teenagers honestly believe that the *ultimate authority* in the school superstructure is a place that both kids and teachers must certainly avoid. They judge teachers' experiences with the *office principal* in terms of their own negative encounters with the school's chief executive.

And some *students* actually believe that *they* can get a teacher in trouble the same way they always try getting each other in trouble. Once I was assigned during my prep period (*PPSA*-Planning, Preparation and Special Assignment) to an absent teacher's study hall in the cafeteria. This last-minute notice represents the *Special Assignment* aspect of the designation' *PPSA*.

Upon entering the mass study hall, I observed that two rascally seventh graders (who didn't know me personally because I was an eighth grade English teacher) had taken a pen from a third *student*, who was vigorously chasing the two petty thieves around cafeteria tables. I halted the first young hooligan, grabbed the pen from his grasp and handed the writing utensil back to the third kid, the very grateful victim.

"I'm going to the office!" the first kid yelled in my direction. "You hurt my hand!"

"Sit down!" I commanded.

"You hurt my friend's hand when you squeezed it!" the second young hooligan barked. "I saw you do it. We're gonna' get *you* in trouble!"

"Sit down at a table, get a book out and start studying!" I sternly insisted.

The two offenders angrily walked-out of the cafeteria against my permission and sauntered down the corridor in the direction of the main office. I asked the third *student* the names of the two obnoxious agitators, and after fifty other *students* in the mass study hall finally settled-down, the teacher wasted ten minutes filling-out two Office Referral Cards describing in detail the incident that had occurred. Then I had to take roll of the other fifty unfamiliar *students* that had been assigned to the cafeteria study hall during my *PPSA* period.

Kids will do almost anything and go to extremes to reduce *you* (the teacher) to their level. And once they have succeeded in making *you* (the teacher) their pal, they then feel they can get away with any antic because you are now their friend (or special enemy) vegetating on their level.

The two silly *students* in the cafeteria mass study hall were playing a stupid game and resented the fact that I had intervened in their fun. The young violators then conspired and contrived a story making me into the villain who was abusing them and their rights. They maintained to the principal that I had used excessive force in repossessing the pen that they "had borrowed" from the third *student* and that the school administrator should punish me for using physical force while reclaiming the pen that the first kid had resisted surrendering.

A half-hour later, the young rogues returned to the cafeteria with their heads crestfallen. Their little charade had ended in two days of "Office Detention" because *they* had left the cafeteria without a pass and without the teacher's consent and had strolled-down to the main office unsupervised after the late bell had rung.

Anyone working in the main office (including its secretaries) gets into the authoritative "telling mode", and *students* and teachers are expected to instantly transform into the "listening and obeying mode" whenever an office announcement is made. The secretaries assume that they are an integral part of the omnipotent office regency. They boldly tell teachers of changes in *their* daily assignments during teacher prep' periods when a substitute could not be gotten that day for an absent instructor. They *tell* teachers that certain complaining parents had called, and the office secretaries *tell* teachers that they can't be paid until next week's lesson plans have been submitted to the central office.

Secretaries will also *tell* teachers over the intercom to send *students* to the Main Office to pick up messages from parents, and the office clerks have become so independent that they refuse to do favors like running-off tests or worksheets for teachers. When I first started teaching back in 1965, an office secretary would always be cooperative and available in a "work do-now". She would gladly type up an exam', run-off dittos (this was before *Xerox* copying machines existed in the Main Office), or the courteous young lady would type a letter of *student* commendation or recommendation for the teacher to be sent home to mom and dad. All of that cooperation has changed over the years. The Main Office secretaries are now independent of teacher functionality inside the school, and they have become an extension of the principal and the vice-principal's voice of authority.

The blind obedience that the office secretaries have to the school administrators is akin to the unwavering loyalty that Patroclus had exhibited for Achilles in Homer's *Iliad.* Having become a part of "the royal *aristocratic* court of the school," the secretaries are happy campers thriving in the lower echelon of "the Educational Aristocracy". Some of them have even become intoxicated with the imperial power the main office frequently commands.

The school structure is stratified like a pyramid matrix. The superintendent and the board of education are at the top. The principals are on the second strata; the vice-principals are on the third ledge; the supervisors and guidance counselors are then positioned below the head honchos, followed by the office secretaries to complete the Educational Aristocracy's portion of the matrix. Then below those lofty shelves are the teachers, the janitors and finally the cafeteria brunhildas. Remember, as that school district superintendent had once told me, "Rank has its privileges!"

The public must understand that schools exist for *students,* and it is the teachers' who have been entrusted to educate the community's youth. The school is there for education, and the teachers are the only ones in the building that do the educating. The modern-day public-school instructor is hindered because he or she must often be his or her own clerical staff. Teachers' type-up their own tests, exams', quizzes, work sheets, progress reports, announcements, and warning and commendation letters.

The *students* invariably suffer when a good portion of teacher out- of-school time is dominated by performing pedestrian "secretarial work". Getting secretarial assistance for encumbered teachers with heavy workloads is as likely as D.H. Lawrence's *Lady Chatterley* evicting her lover from her infamous boudoir.

And don't expect frugal board of education members (who budget and squander hundreds of thousands of taxpayers' dollars on special interest school pork barrel projects often awarded to relatives or contractor/friends) to hire one secretary for a staff of a hundred or more teachers. The average high school has upwards of ten secretaries busily tapping computer keys. The superintendent has one, the school board administrator has one, the principal has one, the vice-principal has one, the head of the *Child Study Team* has one, and the guidance department has several loyal clerical workers, too. But the hundred high school teachers that have the essential task of educating the district's *students* don't have one secretary to share amongst themselves! Forcing teachers to perform their own clerical work is like making Frank Lloyd Wright waste his creative time designing outhouses.

The teacher handbook stipulates that school announcements will be read from the Main Office twice a day, once during homeroom and once during the end of last period. It all sounds rather innocent, pure and faultless, doesn't it? Sometimes the intercom doesn't work properly, emits lots of static, and occasionally only every other word is audible. Sometimes *students* that are assigned by the office to read the daily announcements laugh or make light of what they are doing. This immature silliness causes homeroom and last period teachers instantaneous discipline problems for needless interruptions that attempt to edify insignificant (to most of the *students*) after school activities that pertain to diverse segments of the *student* body.

On several occasions the office secretaries neglected to turn-on the office intercom, and then unknowing *students* read the perfunctory *Pledge of Allegiance*, the generic "thought for the day" and the morning announcements, and no one in the school's classrooms ever heard them spend five minutes going through the entire script.

Sometimes, the office secretaries (who are too busy processing *student* homeroom attendance cards and Office Discipline Referrals) don't begin the morning announcements until the end of homeroom period. The dismissal bell to first period automatically rings, and the muffled announcements screech through hall speakers and contribute to general turmoil as restless *students* block and knock each other into lockers, playfully shoving peers into one another, and gleefully begin clobbering each other with loaded gym bags, or with heavy back book packs.

Many times, the school intercom produces more harm than it does service. It sometimes sounds like a submarine submerging when its shrill whistle blasts and interrupts a placid classroom atmosphere when the *students* are finally busy concentrating while taking a grammar test or a literature exam'. Sometimes the rude intercom distraction occurs during an intense discussion that disrupts a lesson's continuity. So, a simple device such as the office intercom can become a daily intrusive annoyance.

Sometimes fifty *students* (I called it the "Listless List Catalogue") are summoned to *the office*. Students are called down to retrieve a lost book, or to be reminded to call their mothers before leaving school, or maybe to take the school bus home because mother is too busy that afternoon. The Main Office also summons derelict *children* over the intercom to pay back lunch money that had been borrowed from the office, to pay debts owed for class trips, for school insurance, or money for yearbook pictures, or for a variety of other trivial reasons including overdue library books. The important concept here is that office adminis*trivia* takes precedence over classroom academic education.

Many times, the flustered (or perhaps apathetic) office secretary will call over the intercom the names of *students* that she herself had typed-up on the absentee sheet that same morning. And many times, during the end of eighth period, the boring announcements will commence right before the final dismissal bell. Try keeping a class in their seats listening attentively to irrelevant minutia three minutes after the final dismissal bell has rung.

The principal's secretary proudly prepares the school budget, a document that is sacrosanct to administrators. She is also the general keeper and custodian of the Main Office's records. If a teacher needs information about any club activity or bank account, then detour around the principal and consult his competent secretary, for in many instances, her knowledge of office matters surpasses her superior's. And the informational office guru probably is entitled (by virtue of job performance) to the bulk of her boss's obese salary.

However, be forewarned that the principal's secretary is also the seasoned Office Manager who has converted her bailiwick into a matriarchal commune, and she covets her authoritarian dominance by confidently making some of the important determinations her boss gets paid to decide. The principal doesn't mind sharing certain confidentialities with his trusted personal secretary, for her efforts often alleviate the need for him performing certain aspects of his or her job description.

Teachers are advised to avoid going behind the office counter because sensitive confidential information pertaining to *students* or instructors might be sitting upon a secretary's desk. The secretaries have access to the school's biggest secrets, yet the *professional* teaching staff does not. And *student* office pages are often helping the secretaries with their clerical work and standing right next to the confidential records that teachers are forbidden to see.

Upon entering the main office's portal from the diminutive teacher mailbox room, an instructor in a rush (and in dire need of secretarial assistance) will have to wait his turn in deference to a *student* whom the office secretary prefers to recognize first. Because the principal's secretary runs the Main Office with Spartan efficiency, and organizes administrative data, agendas and schedules, she also knows plenty about the personal records of school personnel. She often perceives herself as the indispensable cog in the office wheel. This affords the stern Office Manager the license and privilege of ignoring *subordinate* teachers and acting as the official representative and extension of the school administration.

The school executives appreciate the capabilities that their Main Office secretaries demonstrate, and they allow *them* plenty of latitude in lightening the torrent of *administrivia* that plagues *their* everyday existence. The real problem in education arises when office adminis*trivia* is given priority over teaching and learning in the school's classrooms.

Teacher requests are often put on hold so that more Main Office attention could be directed toward the collection of raffle ticket money for the junior class fundraiser, for the counting of *free lunch* vouchers, or for table seating diagrams for the senior prom. And then in early November, the faculty is informed that no teacher work can be performed by the secretaries because the office clerks are too preoccupied preparing the *Magna Carta* of school documents, the mighty school budget. "Don't make any office requests next week because the secretaries will be too occupied with the budget," teachers are informed via a memo' from the principal.

From all of the office pomp and circumstance comes one negative result: when the interests and needs of teachers are neglected, in the final analysis, it is the kids that ultimately suffer the consequences. Teachers need clerical help and/or classroom aides to assist them in the performance of clerical duties like correcting objective tests, recording grades or running-off class materials. And the hundred or more teachers must share one *Xerox* machine that always seems to break-down when *you* (the teachers) have a hundred and fifty sheets to duplicate for classroom distribution.

A working faculty of a hundred teachers has no secretary, but each administrator and almost every guidance counselor has the luxury of at least one clerk who comes complete with shorthand, computer screen and steno pad. It doesn't take long for teachers to see the light at the end of the tunnel. Evolve into the Educational Aristocracy or remain *subordinate* to office fiat and be valued below executive adminis*trivia*. The *Concept of Office* reinforces the lowly status of the teacher in the well-defined educational pyramid every single day of the school year.

Chapter 5
"Little Things Add' Up"

If an educator's coffee was cold at breakfast, or if the toaster had burned your English muffin, then the teacher might as well stay home that morning. When a public-school instructor's mind is just a tad out of kilter, or when he or she is not absolutely feeling a hundred percent mentally and physically, then the teacher is vulnerable to anything that might incidentally occur in the workplace. Not being a hundred percent with a fuzzy mind means that *you* (the teacher) are more prone to lose your temper with a *student*, with an administrator or with a parent. You are more inclined to jeopardize your entire teaching career by accidentally saying something vague that could be misconstrued by a *student* or by his or her parents and then brought to the attention of administrators. That one little thing could easily snowball and explode into a career-threatening episode. That single last event that coincidentally irritated the teacher could be the straw that breaks the pedagogue's camel's back.

It used to tickle my fancy when every morning like clockwork in 1965, an elderly teacher named Larry DeLancy would pass me in the school corridor and say, "Just think John. You just have thirty more years of this abuse until you retire!" At first, I interpreted the daily remark as cynicism laced with sarcasm. But as time meandered onward from 1965 to 1999, I found myself making the exact same remark to a fledgling educator just embarking on his challenging public-school teaching career.

Let's examine some reasons why dedicated teachers lose their enthusiasm (and become cynical) but stay in the profession because they have become very good disciplinarians and effective instructors and classroom managers over the years. Their general cynicism and pessimism are a result of thousands of minor irritating events that accumulate in *their* consciousnesses over a period of three and a half decades. Those little things over time really add up. And when you've seen everything once too often, it's time to hang-up your teaching certificate on the den wall and apply for pension benefits.

Now let's say a particular teacher's all revved up telling a second period English class exactly how Samuel Langhorne Clemens acquired the pen name Mark Twain when a voluptuous office page enters your sanctuary and deposits the school's absentee sheet on the teacher's desk. Just try expounding on the merits of Mark Twain when sixty hypnotized eyes follow the curvaceous intruder's body as she playfully traipses in and out of the room every second period, five days a week, thirty-eight weeks a year.

And then there is the page dispatched from the Main Office that enters the classroom and interrupts the teacher while he is telling his disciples how Mark Twain went west to try his hand at gold prospecting. "Mr. Wiessner, the Guidance Office would like to see Tom Durham," the interloper states without the courtesy of ever saying "excuse me".

"Who in the Guidance Office wants to see Tom Durham?" I requested knowing.

"The head of the department!" the distressed young man returned amidst a wave of *student* giggling.

"For your information," I stated, "Tom Durham is a *student* of mine third period. This is second period and he's not in this class!"

No sooner did I get back to Mark Twain journeying to California to pursue a viable career in newspaper journalism that a Guidance Office page entered my classroom. "The *office* wants to see Joe Conway. The Guidance Office wants to see him because Joe was absent the day the Guidance Department gave the IQ tests," the dispatched page informatively revealed.

Everyone in the class instantaneously picked-up the subtle message. *Students* can *tell* teachers what to do if they become office and guidance pages. 'I could *tell* (dictate to) my English teacher exactly what needs to be done if I become an office page,' the vernal dreamers naturally hypothesize.

The significance of English literature in the form of Mark Twain's biography is instantly reduced to rubble when a Guidance Office standardized test is given priority over a valuable classroom lesson. And if I was administering a grammar test on Chapter 5 or a quiz on the past fifty vocabulary words, then Joe Conway would have to leave my test-in-progress and go to the Guidance Office and take *their* test, which they obtain from an educational testing company. Kids quickly pick-up on these telling and obeying relationships within the great educational pyramid and quickly determine what an inferior level the teachers occupy. And all of this chaos happens because Joe Conway didn't come to school on the day the IQ test was distributed to *students,* and English class had also been suspended that day because of that special school testing priority.

The *students* understand that classroom activity is secondary to office discretion. It really doesn't matter that the English teacher spent three hours the night before reading all about Mark Twain. It really doesn't matter that it required three hours to prepare and type up the teacher-made Chapter 5 grammar test. The guidance director spent three minutes opening the standardized IQ test packet from the educational testing corporation, and it was absolutely imperative that Joe Conway leave the English seminar and take the guidance test immediately so that the essential data results could be placed in the *student's* confidential folder.

Teachers eventually become numb and immune to such typical *subordination* of both his/her subject and himself or herself to arbitrary office decree. Some teachers become cynical and eventually gravitate toward becoming openly sarcastic. Others simply listlessly accept the demands of any office person or of any surrogate *student* page sent as an office courier. The *Concept of Office* is perhaps the greatest external eroding force that rapes beginning teachers of their integrity, and it conditions them to be trained robots programmed to honor any and all *administrivia*, regardless of how meaningless it might actually be.

Even a small distraction like the classroom wall pencil sharpener can be annoying. Its raspy grind might permeate a serene classroom atmosphere that might have required fifteen minutes for the teacher to establish after a surprise fire drill. The restless *students* and the "attention deficit *students*" now have a new focal point to actively distract them. After seeing and hearing thousands of pencils being sharpened and causing thousands of diversions over thirty-four years, a teacher begins to wonder about his or her place in the entire educational universe and seriously contemplates early retirement.

One way to solve the pencil sharpening problem is to insist that *students* sharpen their pencils upon entering the room before the late bell rings, but what about those *students* that enter after the late bell and must be recorded as tardy? What about those ornery *students* that break their pencil points, either accidentally or deliberately? Even the faithful pencil sharpener could have a toll on a teacher's emotional health over a thirty-four-year period.

During my career I have intercepted at least five hundred notes casually being passed between *students*. Most notes contain similar themes that focus upon upcoming parties, upon *student* enemies that a vengeful *child* plans to pulverize, or upon prospective boyfriends or girlfriends. Here is a typical note that I intercepted while teaching a junior English class.

Alicea,

Hey, could Wiessner be any more fun? He thinks he's so funny! Why does he talk so fuckin' much? What are ya' doin' Saturday? I have to go to Jennifer's stupid show. I'm scared. Her band is gonna' suck, so you should come with me in case I get into a fight. You probably have to work though, huh? Does Frank know that Steve was over your house? Tell Julie to grow some tits, will ya'!

Tracy

Now how can O. Henry or Jack London's literature compare with erudite nomenclature like that? After reading five hundred similar dysfunctional notes, the teacher begins pondering, 'Why didn't I go into guidance? Why didn't I become an administrator, or perhaps a mediocre supervisor?'

Classroom bulletin boards could constitute another source of teacher discomfort. They are supposed to supplement and brighten the room's dull, rectangular, tan-painted cinderblock appearance and inspire *student* interest in an upcoming project, activity or lesson. For what little they accomplish, high school bulletin boards are mostly all show and little go. If they are constructed during a classroom period, then the enterprise renders itself a distraction to the essential lesson being explored.

But some teachers have more time to devote to bulletin board assembly than others do. If a teacher is fortunate enough to have a study hall in his or her classroom or homeroom, then the chore could easily be completed then and there. But most teachers must apportion time to develop their classroom bulletin boards either before or after school. Doing bulletin boards is the downside of having your own classes in your own classroom.

After a newly designed bulletin board is intact, its longevity might be in jeopardy. Aggressive *students* with curious, devious minds might arrive in an empty classroom two minutes before the teacher or other *students* make their debut. It is true that idle minds are the devil's workshops, and laziness could quickly and easily transform into destructive overt behavior.

Carefully stapled letters on classroom bulletin boards may either be removed or rearranged to spell-out embarrassing lewd slogans. Beards, goatees and monocles may suddenly complement the portraits of distinguished American and British authors. Many *students* are masters at enacting *destructive creativity*.

Some defacers will combine their artistic genius with a dash of literary wit. Those saboteurs have the unique capacity to manufacture an immoral-but-nevertheless rather innovative dirty expression. The classroom teacher is always on the lookout for bulletin board vandalism because the objects require a great deal of patience and imagination to carefully assemble. Regrettably, two unscrupulous and inconsiderate villains could in seconds obliterate a skillfully crafted bulletin board that took two hours to organize.

As an avowed English teacher, I had always kept thirty-five dictionaries on the heater shelf under the side windows. At least three times every year a *student* (usually a girl) approached me with an opened dictionary in her palms. Observing the girl's prudent gait and the stoic expression exhibited on her face, I automatically suspect that the concerned *student* wishes to show me some risque prose scribbled inside. Instead of desiring to report an indiscreet moral infraction, most kids that do this kind of revealing activity simply want to see what kind of response the written dirty phrase will elicit from the teacher.

When confronted with the esoteric passage, "Fuck you Wiessner!" I normally say to the curious *student* doing the reporting, "If the author of *that* expression really meant those words," I nonchalantly replied each time, "then he or she would say it directly to my face rather than just jotting it down inside some remote dictionary! *Students* that write *in* or *on* books will never be able to author them!"

Hearing my strange monologue, the *stunned student* usually would gape at me for a moment in pure astonishment, and then realizing that I had not been fazed by the "Fuck you Wiessner!" obscenity, she would walk back to her desk blushing in a wonderfully baffled state of mind.

Student desk slates would be another area that could frustrate a teacher who diligently tries to keep a classroom neat and orderly. Frequently, because of space utilization and space economy, a teacher must share his or her classroom during his or her lunch period, cafeteria period, and/or *PPSA* period with other pedagogues. This sharing usually winds up with one teacher blaming the other for lewd writings and drawings on desk slates or for the apparent mutilation of bulletin boards.

If one delights in reading X-rated poems, then the tops of *students'* desks are good places to direct one's attention. If illustrated pornography stimulates one's libido, then a variety of grotesque, distorted and exaggerated reproductive organs are at one's immediate disposal.

Many honorable chaste *students* still demonstrate some adherence to "old Puritan morality" virtues and attempt erasing the licentious drawings before the patrolling teacher can observe the naughty artwork and blame *them* for creating it. Other less prudish *students* will conversely add their own perverted impressions to the original obscene drawing, thus producing an entirely new rendition.

It is very disturbing to witness innocent high school and middle school girls blush when first recognizing the lustful desk illustrations, but it is equally distressing to witness other young females adding their own personal, imaginative decadence to the already bizarre sketches. It would take plenty of brainwashing to convince me that morality (or moral standards) is not presently on the decline in the *United States of America*.

When viewing vulgar graffiti scribbled upon lavatory walls and upon classroom desk slates, one still wonders whether schools are really academic institutions where knowledge and tradition are imparted, or whether American schools are simply places where the fruits of centuries of sexual suppression are being harvested.

The noble educational philosopher John Dewey is reputed to have declared, "Children learn by doing!" I have often wondered if Dewey's dramatic statement pertains to the public-school teaching of human reproduction and sex education. Perhaps Sigmund Freud had a better handle on teenage development than John Dewey had.

When a teacher brings the repulsive desk drawings to an administrator's attention, he or she receives the feeling that the teacher in charge must patrol the classroom aisles more regularly and that the cleansing of the trash language from the desk slates is solely the room teacher's responsibility. After a while, a teacher realizes that he or she is actually indicting himself or herself by sending derelict *students* to the office or reporting incidents of vandalism to school property. The administrator comes back with the patented answer heard all-too-often, "You should have done more to prevent this from happening! Try being more alert next time!"

When telling the school custodians about the need to cleanse the graffiti-riddled desks, the day janitor claims that he's too busy to help the perplexed teacher out and that the night janitor has more free time to devote to the enterprise. The night janitor doesn't speak English and pretends he "no comprende" what the teacher is attempting to tell him. The administrator contends that it's the teacher's *duty* to keep the desks and bulletin boards presentable, even if the defacing had occurred while another teacher was working in the classroom.

And so, each morning, I would predictably arrive at school an hour early and then personally clean-off the thirty student desks situated in Room B-11. 'I can't injure myself opening a window before 7:45 a.m., the official starting time of school,' I would tell myself. 'Simply because I'm not insured for disability workman's compensation before the actual beginning of the teacher-school day.'

Janitors, cafeteria workers and school bus drivers are quick to perceive the futility of the modern-day *educator*. Janitors follow the lead of the Educational Aristocracy and *tell* you (the teacher) to close and lock your classroom windows at the end of eighth period. The cafeteria brunhildas *tell* you to chastise certain undisciplined *students* that give *them* trouble in the serving line. Office secretaries *tell* you to cover an absent teacher's class during your *PPSA* period. Bus drivers *tell* you to admonish certain *students* that terrorize other *children* on their separate bus routes. *Student* office pages enter a teacher's room and command that *you* obey an office's decree, whatever *it* might be.

The teacher is the *Vital-Non-Entity* functioning within the school infrastructure. It is ironic that the teacher, the one that is entrusted to educate *children,* is a powerless microorganism who is vainly horizontally crawling around the base of the school pyramid. Other building employees quickly recognize the teacher's demise and don't hesitate following the example of the supreme Educational Aristocracy, and they soon get activated in their new-found *tell* command modes.

Teachers should only be expected to act within the limits of their job description. Teachers should only be expected *to teach*. Farmers only farm, doctors only doctor, lawyers only lawyer and accountants only account. Why must teachers sell insurance to homeroom *students* for insurance companies, collect lunch and milk money in elementary schools, monitor the halls and guard the cafeteria, along with several dozen other assorted assignments in addition to loyally teaching six classes a day?

The taxpayers contend that these sundry functions are all a part of a teacher's daily *duties*. My response to *that* suspect jargon is quite pragmatic in nature. The extensive diversification of a teacher's responsibilities makes him or her about as specialized as a prehistoric *Neanderthal Man*. This multi-role "many hats" image is a genuine smear to teachers all across America.

It comes as no surprise that the public hypothesizes that "anyone can teach". When the cafeteria ladies see a teacher patrolling the aisles and telling *students* to pick-up random papers dropped under the tables, they say to each other, "I can do that! Teaching is really an easy job!" And they are entirely right in their assumptions and in their deductions, according to what they are observing.

The teachers have the most vital role in the school, and *that* is educating the next generation of Americans. But the important dynamics that go on in the classroom are constantly *subordinated* to office *administrivia*. A cruel mixture of office-generated paperwork and other control mechanisms like *duties* outlined in the *Teacher Handbook* demarcate boundaries with which the faculty must obediently comply. Adminis*trivia* is a method used by the office to keep teachers deluged with trite concerns so that the real educators will not have ample time to focus upon the glaring inefficiencies of lackluster school administration. If teachers courageously object to performing unprofessional tasks like cafeteria duty and Office Detention duty, then they risk being accused of *insubordination,* and potentially, the loss of "job security".

So, administrators encumber teachers with a hundred and thirty or more *students* stationed in six teaching classes, a homeroom class, attendance cards and attendance pads. Instructors are then provided roll books, lunch slips for lunch counts and for "free lunches", *PTA* membership forms, and also absentee student homework sheets.

Then teachers are besieged with *student* family vacation homework forms to fill-out along with a neat stack of blue or green Discipline Referral Cards. Finally, the school's faculty members are assigned early morning bus duty, after school bus duty, cafeteria duty, hall duty, lavatory duty, Office Detention duty, In-School Suspension duty, report cards, warning letters, progress reports and curriculum development assignments in addition to having the responsibility of teaching and evaluating *students* and the correction and grading of homework.

It is no wonder that teachers suffer from battle fatigue, from high blood pressure, from disillusionment, from hemorrhoids, from chronic bowel disorders, from heart disease, from midday indigestion, and finally, from job burnout.

Public school teachers have for too long been *generalists* in an age that both demands and rewards *specialists*. They have for the past century loyally performed a variety of *non-professional duties* under the false pretenses of "professionalism and duty".

When the role of the teacher finally evolves into a *specialist* exclusively engaged in the art and science of teaching, then the American teacher will at last be in harmony with the *specialist* theme prevalent in the twenty-first century. Some miraculous day teachers will finally discard the rusty shackles of century-old exploitation and for the first time reflect the self-dignity and the community respect that the designation "teacher" so rightfully deserves. Until that distant day arrives, teaching will still be an occupation and not a profession.

Chapter 6
"A Teacher Mentor"

Every so often, an impact person (other than a parent) enters your life. You don't know when or where that person might appear to give guidance until he or she shows up. But that very special individual possesses dynamic qualities that effectively have a lasting impact. The Godsend person will ultimately inspire the beneficiary, and his or her influence will dramatically affect the remainder of the lucky recipient's tenure on this planet.

In the summer of 1960, I was privileged to come into contact with a retired high school mathematics teacher, Mr. Charles B. Sipley, who had a profound positive lasting impression upon my general attitude towards the world. Mr. Sipley taught me the most valuable lesson of my young life. Forget self-esteem! The patient man taught me how to overcome failure and self-imposed emotional adversity, and concurrently, the man injected a healthy dose of resilience and confidence in my character.

In early 1960, my family had moved back to New Jersey from Levittown, Pennsylvania. My folks had an opportunity to purchase a home and a farm market and finally own a viable business. I had to transfer from *Bishop Egan High* in Pennsylvania to *Edgewood Regional High School* in Tansboro, New Jersey.

Coming from a strict Catholic school tradition, I had excellent background in English and also in social studies. I was very adept at comprehending standardized grammar, oral expression, spelling, vocabulary, punctuation, literature and writing. Language Arts, History and Geography came exceptionally easy to me.

Conversely, after I had transferred into *Edgewood High,* I soon discovered that I was extremely weak (compared to other *students* in the college prep' curriculum) in both science and advanced mathematics. Each day at *Edgewood* seemed very paradoxical to me. I would breeze through English, History and World Cultures' classes and then dismally suffer through Trigonometry and Physics.

My mind and heart were in turbulent quandaries, and my spirit shifted several times daily from the positive end of the achievement spectrum to the negative terminal. In late May of 1960, I found-out from my guidance counselor that I had failed Trigonometry. I was not allowed to graduate on stage with my class, and that punishment greatly disturbed me. I felt I had never had adequate preparation in my parochial school background in Algebra and that I could not fairly compete with the other public-school *students* on a level math' playing field in Trigonometry.

In 1960 at *Edgewood High*, if a *student* failed one major subject, that person had to attend summer school for remedial instruction. I was extremely demoralized and confused. I honestly believed that I was destined to be an incompetent failure for the remainder of my life and that my future had been adroitly sabotaged by Mr. Andrews, my strict *Edgewood* Trig' teacher. My English and Social Studies teachers were always touting me as one of the top *students* in the high school, and my Science and Trig' teachers evaluated my lackluster performance as being grossly inferior and situated far below mediocre.

Since I was not permitted to graduate with my classmates, I had a serious choice to make to finally obtain my high school diploma. I could either attend summer school at *Haddonfield High* (twenty miles away from my home) or I could seek-out the services of a qualified tutor. I had heard about Mr. Charles B. Sipley from a friend, so I gave the retired teacher a phone call, explained my dire situation, and I was thrilled to learn that the man would accept me as his *student*.

When I first met Mr. Sipley face to face at his home, I was deeply impressed. The retired teacher was not a huge man, but he possessed a strong constitution that seemed to transcend physical prowess. My soon-to-be mentor had a powerful inner strength shrouded in a hard outer mantle of Old-World values that somehow directly and immediately communicated with my inner-core-being. Mr. Sipley could motivate, inspire and influence me. Charles B. Sipley was confident that I could succeed, and he would not accept "No, I can't do this!" as an excuse. The Trig' guru soon masterfully transmitted that elusive confidence factor along with that special inspirational certainty to me.

Initially, I was reluctant to open up my soul to my mentor, trying to conceal and shield my shame and disgrace at failing high school from *his* scrutiny. After the first several tutorial sessions, under his calm, strong demeanor, I began to finally decipher the enigmas and codes that had previously made Trigonometry a total mystery to my hungry cerebrum.

With Mr. Sipley's encouragement and expertise, I soon became proficient in the fundamentals of sine, cosine, tangent, co-tangent, secant and co-secant. I soon understood the definite relationships between complicated mathematical formulas along with the six basic trigonometric functions. Learning advanced math' suddenly became easy, and soon it also became fun.

In four short weeks, I knew Trigonometry as well as the average *student* of that subject, and after the eight-week tutorial was over, I had a terrific command of the advanced mathematics, thanks to my sympathetic, patient-but-tough mentor. Mr. Sipley *expected* me to succeed and to master Trig', and I had no alternative other than to fulfill *his* lofty expectation. His daily demands allowed me no wiggle room from his strict regimentation.

In early September, I made a visit back to *Edgewood Regional High School* with a "Letter of Recommendation" signed by Mr. Charles B. Sipley. The neatly handwritten missive stated I had mastered the fundamentals and the mechanics of Trigonometry and that I should "receive a minimum *adjusted* grade of B for the course". I proudly took the note to the Main Office, and a secretary showed it to Mr. Pinkerton, the *Edgewood* principal, who then shuttled me up to Mr. Andrews' familiar M-Wing classroom.

I handed the stern pedagogue Mr. Sipley's complimentary letter, and after reading its benign content, Mr. Andrews became quite skeptical and said that the note could have been a clever counterfeit and that I still had to pass *his* awesome final exam' "to officially graduate". The mean-spirited fellow chuckled as *he* directed me to park my body in the last desk near the side windows, the same desk I had occupied as a failing student up to June 15th of 1960. Then Mr. Andrews handed me his toughest final examination as the twenty Trigonometry *students* in the new senior advanced class chuckled and snickered at the Promethean task I was undertaking.

It took me a mere twenty minutes to solve all of the formerly complicated mathematical riddles, and after spending an additional five minutes checking over the more difficult test items, I marched up to the teacher's desk and handed the pedagogue my exam' papers. Mr. Andrews appeared momentarily shocked by my new cocky confidence that I was proudly demonstrating.

The astonished Trig' teacher intensively scrutinized my paper, closely eyeballing every single answer with his mouth agape. Instinctively, I knew that I had gotten every problem correct, but the obstinate, disbelieving advanced math' instructor did not put any grade on my test paper. Instead, he scribbled his name on Mr. Sipley's letter and addressed his comment to Mr. Pinkerton, "Give this former *student* a final grade of C on his report card."

Andrews handed me his notation jotted on Mr. Sipley's courteous letter, which I carefully read with an element of

45

resentment. I looked the instructor straight in the eyes, and somehow, his former formidable dominance no longer intimidated me. I felt that I had grown into a man at *that* precise moment. I felt like viciously punching the inflexible martinet in the face, but I restrained myself from committing violence and thought, 'I'm gonna' attend *Glassboro State College* and become a teacher. Then I'll be able to help kids learn instead of trying to destroy their egos like some teacher I know!'

I accepted the *altered* letter, promptly brought it downstairs to the Main Office, and soon a polite secretary inserted a "C" for Trigonometry onto my report card and then expertly typed that grade onto my *Edgewood High* transcript.

I shook hands with Mr. Pinkerton, who like Mr. Andrews, seemed diminished in stature and in potency now that I had also escaped *his* jurisdiction. I departed the high school with that chapter of my adolescence finally being closed behind me. I imagined a happy future that would be devoid of annoying obstacles like Mr. Andrews and Mr. Pinkerton.

In retrospect, failure was a good experience for me. It provided me with determination to prove to Mr. Andrews that I could overcome the rigors associated with *his* most challenging subject. I believe that today's educators (including myself) are wrong when they pass undeserving *students* along and keep them rising on the academic escalator while simultaneously attempting to insulate lazy kids from the reality of failure. Thanks to Mr. Charles B. Sipley, I had gained the skills I needed to effectively show Mr. Andrews that I was tougher than *his* toughest Trigonometry test items.

Mr. Sipley was definitely an impact person who had entered my life at a most opportune time and had kindly rescued me from despair. It was because of my mentor's extraordinary example that I had vowed to become a public-school teacher and help others as he had so wonderfully assisted me. Mr. Charles B. Sipley extended to me hope once I was able to have faith in my ability. He salvaged my spirit at a time when I seriously doubted my own potential and my own self-worth.

I decided to wait a full year before matriculating into *Glassboro State Teachers College*. During the twelve-month interim, my father got me a job as a welder's apprentice at *his* winter place of employment, Martin and Quade Stainless Steel Fabricating Company in Norristown, Pennsylvania. I quickly realized that I needed a good education to learn a profession because I had no desire to breathe in factory welding fumes for the rest of my working life. And besides, I did not savor the long hour and fifteen-minute commute from Elm, NJ to Norristown PA every workday.

My assigned job at Martin and Quade was to operate a large seam-welding machine. Bulky sheets twenty-foot-long were mounted and then clamped upon *my* machine. The fabricating machine next folded each sheet into a circular tube ten inches in diameter. After polishing off the first batch of fifty stainless steel pipes, the plant inspector came to my workstation to examine the craftsmanship. He found many defects in the quality of the seams I had welded, and my first instinct was that I had not followed directions and that I would be immediately dismissed from real-life employment. Instead of rebuking my ineptness, the foreman told me that I had to seam-weld the tubes a second time, which I carefully did. Fortunately, my second production easily passed the scrutiny of quality control.

In the past, American *free enterprise* has always emphasized individual accountability, responsibility and productivity. It is beyond my comprehension as to why modern public schools do not demand similar performance characteristics from *students*. Instead, twenty-first century American education deviously uses the terms accountability, responsibility and productivity to describe the role of the teacher and not the function of the *student.*

Today's teachers are asked to experiment with innovative instructional methods and to *adjust* the curriculum to the needs of each *student*. Always, the teacher and the system must accommodate the *student* when the situation should be the opposite and reflect the way the real economic world operates. And if the *students* fail to learn, under the current system, it is now the teacher's fault for being ineffective. If a *student* fails to achieve a standard, the teacher is at fault and accountable and should be the one feeling guilt and shame. What a travesty modern education has evolved into since my invaluable learning experience (from failure) at *Edgewood High!*

When I was operating that seam-welding machine at Martin and Quade, the shop stewards didn't care how that activity was satisfying *my* emotional and psychological needs. All industry in the American economic system would suddenly collapse if the board of directors of all major corporations all at once decided that production should be geared to "meeting the emotional and psychological needs" of each worker and be adjusted to the needs of *each* employee.

In today's American public schools, the needs of each *student* vary considerably, and each *student's* specific needs cannot be accurately identified. To insist that the curriculum must be

47

transformed to accommodate each individual *student* is both a sham and a charade, especially when the competitive American free enterprise society that educators are preparing the *students* to enter functions in a completely different and more demanding dimension than the public schools do. The current "meet each *student's* needs" philosophy espoused by our U.S. public schools is counterproductive to the needs of *our* competitive American free enterprise, quality-control economic system.

Instead of adequately preparing kids for the rigors of the real-world job market, public schools are attempting to mold and create a false reality by making *the system* conform with the whimsical utopian fantasies geared to what liberal utopian, quixotic, college professors think the future American society should be. By teaching young people that happiness is paramount in human endeavor and should easily be experienced and achieved in any classroom activity, and by advocating that quality production, healthy competition and failure are secondary values of human enterprise, our schools are committing a grave injustice to the future.

The present educational philosophy is slowly eroding away the vital main cogs that hold together the industrial wheel of our great American free enterprise economy. Giving kids A's and B's for doing mediocre work and C's and D's for doing inferior work is analogous to Martin and Quade paying *me* for welding and producing non-usable stainless-steel tubes.

Mr. Andrews had performed a valuable favor by failing me, and Mr. Charles B. Sipley did me a much bigger favor by becoming my caring mentor. The Martin and Quade shop foreman helped my development by telling me that my job performance was unsatisfactory and then giving me a second chance to succeed. Those three men helped me emotionally grow and mature by being truthful about my deficient performance, and by making genuine demands and not providing false praise, the three individuals contributed to me becoming a stronger and wiser person.

Compare Mr. Andrews', Mr. Sipley's and the shop foreman's methods with those that are currently being practiced by teachers in American public-school classrooms, and you will quickly understand why American education is failing our civilization. Schools are dishonestly passing *students* that are under-performing. Thank you, Mr. Sipley, for showing me the light. Yes, forget the *self-esteem* that educational psychology keeps preaching! Overcoming failure is indeed an extremely valuable learning experience that constructively builds *self-confidence*.

Chapter 7
"The College Academic Experience"

I certainly had a cross section of diverse professor personalities during my four-year teacher college preparation. Some profs' were austere and pompous, others were liberal charlatans, and many of them were quite eccentric in his or her unique way. In retrospect, most of my college professors certainly didn't appear to be ordinary members of mainstream America.

After registering in the college's main building with its "majestic golden dome", I noticed that only the professors' last names had been provided on my weekly schedule, so unless one knew a particular instructor, the incoming freshman didn't know whether the teacher was a male or a female.

A good former high school friend of mine also attending the college had almost the same class schedule as I had. The first day of fall semester, I had inadvertently left my schedule home in the rush of excitement to drive my father's blue pickup truck twenty miles southwest to the picturesque college campus. Remarkably, I managed to remember the time and place of my first 8 a.m. class and waved to my friend Tim Amoro sitting on the opposite side of the classroom. After the dismissal bell for "The Fundamentals of School Organization," I met my friend and started-up a conversation.

"Where's the next class, Tim?" I asked. "I left my schedule at home on my bedroom desk."

"English," my hometown acquaintance answered.

I alertly remembered that English was *my* second class of the day, also. "Your schedule is almost identical to mine," I amiably stated, "so I'll just tag along if you don't mind."

After seating ourselves inside the crowded second period classroom, the professor took roll from his master list. I felt rather uneasy when I recognized that my name had not been called. I raised my hand after the distinguished, mustached professor asked, "Is everyone present and accounted for?"

"Are you Professor Sankin?" I innocently inquired. "I believe that my name was not called!"

The class then spontaneously broke out in raucous hysteria. The abashed male professor's thick eyebrows slanted-down at almost forty-five-degree angles, apparently expressing his displeasure with my innocent inquiry. "My good fellow," the chagrined sage began. "I certainly am not Professor Sankin. I am Professor Stevens. I happen to be a man the last time I checked myself in the mirror. Your Professor Sankin happens to be a member of the opposite gender. Since you are not supposed to be in this room," Professor Stevens rankled, "I strongly suggest that it would be in everybody's best interest if you proceed immediately to Room 217!"

Boisterous laughter could be discerned as Professor Stevens terminated his stern, deriding dissertation. I recall thinking at the time that I wished some faster mode of transportation would be available other than that provided by my two lower appendages. I frantically rushed out of Room 212 red-faced, slightly humiliated, and almost sweating real bullets.

I finally located Professor Sankin's class situated down the second-floor corridor, and unfortunately, my belated entrance had awkwardly interrupted her solemn lecture. The class remained hush as the austere, elderly woman tacitly surveyed the rude intruder's trespassing body from head to toe. The matronly, gray-haired lady motioned for me to occupy the last remaining desk, which was next to the window overlooking the scenic campus green.

Professor Sankin had the distinct habit of carefully enunciating every syllable of every word. The lady's small, oval-shaped mouth exposed her very active tongue continuously lubricating a *Lifesaver* wedged underneath it. The old dame had a warty face that would make any non-blind frog leap with terror. Her screechy voice was either shrill or squawky, depending on her articulation, and when Professor Sankin hit a high pitch, a clanging burglar alarm would have seemed more melodious and appealing to the ears.

While managing to get mostly B's and C's on Professor Sankin's labyrinth-length *objective* tests, I was baffled by the professor's harsh criticism of my writing style. The instructor *subjectively* described my compositions as being too "wordy" and too "flowery", with me using "too many adjectives and adverbs," and I was assured of a D or an F on every essay and theme that I submitted, no matter how meticulous their organization was.

'I know I have writing and language arts' talent,' I thought. 'Creative writing and journalism are my strong suits. Professor Sankin is trying to stifle my special aspiration to become an author. She's deliberately breaking my testicles in this Fundamentals of Communications, 101 class!' I concluded.

Professor Sankin's attacks on my themes were comparable to how the *U.S. Marine Corps* trains its prospective soldiers. First, the recruit's spirit is broken-down to demoralize his confidence, and then the novice is built-up according to accepted standards practiced by the harsh drill instructor. My creativity had to be sacrificed to allow for the rebuilding of my mastery of basic writing mechanics.

Coincidentally, the girls in the freshman English class were all receiving B's and C's on their compositions, while all of the frustrated male peons were *earning* D's and F's. In fact, it was the two freshman-year D's I had *earned* from Professor Sankin during my first and second semesters that compelled me to switch my college major from High School Teacher of English to Junior High School Teacher.

'Professor Sankin isn't the first teacher trying to destroy my future with her dumb, little dictatorial power game!' I stubbornly thought. 'Somehow I'm going to graduate from this place and defy both Mr. Andrews and Professor Sankin!'

In defense of my injured ego, I mentally thanked Miss Sankin for introducing me to the unwritten rules of *student* survival on the perilous college frontier:

1. Never challenge the professor (even though he or she insists that he or she likes it).

2. Be courteous (falsely if necessary) and nice to the professor (color your nose brown).

3. Pretend to thoroughly copy-down everything the sagacious professor utters (for he or she speaks an English dialect known as gospel).

4. Ask questions that compliment (not complement) the prof's basic knowledge. Don't make the professor think more than he or she actually wants to.

5. Avoid using the pronouns *I, me,* and *my* when asking a question (be humble and *subordinate* at all times).

In addition to the above educational commandments, I soon discovered that other secondary understandings would enable me to "play the game" and get better grades (while I consciously exploited the "*subjective* factor" in my teacher evaluation).

1. Work or study with other *students* in the class and always be cooperative (learn to kiss-up and flatter the teacher along with his or her favorite *students)*.

2. Buy the college outline series to the course (authored by the professor) at the campus bookstore and make sure the

professor observes you reading his or her companion book specifically geared to the course.

3. Cheat whenever necessary or when it is expedient.

During my freshman year, in keeping with a Human Behavior and Development course requirement, I was assigned to visit a nearby elementary school and thoroughly observe a "single unique *student*" (translation: discipline problem) and then diligently copy-down every disruptive thing he or she did in the sixth-grade class. Next, as a course requirement, I had to write a "Case Study" term paper on what I had noted and attempt to explain the *child's* aberrant behavior while proposing solutions demonstrating exactly how I would rectify the insolent misbehaviors if I were the targeted *child's* teacher. "Choose a candidate whose deportment slightly deviates from the norm!" our erudite professor lectured.

At the time, I believed that such a selection would add color and variety to my report and make it more intriguing to compile. It was really hard choosing a selected *student* since half the members of the raucous class demonstrated a definite affinity for naughtiness. Three times a week for an entire semester I watched fiendish *students* perform their repertoire of juvenile pranks and assiduously recorded the teacher's very apparent frustration for lack of an antidote to remedy the erratic, idiotic antics and semantics.

The *children* were showing-off to me by chewing gum, passing notes, being defiant to adult authority, engaging in name-calling, blaming each other for unruliness and squealing on one another instead of listening to the directions of the perplexed teacher. This was my first insight into classroom dynamics as an independent observer assessing the many adversities that seriously blight the modern American education process.

'Instead of we must understand the *child*,' I critically thought, 'the philosophy of education should be 'the *child* must understand'!' Teachers are the prey of merciless adolescent predators that are protected by law, the school system's philosophy and the society. The only defense the teacher has against young anarchists is "educational psychology", which in reality is as effective as trying to down a charging rhinoceros with an empty water pistol.

'Education should be based on what a *child* needs to know and not on what a *child's* needs are, which vary from kid to kid and are not specifically identified!' I logically concluded. 'Serious consequences should await the *child* that refuses to understand and respect adult authority in a school building.'

Gym class was probably my favorite freshman curricular college activity. Coach Holmes seemed to fancy me because my personality stood-out like a sore thumb, and my general lack of athletic coordination managed to always capture his keen attention. I usually showed-up during roll call arriving several minutes tardy from the locker room. In late September I had not yet obtained my brown and yellow college gym suit and instead wore my old *Edgewood High* green and white outfit to class. When I finally bought a brown and yellow gym uniform and wore it to class, Coach Holmes had my gym locker secretly opened, removed my green and white shirt and trunks and directed the class to leave the gym and assemble outside on an athletic field.

The imaginative coach ignited my high school uniform with a cigarette lighter, and the enthusiastic gym class began to chant in response to the ritual "Up in smoke! Up in smoke!" The other freshmen sounded as if they were members of a primitive jungle tribe worshiping and extolling the practice of arson. Their dissonant medley then transformed into an impromptu ceremonial dance, and the assembled fellows merrily hopped and skipped around my smoldering forest green *Edgewood High* gym apparel. Little incidents like the tribal dance, towel fights in the shower-room and the overall congenial looseness of Coach Holmes' informal gym class made it my favorite freshman curricular enterprise.

Looking back on my college preparation, I envision an asylum of wacky liberal and eccentric professors trying to rearrange my impressionable mind. Caustic Mr. Rolphs taught sociology and anthropology. The fellow was a restless, neurotic speaker who oscillated from one side of the classroom to the other as if he was a person with diarrhea seeking entry into an already-occupied lavatory stall. Professor Rolphs' speeches were saturated with vitriolic condemnations of traditional institutions and their continuous failure to solve the country's many domestic dilemmas. Rolphs made 'Blame America first" a common understanding forty years before the motto became popular on various radio talk shows.

Most of Professor Rolphs' lessons would envelop arguments questioning the existence of God, the limitations of our breast-oriented civilization, and the inadequacies of *our* evil, materialistic keeping-up-with-the-Jonses' disorganized culture. Rolphs and his exaggerated vituperations wouldn't last a marking period in the average American public school, but a liberal dissident endorsing a quasi-Communist/Marxist ideology could easily thrive on most college campuses and be regarded as a beneficial and a meritorious professor who promotes freedom of thought and freedom of speech.

I witnessed a half-dozen virtuous girls at various times storm-out of Rolphs' sociology class weeping after engaging in a bitter emotional debate with the professor over the virginity of Mary or the divine nature of Christ. Although Rolphs repetitiously indicated that his sole purpose was to stimulate constructive open-mindedness in "the marketplace of ideas", it was plainly obvious that his podium provided a convenient soapbox where the professor could perpetuate the doctrines of Marx, Engels, Lenin, Stalin and Rolphs.

I concluded in early 1962 that many frustrated thespians, actors and scriptwriters masqueraded as college professors under the false guise of deftly advancing "academic freedom". The liberal lecturers experimented with *their* uninspiring rhetoric and used it on their captive audiences, and as indicated in the case of Professor Rolphs, many professors thoroughly enjoyed playing the role of Devil's Advocate while probing the minds and eroding away the traditional values of their insulted and/or fascinated captive listeners.

As long as *academic freedom* is the benchmark of liberal arts college courses, professors feel quite comfortable incorporating *their* own radical liberal views and creeds into each lecture in order to challenge conventional (traditional) wisdom. And the majority of college *students* going through a rebellion against adult authority in their own personal lives find the bizarre and extraordinaire new forum approach refreshingly fascinating. The receptive learners associate *bizarre* and *extraordinaire* with freedom of speech and with individual expression guaranteed under the auspices of the *First Amendment* to the *Constitution*. Any blitzkrieg of traditional moral or religious values is categorized as "authentic intellectual investigation", and therefore, those professorial assaults are revered and tolerated by vulnerable *students*, while being condoned by colleges and universities and perpetuated by radical professors.

So, when someone like Professor Rolphs gets his or her jollies by blasting the maternal instincts of motherhood or the infallibility of the Pope, he or she is only performing his or her job description. The exposure to historically failed left-wing ideas will surely introduce *his* or her *students* to a vista of new perspectives that will undoubtedly widen their horizons and make the subjected recipients think and behave like avowed atheists and like loyal American Communists and Socialists.

Dr. Peaferm was a strange economics professor who appeared to be more interested in his private stock portfolio than in the balance of international trade, in the guns versus butter debate, in the perils of inflation or in the rising cost-of-living index. His drab, drowsy monotone (even during his most enthusiastic oral presentation) eventually sent the most avid *students* on one-way excursions to Slumberland. Dr. Peaferm's boring lecture method could never cut it in a public high school, but a fellow of his unremarkable caliber could easily flourish in a typical college classroom environment.

The highlight of Peaferm's economics seminar was a co-ed that Bob Abrams (a fraternity friend) had labeled and code-named Tokyo Rose. Bob and I would sit in Peaferm's crowded lecture hall and watch Tokyo Rose systematically squeeze the pus out of her facial and neck pimples. This daily ritual would make us revel because it added a new dimension to an otherwise very dull and dismal class.

In a way though, Dr. Peaferm's style was different and unique. Peaferm had no axes to grind or dragons to slay as Rolphs and Sankin truly had. Peaferm was more interested in *Standard and Poors* than he was in raising the standard of the poor by sharing the limited wealth and resources of the average middle-class American. Despite his nauseating mediocrity, Peaferm's monotonous course was ostensibly different in the sense that he wasn't riding a white charger looking for the *Holy Grail* or crusading for the downfall of selfish, greedy capitalism while simultaneously championing the noble pursuit of generously sharing the world's wealth.

And then there was Dr. Su, a petite Chinese lady who dressed in 1962 as if *WWI* was still in progress. Dr. Su's class was titled Teaching Methods I, but it would have been more appropriately named The Evils of Mao Tse-tung. Dr. Su spoke with a heavy Oriental accent, despised Red Chinese Communism with a passion, and she always mispronounced my last name Wiener (as in grilled hot dog) instead of Wiessner.

One day before class, a friend (during a moment of jocularity) scribbled on the front blackboard, "Do not erase-Dr. Wiener". Before I had a chance to exit my desk and remove the prosaic verse, Professor Su swiftly entered the room. She automatically grabbed an eraser and then momentarily hesitated as the petite woman somberly studied the message scrawled upon the black slate. She then innocently prattled, "Ah so, class! Dr. Wiener say I should not erase board, so I just lecture today and not write notes with chalk for you to copy." The class slipped into a minor state of pandemonium in response to her shallow perception and reaction to my good friend's juvenile prank.

On another occasion, I had cut Dr. Su's class to engage in an impromptu softball game on the baseball diamond adjacent to her corner second-floor classroom. Dr. Su stepped to the back of the room to open a window and observed me gallivanting on the baseball field below. "Wiener!" she imperatively bellowed. "You come up here this instant to my class!"

Although I had distinctly heard her piercing soprano voice, I ignored the diminutive lady professor's command, pretending not to hear the oral dictum. Dr. Su re-evaluated her impetuosity and exclaimed to the already hysterical class, "Maybe that isn't Wiener down there after all!" A thunderous burst of laughter blared-down to the baseball field from the upstairs corner classroom window.

Dr. Attleburg taught the subject of Mental Health and had a gruff looking square face that qualified her to enter and win any ferocious dog show as a female pit bull. The professor's wrinkled countenance was a portrait of emotional anguish, and her tainted breath exuded an odor akin to a dried-up Manhattan. The instructor's anomalous lectures sounded very much like humdrum epistles originating from the lips of a peevish tavern patron about to fall off of her barstool.

Dayton, a black *student* in Dr. Attleburg's nondescript seminar, sat in the fifth seat in the row to my right, next to the sidewall. Dayton worked nights on the back of a garbage truck, was extremely fatigued during the daylight hours, and would always lean his body against the wall and fall asleep during the climax of Dr. Attleburg's uninspiring dissertation. The lady professor was elaborating about the need for love, forgiveness and sympathy in *our* interpersonal relationships as if she was giving a guilt-laden testament at an Alcoholics Anonymous meeting. Feeling depressed, I then quite mischievously removed and opened a safety pin from my pocket and next quite methodically pierced Dayton's pants and leg with it.

Dayton howled as his reflexive reaction to instant pain sent both him and his desk crashing onto the polished wooden floor. Dr. Attleburg continued her lazy lecture as if nothing at all extraordinary had occurred. I wondered how such a numb person could be an authority on the manifold operations of the human mind after she had been completely oblivious to stark reality. But people of her ilk thrive in education, especially at the college level. They draw *lush* salaries and help pollute the educational canal by grotesquely supporting the advancement of non-learning.

Dr. Attleburg's favorite maxim was, "There's a rather big difference between teaching thirty years and teaching one year thirty times!" The most lamentable aspect of her impious oratory was that

Dr. Attleburg had been uttering the impressive proverb ever since her initial year of professoring.

Speech with Dr. Lane was another class I had to attend. On the first meeting of the September session of my junior year, I sedately sat in my desk awaiting the instructor's arrival. An older gentleman who I had presumed was also pursuing a teaching degree sat next to me. The self-proclaimed *Korean War* veteran initiated a cordial conversation. I soon discovered that he was very critical of the speech professor who was designated to teach *our* course. The elderly man used the terms "lousy" and "hideous" in his negative depiction of Dr. Lane.

I explained that I hardly knew anything about Dr. Lane except that the speech teacher's unorthodox behavior was rumored being "a bit on the eccentric side". Five minutes elapsed and then the distinguished-looking *Korean War* veteran sitting next to me arose and announced to the class that *he* was the inimitable Dr. Lane.

On the class's second session, Dr. Lane made what he considered to be "a spectacular entrance". The nutcase had scaled the tall oak tree that had grown parallel to the main campus building, crawled out onto a sturdy limb and then clumsily swung his slender frame inside an opened second floor window.

Dr, Lane's interpretation of the meaning of the word *creativity* was doing something excessively peculiar or something unexpectedly sensational. His mannerisms were predictably unpredictable, and one could only expect the unexpected from him. However, even climbing through opened second floor windows, standing, gesticulating and lecturing from atop the teacher's desk, and then boisterously shouting slanderous obscenities for no apparent reason at all soon became tedious and unimpressive after I became accustomed to their constant enactments.

Professor Flank taught History and Issues in United States Government. His lectures were as dull as an eight-inch-thick razor blade. Flank reveled in discussing American social disorganization, world chaos and the general frailness of the culturally retarded human species. Somehow, his Marxist "blame America first" quips always seemed devoid of integrity, sincerity, honor and courage.

One winter day, while delivering a vitriolic critique on American imperialistic military/economic institutions, Dr. Flank's nose began bleeding. Feeling the slight trickle escaping from his nostrils, the hypercritical professor dabbed his nose with a handkerchief, but the flow of scarlet became even more profuse.

Flank glanced down in horror at the quantity of blood accumulated inside his handkerchief, and feeling exceedingly frightened and embarrassed, the sophist's normally florid face turned as white as a lily. The distressed professor swiftly canceled the remainder of the pathetic lesson, dismissed the class and hastily departed the scene looking as if he was a wounded infantryman searching for the services of the nearest Florence Nightingale.

Professor O'Connor was a very outspoken leftist that thought his essential destiny in life was to expose the myriad faults and insidious weaknesses of our corrupt American socio/economic structure. The intellectual establishment (college deans) regarded O'Connor's attacks on U.S. institutions as productive and scholarly just as long as the axe-to-grind crusader lectured his way through issues like American racial prejudice and evil U.S. capitalistic exploitation both at home and abroad.

But dye-in-the-wool Professor O'Connor began skating on thin ice when *his* pseudo-intellectual investigations revealed instances of perverse homosexuality among other notable members of the college faculty. Although he was one of the *students'* favorite professors, O'Connor soon became the object of detestation of his envenomed influential colleagues on the faculty. In an incredibly short time, Professor O'Connor earned the disfavor of the college administration that suddenly abhorred *his* inquiries into his fellow instructors' bedroom habits rather than focusing his channeled attention upon what was wickedly wrong with America.

O'Connor's bold muckraking and whistle-blowing activities drew area newspaper attention to the local college campus, thus casting a dusky pall that immediately eclipsed all of the favorable publicity that the school's deans so sanctimoniously had labored to build. O' Connor's flirtations with attempting to right all wrongs (including social injustices and sexual perversions) became an uncontrollable obsession that eventually led to his demise, and the maverick professor did not heed the admonitions of the school's executives about what was deemed inappropriate on the college campus.

Professor O'Connor could best be described as a combination of Upton Sinclair and *Don Quixote,* and he appeared quite oblivious to the hatchet of doom being held over his self-righteous head. His determination to identify and expose all evil ruined his career. O'Connor was denied tenure, not because of his incompetence but because his mouth had oracled bad publicity about the school.

It was perfectly all right for O'Connor to subvert and indict the *United States of America*, but when he made it too personal by demonizing the college's good reputation, then he was abruptly dismissed from educational service. The prestigious image of the academic institution was much more important than the necessary criticisms prolifically directed at immoral America.

Professor McIntire was an English prof' and an acknowledged expert on William Shakespeare's work and life. McIntire relished several of my literary contributions that appeared in the campus newspaper and in the school's literary magazine. The strange fellow was a jolly sort of man who seemed to be knowledgeable and conversant in almost every subject. McIntire was rumored to be a "gay instructor", and to listen to his unique speech patterns, which featured a distinct effeminate twinge, I had good reason to place credence in the abundant hearsay. On one occasion inside the *Student Union*, Dr. McIntire politely invited me over to his abode for cocktails to discuss the element of *romance* existing in Elizabethan British Literature, but I took a rain check when the pedagogue intimated that only the two of us would be "romanticizing" at the proposed intellectual symposium.

In all fairness to my college education, I had several dozen other dedicated professors that contributed positively to my professional development. To them and their selfless dedication, I will be eternally grateful. But the professors I have just described somehow seem to stand-out in my mind for several very obvious reasons. The most discernible one is that instructors of their deleterious kind prolifically populate every college and university faculty in America.

Chapter 8
"College Cheating"

I was shocked my freshman year to find that cheating was quite rampant in college classrooms. It manifests itself in the re-copying of another *student's* homework, in reproducing term papers written on other college campuses, in having theses or term papers ghost written for you, or in simply "borrowing" answers to objective questions while taking a professor's difficult exam'.

Soft and unassuming proctoring of college tests only encourages lethargic-but-alert *students* to cheat. The *student* is practical and rationalizes that the final grade (no matter how it is acquired) counts much more than the mostly irrelevant knowledge and facts gained in a course. The professor might have certain biases against *students* for being smart, for being handsome, for being too inquisitive, for being black, for being popular or for just being a male or a female. "Cheating is not dishonorable," I recollect another *student* matter-of-factly telling me. "It is merely a means to an end, the end being a satisfactory grade and ultimately, a decent paying job after graduating from this hellhole!"

That *student's* explanation of and justification for cheating exemplifies the ugly transformation occurring within our great American society. The culture is undergoing a steady transition from *absolute* moral values to *relative* moral values. Things are not right or wrong anymore, and an arbitrary eighty-percent gray area existing in between has been deftly created by lawyers, by television commentators and by ultra-liberal college professors, many of whom often cowardly turn *their* feckless academic backs on *students'* blatant cheating within their midst. Cheating is now understood by *students* as acceptable if the misdemeanor can be justified in terms of the individual's emotional and/or future career *needs* along with his or her "pursuit of happiness" as specifically defined in the *Declaration of Independence.*

I didn't engage in college cheating until my junior year, but I quite vividly remember my freshman philosophy final exam' given in the college's main cafeteria. A hundred and fifty freshman philosophy *students* had been massed together like a gaggle of rambunctious geese. The professor's examination was really tough, but I managed to stumble through the hundred and fifty objective items based on three nights of dire cramming.

Whispering questions and low-spoken answers sallied back and forth among anxious *students* seated at my table as if test multiple-choice prompts were bullets ricocheting off walls at the *OK Corral*. "Kant," "Nietzsche," "a priori," "Plato" and at least a hundred other correct responses were lowly and liberally verbalized by seven other *students* seated around me.

Some of the "A, B, C, D and None of the Above" objective answers swishing by conflicted with ones I had circled on *my* exam', and although I soon recognized that my selections were incorrect, I gallantly refused to alter them under my own personal honor code. While the massive cheating disgrace was evolving, the lax philosophy professor was casually analyzing the obituary, sports, *Metro* and editorial pages of the *Philadelphia Inquirer*.

I soon wised-up to the grim reality of cheating. The seven *students* that were doing it at my table received A's and B's for final philosophy grades, while I emerged with a lowly C for being naively honest on the final exam'. 'Four more correct answers and I would have gotten a B on the exam', and a B instead of a C for the challenging course's final grade,' I remember thinking.

And now, later on in life, most of the indulgent freshmen that had unethically exchanged answers on that philosophy exam' are prestigious college professors, department supervisors and eminent school principals and superintendents. All of that had happened since 1962 while currently, I still remain a lowly English teacher.

On one inglorious occasion during my junior year, I did find it necessary to engage in the immorality of cheating. It was during the end of the first semester, and my section was cursed with the whammy of having Professor Trenoff as our demanding instructor. He was a short fellow that wore horn-rimmed glasses, had an enormous Napoleon Complex and was truly very sensitive about his diminutive stature. The guy's unappreciative Ed. Psych *students* non-affectionately and secretly called him "the mole".

Dr. Trenoff was undoubtedly an authoritarian dictator. The academic despot demanded the class's attention, and he seemed to exude animosity toward any male standing over five-feet-six inches in height. When walking past Trenoff in the classroom, I would deliberately slink-down so as not to accentuate my lankier altitude.

One day a *student* with sincere intentions attempted to record Professor Trenoff's "Educational Psychology in the Junior High School" lecture on a concealed tape recorder. Upon discovering the hidden device, the short, paranoid instructor became rather furious, grabbed the recording device and then confiscated the attached microphone. The *mad professor* scolded the petrified *student* for not asking expressed permission to tape *his* profound utterances. The most horrifying feature of the entire comedy episode was that the title of Professor Trenoff's course had the fabulous words *Educational Psychology* in it.

Trenoff had more hang-ups than the corner dry cleaners, and yet he was teaching required courses like" Educational Psychology in the Junior High School". He and his lecture method wouldn't last a marking period in the average American middle school or junior high. The notorious "Peter Principle" is more evident on the college level than anywhere else in the American educational spectrum.

Besides the professor's extremely repulsive, affronting disposition, Dr. Trenoff prided himself' on preparing and giving his prodigies incomprehensible exams. His true or false questions were lengthy, arbitrary and nebulous, and the tyrant's multiple-choice items were bewildering in their seemingly contradictory content. Guessing often came nearer to the desired answers than logic did.

The bulk of the class came into the final exam' with D and F averages. It was imperative for the course to be passed, or it would have to be made-up during the summer session, and only Dr. Trenoff taught Educational "Psychology in the Junior High School" during the summer session.

Dr. Trenoff often attempted to exude his tremendous cleverness, and I recall him haughtily addressing the class, "I have heard a rumor circulating around the campus that several of you are conspiring to steal my final examination. Well," the Professor contemptuously continued his narrative, "I have good news for you potential felons. I have the exam' hidden in a safe inside my home, and confidentially, only I, along with my devoted wife, know the secret combination."

As Dr. Trenoff arrogantly spoke, I detected twenty-five other *students'* larynxes swiveling up and down as if they were hyperactive yo-yos. While Trenoff was making his intimidating and caustic remarks, one prominent thought dominated my mind. 'Trenoff is unfair and his exams' are unfair,' I concluded. 'Why should I be victimized by those two inherent evils?' Attila the Hun in all his wicked ferocity was probably more ethical and compassionate than either Dr. Trenoff or his diabolical tests were.

I still recollect the intense sensation I had felt on a frigid Wednesday night in January. Patches of ice dotted the frozen ground near the main campus lecture building. Bob Abrams (who is now an esteemed high school superintendent) and I surreptitiously used an unlocked janitor's door to enter the campus's main building. No *students* were allowed inside after 10 p.m., so our encroachment was a reprehensible breach of sacred school regulations.

Bob and I stealthily slinked and rambled from corridor to corridor to evade night custodians and watchmen as if we were characters acting in a B mystery movie. Abrams and I couldn't have been better prepared to execute our heist if we were both honor *students* at the Jolly Roger Thief Academy.

Bob and I both wore rubber-soled tennis shoes, black trousers, shirts and jackets, and we carried a collection of useful tools to aid us in our stealthy commando mission. One of Bob's acquaintances had been a school janitor that had consented to letting him borrow the master office key as a favor returned. Abrams had duplicated the key at a local hardware store and then returned the original to the cooperative custodian. With a metallic click, the office suite's lock was successfully turned.

Bob had furtively visited Dr. Trenoff's office the day before, so he had a good idea of where everything was situated. Even though Trenoff had claimed the exam' was hidden in a safe at home, Bob thought that there might be a remote chance of acquiring it (or part of it) inside the professor's sacred office. "Some professors are absent-minded," my fraternity friend confided, "and Trenoff is so clever that he might've unconsciously outwitted himself somewhere along the line!"

The best we had hoped for was that a few useful notes relating to the final exam' might be found inside a desk drawer, or possibly discarded in a metal trashcan. Two things were certain on that cold, dark January evening: Abrams and I were both desperate and in danger of failing the despicable professor's course, and neither of us knew what the hell we were doing masquerading as thieves searching for a long-shot lucky discovery. Bob methodically closed the squeaky door behind us, and then we melodramatically turned on the beams to our trusty flashlights. Our eyes hurriedly scanned the cluttered receptionist's desk inside the office suite.

Dr. Trenoff's partitioned cubicle was located directly behind the first series of offices. We clambered-up the flimsy barrier and adroitly crawled without lit flashlights along the narrow dividing ledge separating the Psychology Department from the Educational Curriculum Department. That was the only time I remember praising thrift in education, for the offices were "open-spaced" without any expensive acoustical tile ceiling hindering our mobility.

Abrams and I finally reached Trenoff's personal enclosure, and when Bob made his descent, his foot banged into a metal waste can that rattled and then thudded upon the floor. Sweat beads clustered on my forehead when a beam of light refracted through a glass door and into Trenoff's office. I felt as if I was a San Quentin fugitive on the lam suddenly caught in a police dragnet. 'This is it! Expulsion!' I frightfully conjectured. We both instinctively tightly held our now-closed flashlights in the dark.

The night guard entered the office suite and paced down the narrow hallway. The wary watchman then turned the still-locked doorknob to Trenoff's office. Apparently satisfied with his perusal of the quiet area, the night guard redirected his flashlight beam and then ambled his way back to the receptionist/secretary's desk, and much to *our* relief, exited the suite of offices.

"That was too close for comfort," Abrams nervously whispered. "I think I crapped my dungarees!"

"It was too close for *me* too!" I neurotically replied before inhaling another deep breath.

Bob and I exhaled sighs of relief as if we both had been spared from being exterminated in an atomic explosion. We then proceeded with enacting our covert *CIA*-type operation. Bob turned-on his flashlight again, and I cautiously imitated his stellar example. Absolute astonishment immediately overcame our very-real anxiety.

Dr. Trenoff's final exam's master key was neatly sitting there upon his cluttered desk, right before our very eyes. "Look!" Bob gasped in an amazed low voice. "The holes for the A, B, C, D and None of the Above correct answers and also for the corresponding True and False questions are punctured on this master grading sheet!"

"Maybe Trenoff is trying to outsmart us and set us up!" I skeptically answered. "Maybe this is a dummy answer sheet designed to trick us into cheating and foolishly putting-down the wrong answers! It might be a treacherous trap!"

"Then Trenoff could not only fail us but also have our asses booted out of college!" Bob worriedly observed and exclaimed. "We might even have to face criminal charges for breaking and entering into his office and stealing the wrong answers to an exam'! Then I'll never have the chance of becoming a high school superintendent!" my ambitious friend gasped.

After exchanging those fearful speculations, Bob and I copied-down on a sheet of notebook paper the punched answers on the master key, and then we meticulously placed the pencils, papers and master answer key back into their original positions on Trenoff's dusty desk. We then surreptitiously executed our careful departure from the dark office suite and next, from the main campus building with the utmost dispatch.

"Do you have all the answers copied-down on the notebook paper sheet?" I neurotically asked in a slightly squeaky voice.

"Yeah, let's get out of here in a jiffy!" Bob answered. 'Let's hope we scored a touchdown!"

Two days later, the class assembled in Dr. Trenoff's musky room to suffer taking *his* final exam'. Blood was surging through my neck's veins and arteries as the despotic pedagogue distributed his awesome final evaluation, which happened to be ten pages in length.

Bob and I had devised an ingenious cheating method; that is to say, if the loathsome Dr. Trenoff was administering the same test that precisely corresponded with *our* illegally obtained answers. On our Number 2 pencils, Abrams and I had made a series of vertical craters on each side representing "True and False, A, B, C, D and None of the Above Multiple Choice" answers specifically for the two major test sections. The correct responses to the entire exam' could be easily surveyed by rotating the yellow pencil in a clockwise direction. 'I hope Trenoff doesn't make us use *his* own Number 2 pencils and not *our* own!' I feared as my heart savagely pounded inside my chest.

As I initially skimmed through selected items appearing upon the comprehensive psychology exam', I identified several problems to which I knew the proper answers. The test items appeared to harmonize perfectly with the punctured pores that had been pierced on my yellow Number 2 writing utensil. I winked over at Bob, who then returned my tacit signal. 'How could any professor be so shrewd and yet so stupid?' I nervously mused.

True, dear old Dr. Trenoff had probably avariciously hauled the physical exams' home and then slyly stashed his intellectual cache in his airtight safe. But despite all his precaution, the wily professor neglectfully forgot his all-important answer key upon his office desk. 'Bob and I didn't even have to go through the travail of researching the answers as we would have had to do if we had pilfered the actual exam'!' I confidently imagined as I triumphantly finished the lengthy examination.

The ever-alert Dr. Trenoff smelled something rotten in Denmark, but his senses of perception and suspicion were leading him in the opposite direction of Copenhagen. His internal compass was out of whack, but the obnoxious instructor couldn't detect exactly what was wrong or what was transpiring.

Cheating for Bob Abrams (who later in life did indeed become a distinguished school district superintendent) and my other *Lambda Phi Sigma* fraternity brothers was a lot easier and less risky during our senior year. The fraternity members had become friendly with several attractive fair damsels employed in the college's copying machine rooms, and through our important contacts, *we* had immediate access to any test or exam' issued by any professor.

From my own personal experience, when I finally became a teacher, I was able to easily recognize the telltale signs of cheating and the overt behaviors that cheaters exhibit. Unfortunately, when public school teachers are too observant and too vigilant, they do catch *students* in the act of illicitly obtaining answers. This detection often leads to other more severe problems when *students* deny that they had been cheating. It then becomes the teacher's accusation against *their* lying, and when loyal parents come to the defense of their guilty offspring, matters become even more complicated. Other *students* then come to the defense of their unexpectedly caught friend and falsely testify to the principal that "so and so" was not cheating and that there is a definite personality conflict between Mr. Wiessner and the accused violator.

I have known teachers that have spent hours documenting and justifying to principals and to parents exactly what they had observed in terms of a *student* cheating, and quite frankly, who needs that sort of time-consuming hassle? It's a lot easier to not rock the boat and to ignore what you can't prove because of the matter then becoming your honorable word against a *student* and his or her friends' assertions. Been there! Done that! And truthfully, I never want to endure it again!

Chapter 9
"Becoming a Teacher"

I must confess, my freshman and sophomore college years were devoted to social and fraternity concerns and not strictly to academic pursuits. I was satisfied with mediocre grades and a steady stream of warning letters, which I intercepted at my parents' home mailbox. In my junior year I became more ambitious about my professional preparation and subsequently my grades improved appreciably.

"Our freshman class had over a thousand students," I related to Bob Abrams in the middle of our third year, "but now as juniors we're, down to less than five hundred."

"That's right," Bob concurred. "That's how colleges make their money. They know that eighteen-year-olds come here to drink beer and to party. Remember those crowded freshman lecture halls?" Bob reminded me. "Some of them had a hundred and fifty kids. Now as juniors, each of our classes has only around twenty-five *students*."

"That's right on the money," I admitted. "The deans know that over half the kids are gonna' drop out during or after freshman year. It's simply a sorting game, and we're lucky enough to have survived the elimination axe."

One unfortunate aspect of teacher college training was that the candidate did not get the opportunity to stand in front of a public-school class of vigilantes until his or her junior year. Some of my best friends had invested two years of their time studying in the teachers' program before they realized it was not meant for them.

During my junior year, I had *Practicum*, where I made classroom observations of *students* and lessons at a nearby South Jersey Junior-Senior High School. I also worked on classroom and hall bulletin boards and assisted the instructor with correcting tests and compositions and then recording the grades. The last five weeks of the three-month intensive course introduced me to the art and science of teaching eighth-graders.

I'll never forget my first lesson. I had as my audience twenty-five fourteen-year-old *students,* and I was rather nervous because my college coordinator would be present in the back of the room to witness and record my educational debut. I monitored the hall traffic during the change of classes from homeroom to first period.

I then greeted the *students* as the teens entered the room, and I was all pumped-up about teaching the kids about helping verbs, verb phrases, about direct and indirect objects following action verbs, and about the subtle distinctions between predicate nominatives and predicate adjectives following linking verbs. After the late bell rang, I confidently entered the classroom and then formally introduced myself to the class.

When I turned my back to neatly print my name on the chalkboard, I discerned a loud thud and immediately spun around. A desk had been knocked over and two free-swinging fourteen-year-old gladiators were pulverizing one another, their bodies rolling around on the tiled floor. Honestly, I was momentarily dumbfounded by the unanticipated chaos. I glanced to the back of the room at my college professor, and he was still seated inside his desk feverishly taking notes on the battle that was transpiring in *our* midst. I had to intervene in the brawl quickly or else risk a bad *lesson evaluation*.

I hastily moved to the center of the classroom and jumped between the two aggressive combatants, both of whom were now standing and still showing plenty of energy. My dignified appearance in *their* presence was greeted with a stiff right-cross punch to my jaw and an errant swift kick to my groin. I finally managed to separate the two adversaries using superior brute force and then reported the altercation to the main office over the intercom.

I then intelligently sent each *student* pugilist down to the vice-principal's office three minutes apart. I glanced again to the back of the room and my impressed college professor was still preoccupied jotting-down notes. It was then that I first realized that college coordinators and school administrators want teachers to break-up fights and had no desire to be involved as either a boxing or a wrestling referee during the classroom crisis.

So, after regaining my composure, I painfully taught my first official lesson to the class, which required another ten minutes to finally settle-down. Throughout the entire grammar exercise, my jaw, groin and right knee throbbed with excruciating pain, and I felt as if I was a wounded war casualty. At the end of the class period, my college supervisor commended me on effectively stopping the fight and stated that the overall content and development of my first lesson generally was satisfactory.

After a full week of instruction, I also soon realized that I could not lecture fourteen-year-olds for forty-five minutes and expect them to stay even-remotely mentally focused. If I imitated the *lecture* teaching method of my college professors, my career would have been doomed to failure from the outset.

I quickly adopted the teaching style of discussing and introducing the general lesson the first ten minutes of class. Next, I would amble around the room and help the pupils with their related textbook exercises (or accompanying worksheets) for the following twenty-five minutes and then assign homework and assist with the extended learning activity the last ten minutes of class. This teaching model was supplemented with assigned student oral reports, lively panel discussions, black board drills and library research activities.

"*We* want to teach kids to be independent," my college coordinator related during a scheduled evaluation conference. "Remember that each *student* is an individual and that the teacher is principally responsible for *learning*," he preached without a pulpit. "It is both the teacher's function and obligation to motivate the *students* to want to learn more about a particular subject."

I had always believed that *a student* was "a young person that *studies"*. I kept mum during the discussion with my supervisor but was thinking to myself that some *students* had no desire to learn, were *not* self-motivated, and they didn't want to be in school in the first place. Some kids only came into the building to keep warm and to eat snacks and junk food in the cafeteria.

But the philosophy of education maintained that the teacher was responsible for both *teaching* and *learning*. In fact, the teacher is not only responsible for *students'* academic progress but also for their sociological growth. As this self-defeating trend continues from the mid-1960s up to the present, *students* acquire more *rights* and enjoy the *privilege* of being less responsible, and conversely, the teachers have more accumulative responsibilities and less authority exercised within the school superstructure.

When teachers are reminded by college professors, administrators and supervisors to *motivate students*, those *tellers* really mean some kids don't give a hang about learning academics and will show a pronounced propensity for destroying and opposing most constructive activities that the teacher attempts employing. By telling teachers to find things in the curriculum that kids can do, administrators and college professors are propagating a gross fraud upon the teacher and also a gross injustice to the American public. This practice is similar to ordering a Congressman from an urban ghetto district to rectify all of the social vices that contaminate his constituency. Ascending *Mt. Everest* in a wheelchair would be an easier task than achieving learning in the curriculum by *motivating students* that lack individual incentive. Until teachers use natural motivations such as rock and roll and rap music, dating, hot cars, sexy videos and R-rated movies to motivate *students* with *their* age-level interests, education, teachers and schools will be harnessed to their present status quo performance.

As a junior *Practicum student,* I watched a foremost college professor being interviewed on my parents' black and white television. The news commentator innocently asked, "I guess in this modern age, effective teachers have to know more than they did twenty years ago?"

The lofty educational guru replied, "We're getting away from the idea that a teacher must be a know-it-all encyclopedia of knowledge. Instead," the contemporary wise academic shaman continued, "teachers are now the facilitators in a classroom and dynamically make learning happen. Today, subject matter is not quite as important as how *students* research and acquire information is."

'Yeah,' I thought. 'You just try to tell *that* rather suspect, controversial jargon to either Dr. Trenoff or to Professor Sankin!'

Most problems in education boil-down to the simple fact that many *students* (probably around twenty-thirty percent) are not self-motivated to learn. That same twenty-thirty percent segment causes daily havoc in public-schools all across America. Their parents indulge them, entitle them and defend them to the hilt, but mom and dad have been negligent in instilling the proper attitudes for respecting teacher authority and for valuing and learning academics. And the college professors and the school administrators put the onus on the teachers' backs to reverse this social turmoil created by this insolent, non-productive twenty percent riffraff, who by virtue of peer pressure, cause other normally good kids to mimic *their* rebellious rudeness.

The society's unreasonable expectation of teachers in America is education's great unreachable star. If derelict parents were doing their adult responsibility, then schools would not have to provide physical education and free lunches. If parents were doing their jobs, schools would not have to teach driver education, home economics, family living and sex education. What ever happened to the importance of core curriculum academics? They've been relegated in status in deference to sociological education as school responsibility for learning increases and as parental guidance (and broken families) decreases. And the beasts of burden that must tote the extra heavy load and achieve the impossible are the donkeys the public calls "overpaid teachers".

My college idealism quickly disintegrated during my first real exposure to teaching in a public school. I soon became aware that many *students* in eighth grade couldn't read on a fourth-grade level, but still I had to provide textbooks written on an eighth-grade level to endeavor relating to fourteen-year-olds possessing fourth grade reading and writing proficiency skills.

I soon understood that teachers weren't exclusively to blame for the faults of American education. The system allows *students* to be rewarded and passed along to the next level without them demonstrating either motivation or achievement. Sociology now governs American public schools and not academics, and the good *students* are thrown into the stew and only really excel when they are fortunately collated into advanced placement college prep' courses with the twenty-thirty percent riff-raff being filtered out.

My senior year placed a degree of stress on my mind. I had to raise my cumulative average to a respectable high B level. I felt compelled to get a good grade in *Student Teaching*, and I was under a good deal of pressure from my parents to secure a teaching position and finally become a productive member of society.

My *Student Teaching* stint was very unique when contrasted to my Junior/Senior High School junior year *Practicum*. I was assigned to a small rural country schoolhouse, which was a throwback to the early 1900s. I had a class of twenty-four pupils, but one-third of them were sixth graders, a third were seventh graders, and the remaining eight were hormone-wired eighth graders. My cooperating teacher was rather old-fashioned and was on the last leg of a lengthy teaching career. Her ultra-strict teaching style seemed as archaic as cuneiform writing, and the old dame's appearance would have qualified her to pose for a Matthew Brady *Civil War* photograph. Mrs. Miller was not the easiest person to get along with, and she ruled her classroom domain with martinet austerity.

Mrs. Miller was quite reluctant to turn the reins over to me, and she nearly fell out of her girdle when one day I gave the class a short health lecture on the increasing widespread use of marijuana among teenagers and its inherent dangers. After that trauma, Mrs. Miller made certain that my every lesson was under her doubting authoritarian surveillance. She did not want her clan of backwoods angels corrupted by some wet-behind-the-ears college *student* exploring subject matter of debatable, ethical propriety.

Whenever my college coordinator would arrive to observe and evaluate a lesson, the two dozen kids would try their hardest to be attentive and receptive. The class and I had devised our special internal communications system, especially to be utilized when my college mentor Dr. Ash came to assess my performance. When *students* in the class knew the correct answer, they would raise their left hands, and if they didn't know the correct response, then they would raise their right arms.

My college coordinator believed I was doing a tremendous job because all of the *students* had their hands up all of the time. My questions asked were eliciting fantastic and amazing right answers. "You appear to be quite effective, and your enthusiasm has definitely *motivated* the students," Dr. Ash complimented and attested. "But you should try to promote inductive thinking rather than deductive thinking. Try to get your *students* to think divergently rather than answering questions that elicit and engender simple convergent thinking and particular factual responses."

Of course, Dr. Ash's suggestion was diametrically opposed to Mrs. Miller's old-fashioned teaching strategy, so if I employed the professor's recommendation, then I was destined to get a C or less from Mrs. Miller as her part of *my* final grade. I luckily completed *Student Teaching* with the grade of B, which was mutually agreed upon by Mrs. Miller and Dr. Ash. I found some consolation in Dr. Ash's testament, "The best public-school teachers were B and C *students* when they had attended college. Eggheads with A averages usually don't relate their stilted lingo too well to public school kids!" Dr. Ash claimed. "B and C students tend to have more balanced personalities than an A average college *student* does!"

Looking for my first teaching position in April of '65, I traveled the length and breadth of New Jersey while maintaining a tedious agenda of interviews with building principals and school superintendents. I learned several important rules very quickly during those intensive conferences. I was expected to act humble and not be too aggressive, opinionated or knowledgeable. Otherwise, I would be regarded as immature and dangerous to the status quo, artificial tranquility that superintendents and administrators get paid to guard and preserve. I learned to allow the *super* to control the tempo of the discussion and that the receptive interviewee should show a sense of desperation by maturely communicating to the interviewer that *he* needs the position to satisfy enormous debts that the expense of his college education had accumulated.

School executives generally like feeling they have *their* staff over a barrel and that the coveted job *you* maintain is your sole lifeline to economic survival in this cruel and merciless world. Job security (notice I deliberately abstained from stating *professional* security) has for the last century been an effective way for administrators to keep teachers herded together like cattle in *their* dependent, educational corrals. If a non-tenure teacher exhibits too much independence, then an administrator could easily exercise his or her prerogative and pull the iron lung's electric cord out of the wall socket. A non-tenure teacher can easily be terminated, and a tenure teacher can easily be manipulated and harassed.

Coercion is a pressure especially felt by non-tenure teachers. Fear of job jeopardy is not verbally conveyed by administrators, but it is implicit and felt in most relationships between beginning teachers and their employers. Vertical downward pressure can be very easily applied by school executives that are perched atop the local educational pyramid. Only the educational sultans are entitled to prestige, to elite status and to public kudos in this demented massive bureaucracy. Remember the aphorism, "Rank has its privileges!"

The job interviewing routines I encountered lacked both scientific and consistent application. Each of the dozen school executives that interviewed me pursued different subjects and distinct personal interests. One superintendent became enraptured reviewing his *World War II* exploits, and another *super* conversed extensively on his fondness for shrubbery and for gardening. The dialogues always meandered from the areas of educational substance and the intended center of gravity.

'This process would be much more professional if superintendents would get together and devise a list of fifty questions to ask teacher candidates,' I speculated. Instead, the interviews degenerated into tavern conversation tangents without accompanying mugs of beer. After twelve lengthy interviews, I felt as if I had been on the late-night TV talk show circuit rather than traveling the state of New Jersey as a prospective teacher seeking *professional* employment.

I finally received a "Position Offering" in the mail, but it had come from *Edgewood Junior/Senior High School*, which needed a seventh-grade Social Studies/English teacher. "I don't really want to teach on the same faculty as Mr. Andrews who had failed me in Trigonometry!" I told my disappointed parents. "I'll wait a week or so before I respond to the superintendent."

Even though I was nearly hitting the panic button, I judiciously decided to wait seven days for another "Position Proposal". My eligibility for the *Vietnam War* escalation was a real consideration, and I would be exempt from military service if I could secure a forthcoming teaching position.

Luckily, I received a second offering from a neighboring school district, and I hastily signed the contract to teach a self-contained sixth grade class seven different subjects. And over the summer time, I later received a notice from the school system's board of education that my salaried first year contract of $4,900.00 had been generously raised to $5,050.00. "Wow!" I exclaimed to mom and dad. "Teaching's really a terrific profession!" I emphatically stated. "I haven't even done anything yet, and already I'm getting a hundred-and-fifty-dollar raise!"

I had been *trained* (I use *that* word deliberately for it is regarded as a dirty reference in American education) and had been certified to teach junior high school and not sixth grade, which required an "Elementary School New Jersey State Teaching Certification". I soon discovered that sixth grade was a rough situation where the teacher was in charge of twenty-five rascals all day long, every single day of the hundred-and eighty-day school year.

On the other hand, a junior high school instructor taught two or three subject preps' to five or six different classes, and had a daily workload of a hundred and thirty *students*. A junior high school teacher would be much more *specialized* than the ordinary elementary school instructor was.

Now finally, my time was at hand. My educational blossom was about to bloom. Like most fledgling teachers, I felt like I was fully qualified to inspire young minds with the intense fire blazing within my activated soul. Little did I know that the junior devils I was about to encounter were accomplished miniature firefighters whose behavior often would extinguish *my fiery motivation.*

Chapter 10
"The Copernicus Play"

My first sixth grade class was an amalgamation of rather weird and peculiar characters. Jack Dobbs was a skinny string bean of a kid who was extremely hyperactive. He had the memory capacity of an amnesia patient, and about the only thing that Jack Dobbs could skillfully remember was how to forget. The young scoundrel would unconsciously mumble and repeat just about everything I would say in class, and eventually I strongly believed that nature had originally intended young Jack to be a chattering parrot. After a while, the annoying imp's constant repeating had the effect of an echo caught reverberating inside a circular, maze-like canyon.

About mid-September of 1965, the class and I had finished authoring an original play titled *The Trial of Copernicus*. Jack's role was quite simple. All Dobbs had to do was scurry like a maniac out onto the auditorium's stage while brandishing a wooden sword covered with tin foil and then vociferously shriek, "You are insane! You are insane!" to the suddenly startled *Inquisition* judges. After delivering his *Academy Awards* deserving lines, Dobbs had to then hurriedly exit the stage.

A throng of anxious parents and guests gorged the auditorium on the night of the sixth-grade play. Everything went rather smoothly as the first several scenes unraveled. Then it was Jack Dobb's turn to enact his marvelous bit-part. Knowing the kid's propensity for forgetfulness, I stood backstage and repeatedly coached him until his grand entrance onto the set was imminent. The dramatic moment finally arrived, and as I shoved young Jack Dobbs out from behind the royal blue curtain I twice whispered into his ear, "You are insane! You are insane!"

Jack darted-out onto center stage, paused momentarily and then remained stationary as if *he* had transformed into a petrified rock. Then the confused lad came dashing back to me and asked, "What do I have to say?"

"You are insane! You are insane!" I was rather perturbed and squawked those three words while rotating and then pushing the junior thespian back under the overhead spotlights in the direction of center stage.

After I magically whirled Dobbs around and launched him toward Copernicus and the seated *Inquisition* judges, Jack scampered onto center stage and bellowed to the six hundred amused people in the audience, "I am insane! I am insane!"

The audience amply appreciated the lad's spectacular elocution, thinking it either an imaginative ad-lib or a creative comedy line that had been cleverly inserted as part of the script. Despite his cerebral denseness, the boy eventually found a reliable niche in American society. Ten years after the Copernicus play incident, Jack Dobbs became the manager of a large department store, earned a handsome salary and made *his* valuable contribution to our dynamic free enterprise economic system.

Billy Sliben was a hefty kid with thick-lens bifocal glasses. He had mammoth buckteeth that looked like elephant tusks. The chunky boy's speech delivery was hampered by an erratic stuttering and slurring handicap. Billy was unlike most lispers shackled with a severe speech impediment. He was an extrovert and was not at all inhibited by his obvious oral communication difficulty. When it came to the art of conversation, Billy Sliben was overindulgent.

During class "Snack Time", I would allow Billy the opportunity to stand before the class and tell a few silly jokes simply to satisfy his ego *needs*. A Jackie Gleason or a Bob Hope he was not. Not being loquacious but thinking that you are can represent a serious conflict between reality and fantasy.

I scheduled Billy's father for an after-school parent-teacher conference where I planned to discuss Billy's chronic speech hindrances in depth. His father, a burly fellow, sauntered into the room. "I am-am-am Mis-ss-ter-rr-rr Slib-bb-bb-ben!" he stuttered.

'Holy mackerel!' I thought. 'How can I effectively discuss Billy's severe handicap when Mr. Sliben's speech impediment is ten times worse than his kid's is!' I rationally considered. 'Mr. Sliben makes Billy sound like Cicero!'

Billy Sliben was given the role of being a silent judge in the Copernicus play to spare him the embarrassment of becoming nervous and then stuttering, lisping and slurring his way through either an easy or a challenging line or two. I just couldn't risk giving him a speaking part, so implementing sound teaching strategy, I had "Young William" also help-out on the stage crew.

Leonard Caro was a pugnacious bully who always liked instigating altercations and then meanly injuring other *students*. Lenny's sadistic personality was about as charming as that of a condor, and his favorite historical idols were vinegary hombres like Al Capone, Jesse James, Snidely Whiplash and Adolph Hitler. Lenny was an abused *child* who often imitated his father's overt nastiness. His dad was a ruthless ruffian that nightly pulverized his wife and then mangled his children to psychologically compensate for *his* frustration of failing monetarily in the *adult world* (and of also being very addicted to alcohol).

In one bitter family quarrel, Mr. Caro, in a fit of utter rage, tossed the family television set out a closed window. The unique aspect of the family dispute was that the argument had taken place upstairs, and the television was effectively demolished when it collided with the ground twenty feet below. The visual device would never again monitor such television favorites as "Love of Life", "As the World Turns", "Search for Tomorrow" and "Father Knows Best".

Kids that come from home environments like Leonard Caro's have the card deck stacked against them right from the starting gate. It is extraordinarily difficult for them to overcome the overwhelming odds that are against them and then suddenly and miraculously mature into normal self-sufficient adults. Apples don't fall far from family trees, and in a barrel of apples (a class for example), it is the rotten apples that make the good fruit decay. Even the most optimistic person never hears of the healthy apples curing the decomposition of a blighted one.

But in keeping with the tenets of American education's "teach and motivate" *democratic* spirit, it was *my* supreme duty to tolerate and attempt to rehabilitate Leonard Caro. A totalitarian state would have a much simpler solution: remove the child at an early age from his father's negative influence; make the state responsible for Leonard's welfare and development, and have the "major discipline problem" exposed to the finer values that the government and the society are attempting to perpetuate.

In our befuddled American "democratic system" of education, the verbally abusive parents are allowed the privilege of continuously corrupting their children. In reality, the kids' value systems are basically formed prior to attending kindergarten. A vicious cycle has been initiated where the abused *students* emulate the bullying traits of their dysfunctional parents, and then school administrators pompously tell teachers at faculty meetings that *they* have been designated to alter the course of those irreversible contingencies. Squeezing the Atlantic Ocean into a Dixie cup would be an easier assignment than being commanded to change chicken feces into chicken salad.

But still, a cherished slogan that's often espoused by public school administrators is, "Anyone can teach the gifted *students*.

They will learn in spite of you. The disadvantaged *children* and the slow learners are *your* real challenges in education."

Administrators neglect to mention that at least twenty-five percent of today's *students* are actually "special needs" *children* that are mainstreamed into standard classrooms all across America, and that another twenty-percent could be easily classified as "special needs" *students* with learning disabilities, with attention deficit syndromes and with very evident emotional problems. And when these special needs *students* are placed into regular classrooms for socialization benefits, discipline problems manifest themselves, and academic excellence disintegrates into simply "keeping the lid on".

The above administrative contemporary logic is as porous as a ruptured sieve. A teacher might have daily a diverse combination of twenty-five or more heterogeneous individuals, many of whom might lack courtesy, respect, tolerance, trust and desire, with five brutal bullies tossed into that wild mix. Twenty-five to one are atrocious odds at any racetrack. Put five Lenny Caro-types into any classroom dynamics and then be told "Motivate these *students*" quite frankly represents a very unreasonable situation. That is precisely why so many demoralized former teachers are now public-school administrators, misguided liberal college professors, and idealistic one-on-one guidance counselors.

Leonard Caro was also a talented thespian involved in the Copernicus play. I couldn't trust Lenny to normally act in a tolerable manner, so naturally I assigned him to the climactic fight scene. In the midst of one half-decent after-school rehearsal, Lenny certainly jazzed things up a bit. Upon cue, he was instructed to lead his band of villagers from stage left to act out "a mild scuffle" with sword-wielding *Inquisition* guards. Lenny smashed Copernicus (who was supposed to be on *his* side) with a blunt uppercut to the jaw that would have made Mike Tyson grimace with pain. The bleeding recipient (Copernicus, Bobby Miller) was speedily taken to the school nurse with a bloody nose and a swollen mandible.

After the other teacher/assistant director escorted the wounded main character out of the auditorium, I had trouble controlling my temper concerning Leonard's unwarranted assault. I un-gently grabbed the young bully by the shoulders and really reprimanded him. Reflection and discretion would have advised me wiser than instinct was capable of doing.

Leonard Caro had been clutched (and battered) by his father innumerable times before I ever graced his shoulders with my fingerprints. The angry kid wrenched himself free from my grasp and then bolted out of the auditorium quicker than an antelope fleeing a raging brush fire.

"You could be accused of corporal punishment," the returning teacher from the nurse's office told me. "I've seen other teachers lose their jobs under similar circumstances, and it usually happened when *they* tried to give the kids something extra like putting on this crazy Copernicus play. Incidentally John," the empathetic teacher continued, "Bobby Miller has a broken nose!"

"Thanks a lot!" I answered in a state of shock. "A kid like Leonard Caro can get me fired when I was only trying to set him on a straight and narrow path. If someone like Leonard or his nutcase father can get me fired, then my job is not worth too much to begin with. Now, is it?" I rhetorically argued to my more experienced colleague.

The only hope for a *student* like Lenny would be for the teacher to take the class on a field trip to Lourdes, France and then hurl *him* into the holy lagoon and say a hundred rosaries while praying for an absolute miracle. After escaping my verbal wrath and my physical grasp, Leonard exited a building door, left the school property and ran through the honking horns of passing motorists across the street. I immediately reported the incident to the school principal.

I was in the principal's office explaining what had recently transpired on the auditorium stage when the desk phone rang. The office secretary informed the administrator that the chief-of-police was on the other end of the line.

Leonard had left the school premises after assaulting another *student,* sprinted across the street to police headquarters, and had reported his teacher for "child brutality" because I had grabbed him by the shoulders. Leonard had memorized one critical precept from his bullying father. "If any teacher ever lays a finger on you, it's against the law!"

'My career could go up in smoke all because of a rash five second impulsive reaction!' I sincerely regretted to my conscience in the principal's office. "I must have better self-control!'

Luckily, the police chief had recognized the illegitimate nature of Leonard's demand and returned the boy to school jurisdiction. That event had occurred back in October of 1965.

Let's be practical. A swimmer is of no use without water, a book is of no use without a reader, a transmitter is of no use without a receiver, and a teacher is of no use without *students* that care to learn. Teachers need to be vindicated by the public instead of being vilified, need to be defended instead of offended, and need to be supported instead of being perpetually criticized.

Many *students* come to school and attempt to drag the teacher down to their social level, and if and when they eventually succeed, the teacher suddenly finds *himself* (masculine by preference) in deep trouble. No teacher that I have known over my thirty-four-year career ever came to school in the morning thinking 'I'm gonna' hit Leonard Caro!' But when Leonard managed to get me onto *his* shelf, I became vulnerable, and my attempt to discipline him automatically put my job security and my teaching career in instant jeopardy.

My sudden encounter with Leonard Caro and a hostile parent conference thereafter put me under intense emotional stress. I came to school the following morning quite fatigued from a bout of insomnia. My face was pallid and my nerves were quite jangled, yet I still had to teach those seven subjects and pretend to be unfazed as if nothing negative had ever happened the day before.

After school bus duty, it was again time for the Copernicus play practice. The first act went by smoothly without nary a miscue. I had the *students* occupy seats in the auditorium's two front rows so that I could commend them on their stellar effort and then review the areas of strengths and weaknesses. As I was addressing the kids, I noticed that a stage prop' had fallen over. When I stooped-down to pick up the grotesque azalea crayoned onto cardboard, everyone seated in the large chamber discerned a very loud crack.

A terrible pain shot-down my spinal cord. I soon realized that I could not assume an erect posture. My bending over had terribly knocked something seriously out of whack. I summoned two stout sixth graders and had them transport me down to the nurse's dispensary, my arms draped over their shoulders.

"I'll take care of the second scene," my sympathetic teaching colleague/assistant director intrepidly volunteered. "Hope you're feeling better when you come back from the nurse's office!"

For a full month, I was in agony and under a chiropractor's care. I was crunched and sandwiched from all angles and at times assumed the many positions of an accomplished triple-jointed contortionist. "All of this," I quipped to my teaching associate/assistant director at an after-school play practice, "and it's Lenny Caro that needs to be straightened-out and not me!"

The advantages of being a first-year teacher are that you (the instructor) possess a freshness of spirit and have a proclivity for experimenting with new ideas like the Copernicus play. The liabilities connected with a first-year teacher are that you cannot accurately measure student potentials and limitations and that the novice instructor does not exercise consistency in discipline.

An effective veteran teacher knows that discipline is not verbally chastising deviant or defiant *student* misbehavior. True discipline is when the *student* actually thinks to himself': 'Perhaps I really shouldn't be doing this!' Correcting and chastising out-of-control *students* is really the definition of the absence of discipline. So true discipline is really *student* self-discipline!

Attention spans among elementary school children cannot be guaranteed beyond ten minutes at a time. And the lower-down that an instructor goes in terms of grade levels, the more teacher skill is required where a variety of activities must keep primary grades' *students* interested in each subject area from 9 a.m. until 3 p.m.

After six weeks of intensive rehearsals, in late October, the Copernicus play was finally presented to a packed auditorium of proud parents, ecstatic relatives and happy guests. Jack Dobbs accidentally delivered his hilarious "I am insane! I am insane!" spoken lines, which were the most delightful and sensational elements of the hour-long performance, his bungled words receiving the most audience applause. And the most surprising thing about Jack Dobbs' brilliant miscue was that it was spontaneous and had not been rehearsed once during the six weeks of serious, meticulous play preparation.

Chapter 11
"Other Members of the Class"

One cold morning in early January, I was lecturing my sixth graders on the wrongs of being tardy to class while loitering in the halls and also, I was criticizing the habit of certain *students* always asking me to visit the lavatories ten minutes after the class had just begun. I was really fuming because several of my more-ornery charges had been constant violators.

Soon, I made the transition from drill sergeant to classroom *facilitator* and got the *students* industriously working on their general science worksheets before assigning the *children* their upcoming astronomy projects. Everything seemed to be copasetic.

After my stern lecture on the need to be punctual and the need to be cooperative in not abusing lavatory privileges, with relief I detected a palpable hush in the classroom. But then a very filthy malodorous stench pervaded the air.

'Someone has just crapped themselves!' I theorized. 'My tough lecture on abusing the bathroom privilege must've scared the living feces out of one of the kids and now it's all backfiring on me!'

I hoped that the foul cesspool-like odor would dissipate, but the nauseating putrid smell lingered and seemed to be growing in magnitude. I knew someone had discharged a large quantity of waste material, but which *student*? I had to act quickly because some *students* began giggling and snickering and others started holding their noses and simultaneously pointing their index fingers at each other in mock accusations.

Each kid had instantly transformed into an adolescent Sherlock Holmes trying to trace-down the source of the terrible, disturbing scent. I regretted that I had just taught the class the four main steps in the scientific method of reasoning: observation, hypothesis, verification and conclusion. The kids were now preoccupied with the observation phase and were randomly hypothesizing which one of them had abundantly crapped themselves. Jenny Martin had her thumb and forefinger simulating a clothespin over her nose, and the observant girl blurted out "Look!" as she then pointed to the floor. A dreadful mound of excrement had fallen onto the polished wood.

Margaret Stone, a bashful black-American girl, suddenly went zooming from her desk and dashed out of the classroom as if she were being chased by ugly-looking space aliens. Apparently poor Margaret had a stomach virus and also had a dire need to utilize the lavatory facilities five minutes after the class had just returned from the bathrooms, but my harsh speech had dissuaded her from asking permission to revisit the facilities.

I hastily instructed the revved-up *students* to line-up in the hall, and then I urgently buzzed the office secretary over the intercom to immediately dispatch a custodian with a mop, scented disinfectant and a bucket to my upstairs classroom. I speedily organized a kickball game out on the playground and then sent a *student* to the office to disclose to the principal that I wanted to see him as soon as possible outside.

"What's wrong?" the harried administrator asked after hustling-out to the playground. "What's the emergency?"

"One of my *students* Margaret Stone is missing in action!" I answered. "She had a bowel accident in class and ran out of the room in shame. I have no idea where she is right now!"

The principal, vice-principal, guidance counselor and the Child Study Team conducted an all-out search of the property's three separate elementary school buildings. The principal finally discovered Margaret Stone imitating *Quasimodo,* and the girl was acting like a hermit hiding in the middle building's bell tower, evidently completely mortified by her memorable contribution to science class that day. Her mind had elapsed into a defensive-but-aggressive behavior mode, and the humiliated girl resisted all attempts at administrative rescue as if poor Margaret Stone was the *Hunchback of Notre Dame* fending off the soldiers of Paris.

Bernie Mitchell was a husky kid that wore glasses with a set of lenses that were so thick they looked-like they belonged in the *Mount Palomar* or in the *Hubble Space Telescope.* The sticky boy profusely sweated in all seasons as if he was a pig locked inside a sauna bath, and he incessantly drank water like a parched pachyderm distressed with a bad case of diabetes.

Once I caught young Mitchell filling-up at a hall water fountain and joked, "Bernie, don't throw a pen in that fountain unless of course, it's a *fountain* pen!"

The *child* turned his head while slurping away and answered, "What the fuck's that supposed to mean!" So sometimes, it doesn't really pay to try and humor *students* (even sixth graders), and saying as least as possible to any of them usually constitutes the best policy to pursue.

Bernie's torn and tattered black and white marble-covered composition book resembled an archeological enigma laden with cryptic passages. But instead of having Greek symbols or Egyptian hieroglyphics, I imagined that young Bernie Mitchell's written work was indecipherable "lower-glyphics", instead. The Rosetta Stone would have been more legible and much easier to interpret than the *child's* insane scribbling.

One day I made a fatal verbal error and addressed Bernie by stating, "I understand you're Bobby Miller's cousin!"

The stocky defensive kid replied, "So what's it to you!"

I knew I had a real character on my hands, so I simply complimented Bernie Mitchell by saying that Bobby and he were two of the finest kids in the entire school.

In March of '66, my pregnant wife accompanied the class on a New York City field trip. We had four buses to accommodate the five sixth grade classes, their teachers and parent chaperones on the hundred-and-ten-mile Big Apple excursion. The buses separated in midtown Manhattan, and in different rotations, toured the *Statue of Liberty*, *Times Square* and *Broadway*, the *United Nations Building* and the *Empire State Building*.

Parents as chaperones on field trips are sometimes as frightening as an actual guillotine demonstration. The sign on the bus read: "No Smoking", but still several maternal betrayers set a bad example, lit-up cancer sticks and inhaled and exhaled nicotine and tar contamination as second-hand smoke. How do you politely reprimand derelict parents in front of their own delinquent kids and live another day to tell all about it?

On the Manhattan field trip, the *students* were often more dependable than their problematic parents were. One mother delayed us for an hour buying birthday gifts at *Gimbels* and at *Macy's*. Another mother met-up with her sister on Fifth Avenue, and they were trapped inside a stalled skyscraper elevator for an hour, so we had to wait an additional fifteen minutes for them to arrive back at the bus. For every aspirin I've taken on field trips because of raunchy kids, I've taken two for the eccentricities of their nomadic, narcissistic parents.

Word reached us that a parent chaperone on another bus had collapsed around *Times Square* from a cardiac arrest and had to be rushed to the nearest hospital. That tragedy really put a damper on the trip, and everyone entered into a more solemn state of mind when we eventually boarded the four buses for home. But being solemn and somber to most kids is only a temporary phenomenon.

On the way out of New York City, *our* bus was caught in a massive traffic jam smack-dab in the middle of the *Lincoln Tunnel*.

"Thank goodness we have air conditioning on this bus!" I related to another teacher sitting directly across the aisle.

"At least we have some cool air that's still circulating!" the other instructor replied. "Thank goodness that we should be safe at home in three hours."

It appeared nice and comfortable inside the old *Public Service Bus* despite the pollution fumes and the inconvenience of being in city traffic gridlock in the middle of the *Lincoln Tunnel*. Without my immediate notice, a little scoundrel in the rear of the vehicle opened *his* side window. Nasty gas, truck and tractor trailer exhaust fumes seemed to be sucked inside our bus as if someone had evilly turned-on a giant vacuum cleaner. I rose from my seat, rushed to the back of the bus and slammed the window shut.

The culprit was Bernie Mitchell, who was perspiring like a sweat hog in heat. After cooling-off from my outrage, I stepped to the front of the bus and attended to my choking wife, who by that time was filling her second bag of vomit. That was the first and the last field trip my wife had ever accompanied me on. Upon returning to the school, we learned that the parent chaperone that had suffered the heart attack from the third bus had died in a New York hospital.

Gaylord Zink was a stealthy black American boy that had an office discipline file thicker than that of most of the teachers on the staff. His defiance and rancor were attributed to a broken home (with no father around), which was complicated by extreme poverty and a loose, immoral, alcoholic mother. Any person who thinks that *those* debilitating factors can be reformed is first a fool, second a dreamer, and third a teacher.

Gaylord had very inharmonious peer relations and was a total loner. He spent a good deal of the day leaning over and looking up girls' dresses in the classroom when he wasn't looking up them at the base of the stairs. Gaylord never looked me in the eyes, and he was the type of volatile kid *you* (the teacher) just couldn't trust even when you were staring the stealthy kid flush in the face. There was seldom any direct eye contact.

Gaylord Zink could fabricate a lie better than any professional convict could. The boy's inferior home environment had prescribed his destiny, and *that* circumstance seemed unalterable, no matter how hard I tried giving him classroom responsibilities, like distributing notebook paper or cleaning the erasers after school.

One day, Gaylord asked permission to go the Boys Room. I thought, 'Maybe this kid really needs someone to trust him. I have established a fairly decent rapport with him.' I responded to his request, "Sure Gaylord. Meet the class outside in five minutes for a game of dodge ball!" As I was leading the sixth graders to the playground, I observed a blizzard of confetti spiraling-down from the second-floor Boys Lavatory. Although 1965 was still before the days of widespread ecology and recycling, I quickly recognized that something was rather inordinate. I glanced-up at the bathroom's exhaust fan and saw mischievous Gaylord feeding notebook paper into the spinning fan blades, which were chopping the sheets up and then blowing the litter outside, simulating a sort of snowstorm.

Several appalled women teachers reported and complained to me the following month that Gaylord had stationed himself at the foot of the stairwell and then looked up *their* skirts as they ascended the black metal steps. I referred the youthful voyeur to the valiant Child Study Team, and the committee of idealistic visionaries revealed that young Mr. Zink had been under *their* professional scrutiny for four years. The same deranged "spying symptoms" had been documented by six other female teachers, and the misbehaviors had been comfortably filed-away in *his* confidential *student* folder.

And so, ten years later, when I read about an area sex predator in local newspapers, I immediately recognized the name. Teachers can often accurately predict who future law-violators will be, and conversely, some of the wildest and most defiant kids I had ever taught in my thirty-four-year career later in life became by-the-book policemen in the town.

Greg Chad was a rowdy rascal that occasionally would attempt performing a sensational feat to demonstrate his daring to his classmates. Greg had to be closely watched every minute during the second half of the lunch period while I was assigned on recess playground duty. Climbing fences to clamber-up trees on adjacent private property and leaping off of monkey bars or knocking other kids off of playground equipment were some of Greg's most favorite pastimes. And the ugly part of the whole scenario was that *I* was responsible for his adventurous activities and would ultimately be held accountable for Greg Chad's reckless, *irresponsible* behavior.

Greg was notorious for his Tarzan-like acrobatics during lunchtime, which he also practiced before and after school. The kid was always testing his physical prowess and also the teachers' emotional limits. The *student* was certainly more *daring* than he was *darling,* and in the process, young Mr. Chad possessed the balance and grace of an overweight hippopotamus.

One dismal late March afternoon, the inevitable happened. Greg Chad plummeted from the top of the monkey bars (despite frequent warnings) and fell victim to the forces of gravity. The accident waiting to happen finally did happen. The *child* crashed onto the ground like a speeding meteorite, and *he* finally learned exactly how the law of gravity operated.

I ran over to see if the daredevil was all right and observed that moaning Greg had dislocated his right elbow. So, I dispatched a fleet *student* courier to advise the nurse and the principal of "the playground accident". She, the male principal and the rescue squad all arrived on the scene simultaneously. Greg was taken to the hospital with a fractured arm and a dislocated elbow.

The alarmed principal summoned me to his office after school. "You should endeavor in the future to prevent such terrible accidents," the head honcho sanctimoniously lectured. "After all, you are a *professional* person, and playground duty is one of your chief responsibilities!"

Shrewd school administrators use the cliché "professional" when addressing teachers because they realize three vital concepts. Teachers are seldom regarded or treated as *professionals* by anyone anywhere. There is nothing at-all *professional* about the playground patrol, or about any other non-classroom *duty*. Finally, teachers so strongly desire to be *professional* that they are very sensitive and paranoid about being referred to as "acting *unprofessional"*.

Another problem that a teacher might have on playground duty is a disoriented stranger wandering onto the school premises to harass kids, to entice them with offering drugs, or to solicit the girls with candy. And then there are child custody cases where teachers have to fear an estranged parent showing-up to kidnap their biological son or daughter and then ferry the child out of state.

One day, as the *students* were returning from the playground, a wild rumor was circulating amongst them that a "crazy man" had offered a girl candy and had tried to grab another one of the young ladies. Several *students* had conveyed to me the alleged attempted mugging, and I presented them and their testimonies to the school principal to ferret-out the details, and as usual, the school executive was busy talking and arguing with an irate parent on the telephone.

Instantly, the halls were flooded with teams of gendarmes searching every nook and cranny of the building for the elusive suspect. My ears and eyes detected a rumble at the end of the second-floor corridor, and as I further observed the disturbance, I noticed two local patrolmen escorting a third party down the black metal stairs and then out of the building and down to an awaiting police vehicle.

After conducting an initial interrogation, the embarrassed cops discovered that they had impetuously arrested one of the school janitors. The poor fellow was an Italian immigrant who spoke only a few words of English. The policemen's better judgment had been befogged by the thrill of the hunt.

Teachers are often confined with *students* for hours on end and frequently cannot get to the lavatory when nature calls. Because *students* must be supervised at all times, a teacher just can't leave his or her classroom and utilize the facilities at his or her leisure. Many times, I had endured wicked abdominal discomfort or kidney/bladder pressure so that I could complete my professional responsibility. It is embarrassing to have to call the office and request a teacher in the faculty room to take your place. The *children* immediately know what's going on with your bladder, or with your' bowels.

But many teachers I have known have hemorrhoids and chronic intestinal difficulties, much more so than members of other luckier professions that can enjoy the "freedom to eliminate waste materials" at their own discretion and convenience. In teaching, you learn to go when you have an opportunity to go, and not necessarily when simply you have to go.

And now here's where school administration is a major part of a teacher's daily dilemma. Principals and vice-principals are accomplished public-relations-experts that cram local newspapers with themselves handing awards, trophies and academic certificates to deserving *students*. The administrators' propaganda is focused on praising the smooth operation of the school, and the gullible public concludes that public schools are wonderful places to work-in and that teachers have the easiest jobs on the planet. A false equation is transmitted to the local population, and it states that 'Good School Administration Plus Easy Teaching Situation with Good *Children* Equals No School Problems and Fully Ideal Teaching/Learning Conditions.'

"Teachers only work seven hours a day," the erroneous public thinks and gossips without taking into regard the preparation and the typing of lessons, lesson plans, and tests along with the correction of compositions, homework, quizzes, and marking period exams'. And as far as money is concerned, I have always resented the public criticism that teachers have all summer off.

First of all, teachers have no paid vacation or paid holiday time. They are under contract to teach and to be at school 183 days a year with not one paid holiday or one paid vacation day. That's the stark, honest truth, and the full hidden crux of the matter. True, teachers have holidays off and summers off, but it is always without pay.

The sixth-grade cafeteria/playground duty was *not* a pleasant daily sacrifice. I found myself standing in the center of a whirlpool of vernal munchkins swirling all around my presence while praying that the *student* mortality rate would remain at zero. Three intrepid teachers in addition to myself were assigned to the horrendous detail, and we were delegated to supervise a hundred and fifty boisterous hyperactive junior humanoids. The concerned principal insisted that *we* organize games and have "structured activities" to keep behavioral disorganization and the flow of running traffic on the playground to a minimum.

Duties are perhaps the greatest insults to teachers' dignity. The non-professional assignments contaminate the public's perception of what a teacher is and does. Watching kids trample, maul, molest and test each other's mettle requires little expertise. It (sociological interaction) is as remote from the process of education (academics) as the planet Pluto. Anyone can perform those *supervisory* functions: a butcher, a baker or a tallow chandler. Until aides with sixty college credits are hired to perform all non-professional *duties* in the school, teachers will remain criticized as being sociological *generalists* and will never become academic *specialists*.

Of course, building administrators and school board members are the beneficiaries of the instructors' well-concealed grief. The educational aristocracy receives the praise and the accolades while teachers reach for the *Rolaids*. Although I have always despised mandatory teacher duties, they still are a big ugly segment of daily *educational* reality.

Educational psychology may work most of the time in the controlled classroom environment, but when *you* (the teacher) are trying to get the attention of two hundred raving maniacs with an ineffectual microphone in the cafeteria, *you* (the teacher) better have more than psychology in your strategy arsenal. Despite the nice, utopian propaganda prospective teachers are spoon-fed in college, most twelve-to-sixteen-year-old *students* are too immature and fickle to show rational individuality, and they are more influenced by peer pressure than motivated by a choice distinction between right and wrong. And clinical studies have lucidly shown that a person's brain does not reach full development until after the individual reaches the mature age of twenty-one (so much for teenage sophisticated decision-making ability).

I quickly learned with my first sixth grade class not to make *their* problems my problems, or else I would soon be on a one-way trip to the funny farm. If Bobby Miller came up to me in the cafeteria and reported that his cousin Bernie Mitchell was picking on him and calling him names, I would never reprimand the accused instigator. Instead, I would say to the plaintiff, "Bobby, what do you say I sit you over there with that table of giggling girls? Then you won't have to worry about being assaulted by Bernie!" The *student* attempting to get the other kid in trouble would reexamine his alternatives, and then develop the following generalizations. 'The teacher can't be bothered with my picayune conflicts. I don't want to ever sit with the gossiping girls. I'd better learn how to get along with cousin Bernie.'

The adult that takes personality conflicts between kids too seriously is then complicating his or her life with childish discordance. If two *students* get into an imbroglio in the cafeteria or on the playground, the friction between the two usually diminishes to a faint memory after several weeks. But if parents take sides and ally with their offspring, the adults probably will become eternal feuders while the original wrangle is completely erased in their *children's* minds. Fights between *students* reach a head and are generally only temporary violent events that in time, fade in scope and sequence. But disputes between parents because of their *children* quarrelling often leave open wounds that are slow to heal. That is why I learned not to overact to transient *student* battles.

Jenny Gibson was a flirtatious girl that liked more mature high school boys. Twelve-year-old girls tend to be two years more physically advanced than their male peers are. It was no wonder that Jenny Gibson was attracted to several sophomore-aged young men. I was shocked when I learned that Jenny had become pregnant as a sexually active sixth grader. Somehow the class as a whole lost its general innocence when that reality had been whispered.

Rick Derks was a short, thin boy that had a chronic absentee problem. Rick could scarcely read or write, and he valued education about as much as he valued ostrich plumes or ladies' perfume. Out of curiosity, I inquired one day, "Ricky, what do you do when you don't come to school?"

"I go fishing!" the lad guiltlessly returned.

"Does your father know that you go fishing when you're supposed to be in school?" I curiously asked.

"He's the one that takes me!" Ricky proudly and shamelessly announced. "We always go to the lake together and then drink a couple of beers."

Tom Bailey was another frisky lad who also cared little about reading, writing and arithmetic. One afternoon while the class and I were reading and discussing *Junior Scholastic* articles, pesky Tom raised his hand and asked, "Mr. Wiessner, what do the letters r-e-s-i-d-e-n-c-e spell?"

My curiosity had been stimulated, so I stepped over to Tom's desk to determine why he desired to know that particular word's functionality. I was mildly shocked to see Tom filling-out a mail order coupon for a shotgun he wished to order from a hunting magazine. I instinctively confiscated the coupon, ripped it up and tossed the remnants in the metal trashcan.

In late May, I had heard a commotion occurring out in the hallway near the *student* lockers. Tom Bailey was showing-off his new mail order shotgun, which I immediately impounded as evidence. "I only wanted to let the other kids see it!" he shrieked in protest.

It really scared me back in 1965 that I lived in a society where a person that could hardly read or write could have access to weapons and munitions through the mail. Certainly, the mail order business has changed since then, and I guess some good laws with a basis in common sense have been passed and implemented. But it really struck me at the time that an illiterate minor could falsify his age on a coupon, and as long as he had the money, could easily acquire a shotgun through the mail.

In sixth grade that year, our school conducted a federally funded reading program after normal hours. Low reading scores had identified Tom Bailey as a candidate to participate in the program, and I was assigned as *his* special tutor. Although young Bailey had the academic mentality of a thorny cactus, his doting parents made sure that he had at least two twenty-dollar bills stashed inside his wallet at all times. Once Tom challenged me, "Mr. Wiessner, I'll bet I have more money in my wallet than you have in yours! Winner takes all!" I refused to take his bet because the twenty-five bucks in my wallet happened to be all the money I had until my next bi-weekly paycheck.

Tom Bailey never really valued the cash in his wallet because it had been easily obtained and given to him, and the boy never had to earn it. Easy come-easy go seemed to be his perception of money. After the rigors of the regular school day, Tom would trek over to the corner pizza parlor and procure two large tomato and cheese pies and four quarts of *Pepsi Cola*. Bailey was really generous with his parents' subsidy. He fed all six *students* and the teacher in the federally funded reading program every Tuesday and Thursday afternoon. The ironic part was that although Tom could not recognize either the word *cheese* or the word *tomato* in print, the nouns *pepperoni* and *anchovies* were frequently implemented functional terms in *his* speaking vocabulary.

Ten years later, I came across Tom Bailey stumping through the woods behind my home. "Hi Mr. Wiessner," Tom greeted. "It's the first day of rabbit season and I'm gonna' bag a few!"

My brother-in-law was with me, and after I described Tom's history with my sister-in-law's husband along with the sixth grade shotgun incident, *we* felt compelled to post our grounds with a plethora of "No Hunting" signs.

"Do you think Tom Bailey will be able to read the language on these signs we're posting?" I asked my brother-in-law.

"He should be able to recognize the signs even if he can't read the words on them!" my brother-in-law aptly answered.

After a few months laboring inside the classroom, I realized that it was the *children* that were doing the testing and not the teacher. Kids will smite you with anything from hog calls to cat meowing when your back is turned. A few *students* will spill ink from their pens and etch the blue substance onto desks. Other *children* will squirt each other with concealed water pistols and place chalk in the grooves of the erasers so that the unsuspecting, conscientious teacher will be squeaking white lines onto the chalkboard when he or she is attempting to erase notes and words. If that happens, I'll tell the class, "Someday we will have magic erasers that will put words on the blackboard instead of taking them off. The *student* who had put chalk in the eraser must be the one that will invent such a wonderful device!" So, before I ever erase a board, out of habit I always would check the eraser first to inspect it for chalk in the grooves.

Another headache of which teachers must be wary of is when an adventurous *student* (or *students*) decides to entertain the class at the teacher's expense. He (masculine by preference and by probability) will place a vertical thumbtack on the teacher's chair so that when the weary instructor pulls his or her chair out from under his or her desk (especially eighth period when your resistance is low). your butt will be painfully penetrated.

Once, I sat on an eighth period thumbtack and then observed the mass disappointment on the faces of interested cherubs in the class when I neglected to leap out of my seat while experiencing agony. I simply sat there and endured the pain. All the while, pretending that nothing was unusual. I didn't want to give anyone the satisfaction that a nefarious *student* had *gotten a rise* out of me.

Once, I had six *students* up at the chalkboard doing arithmetic problems, and one of them had a small, cute stuffed animal that was designed to make offensive farting sounds. Naturally, I had to trace down the source of the annoyance and then take disciplinary action after becoming aggravated by the recurrent, surprise nuisance.

And then *students* test the teacher by merely raising their hands and asking permission to go to the lavatory just to "feel you out" and measure your reaction. All the other kids' ears suddenly prick-up, and how *you* respond to the inquiry will establish a pattern for the entire day, period or school year. I usually only allowed *students* to go to the bathroom once a marking period, and it had to be "an emergency". Of course, that particular enforcement required more record-keeping on my part so that the once a marking period privilege was not abused.

"You all have plenty of time to visit the bathroom to or from lunch period, to or from gym class, or when I take *you* twice a day!" I would tell the fidgety class. If a teacher doesn't establish that kind of firmness the first two weeks of school, then the perceptive *children* will invariably exploit your kindness and take advantage of the instructor's patience and benevolence.

And then the *students* will constantly ask for hall passes to visit the nurse, to converse with a guidance counselor, or journey to the office to register a grievance against another *student* or to call mom at home or work. A teacher will always have *students* that want to roam around the halls or fool around in the lavatories. And if an individual leaves your class (even with a pass), he or she is basically unsupervised, and *you* are liable for anything the *student* does outside the classroom ranging from vandalism of property, to graffiti scribbled on walls, to leaving the building. If you aren't on your guard and quickly learn how to say "no", or the words "later on," then the entrance portal to your classroom will seem like it's a major big city department store's revolving door.

Chapter 12
"Bureaucracy, Teachers and Parents"

Supplies in the elementary school were about as rare as Australian platypuses floating upside-down inside Mt. Etna. I was quite disenchanted with the inadequate means of materials' distribution and the lack of available inventory, which hindered my classroom needs and also my teaching effectiveness. The school board had been frugal the year before because the members had made a major concession to pay each teacher a hundred-and-fifty-dollars more plus already established salary guide increment raises.

The supplies' storeroom was partitioned into a makeshift room behind the auditorium's rear black curtains. I had to resort to petty larceny to satisfactorily meet the educational needs of my sixth grade *students*. I became a trifle hostile with the janitor's procrastination after I had ordered emergency supplies (construction paper, paint for props, staples) for the Copernicus play and was told, "You have to wait until the beginning of next month!"

After school, I would stay in my classroom under the pretense of assiduously working overtime. I would then stealthily sneak down to the supply room behind the back black curtains and employ techniques I had learned while pilfering Dr. Trenoff's master answer key final exam's correct responses. I became an educational *Robin Hood* stealing from the parsimonious board of education and redistributing the materials to the poor deserving *students*.

Some good advice for beginning teachers is to become chummy with the head custodian. A new teacher's requests will be expedited if he or she likes you. An antagonistic or a disgruntled janitor can stall your written requisitions in deference to servicing his or her favored teachers first.

I recall some of the other faculty members that composed the elementary school's instructional staff, and a few of them were dysfunctional, or perhaps staying around *the profession* a little too long. I worked with many competent educators, but I must honestly admit that a few were misfits and charlatans.

Miss Borona was an inelegant spinster that had seen better days in the classroom. She was oblivious to anything and everything in her *academic* realm but couldn't adjust to the new *sociological* education of the sixties. The days of polite, fearful, submissive and respectful *students* of the 1940s and '50s had passed. Miss Borona stood in front of her late sixties' *students* verbally reviewing the full spectrum of her past academic fantasies and also recalling her vast world traveling experiences.

While the rattled woman lectured her inattentive class, nefarious boys detached the sliding closet doors, sawed the legs off of several wooden desks and dismantled other desks by removing important main screws. So much damage existed at the end of one school day that Miss Barona's classroom appeared as if it had been rammed by a belated Japanese kamikaze pilot's plane.

Ben Martin was an affable guy that seemed to like kids. His problem was that he was too damned friendly with them. Ben would casually chauffeur the darlings around to roller derby matches and skating rink parties, usually at *his* own expense. His biggest weakness was that his love for *children* was not just a random extension of his dedicated professionalism.

Mr. Martin would invite sixth grade boys to his apartment and even showered with a few of the more cooperative post-pubescent ones. Several concerned parents reported word of Ben Martin's deviant eccentricity to the administration. Martin agreed to resign only after being assured that a favorable recommendation would be received from the school executives. And *you* probably thought that most pedophiles were Catholic priests!

Ben got another elementary school teaching position in a distant South Jersey school system, and the naïve residents in that town thought that Mr. Martin was a newly transplanted pillar of the community. Another teacher that had problems similar to Mr. Martin's was allotted severance pay from the board of education until he could obtain employment elsewhere.

Harry Elson was a jolly fellow that taught impressionable fourth graders. He talked to me about "the princesses" in his class as if they were his harem, and Mr. Elson was their sultan. Several alert parents complained to the principal about Harry's overfriendliness with their daughters. Harry managed to stay on the faculty two years before the administration mustered-up enough gumption to fire him just before the man received tenure. The worst part about people like Miss Borona, Ben Martin and Harry Elson existing on *your* faculty is that their ineptitude reinforces the community myth that anyone off the streets could enter a building and teach. Their reputations negatively reflected on the public's image of the remainder of the staff.

Dean Hagbart had a master's degree from a leading university, but it was in liberal arts and not in education. Dean only wanted to teach sixth grade for two years so that he could save money needed to acquire his doctorate. Hagbart's classroom was disorganized, noisy and his *students'* behavior was generally chaotic and wild.

Dean was especially weak in English skills, so I tutored him in the fundamentals of communication that I hadn't learned from Professor Sankin. I was amazed that a person could obtain a master's degree from an accredited college without knowing an adverb from a conjunction, a comma from a coma or a colon from an intestine. In November of '66, Dean's class was rehearsing a new rendition of the ancient Greek play *Prometheus Bound*, but the racket penetrating through the wall from next door sounded more like *Edifice Wrecks*. Despite his deficiencies in English and in teaching skills, Dean is now a prominent curriculum coordinator drawing a handsome salary up in North Jersey.

Darren Jensen was a pretty good teacher who maintained excellent classroom discipline. Darren's main problem was that he was divorced, and he tended to be a little too flirtatious hanging around area bars. One morning, I heard a loud racket coming from another classroom down the hall.

A motorcycle guy wearing a black leather jacket had walked into the building, found Darren Jensen's classroom and entered it unannounced. The intruder went berserk and savagely knocked both Darren Jensen and his wooden lectern to the floor, and then started ferociously punching the targeted victim in front of the screaming, hysterical class. "That's for hitting on my wife!" the crazed trespasser kept repeating until several teachers and the principal rushed into the raucous classroom and removed the violent interloper. Jensen pressed charges against his hostile assailant, but the school principal was reluctant to also do so after considering the general circumstances leading up to the aggravated assault and classroom battery.

I did notice one thing, though, back in 1966 pertaining to certain members of the faculty. Those new instructors that had graduated from teachers' colleges seemed to have better discipline-control and utilized superior teaching methods and better visual aids than those teachers that had graduated with academic non-teaching degrees from various colleges and universities.

A few faculty members that have already been mentioned were suspected womanizers and alleged pedophiles, but the irony was that several of those bizarre deviates were also decent teachers who were dismissed back in the mid-'60s because of their unorthodox lifestyles and not because of their lack of teaching ability.

But who was instrumental in hiring Ben Martin, Harry Elson, Dean Hagbart and Darren Jensen in the first place? How can the teaching profession be indicted for having unfit personnel in its membership when teachers do not do either the hiring or the firing? How does deadwood manage to get tenure? Weren't certain questionable teachers observed, monitored and evaluated for a three-year probationary period prior to receiving tenure?

It is not the fault of the teaching profession or their unions that incompetent or morally loose people are hired and then play havoc with children's impressionable minds. It is because of the inadequacies of school administration that third-rate impostors abound in school systems all across the country.

Certain standard procedures should be employed nationally to ensure that the most qualified candidates secure teaching positions. Prospective teachers should respond to the same list of objective and subjective questions no matter *where* they apply for a position. In the present scenario, administrative interviews are not uniform or consistent from district to district, from county to county, and from state to state.

Boards of education should not be rubber stamps for administrative recommendations. Board members assume too much when they believe that principals and superintendents know everything that they're supposed to be doing. Teaching candidates ought to be intensively queried by a panel consisting of administrators, school board members and veteran representatives from the local teachers' association. No prospect should be hired without the unanimous approval of all three factions. Teachers would then believe that they have more say in deciding important matters like faculty additions or replacements, and the combined interviews of teaching candidates reacting to three separate points of view should improve the current poor hiring track record of autocratic school executives.

Aspiring teachers ought to spend a two full year "internship" working in at least four different public-school systems before being qualified and certified to teach in any elementary, middle, or high school. This could save school districts millions of dollars annually because the teachers in training could devote half of their school days performing *duties* and other non-professional teacher responsibilities that take-up a lot of the regular teachers' time and daily energy.

School administrators that anticipate teacher employment vacancies the following year could observe first-hand student teachers in *their* buildings conducting whole series of lessons and subject units. Teachers would then only be teaching and not performing non-professional duties, and the student teachers would be learning their craft from a variety of mentoring educators, and school districts would be saving tons of money, too.

As it is now, plenty of struggling beginning teachers (in need of suggestions and assistance) seldom receive adequate advice from building administrators, who want little or nothing to do with classroom teaching. It is usually a sympathetic veteran teacher that steps in and provides the necessary advice, special mentoring and quality guidance to the faculty rookie.

Some faculty members are actually counterproductive to teachers acquiring power in the nation's school systems and achieving dignity in *their* chosen profession. These harmful individuals are fixtures inhabiting most elementary, middle and secondary schools, and the detrimental individuals are often sarcastically described as being "Super Teachers". Although a Super Teacher can't leap a tall building with a single bound, he or she thinks that the school could not operate properly without his or her important daily input. Super Teacher has an impeccable attendance record, comes to school every single day despite having the flu or a bad case of bronchitis, and will only take half of a personal day for the funeral of a spouse or a parent. And many Super Teachers instinctively mimic the attitude and personality traits of the school principal in what I call the *"Chameleon Effect"*.

Super Teacher will immediately report to the administration what is going on in another teacher's classroom and will tell the principal *who* has left the building early without really knowing why that person had to depart in a hurry (with or without permission). Whatever Super Teacher does, he or she regards his or her effort as being inspired work of a superior quality that transcends the labor of every regular instructor on the faculty.

Super Teacher solemnly pledges that he or she would not strike if a showdown becomes imminent during contract negotiations between the teachers' association and the board of education. Super Teacher will abandon his or her colleagues on the battlefield while aiding and comforting the enemy (administrators and the school board).

Administrators and school board members depend on Super Teacher for intelligence gathering about other *less super* faculty members, for enacting Benedict Arnolding, and for maintaining the general mediocrity that thrives in the school system. Teachers that use imaginative new methods are regarded as dangerous by Super Teacher, by the board of education, and by narrow-minded parents that call the "power base", all the time complaining about "that new, dangerous teacher"! Super teacher is as trustworthy as a rattlesnake and often is a liaison informer that really has his or her heart's desire set on someday becoming a royal, aristocratic administrator.

Super Teacher thinks that the movement towards teachers' rights is radical in motivation and that it jeopardizes his or her important administrative relationship in the school building. These old guard leftovers see no connection between the increase of teachers' salaries and the rise of teacher militancy, and he or she only goes to teacher association meetings to learn information and gossip and then relay faculty news to the receptive administration.

If it were exclusively up to the local board of education, teachers would be manipulated pawns on the administrative chessboard getting rooked by *their* petty feudal overlords with teacher serfdom and with futile non-navigable channels to redress legitimate grievances. According to Super Teacher, no unique problems exist in his or her classroom, and he or she cannot comprehend why other teachers have plenty of difficulties and numerous complaints.

Super Teacher is mercenary and enjoys the role of informant as a loyal administrative clone. He or she insists that *they* teach because they simply love it, and not because they have to do it out of financial necessity. Super Teacher is often a woman whose husband owns a prosperous local business. This kind of Super Teacher regards herself as being well-anchored in the upper echelon of local society, and her profit-oriented spouse has many financial ties with prominent businessmen serving on the board of education.

Petty strife was prevalent when I had worked in the elementary school. I often felt like a rooster in a chicken coop waiting around for another rooster with whom to converse. Women teachers bickered over pencils, chalk, assemblies, rulers, erasers, crayons and duty assignments. They gossiped about other teachers that were not in the faculty room at the time, about problem *students*, about the problem parents of problem *students,* and about what petty events were happening in the community. The faculty room often sounded like a cacophonous beauty parlor instead of an area designated for professional pursuits and conversations.

Some administrators I had worked under seemed to tolerate teachers quarrelling over petty concerns. They knew that a fragmented faculty will never organize against them and will offer little resistance to executive edicts. By disagreeing amongst themselves, teachers will focus their energies on each other's weaknesses and not seriously scrutinize and criticize administrative inefficiencies. The feudal aristocratic school barons were well-aware that the best way to control and conquer their faculty was to keep the potential enemy divided and battling each other.

Nature has invented a mechanism for eliminating the weakest species, so in the ongoing evolution, only the strongest and the fittest survive. American education knows no similar technique. In public schools, the ineffective instructors often gain tenure, because other weak-but-ambitious, former teachers filter out of classrooms, and the power-motivated social climbers cleverly evolve into becoming bureaucratic school principals and superintendents, into wifty guidance counselors, and into dingbat college professors. The *Peter Principle* has instantly made many former weak, ambitious teachers into today's "dictatorial educational authorities".

Two factors constitute the underlying justification for the need for school administrators. The first is student discipline problems, and the second is ineffective teachers. Take those two factors out of the overall equation and then the public would quickly realize that administrators would have very little to do except attend county roundtable school management meetings. Administrators need student discipline problems just like police departments need crime and criminals in order to stay in business, and school executives need ineffective-but-ambitious teachers to breed a new generation of school administrators.

Most ten-to-twelve-year-old boys don't have a realistic male role model with whom to identify until they reach junior high on upper middle school. Some emotionally scarred boys coming from negative home environments get to be further badly influenced by the likes of Ben Martin, Harry Elson, Dean Hagbart and Darren Jensen. Those youths are deprived of wholesome male images because women teachers dominate elementary schools, especially the primary grades, and the male role models available to already troubled boys often aren't the most desirable mentors.

When I was saddled with twenty-five unique personalities in my sixth-grade experience, I had to have tricks better than those of an accomplished prestidigitator maintained to preserve some semblance of discipline among my tempestuous young broncos and among the less vocal fillies. After an hour of doing subject worksheets, those wooden desks become mighty hard, and it requires great skill and persuasion to keep the *students* interested and occupied for a full seven hours of concentration. My three years laboring in elementary school proved to be good training for teaching high school and junior high later in my career.

It requires a veritable *Mandrake's* magic to coordinate twenty-five diverse minds and continue maintaining a constructive learning activity over a week's span, especially with seven or eight *students* absent daily, and others stepping in and out of the room for a variety of reasons during that five-day time frame. Parents with three young, pesky vipers at home go bananas simply trying to get their kids to do homework, to eat properly, or to go to bed. And during the summer vacation, parents can't wait for September to arrive so that they can safely drop-off their precious *children* and leave them in the trust and custody of school jurisdiction. Multiply the migraine of three kids in the family by eight, and you'll have accurately tailored the daily responsibility of the average elementary school teacher.

High school teachers have the luxury of getting by a standard forty-five-minute time capsule by reading and discussing the textbook, by lecturing, and by conducting question and answer sessions with *their* five or six daily classes. But elementary school teachers must supplement *those* aforementioned teaching techniques with plenty of other types of activities just to keep the self-contained class interested and to keep the individual *student* motivated.

In junior high and in high school, a discipline problem *student* is in and out of a teacher's daily responsibility in a forty-five-minute period, but in elementary school, that little agitator is bothering the instructor's dwindling patience all day long.

Chapter 13
"A Mistake in Judgment"

Teaching in an elementary school is far from being an elementary task. The task challenges an instructor's intellect, its emotional strain saps his or her energy, and at the end of the day, public school teaching will either have the purveyor of learning standing exultantly on top of a mountain or sitting depressed and disenchanted at the bottom of a psychological valley.

An assembly line factory worker putting component parts inside television sets can point to a corner of the shipping department at the end of the labor session and say, "I have worked on five hundred units today!" The teacher working with intangibles like concepts, objectives, motivation, theories and children's minds asks himself or herself the frustrating question, 'What did I accomplish today? What did the kids learn?' Unlike the products manufactured by factory employees, the fruits of teachers' endeavors are not cartons on skids transported by forklifts to a shipping corner. Kids are not products.

While speaking with members of the community, I had to marvel at their misconceptions about teachers, which were about as clear as London metropolitan airports on a foggy night. Many citizens hypothesized that high school teachers made more money than elementary school instructors because the subjects *they* taught were more advanced and that high school teachers had to master much more sophisticated, curriculum matter than elementary school teachers had to acquire.

Actually, it is more important for a teacher to know his or her *students* than to completely know the subject matter he or she must convey. Another popular erroneous community assumption was that teaching is easy because the only thing the teachers have to do is command the obedient *children* around and then watch them feverishly execute the given instructions. The truth is that a blue-collar worker basically performs the same tasks over and over throughout the year, but a teacher has a hundred-and-eighty-day annual assignment that gets more difficult from the first day in September to the finish line in June.

I made one of my biggest teaching blunders during my second year of elementary school instruction. I was still under the ethereal influence of what my college professors had *lectured* and advocated. "Challenge your *students* to think!" they would boldly articulate. "Tell them the truth!"

Back in 1966, most areas of cultural thinking were very compartmentalized, and society was similar to a library file catalog containing many drawers. People had more mental prejudices than they have today, and church groups and their moral values were more involved in education than they are right now. Rural communities viewed taboo subjects along with controversial issues as being "too delicate" or "too offensive" for elementary school discussion. Religion, death, race, politics and sex were among those forbidden territories in which teachers should never wander into. I had taught in an ultra-conservative community with reactionary middle-class values, so instinct should have cautioned me to evade any implication in, or any exploration into, one of those taboo areas.

If a *student* showed interest in the puberty rites of African tribesmen, then my internal compass should automatically read "Danger zone! Red flag!" and then deftly deflect his or her inquiry into something less controversial. "Avoid taboo subjects as if each was an incurable leper," a sage elder teacher had once told me. That sound advice holds true today, just as I should have heeded and honored its veracity thirty-seven years ago. But I had naïve, gullible inclinations and was still on some idealistic crusade inspired by my ethereal college professors.

An enthusiastic girl that also happened to possess a gifted intellect asked me, "Mr. Wiessner, where did I come from? How was I formed?" I evaluated child's sincere motives in asking the very curious question.

At first, I retreated from the bold inquiry as if I was a true coward. After I attempted taking evasive linguistic maneuvers, other perceptive *students* took-up the smart girl's very relevant question and pleaded with me to be honest and direct because their parents had told them such remarkable fabrications as "the stork delivered you", or "you came from Heaven", or "go ask your teacher".

The expressions on the *students'* innocent faces seemed to be thirsting for accurate knowledge, and for once, the room had turned as silent as the moon's surface. 'How could I (the ultimate educator) deny them the privileged, hidden knowledge of their wonderful origin?' I foolishly speculated and imagined.

As my attention further scanned the room, receptive ears and piercing eyes faced my presence. I tried detecting one iota of misbehavior to blame a change of venue upon, but could not discern one small sign of disobedience. 'Is not their hunger and thirst for knowledge genuine?' I faultily thought. 'How can I call myself a bona fide teacher and then conceal from them a definite truth they feel they need to know?'

Then, I pondered the thought some more. 'Aren't matters like venereal diseases and teen pregnancies direct results of ignorance and the lack of knowledge? Isn't perhaps the most central question that humans can ask themselves at a young age the rather important subject of 'Where did I come from'?' I plausibly considered. 'If I can't give the class a religious or a cosmological explanation, certainly I should be able to tell the truth and provide *them* with a basic biological description of how every person on the planet had his or her beginning as a human being!' I was inclined to cast discretion (and almost my fate) to the wind.

At first, I attempted to explain the facts of life in nebulous terms like birds and bees and ovaries, and fertilized seeds, but the *students'* questions soon became more specific and detailed. I tried my best not to deviate from scientific facts, but something deep-down inside told me that this most recent discussion would surely yield a number of indignant parental protests. But I persevered through the crucial ordeal and thought I had done a pretty excellent job under the very trying circumstances.

Much to my relief, the generic fifteen-minute improvised discussion of eggs, sperms, embryos, ovaries, and testes finally concluded, and the smiles on the *students'* countenances all appeared to reflect satisfaction with my general candor. I felt that I had triumphantly vanquished the totally evil quartet consisting of superstition, fear, rumor and ignorance.

The next morning before school, a group of petulant parents packed the main office as if the moms and dads were neurotic boxcar cattle. The assertive adults were demanding my immediate resignation, commanding the besieged principal that their sons and daughters should be transferred to a "more mature teacher", and in the process, the incensed objectors were bombarding the beleaguered school executive with as much verbal artillery their obsessed mouths could vociferate.

A comrade hailed me in the upstairs hall when I was on my way downstairs to the office to run off a worksheet. He had known of the crazy donnybrook transpiring inside the principal's office and advised me to "Stay away from the Salem witch-hunt in progress! Irate fathers want to decapitate you, and the fit-to-be-tied moms want vengeance by having you tarred and feathered and then immediately canned!" my fellow teacher anxiously related.

I had trouble reconciling in my mind what all of the parental disdain was about. While *their* precious *children* were entering puberty, those bellicose parents wanted their offspring to believe that the stork had delivered them and that the *Immaculate Conception* was a "bright idea" the Virgin Mary had formulated. "The fathers are foaming at the mouth and all look like they need rabies shots right away," my colleague nervously confided.

"All they want me to do is give their kids a lot of irrelevant facts and stay away from anything of substance that requires real thought or real explanation," I stubbornly answered. "They just want me to keep the lid on tight, and also to artificially give the appearance of knowledge being imparted!"

The next week was a real tribulation for me to endure. I had five separate conferences with school administrators including the superintendent, and my superiors all made me feel as if I had been an unprofessional, vile monster that had egregiously violated my "professional ethics". Their steadfast position was that "sex education is not listed in the sixth-grade curriculum", and if anyone on the staff were qualified to teach it, then that person would be the school nurse, or perhaps the Health and Phys. Ed. instructor.

'My God!' I thought while being the object of the severe administrative rebuking. 'Here I am, the main character in a contemporary Scopes Monkey Trial without any famous Clarence Darrow around to defend me!'

When I exited the last horrible conference, I felt like a resident of either Sodom or Gomorrah waiting for fire and brimstone to abruptly descend on my physical being. 'Move over Lucifer!' I mentally contemplated. 'You have company in hell!'

I could not comprehend the parents' Jonathan Edwards-Cotton Mather type demeanor. I had been taught in college that Inquisitions were outmoded medieval phenomena, but I can assure you they do occur periodically in school principals' offices without the involvement of Copernicus. 'I mean, let's cheer for the dragon against St. George,' I privately sulked. 'And while we're at it, how about cheering for the Russians to beat us to *Mars*!'

Public schools are often citadels of hypocrisy. College professors tell prospective teachers to challenge *students* and to not shy away from what *they* genuinely care to know. I discovered quite readily that sensitive school subjects such as religion, politics, sex and race could get someone catapulted into the hot seat or rapidly fired in a New York second. Forget about eradicating local ignorance and national injustice. The public school I had taught in practiced a fantastic sleight-of-hand trick where the institution reflected the impression of constant revision and curricular change, but always somehow remained the same during my thirty-four-year tenure.

The school administration worshiped mediocrity, and the status quo, and then protected those sanctuaries like Beefeaters guarding the *Crown Jewels* of England at the *Tower of London*. True "freedom of thought" and the "freedom of expression" are merely goals stated in the curriculum books, but those noble objectives are seldom practiced because of the fear of hostile parental backlash. "Play the game," "Don't swim against the tide!" and "Stay between the lines!" soon become the cautionary watchwords of teachers.

I knew little about the *ACLU* or similar organizations that might have defended my "academic freedom". So, I tried forgetting about the parent rebellion and amazingly, in a matter of a month, the situation seemed to invert itself back to normal. At the end of my second year in the system, the educational gods smiled favorably on me. The parents that were my most vicious critics miraculously transformed into my staunchest supporters. The administration offered me a third-year contract, which indirectly forgave me for my reckless "error in judgment".

So ever since 1966, every time a *child* hungering for enlightenment about sex, population control, teenage pregnancy or sensitive matters that engendered political controversy, my ever-present instinct to survive surfaced and dictated to my suppressed, conditioned conscience, 'Let the kid starve!'

Adam and Eve ate the forbidden fruit of the Old Testament *Tree of Knowledge,* and mankind has been cursed and punished ever since. I offered significant knowledge to satisfy the mental appetites of curious sixth grade *students,* and I almost was banished from the non-paradise known as elementary school teaching. How ironic!

Despite the fact that I had addressed the class in strictly scientific language, my reputation in the community thirty-seven years later is still frayed from that 1966 incident. Disregard the fact that I had developed and taught hundreds of unique lessons in that lengthy time frame. Forget the fact that I have taught over four thousand *students* in my three-and-a-half-decade career. Local posterity will always remember me as the naïve teacher that stupidly taught the forbidden "ten-minute sex lesson".

Chapter 14

"Summer Employment"

In December of my third year of teaching sixth grade, a fellow teacher reported that I had been nominated for president of the teacher's association for the 1968-'69 school year. I reluctantly consented, stating that I was still a non-tenure teacher and that perhaps I should wait another year before I declared my candidacy.

"A lot of teachers think you're ready for the leadership position right now," Mr. Renbeck declared. "They truly admire your audacity and think that you're the most outspoken teacher in the entire system, and also, the troops believe that you're not-at-all afraid to proudly stand-up to the administration."

"Thanks," I non-passionately acknowledged the compliment. "But I think I'd rather be vice-president of the association until I get tenure. But put my name on the ballot for president anyway, and get the word out that I would really prefer to be vice-president."

I was honored and flattered that my colleagues thought enough of me to represent them against the potent administration and the board of education. Several weeks later before school, my butt was parked on the hopper in the upstairs Men's Teacher's Lounge. I was dealing with a touch of constipation when Rob Renbeck's voice filtered through the closed bathroom door.

"Guess what John!" Rob Renbeck rhetorically began. "I'm the curator of ballots for the teacher's presidential election, and remarkably, you're the only person that hasn't voted yet!"

"Is the election close?" I worriedly asked while recalling my infamous "sex lesson" and my disfavor with several board members and parents that had kept extended grudges. "I have my doubts about wanting to be president right now."

"That's why I'm here!" Rob replied. "You're tied with Ed Donohue with seventy-nine votes each. What's your pleasure J.W.?"

Like a squashed coward I voted against myself', and that's how I lost the election by one vote. I served as vice-president of the teachers' association for the next five years until 1973.

I distinctly recollect those first teachers' association dinner meetings, which were somewhat akin to Taras Bulba or Attila the Hun rowdy smorgasbords. While Ed Donohue tried obtaining order with his gavel, glasses were clicking, silverware was clanging and rickety wooden restaurant chairs were scratching against the floor. Raucous debates over petty concerns prevailed, and little in the way of professionalism was observable. The association lacked strategy, organization, policies, bylaws, direction, focus and power.

The one true satisfaction I had gained over the course of my teaching career was witnessing the teachers' association mature into an effective body of concerned educators that realized genuine improvements in our school district would only result from a staunch, consolidated solidarity exercised by the professional staff.

"Teachers associations have for far-too-long been sleeping giants," I told President Ed Donohue. "And members should not be the obedient serfs of omnipotent administrators and their comrade school board members. The rules of engagement are changing. Next year, we'll have our first official, state recognized, negotiating team, and then we will not have to beg the board of education for meager hundred and fifty dollar raises!"

"You ought to write a book about all this crap!" Ed casually suggested and jested. "I have confidence that you can!"

"I think that someday I will!" I audaciously answered. "I'm gonna' call it *Teacher Serfdom in America!*"

"Make sure it's published after *you* get tenure!" Ed grimly advised. "I'm being harassed by the superintendent and being called-down to his office every day after eighth period to discuss a lot of trivial nonsense!" the high school Latin and English teacher divulged.

In the spring of '68, the superintendent and the principal did not renew the contract of a third-year teacher, Ed Pevkis. Everyone on the staff believed that Pevkis was a terrific teacher, so Donohue and I circulated a letter of support with a hundred and eighty teacher signatures and delivered the missive to the superintendent's secretary inside the recently constructed high school building.

The superintendent was angry that a copy of the letter had also been sent to the board of education. So, "the super" harassed the association by calling in (over the summertime) all hundred and eighty teachers that had signed the letter and then aggressively interrogated and harassed the hell out of the membership while questioning each teacher's "loyalty to the system".

Fortunately for me, my last name began with W, and I was at the end of the list and not called in until the beginning of September.

"You know the administration had stood-up for you when you were on the ropes last year about that suspect sex lesson!" the red-faced superintendent reminded me.

"Thanks," I replied. "I definitely made an error in judgment!"

"And you're up for tenure next year," the superintendent indicated.

"For your information," I told the forgetful chief school executive, "I got tenure last week after I had completed the first day of school in the beginning of my fourth year!" I assertively related to the surprised, aged, baldheaded philosopher who thought that he was Socrates reincarnated. "And I want you to know that I don't react favorably to intimidation!"

"You may leave now!" the superintendent announced in a rather peeved, superior tone of voice.

Another aspect of "Teacher Serfdom" is that most male teachers and some female ones must annually find summer employment. Several of my male friends found lowly July and August jobs earning minimum wage installing chain-link-fences while working alongside *students* they had taught the year before. Several female teachers worked as waitresses, substitute bank tellers and convenience store clerks during the summer months. One teacher revealed that he had worked for a foreman (on road construction) that had been a slow-learner *he* had instructed in remedial reading five years back in 1963. "*He* now knows how to install guardrails and how to pour cement even though *he* couldn't read a damn sentence in plain English," my rather flustered instructor friend petulantly commented.

Since teachers' salaries back in 1965-'68 guaranteed them little more than subsistence living conditions, I needed to find summer employment to supplement my anemic wages. After surviving my first year in the grizzly educational arena, I worked for my father-in-law, a tough Sicilian taskmaster who owned and operated a four-hundred-acre farm growing mostly peaches and apples. He also grew twenty acres each of tomatoes, peppers, corn and zucchini squash, which were then sold both wholesale and retail at *his* prosperous packinghouse and farm market.

My father-in-law considered himself a self-made man, and his tough demeanor often made Simon Legree look like Little Orphan Annie. My new boss's commercial farming operation required the employment of seventy migrant workers during the height of the summer harvest season. My background had been limited to displaying and retailing fruit and vegetables at my parents and my grandparents' farm markets, but my obstinate father-in-law insisted that I needed to learn all aspects of *his* farming empire and not focus exclusively on *his* farm market.

My father-in-law and I planted five acres of staked tomatoes, but then he realized that the rows were too close together and the spaces between them were too narrow to cultivate with any of his tractors. "You're gonna' have to use *this* contraption to cultivate the tomatoes!" my father-in-law indicated as he showed me a garden hand-tractor/cultivator inside his tin storage shed.

I looked closely at the rusty garden furrowing machine, which appeared as if it had been leased from the *Smithsonian Institute*. "You gotta' be kidding!" I exclaimed. "This is entirely unrealistic!"

"That's *your* own personal tractor!" my summer boss answered without cracking a smile. "Now get busy cultivating those five acres of staked tomatoes with this rotor tiller!"

The device was not easy to manipulate and steer. I had to press down firmly on the throttle with my right hand while attempting to guide the mechanism along all fifty long rows situated between the staked tomato plants. 'Oh, the marvels of this wonderful age of technology!' I futilely thought, glad that I didn't have to keep the excessive weeds out of the field with a hand hoe. The task took me a half-day's exhaustive physical labor to complete, and I grumbled and cursed incessantly as I traversed up and down the skinny, sandy weed-infested lanes.

At the end of the workday, my body ached from head to toe. My hands were a series of blisters formed around and between each callus, my legs hurt so much that they felt as if my feet had been embedded all day in concrete blocks, and my calves were swollen to the size of cantaloupes. What a *harrowing* experience that five-acre cultivation job was!

The farm packinghouse's cold storage had a capacity of five thousand forty-pound boxes of tree-ripened peaches to be temporarily held inside before sending them via tractor-trailer transportation to New York, Boston or Philadelphia wholesale food distribution centers. My assignment was to haul the peach crates on wheeled skids in and out of the cold storage. I had to stack the forty-pound boxes from the floor to two feet over my head one by one. "Here's a jacket for you to keep warm inside the cooler!" my father-in-law said as he handed me an Eskimo parka. "Try not to catch a cold and get sick! You'll be more lucky next year when I plan on buying a forklift!"

Forty-nine forty-pound boxes of peaches were loaded one by one on skids by stackers after the fruit had been sorted by hand and size-graded by machine, and I was the source of energy that had to pull the two-thousand-pound loaded skids into the frigid cold storage and then stack them. When a tractor-trailer arrived, I had to un-stack the boxes onto the skids and then haul them outside the cold storage to be hand-loaded loaded onto refrigerated trucks. 'I feel like a crippled locomotive pulling these two thousand-pound loads in and out of the cooler!' I realized and mentally complained. 'Walking across the *Sahara Desert* on stilts would be less exhausting!' This was before forklifts and square bins became popular in farm use, so I had to perform the work of a forklift with a hand-jack and then load and unload the skids.

One hot July day my father-in-law and I were out in one of his peach orchards. A terrible summer drought had plagued area farms, and the peach trees needed watering. A shallow stream ran through that part of the farm, so my father-in-law and I rigged up a fire hose to an irrigation pump because the stream had gone almost dry. I had driven to the project scene in a chopped-down flat-bodied rusty old truck with a one-thousand-gallon water tank mounted on its rear. My job was to clamber-up the back of the truck and then hold the fire hose inside the opening on top of the giant plastic vat until it was completely filled with a thousand gallons of water.

Everything seemed to be going okay until my father-in-law opened the valve and then water spurted and then gushed into the enormous plastic container. The pressure became very intense, and I struggled with every ounce of strength I could muster to keep the powerful fire hose from popping out of the mammoth tank. I found that I could no longer control the great downward thrust. The fire hose slid from the tank's opening, and I stretched and exerted every muscle attached to my anatomy to squeeze the hose back inside.

The fire hose's resistance was too indomitable for my futile effort to control. Soon I staggered backward and awkwardly wrestled with the pivoting hose that somehow wrapped around my body like a boa constrictor going amok. I clumsily danced around upon a ladder near the top of the colossal water drum while water flares shot out in all directions as I wildly grappled with the powerful fire hose's force.

Laughter abounded among four migrant workers and my father-in-law, who were mirthfully witnessing comedy in the making. My audience of five found my travail very amusing as the spectators attentively appreciated the zany antics that were transpiring. I ungracefully stepped-down from the ladder and next swiveled about the huge plastic barrel as if I was a drunken tightrope walker losing confidence in his balancing act. Hercules must have had an easier time grappling with the nine-headed hydra.

After a minute that disguised itself as a century, the awesome water burst was shut off at the irrigation pump, and I then disgustedly threw-down the limp hose onto the truck's platform. The four Puerto Rican migrant laborers, who incidentally were gregarious enough to give me a mock round of applause, ecstatically celebrated my frustration. 'Agriculture is definitely not in my *field*, and certainly not in my orchard!' I angrily concluded.

I was undaunted by my most recent challenges. I truly believed that in the end my fortitude would prevail, and I would finally be allowed to manage the farm market. One sultry day in late July, my father-in-law decreed that I should pick ten half-bushel-baskets of Jersey sugarplums. Armed with basket straps, ten empty half-bushels, a wooden picking ladder and my desire to live, I joined-up with a team of six migrant workers who also had been assigned to pick ten baskets each. Everything was going smoothly, and I climbed up 'the ladder of non-success' and was 'plum loco' actually enjoying the act of 'plumming' as my mind had fancifully labeled the laborious assignment. 'I thought that plumbers made more than $1.25 an hour!' I mentally joked in relation to the farm workers' (and mine) minimum wage at the time.

I noticed that the finest, plump, purple plums were either roosted at the top of my tree or at the extremity of the highest limb. I left the safe ladder rungs and clambered-upon a sturdy limb with the half-full, half-bushel hooked to straps around my chest. I felt like I was the master of my environment as I invincibly hopped from limb to limb as if I was a jaunty chimpanzee. 'Peter Piper picked a peck of plump purple plums!' I ecstatically amused myself.

Plum picking could become rather monotonous after a while, so I imaginatively pretended I was a 'fruit sheriff' arresting wanted criminal plums several at a time. A huge luscious-looking overhead plum (with an alluring purple midriff at the top of the tree) instantly caught my attention. I confidently reached-up and extended my left arm to its maximum reach. 'And to think that Charlie Darwin thought that our human ancestors were tree dwellers!' I mused while mentally alluding to my 'limbering-up' activity.

My outstretched fingers finally touched the magnificent plum's circumference, and then all of a sudden, I lost my equilibrium and hung diffidently from a weak tree branch for at least ten seconds. The contingent of migrant workers heard my shrieking from their ladders, turned in my direction, and then began laughing hysterically at my very precarious predicament.

My endurance and my stamina were swiftly diminishing, and when I gaped at my wrists, I observed crimson blood trails trickling down towards my elbows. I closed my eyes, hoped for the best, and then let go of the tree branch from which I had been dangling. Luckily, I didn't carom off of any limbs in my swift plummet to the ground. Upon making impact with *terra-firma*, my legs buckled, and I rolled down an embankment with the picking basket still attached to my chest, with my clumsy tumbling finally stopping two feet from an irrigation pond. The juicy essence from the crushed plums had rolled onto my face, since gravity had forced the purple fruit downward from the smashed half-bushel basket that was still tightly strapped to my bosom.

The migrant workers cackled convulsively at my latest difficulty, and then they exchanged mirthful phraseology in their Spanish dialect about the hilarious spectacle they had just witnessed. I escaped the misadventure slightly embarrassed and humiliated from my unexpected plunge. All I really needed was a little gauze, two band-aids and a reconstructed ego to valiantly enter into battle again the next morning.

Another farm incident that is still lodged in my memory occurred at another old reliable irrigation pond located at the intersection of four peach and nectarine orchards. My father-in-law desired to inspect the composition of a well pipe that had been designed and constructed to protrude from the ground. He directed me to hold the well pipe steady while he gingerly lifted it from its underground shaft to make sure that the pipe was not leaking.

I couldn't believe my eyes as my boss kept lifting and raising the seemingly endless aluminum tube from the ground. The process reminded me of a magician pulling an infinite string of handkerchiefs from a hat. As I glanced skyward, I realized that I was supporting a wobbly vertical aluminum irrigation tube that must have been twenty-five-foot high. A swirling summer wind gyrated the lengthy tube back and forth as I desperately attempted to keep it steady and perpendicular to the ground. My brawn was easily overwhelmed, and then the wobbling aluminum tube fell to the ground with a dull thud.

The reaction force in the opposite direction sent me somersaulting down the embankment and into an irrigation ditch that emptied into the small pond. After verifying Newton's third law of motion, I emerged from the ditch looking like I was a hog that had spent the afternoon wallowing around in filthy slush. And to add insult to my displeasure, my egress from the muddy ditch was greeted by a tirade of unsavory, derogatory and demeaning comments from my livid father-in-law.

The aluminum pipe to the well shaft had been bent and misshapen from impacting the ground, so it was *our* task to transport it to a repair shop to be realigned. The deformed tube was strapped to a rack in the rear of my father-in-law's pickup truck, and my responsibility was to hold the front section with my arm hanging out of the cab's passenger side window.

As my father-in-law slowly drove the necessary two miles down a major highway to the repair shop, the elongated metal tube swayed back and forth, crunching my right wrist, elbow, forearm and bicep with each banging oscillation. I grimaced in agony but had too much pride to complain about my encumbrance to my already infuriated father-in-law. By the time we reached our destination, my chafed right arm was pulsating with unbearable pain. 'My battered lacerated right elbow is more disfigured than the shaft pipe!' I soon realized.

My right arm remained swollen for an entire week after I had miraculously endured that gruesome punishment, and my mind was convinced that the wrath of all my enemies had to be avenged tenfold for all of the agony I had experienced from the overall ordeal. But I showed my grit and determination and managed to survive my wicked summer anguishing on the fruit and vegetable farm without perishing.

After my first two summers on the farm, I promised my conscience that I would have another more tranquil and less strenuous existence the following June. Another sixth-grade teacher had gotten a summer gig as the manager of a small arcade on the boardwalk in Ocean City, Maryland. "I need a good assistant manager!" he related. "Are you interested?"

"Sure am," I answered. "Anything will be better than that insane gauntlet I had to run through on my father-in-law's peach farm!"

I really liked running the boardwalk arcade, got to know the owner pretty well, and when he needed money to finance other similar operations in Wildwood, Atlantic City and Seaside Heights, New Jersey, I borrowed money and used my savings to buy into the Ocean City, Maryland arcade. I was ready to participate in free enterprise business before the 1968 summer season.

From 1968-'81, I had co-owned boardwalk businesses and arcades in Ocean City, Maryland, Rehoboth Beach, Delaware and Atlantic City, New Jersey. I was like a jackrabbit each year from weekends in May right through October "jumping up and down" the East Coast between the three resort cities. The highlight of each trip was the seventeen-mile ferry-cruise excursion across *Delaware Bay* from Cape May to Lewes, Delaware. I estimate that I had taken the short voyage at least seven hundred times between '68 and '81, transporting merchandise, tee shirts, arcade prizes and finally loose *(non-carton)* stuffed, plush animals between my Jersey home and the three popular, summer, seashore destinations.

The price of the crossing was quite cheap back in '68. I recollect spending a mere five dollars to cross the bay with a car full of merchandise (today the expense is fifty dollars from April-October for driver and car). I recall that fellow passengers would request to buy stuffed animals from me and I would refuse, telling them that "the plush" (boardwalk slang) happened to be arcade prizes that had to be won and not purchased.

I would jam as many *ferry furry creatures* inside my green *Pontiac* station wagon as I could. And when curious ferry riders would gawk at all of the bears, giraffes, cats, dogs and elephants crammed inside my vehicle, I would yell-up to them on the main deck, "Now you know why *they* call these things *stuffed* animals!" That comment would always elicit a chuckle or two.

I would habitually leave my Jersey home at six a.m. and still have sufficient time to board the *Cape May-Lewes Ferry* for a seven-thirty departure. I enjoyed many bacon and eggs breakfasts on the boat during the hour and fifteen-minute leisure bay crossing. My memory recalls that one foggy morning in late September, the captain had made an error in judgment and the almost-empty ferryboat wound-up on the wrong side of the jetty on the Delaware side. We were nearer to Cape Henlopen than to Lewes, and the general atmosphere was similar to being on a mysterious lost ghost ship adrift at sea.

Occasionally, I would encounter local people on their way south for business or for vacation. One time I struck-up a conversation with Egg Harbor City undertaker Larry Winberg (who had attended *St. Joseph High* with my wife). He was on his way to Delaware to pick up a new client, and another time I met Mike Palmieri, owner of the Farmers Daughter Market going south to procure a load of early season cantaloupes.

Sometimes my being a conscientious person backfired. One busy Friday, just before *Memorial Day,* I stopped at a New Jersey bank to deposit my wife's and my teacher checks. I had the green station wagon loaded to the gills with arcade prizes, and my wife was my passenger. I thought that one of my back tires was low, so I pulled over on the *Garden State Parkway* just before Cape May.

Richard and Teresa Lanza (blueberry farmers from my town) pulled-over and asked if my wife and I needed help. I thanked them, saying that the tire would be "all right". When Joanne and I arrived at the ferry terminal, the Lanzas were the last car able to squeeze aboard the final ferry to Delaware. As a result, I had to drive the entire distance to the *Delaware Memorial Bridge,* and then motor down the *Delmarva Peninsula* to Ocean City, Maryland. A three and a half-hour-trip suddenly transformed into a nine-hour-nightmare. "All of this craziness because we're schoolteachers and need summer income!" I protested to my wife.

"Keep your bleary bloodshot eyes on the road!" my wife retorted.

I was in town one 16th of July, a local carnival feast day. I needed to buy a new portable TV for the apartment in Ocean City, MD. My mind remembers being under duress trying to get around the crowded town streets and to Colonial Electric. Louis Valenti (an old-time friend) sold me a set, which could just squeeze into the already packed front bench seat between my wife and me.

Driving down Twelfth Street, I ran over a board that had protruding nails. I felt my steering wheel wobbling, so I proceeded to the Frank Farley Rest Area on the *Atlantic City Expressway* and filled-up the left front tire with air. The same thing happened near Pleasantville, where I exited the *Expressway* and repeated the inflation procedure at a local gas station. I filled the tire twice more, once on the *Garden State Parkway* and finally again in Cape May.

When I finally arrived at the *Cape May Ferry* tollbooth, I turned-up the volume on the car radio and paid the collector the exact amount so that she could not hear the air sizzling originating out of my left front tire. Then my green station wagon boarded the boat. My wife and I sat in the vehicle until the tire went flat, stepped upstairs and had lunch, and when the ferry was in the middle of the bay, I reported my "newly discovered dilemma" to the ship's captain.

After the boat docked in Lewes, two burly ferry employees came to my assistance by inflating my maligned front tire with air-sealant. I departed the vessel and safely made it to Ocean City, Maryland without incident, and to this day, I must laugh to myself every time I think about how I had made my very aggravating flat-tire nightmare the problem of the *Cape-May Lewes Ferry* personnel.

"All of this insanity would never be happening if I wasn't an impoverished schoolteacher in need of extra summer income to make ends meet!" I reiterated to my wife after arriving at the 410 South Boardwalk arcade. "Life is almost too difficult to endure!"

"Remember, you aren't a schoolteacher!" my wife replied. "You teach kids and not schools!"

The following spring, a very important school referendum was taking place in the town where I was teaching. A bond issue was up for public approval for a new elementary school to be constructed in order to alleviate overcrowded conditions in the archaic, early 1900's school buildings being used.

My wife had just delivered our second son. Since she was still weak from her delivery, and since I was still commuting back and forth on weekends to Ocean City, Maryland and Rehoboth Beach, Delaware, we had secured absentee voting ballots. My wife and I had voted independently, sealed our secret ballots in envelopes, and then I mailed the documents at the town post office on my way south to the all-too-familiar *Cape May-Lewes Ferry*. Alfred Hitchcock couldn't have planned a more suspenseful drama (or should I more accurately state, "trauma")?

Voting is a sacred franchise, and each person's selection should remain an individual's secret choice. But everyone in the town seemed to know that *our* two ballots would determine the fate of the new elementary school building project. Our voting slips had been improperly sealed, and my wife's and my absentee votes were invalidated. The bond issue was defeated by one vote, and our two votes had been disqualified.

Up to this day, my wife and I are still blamed for the defeat of the bond issue. The board of education and the townspeople not only know me as the teacher that taught the infamous "sex lesson" but also as the teacher that voted down the new school building, which eventually was finally built five years later.

Late during my tenure year, I had heard that a vacancy would be available for a high school teaching position. Since I wanted out of the elementary school scenario, I applied for transfer within the district. The elementary school principal and the high school principal confided to me that I had the vacancy locked-up, so I left for the summer to Ocean City, Maryland thinking that my new job as "Permanent Substitute" in the high school was secure.

In early July, the superintendent's secretary called my place of business in Maryland and informed me that the *super* wanted to interview me about my upcoming New Jersey teaching assignment.

"I've already submitted a formal letter explaining my intent," I maintained, "and I've already been lengthily interviewed by the superintendent before I was given the sixth-grade teaching job. And besides that, the high school principal has already interviewed me!"

"Sorry, but *he* insists that *you* come in and see him next Wednesday afternoon at two," the superintendent's secretary apologetically related. "Remember, he's the boss!"

I was pretty damned angry because I had to leave my boardwalk business enterprise and had to be inconvenienced for a mere transfer inside the school district when I had already been interviewed for the position by the high school principal. 'Administrators don't like it when teachers have their own businesses in addition to being a humble employee who is *subordinate* to their whims!' I concluded.

The hundred-and-seventy-five-mile excursion from Ocean City, Maryland to my town in New Jersey took three and a half hours. On the way back to Jersey, I recollected how the superintendent was a good friend of my father-in-law. Once I had to take a personal day from teaching to have a root canal done to correct a serious tooth-gum abscess problem. I stopped into my father-in-law's home on my way back from the Haddonfield oral surgeon. The superintendent was sitting at the lunch table after *he* had stopped by to get some spring tomato and pepper plants for his garden. "Why aren't you at school?" the head school executive asked me.

"I'm just returning from the dentist and had to take a personal day," I mumbled from my swollen mouth filled with gauze.

"Couldn't you have taken half a personal day instead of a full one?" the out-of-touch superintendent seriously remarked.

"No; I had oral surgery and my mouth is really swollen!" I explained. I thought of saying 'Why aren't *you* running the damned school like you're supposed to be doing instead of sitting here drinking coffee and eating doughnuts while doing your personal business getting tomato and pepper plants for your garden?' But then I intelligently refrained from making the caustic commentary.

I arrived from Maryland for the scheduled conference at the superintendent's office a half-hour early. The self-important school chieftain invited me into his air-conditioned office, and after twenty minutes of insignificant chitchat, the interview was over. On the drive back from New Jersey to Ocean City, Maryland, I stewed about how I had wasted an entire day and three hundred and fifty miles of travel in heavy shore-bound traffic for the sake of a twenty-minute routine "power game bull session".

When I arrived back at 410 South Boardwalk, I was shocked to see that the store doors had been closed and the lights were out. 'This is highly unusual!' I reckoned. After I entered the establishment, I stepped to the back office, and I soon discovered that money had been purloined and prizes had been pilfered from the storage shelves. The total loss came to an excess of a thousand dollars (about ten thousand bucks adjusted into today's money). Several brazen culprits in my employ had made-off with their loot, blew town, and never returned to the scene of the crime. And so, I'll never forget the "power game interview" to preserve a forty dollar a day 1967 teaching job that cost me in excess of a thousand bucks plus traveling expenses, and a day's business to boot.

But my title as an educator was about to change from elementary school teacher to an esteemed high school permanent substitute. I had contemplated making a move to the high school for three years, and now was my chance to work with more mature *students*.

Chapter 15
"High School Permanent Sub"

A cynic is one that finds fault with most everyone and most everything. Cynics are negative and pessimistic. People that are cynics feel impotent and dependent in a state of affairs they view as unalterable or permanent. A satirist pokes fun at hypocrisy and hopes that circumstances will get better. Not only does a satirist believe that conditions will eventually improve but he or she goes about the chore of exposing foibles and bringing injustices and ambiguities to the public's attention to make others aware of *alterable* conditions. American education is a self-satire where this work's author merely has to describe a litany of events that have occurred during his teaching career.

I felt jubilant making the transition from the elementary school doldrums to the resplendence of the local high school. The lower grades had many accessory duties I despised like answering the fire phones, keeping class attendance records in a logbook, collecting milk money and having to schedule and then record two parent/guardian conferences for each *student*. Elementary school teaching involved plenty of trite clerical record keeping.

But some of the duties assigned to high school teachers were similar to those apportioned to elementary school instructors. Teachers still had to write the following week's lesson plans and submit them to the office secretary by Thursday morning. Instructors still were assigned morning and after school bus duty, and homeroom teachers still had to collect picture and insurance money from *students*.

Duties balanced-out between elementary and high school because most high school teachers had an after-school activity, a sport to coach or a *student* club. And most of the faculty members were commissioned with cafeteria duty, Office Detention, In-School Suspension (for a forty-five-minute school period), study hall duty, lavatory duty and hall duty between the changing of classes. All of those additional duties levied a great burden on the teachers that all originally had become educators because they solely desired to civilize the next generation inside classrooms.

School board members and parents have long considered duties as assignments that are and were indicative of teacher dedication. And as far as administrators were concerned, teacher duties were synonymous with apple pie, mother, baseball and *duty* toward God and country.

But duties cause educational inefficiency to thrive like a pestilence in American public schools. Being pedestrian in function, grueling duties fleece teachers of self-esteem. Teaching his or her classes is paramount in an instructor's mind, and that's why he or she comes to school each day. And most teachers that get in trouble for grabbing a *student* or insulting a *student* lose their tempers while on these *non-professional* duties. I soon discovered that high school teachers quickly become disillusioned when they experience *student* abuse and disrespect as they handle non-teaching duties in addition to having a homeroom and teaching five or six periods with twenty-five kids in each one.

Most of the time the art of teaching is an enjoyable experience if the *students* are receptive and cooperative. As a permanent sub', I understood how those leeching duties inclined many good teachers to raid the medicine cabinet each evening. Duties erode teacher enthusiasm and hurl an instructor into volatile *student* mass situations like the cafeteria and the school parking lots.

Duties in general cheapen both a teacher's self and public worth, corrode one's self-image, and frequently create bad vibrations between himself (herself) and pupils prior to dealing with the same *students* that misbehaved in the cafeteria again in the classroom. Duties generate massive inefficiency (because teachers could be doing professional responsibilities instead of duties in the interim), and they are debilitating irritations in that they have nothing to do with the art and science of teaching.

As a high school permanent substitute teacher, I soon learned that high school *students* weren't that much more academically knowledgeable as sixth graders had been. They were only bigger kids and some of them were much more defiant.

I was amazed at how deficient high school kids were in basic history and geography common knowledge. Only about forty percent knew that Thomas Jefferson was the third U.S. President, and only around twenty percent could find Iraq or Iran on a globe. But things are getting worse instead of better as our American culture continues to "dumb down".

In 1950, the average American fourteen-year-old had twenty-five thousand words in his/her speaking/reading vocabularies, and in 2000 the average fourteen-year-old used and understood only ten thousand words despite all of the new technology at his or her disposal. Computers are actually contributing to the "dumbing-down of America". I witnessed this "dumbing-down" occurring from the mid-'70s up to my retirement in June of '99.

The permanent substitute had to replace the regular teacher that had been absent from school that day. If a teacher took sick midway in the school day, or had to leave the building because of a family emergency, I would take his or her place if I were available. Since I was a certified teacher, *students* were guaranteed that they would not be exposed to a weak outside substitute with only sixty credits (many of them not even in teaching methods) coming in and compounding their "dumbing down".

Bill Catello was the other permanent substitute on the high school staff of eighty-five instructors. Bill was ready to retire with thirty-six years of experience under his belt, and he was one of the finest individuals I've ever had the pleasure of knowing. He was from the "old school" and had served on the same faculty as Mr. Charles B. Sipley. I admired Bill because he was gracious, had firm values, knew how to take a stand, and would verbally joust with another teacher to the end if *he* believed he was right. Teachers of Bill Catello's character in this "politically correct society" are now as rare as Buddhist pagodas in downtown Moscow.

Bill Catello had the willpower of a devout Jesuit, and every facet of his suave temperament exuded strength and Italian/American determination. He possessed a deep old-fashioned virtue that at times was passive and beaming, and at other times angry and annoyed at the "dumbing down" of *students*. Mr. Catello also abhorred the whimsical idiosyncrasies of administrators and could see through the Educational Aristocracy's personality veneers as if the boyars' foreheads were transparent.

My aged partner came from an educational era when right was right and wrong was wrong, and there wasn't any eighty percent gray area in between that's being promoted by school executives, by lawyers, by talk show hosts and by politicians. His accent revealed a tough person of Italian descent that called a spade a spade. Bill certainly was not "politically correct" in the late 1960s, and he was both admired and despised because of it.

Bill Catello told me that education was "turning phony" and that administrative diplomacy with irate parents was taking away teacher authority in the classroom. "When I was a young teacher," Bill revealed, "I could get a misbehaving kid suspended on my own. Now I have to write a report to the principal, who then acts like a judge. Teachers are no longer respected by parents and kids because *they* know we have no authority like we did have back in the '40s!"

And Bill was absolutely right. If a *student* steals, the teacher is supposed to be diplomatic and tell the parent during a conference, "Johnny can't keep his hands on his own property!" If a *student* lies, the teacher will say, "Johnny has quite an imagination and is always stretching the truth!" If a *student* is caught cheating, the teacher will say almost apologetically to the parent, "Johnny's eyes wander when they aren't supposed to!"

Bill Catello was a guy that wouldn't have any part of widely practiced fake diplomacy. He would say to a parent something blunt like, "Your kid is a thief, a liar and a cheat, so what the hell are *you* going to do about it?"

"Telling it like it is!" is a no-no in modern American education, but back in 1968, Bill Catello never searched or groped for cliches, or platitudes, or euphemisms when truth was at stake. Bill's refusal to surrender or compromise his convictions made him (in my eyes) a tower of strength on the high school faculty.

When two teachers were absent, I didn't mind taking the more challenging or demanding assignment. When only one teacher was absent, I insisted on taking the detail because Bill was old and his health was beginning to decline.

I would observe Bill Catello sitting in the teacher's lounge, trying vainly to keep his eyelids open and half-listening to idle conversation. Next, he would doze-off into a placid slumber for ten minutes or so, and then wake up. Bill's face was pallid, and when he took a catnap, a massif of wrinkles on his countenance displayed a man that had lived a good hard life.

William Catello was a tribute to his profession. But old Bill never lived to see a happy retirement. He died of cancer over the summer months, and three years after his passing, the high school football stadium was named in his honor. I don't think I've ever admired any other teachers as much as I had revered distinguished Bill Catello and Charles B. Sipley.

When driving early to the high school each morning, I wondered whether I'd be a History, English, Math' or Science teacher that day. The suspense always intrigued me. Each morning, I strolled into the Main Office feeling as if I was a secret agent getting my next "Mission Impossible" assignment.

After receiving my command instructions for the day from the head secretary, the next full hour was spent feverishly researching the needed material I had to teach. The permanent sub' job was fascinating because I had to keep up to date on the latest knowledge advancements and teaching methods in all areas of the curriculum.

The biggest challenge facing any substitute teacher is winning *student* confidence and initially convincing classes that *you* are knowledgeable in the subject area and that you aren't just there to be babysitting. Whenever an unproven substitute enters a classroom, the *students* run him or her through an obstacle course that they call "the kill", and that's exactly what they'll try to get away with until the sub' gains their respect. The fact that the regular teacher is out and that a temporary warm body is in the room lays the groundwork for attempted disruption and rabble-rousing.

Some *students* take sadistic satisfaction in emotionally torturing a substitute. I have seen some of the best *National Honor Society students* in the school turn colors and "kill" an unwary unskilled substitute. It is like taking a taxicab driver and then putting him or her into a chariot pulled by twenty-five wild stallions. If the driver cannot maintain mastery over the Titanic steeds, then the reins of control are relinquished to the equines, whose objectives are to rebel, destroy authority, and gain control. Then the sub' is at the mercy of kids that don't know their limits, or who are incapable of producing constructive self-guided work. If the sub' is pusillanimous and can't command dominance or communicate the subject matter, then the *students* will unleash their own version of how to decimate a substitute in one easy lesson.

Gym classes were without a doubt the toughest assignments. The classes were overpopulated with anywhere from fifty to seventy-five *students* in each forty-five-minute period. Fights would erupt in the boys' locker room, and kids would steal the belongings of others. Soap and towel battles would prevail in the shower areas, making the confined locker room section of the school sound like *Mount Vesuvius* destroying Pompeii in 79 A.D.

Several boys thought they were ventriloquists and saturated the air with tropical birdcalls, amphibian frog sounds or domestic animal noises. Their jungle friends would forewarn them of my approach, so that the sources of hooting, cawing, croaking and mooing could never be identified.

The activities for the day had already been outlined in the gym teacher's lesson plans. Despite the fact that the *students* had already been divided up into squads, the kids' behavior in the locker rooms before and after the gym lesson gave me no peace of mind right up to the moment I reached my lunacy threshold when the final dismissal bell finally rang at 2:20.

I actually preferred the girls' gym classes better. The young ladies were much more sedate and refined than were their male counterparts. They were generally more cooperative than the counterpart boys were, and the girls thought it cute to have a male instructor for the day. Thank goodness I never had a fight or disturbance in the girls' locker room back in 1968. I would have felt funny entering their dressing and undressing sanctuary. But all along, I knew that being the teacher in charge I was responsible for theft, graffiti, vandalism and personal injury.

I dreaded the boys' gym classes mostly because the *student* that I had held in high regard in a formal English class or social studies' scenario would often attempt to get my goat in the informally structured and overcrowded gym class. A transfer of respect did not exist from the regimented, standard, academic classroom to the casual and informal gym setting.

Music was my second least favorite assignment. I knew about as much about conducting a band as I did about me conducting a safari expedition down the snake-infested *Amazon River*. When placed in a situation where the subject matter was too highly specialized, I found that the best solution was to select a reliable student to lead the class through its normal prompts. Potential discipline problems could still be deterred using *that* method. I knew how lessons should happen once a seriousness of purpose had been established. Class commitment to the fabric of the lesson became more important than it was for me to have abundant knowledge of the subject of music.

The spacious band room lacked proper soundproofing insulation. Although the musical medleys played were consonant in tone, they were ear-shattering to say the least. "I'd hate to be the poor fellow next door trying to teach world history," I told Bill Catello.

"Yeah; the *1812 Overture* and the causes of *World War II* really don't seem to go together," Bill chuckled. "And it's a good thing that Napoleon and Hitler never got together, too!" he humorously added.

It certainly would be hard integrating the *William Tell Overture* (which the *students* called "The Lone Ranger Song") with the Boston Tea Party, or *Brahm's Lullaby* with the Battle of the Alamo. Maybe the band director was used to blaring symphonies, but the poor History teachers in the vicinity of the band room were not. My memory can still hear the repercussions of the percussion section.

Home Economics class was another carnival that I was apprehensive about entering. The first time I stepped into a home ec' class to substitute teach, I found senior boys flinging chocolate buds at each other while another cluster of kids was stomping chocolate chip cookies into the floor as if they were mashing juicy grapes inside a wine barrel.

I finally managed to direct everyone to a seat. Each successive class that entered the Home Economics portal had its own assortment of shenanigans, and almost every time I nearly had to blow my cork to establish order. I was surprised to see so many junior and senior boys taking home economics, some of whom were among the worst-behaved in the entire high school. But that was the beginning of "gender-neutral subjects" where the stereotypes of "male subjects" and "female subjects" were being systematically abolished. Those distinctions no longer apply with girls now taking Auto Mechanics and Woodshop, and boys taking Family Living and Home Economics.

In 1968 the only academic requirements for high school seniors were English and Gym classes. Seniors loaded-up their schedules with snap courses such as Home Economics, Family Living, Typing, and Chorus to keep *studying down* to a minimum and to coast through to graduation (dumbing down). If a course or a teacher had the reputation of being "easy", then the *students* had a tendency to gravitate in those directions. All of this "dumbing down" was and is done in the name of "democratic" and "comprehensive school" education. Schools are for all *students,* and not just the academically-oriented college bound kids. And as a result, academically-oriented college bound seniors have the opportunity to take "electives" in non-academic areas so that the curriculum does not *discriminate* (a non-democratic word) against them.

Guidance counselors assert that when college-bound academic *students* take the easy electives, their experience base is broadened, but the unvarnished truth is that seniors took the "electives" because *they* didn't have to intensely study and pass supplemental academic subjects in the areas of Literature, Science and World Cultures. So, public high schools are not exactly exclusively lyceums for college-bound *students* learning academics. In reality, they are sociological places where mediocrity flourishes.

The selecting and the taking of "electives" are integral parts of "democratic education", and the practice clearly illustrates how our high schools are satisfied with pursuing only *average* performance. The more demanding teachers find themselves continually compromising their academic standards because *they* are under pressure from administrators (who are under pressure from irate parents) not to fail too many *students.* Quantitative (and not qualitative) flaccid education reigns supreme in most typical American high schools.

Before the introduction of "electives" as a product of "democratic education", lethargic *students* sat in their desks and dawdled their time away not caring whether *Monticello* was a masterpiece in architecture or a bordello in Naples. Apathetic high school *students* would yawn in World Civilizations class, doodle in European Literature class, or sleep in History of Art class, and then be in jeopardy of failing at the end of the year. By channeling unmotivated *students* into more moderate (and less academically demanding) classes like Woodshop, Refresher Math', Sewing, and Family Living, Over the past amazing half-century, American high schools have accomplished several significant flimflams.

First of all, the schools have successfully pacified the teachers of Science, Math', Literature and Social Studies that had to contend with the lazy Rip Van Winkles sitting there all day, or deal with the obnoxious saboteurs that tried daily to disrupt *their* formal lessons. Now, when teachers come into contact with those kinds of *students,* the course standards in Remedial English or in Refresher Math' are a lot lower than in British Literature or in Trigonometry (remember what Trig' had done to me!).

By promoting "electives", the U.S. high schools have gotten unmotivated *students* into easier classes that are activity-oriented. The kids are more mobile, move freely around woodshops and metal shop work tables, and also in Home Economics classes, and the kids don't have to sit in a desk for forty-five-minute intervals where they must think and concentrate. The *students* get to move their fingers in Computer Class, get to thread needles in Sewing, get to saw boards in Woodshop, and get to toss chocolate buds in Home Economics. They can move around almost at will and with impunity, so in an elective course, the *students* don't have to take any grief from a strict, content-oriented academic subject instructor.

The American educational myth of the "comprehensive school" has been preserved with the offering of "electives". All *students* are now "democratically entitled" and privileged to receive a well-rounded education, including those college-bound kids taking Sewing and Home Economics, and those factory-bound *students* trying to stir mashed potatoes with a colander.

In a nifty manner, American high schools have made the concept of "democracy in education" more fluent. Under the old curricular format, certain *students* napped or rebelled, while others participated and contributed. It was too glaringly obvious that "equal opportunity to learn" wasn't working because certain *students* had no desire to learn academics.

When course "electives" were instituted, subject requirements became watered-down, and even though true learning was happening on a lower level with "choice subjects", schools were not being destroyed by teenage thugs because now they're preoccupied having fun in "easier, move around" elective courses. And now with easy electives, the overall inadequacy of the total school curriculum is better concealed from public scrutiny.

Elective Home Economics class was definitely a very interesting assignment. One day, while I was permanent subbing in an advanced cooking class, two *students* were making waffles in a toaster. The electrical device began smoking, and sparks shot-out of it as if the *Fourth of July* was being celebrated inside the device. Quick thinking and good reflexes told me to disconnect the kitchen mechanism and then toss it out the opened window before I had a chance to honor my second impulse, which was to frantically pull the wall fire alarm.

The faculty would always pay particular attention to when either Bill Catello or I had been assigned the Home Economics Advanced Foods class. Bill and I would always have the culinary prodigies whip-up exotic pastries and delicacies and then forward them to our appreciative colleagues sitting in the faculty lounge.

On one occasion in Home Economics, I was conducting a lesson on proper table settings. A *student* got-up from his seat, walked over to the sink and started filling a glass of water to drink.

"Excuse me!" I protested. "You didn't ask permission to do that! Could you kindly have a seat?"

"Mrs. Carter always lets me do it!" the lanky boy protested. "Why do you have to give me a lot of shit?"

"You just earned yourself an Office Discipline Card for using foul language!" I informed the insolent violator.

This is a major problem that substitutes encounter. Your methods and expectations often do not coincide with those employed by the regular teacher. That difference was usually the first item I would stress after entering a classroom. "I am not Mrs. Carter, and my ways of doing things may be different than her ways are. Do as I say until your regular teacher returns!"

If a *student* successfully made headway with something like: "Mrs. Adams lets me pass-out the paper each day," or "Mr. Evans only uses notebook paper and not the composition paper you're passing out!", then the substitute is allowing the lid of a Pandora's Box to open. The last thing he or she should do is to honor the *students'* objections. The sub' is then unknowingly transferring decision-making power to the *students*, many of whom have in mind the sole objective of undermining the substitute's presence inside *their* classroom. Mr. Evans and Mrs. Adams have hundreds of classroom management differences from the substitute's instructions, so in order to keep control, the sub' must assert his or her authority/dominance right from the start. Basically, in conclusion, you are definitely on your own if you are a high school Permanent Substitute. Having a jar of aspirins, along with a bottle of water handy represents sound, sage advice.

Chapter 16
"Bill and I Get It Done"

Bill Catello and I were all over the high school doing "our thing" as permanent substitutes. Before there were computer classes, typing and steno' classes were the vogue in 1968. Those classes were generally smaller than major subject ones and had twelve to eighteen *students*, mostly cooperative girls preparing for futures as office secretaries. The classes were more relaxed than the formal academic ones were, and I enjoyed visiting them immensely.

I would make-up and dictate imaginary business letters to the girls, and they would take the words-down in shorthand and then transcribe their notes into "block form" typed letters. I actually had the girls fooled into believing that I knew stenography. The young ladies had textbook exercises written in steno'. The important part of the lesson was for them to read their translations out loud. In the meantime, I had the skinny paperback answer key neatly tucked inside my text, and only I knew it was there. The girls really thought I knew my stuff when I would correct, "That last word was p-r-e-s-e-n-c-e, not p-r-e-s-e-n-t-s, Miss Jackson!"

One of the most embarrassing moments of my entire teaching career came while I was permanent subbing a steno' class. I was calmly dictating a business letter to be later typed, and fifteen receptive girls were busy copying-down my eloquent oratory. I leaned back in my serious pensive posture while majestically sitting in the teacher's black, comfortable reclining chair. My seat was the swivel kind that could assume more positions than a barber's chair. The fingers of my two hands had formed a perfect church steeple under my nose.

Without warning, I suddenly swooped backwards, did a back tumble onto the floor that would have gotten me a job at *Ringling Brothers Barnum and Bailey Circus*, and then landed squarely on my spine. The roller swivel chair rocketed into a nearby *student* desk. The girls in the steno' class roared with laughter at my unplanned stunt, and ever since that trauma, I have had a phobia for reclining swivel chairs on rollers, especially in normally placid steno' classes.

"It's not easy 'floating' all over the high school on a different assignment each day," I told Bill Catello. "It's borderline madness!"

"Well, J.W.," Bill pleasantly replied. "Ya' know what they say at the town sewage disposal plant, don't ya'! Shit *floats!"* he jested.

While permanent subbing in all wings of the high school, I couldn't get over all the unnecessary distractions that were interrupting classes. Try teaching an intense grammar lesson when a school maintenance man is snipping-away at non-pruned yew bushes under your side windows. It's *shear* (sheer) madness! Try leading an intellectual discussion on Ralph Waldo Emerson's love for nature when a local contractor is noisily putting down asphalt for two new tennis courts just outside your side windows. Try teaching about the arid conditions of the *Kalahari Desert* when the illustrious high school maintenance crew has the irrigation sprinklers splattering torrents of water against your classroom's windowpanes. Try elaborating to a health class the need for vigorous exercise when a corpulent maintenance worker sitting atop a power lawnmower buzzes back and forth by your room's windows. The sub can close the blinds and cancel-out the visual effects, but somehow the din from the intrusive spectacles penetrates into the classroom and presents itself as another non-welcomed vexation.

While serving as permanent subs', Bill and I knew we could expect about as much assistance from non-professional school employees as we could expect Esther Williams to doggy paddle across the length of the *Bermuda Triangle*. On one memorable occasion, several school maintenance men were diligently repaving a cement sidewalk that connected the courtyard entrances to two school wings. An entourage of twenty *students* on their way from the C-Wing to an Industrial Arts class in the E-Wing momentarily thought that they were Hollywood celebrities at *Grauman's Chinese Theater*. I watched the twenty scoundrels from a B-Wing classroom as they embedded their footprints in the wet cement while the maintenance workers continued their task on their knees and eventually covered-up the senseless, moronic vandalism that the *students* had imaginatively created.

When I notified the office of what was in progress, the assistant-principal sped-down the C-Wing corridor and then burst-out of a rarely used side door entrance like Secretariat zipping-out of the *Aqueduct* starting gate. Missing a concrete step, the assistant-principal ungracefully tumbled onto the ground. The result of his haste was a twisted ankle on his right foot, and a right shoe covered with dog feces (German shepherd, I believe). Since *that* was the age before video security cameras, the young vandals had all managed to escape the crime scene without ever having to fear the threat of experiencing administrative prosecution.

Bill and I often talked about something that bothered the both of us. Student teachers assigned to monitor study halls were often reassigned to cover the classes of absent teachers in subject areas that were out of the apprentices' college specialty. When a good number of teachers were absent, *the office* staff would juggle teachers, other personnel and schedules around to utilize the strongest on-site people in the most potentially dangerous situations, especially those areas having the worst behaved *students*.

Oftentimes, instead of having the full schedule of one absent teacher, my daily agenda might include three Math' classes, one English class, one Science class and then cafeteria duty (that never appeared on the main absent teacher's daily schedule). This type of manipulation was often done to spare the weaker, outside substitutes the shock of being exposed to the hazards of cafeteria patrol along with the trauma of a viperous eighth period General English class inhabited mostly by young hooligans and terrorists.

Each class I would visit seemed to have at least one *student* that attempted haranguing me with a battery of baneful questions because he was "bored" with the subject matter. In one junior U.S. History II class, I asked, "What were some causes of the *Civil War*?"

An aggressive punk that was frantically waving his arm was called upon. "I don't want to talk about the stupid *Civil War!*" he objected. "Why don't we talk about sex and about getting laid?"

Some kid will come out of nowhere and endeavor to sabotage your lesson with some torpedo-like nonsense. After a while, I became immune to such blatant indiscretions. I knew from Dr. Trenoff's educational psychology class that this brazen *student* had a reason, a motive for his impudent inquiry. As an educator, I had to earn the young jerk's respect. Only a Republican conservative would purport the impetuous query, 'Why do I have to put-up with this stupid, uncouth idiot's nonsense?'

I immediately sensed that the young wise guy's verbalizations were malevolent in nature. I had also been conditioned by the sixth grade "sex lesson" fiasco, so I scowled back to the instigator, "Mr. Gordon's lesson plan indicates that I am to cover the causes of the *Civil War!*" I emphasized. "As a permanent substitute, I am only empowered to do what Mr. Gordon's lesson plan instructs me to teach. Sex is not mentioned anywhere in Mr. Gordon's lesson plans for today!" I deftly deflected and elaborated. "And furthermore, only *people* can be *stupid,* and not major events like the *Civil War!*"

The feisty, smart aleck was not appeased by my logical rhetoric. The jaundiced heckler scoffed in a sassy tone of voice, "How did all of the people that fought in the *Civil War* get on the Earth?" he asked. "By sex, didn't they?" he clarified.

The *student's* obnoxious wit was quite obviously designed to abash me in front of *his* temporarily perceptive classmates. I answered the imbecile in a bland tone of voice, "Okay, you win! Since I am not an expert on the subject of sex," I said, "I'll allow *you* ten minutes to *elucidate* on the matter, for surely *you* are more informed than I am on the delicate subject!"

The prospect of standing and addressing his peers instead of insulting me while sitting-down seemed to silence the *student* and strip him of his ridiculous audacity. Another *student* raised his hand, and after being recognized, he sincerely asked, "Who did *Lucy date* anyway?" in response of me uttering the word *"elucidate?"*

After the class stopped laughing, the *Civil War* analysis proceeded rather smoothly. The entire lesson's success depended on my skill at handling the first *student's* arrogant comments. I had pity in my heart for the unprepared women outside-substitutes that had to encounter similar abuses. Being thrown into a deep lagoon with a school of hungry piranhas might be a more fortuitous fate.

Mrs. Burns was a demure history teacher that kept a hybrid African plant situated on her classroom windowsill. One very dismal early day in March, the botanical wonder unexpectedly died. Mrs. Burns suspected that herbicide (either plant suicide or plant homicide) had been involved, so she commissioned Bill Catello and me to solve the "mysterious death".

Bill and I took the lifeless specimen for post-mortem analysis, and we requested an unofficial autopsy from Mr. LeFey, the main chemistry teacher. LeFey's investigation revealed that the imported African plant had died from an overdose of uric acid. "Apparently, some *student* took a heavy piss in the plant's container!" LeFey hypothesized and related.

"Although the deceased vegetation resembles a greenish-brown fire hydrant," I stated and laughed, "I haven't seen any handicapped dogs limping around the school property, so *that* rules-out perverted canine activity!"

"What about that mangy, ferocious German shepherd the kids let into the building last week that terrorized the entire A-Wing?" LeFey reasonably asked.

"No;" I don't think that *that* mutt was smart enough to have a grudge against Mrs. Burns," I coyly answered.

"Maybe one of the kids with a conscience will come forth and rat on the culprit," Bill merrily suggested. "J.W., you should know a few decent *students* on the Student Council that might have valuable information about Mrs. Burns' deceased vegetation!"

I endorsed Bill's recommendation and sought adolescent testimony to solve the intriguing case. I interviewed a trustworthy honors' senior on *Student* Council about the strange, incidental African plant's death. The senior intimated that he thought the new foreign exchange *student* from France had committed the crime.

"What makes you think that?" I curiously asked.

"The senior honors' *student* had trouble maintaining dominion over his meditation. "Because the French girl's been saying *oui oui* ever since she's gotten here!" the kid belched and then walked away, laughing hysterically.

The school librarian then reported to me that many of the plants in her hallowed domain were also dying. I approached Mr. LeFey, who was beginning to relish his new role as "Chief Medical Plant Examiner for the High School." After Coroner LeFey conducted a comprehensive soil analysis of the deceased library plants, it was determined that those items had also died from an excess of uric acid. Mr. LeFey concluded that too many *students* in the school possessed "*piss*imistic attitudes towards their future Alma Mater".

Woodshop was another area that Bill and I didn't mind supervising. We were not certified in that specialty, so the *students* were prohibited from using power tools. They could only use hand tools, read boring textbooks, and then answer questions from the end of the chapter. Although the *students* couldn't use power drills and the electric saws, the kids really impressed me with their desire to use their hands.

The same *students* I had observed taking siestas in English and in history classes were skillfully and proudly manufacturing wooden cabinets, gun racks, jewelry boxes, birdhouses and duck decoys. I was amazed at their initiative and sincerity of purpose, and I couldn't help thinking that *their* schedules should have been loaded with "hands-on" vocational shops where they could dabble with their fingers and rotating wrists all day long. As it was, the young rascals would either sleep their way through academic subjects, or imitate the behavior of the *FBI's "America's Most Wanted Criminals"*.

Chapter 17
"Educational Socialism"

While permanent subbing in woodshop, I noticed how much the *students* enjoyed working independently, deriving tremendous satisfaction from self-achievement. But *educational democracy* attempted to cultivate the concepts of *sharing* and *cooperation* to disguise *student* ineffectiveness (lack of individual achievement) in the name of group accomplishment. However, the *students* in woodshop always seemed to value individual achievement over group accomplishment.

Study the great contributors to civilization: Aristotle, Archimedes, Galileo, Buddha, and Thomas Edison to name a few. Those great men preferred to think and be alone while learning, discovering, exploring and inventing. Thomas Jefferson preferred to be alone when he authored the *Declaration of Independence* to capture the magnificent inspiration that dwelled within his soul. On a lesser plane, I am alone without human distraction or assistance (and prefer to be alone) as I write these words appearing upon my computer screen. The phone is off, the stereo is off and the television is off. The only things "on" are *my* mind and the silent computer. No one is helping me or telling me what to do. This is why "independent study" is the best thing academic schools could teach *students*.

College professors, curriculum coordinators, supervisors and school administrators coerce teachers into spending precious weeks experimenting with "cooperative education" to foster "democratic values" in their classrooms. The theory is that the *students* should work in various groups and then *share* ideas with their teammates. The idea behind *cooperative education* is that "verbal social interaction" significantly contributes to the successful development of conscientious, well-prepared citizens.

I believe that *group work* supports my hypothesis that schools have become sociological places and have drifted away from being academic institutions. *Students* squander valuable class periods deciding what they're going to study as a group project, how they're going to study their topic, and then determining who's going to do what in the group (role assignment). Education calls *this* process "group planning, group assessment and self-evaluation". A teacher in an "instructor-guided-lesson" can cover a textbook chapter in a week, but a class divided into cooperative learning groups requires three weeks to complete the same chapter. Is *that* being efficient?

In this new arrangement called "cooperative education", the teacher is reduced from being the authority person guiding the class through a lesson, and now his or her new function is to wander from classroom group to group being a resource person known as a "facilitator". The new emphasis is on the *group* (instead of the individual) determining its own goals, roles and methods.

Now here's where quality time-on-task education suffers. The groups waste time bickering, debating, selecting, compromising, and talking while *student individual will* is surrendered in order to conform to majority opinion. When teachers are compelled to divide classes into groups to engage in "cooperative learning", they are adhering to an educational trend that postulates "getting along with others" (in a contrived pecking order) transcends the need for "individual academic achievement".

And so public high schools produce many *students* that can't read and can't write because someone in the "cooperative group" had done those things for them, since those other conscientious *students* wanted to get good grades for *themselves* on *their* report cards. Schools are now producing graduates that are unskilled, untrained, and unprepared, and unless they're going to college, the seniors are bound for and being herded into minimum wage employment. But despite those horrendous facts, administrators are edified to know that the graduates have learned how to get along with one another in cooperative groups. The "group technique" in American education has dismally failed because it has been (and is) producing a society of doltish gossipers and not a nation of independent thinkers.

When *students* are divided into groups for "cooperative learning", the stronger-willed ones and the more intelligent ones will naturally dominate the group's power structure. The more dynamic *student* leaders tend to be ambitious and are concerned about doing well because they *selfishly* want to earn a good grade for *their* group contribution. The more industrious *student* leaders not only determine the direction the group will take but also wind-up doing the bulk of the work for the lazy *students* in the group that lack sufficient motivation to achieve on their own.

When a scenario exists where the better-motivated *students* produce work for the more lethargic ones, and when the less motivated *students* profit from the labor of the more motivated gifted-*students*, then the end-game is *educational socialism* and not *educational democracy*.

Democratic education (as interpreted by educational psychology) has led to a very dangerous notion that "*students* should be equal". *Student* differences are minimized in today's public schools regardless of individual ability. Excellence is sacrificed and mediocrity results when both ends of the educational spectrum (A and F *students*) are forced to gravitate toward a *sociological* median.

While the needs of the group are magnified, the input of the individuals that contribute the most is devalued in terms of individual reward. The smarter *students* then become subordinated to the needs of the group and must tow the weight of the weaker non-motivated *students*. By craftily interplaying psychological and philosophical terminology like "cooperative learning," "*democratic* education" and "sharing," the truth becomes both blurred and nebulous in the eighty-percent gray zone, and it is increasingly more difficult for the average citizen to distinguish. And so, *socialism* (group work) is advanced and stealthily masquerades around disguised as *democracy* (individual pursuit) in education.

I have been and am disturbed that if the practice is indeed *socialism*, then it ought not be labeled and marketed under the title *democratic* education. We have drastically wandered from our original American *Constitutional* precepts (individual pursuit of happiness and individual rights) as prescribed by our Founding Fathers both in our society and later instituted in our public schools. This socialistic deviation from true democratic principles has certainly weakened our national moral fiber.

Being politically correct and being influenced by sound-byte messages in American society have taken precedence over individual sacrifice and individual accomplishment resulting from hard work that is directed toward *a personal goal*. Smart *students* are labeled "nerds" and "geeks" and "freaks" by their dumber peers, and the academically gifted teens are also labeled "selfish and greedy" by the educational powers-that-be because some smarter *students* refuse to *share* their knowledge with their unmotivated intimidators.

Our society and our public schools are losing their sense of purpose, are shrewdly hiding their many weaknesses, and are maliciously destroying the foundations of our American culture. By attempting to accommodate the needs of those *students* that cannot measure-up to the rigorous standards of *individual pursuit of happiness*, individual free enterprise, the American dream, and the pioneering instinct as ordained by Thomas Jefferson, public schools have adopted the course to use socialistic methods to attain democratic goals. Today's teenagers misconstrue the pursuit of pleasure as the definition for the "pursuit of happiness". As a result, our American culture is becoming more hedonistic than intellectual.

One day, I was in the B-Wing permanent subbing an English class. The instructor across the hall had an energetic student teacher. My advice to the female apprentice was that she should divide the class up into groups when her college coordinator came to observe her lessons. "Just continuously strut around the room pretending you're ingeniously guiding the kids through the lesson and be sure to converse with the group leaders," I suggested.

True to form, the young lady received the grade of A in her student teaching seminar, and the two other student teachers in the school at the time that had employed the same "cooperative learning" method also received A's. Two other student teachers the following semester utilized practices such as textbook reading and discussion, student oral reports, individual seatwork, teacher lecturing, and other teaching styles that required *individual initiative* on the part of the *students,* and those student teachers received the average grade of B from their liberal-minded college coordinators.

A colossal hoax is being perpetuated upon the American public. It is quite ironic that the trusting public elects board of education members to be responsible for *quality education* to be practiced in public schools. By flirting with the perils of "democratic education", "cooperative learning", "the American comprehensive high school", and "progressive education", schools have been sacrificing quality for quantity, substituting individual achievement for group adjustment, replacing competition and free enterprise for the sake of *student* socialization, and eliminating academic teaching standards to promote sociological education.

Billions of dollars of taxpayers' money are annually being wasted all over America in the worst conceivable boondoggle since the stock market crash of 1929. The Better Business Bureau should really investigate American public schools, for in terms of false advertising claims, it is the biggest fraud this side of Piltdown Man.

Everything academic in American schools must now play second fiddle to *student* sociological development. Academic disciplines have been demoted in rank for the worship of football, band, soccer, basketball, clubs, societies, councils and specific committees like "yearbook" and "conflict resolution". *Students* are continually excused from regular classes to engage in inter-school sporting events at distant towns, to practice for plays, shows and assembly performances with the band and chorus, to attend Student Council meetings, or to take exotic field trips to cookie factories or to beauty culture schools.

The clever, more academically gifted *students* are quick to theorize the true character of the situation. They keenly know that extra-curricular activities take priority over academic curricular classes, that baseball and girls hockey supersede science and literature, and that the award-winning school band is much more important than Algebra, Geometry and Trigonometry.

Democratic education has added to the daily quandary of the modern-day public-school teacher. Not only is he or she stripped of dignity by poor community attitudes toward his or her *profession,* but also veteran teachers are cruelly subjected to having to watch their coveted academic subjects losing prestige to *democratically* (socialistically) slanted *student* activities and electives. Objecting to the Minotaur known as "activity-oriented education" is like trying to extinguish an inferno by throwing gasoline upon the flames. The more that academically-oriented teachers fight the extremely suspect curriculum "Socialistic" changes, the greater the administrative resistance becomes.

The Educational Aristocracy will give teachers a litany of implausible justifications for the "comprehensive school" and for "democracy in education", and Bill Catello and I often felt as if we were wounded captives in a zany concentration camp where none of the brainwashing techniques were working.

High school bands, winning football teams and victorious soccer squads occupy dear spots in administrators and board of education members' hearts. The "Aristocracy" knows that if the football team wins a championship, or if the band wins interstate acclaim, then the public will judge the whole high school as being a good one without ever considering any academics. The school trophy cases are loaded with awards for band, football and other extra-curricular activities, but few academic awards are ever received or on public display.

More town residents read the high school sports pages in the local newspapers than the school honor roll that is published in the same edition. That is, of course, unless *their* son or daughter's name is on the school honor roll. It is a sad testament of American society when a high school's reputation depends on the successes of its sports' teams and its marching band and not on its academic excellence. Why don't public schools have Academic Leagues and intellectual competitions just like *they* advocate sports and band rivalries?

And so. when *students* are yanked out of academic classrooms to participate in a sports' event, to march in a band competition rehearsal, or to attend a conference on a future career in recycling paper, metal and plastics, the teachers should remember one thing. The *students* leaving their classrooms are now ambassadors leaving the building to give their school a good name in another community. Forget the literary attributes of O. Henry or the cynical humor of Mark Twain. Forget the diagramming and analysis of complex sentences with adjective, adverb and noun subordinate clauses. The school's image comes first and foremost, and academics must be shrewdly *subordinated* just like those prevalent subordinate clauses are inside complex sentences.

Perhaps the worst ordeal that Bill Catello and I had encountered as permanent subs was a terrible mental excruciation known as "In-School Suspension". When the entire faculty was present on any given day, the dreadful assignment was conferred on Bill and me. We intelligently alternated the coverage every other period of the eight-session-day. The monotony of eight consecutive periods of In-School Suspension duty would be sufficient boredom to hypnotize Franz Mesmer or Sigmund Freud.

The teacher on duty was confined to a small office with anywhere from one to eight *students* that had been suspended from school. Once, there were a dozen of us crammed into the tiny room as if *we* were ordinary sardines. That day Bill and I felt like *we* were squashed commuters sitting for forty-five-minute intervals on a crowded New York subway during rush hour.

The *students* weren't allowed to talk, and Bill and I weren't permitted to speak to them, so in effect, the permanent subs' were being punished by the administration, too!

"Bill, I really could've used the time today to do research in the library, or relieve other teachers proctoring tests, or give breaks to those unfortunate teachers serving on demoralizing cafeteria duty," I complained after school that day. "And to tell you the honest-to-goodness truth, Bill," I joked, "I'd rather proctor than gambol!"

"Yes, even cafeteria duty or a mass study hall would be better than suffering through a whole day of In-School Suspension with a dozen chronic violators!" Bill agreed. "It's safe to say that there's very little professionalism in this profession!"

In-School Suspension duty was the administration's way of safeguarding taxpayers' dollars by keeping Bill and me occupied. Usually, regular, every-day, classroom teachers were assigned to share the horrible duty on their daily work schedules a period at a time, but since no one was absent, Bill and I had been put on the detail. The duty had no educational or therapeutic merit to the *children* sitting and vegetating in that tiny office. It was as psychologically rewarding to them (and to Bill and me) as cutting one's toenails with a can opener, or voraciously eating *Jell-o* with curved chopsticks.

Bill and I also got to perform another unappealing duty for high school administrators known as "Office Detention". When a *student* is defiant in class, or curses, or gets into fights, a teacher will write out a blue or green Discipline Referral Card and then send the impudent varmint down to the vice-principal's office. But the offense might not have been serious enough to warrant In-School Suspension. After receiving the cursory lecture from the assistant-principal, the *child* might be given a week of after school Office Detention by the general office.

Now here's the hitch. The school executives can't be bothered doing such a lowly task as supervising the Office Detentions that *they* have assigned wayward *students* to sit in. So, every teacher on the staff (including the permanent subs') is scheduled to have after school Office Detention shared on a rotating basis (duty without additional pay, of course).

Just like In-School Suspension, Office Detention offers little corrective or reformative value for the *students* while its implementation simultaneously punishes the assigned teacher on duty. Usually, the same fourteen-to-seventeen-year-old *children* that were sitting in Office Detention in September are still there getting splinters in their butts in June.

And yet a core of the same fifty-to-seventy-five *students* are constantly disrupting the average-sized school, smoking in the lavatories, tossing food in the cafeteria, or insolently badmouthing teachers. All of the superintendent's psychologists and all of the superintendent's men can't make this contingent of Humpty-Dumpties productive again. Trying to paddle a kayak up Niagara Falls would be less frustrating than attempting to daily rehabilitate those seventy-five black sheep existing in the educational herd.

Bill and I really couldn't blame the vice-principal for being ineffective in dealing daily with the seventy-five troublemakers because he or she too had little authority or few available options in disciplining them. I don't advocate smacking kids around, but I do endorse a police presence in the school to arrest disruptive *students*. The kids know that the vice-principal or a teacher cannot lay a hand or a finger on them. So, after the vice-principal verbally rebukes the violators, the troublemakers prance back to their respective classrooms telling their peers "He didn't do nothin' to me!" In urban ghetto schools, the core of seventy-five disruptive *students* might pertain to the more earnest ones that aren't yet juvenile delinquents.

And the overcrowded school cafeteria is the major trouble area in the entire building being the ultimate romper-room for frolicking post-pubescent instigators, their misbehavior instinctively reacting to their own hormone imbalances. Hippocrates would have abandoned medicine at the beginning of his career if he were presented with half the daily aggravations that are experienced by teachers in the comprehensive, *democratic,* contemporary American high school.

As permanent subs, Bill and I also had to check the boys' lavatories whenever we could, and make appearances especially during the change of classes. The detail did entail potential dangers. One day I walked into the boys' C-Wing lavatory and noticed a cloud of smoke thicker than Los Angeles smog. A *student* with a cigarette butt between his fingers instantly flung it into a toilet and quickly flushed away the evidence.

"Okay, let's go down to the office!" I related to the *student* whom I didn't even know.

"I didn't do anything!" the violator protested. "You don't like me! You're pickin' on me!"

"Yeah, he didn't do nothin'!" four of the anonymous *child's* anonymous friends testified in a familiar double-negative.

Soon, I was embroiled in a clamorous, passionate quibble with five conspirators that were denying what my mortal eyes had seen. I almost came to punches with the antagonistic, anonymous violator as I escorted him out of the lavatory to the Main Office. Meanwhile, five minutes had elapsed, and my next class, which was located at the other end of the school was being unsupervised. If a fight had erupted inside *that* classroom, then *I* would have been responsible for any and all injury or for property damage. And because of that lavatory incident where I was forced to play prosecutor to the administration, that's why Bill Catello and I never again took the aggravation of lavatory patrol too seriously.

As a permanent sub', I developed a great admiration for my teaching colleagues that were still trying to keep academics alive in American education. Sometimes I had to know and teach about Avogadro's number, Schleiden and Schwann and colloidal suspensions all in one day to avid physics, biology and chemistry *students*. Several times, bright *students* had caught me in the middle of a contradiction as I stumbled through highly specialized subject matter. I immediately confessed, "I don't know this concept too well. Please help me!" and the more sympathetic college-bound *students* were equal to the task and did come to my assistance. I found that if I tried being too pedantic, then the more gifted *students* would aggressively challenge my intellectual bluffing and then hack away at the glib façade I was weakly reflecting. *Harvard*-bound *students* could leave a garrulous substitute teacher (deficient in knowing specialized facts) feeling as helplessly naked as a fool wearing his or her birthday suit to a masquerade ball.

Bill Catello was right on target in his general assessment. Schools were no longer places where *students* learned how to read, think, and write. "Schools are now twelve-year vertical holding platforms where *students* are supposed to learn how to get along with one another so that the school building is not damaged or destroyed!" Bill strongly maintained.

And Bill was absolutely correct. Consider the relegation of the term "academic" in our American society. *Academic* is presently used in a rather negative way, and it is synonymous with the word "unimportant". If a football team is leading its opponent by thirty points with two minutes left to play on the official scoreboard clock, the television announcer will lethargically state, "Well fans, the rest of the game is *academic!*"

Core curriculum teachers are no longer valued because their academic subjects have lost importance and status to extracurricular activities and also to easy electives that the public seems to value more than individual performance in hard-subject pursuit. So, as Bill Catello so eloquently articulated, the thousand *students* in the high school are in a holding pattern until society is ready to absorb seventy-five of the more chronic troublemakers after a dozen years of non-academic performance. And the American public can thank the menaces of modern educational philosophy and psychology for the disintegration of academic scholastic standards, for declining *SAT* scores, and for *democracy* (Marxist-type socialism) in our nation's public schools.

Chapter 18
"The High School Faculty"

Tim Carley and Bob Gordon were close friends and almost inseparable amigos on the high school faculty. Tim taught both U.S. and Ancient History courses in a room that had been originally designed as part of a larger family living classroom. A toilet that was once inside the family living room had been partitioned-off and soon became a part of Tim's Social Studies' office. An entrance door to the office and its accompanying toilet separated the porcelain fixture from Tim's History classroom.

The availability of the toilet proved very *commod*ious to Tim. Whenever a *student* with weak kidneys asked the history teacher if he or she could visit the lavatory, Tim would open the door to *his* office and announce, "Sure! Use the facilities right here in my office!" The History mentor would then open the door to his *office* exposing the glistening hopper to the view of the appreciative class.

The *student* seeking biological relief would consider the thought of embarra*ss*ing noises emanating from *the office* into the classroom and would then become discouraged from attempting to conveniently answer nature's call. Tim Carley was seldom plagued with continuous annoying *student* requests to leave the room and use the bathroom facilities.

One day when Tim was enlightening his second period World Civilizations *students* on the brilliant attainments of the ancient Mesopotamian culture, a temporary classroom silence was created when everyone in the room heard a distinct gurgling reverberation. All heads turned left as the office door opened, and then out stepped the unabashed Bob Gordon. He casually waved a cute salutation to Tim and *his* World Civilizations class, acting totally nonchalant about the impropriety of *his* "unprofessional toilet flushing conduct". Tim Carley's face turned redder than a beet as the mixed male and female class snickered and chuckled for a full five minutes.

On another occasion, wily Tim Carley and Bob Gordon were chaperones on the senior class Washington Trip. The two teachers supervised rooms and randomly searched *student* luggage for booze that might have illegally been smuggled into the motel. After confiscating six pints of alcohol in true Eliot Ness fashion, Bob and Tim generously re-distributed their plunder to the ten faculty chaperones on duty as a well-deserved "Washington Trip fringe benefit". And so, the grateful teachers had a small all-night party at the expense of some irascible-minded *students* attempting to pull a fast one on the chaperones.

On that same Washington Trip, Tim and Bob had a photo' taken of them sitting with a manikin of Lyndon B. Johnson at a District of Columbia wax museum. A mock newspaper headline along with the photo' was published at a novelty store and the item read, "Local Teachers Confer with President Johnson". The front page of the mock newspaper was conspicuously hung on a central bulletin board in the main high school corridor. The unique piece of journalism lingered there for two whole months without it ever being noticed or scrutinized by sleepy *students* changing classes. Then I decided to bring the unique newspaper picture and caption to a talkative *student's* attention, and it wasn't long before the thumb-tacked poster became one of the featured points of *student* interest while "*the herds*" were passing and then stopping to gander at the hall newspaper headline spectacle between classes.

Bob Gordon was notorious for playing pranks at teacher parties. Once, while Mr. Gordon was attending a rollicking Friday night affair hosted by Math teacher Jim Kyle, Bob tested the alcoholic capacity of seven fish swimming about in Jim's aquarium. When no one was looking, Mr. Gordon poured a large quantity of vodka into the fish tank to scientifically study how the intoxicant would influence the swimming patterns of the victimized marine-life.

The next morning, the teacher that had thrown the big shindig the night before discovered his seven fish floating on top of the water instead of in it. The following Monday at school, I consoled the depressed party host by saying, "Well Jim, I guess there isn't too much validity to the statement *he drinks like a fish*! I believe someone with unscrupulous intentions must've poured vodka or gin into your aquarium! What a way to get *tanked!*"

"Thanks a lot!" the despondent teacher disgustedly answered. "Your kindness *underwhelms* me!"

At another wild faculty party given by host Jim Kyle, Bob Gordon raided the bathroom medicine chest. He secretly confiscated our friend's razor blades leaving only one behind, which the trickster mercilessly warped out of shape and then somehow managed to insert the twisted shaving blade into Jim Kyle's razor. On Monday morning, the aggravated teacher that had just lost seven aquarium fish the week before showed-up at school with a face that appeared as if it had been shaven by a power lawnmower.

"Well Jim, at least you don't have a five o'clock shadow! Anyway, that was a great happening at your place Sunday night!" I commented as I stared at the variety of nicks and gashes that gutted Mr. Kyle's ruddy countenance.

"Somebody else is gonna' throw the next damned teacher party," Jim glumly answered. "Frankly, I've had it hosting this damned unappreciative faculty!"

Bob Gordon always had a prank or two up his sleeve. The main corridor of the high school had two attractive planters attached to a wall with neatly arranged displays of artificial flowers in them. Bob surreptitiously noticed that certain overhead spotlights ideally beamed shafts of light directly into the flowerboxes.

In January of '68, early each morning, Mr. Bob Gordon would clandestinely deposit several pounds of dirt into the flowerboxes before any administrators were inside the building. After two weeks passed, Bob was ready to initiate phase two of his devious scheme. Mr. Gordon planted pumpkin and sunflower seeds into the freshly transferred soil. Several weeks later, *student* passers-by stopped and incredulously peered at the remarkable planter, which had a splendid array of real natural vegetation and vines growing above the dwarfed synthetic greenery.

In conjunction with the late '60s ecology fad, Bob Gordon and Ron LeFey took two conservation-minded biology classes on a school-sponsored three-day camping trip to a lake located twenty miles from the high school. Tim Carley and I drove-out to the lake the second night to see how the contemporary Henry David Thoreaus were doing. When we arrived at our destination, larking *students* were chasing each other through the briars while others were already paired-off and passionately necking under tall pine trees. Tim noticed a mixed group of *students* dash into the woods, and the errant *students* immediately vanished to avoid the detection of the two old-fashioned, newly arrived conservative visitors.

"I hope those *students* don't eat any poisonous mushrooms!" Tim exclaimed after witnessing the sudden exodus into the forest.

"I think the *students* are more interested in basic biological pursuits than in honest intellectual ecological inquiry!" I replied.

About the only souls in the immediate environment that Tim and I could locate were Bob Gordon and Ron LeFey, the organizers of the frolicking nature study junket. The curfew was supposed to be ten o' clock, but the dials of my trusty *Timex* accurately read 11:30.

"The *students* are really infected with the pioneering spirit now," I jested to Bob and Ron as Tim laughed his rear end off. "What happened to the various Conestoga wagons?" I joked as I watched silhouettes darting in and out of the distant foliage.

"It looks like a screwed-up primitive Sadie Hawkins Day with a surplus of Little Abners and Daisy Mays," Tim Carley added while still laughing. "But it's about equal the number of boys chasing after girls, and the number of girls chasing boys!"

Bob Gordon was more optimistic than we were and attributed the excessive chaos that we were witnessing to something else. "Guys, it's just the first time these *students* have had any freedom on their own," he defensively generalized. "They simply don't know how to act when not under their parents' domination!"

"I'm glad I'm only a Social Studies teacher and don't have to teach *wild life!*" Tim amusingly interrupted his favorite faculty pal.

"These sensational *student* shenanigans do look a little Saturnalian to the, pardon the expression, to the *naked* eye!" I calmly stated to the two embarrassed and slightly chagrined camping chaperones.

With two reinforcements from the high school faculty on hand, Bob and Ron, with the assistance of Tim and myself, rounded-up the revelers and herded them back into their respective gender-separated, designated cabins.

But before the reveling *students* had been officially returned to their particular corrals, Bob Gordon had taken the time to smear butter on all the bunkbed sheets inside the four *student* cabins of the kids that had been assigned to *his* custody. After his *students* tramped into their respective cabins for the night, devilish Bob sternly entered each logged building and reprimanded his underlings (a cabin at a time) for their aberrant conduct cavorting around in the majestic pine-barrens forest. "I didn't appreciate your Pan-like goofing off one bit!" he yelled-out in relation to the *students'* wild gamboling. "Now get to bed in a hurry, and I don't want to hear one peep outa' any of ya' for the rest of the night!" the chaperone vehemently snarled.

The *students* under Bob's care obediently washed-up, and when they soon slid under their bedcovers, a low chatter could be discerned outside the cabins as the victimized *students* accused each other of skullduggery. Bob Gordon pretended to be angry after hearing the *student* recriminations being volleyed back and forth. He opened the cabin door and rebuked the chatterers, "What's wrong with you imbeciles!" his voice loudly boomed. "I just yelled at ya' for foolin' around in the woods! Don't you kids have any sense of shame?" Bob screamed at his doubly startled prodigies.

When Bob left the third cabin after hollering at his *students,* Tim Carley declared, "Well Bob; I'm sure glad to see that you know how to *butter-up* your advanced learners!"

"You leave little *margarine* for error!" I added referring to the excessive butter *spread* in the bed sheets.

"Those squawky kids will blame each other all night long and never suspect that Mr. Gordon would play such a dastardly prank!" Ron LeFey laughed. "Nice job, Bob!"

"Yeah, it's almost like honorable Smokey the Bear moonlighting as a petty arsonist, or George Washington turning turncoat for the redcoats!" the self-amused sophomore History Teacher stated. "Somebody's got to get back at these kids for all the crap they pull on us!" Bob Gordon opined and summarized. "So, therefore, I've just deputized myself a one-man vigilante committee!"

Being an accomplished prankster sometimes has its pitfalls as Bob Gordon once found out. Every *Halloween* the sophomore social studies' teacher would unexpectedly dart into a classroom where I would be permanent subbing and Mr. Gordon would be wearing a dreadful-looking Dracula mask. The unexpected intrusion would startle the wits out of even the most bored and phlegmatic *students.*

I thought that Bob's *Halloween* caper was amusing, so I always kept a Frankenstein mask in the desk of the room where I was subbing. And towards the end of October, when the *students* would be busy taking a test or doing a worksheet, I would get the mask out of the desk and quickly hide it under my sport jacket. Then I would put the mask over my face in the back of the room and stroll around until the first *student* (usually a female) would see me, become frightened, and then frightfully let-out a shrill shriek. So, when Bob Gordon would unexpectedly enter the same classroom a day later while wearing the grotesque Dracula mask, the *students* believed that the entire faculty was dramatically going off the deep end.

The laws of karma, however, have a way of boomeranging when one least expects a negative consequence to happen. One *Halloween* afternoon Bob Gordon was casually driving his red *Volkswagen* home from the high school. The sophomore Social Studies teacher had the bad habit of attempting to scare adults he knew with his hideous Dracula mask (besides startling his beloved *students*).

Bob's red *Volkswagen* was approaching a very friendly school-crossing guard that always enjoyed waving greetings at motorists and exchanging pleasantries with pedestrians. When the red foreign car neared the woman traffic director, Mr. Gordon donned his frightening Dracula mask.

As the red *Volkswagen* slowly passed by the pleasant crossing-guard, Bob let out a ferocious growl that immediately stunned the woman. However, as Bob removed his mask to reveal his true identity to the shocked guard, his small vehicle was still advancing forward keeping pace with the slow-moving road traffic. A town garbage truck turned the intersection corner and Bob's red *Volkswagen* plowed into it as Gordon was preoccupied exposing his true identity to the amiable crossing-guard. The total damage amounted to four-hundred-dollars and ironically, the next day at school, Mr. Gordon told everyone in the faculty room that his costly impractical joke turned-out to be a "smashing success".

Jim Kyle wanted to get even with Bob Gordon for drowning *his* seven tropical fish, and also for mercilessly warping his only remaining razor blade. Bob was a big citizen-band-radio operator and would talk incessantly over his *CB* with big-rig truckers and other radio-talking enthusiasts.

One March evening, Tim Carley, Jim Kyle and I pulled-up in front of Bob's condominium with a walkie-talkie that was electronically set to communicate with Bob's *CB*. We patiently sat in Tim's car, and Jim disguised his voice with a handkerchief while conversing with Bob. But Mr. Gordon was slightly paranoid and thought that other *CB*ers and the *FCC* might be monitoring his transmissions, so *he* practiced keeping all his conversations over the airwaves clean and totally free of perverted, foul language.

Jim's walkie-talkie in the car could send and receive to Bob's *CB* inside his condo', but no one else could hear Jim's transmissions except Mr. Gordon on *his* receiver. All other *CB*s were out of range and could only hear Bob Gordon speaking, but talking to no one that was communicating back.

"Well Bob," Jim courteously said over his walkie-talkie. "How the hell are ya'!"

"Hey, who is this anyway?" Bob barked into his *CB* microphone. "Watch your language!"

"I've been listening to your lousy bullshit over the *CB* for years," Jim indicted, "and everyone I know thinks you're totally full of crap. Why don't ya' just piss-off and leave everybody the hell alone!"

"Hey, what's your handle?" Bob demanded to his entire *CB* audience listening to him. "Who are you?"

"Do I sound like a pot? I don't need a damned handle! And I don't like talkin' to stupid assholes," Jim enunciated into the speaker through his handkerchief while Tim and I were biting our tongues to avoid splitting our guts. Of course, Bob was the only one who could hear Jim's inflammatory oratory. "I thought you had balls, Gordon!" Jim coarsely accused. "You're probably even friggin' scared of the damned *FCC!*"

"You can lose your license talking foul language like that!" Bob yelled to everyone out there operating a *CB* on or near his popular frequency. "Stop with the obscene language already!"

The three of us sat in Tim Carley's car and laughed our rear ends off as we watched Bob Gordon's silhouette pacing back and forth in front of his sheer drapes. After a few minutes, other *CB*ers were calling Bob and asking him why he had been talking to himself. Tim backed-up his auto', and after we left the condominiums' asphalt driveway, the navigator put his headlights on and drove Jim and me to the nearest tavern to enjoy some good roast beef' sandwiches and several cold mugs of tasty brew.

A guidance counselor with Afro-style curly hair named Mark Singleton looked just like a junior *student,* Ken Tomasini. So, every time Mark would come into the faculty lounge and plop-down into a chair, Bob Gordon would sit-down right next to the guidance counselor and say to me, "Hey J.W., do you know a *student* named Ken Tomasini!"

I knew that Bob was actually referring to the physical similarity between Mark Singleton and Ken Tomasini, but Mark thought that Mr. Gordon was simply engaging in *his* typical zany frivolity.

"No Bob," I would say with a stoical expression upon my face. "Tell me more about this amazing *student,* Ken Tomasini!"

Bob Gordon would always talk about imaginary places whose names *he* would creatively make up. "Well, J.W., for your explicit information, Ken Tomasini has been accepted at the prestigious Driftwood Naval Academy up in East Squirrelsneck, Pennsylvania. In fact, John, I have an uncle who teaches Ornithology up at the Academy; Professor Bill Ballpack!" Then Bob Gordon turned to Singleton and said to the preoccupied look-alike guidance counselor, "Say Mark, do *you* know a kid named Ken Tomasini!"

"No, I don't!" Mark honestly answered while holding a morning newspaper in front of his face. "I'm in charge of all the *students* whose last names range from A to G!"

"Oh, okay!" Bob solemnly-but-facetiously answered. "I meant to tell ya' that Ken Tomasini's been accepted at the Driftwood Naval Academy up in Squirrelsneck, Pennsylvania!"

"Ya' don't say!" Mark Singleton reflexively replied while still reading the newspaper. "Never heard of *that* institution!"

I was holding-back laughing so hard that I thought my kidneys were going to burst. I got-up from my chair and made a beeline for the Men's Lavatory just in time to make it to the urinal.

Dean Miles was an affable general science and environmental science teacher on the high school faculty. Miles possessed an abundance of trust in his *students* and was always optimistic with the glass being half-full all of the time instead of always half' empty. Mr. Miles firmly believed in a permissive classroom atmosphere where *students* could ramble around from experiment to experiment, giving their input and advice to their comrades. "*Student* freedom is necessary for kids to grow-up becoming mature thinkers and eventually realizing their own potential, and also achieving their own destinies," Dean once preached to me in the faculty room.

"That approach works with small classes with honor *students,"* I answered, "but I don't think it would be too practical trying it with unmotivated general *students*. Say Dean, what college department are you in charge of anyway?"

A narrow creek ran parallel to the high school property, and the recent ecology trend in late '60s education promoted the preservation of the natural environment. Dean Miles ambitiously organized a *student* clean-up program that would purge the stream of ugly litter and debris. Assisted by a crew of conscientious, select science *students*, Miles and his reluctant disciples diligently converted the half-mile-long murky creek and its bramble banks into an attractive brook-like setting.

"Do you now see what a team of motivated *students* can accomplish?" Dean Miles informed me at lunchtime in the faculty room. "All I had to do was establish the goal and then set *the kids* free to attain it any way they wanted!"

"I don't trust human nature quite as much as you do," I suspiciously maintained. "Over the summer, the stream will again become polluted with litter despite the fact that your recruited environmental *students* have wonderfully cleaned-up the place three times each week."

"I'm even having trash barrels installed every hundred feet to cut-down on the random litter!" Mr. Miles proudly related.

Three days later, before school, some of the more humanitarian *students* transported six full-barrel-waste cans from the sides of the creek and then maliciously hurled the metal cylinders (loaded with debris) into the formerly pristine stream.

Tim Carley and I parked our cars in the teachers' lot between the high school and the creek and then walked over to talk with Dean

Miles, who suddenly appeared quite disillusioned. The metal trash receptacles were bobbing up and down in the shallow water. I suggested to Mr. Miles, "Maybe the *students* are studying Virginia Woolf's *Stream of Consciousness* literary technique in senior English. You know: the state recommended inter-disciplinary approach combining English with Ecology!"

"Yeah Dean," Tim Carley pitched-in his glorious opinion. "The *students* might be integrating English Literature with Ecology!" he offered. "Whoever did this to *your* stream has really gotten *into the swim of things*, wouldn't you say?"

Dean Miles did not savor Tim's remarks or my commentary very much. The stealthy *student* vandalism triggered-off a good deal of faculty banter that Mr. Dean Miles had to suffer. Poor Mr. Miles had to endure recurring jesting from his peers about *his* major twentieth century contribution to the advancement of American education, "The Barrel-Stream Concept of Learning and Talking Trash!"

Tim Carley had a reputation for being a fair-but-tough History teacher that did not tolerate *student* dereliction. One fine morning, he stepped from his home to his car to find several gallons of paint splattered on the hood and trunk. By coincidence, the History instructor had failed several *students* the previous marking period, and Tim interpreted that the horrible vandalism had been deliberately targeted at him. The school administration didn't want to get involved in the case because the destruction had not occurred on school property. So, Mr. Carley had a good idea of exactly who had performed the dastardly acts, but the suspected perpetrators had influential parents and relatives in the community, and also direct connections with certain school board members.

Miss Presti was another victim of *student* retribution. The English instructor had made the mistake of not locking her car in the B-Wing parking lot. When she returned to the parking lot after school, she found a dozen egg yolks staining the upholstery of her new sedan. Another time, Miss Presti was having nighttime conferences with concerned parents on Teacher/Parent Conference Night. When she returned to her car after thirty exhausting ten-minute conferences, all four tires on her auto' were deflated. Destructive *students* ought to find more constructive ways to *air* their opinions and frustrations.

John Taylor taught Math' and had the displeasure of walking out to the parking lot after school one Wednesday only to find a gaping hole in his car's rear window. Another time John's auto' wouldn't start because a number of wires in his engine had been mysteriously disconnected and severed.

Mrs. Batten was a scattered-brained instructor and only lasted at the high school for several years. I can't remember precisely which curricular department the hefty woman was in, but during a transition of class periods, I was sitting on a sofa in the teachers' lounge when Mrs. Batten abruptly exited the Ladies Room. The female pedagogue must have been in a rush because a new roll of toilet paper was hanging-down from the back of her dress, and the T.P. was rapidly unraveling as she departed the Faculty Room, with some of the white tissue sheets being sheared-off as she madly closed the main door leading into the outside corridor. Exactly what transpired as the chubby woman hastily sped down the crowded hallway to her next class remains a mystery to this day.

Phil Tweston was a well-mannered man that demanded strict self-discipline from his junior and senior English Class *students*. The *students* mischievously called the veteran teacher "Stone Face" after some of Phil's literature classes had read Nathaniel Hawthorne's classic tale "The Great Stone Face". Mr. Tweston was commonly feared by *students* and was quite notorious in the high school for catching a bored *"disciple"* staring at the wall clock. Phil would first point to the classroom timepiece and then aim his index finger at the aberrant *student* while austerely stating to the fully shocked, non-scholar, "Time passes! Will you?"

One Saturday night in the late 1960s, before the creation of 911, Phil was sitting in his living room with his wife when the town rescue squad burst into his house with a stretcher and accompanying respiratory apparatus. The intense on-a-mission paramedics were very seriously responding to a crank phone call about an emergency heart attack victim at Phil's residence. After the incident, Mr. Tweston confided that "Someone should never live in the town in which he or she teaches." Phil, along with other teachers, also frequently complained about anonymous phone calls at all hours in the early morning. And this was in the early '70s before American society became even more dysfunctional than it is today.

Jack DeCicco was really revered by other faculty members, mostly because he had taught most of them (or at least one of their parents) through rough times during the '40s and 1950s. The French and Spanish master was a carryover from the past who had instructed his foreign language *students* on the same staff as veteran teachers Bill Catello and Charles B. Sipley. I always enjoyed listening to Jack DeCicco's stories that focused on the way things were in the past.

One time, Jack related that he was on his way home from teaching at the old high school in the 1940s when he was stopped on the highway by state policemen and told to get out of his car and help firefighters combat a raging forest fire.

"Didn't you have a choice in the matter?" I asked Jack. "I don't think that today the state police could get away with making someone involuntarily do something against his will!"

"Back in those days, it was part of a citizen's civic responsibility to chip-in and help whenever requested to do so by someone in authority!" Jack respectfully replied. "And that's the way it was in the old days! People respected and obeyed authority and gladly assumed responsibility when asked to help out!"

I always regarded Jack as a noble and distinguished man, and it was sad that he was close to retirement in 1968. He still possessed a great fervency for his foreign language subjects and also for the art of teaching. But unfortunately, for Mr. DeCicco in 1968, times were changing and *students* were changing too with the *Vietnam War* protest movement gaining momentum. In addition to being gray-haired and quite elderly in appearance, Mr. DeCicco was short in stature and a trifle bulging around his waist.

When Jack was assigned to the doom of cafeteria mass study hall patrol, several of the more fiendish male demons hibernating in the mass educational study hall wasteland showed little homage for either age or decency. They would deliberately call Jack "meatball" and "old geezer" whenever he walked by the *students*' tables.

When I was permanent subbing on cafeteria mass study hall duty with Jack, I would shudder upon hearing the ugly, adolescent disrespect being mumbled and muttered in *his* direction. The man had dedicated his entire adult life to the education of youth, and some of those audacious imbeciles in the mass cafeteria study hall (around eighty kids) were brazenly ridiculing the fine teacher that had devoted *his* entire professional energy to *student* betterment.

I had to control myself and show cool self-restraint because my first instinct was to grab one or two of the juvenile fools and bash their skulls against the cafeteria's tan-painted cinderblock walls.

Either Jack or I would eventually escort two or three of the impudent clowns down to the vice-principal's office and write-out Discipline Referral Cards on the uncivilized renegades. The punks would then receive two or three days of Office Detention. And of course, some unfortunate teachers would have to be punished after school sitting and suffering in the atonement room for forty-five minutes with them.

Jack DeCicco despised both cafeteria duty and the mass study halls because he only wanted to teach good kids in French and Spanish classes of fifteen or so *students*. He even requested an extra teaching period to avoid the horrendous "mass duty periods", and the administration finally granted Jack's wish the last two years of his distinguished teaching career.

Jack once told me something relevant during a teacher lunch period that has stuck in my mind. "Years ago, the teachers didn't have community respect back in the '40s and the '50s," he began. "But at least the *kids* respected *us*. They saw the value of education while their parents mostly worked with their hands in local factories and resented teachers since they thought *we* never got our hands dirty," Mr. DeCicco noted. "Today, public-school teachers neither have community respect nor *student* respect, either! That's the biggest major difference between 1948 and 1968!"

Jack then told me that even in the "old days", a teacher's life was never "peaches and cream". He had been assigned *to volunteer* and collect gate money for high school football games without pay as part of *his* professional *duty* as a teacher. Cash wasn't too readily available in the late '30s and early '40s. And when Jack first started teaching, the board of education paid him and his colleagues in *script*, which was a promise of salary that was honored by town pharmacists, barbers, doctors, retail stores and other businesses and services during the tough times before and during *World War II.*

Mrs. Finnian was another teacher on the high school faculty who was ready to retire. Her starting salary was $1,200.00 and was paid in *script,* or a board of education "I owe you!" as she called it. To secure a teaching position in the system, Mrs. Finnian had to orally agree to purchase a new automobile from a school board member that also coincidentally owned a local retail car dealership. The acquisition had cost Mrs. Finnian an entire year's salary, but that's the way educational politics worked in small towns during (and right after) the 1930s *Great Depression.*

In 1968, Mrs. Finnian had failed several *students* second marking period in Math' and in Algebra. Upon entering her B-Wing classroom between the changing of classes, the elderly woman noticed that her grade book and her attendance record book had been pilfered. And upon going to the teacher parking lot after school, Mrs. Finnian's car would not start. It was soon towed to a town garage and the mechanics found a mixture of sand and sugar in the gas line.

The administration did not want to get the police involved because of the bad publicity a police report would generate in local newspapers. So, victimized Mrs. Finnian had to quietly absorb the expense for the damage to her car's engine herself' and also re-do her roll book and her attendance record journal for the reticent-but-authoritarian administration.

European *students* that immigrated to America were amazed at the amount of irreverence directed toward teachers by rebellious and obnoxious kids that had grown-up in this country. Bill Catello summed it all up rather nicely. "J.W.", he moralized. "We can thank the community for the remnants of teacher serfdom we now experience daily, and we can thank educational psychology for the disrespect *we* get from *students*. The rules of the game have changed since when I started out in this *profession*," Bill articulated. "Teachers must respect and must be courteous to all kids, but all kids don't have to reciprocate! It's no longer a level playing field!"

Over the years, school authority has been transferred from teachers to school *specialists* like principals, vice-principals and guidance counselors. The teacher is still a *generalist* as he or she was back in the 1930s. But now teachers are the vulnerable prey of certain nasty *students,* of certain irate parents of nasty *students,* of cloud-nine college professors, of amateur school board members, and of bungling/public-relations-minded school administrators. Some may consider my position on this matter as being "cynical or unprofessional," but I maintain that teachers have never been professional people during the last century in the taxpayers' eyes.

The daily activity of being permanent subs' was an immense challenge to both Bill Catello and me. We both preferred the euphemism "special assignment teacher", only because it sounded more professional than the appellation "permanent substitute" did. Bill was getting weaker with each passing day, so he decided to call it quits and retire before cancer made him "die on the job", as he put it. In June of 1970 the frugal-minded board of education and the administration agreed to eliminate two of the four permanent substitute positions in the school district. "One from the elementary school and one from the high school *must* go!" the principal told me.

I saw the writing on the wall, that soon, all four permanent-sub' teaching positions would be eliminated. 'It was a real innovation of this school system having four certified teachers as subs', and now it's being junked for the sake of saving taxpayers' dollars!' I realized and concluded.

I also finally surmised that teachers were regarded as expendable entities regardless of one's worth to the system, regardless of one's personal dedication, or regardless of one's total contributions. The administration and the board of education believed that replacing any teacher was as easy as removing a dead light bulb and then twisting a replacement into the temporarily empty electrical socket. 'No matter how a person looks at it, in the end, the teacher will get *screwed* (or unscrewed),' I logically concluded.

Chapter 19
"The MEATs"

The teachers on the high school faculty felt a great deal of anxiety and stress from always having to be perfect role models and knowing that at any time, a parent or a *student,* or a *student* conspiracy could fabricate some outlandish lie and get an instructor suspended. The men teachers had our own fraternity, which met (usually at bars) several times a year both in our town and out of our community. The MEATs *dis*organization was our unprofessional fraternity, and the acronym stood for "Men's Epicurean Association of Teachers". The MEATs happened to be a convenient safety valve where the male faculty members could let-off steam, and it was a terrific escape mechanism from the rigors of teaching.

The MEATs had nothing to do with the local teachers' association, with the *New Jersey Educational Association,* or with the *NEA.* The loosely configured "teachers' fraternity" rabble was an appropriate emotional outlet because it afforded the men teachers a chance to have male bonding, to commiserate, and also to get away from the mental anguish associated with perpetual educational pressure. Our beer and venison bashes unveiled our hidden carnivorous natures and gave us a way of basically thinking and behaving like primitive *Neanderthal Men.* Some of the guys on the high school faculty were accomplished forest hunters, so boar, deer and bear meat were often on the dinner menu.

In 1972-'73, I was President of the MEATs and conducted the general meetings. I was also the vice-president of the district's teachers' association at the time, and the one thing I didn't like about the MEATs was the fact that the school administrators had helped found the organization before I had commenced with my teaching career in September of 1965. I had always been suspicious of school administrators "in the organization", fearing that their primary motive for membership was a means of intelligence gathering about male faculty members. Some town board members didn't exactly savor *my* opposition to their directives during teacher contract negotiations, and I really didn't need any principal or superintendent spouting-off about how I had acted grossly "unprofessionally" at the MEATs' unprofessional dinner meetings.

New male teachers in the district had to be accepted into *our* social rank by an initiation ceremony. The men teachers all recognized that we needed such an ignoble organization to temporarily lose our identities, get plastered, and behave unprofessionally just like the community attitudes had always perceived us as being and doing.

Each prospective first year teacher was given a topic for a "ten-minute formal induction speech" that had to be somberly and soberly presented to the group of eighty-or-so educators seated in attendance at the first of two annual MEATs' feasts. Each new male teacher had a sponsor, who would lead the candidate from the restaurant's bar area to the secretive meeting room. The Board of Directors and Officers had carefully constructed and previously distributed speech assignments for the novices' final acceptance into the prestigious brotherhood. Here is a typical speech topic for a junior high school English teacher.

"Your subject is as follows: An intensive dissertation on the relevancy of subjects and predicates (as opposed to nouns and verbs) in this age of technological transformation and cultural upheaval."

A social studies teacher might be given the subject: "The need for non-tenure teachers to get directly involved in national and local social and educational controversial issues."

A science teacher might draw the premise: "The necessity of permissiveness in an unstructured high school laboratory classroom in order to teach *students* the value of independence, responsibility, rebellion, and anarchy."

A new high school literature teacher might have the speech topic: "The significance of the development of thespian and lesbian appreciation in education ranging from the gay nineties to the modern gay community."

Each new male teacher received a letter of invitation outlining his speech. Here was the official cover letter sent to all candidates:

> "The MEATs speech committee, after contemplative investigation, has agreed upon the subject appearing at the bottom of this page as the most applicable to your ten-minute formal presentation to our noble organization. Good luck on your upcoming dissertation.
>
> "Your oratory must not exceed fifteen minutes, nor should it constitute a mere nine-minute rhetorical utterance. All fledglings seeking membership into this esteemed organization should pay particular attention to your poise, dignity, confidence, and mastery of content during your presentation, along with other pertinent ramifications. We suggest that you practice as the ancient Greek Demosthenes

had done by putting pebbles in your mouth to improve your elocution and your enunciation."

"Finally, you will be addressing knowledgeable professionals having eminent and distinguished reputations. Our organization is comprised mostly of dedicated educators that have proven themselves worthy of the title of public-school instructor. Be prepared to defend awkward intellectual positions that you might inadvertently propose or maintain, and above all else, don't act like an arrogant asshole. Your social acceptance into our most reputable association depends almost exclusively on your competency at defending your generalizations and hypotheses delivered on your assigned topic. Be prepared to answer questions advanced by the Officers and by the Board of Directors after you communicate your speech. Any hint of frivolity on your part will not be tolerated and might result in you being ostracized from the faculty."

An incoming Spanish teacher was given this speech topic:

"You are to present a provocative comparison and contrast of the structural analysis, etymology and evolution of frequently used Spanish and English expletives and obscene exclamatory nomenclature. Your fundamental focus should be on past history, current trends, phonetic patterns and tonal accents as opposed to traditional Spanish European vernacular."

"Also, please come to the meeting prepared to attack and critique all new innovations in the teaching of Spanish in the curriculum that have surfaced in the last twenty years. Finally, you should include in your presentation a justification of the need to teach Spanish to *students* in a community that espouses a WASPish, Anglo-Saxon tradition and heritage."

The greenhorn teachers spent hours of honest research and mirror-practice perfecting their speeches. At the initiation meeting, each candidate's sponsor (at twenty-minute intervals) escorted him from the bar into the stone-silent, general meeting room. After the department area sponsor introduced the novice to the MEATs' conclave, the newcomer to the district would initiate his lecture.

All MEATs' members would sit attentively and pensively listen to the monotonous articulation for the first five minutes. But then the MEATs' members would begin talking among themselves' while the new teacher was struggling through his oral presentation. Soon, everyone seated in the room was ignoring the anxious, standing speaker's sincere words.

As the stunned newcomer labored on with his oration, intermittent burps and belches, and also occasional loud farting, interrupted *his* sentences. Despite the chafing distractions, most of the shocked neophytes would persevere on until the conclusion of *their* enlightening discourses. Then, heckling and jeering would ensue, and several of the more muscular MEATs' members would rise from their chairs, grab the new candidate and threaten to pulverize the pledge, much to the boisterous elation of the membership.

Once, the MEATs even had two local uniformed policemen enter the meeting during a speech presentation, with a barking German shepherd baring sharp fangs. The local cops put the worried candidate in handcuffs, made a pretend arrest, and finally conducted the shocked, rejected, fuming speech-giver out of the smoke-filled meeting room.

After a speech was finally delivered, the novice was shown a large hypodermic needle, which the President had earlier told "the candidate" would be used to inject a potent stimulant into *his* sensitive buttocks. The MEATs' candidate was also shown a large club and had been foretold that the awesome weapon would also be used against him if *he* did not fully cooperate and give a truly professional presentation. The pledge would then be blindfolded and instructed to bend over, firmly gripping the seat of a restaurant chair. He would then be stuck in the buttocks with a pin, which the anxious pledge naturally suspected was the giant hypodermic needle.

Next came the highlight of the MEATs' initiation ceremony. Bob Gordon and Tim Carley poured red food coloring onto a feminine sanitary napkin and then placed the wet fabric into the blindfolded pledge's mouth. Jack DeCicco (the smallest MEAT member) next lifted and held the aforementioned giant club above *his* head. The blindfolded candidate was told to again bend over.

As the assembled male teachers all yelled "One, two…" sweat beads would be cascading down the pledge's forehead during the extended hesitation. On the count of "three", Jack then slammed the huge shillelagh against the leather seat of another chair other than the one the blindfolded candidate had been tightly holding.

The most laughter was derived when the newcomer was instructed to "take the blindfold off and also remove the *handkerchief* out of your mouth". The staggered, first-year teacher would incredulously gape at the red-stained feminine napkin sitting in the palm of his hand. The newly initiated teacher would next join his colleagues in harassing the incoming prospect, who would soon be escorted into the room by *his* department sponsor.

As President of the MEATs, I had the distinct honor and the unenviable task of controlling the avid, half-inebriated beer guzzlers while attempting to preside over the meetings. My concluding remarks to the membership had been designed to make absolutely no sense at all. However, it was well-received and went like this:

My fellow processionals:

I would like to extonate to you, my trulifinated colleagues, the salutrified experience it has been for me to be enulbed as el presidente of this trankanimous organization. This sobravenous group behoones me to be very podulent and pedistic about our civic troduncidies.

While you hornts and you cubinators have been blitumated in *men*struation, I have been sedunting about the future mentronals of tomorrow, which will certainly allutinate our present circumcisions.

With such a relantrified faculty, ajending in consulfinating challenges, I am confident that the hermotudes of our civilization will certainly be donafied.

The ventrunal nature between teacher and *student* couldn't be more robundant and dudly reperdidified. It can almost be vernificated that without being fully kakrinated into our produngeous society, the dumb-ass citizens of tomorrow might be doomed to being ad-hutinrotted. Now I hereby thank the MEATs for your gruntudinous attention, and I hope I have merited your metronical conjuence.

I'll never forget the time I organized a Saturday noontime spring MEATs' fishing expedition to a salt-river-inlet that was fed by the *Atlantic Ocean*. The fellows showed up en-masse, many of them not knowing a fishing rod from a lightning rod. After the six dozen of us consumed gallons of homemade Dago wine and cases of *Budweiser* along with other potent intoxicants, the male teachers were more prepared to lampoon than to harpoon.

Several of *our* aberrant fishing lines became entangled with those of three more skilled and more serious fishermen that frequented the isolated beach every day. Then, one of the more extroverted MEATs' members demonstrated his casting prowess and suddenly his line intersected with those of the three serious regular anglers, right after they had spent fifteen minutes unscrambling their lines from the first major entanglement. After *they* finished unwinding and unraveling the incredible knots, the trio of disgruntled fishermen evacuated the sandy beach and left the MEATs stranded there to contend with each other's high jinks. The MEATs continued our merriment, drank some more, and a few of us even danced around on the hot sand to accordion music provided by one of our newest inductees, which scared every fish within a five-mile radius far out to sea.

The MEATs provided the men teachers the opportunity to abandon the tensions associated with the demanding role of being school teachers, and the club gave us a license to act imperfectly and unprofessionally in secluded places existing far from our base of employment. It was a way for us to have some connection with the manner in which "regular civilian people" enjoyed themselves.

I recall a minor vendetta brewing between two members of the MEATs' fraternal order. Many of the various department fellows took sides in the friendly quarrel, which soon escalated into intense one-upmanship between the two competing camps.

Cars in the school parking lots were found stuffed with crinkled-up papers, which at first impression, some instructors suspected had been done by naughty *students*. Bob Gordon was getting long-distance phone calls to buy Florida swampland real estate and investing in defunct alligator farms. Tim Carley received inquiries at his home phone over falsified newspaper want ads published in *his* name advertising to sell "pedigree dogs, thoroughbred horses and collectible skunks".

The escapade expanded and more faculty members were soon affected by the imaginative pranks. I was summoned by a secretary over the intercom to the Main Office to answer a phone call before my lunch period. A salesman from Colorado wanted to sell me a bulldozer and a steam shovel, and the fellow became rather angry when I informed the long-distance caller that *we* were being "innocent victims in a mass practical joke". Joe Sacci (a music teacher) woke-up one morning and found over a hundred dead blackbirds and sparrows strewn all over his front lawn.

But the issuance of junk mail was perhaps the biggest craze. Men teachers were scanning every available magazine and newspaper and clipping-out coupons guaranteeing free information on any product "with no obligation". Then *we* would print another staff member's name and address in the information blanks instead of our own.

Some days, I would step to my teacher mailbox and discover forty pieces of junk mail, and then go home and find forty more waiting for me in my driveway mailbox. And the problem was growing to monster-proportions because all our names were being placed on other company mailing lists all the time.

Teachers were getting mail addressed to crazy names like Sir Loin' Kyle and Missed Her Carley. And the junk mail was coming from unknown hamburger franchises, from legitimate taxidermy schools, from locksmith institutes of higher learning, and from established butchering academies. Jack DeCicco (a diminutive man) received at least five "Big and Tall Men's Catalogs" every week. Ron LeFey drove his car home from school one fine afternoon and found that a "test-drive camper" had been left in his driveway for a "free week's trial demonstration". And three years after the height of the junk mail deluge, I was still receiving vestiges of the wild male faculty members' royal caper.

John Rizzo was a personable Driver Education teacher. John and I were appointed by the MEATs executive committee to go to a local slaughterhouse and pick-up a hog for the next annual end-of-year pig roast. John Rizzo and I were innocently standing in the meat-house's receiving area and talking about what kind of hog we would be getting when a trap door opened behind Rizzo, and suddenly, a tremendous pork belly (slit down the middle) came rolling upside down toward us on a chain rotary.

The fresh, out-of-the-freezer, recently severed pig was speeding directly toward Rizzo. John turned around, saw the suspended animal heading his way and let-out a primitive scream that would have scared the heck out of Frankenstein. The gigantic pig had blood oozing out of its nostrils and had just been carved open by skilled meat butchers.

At the end-of-year pig roast, Zeke Shullmon, a junior high Science teacher, entertained the assembled MEATs. Zeke showed us images from a slide projector of past MEATs' banquets, with certain members vomiting in toilet bowls or having simulated sex with a rubberized woman dummy used in health classes to demonstrate artificial respiration. That particular meeting was perhaps the most clamorous one ever for our illustrious organization.

The high school vice-principal tied one on good that afternoon. First, he mixed the salad by putting all of the chopped-up lettuce, radishes, pickles, green peppers and onions into a new clean waist-high trashcan. Then he liberally poured a gallon of oil and a gallon of vinegar into the mix, put the trashcan lid down onto the container, lifted the metal can upside-down over his head and blended all of the delicious salad ingredients together. Actually, that was the best salad I had ever tasted.

Next, the feeling-no-pain vice-principal put the decapitated pig's head on his own crown and stuck bones in his nose and mouth, looking very much like a cannibal out of *Robinson Crusoe*. The school administrator and I soon got into a heated argument over "teachers' rights" and "educational philosophy", and the school executive stood-up and wildly took a swing at me. I ducked down and his fist penetrated a wall of the civic club we had rented for the *MEATs*' party. The fellows then moved a piano over from an adjacent wall to cover-up the hole that had recently been formed.

The following Monday morning, the high school principal called me into his office. I thought I was going to be interrogated about the punctured hole in the clubhouse wall. Instead, the principal was upset that I was violating the school's teacher dress code by wearing a '70s leisure suit with an open collar and no tie.

"I want to see you wearing a tie to school," the straightlaced principal (who was not at the most recent *MEATs*' feast) insisted.

"Leisure suits are now in style," I argued. "And ties aren't worn with them. Check any men's fashion catalog to see what I mean."

"I still want *you* to wear a tie at all times," the irate principal rankled. "I have nothing against leisure suits, but if you want to wear one, then you must wear a tie, too!"

"Ties strangulate blood circulation to the brain," I intelligently replied. "Do you want me to suffer a massive stroke?"

"Wear ties!" he angrily maintained. "If you don't, you'll be regarded and treated as being *insubordinate!*"

"Ties *are* symbols of *subordination!*" I fired back. "And besides, the women teachers don't have to wear ties when *they* wear suits! It's gender discrimination against male teachers!" I shouted. "Yes, that's what you're advocating with this stupid tie thing! You're playing a silly power game, that's all you're doing!"

"Wear ties!" the principal nastily yelled as his face turned red. "*Wear ties* I said!" He repeated in a maniacal tone of voice.

"I can only wear one tie at a time," I laughed in response to *his* crazy, animated anger.

"Why are you so stubborn!" he challenged. "Why can't you just wear a tie as a favor to me instead of being so obstinate!"

"Do you see this gold necklace!" I exclaimed to the uptight principal while pointing to an expensive piece of jewelry hanging down from my neck. "This golden necklace cost as much as fifty ties, so the next time *you* see me wearing a leisure suit with this golden necklace around my throat, just pretend you're looking at me wearing fifty ties!"

"Very well then, you can leave now!" the principal ordered. "I only wish that you were more cooperative!"

"You mean more subordinate!" I answered as I rose from my chair and then left *his* comfortable, beautifully decorated office.

The *MEATs* to the male teachers happened to be comparable to a twice a year *New Year's Eve* party where everyone (except the high school principal) could deviate from stiff rigid "professional behavior," discard our inflexible public image, and then explore the suppressed *Mr. Hydes* that dwelled deep inside of us. Over the years, our membership has gotten older and has mellowed. The members from the early 1970s are mostly now married, have wives and families, or are retired or dead. The '70s *MEATs'* camaraderie has lost much of its former momentum, zaniness and spunk, and by 2003, it existed as a faint memory of a happy, bygone era.

John Magliari was a new member entering into the *MEATs* fraternity. But I distinctly remember John (who had arrived from Argentina and was actually shorter than Jack DeCicco) from the first day of school in September of '69. I was a permanent sub' standing behind the counter in the Main Office, seeing if any teacher had been absent when Magliari soon entered to put a check next to his name on the teacher sign-in attendance sheet.

"Are you an administrator?" John curiously asked, seeing that I was hanging around in the Main Office.

Before I had a chance to answer, or even introduce myself as a permanent sub', the principal came out of his office and disclosed, "Mr. Magliari; I'd like to talk with you a minute!"

That September day, I had little to do and was becoming bored. No teachers were absent, so Bill Catello and I walked around the building and gave teachers on cafeteria or on study hall duty fifteen-minute breaks to freshen-up, or to use the facilities. When I stepped into an A-Wing classroom, I was about to introduce myself to John Magliari, but he beat me to the punch.

"Oh; *you* are one of the school principals!" falsely observed and stated the newly-hired ESL instructor, who had expressed those rather worried words in his broken Argentine accent. "Just sit in back of room and observe my lesson if you'd like!"

I stepped to the back of the room, watched John's entire lesson, and then told him *he* had done a "satisfactory and almost excellent job". The rookie instructor thanked me for my compliment, and still thinking that I was an administrator, John invited me to come-in anytime I needed to write-up an official lesson observation report.

A month later, in the faculty lounge, Bob Gordon told John Magliari that he had heard that the principal was going to observe the jittery teacher the next period, which was only five minutes away. "You'd better use the bathroom now. I know I would if I were you!" Bob advised the recently hired English-As-A-Second-Language teacher. "I think you should empty your radiator!"

"That's a very good idea!" the new *ESL* teacher acknowledged.

After John Magliari entered the Men's Room (which was really part of the faculty lounge), Bob Gordon, Tim Carley and I slid the nearby *Coke* machine from a side area to the lavatory door, which needed to open outwards for someone to exit.

After John had finished doing his washroom business, he attempted to open the bathroom door, but couldn't because of the huge, heavy obstacle in the way. The beleaguered fellow began pounding on the door and screaming and begging, "I need to keep my job! Let me out of here! I have to be observed by the principal!" John was screaming.

I had the next period off, so I walked-down to the A-Wing to get John's next class settled. Two minutes later, Bob and Tim moved the heavy *Coke* machine back to where it belonged. Magliari rushed-out of the Men's Room and sprinted like a wild man down the C-Wing to the A-Wing. He entered the classroom and was very relieved to see no principal seated in the rear. Then, he thanked me for "watching my class!" John did not realize that I had been one of the conspirators and perpetrators who had blocked the Men's Room door with the bulky soda machine.

On the first Friday night in early October, several MEATs members and I determined that we needed to "un-traumatize" John Magliari, so in the interest of camaraderie and male teacher fraternity, we decided to treat the new ESL teacher to a "boys' night out". I drove my three enthusiastic passengers over to a distant tavern in Turnersville, where we enjoyed downing several mugs of beer and devouring delicious ham sandwiches. Next, we excitedly motored twelve miles further west to a strip-joint on Admiral Wilson Boulevard in Camden, a destination where we believed we would not be recognized by anyone. After paying a hefty admission fee, the four of us were having a great time, but when the third stripper appeared and paraded down the catwalk, the three veteran tenure teachers realized that the well-endowed female was a *student* we had each taught six years before. Afraid of violating the sacred "moral turpitude clause" in our signing contracts, the three of us were sweating bullets while being absolutely scared at being identified. The trio tilted our baseball caps down to shade our eyes while we kept-on feeding a puzzled John Magliari fresh dollar bills to stuff-down the stripper's skimpy panties. To tell the truth, that experience was the last time I've ever visited a tawdry strip palace.

The following fall, I organized a little MEATs' hunting trip to a small game preserve not far from Gettysburg, Pennsylvania. Bob Gordon was a skilled taxidermist who promised to stuff any animal that one of us might bag. John Magliari came along on the hunting expedition, and my brother-in-law was a guest member of the hunting excursion.

I had shot a white ram on the expedition, which Bob Gordon later mounted onto a large plaque that now hangs from a wall in my den. Right after my shooting the ram, my brother-in-law was on the other side of a hill. He fired several shots from his rifle, and before John Magliari or I knew what was happening, a wild boar with sharp tusks came snorting over the crest heading right towards Magliari and me.

John and I dropped our rifles, swiftly dashed to the nearest tree, and then we started scaling the oak as fast as we could. The ferocious, wounded beast slammed its head into the base of the oak, nearly knocking John and me off our respective limbs. When the MEATs' hunting trip had ended, I had shot the ram, my brother-in-law had killed the boar, Bob Gordon had gotten a deer head trophy, and John Magliari had successfully killed three blackbirds while unskillfully shooting at a wild turkey.

I had always liked John Magliari. He came over to my home along with Math' teachers Jim Smythe and John Senna, and we played cards in my carpeted basement and enjoyed more than a few beers together. John would even accompany me down to Ocean City, Maryland on April weekends and help me set-up the arcade prizes on the shelves at 410 South Boardwalk.

Being an *ESL* teacher, John Magliari always had small classes with around *ten* or less *students* in each one. Then the administration assigned the shy young man cafeteria duty and also a difficult study hall loaded with eighth grade hellions that John had trouble disciplining. "I can't control those crazy kids!" John openly cried one evening at my house. "In Argentina, the *students* always respected the *teachers*. Here the kids try crucifying me every day!"

John went to the administration and asked for small classes to teach rather than be abused in the cafeteria or having rolled-up paper balls hitting him in the back of his head when he was facing the opposite direction in the hard-to-handle eighth grade *study hall*. John Magliari was never re-assigned and subsequently went into a deep state of depression. "Learn how to keep the lid on!" he was told. "You're a teacher and you have to be able to control *students* in all situations!" was *his* advice received from the administration.

John's unfortunate fate was chronicled in the local newspaper with a headline: "Local Teacher Shot to Death". The article described John and his exemplary teaching record. Administrators stated that his work was most satisfactory. The newspaper never reported the truth that John Magliari had shot and killed himself because he had become despondent about not knowing how to cope with or how to control the malicious, non-*ESL students* he had encountered both in the cafeteria and in the eighth-grade study hall. John was one of three district teachers that I knew who had committed suicide.

Chapter 20
"A Nightmare Vacation Trip"

During my fifth year of teaching, my wife and I had taken a three-day mini-vacation to West Virginia. We stopped at Harpers Ferry, the sight of John Brown's raid, and the venue was also a historic landmark rich in *Civil War* era heritage. Then, my spouse and I proceeded south on scenic Skyline Drive through the Blue Ridge Mountains to Luray, where we had planned to tour the famous underground caverns. It was getting a bit dark, and a heavy mountain fog began gradually settling along the elevated highway.

I instinctively turned on the headlights to forewarn oncoming traffic of our presence while nervously holding and blasting my horn around each successive curve and bend.

"Your headlights are becoming dimmer!" my observant wife related. "You got to get to a gas station in a hurry!"

"You're right!" I concurred. "And now my horn has the blast of a dying mouse caught in a trap!"

Luckily, my expert driving had safely gotten us through the dense fog to Luray where we tarried for the night at a well-appointed motel situated right near the acclaimed caverns. The following morning, we toured the beautiful subterranean hollows and consumed a casual lunch. Then Joanne and I returned to our motel, packed our bags, paid our debts, and put all of our belongings inside the car trunk.

"Oh no!" I moaned to my wife. "The engine won't start!" The ignition kept making a pathetic groaning noise that sounded as if it was suffering from a severe case of laryngitis.

I paced to a nearby phone booth, leafed through the yellow pages, located a certain number, and spoke with a service station mechanic. After an hour of patient waiting, the repairman arrived at the scene of distress in his tow truck. After examining my wife's car's engine, the expert's diagnosis was that I needed a new battery cable.

"Do you have one to spare on your truck?" I inquired. "If not, can you get one?"

"We sure do have one, sir," the jolly fellow with a strong southern accent replied. "I'll need to charge up the battery after I change cables. The whole deal will only cost you thirty-five bucks for parts, labor and installation!"

After the defective battery cable had been removed and the new one installed, I gladly paid the good-natured mechanic for his polite service and generously gave him a five-dollar tip.

I proceeded out of Luray and drove through a piedmont section, my route gradually heading-down from the mountains toward the valley below. We stopped at several places of interest along the route including a gift shop and a farm market. It was autumn, and the tree leaves in and around the beautiful *Shenandoah Valley* were turning to spectacular brown, red and yellowish hues.

"Isn't the scenery magnificent?" I asked Joanne. "This is one of the prettiest sights in America!"

"Yes, and this is the vicinity where Johnny Appleseed is said to have planted all those apple trees! We read a story about John Chapman in school!" my wife, a third-grade teacher, added. "You're right John! It's quite a fantastic panorama!"

It was late afternoon, and twilight was slowly descending upon the region. I flicked on my headlights to prepare for nocturnal driving. The radio announcer's voice sounded as if he was going unconscious while suffering from life-threatening yellow fever. My devoted wife turned the station selector dial, and the next speaker sounded like a hospital patient lying in traction, broadcasting from a very distant intensive care ward.

"There's a gasoline station just up ahead!" my alert spouse noticed. "Let's stop and see if the new battery cable is loose!"

Luckily, my automobile sputtered to a halt just beyond the entrance to the garage. Several flabby, grease monkeys came ambling over and then helped me push the green *Pontiac* into the service station bay. I was quite thankful for their assistance.

After raising the hood and generally inspecting the motor, the chief neurosurgeon evaluated, "Your car needs a new battery!"

"Install it!" I automatically commanded. "My wife and I are on the brink of mental and physical exhaustion. Just install it!"

The battery transplant was successfully completed without the use of any special anesthesia. I forked-over the thirty-seven dollars for the new battery, a reasonable sum even by 1970 standards.

"Thank goodness the car didn't stall-out in the middle of nowhere!" my wife attested. "That sort of wicked disaster would be totally devastating!"

"I hope this new car isn't a lemon, even if it is a belated wedding gift from *your* father!" I answered.

"Just drive and keep your negative comments to yourself!" Joanne sarcastically chastised.

My wife and I waved to the accommodating service-station technicians and re-embarked on our northern itinerary, all the while believing that the electrical difficulty had been effectively corrected. Several hours of carefree driving elapsed, and we were heading northeast toward Harrisburg, Pennsylvania. A road construction project got us detoured onto a lesser traveled thoroughfare that had scarcely any traffic moving in either direction.

"You must've made a wrong turn somewhere!" my upset wife declared. "I wish you'd pay more attention to what you're doing!" she rambunctiously criticized.

"I don't remember seeing any additional detour signs!" I calmly responded. "There's hardly any other cars on the road we're on, and it's pitch black out. It's almost as if we've drifted into some mysterious *Twilight Zone!*"

"Just stop talking and drive!" my wife exclaimed and insisted.

I nearly swallowed my tongue when I perceived my headlights again dimming and then flickering on and off, doing an animated dance across the deserted two-lane highway. My wife was indeed a nervous wreck about to become an asylum patient. Apparitions of looming disaster haunted my all-too-shaken cerebral processes. We intensely discussed being marooned on a forsaken country road that was infested with bears, skunks and bobcats.

By a miraculous stroke of good fortune, the green *Pontiac* coupe coasted down a hill and into a quaint village that featured a small service station. The gas station attendant was very cordial and cooperative. He opened the hood, browsed the engine with the aid of a "trouble light", and then intelligently traced the origin of the problem down to the distributor. My wife was almost in shock from the series of car-repair crises we had been experiencing, and our only desire was to get back on the road as quickly as possible and make it to New Jersey at any expense.

"I just happen to have the necessary part in stock!" the gas station guru stated in a cute Pennsylvania Dutch accent. "It's used, but it'll work perfectly!"

The benign fellow performed the needed distributor exchange, charged-up the recently acquired battery, checked the replacement battery cable at my request, and next merrily charged me ninety dollars for his labor, expertise and parts.

"How can we get onto the *Pennsylvania Turnpike*?" I asked. "Once we're on *that* highway, I know exactly how to get home!"

"Go down three miles and make a right at the fork in the road," the obliging fellow instructed. "Then go three more miles and ya' can't miss the big green sign."

"Thanks for fixing our car!" my wife exclaimed with a sigh of relief. "I've spent worse three-hours just sitting in the hairdresser's getting a permanent!"

After a half-hour traveling east toward Philadelphia on the *Pennsylvania Turnpike,* my headlights again began to dim and then flicker. Almost having conniptions, and almost being a total basket case, I fortunately was able to pull into the next service plaza. The night mechanics on duty were cheerful blokes, and they ingeniously hypothesized that my car's ailment was electrical in nature.

"Do what you need to!" I humbly insisted. "All I want to do is drive back to Jersey alive! We should have taken the trip in my *Triumph Spitfire* sports car!" I told my already traumatized wife.

I just had to marvel at the mechanics' mental alacrity. Two servicemen put new spark plugs in, changed several crucial wires, adjusted the points, and then retested the battery after charging it. I realized that the car probably didn't need a few of those added items, but I was so stressed-out that I didn't care how much the parts and labor would cost. I just wanted to get home and escape the living nightmare my wife and I were trapped in.

"Your oil is dirty!" one mechanic brought to my attention. "I think you ought to change it just to be safe!"

"Go right ahead!" I reluctantly agreed. I was on the verge of a mild coronary, but now the engine wizards had to verbally degrade the quality of my engine oil and virtually accuse me of being derelict in maintaining my wife's undependable car. But being reasonable, I did not dispute their claim or challenge their mechanical knowledge.

"Anything you have to do to make this tin pig run better!" I answered as my wife gave me a terrible frown as I critiqued the automobile her father had given us. I even consented to the men adding two quarts of anti-freeze and a pint of transmission fluid just to make the car run more efficiently.

"They could tell me I need a new cigarette lighter and I would insist that they put one in," I revealed to my annoyed and impatient wife. "Neither of us smoke, but I would still have *it* done just to have peace of mind!"

"It was your idea to go on this relaxing trip!" my spouse reminded me. "Have you got any other great ideas? How about skydiving?"

We made it to Philadelphia and gladly passed over the *Walt Whitman Bridge* into New Jersey. About three miles from our home, the lights again began losing their illumination. I turned into our driveway, shut-off the ignition, took several deep breaths, and then began unloading our suitcases and souvenirs from the jinxed car.

The following morning, I just managed to get the engine started. Then I drove the accursed auto' to the local garage mechanic. He inspected the engine without the aid of a sage *Ouija Board* and immediately determined that the fan belt that cranks-up the alternator had snapped-off, and its absence was paralyzing the car's entire electrical system, especially at night when additional power was required to operate the headlights. The fan belt cost me $3.98 plus labor, but the point is that I had spent almost three hundred hard-earned dollars in parts and labor for a vital $3.98 part.

A dozen pleasant mechanics had seen the same thing and had come-up with the wrong theories as to why the lights were flickering. But only the last hometown automobile guru had the ability to pinpoint and finally alter the deficiency. All of the "mechanics" I had encountered were courteous and amiable, but only one of them knew exactly what he was doing.

"I now know that education isn't the only field where incompetent performance flourishes," I told my wife at the supper table. "This country needs more knowledgeable automobile mechanics."

"Be quiet and just eat your lima beans!" Joanne answered back.

But then a revolutionary thought occurred to me. In speaking with each of the "mechanics", I had learned that they all had graduated from high school, even though they were inept at diagnosing engine problems. But they all also had congenial dispositions and temperaments. But *their* bungling had cost me in excess of three hundred dollars in unnecessary expenses. Then it all came to me like some supernatural revelation.

"Incompetent performance in high school education is the genesis of the irresponsibility we had experienced with the untrained garage mechanics," I informed my uninterested wife. "They learn how to socialize and get along with each other in high school classrooms, but their inadequate educations grossly unprepared them for their future occupations. We have to begin assessing the true damage schools are doing to young people!" I argued.

"Now that you've eaten your lima beans," my spouse uttered, "you can now start on your broccoli!"

"Joanne, of what value is a society of friendly workers that can't produce, that cost others valuable time and money, and that lack sufficient skill in performing their jobs?" I wondered and then asked. "Of what benefit are nice guys that make a motorist pay over three hundred bucks for an ordinary four-dollar fan belt?"

"Don't forget your mashed potatoes," my concerned wife reminded me. "I had to mash them all by myself because *you* were at the auto' mechanic's garage!"

The real education in America is not being done by public schools. It is done by large corporations like *IBM, AT&T, Microsoft, General Motors and GE.* Those companies *train* (there's *that* evil word) prospective employees to perform highly *specialized* tasks. The thrust of corporate America is to turn a profit for stockholders, and company executives realize that highly *trained* workers contribute to the prosperity of the firm and to the stability of the country when they *train* (teach) people to do specific jobs.

High schools could best serve non-college-bound *students* by setting-up curricula with large and medium-sized corporations to begin *training* the future blue-collar workers that are presently vegetating in academic English and History classes, and also terrorizing teachers in Home Economics, in the cafeteria, in mass study halls, and in family living classes.

An incredible Great Barrier Reef separates the concept of "child-centered curriculum" with its liberal expectations from the tough standards that are demanded of employees by corporate America. While pursuing the *Holy Grail* of *democratic* education, public schools are performing a terrible disservice to this great nation. The *child-centered curriculum, democratic* sociological (Marxist) education, the lack of tough academic standards, along with the promotion of "cooperative learning" are really the antitheses of orderly self-responsibility and self-accountability. Just imagine the fate of American corporations if the companies valued and practiced "worker-centered production", and next espoused "psychological, cooperative production" among employees, instead of currently advocating "democratic rights on the assembly line", and "sociological, non-academic bottom lines" as is the trend.

The *"democratic* comprehensive high schools" are producing non-college-bound graduates that are grossly unprepared to be absorbed into the mainstream of the American free enterprise system. A future citizen needs food in his stomach before needing to "socialize". He or she needs clothes on his or her back before he or she needs to get along with others in cooperative groups, and *students* need secure jobs based on adequate *training* before they need a devalued piece of parchment inscribed with the official school emblem.

Chapter 21
"The Need for Competition"

Cooperation is emphasized in American public schools while competition is generally discouraged. Competition is even being downplayed amongst the most gifted *students* because educational psychology maintains that competition breeds selfish, arrogant adults that only care about themselves and not about the needs of the less fortunate. Everyone involved in education has to get back to the idea that competition is a worthwhile pursuit that is consistent with our great free enterprise system of economics. That is why it is so important that public school philosophy pragmatically follows the proven *free enterprise* economic model rather than the current ineffective political *democracy* model of education that impractically squanders billions of dollars annually.

Industry is keenly aware of the need for competition as the true instrument of societal prosperity and personal improvement. Surely *Nissan* and *Toyota* have forced *General Motors* and *Ford* to manufacture better cars, or else go the way of the dinosaur. But our schools just don't get it! Rivalry is the key to individual self-sufficiency and to corporate progress everywhere in America, except in our public schools.

As it is, our schools are eroding-away the one essential tradition that has made America great. Why should *students* attempt to excel if they are working in a *democratic*, sociological educational system that accentuates grade inflation and promulgates the status quo? The entire average high school's curriculum is gradually drifting away from academic competition and gravitating toward a median that promotes sociological growth under the guises of *democratic* education and cooperative learning. Instead of *group adjustment,* schools should be emphasizing *student* exploration of individual potential, tough grading standards, and rugged individualism.

In short, educational philosophy must reflect the true values of American tradition. Americans are more materialistic than they are aesthetic. Our traditions have supported the premise that success has more to do with individual "pursuit of happiness" than with group adjustment to happiness. Success in the real world has more to do with individual competition than it does with group cooperation. The concept of *Utopia* can never be achieved on a Marxist, general societal level, but Utopia can be accomplished on an individual productive level through basic hard work and sacrifice.

185

Philanthropists had to be selfish to accumulate fortunes so that they could then become benefactors of society and effectively contribute to the stability of our great "economic civilization". The wealthy are the biggest contributors to American government paying over seventy-five percent of federal income taxes. When schools begin teaching *students* how to better their own lives economically, then this country will again be steadied on the right track. But high schools persist in putting the proverbial cart in front of the horse!

The United States defeated the Soviet Union in the *Cold War* because of our free enterprise economic system and not because of our idealistic educational system that promoted *group assimilation*. The Russians shot a cannonball across America's bow when the Communists sent-up the first *Sputnik* in 1957. The U.S. knew it was in a do-or-die competition for survival, so we got tough, developed a space program, and scientifically put the first man on the moon. But it was the threat of *competition* from Russia that brought-out the best in America! Competition is good, and as long as educational psychology sees *student* academic rivalry as being the opposite of societal needs, our educational system is doomed to mediocrity.

For over half a century, our misguided American schools have been implementing *democracy,* but despite all of this energy and expense, crime and delinquency run rampant, drugs, AIDS and alcohol are destroying city and suburban teens, and American society as a whole is degenerating towards disintegration.

Why do kids join gangs and experiment with dope? It is because the *group pressure* exceeds the will of the individual's conscience. And what do schools teach *students* to do? They teach kids how to sacrifice individual will for the sake of *group conformity*. Peer pressure can make almost any *student* yield to temptation and surrender to bad habits. A teenager's friends at age fourteen are more influential on his or her development and choices than his or her own parents are. Have the wrong friends, and then a *student* is easily led down the wrong path, and *cooperative learning* in a group is partly responsible for that peer pressure social phenomenon. In essence, each American teen must have the wherewithal to bravely find his or her own path.

In the classic science fiction novel, *The Time Machine,* H.G. Wells suggests that it is man's aggressiveness, along with his sense of competition (geared to his need for self-survival) that drive individuals to invent, to create, to explore and to discover. The wonderful novel teaches that it was because mankind became *too secure,* too happy and too contented that caused the inferior Eloi race to evolve and be exploited and massacred by the heartless-but-superior Morlocks.

As long as school systems ignorantly pursue making *students* socially secure and happy, our civilization will be drifting towards complacency and starting to author its self-destruction. It is a testament of history that empires and civilizations usually decay and decline from within and not from experiencing external attack. That's what happened to Russia, to Rome and to ancient Persia, to Egypt and to Mesopotamia. If we as a nation lose our original sense of purpose as outlined in the *Declaration of Independence,* which is currently being undermined by radical interpretations of the *United States Constitution,* then we are surrendering the essential principles that made this country the envy of the world. As long as psychology and sociology govern law, culture, and education, the predictable decline of this great nation will continue to accelerate.

Education in America should reflect the values of the adult world. If high school *students* earn good *academic* grades, the school systems should reward their achievements with pay, and the money earned from good high school grades could be set aside for future college tuition. All kids understand money, but many teenagers find high school irrelevant and the philosophy of learning for the sake of learning alien to their natural survival instincts. Teenagers as a whole don't buy the current false teachings that maintain, "You are here for a non-future because we are not training you to do anything but sit there." Those non-motivated *students* that can't cut stiff competition in academic courses should not be allowed to take them.

Only the best *students* should be paid for attaining honor roll averages in valid *academic* courses that have not been diluted to accommodate mediocre and unmotivated *students*. In other words, difficult academics should be the *privilege* of the motivated minority and not a *right* of everybody. When *that* important transformation happens, there will automatically be more *privileged students* because teenagers will recognize that achievement is rewarded by the high school and that the institution is more attuned to the way the real-world functions.

Educational psychologists tell school systems that *children* learn from the *concrete to the abstract.* First of all, high school teenagers are not *children.* Secondly, if teenagers were put on the board of education's payroll, then they could plainly see the relationship of achievement and academic excellence on a *concrete* basis rather than be perpetually puzzled by the nebulous abstraction of "psychological reward" as opposed to the easily grasped concept of "monetary reward" being set aside for college expenses.

Get psychologists and the counterproductive influence of psychology out of education, and soon the ponderous institution will automatically improve. Future teachers must stop hearing the mantra that "Intrinsic rewards are more desirable than extrinsic rewards (money)". When Jesus spoke to the masses, He used parables to express His intent. The masses could not grasp His abstract moral principles. So, Jesus used *material* references such as sheep, shepherds', mustard seeds and good Samaritans to represent His abstractions to His *mass* audience. Jesus did things right by truly using parables and going from the concrete to the abstract.

Students today are a part of a mediocre *Mass* America. They need reality education and not intrinsic, *democratic*, sociological, and psychological preparation for an abstract ideal society that *they* have to magically build without any particular training or skill. It is about time that education gives both form and substance to the word *reward* instead of emphasizing an elusive phantom known as "intrinsic reward". Then, all *students* will finally *visualize* the profound concept of *concrete reward* when the matter is given a material image in the form of money provided for valid *academic* achievement, with the accumulated dollars being set aside to satisfy future college debts.

Grade level norms must be re-established and strictly enforced. Tenth graders should not be reading on a seventh-grade level, and seniors ought to maintain a B average in all academic subject areas. Teachers should be allowed to enforce rigid standards that don't use grade inflation to dilute educational quality for the sake of quantity (passing everyone). But the educational power structure avoids grade level norms because precise grading standards would accurately reflect the inadequacies of the present sociologically oriented *democratic* comprehensive public schools. At present, true grade level norms in various core curriculum content areas are cleverly disguised and camouflaged by enigmatic standardized test results using difficult-to-interpret terminology like "stanines" and "relative skill competency".

Critics promptly state that grade level norms would deprive school systems from having their own unique and individual curriculums, which incidentally hardly vary from high school to high school throughout the country. Educational pundits insist that grade level norms would have teachers teaching for standardized tests and not for the individual instructor's personal goals and objectives. So why can't teachers pursue both the standardized tests' goals and their own goals simultaneously while devising lessons that support both?

The miracle of television along with the radio and motion picture industries have more than erased "regional uniqueness" throughout the United States. When I was a teenager, people in the Dixie states sounded very different than northerners did, but today the speakers on radio and *CNN* television news shows originating from Atlanta sound exactly like those *Fox* announcers in New York City. Kids in Palo Alto, California watch the same *CBS* cartoon shows and *MTV* broadcasts as kids in Emporium, Pennsylvania do. Teenagers in Kalamazoo get on the same color and model school buses as kids in Poughkeepsie. We don't need to preserve our local eccentricities as much as we need to reinforce our national commonalities, interests and beliefs. In the current reality, Socialistic education translates into delusional artificial education.

It is true that local customs have given way to national *mass* conformity, but the educational establishment is generating more of this *"mass* mentality mediocrity" under the cloak of *"democracy* for individual *student* development" and under the whimsical disguise of the "comprehensive (code jargon for not being strictly academic) high school".

Educational gurus flirt with flimsy theories like "The child needs an educational environment where he or she can *create* and *experiment"*. American education contains more fantasy than an anthology of *Mother Goose* nursery rhymes, and it is really very much akin to a *Grimm* fairy tale.

Educators really mean *re-creation* and *re-experimentation* when they talk about *student* "creation" and *student* "experimentation". The exploited *students* aren't really creating or experimenting anything at all, but they are merely re-enacting what mankind already knows, and the afflicted learners are merely repeating demonstrations that have been performed by numerous scientists and authors millions of times in the past.

Classroom learning (as teachers know it) is really *students'* re-discovering and not discovering, and also *students* re-creating and not creating. Sir Isaac Newton and Albert Einstein were examples of *discoverers,* and William Shakespeare and Mark Twain were examples of *creators.* Anything that *students* do in the classroom is really only imitation of what past true creators and true discoverers have already accomplished. So, in that respect, *students* (no matter how talented) are not true creators or true discoverers at all. They can only be re-creators or re-discoverers, or else they would be recognized *masters* instead of ordinary *students*.

Experience is often not the best teacher, as many often believe. A *student* could do something wrong a hundred times and have plenty of experience without ever performing a particular task successfully. True creativity (like authoring this book) and true experimentation are a lot of hard work and should *not* be easy chores that can be easily achieved by simply following a procedure that has been duplicated millions of times before. Big projects, writing books and great accomplishments require years of dedicated labor. *Failure* is an inescapable characteristic of true creativity and also of true discovery. Schools expose *students* to certain learning devices, and after several superficial tries (designed to build their self-esteem), the learners succeed in completing a certain elementary task. Educators prematurely and falsely label what the *students* have done as *discovery* and as *creativity*.

Most authors have to go through dozens of painful publisher rejections before their works are eventually available to the public. Scientists must develop tests that fail hundreds of times before that one experiment achieves an objective, or accurately diagnoses a disease. It was Thomas Edison who had eloquently said, "Discovery (a genius) is 1 percent inspiration and 99 percent perspiration." True creativity and true discovery involve years of difficult research, hard work, and plenty of rejection and failure. When learning is made (or disguised) to come easy, kids get the wrong impression of what adult life and real success are really about.

By isolating *students* from failure in public schools, educators are insulating and protecting them from what they need to know most: how to adjust to failure and rejection, and how to reconstruct the spirit after failing so that *confidence* is built, and not *self-esteem* being continually reinforced. *Democracy* in education and modern school psychology are obsessed with the objective of eradicating failure from a *child's* experience in order to make watered-down learning come easier to him or her. By eliminating the *student's* "right to fail", individual accountability is being sacrificed for the propagation of *student* irresponsibility in school, at home, and ultimately, in the society.

But to accommodate administrators, college professors and school psychologists, *academic* tasks have been reduced to simple sociological experiences. And after a *student* has completed a task that has been performed millions of times before, educators proudly declare that the *child* (even if he is eighteen with a beard, a tattoo and long bushy sideburns) has dynamically "created" or "discovered".

American education makes a big mistake when it gives little Johnny Jones in the first grade of Happyville PS #1 the same credit for discovering that 4 + 3 =7 as we do Christopher Columbus for discovering America or Marie Curie for discovering radium. If we mean learning or *re-discovering* when we say *discovering*, then I insist it's time for educators to call a spade a spade.

Leonardo DaVinci and Michelangelo were bitter rivals, and that *competition* motivated each to attempt out-creating the other. True *creativity* is basically a selfish enterprise and has little or no sociological implication. I often wonder if Picasso painted because he wanted *to share* his fame or his inspiration with other less-motivated painters, or if Thomas Edison was inspired to invent while being motivated to *share* his ideas with other less-motivated or less-gifted idle dreamers.

The truth is that most great contributors to civilization preferred to think and to work alone and not in groups. This is why only advanced *academic students* should be involved with *creating* and *experimenting* because they are the only *students* in the high school remotely capable of ever creating and discovering anything. American education slyly conceals its own failures by disguising them in fancy terms like discovering, creating, sharing, cooperative learning, and self-esteem, all of which have little or no application in the dog-eat-dog real world that's really out there after graduation.

The American educational idea' of *sharing* (as generated by airhead college professors and impractical school psychologists) is actually more Marxist (share all wealth) than it is Jeffersonian (individual pursuit of life, liberty, free enterprise, happiness).

Kids are babied and doted-on by parents that want to be their child's friend. Schools don't demand too much of the already-spoiled *students*. Teachers are compelled to dilute their *academic* courses to accommodate dim *students* that have sound-byte minds that give-up too easily on hard items that require time, hard work and energy to solve or complete. Schools discourage individual competition and encourage sociological cooperation and group activity to keep slow-learners and unmotivated kids riding on the old "academic escalator".

High schools only ask of *students* to participate according to their ability and don't demand excellence by raising the bar. "*Students* must be understood and given assistance and support to build self-esteem," the Educational Aristocracy preaches to teachers. "The curriculum must be adjusted to meet each *student's* individual needs." Now let's pause for a minute, take a deep breath and analyze what evils are actually being perpetuated all across America.

"From each (*student*) according to his ability; to each (*student*) according to his needs." Does *that* explanation sound familiar? This country's educational system has gone completely topsy-turvy! The slogan for dialectic materialism (Communism) has become the hallmark of American *democracy* in education. This is George Orwell's *1984* revisited.

That eighty percent gray area that psychologists and *Constitutional* lawyers have created has erased most of the distinctions between right and wrong, between good and evil, and between smart and dumb. Love is now mirrored hate; peace is war, truth is falsehood, and *democracy* is the same as socialism. Nothing has clear distinct definition anymore. Everything is, well everything! So that is why it is so easy for liberal educational philosophers and psychologists to deviously corrupt the entire American public school educational system without ever firing a single shot.

A turtle hardly seems to move at all. But after wandering for fifty years in a certain direction, that tortoise will definitely be far from its original starting point. And that is exactly what has happened to American education in the last half-century. It has moved slowly, step by step, until school curriculums are more socialistic than *democratic* and more sociologically cooperative than academically competitive. The unwary public has not felt this fifty-year pendulum shift because it has been happening too gradually, too slowly, yet being implemented very deliberately.

Other nations and terrorist organizations believe that our country's resolve is turning soft because our schools are not demanding *student* excellence and *student* academic accountability. The powers-that-be in American education are too idealistic, too impractical, and too conciliatory, and as a result, the *students* of today are too wimpy to academically compete, and the parents of tomorrow will be too wimpy to economically excel. Soon, this toxic infection will reach lofty places like *Harvard* and *Yale* where grades and subjects will have to be watered-down to accommodate the wimpy nature of the high school *student* pool that will be filtering out of watered-down high school programs.

The frail theories of American educational philosophy are as naïve as a grateful Caesar giving Brutus a shiny new cutlery set as an *Ides of March* appreciation gift. Besides grade-level norms for academic college-bound *students,* high schools desperately need a workable two-track system that sorts-out and separates vocationally oriented students from those going on to higher academic education. Each county should have at least two vocational schools where high school *students* could learn viable trades.

A two-tiered or two-tracked system has been attacked by the educational power structure for being un-American, *undemocratic,* un-comprehensive, and unethical. But this vocational advocacy is what is actually necessary to promote the true American way of life that is fundamentally based on competition, on free enterprise, and finally, on individual achievement.

After eighth grade, *students* should be given a battery of tests, and on the information gleaned, be channeled into two curriculums: the local academic high school and the county vocational trades' high school. Grade level norms could be enforced in the academic high school and more readily evaluated than at present. Local high schools would then be more academically efficient. The brighter kids could work independently in experimental labs'. The *students* that have been sorted into the county vocational curriculum could learn skills and trades applicable to their later adult lives and then graduate to become productive members of society.

Teachers in the academic high school would not be completely baffled by such enigmas as "motivating" *students* to learn in a "*democratic* comprehensive high school", and also, adjusting grades to accommodate "*student* self-esteem". Discipline problems would then all but disappear.

The dual tracked system would not deprive any *student* of his or her freedom of choice. The new two-tracked curriculum would be flexible enough for a *student* in the trades sector to switch back to the *academic* college preparatory sector if he or she could pass a basic language and Math skills academic entrance examination and then successfully migrate into the other more demanding curriculum.

Vocational *students* should not be stigmatized or discriminated against. A *student* in the academic college prep' curriculum could also make the transition to the trades program if he or she so desires, up to the start of the senior year. We know that a good plumber or a well-*trained* electrician could make a lot more in the American free enterprise economy than a good teacher or a good nurse could. Let's start valuing trades education in conjunction with *corporate training* to make American education become more cost-efficient.

As the curriculum now stands, easy general high school electives only pay casual lip service to true vocational specialist preparation. Instead of putting the onus for learning for all *students* squarely in the laps of *academic* high school teachers, American high schools and county vocational schools should teach teenagers about the wisdom associated with true freedom of choice. Teenagers must learn the indispensable value of true individual responsibility, of personal decision-making, and of individual accountability for his or her grade performance along with his or her individual behavior. The ultimate decision of whether to be in either the academic or the vocational trades curriculum, or to stay or to transfer from one to the other, would be his or hers to make based on the *student's* overall performance and general behavior.

As it is now, parents put pressure on school guidance counselors to place their sons or daughters in *academic* college prep' courses, and when all the kids can't make the grade, the teachers feel pressure from administrators, and then the instructors practice course dilution and grade inflation. When too many *students* fail a course, it is now judged as the teacher's fault. College is not for everybody! We must elevate vocational training education to be on the same plane as the academic high school. The stigma connected with vocational education as not being equal to academic preparation must be erased.

Upon graduation eligibility, the vocational diploma and the academic high school diploma should be given equal status. The achievements of each *student* along with the *student's* class rank should be indicated on *both* diplomas, so that prospective college admissions officers will know the exact credentials of the class Valedictorian and be able to distinguish him or her from the class vagabond in the academic program, and prospective employers will be able to differentiate the class expert tradesman from the class clown in the equal-status vocational curriculum. Presently, a future employer can't decipher anything significant by reading or examining a devalued high school diploma.

College education is no longer synonymous with earning capacity, so why should the silly myth be perpetuated that a college education is advantageous and more prestigious than a degree from an advanced post high school trades' academy?

Americans live in an economic society where garbage collectors (excuse me, sanitary engineers) earn more money than beginning teachers receive, who actually have to put-up with more garbage (from administrators and from rowdy *students*) than trash collectors do. Absolute *democratic* freedom without individual accountability (or the assumption of individual responsibility) translates into anarchy, and that's where the present educational scenario is leading this great nation. Educators need to formulate a more practical and cost-efficient model of *democratic* education and abandon the sham that is now gradually bringing our great American civilization to its knees. In its present pathetic form, *democracy* in education is actually functioning *socialism* in public schools. Free enterprise and fierce competition are what has made America the greatest civilization world history has ever known, and those two wonderful aspects must (in the future) again become the hallmarks of our American public schools.

Chapter 22
"The Problem Child"

In August, the principal phoned me down in Ocean City and informed me that the letter of application I had submitted for a position vacancy in the junior high school had been accepted and that I would be coming back as an eighth grade English teacher the following September. Over the summer months, I operated the Ocean City, Maryland boardwalk arcade business and still managed to read and outline all of the stories in the eighth-grade literature book and master all of the more complex exercises in the grammar text. I was all set to be a junior high school English and social studies teacher, which was a position that I had maintained from 1970 until my retirement in 1999.

Every teacher fully knows that each *student* he or she comes into daily contact with is his or her own unique case study. During the 1970-'71 school year, I had an incredible, nightmarish one-hundred-and-eighty-day adventure with a certain immature deputy of destruction. I shall codename the *child* Joe Dodge, a *student* who could expand any teacher's ulcer, shatter any nerve cluster, or harden the most flexible artery.

It is fairly difficult on the first day of school to distinguish individual *student* behavior patterns with a hundred and thirty cherubs assigned to your custody. Teachers are preoccupied acclimating to new *students* and new classes, and dispensing with procedures like distributing textbooks and reviewing class rules dominating all the instructor's time and energy. But as the academic year churns onward towards the end of September, the clarity of each *student's* character and behavior becomes more perceptible when it is contrasted with the character and behavior of his or her peers.

Joe Dodge at first blended-in with his classmates, but it wasn't long before I became acutely aware of his reckless abandon and his shortage of respect for teacher authority. Less than two weeks had elapsed when Joe's authentic nastiness flung itself in my attention's path. I was in the midst of dramatizing a crucial point in literature while reading a passage aloud from Washington Irving's "The Legend of Sleepy Hollow" when I soberly noticed that Joe was not being one bit receptive to my ambitious, animated presentation.

"Joe, don't you like this story?" I began. "It's one of the most classic novellas ever written!"

"I hate this fuckin' class, I hate you, and I hate this fuckin' subject!" the *child* rudely protested.

"Gee Joe, I'm sorry I asked you about the story," I mock apologized. "Now I'll have to write-out a Discipline Referral Card and send you down to the vice-principal's office for your using inappropriate language."

"I don't give a shit what the fuck ya' do!" the *student* defiantly barked back. "Just leave me the fuck alone!"

Now resentment and antagonism from *students* of Joe's caliber are very commonplace experiences for today's battle-weary teachers, and I had no intention of ridiculing or humiliating angry Mr. Dodge with my superior command of the English language. Any teacher remembers from his or her college educational methods' courses that young Joe is probably overreacting to some obscure, subconscious phobia, or perhaps responding to a morning argument with a parent or a girlfriend, or possibly feeling the pressure of the galaxy of stresses and strains caused by our cruel technological society. 'Maybe Joe's uncle told him to go thrust his thumb up his rectum and the kid got his thumb dirty?' I conjectured.

Surely, any educator worth his salt will endeavor to explore and remedy the unknown mysterious forces that had triggered the fourteen-year-old *student's* audacious, defiant monologue. Even rookie teachers know from their college professors' indoctrinations that Joe should be recognized as a challenge and that it was my distinct responsibility to earn his admiration by proving to be a dedicated instructor showing loyalty to his pupils. Trust would then eventually result in mutual acceptance and coexistence.

Show me a problem *child* (that's what the school psychologist calls kids like Joe) and I'll show you at least one problem parent or at least one problem parent that is afraid to discipline his or her out-of-control problem *child* that happens to now be your problem *student*.

The first week of October, I caught Joe making sado-sexual hand gestures when my back was turned while writing a verb phrase on the chalkboard. 'So, what if the impish *student* sometimes interrupts my train of thought by babbling and mumbling under his breath!' I thought. 'So, what if his primary daily purpose is to sabotage my well-prepared lesson! Good teachers are able to circumnavigate those minor disruptions and concentrate their total vitality on reforming the obnoxious misbehavior by using the dependable tool of educational psychology,' I hypothesized.

Then, I contemplated circumstances some more. 'I must make a solemn effort to discover what makes Joe tick!' I believed and thought. 'There must be some latent explanation that can give me insight and can account for all of his persistent abnormalities,' I considered. 'Our honored educational system is modeled after our inimitable political system, and every devout, patriotic, American automatically knows that fundamental *democracy* is based on the premise that man's nature is basically good,' I mentally summarized.

A famous syllogism describing the ancient Greek philosopher Socrates immediately came to mind, and my vigilant brain substituted the word *students* for the term "man", and the name Joe Dodge for "Socrates".

All *students* are good.
Joe Dodge is a *student*.
Therefore, Joe Dodge is good!

'Eureka!' I mentally delighted. 'Yes, that is it! How esoteric, and yet so simple!' I plausibly concluded. 'I must use the psychological tool of praise to build Joe's self-esteem and then *that* approach will enable me to excavate the camouflaged goodness lodged deep inside the *student's* heart.'

I decided I should discover Joe's hobbies, interests and goals and focus on them while still managing to teach my other hundred and twenty-nine *students*. I figured I should forge a genuine and enduring friendship between teacher and *student,* and I should temper my rash inclinations to publicly malign *his* dormant decency. 'Even though I feel like strangling Joe,' I theorized, 'I must strongly consider the long-range detrimental effects verbal retaliation from me might have upon the *student's* fragile future welfare,' I convinced myself.

Those angry feelings towards Joe Dodge characterized my guilt and sensitivity at the time, but regrettably, it required a hundred and forty-five days of constant besiegement and frustration until I finally determined I needed to endorse a new set of strategies. My coping mechanisms had all become tattered, frazzled and frayed.

It was a sweltering Indian summer day in early October when my restraint for pummeling and pulverizing Joe Dodge almost wholly disintegrated. I was casually strolling down an aisle between rows of desks while the class (with the exception of Joe) was busy engaged in solving matching questions with answers on a literature worksheet.

I described to Joe the filthy appearance of his desk slate. "Mr. Dodge, just look at the top of your desk and all of the debris under and around it (forgetting that Joe probably didn't know or care what the word *debris* meant). The whole area looks almost like a pigsty!"

I did not anticipate the extraordinary display of paranoia that ensued. Joe Dodge isolated and then capitalized on one particular word *pig* so he convinced himself that he was going to amuse his preoccupied peers by imitating reprehensible pig noises at my expense for the last twenty minutes of the period.

On another occasion I had made the mistake of saying to the lad, "You're as stubborn as a mule!" I was tormented with a barrage of "hee-haws" and "I'm a jackass, I'm a jackass! Hee-haw!" for ten whole minutes until the dismissal bell finally rang.

It reached a point where any verbalization anyone in the classroom made or any sentence in a literature text was converted into some stupid sound or inane onomatopoeia by the repulsive teenage comedian. The class and I were treated to barking dogs, trucks in need of mufflers, impromptu habitual sneezing, and growling dinosaurs each and every detestable forty-five-minute period.

'How can I teach this class anything with all of these very disturbing interruptions?' I wondered. 'How come all the praise and the educational psychology is not working?'

The central problem gradually magnified, when Joe Dodge corrupted other young rascals in the class that decided to mimic the derelict scoundrel's daily escapades. My dilemma was escalating with each successive day. It reached the point where my second period General English class was the culminating event of the school day for the twenty-seven desperadoes in it, and the worst-case scenario eventually happened. The legend of Joe's frolics and his ugly defiance of Mr. Wiessner spread like wildfire among other *students* in other eighth grade sections.

Once a *student* (I use the term loosely) succeeds in hatching daily turmoil inside a teacher's classroom, and unless the instructor has the magic solution to extinguish the expanding inferno, then the mania soon spreads like a dangerous virus to other *students*. The little rogues in other class periods suddenly declare it open hunting season on the already beleaguered teacher.

After sharing my "discipline problem" with several more experienced teachers, I soon discovered that repulsive Joe Dodge was an absolute terror in *their* presence, also. But a faulty tendency among teachers is to 'let things slide', hoping that "tomorrow" will bring some miraculous transformation. However, I was determined to keep digging until I had successfully mined the root of Joe's totally scary personality disorder. Unfortunately, I still reluctantly espoused the educational theology (psychology) that those former college seminars had somewhat inculcated.

The drastic turning point in my deserting of high educational morality and ethics came with the appearance of the following classroom caper. Joe Dodge escalated daily "psychological warfare" by resorting to certain loud biological interruptions, deliberately and loudly passing gas in class (no rhyme intended).

Now, it is embarrassing enough when a *student* lets one go accidentally, but Joe Dodge was performing his repugnant insolence deliberately. It was extremely challenging to attempt engaging in the art of teaching with a foul anal baritone constantly reverberating from the back of the room. And the disconcerting serenade was happening every single day. How does a teacher cope with such disgusting uncouthness from a *student?*

And then one morning a boastful comment was emitted from the totally insolent *student's* malicious lips. "Do you smell anything Mr. Wiessner?" the young punk snorted.

"Okay Joe, that verbalization will represent your third Discipline Referral Card of the week!" I replied as calmly as I could.

"Write the damned thing out and see how much I fuckin' care!" the young wise guy replied.

'How can a clown of his ilk be silenced before, during, and after the *student* has transformed the teacher's sanctuary of learning into an appalling cesspool of oral and anal banter? How can *this* unruly bronco be tamed, and how can my dwindling sanity be salvaged?'

In graduate school classes, I had learned all about *student* oral reports, but quite frankly, that second period class was my first exposure to *student* anal reports. I was rapidly becoming weary of being a martyr to *his* daily recalcitrance. And the class, which was not exactly comprised of Phi Beta Kappa scholars, reveled in the insulting daily derision and requested "encore" performances from the irascible classroom saboteur.

Joe Dodge was pulling the same kind of perverted antics in the science teacher's class where the *student* would emit thunderous quantities of intestinal gas, making each discharge sound like a neurotic machinegun releasing sporadic rounds of ammunition.

Mr. Allen made certain efforts to curb Joe Dodge's queer rituals by asking the *student* to keep a record of *his* gross misdemeanors as the guidance department had recommended. Mr. Allen asked the chronic offender to jot-down *his* latest act of infamy in a journal. After the rattled science teacher managed to restore order, the classroom rivaled the silence of a public (not a school) library. Silly Joe then asked Mr. Allen, "Hey, tell me. How do ya' spell *fartin'* so that I can write it down?"

Chapter 23
"The Parent Conference"

The constant *student* abuse all seemed surreal. Every second period my ego shrank, and my spirit almost entered a stupor from each traumatic forty-five-minute encounter with Joe Dodge. Now the lunatic *student* was giving me the royal double middle finger salute not only when my back was turned but also when I was addressing the problem class. 'I am a professional!' my mind kept repeating. 'Maybe if I ignore this crazy *student* his disobedience will simmer down!' I even pinched myself several times to try to determine if my exposure to the imbecile was real, just to stimulate me back to reality. My confidence was definitely dissolving with each passing day, since the irascible *student* was converting my English class more and more into *his* ludicrous circus.

Every time my class approached being transformed into a travesty, I would hastily write-out a Discipline Referral Card describing the infractions and send the venomous culprit down to the Main Office. On one occasion, the dastardly troublemaker hurled the discipline card onto the classroom floor and stomped all over it in an inane jitterbug of defiance. After the *child* left the room, I sent a second Discipline Referral Card via another *student* down to the office describing Joe's impromptu St. Vitus Disease dance routine.

When Joe returned to my room fifteen minutes later, I had already filled-out a guidance department form during his brief absence and then directed him to see his counselor just to get the junior educational criminal out of the classroom. Then finally, I got the chance to teach the class in a rare interval of tranquility the last ten minutes of the period, for Joe Dodge was one of those *students* that hardly ever missed a day of school when he wasn't suspended.

I had always regarded myself as being a fair-but-strict teacher that treated *students* with courtesy and respect. I was not used to being tormented and persecuted in such a wicked manner. In my prior five years of teaching, I had to contend with a scant number of serious discipline problems, which normally went away after the *student* was given Discipline Referral Cards by me along with Office Detention and In-School Suspension by the administration.

Perhaps his eminence, the educational philosopher John Dewey would have introduced Joe Dodge and the class to the cognitive virtues of Boyle's *Gas* Laws, but being deficient in advanced experimental science, I lacked Mr. Dewey's inventiveness in solving perplexing *student* deviant misbehavior.

Diversified animal sounds and fake intentional repetitive sneezing were indeed very annoying, but then they seemed insignificant when compared with irreverent continuous intentional farting in class. So, I entered my self-preservation "survival mode" while still trying to psychologically analyze the demented motivations for the evil banshee's erratic misconduct.

I requested a parent conference through the guidance department but was informed by the secretary the next day that only the mother would be coming in for the scheduled appointment. I insisted that the *student's* guidance counselor sit-in on the impending discussion if the mother became too defensive and belligerent if normal decorum got out of hand.

The school makes every attempt to have parent conferences sedately *professional* and as cordial and as placid as possible. After being introduced to Mrs. Dodge by the public relations-minded guidance counselor, I dramatically described in detail Joe's peculiar antics ranging from his imitation of a zoo of animals to snapping six new pencils in a row during class. I described how the *student* hostilely flung his desk against a wall and how he mutinously hurled his textbooks on the floor when being corrected for hostilely smashing his desk against the tan-colored cinderblock wall.

I then informed my two listeners how the *student* entertained his peers at my expense by enacting frantic gyrations that appeared analogous to epileptic convulsions. My silent audience simply sat unflinchingly there in the guidance office, and their bleak facial expressions showed little emotion or empathy for my plight. After spending a full fifteen minutes of telling how Joe Dodge persisted in deliberately interrupting my English class, I then listened to the guidance counselor interview the *student's* mother.

I learned that Joe had a motorbike and anything else that his heart desired, and also that his parents had spoiled him rotten, making the *student* egotistically believe that *he* was the center of the universe. Mrs. Dodge maintained that I delighted in picking on her son and persisted in embarrassing *him* in front of the class. "He is a good boy and is misunderstood and mistreated by his teachers," Mrs. Dodge maintained to the sympathetic guidance counselor. "And in your case Mr. Wiessner, you have to find something that Joe likes to do to get him interested in your lesson."

The conference interview revealed that not only did Joe Dodge despise his teachers, but also the *student* did not naturally identify with his doting father (that explained why only the mother had attended the conference).

Throughout most of the strange meeting, the guidance counselor just remained mum like a slothful official at an ice hockey game. And when the conference threatened to turn into a verbal melee, the affected fellow in the middle finally came out of his shell.

"Has Joe's father ever physically disciplined him at home?" I asked, much to my audience's chagrin.

"Mr. Wiessner, please refrain from such personal questions," the professional guidance counselor sternly advised. "You are not a psychologist. We must address the issue at hand and figure out how you and Joe can coexist in the classroom."

Despite Joe's strained relationship with his father, Mrs. Dodge disclosed that her husband had promised her son that *he* would be able to work for his dad in a business partnership after high school (in four years) and have a solid career in construction and heavy equipment operation. The *student* didn't value academics because he thought his future was secure working with, owning and operating big machines. Joe Dodge saw no special connection with the academic abstractions presented in school textbooks in relation to *his* future occupation, which had already been prescribed by his father, who never disciplined his son the *student*.

"Have you taken-away any of Joe's privileges at home because of all of the many discipline problems he's had here at school?" I toughly asked.

"My husband and I don't believe in punishing our only son," Mrs. Dodge divulged. "We trust the school administration with that responsibility should *they* think the action is necessary."

As the confrontational conference rambled on to its conclusion, I had an additional pertinent question to advance to the mother. "Could you Mrs. Dodge guarantee me right here and now that Joe will complete all of his English assignments, behave himself in my class, and show respect towards the teacher and his classmates by remaining quiet? Will he obey my class rules?"

"No, I can't guarantee that!" Mrs. Dodge snapped. "You have to develop a rapport with my son! That's your problem!"

"Mrs. Dodge, are you saying that neither you nor your husband can control your son?" I vehemently bellowed. "Are you saying that both of you are afraid to take action at home against your kid?"

"Mr. Wiessner, please conduct yourself in a more *professional* manner," the suddenly alarmed guidance counselor insisted. "Mrs.

Dodge should not be under interrogation here, and you are not the county prosecutor!"

"Mrs. Dodge," I reiterated, ignoring the guidance person. "Don't expect me to continuously discipline your son if you and your husband are fearful of doing the exact same thing at home!"

"Mr. Wiessner, you may leave now!" the public relations-minded guidance counselor ordered. "This conference is disintegrating into an unproductive shouting match!"

Before I stood-up to leave, I noticed that the flustered woman had suddenly relinquished her arrogant disposition and began sobbing into a handkerchief. Apparently, some of my *unprofessional* questions had hit home figuratively, literally, and also quite realistically. The direct candor that I had directly exhibited is rarely seen in parent/teacher conferences.

When I glanced over at the florid-faced guidance counselor, I perceived that he thought that I had been too harsh with a community taxpayer and that my remarks had stepped over-the-line from good school public relations to unwarranted and un-teacher-like verbal conflict with a concerned, overprotective parent.

As I left the well-furnished Guidance Suite, I did feel somewhat guilty for my uncharacteristic aggressiveness toward Mrs. Dodge, but then I honestly believed that I had unmasked a formerly hidden parental impotency and also plenty of parental dereliction of responsibility that prevailed on the home front.

But causing tears in parents' eyes, showing fury and poignancy, and being blunt and frank are conditions American education frowns upon because those reactions spring from a subjective origin. In all affiliations with antagonistic parents, teachers must remain objective, professional, sophisticated, diplomatic and rational. But what problem *child* (having problem parents) behaves in an objective, or more accurately, in a normal, rational manner?

I was willing to wager that some confounding emotional disorder had been contributing to Joe Dodge's schism with conventional, accepted *student* behavior. But the Educational Aristocracy views as unfavorable the idea that teachers should go on the offensive and penetrate the taboo of being assertive and prosecutorial toward accusing parents. Many wimpy people in American education shield themselves with artificial veneers such as "remain objective" and "act professional". Those charlatans are bewitched with the folly of their own self-deception. Wisdom (and its nature) happens to be more subjective than it is objective.

After the strange parent conference became history, some of the missing pieces to the irregular Joe Dodge riddle materialized into more fathomable factors. The mother, I speculated, was the chief of the Dodge tribe, with her husband playing a subordinate role. The boy, who was tall, corpulent and in need of a brassiere appeared quite effeminate in spite of his brazen bellicose misbehavior. Joe Dodge, I believed, identified more with his dominant, burly mother than he did with his sometimes apathetic-but-doting, recessive father.

I concluded on my way back to my classroom that Joe Dodge resented me because I projected an austere masculine image, which seemingly contradicted the *student's* subconscious contrivance that females should domineer in human relationships involving males. That seemed to explain why Joe got along better with female teachers than he did with male faculty members. But as the school guidance counselor had insisted, I was not a psychologist and therefore certainly was not qualified to make any judgments, assumptions, hypothesis or conclusion about the disruptive *student* or about the disruptive *student's* home life and parents.

One thing was for sure. Joe Dodge didn't hold *academic* education in high regard because he believed that what activities I was doing in the classroom had nothing to do with his future occupation in the construction industry. 'How do I get a bulldozer or a front-end loader into my classroom as a visual aid?' I mused and wondered.

And as for Joe Dodge's abominable attitude toward grammar and literature, abhorrence of academics is quite commonplace in small American towns where the bulk of the successful citizens boast that they had made it big owning their own businesses with only an eighth-grade or a high school formal education.

I recalled one of my more erudite college professors postulating, "The first step in solving a problem is recognizing it." (Pretty heavy scholarly stuff, huh?) Wisdom of that sort has always abounded in American education, but as always, the omitted second step, so vitally needed to scale any cryptic stumbling block like Joe Dodge, was meandering somewhere in psychological infinity. But still, I thought at the time that some practical application had to ascend like the mythical *Phoenix* from all of the bureaucratic nebulousness.

'This kid is surely overprotected and pampered at home,' I decided, 'and he more than likely dictates directives to his parents including his dominant mother,' I deduced. 'His every whim elicits their loyalty, compassion and defense. How can I deal with *his* senseless audacity now that I partially understand Joe Dodge's background?'

Joe Dodge and his weird parents were embroiled in an urgent subjective crisis that needed *their* addressing. But they chose to elude acknowledging the fundamental problem for years. However, I had performed a grotesque teacher mortal sin of the greatest magnitude as far as the administration and guidance department were concerned. I had gotten out of my *subordinate* teacher realm and had focused on the true causes of a *student's* misbehavior. I was being an educational impostor by doing the job of a school psychologist.

And teachers are not supposed to evoke passion or anger from parents. Such assertive conduct endangers the fragile balance that exists between school and community. The school administration diligently labors to preserve the delicate equilibrium between teachers and parents, and I had violated *that* unwritten policy.

"I don't want my son in any special education classes," Mrs. Dodge had insisted to the receptive guidance counselor. "I want him in regular classes! There is basically nothing wrong with my son! Maybe Mr. Wiessner has to change his teaching methods!"

"I think your son should be psychoanalyzed by the *Child* Study Team!" I recommended to the parent while the guidance counselor showed his disdain for my unprofessional conduct and for my "non-provable allegations".

I later dismissed the guidance counselor's noticeable inertness to him slyly playing the complicated psychoanalyst role by remaining reticent while the active participants wallowed in flagrantly exchanging accusations and acrimonious statements. And then the idealistic guidance counselor felt obligated to intervene and take the parent's side because I was the school *employee* and was antagonizing an important taxpayer with my rude recriminations about her innocent son. But then after the meeting terminated, I was more determined than ever to erase the stain of Joe Dodge's stubborn intransigence from my educational soul.

Although I thought I had a better gauge on Joe's diabolical motivations, I had trouble fathoming why none of his previous instructors had had the *student* referred to the *Child* Study Team for analysis and evaluation. Teachers had meticulously written a volume of critical comments, and the paperwork gorged out of the *student's* thick "Confidential Folder", but Joe Dodge's past instructors all were remiss in having *his* mischievous mal-conduct further professionally documented. I soon realized that piles of bureaucratic paperwork, endless conferences and meetings, added to a sense of futility from a lack of progress received from trying all of those demanding factors, discouraged other teachers from pursuing resolution through the school system's ineffective, established channels.

As December arrived, the personal friction between Joe Dodge and myself intensified. The *student* made every forty-five-minute period seem like three eternities. Every time I issued notebook paper for an assignment or composition paper for a final draft, the demented *student* would defiantly wrinkle it up. Then the *child* would imaginatively crinkle the paper into an irregular ball, and he would next either toss the sphere onto the floor or hurl it at another *student*.

If I offered Joe a yellow number two pencil, the malcontent (who never brought materials including pencils to class) would fracture its existence with one ferocious snap. Since Joe was continuously disturbing other *students,* I moved the lad's seat near the side chalkboard where he amused himself for a while drawing deformed *Quasimodos* with exaggerated genitals on the available board. I shrewdly confiscated the chalk from the sideboard ledge, but then the vile *student* had several sticks of his own inside his pants' pockets.

And then, when corrected for his vulgar impudence, the *student* had an inspiration of evil. He crumbled the chalk in his hand into a powdery dust by slamming the limestone against his desk's slate, put the dust on the side chalk ledge, and using the ledge as a convenient launching ramp, the demonic villain blew loudly and propelled a foggy chalk cloud toward the front of the classroom.

Five unsuspecting *students* began choking and coughing incessantly after the artificial cumulus Joe Dodge had manufactured enveloped them. 'This *student* is trying to obtain social attention and recognition,' I logically reckoned. 'The *student* is responding to his psychological *need* for attention and approval in a destructive manner because the transgressor cannot earn attention and approval in a conventional constructive way!' I assessed.

Whatever Joe Dodge's unique sociological and psychological circumstances were, I had now lost all patience and tolerance for the frisky one-*student* demolition crew. I had to find a way to put an end to the prolonged horrible evolution of crazy classroom delinquency. I next deemed it necessary to have Joe Dodge referred to the heralded *Child* Study Team. Surely the *CST* could help me solve my daily dilemma with the heinous, despicable *student*.

I invested at least seven hours of my limited time (preparation periods and before and after school time) to confer with a confederacy of specialists about Joe Dodge's mystic deportment. Some very relevant facts surfaced from the *CST's* intensive investigation. I learned that Joe had been a plump specimen as an infant. The crack jury of researchers also informed me that Joe was frightfully worried and almost terror-stricken as a child at the fear of his parents leaving him or dying.

"When Joe Dodge' sits himself' in your office," I told the Child Psychologist, "the deplorable kid is the real psychologist doing the real analysis!"

'Please, Mr. Wiessner; you don't have any credentials in the area of psychology," I was reminded, "so keep your opinions to yourself!"

I had often heard certain *students* in the halls and in the cafeteria brag about their separate encounters with "the shrink". The *children* would laugh and relate to each other how they had fabricated extraordinary fables that led the entire *Child* Study Team on a bizarre safari from the school jungle into the vast educational wilderness.

From past experience, I seldom worried about the future of *students* like Joe Dodge, for unlike the idealistic college-bound academic pupils, Joe had the uncanny ability of accurately measuring the sympathies and the limitations of adults. Just as Joe had made a farce of the *LDS's* (learning disability specialist) abbreviated classroom observation, he had also adroitly coordinated the *Child* Study Team into a defensive weapon to fend-off the encroachment of teacher jurisdiction. And I winced every time I glanced at that thick, worthless dossier of impertinent facts that the out-of-touch *CST* had so thoroughly compiled.

The squadron of *CST* secretaries had neatly typed and organized the wordy, meaningless *student* folder, and it was brimming with an abundance of destitute facts that were of little value in terms of practical application. In American public-school education, as long as something looks as if it's working (like the *Child* Study Team), its flimsy essentiality is justified with the more mediocre information it can produce.

The *Child* Study team found that Joe Dodge was a lad of normal ability. He sought his need for attention by *challenging* (randomly slaughtering) the authority of his instructors. I chuckled at my naïve flirtation that I should gain the *student's* respect by using psychological tools such as praise in order to elicit positive responses from the chronic violator. I concluded that the *CST's* final report was of little merit and constituted a two-inch pile of jargonized balderdash. 'Joe Dodge is more of a proficient psychologist than I'll ever be with a thousand graduate credits on my transcript,' I regretfully surmised.

I was determined that I would not put-up with his daily harassment any longer. I rejected the notion that my daily presence as a teacher was solely for the amusement and edification of fourteen-year-old idiots like Joe Dodge. I refused to be a sacrificial scapegoat upon *his* altar of contempt. This eighth-grade English teacher had not spent four years in college preparing to be a victim of some uncivilized *student* terrorist's lack of morality.

When Joe Dodge went to hamburger palaces or custard stands, did he bother local businessmen with his frivolous stupidity? Did Joe Dodge behave the same way in the aisles of the magazine shop or the local merchandise store as he did in the school corridors? Of course not! Since I was a teacher, the sly *student* knew from continual home reinforcement and nine years in different classrooms that I had to tolerate his malicious conduct. He knew that the rigid state law prohibiting corporal punishment sheltered him from physical harm.

Quite simply, Joe Dodge had the upper hand in our little war. The vernal maniac had an advantage and could use guerilla tactics while I was handicapped by my professional ethics, my public image and reputation, by the fear of losing administrative support, and by the righteousness of the law. But the school brass, the *CST* and Joe's guidance counselor did not give him credit for being such an adept conspirator and devious manipulator.

I received the impression from the *Child* Study Team that Joe Dodge was a virgin lamb that had to be protected from teacher tyranny. Every instructor that had survived his or her contact with the *student* had reported to the *CST* negative examples of the bellicose fiend's myriad transgressions. I wondered whether the fiasco of a study that I had initiated should be labeled a miscarriage of justice or a comedy of errors.

I was extremely baffled by the futility of relying on a bureaucratic solution. I now understood why Joe Dodge had never before been referred to the *CST*. Other teachers had learned through the wisdom of experience that the necessary steps to be taken were hidden in a hodge-podge of voluminous red tape and senseless and time-consuming documentation of unimportant facts that absolutely achieved nothing.

The theory that it was easier to contend with Joe Dodge's demonic activities than to utilize the recognized avenues of resolution within the school crushed my sense of professional ethics. I realized that I had to carry a ton of grief to be honest to my conscience and also to my convictions. As Joe Dodge's scornful provocations became more accelerated in early January, my former faith in conventional, bureaucratic approaches to this satanic *student* rapidly diminished to the level of zero.

After several heated vocal exchanges, Joe arrogantly threatened to shoot me, much to the elation of some of his fellow classmates. The *student* also predicted that he intended to knock-down my home with his father's bulldozer. The young barbarian also boasted that he had gotten rid of his sixth-grade teacher and that he would either have me canned by the administration or have me go into agriculture as an insane funny farmer. 'Should I treat these haughty utterances as mere hollow threats?' I considered. 'Is this the speech of a child in search of love and understanding?'

Modern American education is riddled with many porous delusions of grandeur. On the one hand, Joe Dodge was a chaste product of his home environment, and his concerned teachers should make every attempt at tolerating his myriad emotional problems. The *child* was not really responsible for enacting his rebellious behavior because the *student* was affected by abnormal doting influences at home.

On the other hand, American education had to pathetically function *democratically*, and Joe Dodge should be granted the privilege (right) of learning regardless of his terrorizing tendencies. The right to learn is the First Amendment in the unwritten student Bill of Rights.

Often *students* misconstrue the freedom to learn to mean freedom to devastate and freedom to do whatever pops into a kid's mind (or mouth). It was extremely difficult to teach in school buildings where *students'* assumed rights were magnified and teacher authority was minimized. *Students* were and are given too many inherent rights glorified under the umbrella protection of *democracy* in education.

However, whenever a *student* is caught smoking marijuana, writing graffiti, smearing feces on lavatory walls, or ripping a sink off the boy's room wall, our naïve system feels that the culprit is not totally responsible for his or her action. Malignant elements in our corrupt society had temporarily contaminated his or her vulnerable mind. Blame society first! Blame America second! Blame the involved teacher, too! But blame the *student* and his parents last!

This is the type of absurd hypocrisy that has been poisoning American education over the last half-century, and its flimsy logic furnishes a safe refuge for thousands of Joe Dodges from Maine to California.

I felt intense hostility toward Joe Dodge, but I had to employ stealth to furtively conceal it. I moved the *child's* desk to the front of the classroom so that I could keep him under close scrutiny while speaking to the class. Joe would remove a ring from his finger and would rise from his desk until he stood inches away from my chin. The *student* then would squint one eye and peer at my face through the ring in a similar manner that a skilled jeweler examines a multi-carat diamond through an eyepiece.

And then, Joe Dodge would imagine that his hands and fingers were authentic pistols. The young punk would make authentic gun sounds and pretend shooting me dead as I attempted addressing the thoroughly amused class.

I sent the instigator with a Discipline Referral Card to the vice-principal, who forwarded the case to the principal, who then directed Joe Dodge to the superintendent's attention. The superintendent was a Socratic-type of philosopher that believed a touch of goodness resided in each of us. When Joe and the *super* got into a dispute, that's when the *student* threatened to hit the head school official with a raised chair. The vice-principal was called in and chased young Joe Dodge outside the school, and that's when the *student* kept yelling, "Fuck you!" every time the stocky *VP* ran out of breath and stopped.

It was indeed a rewarding sight to witness the distinguished vice-principal have negative contact with *my* menacing, incorrigible *student*. I honestly was thrilled that I had succeeded in making my problem the administration's problem.

After a three-day suspension from school, Joe Dodge returned to torment me once more. I kept a close watch on him in all sectors of the building. On days when frankfurters were served in the cafeteria, Joe would purchase extra portions of baked beans heaped upon his tray so that he could have more biological gaseous discharges in my classroom sanctuary the following morning.

When thinking about the Educational Aristocracy, including the *CST*, I believed that more intelligence was vacuum-packed inside chicken soup cans. Thousands of Joe Dodges across the country are masters of the black art of negative psychology, but teachers are told that we must exercise positive psychology as a remedy. If a *student* is deft at distorting reality and then inventive in redefining it in his or her twisted behavioral terms, and if he or she could concoct a chain of pathological lies, then the child's contrived tainted answers to well-intentioned questions naturally will mislead any *CST*.

Interviewing *students* like Joe Dodge and recording the dialogue as fact is similar to feeding erroneous data into a computer. The findings will always be fallacious. Positive psychology only works when the *student* is cooperative, unassuming, receptive, honest, and genuinely interested in the betterment of himself and the world.

If a *student* happens to be a conniving high deacon of the negative psychology cult, then all of the cognitive maps and all of the majestic behavioral objectives cannot prevent a vindictive, malicious *child* from performing his insanity in the great educational arena. Most school systems need fewer child psychologists on their *Child* Study Teams and more professional exorcists.

Joe Dodge had produced in six short months enough venom to make any cobra or rattlesnake envious. The *Learning Disability Specialist* was primitively hunting for evidence of abnormal theatrics, but he exited my classroom in thirty minutes clinging to a gross misconception of my daily reality with the case study *student*. The *LDS's* theory on the matter was quite inadequate. He believed that his presence in the back of the room would have no impact upon Joe Dodge's everyday conduct. During the *LDS's* thirty-minute glimpse, Joe's deportment while the observation was occurring appeared to be quite ordinary. After the *LDS's* departure, then the *student* instinctively returned to being his normal, destructive self.

It all seemed logical from the *LDS's* point of view, and irrational from my perspective. The *LDS* theorized that Joe Dodge and I were having a personality conflict and that our relationship was crippled by mutual discord. But the *LDS* believed that since I was the adult and also the teaching professional, it was up to me to compromise and rectify the problem I was encountering daily with the *student*.

I seriously doubted the veracity of the *LDS's* conclusion. I believed that Joe Dodge was truly an intelligent mental case and also an accomplished pathological liar. I was through trying to use positive psychology to rehabilitate the *student*. My next step would involve non-professional methods to satisfactorily deal with the fourteen-year-old obnoxious maniac.

Chapter 24
"My Way"

The *Child* Study Team's function is to probe the inner depths of the *student's* active emotions along with his/her thought processes and then make appropriate recommendations and methods of resolution to the school administration. Each subject teacher on Joe Dodge's daily schedule was instructed to submit a comprehensive report describing the *child's* academic and behavioral performances in their classrooms. Coincidentally, the opinions of my teaching colleagues (that were vainly attempting to educate mercurial Joe) paralleled mine.

The *Child* Study Team can be described as a burnished hunk of chrome on the educational limousine (teachers reside somewhere in the exhaust system). The *CST* was composed of a scholarly *Learning Disability Specialist* (*LDS*), the school psychologist specialist (*PS #1*) and the school social worker (*SSW*). The *LDS* and the *PS's* salaries vastly exceeded those of the multi-role academic cellar dwellers (the teachers), so those revered specialists too should be considered as being part of the "Educational Aristocracy".

The *CST* was assisted in its important mission by a resource teacher, a speech therapist, the guidance department, and the school medical staff (the nurse). The team of professional examiners was supported by a squadron of secretaries, whose function was to type-up the distinguished bureaucratic panel's findings, reports and suggestions. The army of school personnel had been assembled on that occasion specifically for the purpose of case studying the incomparable Joe Dodge. 'What an ignoble tribute to this age of specialization!' I critically thought.

The panel of Merlins began their vital research by delving into inscrutable Joe Dodge's biographical history, and each unearthed iota was compiled into a very impressive and prodigious manuscript typed-up by the *CST's* secretarial brigade. In keeping with traditional orthodox practice, the *Learning Disabilities Specialist* visited my second period English seminar to observe Joe Dodge's *academic* performance along with the *child's* psychological functions for a second time in an educational setting. Much to my dismay, the wily *student* smelled a rat and managed to outfox the system. The alert *child* sensed that he was being the focal point of the *LDS's* examination, so Joe cleverly reversed his field and again put on a show by exhibiting cooperative classroom etiquette.

If the second *LDS* observation could have been made through a one-way mirror or videotaped by a hidden camera, then a more valid and lucid introduction to the crafty *student's* vehement, outlandish demeanor could have been recorded. I cursed the invalid mockery of truth under my breath as I conducted the grammar lesson on prepositional phrases. I readily knew that the Galahadian innocence of the educational establishment had been cleverly vanquished by the astuteness of an eighth-grade *student* employing his intelligence in a different way than *he* ordinarily had when not being observed. It was obvious that the *LDS's* second observation would not be reliable, scientific, valid or accurate, because the false perception was fallibly based on another meager thirty-minute phony glimpse into the *student's* erratic, unruly behavior.

Later that week, I couldn't stand being viewed through Joe Dodge's cheap tin ring, so I moved the devilish *student's* seat back to the last desk next to the side chalkboard. Joe continued doing his hideous drawing on the sideboard, but at least I didn't have to contend with being looked at through a cheap tin ring less than a foot away from my face. The Art teacher reported to me that demented Joe had disassembled his string diagram in class and then adorned his head with the disarrayed remains while making "Three Stooges' sounds". And the Math teacher told me that the *student* was shoving smaller kids around outside *his* classroom prior to first period.

I began thinking about the *student's* crazy disruptions and then an unprofessional thought registered in my mind. 'Surely, this wretched knucklehead must have some nemesis, some vulnerable Achilles heel!' I pondered. My sanity just might be rescued if I could figure-out the secret magic formula to defuse the warped-minded *child."* The coveted *Child* Study Team/guidance/vice-principal approach had proven to be a short-circuited remedy. I decided to resort to the primeval instinct that inhabits each of us: survival of the fittest. Now it was going to be a dramatic showdown between the *student's* evil instability and the preservation of my mental health.

After a hundred and forty-five days of the fourteen-year-old, oversized monster's pestering nonsense, I resolved to put the shoe on the other foot. I unprofessionally began badgering Joe Dodge at every opportunity, and my new aggressive approach seemed to have temporarily baffled him. I began my foray by calling him "Joey-boy", and after his peers adopted my lead, his hostility seemed to be (for a short time) neutralized.

I soon realized that I could defeat the *child* on his level by making him explode and blow his cool in front of his classmates. I kept sending him down to the Main Office as soon as trouble started, and I would already have the Discipline Referral Card written-out before the juvenile cretin would commence interrupting the class. I would then hand the student the discipline card in *real time* right when he had done something disobedient. And every time the *student* did something inappropriate, I would pretend that I was writing-down and recording the evident violation without saying anything at all to the disruptor.

Students tend to fear the unknown, so Joe Dodge had to be taken out of his comfortable emotional environment where everything was predictable to him. This new method seemed to work better than the cause and effect monologue, "If you do this, then I'll punish you by....., let's say, giving you after school teacher detention." I soon found-out that if a *student* thinks that the teacher is crazier than he is, then the *child's* outer shell could be more easily cracked.

"Joe, have you purchased your round-trip public service bus ticket to Pleasantville, yet?" I asked. "The neighboring town's only twenty-eight miles away!"

"Why the hell should I have to go there?" Mr. Dodge returned.

"Because Pleasantville is where the regional summer school is going to be," I clarified, "and it's only twenty-eight or so pleasant miles away from town."

"I ain't goin' to no fuckin' summer school!" Joe nastily replied. "You ain't gonna' make me! You can't make me go!"

"Well, if you fail English, which you're doing right now, it's either going to be summer school or eighth-grade again next year!" I added (knowing full well that the *student* was too old and big to keep back and that the guidance department would recommend that the *child* keep riding the educational escalator to the ninth floor). What parent in his or her right mind wants a seventeen-year-old jerk with a beard, mustache, sideburns and a tattoo sitting next to their naïve eighth-grade daughter in English class?

"You're full of shit!" the nasty *child* caustically answered. "I think you're full of shit!" he contemptuously repeated.

"And if you can't catch the Public Service Bus to Pleasantville," I continued without being fazed by his filthy mouth, "then you can always hitchhike there."

So, every time I saw Joe Dodge in the hall, in the classroom or in the cafeteria when I was on lunch duty, I would give the *student* the hitchhiking sign. Bob Gordon, Ron LeFey, Tim Carley and just about every other male faculty member would give the *child* the extended moving thumb treatment, symbolizing daily trips to

217

Pleasantville whenever they too saw him anywhere in the building. Larry DeLancy actually caught Joe standing at a urinal in the boys' lavatory, called his name, and then gave the hitchhiking sign while saying "Pleasantville, man!"

I could see a rumbling volcano erupting inside the *student*. His eyes blazed with fire, and his face reflected confusion and alienation. The male faculty members continued their symbolic assailing every day, and for the first time, the tide seemed to be changing. Joe Dodge now had a sourpuss, and frankly, no one deserved it more than he.

Up to that time, Joe Dodge had been the only *student* in my five years of teaching that could outstare me after eye contact had been made. But now, whenever he started fooling around in class, I would pause from speaking and give him the hitchhiking sign, and then the other *students* in the class would repeat my stellar example. Joe would then painfully turn his head and put his large skull face-down upon his desk slate.

One morning, Joe Dodge couldn't take the pressure of psychological warfare any longer. After he gave me the middle finger in class, I was giving him the hitchhike sign in return, and then the livid *child* got-up out of his desk, left the room, walked out of the building and trekked two miles to his family's home. I dutifully reported him to the Main Office as being *AWOL*, and when the vice-principal finally got around to calling the *child's* home, the stupid wandering fool answered the telephone and got himself into additional hot water. His penalty was three days of In-School Suspension where other unfortunate teachers had to put-up with his divine presence all day long.

Joe Dodge's protective mother telephoned just about everyone in the Educational Aristocracy, proclaiming that I had been savagely picking on her angelic son. Mrs. Dodge suggested to the receptive guidance counselor that I should be more patient with her *child* and that it was unprofessional for me to "belittle him in front of his peers". I was not about to compromise my tact regardless of pressure applied by the junior-senior high school's high-ranking officials. I was finally enjoying teaching my second period English class, and this teacher was not going to surrender his psychological upper hand to either Joe Dodge or to his concerned mother.

The vice-principal called me into his office to review what I had been doing to the *student*. "You should ease-up on the boy," the discipline-enforcer suggested. "Your strategy will be difficult to justify without having any solid, educational foundation."

"I do what I have to do to get by," I evasively answered. "If Joe Dodge is a *student,* then I'm Plato reincarnated! If Joe Dodge is a *child* prodigy, then I'm the *Good Humor* man!"

My convictions regarding that particular *student* (out of the hundred and thirty I had to teach daily) had become quite fortified and unyielding, and I was not about to make any apologies or concessions to anyone. I did not even give the vice-principal the satisfaction of knowing my next battle plan.

With the entire school hierarchy aligning against me, I decided to take the conflict to the next echelon immediately after the *child* threatened to dynamite my house with my family in it. But truthfully, I was beginning to derive some pleasure from abandoning my role of being the prey to converting into my new role of being the predator. Joe Dodge's perception of a human relationship was "either-or"; *either* I destroy you *or* you come after me.

One morning before class, Joe Dodge tried intimidating me with the shallow warning that his father was going to arrive at the school unannounced and punch me in the face, and then, dismantle my entire body. That particular threat clearly suggested to me that Joe's barbarity was beginning to become domesticated because previously, the *student* had threatened to beat me up all by himself. Since the mentally disheveled *child* actually now feared me, he felt it necessary to assign the beating-up responsibility to his docile father.

Joe's mother called the vice-principal and complained, "If I was a man, I would come to the school and smack that English teacher silly!" At that juncture, I was confused as to whom was going to maul me: confused Joe Dodge, his subordinate father, or his dominant mother that wished she were a man. But I was undaunted by the reckless threats because I was enjoying the fact that I could now teach the second period class and treat it as if it were an ordinary forty-five-minute session. Whenever the abominable *student* started his pernicious Joe-foolery, I would tease him by waving my thumb in the direction of Pleasantville and by smiling at him while doing so.

Then the administration did something rather unprecedented. The school brass transferred Joe Dodge from my second period English class to a study hall (his third one on his daily schedule). Much to the *student's* discomfort, several teachers in the mass study hall knew all about the hitchhiking maneuver and employed it whenever the *child* started misbehaving. And when the *child* would give the teachers the middle finger salute in return, they would immediately dispatch *him* to the office with a Discipline Referral Card.

It was reported to me that during Joe's new cafeteria period, the misunderstood *child* had acted-up, cutting in line, and causing a general disturbance. Three male teachers sat at Joe's lunch table and just stared at him for five minutes. When the kid became paranoid and yelled, "What's *this* shit all about?" all three teachers on duty gave him an extended hitchhiking gesticulation. Joe Dodge tossed his tray on the floor, scampered out of the cafeteria and left the building against school regulations before he ever could receive another Office Discipline Card.

Joe Dodge's departure from my second period English class represented a major triumph for me. The in-place bureaucratic system had not provided me with a viable solution to the *student's* daily nuisance. However, the ultimate administrative movement of the derelict *child* from my classroom had been enacted under the pretense of a "personality conflict".

I was thrilled that I could now teach my second period English class without the *child's* persistent damaging drivel, but I was infuriated that the administration thought that I had been acting unprofessionally with the aberrant *student*. How can a teacher ever have a professional relationship with an erratic buffoon? Would a doctor continue to treat a patient that tried to murder him on numerous occasions? Would a military drill sergeant continue to train defiant Joe Dodge, or would he instead have the trainee brought before a court martial?

Let's examine the basic facts. I was a teacher and Joe Dodge was a *student*. I was an adult, and he was a fourteen-year-old, hundred-and-eighty-pound wise-ass *child*. I was a rational person, and he was a young educational anarchist with a license to commit anarchy every single school day. Modern American educational *democracy* was dissolving the disparate roles and functions of teachers and *students* by putting *us* on the same shelf and making us equal individuals having a drastic "personality conflict".

My purposes upon entering the second period English classroom were well-intentioned, constructive and well-planned. Joe Dodge's purposes were sinister, destructive and disorganized. And the Educational Aristocracy had described the actions I had finally taken to neutralize Joe Dodge as being unprofessional, unethical and unbecoming. But thank heavens that what I had done had been quite effective for me. Joe Dodge was finally in the custody of other victimized teachers on the staff, and I could now teach second period English without the headache of constant interruptions.

Joe Dodge still had managed to enlist and obtain the support of a cartel of school *specialists* whose patented idealism had blinded them to the hazards of a dangerous *child* causing chaos in the building. All the while, I had been jeopardizing my career's security and tenure as each successive school *specialist* pacified the recalcitrant *student's* unwarranted stubborn pride.

The case study *student* still had an assigned seat in the cafeteria. I was never assaulted by him, by his mother, or by his father. My house had not been bulldozed or dynamited. The child's next tact was trying to act extra-polite to the other teachers on cafeteria duty, some of whom still persisted in giving him the infamous "hitchhike sign". After knowing the *student's* discourteous background, Bob Gordon and Tim Carley were not about to extend any sought-after cafeteria pity in Joe Dodge's direction.

If I had swept the daily nightmare under the carpet, as many teachers do daily with similar *children*, then I could not live with my conscience's principles of right and wrong. But a plague of Joe Dodges is running rampant in public schools all over America, and little or nothing is being done about it. Certainly, the *student* I have presented is an independent case study, and I cannot assert that hitchhiking signals are the solution to our national schools' burgeoning discipline problems. But to the many Joe Dodges that are out there causing malignant chaos, school is a daily festive picnic, and recipient teachers are restive daily targets of the troublemakers insidious, malicious contempt.

Rebellious *children* use the classroom as a place where they can impress their peers by blatantly abusing teachers. The disruptors are heavily shielded from punishment by parents, by guidance counselors, by *Child* Study Teams and by usually apathetic school administrators. And the *students* doing the mischief and the malice are rewarded by getting to eat meals in the cafeteria and by getting to stay toasty-fuzzy warm all winter long. Schools can be paradises for mendacious *children* that wield destructive tendencies and that don't respect or obey adult authority. That's why public schools are becoming more and more sociological holding places than institutions of sincere academic pursuit.

Contemporary educational philosophy needs to undergo vast revision and restructuring. Only a good citizen can constructively contribute to a strong *democracy,* and only a healthy mind is attuned to educational *psychology,* to courtesy, to honor and to respect. Fourteen-year-old Joe Dodge was neither a good *student* citizen nor a good *student* performer, but ironically, the *child's* deceptive antics were insulated and safeguarded under the aegis of educational *democracy* and educational *psychology*.

I believe that it is the teachers' destiny to eventually acquire more power within the general school superstructure. That evolution will be hastened by the need to prevent our academic institutions from deteriorating to the point of collapsing. When teachers manage education in a similar manner as doctors control the destiny of medicine, then true accountability will actually again thrive in public school education.

The Educational Aristocracy must be dismantled and be replaced by panels of teachers, school *specialists* and boards of education qualified in making important *educational* decisions. As in hospitals, administrators should handle the daily business transactions of the school. Just like the hospital administrator makes sure the toilets are flushing and counts and documents the number of scalpels and surgical masks, the school administrator's function should be keeping the bathrooms operational and accurately tabulating the numbers of pencils and notebooks stored in the supply room.

The introduction of school *specialists* (a wasteful layer of middle management) into America's school systems has stagnated the educational stream of consciousness. Their idealistic and superficial perceptions of reality have contaminated and diluted *academics* in our public schools and have substituted harmful sociological development in its place. An excess of fantasy idealism, democracy, sociology and psychology in American public schools has polluted the flow of everyday realism. Enough of these parasitic specialists and Educational Aristocracies!

Education should be returned to the simple relationship of teachers instructing *students* that are actually in the building wanting to learn. Respect, prestige, authority and influence must be diverted from the educational *specialists* to the teachers, who desperately need to be specialists and not *generalists*.

Joe Dodge was later allowed to participate in the eighth-grade graduation ceremony and symbolically receive a blank diploma. The administration had made the concession if the student agreed to attend summer school. But much to my satisfaction, the *student* would not receive his actual eighth-grade graduation certificate until after he took and passed a majestic summer school English course in distant Pleasantville.

Chapter 25

"Joe Dodge Graduates"

When I heard that the school administration was going to allow Joe Dodge to walk on stage and participate in the eighth-grade graduation ceremony, I was more than a little angry. I recalled how I had been prevented from graduating with my class on stage at *Edgewood High School* for failing Trigonometry, and when compared to Joe Dodge's demonic malice, in contrasting my past to the despicable *student* saboteur, I was almost like Sir Galahad when I had been a high school senior. The hydrochloric acid in my stomach must have really been baptizing my ulcers because I was downing *Alka-Seltzer* tablets dissolved in water like crazy all week long.

The fourth tallest eighth-grade *student* in the back row was allowed to walk across the stage and shake hands with a board of education member and then receive a *dummy diploma* from the principal was the notorious Joe Dodge. The six-hundred parents assembled in the audience gave the *student* a warm round of applause, inadvertently congratulating him for accomplishing great turmoil and havoc. Judging by the loud ovation the *child* received, a stranger might have thought that David Letterman or Jay Leno had been introduced.

Joe Dodge had failed two major subjects, but was still allowed to symbolically graduate on stage during the ceremony if he promised to attend summer school. As his corpulent frame promenaded across the stage, an accelerated filmstrip of the *student's* more bizarre capers flashed across my mind. 'What a zany miscarriage of decency!' I thought as I listened to the parents and relatives applauding and twenty members of Joe's family proudly snapping pictures. 'What a tremendous travesty of educational justice!'

I knew the truth. Joe Dodge was much more than a bit psycho'. He couldn't read or achieve on a fourth-grade skill level. The diploma he would receive in September wouldn't be worth the paper it was printed on. And unless Joe voluntarily dropped-out of school after age sixteen, he would go on, ride the high school conveyor belt, and finish in another four years with another worthless unearned diploma.

And as Joe Dodge returned to his position in the back row of tallest eighth-grade graduates, I trembled a bit when thinking about the entire fiasco. The unerring voice of a hallowed college professor echoed in my mind saying, "Education is not an assembly line; *students* are not similar cans of soup; each *child* is an individual!" The ugly thought entered my mind that perhaps sometimes schools should be run like factories with the defective products taken off the educational conveyor belt. Maybe a *student* like Joe Dodge was like a car without a transmission or like a camera without a lens. 'Maybe the Federal Trade Commission should investigate American public schools for selling inferior products (*students* of Joe Dodge's caliber) to the gullible American public!' I imagined. 'Maybe the product (Joe Dodge) is only as good as the natural resource or raw material (home environment) from which it (he) came,' I bitterly concluded. 'Maybe true grade level accountability for *students* would bring much-desired *student* responsibility to education!' I reckoned. 'Maybe emphasis should be placed upon the finished product rather than confusing the public by distorting the entire thirteen-year-process with impressive-but-meaningless terminology!'

I realized that Joe Dodge couldn't be compared to a gallon of milk or to a pint of raspberries in a chain store. Maybe Joe's interests were more attuned to tearing lawnmower engines apart than to analyzing the short stories of Edgar Allan Poe, O. Henry or Jack London. Maybe Joe should have spent the year rebuilding V-8 motors rather than dismantling eighth-grade teachers' classes.

The *student* derived little knowledge from all of the labor expended by his dedicated eighth-grade teachers because the *child* was not allowed to function where he was best suited: in auto mechanics, in woodshop, and in metal shop.

The fact that I had a hundred and thirty *students* to teach prevented me from meeting any *child's* individual needs, let alone Joe Dodge's individual preferences. And so bored *students* sleep and snore while others disrupt in the back of American History classes because *they* don't belong in an academic setting. They belong in auto mechanics or in another "hands-on" learning situation.

The educational hierarchy worries too much about depriving a *student* of a well-rounded education supposedly provided in the comprehensive high school. By not collating and channeling *students* into programs where they actually belong, and by putting them in academic classes that don't coincide with their aptitudes and interests, the "hands-on" type of *student* tends to becomes totally bored and unmotivated. He or she either retreats into his or her shell, or the "hands-on misplaced *students*" use their Carte Blanche to persistently aggravate teachers in academic subject classrooms.

I often wondered whether Thomas Jefferson had the likes of Joe Dodge in mind when the genius was inspired to draft the exalted words to the *Declaration of Independence*. Instead of life, liberty and the pursuit of happiness, Joe Dodge believed in kill, anarchy and the pursuit of educational devastation.

The biggest fraud in education today is that schools are preparing *students* for a "should be" society that does not exist in the real world. We are producing low reading ability *students* that suffer through watered-down academic courses that are not in harmony with the competitive job market that awaits *them* after high school graduation. High school graduates that go directly into industry know little about *efficiency, reliability* and *job performance* because they had been permitted to coast through high school on the easy-riding educational conveyor belt.

Students that evolve from high school into factories generally experience cultural shock when their demanding employers don't cater to their needs as the Educational Aristocracy had compelled the academic teachers to do. This nightmare won't terminate until high schools wake-up to the fact that what they are producing is counterproductive to the needs of our competitive free enterprise economy, and also to our nation.

American education should not be based on the quixotic fantasies of a handful of egg-headed *Harvard* and *Stanford* university professors, Ivory-Tower educational philosophers and "way out there" pseudo-psychologists. School expectations ought to be rigorous and ought to push *students* to the limit in either the academic curriculum or in the vocational curriculum. As it is now, high schools represent the grand antithesis of the great American free enterprise system.

The Protestant work ethic and the tough standards of American industry are not implemented today in American public schools. According to educational psychologists, competition and profits appear to be selfish enterprises that are diametrically opposed to intangible abstractions such as human growth, emotional needs, and *student* gratification. Let's be realistic. If Harry S. Truman had been acting as a psychologist while he was president, we'd still be fighting *WWII.* If Bill Gates had not wanted to become rich and famous and make a great contribution to the information revolution, *Microsoft Corporation* would have never happened.

Psychologists should not have control over the destiny of American education. Teachers should. A high school with a thousand *students* and a frivolous curriculum geared to the needs of each *child* is a school having a thousand curricula with perhaps only eighty-to-a-hundred teachers to handle them. This kind of exotic reasoning is madness! Hercules would get a double hernia just thinking about it.

But academic teachers are forced to perform miracles while trying the impossible and attempting the incredible. And when the results are mediocre, society blames teachers for not being able to achieve the impossible and failing to accomplish the incredible.

Forget about pursuing the prodigious fantasies of illustrious college professor dreamers and their mandarin educational psychologist colleagues. If *students* were simply separated into two categories after eighth-grade (academic and vocational), then most of the maladies of today's high schools could be deftly averted.

And after the Educational Aristocracy shoots arrows into the teachers' feet, the experts blame the public-school instructors for being the Achilles heel of the dismal educational process. "*Students* are not learning because teachers are not teaching!" becomes the standard, patented simpletons' indictment.

Teachers must take control of public-school education so that if and when a school system fails to improve, or if it is evident that *students* are not learning, then it is really the fault of the teachers. But as long as administrators and boards of education run schools, and as long as wacky college professors and "other-universe university psychologists" are at the helm of the educational ark, then American education is doomed to either mediocrity in the short sprint or to failure in the long run.

Whimsical Ivory Tower college professors, removed from the harsh realities of everyday classroom experience, are grinding-out fantastic learning expeditions to distant curricular nebulae. The teachers have been designated as the command astronauts to pilot all the passenger *students* to distant, great unreachable stars. As long as public-school teachers are compelled by Don Quixote mandates to implement impractical new methods that are so absurd that they are non-effective, then the afflicted teachers will be continually held liable for the irresponsible and inefficient American public school educational system.

Health experts would never think twice about vaccinating *children* with unproven serums because of possible detrimental after-effects. So, why do American educators continually inoculate (inculcate) *students'* vulnerable minds with new experimental programs and with "new experimental organizational patterns" that are unproven and lack the necessary years of research and evaluation to truly be valid curricular innovations?

The truth is that the so-called "evolving or changing curriculum" must remain constantly evolving and changing so that it can never be easily evaluated and proven the sham that it truly is. If curriculums were to remain stationary and static, they could be closely inspected and analyzed. Education's inadequacies and deficiencies could easily be identified, analyzed and criticized. That's precisely why the Educational Aristocracy wholeheartedly endorses the ever-elusive "changing methods curriculum".

And finally, in regard to Joe Dodge, he did graduate eighth-grade. It was reported to me in 1979 by a reliable source that the former *student* had moved from New Jersey to Arizona where he worked construction operating a bulldozer. He lived with an uncle that had later passed-away without any indication of illness, and Joe Dodge was one of the man's pallbearers at *his* funeral. An inquest into the unexpected death revealed that the nephew had been instrumental in permanently disposing of his uncle.

I assessed the overall predicament in this fashion. If Joe Dodge were to be an eighth-grader the following school year, I would have to contend with his misery again, along with other "Joe Dodges" that might ascend into my custody from seventh grade. In that respect, getting Joe Dodge's upward advancement to ninth-grade should be perceived as a saving grace and also as a divine blessing.

Upon hearing the sad news of the Arizona uncle's death in the faculty room, I recalled my former *student* pretending to be shooting me with an imaginary pistol during second period English. 'Thank goodness I didn't live in Phoenix or Tucson!' I told my teacher colleague that had provided me with the recent alarming news.

Chapter 26
"Homogeneous Grouping"

American education masterfully projects many quite deceiving, illusionary silhouettes. It does this rather amazing sleight-of-hand chicanery to trick the public into believing that change in education is indicative of change representing improvement in the "academic quality" of both teaching and learning. But as has been stated in this work several times, schools are *not* true academic places. They are sociological holding patterns containing thirteen holding platforms.

Overzealous, highly-esteemed college professors and university *child* psychologists/philosophers definitely influence public school administrators to practice this spurious shifting mobility curriculum, constantly maintaining that "changes in curriculum" translates into "changing American culture for the better". In the end, everything in education must change (except school administration), even if the metamorphosis remains the same in terms of ineffectiveness, inefficiency and lackluster test score results. And when the college entrance exam test scores decline, eliminate the SATs all together.

Euphonic academic catch phrases such as *team teaching, behavioral objectives, learning stations, cooperative learning, mini-courses, modular scheduling, paradigms, homogeneous grouping, heterogeneous grouping* and *the open classroom* have agilely wriggled themselves into education to wholly disguise the sinister metamorphosis of sociological education replacing academic education as the basic purpose of public schools. This impressive-sounding terminology is used to contour a contemporary, shoddy mythology that promotes the theory that constant revamping of methods and learning models enhances the total curriculum. All that the above sophisticated nomenclature actually constitutes is "change for the sake of change".

Despite the ornate, gaudy descriptions, American public-school education has undergone little progressive reform in terms of new programs that produce measurable quality results over the last fifty years. Problem *students* are still severe discipline headaches. Truancy is still a trademark of many urban schools, and a growing number of *students* and *children* are now alcoholics, on drugs and *HIV* carriers. Uppers and downers no longer refer to the shape of exciting roller coaster hills, and *Coke* no longer only means a delicious soft drink.

When I had been teaching eighth-grade English back in the early 1970s, the school system was experimenting with *homogeneous grouping*, which incidentally had nothing to do with gay and lesbian behavior. The fancy educational lingo had found a very comfortable niche in the '70s in high schools and junior highs across the country. But homogeneous grouping had its disadvantages to complement its several strong selling points. Here's how it worked.

Students were classified into ability groups (classes) according to reading ability, IQ, and interest range to establish a commonality where similar *students* were placed in classes with peers of similar reading, subject matter, and IQ status. The main objective of homogeneous grouping had a noble pursuit: *students* sharing a similar ability and/or intelligence range would all progress at a controlled learning pace determined by the teacher.

It all sounds logical and foolproof, doesn't it? The teacher had the option to regulate each subject lesson and assignment to the ability level of the group (class). An Accelerated English class could write advanced term papers, deliver oral reports in front of peers with similar abilities, read more challenging sophisticated literature, or explore complicated topics in all subject areas of the curriculum.

With homogeneous grouping, the slower *students* would not have to fret keeping in cadence with the brighter academic *students*. The slower learning *children* had been classified and deposited into classes with other *students* having similar IQ's and/or academic ability. Sounds like educational Nirvana, doesn't it? It would have been if teachers were wizards and magicians instead of only being four-year college graduates.

Conversely, in traditional *heterogeneous classes*, a group's "section" would have a *cross-section* of *student* talent and ability ranges. The popular theory of heterogeneous grouping was that the smarter more stellar prodigies (usually nerds, geeks and eggheads) would assist the slower, more sluggish plodders along the exciting educational trail. But the main drawback was that the smarter *students* weren't really learning too much while always helping the unmotivated and lethargic underachieving children like Joe Dodge along the wonderful *academic* path.

Enter *homogeneous grouping* as the salvation to replace or supplement heterogeneous grouping in public school curriculums. With the new homogeneous grouping educational model, scrupulous curriculum coordinators could *experiment* with innovative trends being produced by those quixotic college professors and those ethereal university psychologists/philosophers. For instance, we could now have the fabulous "laboratory concept" adjusted to the ability level of each group (class).

In the '70s, all of a sudden, my school system had English labs', Social Studies labs', Home Economics labs', and Art labs' to supplement and complement the customary Science labs'. All of this commendable-sounding phraseology was instituted to make it appear that scientific methodology was strictly being practiced all over the school curriculum.

But school and university psychologists and college professors soon maintained that homogeneous grouping had too many negatives. Blacks and other minorities were often separated (segregated) into slower classes. The brighter classes had too much competition, and intense rivalry abounded for the acquisition of the best grades. Educators were compelled to believe that competition was an ugly remnant from the past that produced selfish individuals that only cared about their own presents and their own futures, and who cared little about the slower *students* (the rest of humanity).

While teaching in the homogeneous learning model, I immediately noticed that the advanced *students* loved it because they found competition a very satisfying pursuit. But the educational powers-that-be found fault with homogeneous grouping because the egos of the brighter academically-oriented *students* were being fueled, but the *sociological* "sharing experience" that *they* needed had been largely removed from the *academic* classroom. The smarter classes had little group dynamics because the accelerated academic *students* could now cover twice the amount of material provided in the grade level textbooks (with homogeneous grouping), and the cream-of-the-crop didn't need other *students* to help them learn.

With the slower classes, group work dynamics was ineffective because there weren't any smarter academic *students* in the class to guide or to do the lion's share of the work for the unmotivated Joe Dodge type of *student*. So, core subject area teachers were forced to teach academics to non-academic *students* that were incapable of keeping *sociological* education going on their own.

Competition and free enterprise had always been revered as hallmarks of our great American culture, but the educational gurus on the college level were influencing both textbook publishers and the Educational Aristocracy with the notion that "competition breeds selfish egotistical *students*" in the more advanced homogeneous "sections". *Student* rivalry was described as a negative social influence making the more advanced teens aggressive, inward, self-oriented and apathetic, especially towards the needs and problems of slower *students* in particular, and the needs of society in general.

The legacy that had made America great (free enterprise and competition) since the revolutionary *Industrial Revolution* had been junked in favor of whimsical objectives and methods that were being generated by quixotic "way out there" college pharaohs (education professors/philosophers) and ethereal, brainstorming university czars (educational psychologists/philosophers).

The new educational models had to reflect what society ought to be (an idealistic future) instead of what American culture really was (the selfish evil menace of free enterprise and competition). But who would be qualified with the best skills to build the idealistic society of tomorrow? The answer is the *academic student*, no matter if he or she is prospering in the homogeneous learning model, or stagnating in the heterogeneous "Marxist, group sharing" learning model.

The brightest minds will eventually rise to the top like cream in coffee. But free enterprise (homogeneous grouping) carried with it the dreadful stigma that mankind is basically selfish and that smart individuals are only concerned with his/her own personal gain. The plight of the less-gifted and the needs of the unmotivated, slow learners (the masses) were apparently being ignored in the homogeneous learning model.

So, some kind of compromise had to be hammered-out because the weaknesses of homogeneous sectioning (and also heterogeneous grouping) were too glaring and too obvious. The formula was then "Masonically" discolored by means of "Educational Alchemy", diluted, transfigured, bottled and marketed to the American public as "American *democratic* education in the comprehensive junior/senior high school".

Now the homogeneous model was more aligned with *democracy* (individual pursuit of happiness and self-sufficiency) than the heterogeneous classroom model was (smart *students* helping slow *children* learn in mixed socialistic classrooms).

Democracy requires that each participating individual has the right to govern himself' or herself', and in effect, be his or her own government. True *democracy* is free enterprise and competition (the homogeneous learning model), and the favorable homogeneous learning model rewarded the individual *student* for his or her *academic* classroom accomplishment.

But unfortunately, academic education had to be corrupted by sociological education (Socialism). Those slower Joe Dodge type *students* weren't learning too much English, Science, Math' and

Social Studies on their own and were turning their classrooms into veritable zoos, circuses and carnivals with their uncooperative behavior (rampant symptoms of juvenile delinquency, insolence, irresponsibility and defiance) and lack of motivation (laziness).

The secret truth is that once the homogeneous learning model went out of vogue in the '80s, it was replaced by American *democratic* education (Socialism; group dynamics, and cooperative learning education). American *democratic* education is really *socialistic* education in disguise.

Now academic *students* must sacrifice advancement of self to help the group (tomorrow's society). The dreams and noble goals of Thomas Jefferson have mutated into the aspirations of Vladimir Lenin. The new theme was that *student* competition is bad; cooperation and sharing are good. Free enterprise breeds selfish individuals; the strong scholar must strive to lift-up the weak *child* to function on *their* level. "Homogeneous grouping (free enterprise and stiff competition) is then not a desirable method; conversely, heterogeneous grouping (Socialism) is now considered a worthy pursuit!" This perilous transition soon became the new educational philosophy of the 1980s.

The security of the group (heterogeneous grouping) won out in the 1980s over homogeneous grouping, and it now takes priority over the development of the individual *student* and his or her pursuit of happiness. The personality of the academically gifted *student* is now hammered to the point where he or she must conform to group dynamics where the mentally superior *students* are expected to lead slower *students* along the primrose path of golden knowledge. In this *New World Order, student* answers should bring honor to the class. Getting along with others is more important than finding out who one actually is and exploring one's own potential (self-realization). Free enterprise must be stifled because it radiated the genius of the individual, and *that* successful individual freedom scenario had been the secret underlying educational theme of the 1980s.

Educational theorists were clever enough to mislabel what they were really doing. They shrewdly avoided using the stereotypical term *Socialism* by calling the exact same thing *democracy,* which just so happens to ripple with patriotism. But a real *democracy* truly values and rewards the accomplishments of the individual.

However, now at high school graduation, each *student* (the Valedictorian and the class clown), regardless of academic merit or academic performance, receives the exact identical diploma. Is this thinking more parallel to the spirit of Karl Marx or to the spirit of

Thomas Jefferson? If we truly had a *democratic* system of education, distinctions would exist on each *student's* diploma indicating his or her academic accomplishments.

An empty diploma devoid of information would indicate to prospective employers that the *student* had bummed his or her way through high school. But democracy (Socialism) covers-up that fact, and no one can or should be able to distinguish between pernicious Joe Dodge and the Salutatorian President of the National Honor Society by examining their diplomas, which appear off the press as carbon copies of one another. The deficiencies of the slower *student* must always be concealed because everyone is afraid of truthfully labeling him or her as a lackluster producer. That practice (the truth) would be too akin to *discrimination*.

Educational grade inflation has made the same diploma readily available to all *students*. The meaningless high school sheepskin has been devalued to the point where it no longer has any prestige, whatsoever. Prospective employers realize that high school diplomas are *equally* accessible to functional illiterates that only achieve on a fifth-grade learning level.

If we truly believe in educational *democracy*, why can't each *student's* diploma state his or her accomplishments, honor roll status, class officer status, class rank status, club officer positions held, and extra-curricular activities? As usual individual accomplishment must be put on the shelf so that the under-achievers that don't deserve *academic* diplomas at graduation aren't *discriminated* against. Please, leave "politically correct" to the politicians and get it out of American education.

I became aware of the many built-in ambivalences and ambiguities of American *democratic* education in the comprehensive high school when I was appointed to a two-year stint as the adviser to our high school's chapter of the *National Honor Society*. I assumed the responsibility at the start of my sixth year of teaching in the system.

The local *NHS* chapter (along with the national organization) was slowly-but-surely deviating from the use of *academic* performance as the most important criterion for induction. I soon became disenchanted with the watered-down caliber of high school *students* being nominated for and being enrolled into the *NHS*.

Even if marks in academic subjects were the sole index for recruiting students into the *NHS*, I soon found out that the *students'* grades were not the only factors involved in eligibility measurement. *Students* were being inducted into the *NHS* for attaining A's and B's in Home Economics, in Typing, in Woodshop, in Sewing and in Art. The grade point averages were now not accurate barometers of the *students' academic* achievement. And in more than a few cases, the non-academic elective subjects amounted to the bulk of some seniors' schedules because their only senior requirements were English and Gym.

By taking the easier Mickey Mouse and *mini*-courses, seniors could maintain high averages. And if the *students* hadn't made it into the *NHS* as juniors, their high senior averages just about guaranteed entrance because of the easy electives the *students* were eligible to take. So, not only are academics being systematically diluted, but also honor and merit are being diluted too with the inclusion of elective courses and extra-curricular activities as new criteria for *NHS* eligibility in the *democratic* comprehensive high school.

Essentially, *honor* is no longer exclusively synonymous with scholarship. The requirements for the *NHS* have been compromised to accommodate more mainstream *students* so that the organization does not reflect an elitist "academics only image". Teenagers that came half a day to school and spent the other half of the school day working in the community in special programs to avert dropping-out were entering the *NHS* for being only part-time *academic students*.

American education was and is determined to incorporate the requirements for the *NHS* brand of *Socialism* into every phase of public-school operations in order to be "politically correct", and the tone-deaf Educational Aristocracy then has the unmitigated audacity to call the horrendous charade it has completed *democratic education*. 'What a corrupt requiem to supplement the philosophies of John Dewey and Horace Mann!' I thought while I was the *NHS* adviser. Several times I casually strolled past the high school's main entrance to ascertain that the overhead name had not been changed to either Donald Duck or Bugs Bunny High.

The whole "democratic comprehensive school" recipe was designed to homogenize (but not in homogeneous groups) the entire curriculum with the entire *student* body, all being executed so that it was virtually impossible to discriminate the honor *student* from the class anarchist. Teachers were told they couldn't fail too many *students* in their academic classes, so the instructors watered-down their subjects and covered only ten textbook chapters instead of twenty-four, so that the less-gifted *students* could achieve at *their* rate of speed. But now, the grade of A was within the reach of even the dullest *students*. Many duller *students* were fantastically receiving "A grades" in Literature or Algebra classes, even though they weren't half as advanced or half as proficient as the true academically gifted *students* were. 'Whose A in Literature or Algebra is more valid?' I wondered.

When homogeneous grouping was in vogue in the early '70s, the *students' A* in the Accelerated Literature or Advanced Algebra class were given more recognition (weighted) than the slower *students'* A's in a homogeneous classes of clunkers having a bevy of Joe Dodges in them. The aim of schools was and is to accentuate and elevate mediocrity to give it equal academic credibility, exclusively done so that it is virtually impossible to distinguish the intellectual differences between bright and average kids.

The "politically correct but potent" "educational powers-that-be" don't want to discriminate against those slower *students* that are only capable of producing (at best) average work. Discrimination (even good discrimination) sounds too much like "prejudice", and the terminology also sounds too much like "stereotyping," the ugliest of taboo words in contemporary American education.

In homogeneous grouping, the smarter pupils were isolated from the *students* with lower reading abilities, with lower subject area proficiencies, and with lower *IQs*. Educational psychologists feared that the slower ability *students* would perceive themselves as being inferior and then consequently consummate that "self-fulfilling prophecy" by failing *true undiluted academic* subjects. Educational psychologists also feared that the brighter *students* would egregiously turn into sanctimonious, arrogant, elitist snobs that easily would outshine their general class counterparts.

An argument could be made in regard to homogeneous grouping, advancing the theory that no such animal could exist because there is already a diverse range of interests and talents within any given classroom group sorted out by *IQ* scores, by reading ability, and by subject proficiency. For example, if *students* were homogeneously grouped according to *IQs,* some pupils with similar intelligences would be able to read and comprehend better than others in the group (class) could. Other *students* might be more proficient in Math' than in Grammar, and some might have special interests (SCUBA diving, steeplechase horse-riding) being diverse from anyone else's in the class. Despite these specific differentiations, in the final analysis, there is more *academic* homogeneity existing within a homogeneous group (class) than there is homogeneity existing in a heterogeneous class.

The junior/senior high school in which I had taught attempted to cancel-out the *elitist bias* of "smart group" from the stigma of "dumb group" by making the 8-3 and the 8-4 sections the "slower groups" and the 8-1's and the 8-5's the "smarter classes". But even the Joe Dodges in 8-6 figured-out that *they* were definitely in the slowest of the *six* eighth-grade sections of twenty-five *students* each.

I observed with fascination how *students* chose to group themselves when in the unstructured cafeteria setting. The kids sat with their friends no matter whether their pals were in a different section or in a different grade. But still, generally the smarter *students* sat with their egghead friends, and the slower *students* sat with their social acquaintances. Aristotle described it very succinctly when the sage generalized, "Birds of a feather flock together"!

The critics of homogeneous grouping argued that the method deprived the slower *students* of being democratized (socialized) with the elitist *students* that certainly would be thriving in the more advanced accelerated academic classes. In the cafeteria scenario, true democracy in action can be witnessed when the *students* have the freedom to group themselves homogeneously. Invariably, they sit with friends that share similar academic, intellectual or interest-based backgrounds. All of the democratic education in the world cannot alter *that* very apparent sociological phenomenon.

The big downside to homogeneous grouping was when I had to be saddled-down second period futilely teaching the 8-6's eighth-grade English. If the 8-6 class was just plain slow in terms of ability, then I wouldn't have minded gearing the subject to the speed of their intellectual capacity and the group's general low reading ability (usually third to fourth grade ability in eighth-grade). But when the 8-6 homogeneous class was demonstrably boisterous, obnoxious, belligerent, nasty and diabolical in addition to being slow-learners and unmotivated dawdlers, then I had all I could handle on my plate in one forty-five-minute period.

In my next year of teaching, I had encountered the incomparable class from hell. Every *student* in the homogeneously grouped class was his or her psychological case study, and each *student* had one or more emotional maladjustment. Max Sennett's zany *Keystone Cops* were more docile and more organized than *that* 8-6 class of homogeneously grouped misfits was that I shall always remember. Joe Dodge was the Lucifer of the 8-6 class devils, but many other junior Satans added to the daily forty-five-minute nightmare.

Chapter 27
"The Problem Class"

My second period eighth-grade English class was quite a diversified menagerie of unique individuals. Besides the lunacy of Joe Dodge, I recollect a certain Robert E., who was a short, wormy *student* with a shrill squeaky voice that often outrivaled the school fire alarm, which in my teaching career, I had to listen to *that* noise ringing over seven hundred times. (Twice a month by state law the school had to be evacuated during a surprise fire drill. Times that by thirty-four ten-month classroom years and tack on student teaching time, and you'll obtain the seven-hundred numerical figure as being the correct multiplication *product)*.

Robert E. was silly, giddy and grossly immature. His trademark was answering back teachers that attempted to correct him. One day, it was raining out during lunchtime, so the teachers escorted the eighth-graders from the cafeteria to the auditorium to watch a film because the *children* couldn't go outside the second half of the lunch period. Robert E. refused to stay in his auditorium seat. After commanding him to "Stay seated" five times, I placed "Bob" in a soft auditorium seat and then sat on his lap for the remaining five minutes of the period. In 1972 a teacher could get away with a comical stunt like that for the amusement of the other eighth-graders, but in the year 2000-plus, I don't think so, and now I wouldn't even consider trying it.

Besides possessing a skinny anatomy, Robert E. had moving eyeballs that slanted-down toward his nose. Sometimes his eyes moved-out in opposite directions when the *child* was facing me. I thought it was strange that Robert's left eye was taking in the side chalkboard while the right eye was looking out the right-side windows. Robert E.'s eyeglass lenses were so thick that his pupils seemed to be magnified ten times their normal size through the convex-shaped surface.

Robert E.'s parents spoiled him rotten to the point where the *child* was now the boss of his house, telling his folks what to do. The *student* owned three shiny motorbikes, and the imp illegally cruised the town's streets at night hoping that the police would chase after him and get their squad car stuck in some dirt path meandering through a nearby muddy woods. The *student's* favorite pastimes were chewing gum, gnawing pencils with his sharp fangs, throwing erasers before class, and goosing the more rounded girls as they paraded past his desk. The child's greatest school achievement was cutting teacher and Office Detentions, and Robert E. was predictably suspended from school on the average of once a month.

One particular second period, I caught Robert E. thumbing his nose at Joe Dodge's raised middle finger. I wrote-out a Discipline Referral Card (green card) and dispatched the *student* to the vice-principal's office. The *student* wished to demonstrate to his idol Joe Dodge and to the remainder of the 8-6 class his contempt for teacher authority. The *child* strenuously tried dislodging my classroom door from its sturdy stopper. The door to my classroom often stuck and sometimes stayed very attached to its floor catch. Robert E. vigorously and vainly endeavored over and over to smash the door shut, but the frustrated lad could not free it from its floor-catch and accompanying anchor lock.

"Better eat less *Frosted Flakes* and consume more *Wheaties!*" I nonchalantly suggested as the *student's* frustration mounted from his repeated bungling of a simple task. Robert E. finally gave-up his futile protesting of slamming my classroom door and mumbled some indiscernible phrases under his breath that I suspected were not too complimentary to society in general or beneficial to me in particular.

The second period 8-6 "holy terror" class was at its finest moment, organized chaos. 'Thank heaven I don't have this asylum eighth period!' I often gratefully acknowledged. 'I wouldn't wish this class on Lucifer!'

Tom C. was another headliner of that hideous 8-6 section. The *student* had a bulging body that was more matured than his mind was. The classroom cinderblock walls seemed to vibrate whenever Tom C. discharged his jolly Santa Claus-like laugh, which probably ricocheted three times around the room. The *student* was not only portly and towering, but he was also neurotic and rambunctious. When the *child* would become bored, he slouched-down in his desk, and his gangling frame intersected and blocked two rows.

Joe Dodge would notice Tom C.'s legs present in either of two aisles, so the inane *child* would get-up without asking permission to sharpen the point of a pencil he had just deliberately broken. Joe would intentionally trip over Tom C.'s leg occupying the aisle and then initiate a pretend argument with his comrade to spitefully disrupt my English class.

One day, the class and I were reading a play in literature titled *The Mummy's Foot.* I was dramatizing certain occurrences within the script to spice-up the ongoing lesson. In the beginning of the play, I simulated the sound of thunder by crashing the metal trashcan against the tiled floor. Tom C. was sleeping, and the snoring *student* woke-up in a hurry after being startled in his slumber, and then after regaining his senses, intentionally falling out of his desk.

During a more crucial part of *The Mummy's Foot*, to entertain the class, I hobbled around the classroom and then around the teacher's desk, dragging one foot behind to mimic a staggering-but-revived ancient Egyptian mummy. Much to my surprise, I heard the class laughing. Tom C. was imitating me and doing a parody of my splendid mummy rendition as the fourteen-year-old nemesis was making the full rotation of the classroom directly behind me. 'I'm sorry I ever woke-up this clown by slamming the trashcan against the floor!' I thought.

In my many misadventures with classes like the 8-6 zoo, I had found that it was almost impossible to be creative because some zany *student* in the group would always attempt to sabotage the teacher's imaginative contribution. 'These *students* can't cope with the challenge of abstracting!' I suspected. 'Most of their mental work would make an echo teem with originality!'

And then, I considered one of my eminent college professors stating, "All *children* are capable of appreciating and demonstrating abstractions!" The *students* in my second period 8-6 class found appreciating anything that happened to be constructive or academic an immense Herculean challenge. One day, I even prayed that a steamroller would run me over and end it all.

And to think that thousands and thousands of prospective teachers are taking gossamer undergraduate and graduate courses, and their ever-scheming professors are calmly telling them to first exhibit patience with the *children* in their custody. Then the future teachers are told they must identify the needs of the *children* and to understand every motivation of each *student* (that is trying to make the teacher into either a homicide, a suicide, or in a worst-situation scenario, even into a basket case). It is always easier to tell than to do, so that's why professors teach and lecture in colleges and not in public schools. The second period 8-6 class would have made Jesse James's gang look like Wyatt Earp's posse doing a *Cinderella* play.

Wanda D. was another specter who participated in that second period house of horrors. I had always felt sorry for Wanda D., for she had a hearing disability. A hearing plug fit snugly inside her right ear. Wanda's often-distracted mind was usually vacationing on an extended mental holiday, and she seldom bothered me or anyone else in the room.

One morning, I was slowly writing an example of an adjective prepositional phrase on the front chalkboard. Suddenly, I heard loud, twangy acid rock and roll music accompanied by intermezzos of static. When I turned around to determine the origin of the disruptive dissonance, I spotted Wanda D. frenetically fumbling with her right hand inside her brassiere. I didn't need radar to hypothesize that the noisy rock and roll music was pulsating from her chest. What I had sympathetically believed was a hearing aid in her ear actually was an earphone for a transistor radio imaginatively concealed beneath Wanda D's blouse. The *student* probably accidentally tugged the connecting wire from the miniature gadget, and consequently, her casual pull diverted the music from her earplug into the radio's speaker inserted under her blouse.

Tim G. was another *student* in that motley problem class. Among Tim's more desirable traits were dirtiness, unkempt spaghetti-like shoulder-length hair, and a totally slovenly appearance. The *student* was extremely deficient in the art of self-control. The *child* was bigger than I was and had made it to eighth-grade with second grade reading and writing skills. But the worst aspect of Tim G's personality was that the juvenile egotist thought he knew more than the teacher did.

Tim G. relentlessly blurted-out garbled babble and incorrect answers without the civility of ever raising his hand. Whenever I glanced at Tim's ghastly sword-like fingernails (with dirt deeply embedded under them), I would either wince or involuntarily blink my eyes. The kid's clothes smelled as if his tawdry garments were washed only once every other month.

After teaching a literature unit on Greek mythology, I asked the class the name of Zeus's wife. My throat choked with mirth when Tim loudly chronicled without raising his hand, "Mrs. Zeus!" The shocking reality of Tim's humorous-but-uncouth response was that he had been sincere in stating his impulsive answer.

On another rather momentous (momentum) occasion, Tim was sauntering about in the crowded corridor and then clumsily bumped into Mr. Snider, one of the junior high's Spanish teachers. Mr. Snider accurately sensed that the awkward collision had been a deliberate one, so the teacher angrily pushed Tim G. against the lockers and verbally admonished him.

Tim G. instinctively crackled back, "You can't touch me! I know my rights! I'm gonna' get your ass fired!"

Public schools today are flooded with *students* that know their *rights* more than familiarity with their *wrongs*. The sooner the

Educational Aristocracy acknowledges and faces-up to this dangerous situation, the sooner schools will be able to effectively grapple with the more overt agents of anarchy (disruptive *students*). These wild and out-of-control *children* are more familiar with *their* freedoms and *their* rights than they are about *their* responsibilities toward the rights and freedoms of others.

On another eventful occasion, prankish Tim G.'s throat shrieked-out the erudite phrase, "Mr. Wiessner, it says inside the front cover of my grammar book 'Mr. Wiessner' (and then the *child* slowly spelled) s-u-c-k!"

I was not embarrassed because I had already been a veteran of such stupid, undignified abuse many times in the past. First of all, I was fully aware that Tim G. certainly knew how to read the word "suck" because I often heard him use some of its rhyming words in conversations with Joe Dodge. Secondly, I knew that the *student* had written the imaginative passage himself because Tim G. had the habit of writing precisely as he spoke. The *child* had a lateral lisp problem coupled with a third person present tense singular number misconception, so when the *student* pronounced certain words, he always neglected to put an "*s*" on the present tense third person singular verb.

But here's the biggest farce in American *democratic* education. Tim B. managed to migrate all the way up into the eighth-grade, and the *child* was basically an illiterate. That's the academic escalator doing its dysfunctional function! If Tim had the fortitude to grind onward, the "roads scholar" would receive the exact same graduation certificate as the class Valedictorian and then voyage-off into our competitive free enterprise economy with a third-grade reading, vocabulary and writing ability. And after the *student* graduates into society, the temporarily concerned Educational Aristocracy will want to forget all about him right when the nasty freeloader really would need *guidance* and direction the most.

I recalled my first college Educational Methods class where the professor stated, "Each child has an innate desire to learn! You must exploit *that* need anxiously flourishing within him or her! And now, here's the basic intellectual contradiction. The educational feudal lords in the triumphant Aristocracy adeptly command to the teachers, "You must motivate your slower *students*. You must find things that those *children* can do well. You must gear your lessons to their special interests." My critical mind soon formulated a sudden inspiration: "Why do I have to continuously motivate lackadaisical *students* who, according to Educational Psychology, all have an innate desire to learn?"

The only way that I could gear my lessons to the 8-6 *students'* special interests would be for me to convert my classroom into a vulgar Roman orgy and thoroughly motivate (arouse) the *children*. And then for fifteen or so minutes, Tim G. would have something to occupy and temporarily sustain his limited attention span, and for a short duration, my relevant lesson would be attuned to the *children's* specialized interest.

The members of the 8-6 class (and its rambunctious grade-level peers) did participate in something impressively imaginative in early April of that school year. It was a brisk lunchtime afternoon, so I decided to let the hundred and sixty *students* leave the cafeteria and step outside into a school picnic table area for some fresh air.

Rumors of a potential fight had been brewing all day between Tim G. and Robert E. Aware of *that* possibility, I had cautioned the prospective warriors during the first-half of the lunch period to not conduct their *student* Armageddon inside the school building or on school property.

As soon as I exited the cafeteria, my fear of a *student* altercation materialized into actual combat. I scurried to the scene of the escalating gladiatorial contest, and I observed that the two junior pugilists (Tim G. and Robert E.) were frantically rolling and squirming-about on the lawn. All of the other assembled eighth-graders were zealously shouting encouragement and cheering the two moronic combatants. Upon reaching the pair of brawlers, I was startled when the two wrestlers instantly ceased all their hostilities. As I surveyed the total silence that enveloped me, a hundred and sixty acne-faced *children* all yelled in unison, "April Fool Mr. Wiessner"!

Barbara C. was another denizen of that volatile 8-6 debacle. The *child* was a persistent chatterbox whose speech could outrace the sound of a *CD* rock and roll album played at triple speed. Barbara C. was a haughty, bratty, combative *student* that would only speak to the instructor if she thought the teacher had made some kind of mistake or error. Then her resentment for authority was quite evident in her nasty rhetoric when the generally apathetic *student* attempted to correct me. The *child* possessed a devil-may-care attitude, and the youthful Amazon specialized in contriving ticklish questions about sex and venereal diseases in a malicious effort to cause the English teacher to drift away from the identification of adjective and adverb subordinate clauses functioning in complex sentences.

One day, Barbara C. got into a bitter dispute with another eighth-grade teacher. At lunchtime, the *student* hastened to the public pay telephone in the main corridor and notified her ruffian parents of her verbal disagreement with the eighth-grade science instructor. The father of the unfair damsel accosted the teacher in the hallway and smashed him with a jolting uppercut to the jaw.

The urbane pedagogue refrained from continuing the altercation. Instead, the wise teacher dashed to the Main Office before his next class and called the police. Then the science mentor intrepidly pressed charges against the pugnacious parent. The judge in charge of the extraordinary case found the father guilty of assaulting the teacher, but had the attacked teacher defended himself by punching the aggressor, it remains to be seen whether or not the school administration would have backed their *employee*.

Someone may ask, "Don't they have special classes for these mercurial and emotionally volatile *students* in your school?" To place an insufferable *student* in an emotionally disturbed class, it must affirmatively be determined that the *child* is emotionally disturbed. The school agency delegated with *that* particular responsibility is the illustrious *Child* Study Team, and after reading all about the case study named Joe Dodge, the reader of this book will understand the futility of teaching a class like the 8-6's and then referring one of them to the impotent *CST*. And besides, before a *student* is classified and placed into a special needs learning situation, the *CST* must have the parents' consent. I doubt whether Barbara C.'s father would agree to such a stigmatized placement of his beloved daughter into a special needs' classroom environment.

In many small towns across America, "educational politics" often enters into the domain of which *students* are placed in which sections. If the *child's* parents happen to be prominent citizens, or if the *student* has relatives that have strong connections (strings) with members of the board of education, or with the town council, then the likelihood of an emotionally unstable *child* being placed in an emotionally disturbed special needs' class is remote. School officials don't want bad vibrations with the entrenched economic and political establishments in their blessed communities.

Another explanation for the existence of a homogeneous class of misfits like the 8-6's is the stinginess and the frugality of boards of education. School needs are often dwarfed by the need for "fiscal responsibility" and "safeguarding the taxpayers' almighty dollars." Teachers are often reminded that they lack the necessary college certificates and credentials to psychologically evaluate problem *children*. Teaching those *students* day in and day out does not qualify teachers to recognize emotional disorders. And when the *Child* Study Team recommends a *student* for special placement, stubborn parents can override the recommendation because they don't want their kid labeled as being inferior or as being special needs' material.

Another junior terrorist that knew all of the evil vines in the educational jungle was Frank P. The *student* was a temperamental Afro-American that thought all of his white teachers were prejudiced against him. He hated being poor, wanted to be a professional football or basketball player, and that far-fetched dream was all that really mattered in the *child's* diminutive mind.

Revolutionary political movements appealed to *that student's* fancy of escaping the abject poverty environment that had spawned him. Frank P. would shove the smaller members of the class around, and the antagonist was the only *student* in the 8-6 section that Joe Dodge was actually afraid to fight. The *child* often boasted that his father could "whup" any teacher on the staff, and that egocentric statement summarized the home environment that had produced him.

I was always reluctant and afraid to take a sick day or a personal day from school, fearing what devastation the 8-6ers would have on an inexperienced substitute teacher. Once I was selected to conduct a morning writing workshop for other faculty members, and a sub' had to teach the bizarre second period circus. I came back to the classroom two hours later and stood in absolute disbelief at the doorway. Hiroshima should have looked so good after the *WW II* atomic explosion.

Fiberglas ceiling panels had been pushed-up from their grooves, the old reliable pencil sharpener had been dismantled, pencils had penetrated other ceiling panels, and much of the contents of my desk drawer had been malevolently chucked out the windows including my blue homeroom attendance cards, my utilitarian paper clips, and my indispensable Discipline Referral Cards.

As I scanned the room, most of my paperback books had been removed from the shelves and scattered upon the tiled floor, while a few had been thumb-tacked onto my backroom bulletin boards. Four desks in the rear of the room had been inverted (although it was English class, perhaps several *students* were concretely visualizing the abstract idea of division of Math' fractions by inverting the desks). Obscene words were printed in ink on the *students'* desks, and a part of the tiled floor had been somehow made to look like rustic wood with an irregular grain stained upon it.

My teacher's chair had been positioned upon my desk, my trashcan had its contents strewn onto the floor, and the "circular file" rested on top of the elevated teacher's chair. The hallowed American flag was sticking out from the now-oval bent trashcan. My beloved classroom looked like it was Fort Apache after a barrage of furious Indian sieges. Such was the explosive factor of that treacherous 8-6 homogeneously grouped second period class.

I reported the destruction to the administration and was told that I had to control the class better so that when a substitute was in my room things would go more smoothly.

"But how can *you* hold me responsible for what happened when I wasn't even there?" I protested to the principal wearing my leisure suit without a tie.

"*You* must clamp-down on those *students* so that this never happens again," I was adamantly told. "No substitute should have to deal with an unruly class like yours!"

I had a few interesting notes written to me by substitutes that had the unpleasant misfortune of teaching the "unruly" 8-6 class. Here are a few.

Mr. Wiessner:

I had the dishonor of teaching your second period class today. The *children* were pretty well-behaved the first five minutes. Then there were several paper gliders thrown from the back of the room, one of which was skillfully caught by another teacher entering the room looking for you.

When we went over the vocabulary words on page 494, I was hit in the back by a piece of chalk. Then some *student* in the building set off the fire alarm. When we came back into the classroom from the phony fire drill, I noticed that the seating chart on your desk was suddenly missing. I discovered it at the bottom of the waste-can after class was dismissed. Your classes' seating charts were all torn-up and are now useless.

I want you to know that I never want to see this class again. You must be an amazing teacher if you could control this pack of wild animals.

Sincerely,

Mrs._____

Another substitute wrote the following note:

Mr. Wiessner,

Joe D. gave me a lot of trouble second period. He wouldn't stay in his seat, roamed around the room, and burped and passed gas repeatedly without any shame. Class pictures were being taken for the yearbook, so that activity took fifteen minutes out of the period when 8-6 was called-down to the auditorium stage. When we got back to the room, the *students* would not stop talking. How do you teach this class every day?

Then at the end of the period we had to evacuate the building for a bomb scare, and boy, was I instantly relieved. The office thinks the caller was a *student* absent from your second period class. You must have *ESP!* You picked the right day to be out! As for me, I need to rethink this entire substitute business!

Mr. J. _____

Every once in a while, I'll intercept or find a promiscuous note from a female *student*. Here's one that an 8-6 girl found crumpled-up on the floor. It was from an anonymous girl in another section.

Mr. Wiessner:

You are so cute! You're such a doll! Every time I see you, I feel like playing with myself. Maybe you can teach me how to go down, if ya' know what I mean!

What are ya' doin' tonight? Maybe you, me and my girlfriend can get a threesome going. Ya' know what I mean! I dreamed last night that you were so hot for my body that you got down on me when I was having my period. It was really groovy! Just give me the time and the place when ya' want to get it on with me and my horny girlfriend!

Love ya',

A Secret Admirer

And to think that teachers have been fired for using one obscenity in a classroom or in a locker room. The same rules and ethics should apply to *students* as the ones that apply to public school teachers.

Jose R. was a contemptuous member of that 8-6 class debacle. Every morning, I had to delay the start of the lesson so that the group could watch the *student* put his Hindu earrings on. When I asked the *child* fashion plate why he had to do that daily process in my class, sensitive Jose gruffly snorted, "I have gym first period and don't want my earrings to get rusty in the shower!" Being a veteran teacher, I accepted his explanation as being a valid one and was very happy to hear that Jose R. took a shower after gym class.

In response to any given question that I would ask the class, very resplendent Jose R. would loquaciously volley, "Me no sabe, Kemosabe!" That marvelous *Tonto* rhyme without reason seemed quite appropriate because with that 8-6 homogeneously grouped section, I often felt as if I was the *Lone Ranger*. When I first heard the *child* utter the inane response, quite frankly, it tickled my fancy. But unfortunately, that one cute statement back in September became the entire 8-6's patented slogan for any interrogatory I asked during the remainder of the school year.

Jose R.'s paternal guardian frequently became intoxicated and brutally flogged the boy whenever the *spirits* moved him (this was before suspicion of such incidents had to be reported to *DYFS*-State Division of Youth and Family Services). So, the Hispanic *child's* father (I reckoned) must have been "a big bruiser" judging from the black and blue marks on the muscular *student's* face and arms.

I was not-too-blessed having Jose in my homeroom. During the morning announcements, the *child* would fiendishly blurt-out such poetic phraseology as "Get bent!" and "So what!" "Screw you!" in rebuttal to the boring monologue blasting through the early morning intercom wall speaker.

Tim Amoro was a high school English teacher on the staff. I really liked Tim a lot, but at least once a week my buddy would beat me to school, open my desk drawer, and then randomly rearrange and shuffle my twenty-five homeroom attendance cards, taking them out of alphabetical order. Some of the attendance cards would be put upside-down, others backwards, and still others upside-down and backwards. I really didn't need that extra aggravation at 8 a.m. having to carefully re-sort the blue attendance cards because my peculiar homeroom was almost as interesting as my lunatic second period 8-6 English class.

Jose R. was very fond of receiving attention from girls of Anglo-European vintage. At assemblies in the school auditorium after the lights had been dimmed, Jose liked grabbing the girls' alluring ponytails or their long tresses. In the halls, his anxious palms were often detected touching some unwary girl's breasts. Because indiscreet behavior of that type is *touchy* in more than one way, the victims of the playful molesting were often quite reluctant to report the vile incidents to teachers. In fact, some of the girls actually liked the romantic attention Jose was giving them.

On a class field trip to an amusement park, a girl did report that Jose had grabbed her breasts inside the Haunted House. I referred the bawdy incident to the head teacher in charge of the field trip because I didn't want to have anything to do with Jose R., with his unstable father, or with administrative bureaucracy and the ultimate resolution of the accusation.

On one occasion, I had caught Jose R. casually giving an eighth-grade girl a free tactile chest examination in the hall outside my room. I felt an urgent need to intervene and quell the flagrant abuse of our austere Judeo-Christian-American morality. I yelled at Jose R., "Get your hands off of that girl right now!"

The guiltless young lady that I thought was being accosted and molested apparently had been enjoying Jose's improvised personal mammogram, and the juvenile female snarled at me and insisted, "Mind your own damned business!"

Jose R. had one bitter enemy in the 8-6 class, and that was Barbara C. The two heckled each other constantly, and Joe Dodge would naturally get into the dispute and side with Barbara, whom he would always instigate when the girl wasn't arguing with Jose. The choice of words in the once-a-week character assassinations was not exactly the civil language Professor Henry Higgins had taught to Eliza Doolittle in *My Fair Lady*.

Jose R. happened to have a dark complexion, and in the warmer months his pigmentation shaded towards black. Barbara C. and Joe Dodge celebrated the seasonal transformation, and the erudite duo blatantly called Jose R. "nigger," which he seemed to like because he always smiled when they used that insulting terminology.

I used the unprofessional tool of blackmail to neutralize Jose R.'s impetuousness with his female peers. Several mornings I spotted Jose locked in amorous embraces with buxom Puerto Rican and Caucasian girls. I had each incident documented and had four undated Discipline Referral Cards already written-up for immediate use in the file cabinet in the rear of the room.

Every time Jose R. would become a little too feisty or irascible in second period class, I would go to the filing cabinet, put the date on the "green card", and swiftly dispatch the *child* to the vice-principal's office. After three green cards, Jose finally calmed-down a trifle in that class. But I found that when my mental survival was the supreme issue at stake, the mere thought of acting "professional" seemed rather Lilliputian in magnitude. Last resort "Green Card blackmail" was a definite, viable alternative.

Kirk P. was another divine marvel of that second period class. He had a hot and cold disposition, and I really never knew whether his *TNT* temper was about to explode, or if he was simply hibernating inside his classic turtle-shell. Kirk's greatest, observable aptitude was to "non-shamefully" sketch nude female figures (I was glad to see that he appeared to have heterosexual tendencies) upon his desk's comic-strip slate.

Once I pointed to one of the *student's* revealing pornographic illustrations and exclaimed, "Kirk; it's unfortunate that your parents are paying good tax dollars for you to draw those hideous pictures!" Instead of being embarrassed, the *child's* gritty reply was: "That's okay, Mr. Wiessner! My old man can afford it!"

In cold February of that year, Kirk P. ran away from home and hitchhiked six hundred miles to Missouri. Upon hitchhiking back from his little odyssey, the *child* got into an argument with one of his teachers. The *student* punched the male teacher in the chest, and the teacher retaliated with a firm poke that rearranged the *child's* ribcage. After a brief exchange of blows, fearless Kirk P. bellowed to the instructor, "Who's your damn lawyer? I'm gonna' get your shitty ass on unemployment!"

Kirk's protective mother thought that her wonderful son's vanity should be vindicated and his inflated ego gratified. She called the school principal about the incident and scheduled a meeting with him and the superintendent. This process is called "transfer of blame" where the parent finds fault with the teacher while the parent had surrendered all responsibility for disciplining *the child* over many years to teachers.

My teacher colleague had been keeping a well-documented oak tag file inventory of Kirk's salacious drawings and written idioms that the *child* had thrown into the trash can after classes and naively thought would never be seen or used as direct evidence against him. The teacher eloquently produced the lewd illustrations at the confrontational administrative conference, and the *child's* delusional mother was shocked at witnessing the "smoking gun".

And to think that my teaching colleague might have lost his cherished job had he not been careful enough to prepare a counter case against Kirk P. beforehand. But when instructors have a hundred and thirty *students* to teach daily, a homeroom of twenty-five potential renegades, and a hundred and sixty *children* all at one time inside the cafeteria, it is hard to keep convicting evidence and records on all of them.

One fine morning, I was reviewing with the 8-6 class for the next day's vocabulary test. One of the words on the list was the action verb *intervene* and its definition was: "To come between." Kirk P. heard the correct definition response, and when asked to use the action verb in a sentence, the *child* was inspired to gush out, "Mr. Wiessner; I *intervened* between my girlfriend's legs last night!"

After seven hardened years of classroom experience, I had gotten used to that sort of perverted *student* response. When teaching a problem class and being exposed to that kind of indiscreet comment, the best policy is to ignore the ignoble remark and to continue onward as if nothing important had happened. If the teacher is gullible enough to succumb to the *student's* deliberate baiting, then the omnivorous class will gain full control of the throttle of the smutty carousel that the innocent *children* have deliberately thrust the idealistic teacher upon. The best advice for teachers is to stay off of the immoral *student* merry-go-round as much as possible.

Chapter 28
"Group Un-therapy"

I never expected any *student* in the 8-6 section to be a mental Achilles, but even if *children* happen to be a trifle short on intelligence or on skill ability, they should at least extend some semblance of respect and courtesy to their caring teachers. When *students* of the 8-6's "moral mentality" are sent-down to the vice-principal's office, they usually return with a defiant smile on their faces, interrupt the teacher's class and announce to their smiling peers that "He didn't do nothin'!" The *children* know from their parents that the school administrators can't lay a finger on them, and most of the 8-6 type *students* fear the assistant-principal as much as Goliath must have feared the diminutive David before the classic slingshot surprise had been sprung.

And when teachers give *students* after school detention, they are really punishing themselves for having to sit forty-five minutes in a secluded room with the treacherous violators. Because of possible transportation problems, *students* must be given notice of detention at least a day in advance, and many *children* often stay home or go to the mall with their parents to defy a teacher-given personal detention. Other potential hooligans spitefully cut the detention to demonstrate their contempt and to cunningly aggravate the teacher giving it.

Diane G. was a plump hussy that nervously swiveled her body back and forth in her desk. She wore plunging V-neck blouses, painted her face with a pound of cosmetics, and flirted with any accessible member of the opposite gender. On her best face-day, Diane G. made Medusa the Gorgon look like Miss America. The *student's* older sister had gotten pregnant in the sixth grade, and it was a tribute to contraceptive devices that the *child* had escaped that fate midway into her eighth-grade year. Sometimes I would have to speak to the class from the back of the room because Diane G. would sit in her desk wearing a short miniskirt with her legs wide open "taking your picture", as Bob Gordon aptly put it.

The sexually precocious *child* repeatedly attempted trapping me by tricking the teacher into deviating from the principal objectives of my lesson. She would ask me questions like, "Why do we have to do this stupid stuff?"

Educational disciples might consider an inquiry of that type a legitimate question, but I had learned to be more attuned to its malignant purpose. The best thing to do as a response is to totally overlook the question, or not be too garrulous in answering it. 'Don't be sucked into a horrible argument vacuum!' I thought. Like the twenty-four other pesky sorcerers in the 8-6 class, Diane G. was all-too-familiar with the first *Ten Amendments* of the *United States Constitution* but generally ignorant of the *Ten Commandments* handed down to Moses on Mt. Sinai.

Jake K. was perhaps the *student* that could best arouse terror in my heart since he never said anything directly to me. The uninterested *child* would slouch-down in his desk and rub his crotch incessantly (maybe this suggests that the *student* was demonstrating some Freudian fetal symbolism, or perhaps Jake simply had jock-rash). The *child* frequently stared blankly at me with a gnarled, snarling expression of discontent on his visage. Sometimes, the frightening gaze would last for the full forty-five minutes, and I often wondered if the *child* was on heavy-duty drugs. Animosity just oozed from the *student's* façade, and as Bill Clinton once alluded, "I felt his pain."

Jake wore skintight dungarees and tight-fitting cowboy boots that appeared to have required the aid of a crowbar rather than a shoehorn to put on. The *child* disliked male teachers, and at times, I observed that his consciousness would slip into a semi-hypnotic state. And then without any warning, the *child's* shrill voice would howl-out, "Stop it! Stop it!" in a terrible, nerve-shattering exclamation. That mad "schizophrenia" compelled me to shudder, and on several occasions, shiver with mild terror at the mere thought of the mysterious subconscious menace that had caused the wild utterance.

Maria R. was at first a shy girl that had recently immigrated to the United States with her family from Italy. She was tiny and skinny and also had excessive energy to burn after the newcomer became acclimated to the *democratic* American educational system. The *student* then frequently whirled around in her desk as if she were an Army tank turret-gunner.

Although Maria was very timid entering the class in September, by December, she just couldn't stop talking and gossiping once she gained some facility with the English language and could communicate with her gabby peers. Yes, the school did have *English as a Second Language* back then, but the program was specifically designed to accommodate the influx of *Hispanic* migrants into the agricultural community. And when *ESL* was finally *democratized,* Greek, Italian, Korean and Chinese *students* that had immigrated to our typically American town had to learn Spanish in addition to a little English.

One day, before the long-awaited *Christmas* break, Maria was putting a simple sentence diagram on the front chalkboard. I was sitting at my teacher desk, which was situated adjacent to the *student*. I heard some *children* laughing, so I turned to see exactly what Maria R. was writing on the chalkboard. I saw beneath the girl's upraised blouse half of her sanitary napkin protruding out of her pink bikini-type underwear.

"Maria, maybe you should take your seat and then I'll finish your diagram!" I politely suggested in order to spare the stubborn girl public embarrassment.

"That's what you think!" the very determined female *student* sarcastically answered. "I know how to do this sentence, and you aren't goin' to stop me from doin' it!" the girl vociferated.

The class broke-out in a roar, and Maria thought they were showing their approval of her challenging my imperative to take a seat. I had again tried sparing the *student* from public humiliation, but the obstinate *child* insisted on completing the simple sentence diagram. 'Maybe I should be teaching the *students* all about simple *diaphragms* rather than simple diagrams!' I mused.

Ted B. was a sensitive *student* that had trouble getting along with his bully peers. Joe Dodge and his cohorts constantly picked-on poor Ted B. and mockingly called him "the professor" because of the *child's* large peepers. To impress his classmates and gain their admiration, Ted B. drew inelegant tattoos on his arms and shoulders. And when the *student* flexed his petite muscle, the vital external genitalia of the drawn female wiggled about in a suggestive fashion, getting roars of laughter from Joe Dodge, Jose R. and Robert E.

Young and scrawny Ted B. really belonged in another eighth-grade section because he actually wanted to learn and improve himself', but fear of rejection from his bigger, mischievous male classmates turned him away from showing any distinct love of subject matter. The academically inhibited *child* had curly hair that was frizzier than an orangutan's furry covering, and his teeth were outlined with a greenish, moss-colored border.

Ted told me one day after class that he was attempting to author a book, and with his guidance counselor's explicit encouragement, asked me to confidentially look at his text and then I could render my opinion about the prospect of him submitting it for publication. Here is the first paragraph of Ted B.'s rather atrocious novel.

"Joe Rader and Ghost"

Joe Rader leaves in the sity. His fater and mudder ones a hotle. His fater does all the bizznus. Won day Joe and frends Jim and Tom they were walk down a paff dat guse passed a hunted house. All sudden you here a booing sounded. It gost sed Tom. Its came frum hunted house, dat on odder side of streat. We wur on the porsh an the door open. We den herd a chane nois. We whent upstair to sea watt dat nois is. Butt the dore slam ans we was loked in.

Ted B.

Ted B.'s first paragraph was not the worst eighth-grade composition I've ever had the displeasure of reading or correcting. The hardest part of this anecdote to accept is that I can't teach eighth-grade English to fourteen-year-olds possessing second grade writing and reading skills. Ted B.'s composition was more akin to creative spelling than it was to creative writing, but on the other hand, a skilled "creative writer" would have had to labor rather intensively to eventually generate the same unique language that Ted B. had produced naturally.

Some of Mark Twain's most popular stories became famous because they contained *deliberate* spelling and grammatical errors as in the famous tale "The Celebrated Jumping Frog of Calaveras County". However, before Samuel Langhorne Clemens deviated from the norms of grammar and spelling mechanics, he knew precisely what those accepted norms were.

If Ted B. had been familiar with the standard English composition rules, then "Joe Rader and Gost" (his tribute to Joe Dodge) could have passed the acceptable language test as a bona fide piece of "creative writing". But there is no *creativity* when it comes down to spelling or homophone usage. Either the words are right, or they are wrong. In that sense, spelling and grammar usage are much like Math' answers. There is only one correct application for each word.

Since Ted B. was sorrowfully lacking in fundamental English writing skills, his "creative ideas" could not be accurately expressed. Good ideas and creative thoughts are meaningless unless they can be adequately presented on paper, or on a computer screen. This is why fundamentals (reading and writing) should be the primary purpose of elementary school preparation and not "concept development".

Students that have demonstrated reading and writing skills should be the only ones writing anything in grades six on down. Those *students* that are deficient in reading and spelling should continue studying those areas before being forced *to create* anything assigned on composition paper. Since Ted B. had not mastered elementary spelling and grammar skills, his creative ideas came across (and could only be interpreted) as crippled, inferior writing.

Occasionally, an 8-6 *student* would *accidentally* produce something interesting or vaguely amusing. For example, one *student* submitted a retelling of the story of Noah landing his ark "on the nose of Mt. *Sinus*" (really, Mt. Ararat), and another 8-6er wrote a brief biography on the life of *"Martian* Luther King".

One day, I had just taught a mini-vocabulary lesson to the 8-6ers. For homework the class had to study all ten vocabulary words, study synonyms and antonyms listed in the textbook for those ten words, and then copy-down the ten text definitions for reinforcement of word mastery. Finally, the *students* had to use the ten words by correctly writing each one in an intelligent sentence. The next day, the *children* turned in the following gems:

1. I have a *bulk* dog.
2. I have to *meditate* yesterday.
3. We are very *pronounced*.
4. The *erratically* is not fixed.
5. Our class went *embarking* to *Philly*delphia.
6. The earth is an *equator* in the center.
7. The police *environs* the house.
8. We had a *vicinity* near us.
9. The art teacher drew an *artifact* in art.
10. I *bulges* when I eat hot dugs.

Number one: *students* that write those kinds of sentences don't belong hibernating in the eighth-grade. Number two: the fourteen-year-old *children* can't come anywhere near doing authentic eighth-grade level work. Number three, if I was to call a spade a spade and fail the entire 8-6 class, I would be indicting myself as a poor teacher that can't communicate the subject matter to the enthusiastic *students*. That is why straight shooters in American *democratic* education are almost as abundant as Eskimo nudist colonies.

The entire American public school educational system has been custom-engineered to conceal from the public the reality of an eighth-grade class like the 8-6's. Homogeneous grouping represented a real danger because twenty-five *students* of Joe Dodge's caliber assigned together into one nutcase class made the problems of American education appear to be too glaringly obvious.

Mix a few 8-6ers into five other *heterogeneous* sections and then cunningly blend-up the stew so that the more serious discipline, emotional and learning problems can't be readily identified.

By not having specific grade-level norms, American education can annually have a Harry Houdini act going on and cleverly escape valid accountability for pathetic groups such as the 8-6's reaching the eighth rung on the public-school ladder. But the teacher's eighth-grade literature and grammar textbooks were specifically written for eighth-graders that could do eighth-grade work, so the instructor must then relate the knowledge in the book to *students* that can't read or write on a third-grade level. As a result, for all practical purposes, academics must be significantly diluted and gingerly spoon-fed to those slower *students* in the *democratic comprehensive* middle, junior high, and high school.

And the sagacious college professors are still *lecturing* to impressionable, prospective teachers: "You must motivate your *students* to learn!" Even if the teacher is temporarily successful at stimulating *student* interest with a group like the 8-6ers, the lack of pupil proficiency will quickly degenerate and soon lead to the lesson's disintegration. Eighth-grade teachers cannot enforce eighth-grade standards and norms with fourteen-year-olds that have third and fourth grade skill abilities. The easy answer to the widespread dilemma is to just keep the educational escalator working and let the ninth-grade teachers worry about it.

Classroom teachers generally wind-up becoming both the goats and the scapegoats of the educational sacrifice. The instructors are the goats because they are commissioned annually to be subjected to the despicable *student* harassment that accompanies *their* vital community function, and *they* are the scapegoats because the teachers are blamed for most of the defects that are prevalent in the enigmatic American educational system. But homogeneous grouping was the true 1970s culprit that formed the 8-6 section, which made the Marquis de Sade's dungeon look like *Mother Goose Land.*

Jenny L. was a slinky, black American miss who every day wore a long black dress that resembled a nun's garb. But that was where the similarity between Jenny L. and a nun ended. The *student* had earned a bad reputation among the junior high faculty because of her frequent quarrels with her past seventh grade teachers. The *child* often argued and answered me back scornfully, was a pro' at cutting classes, and Jenny L. was always in quest of trying to get the instructor in unexpected trouble by twisting specific words or reprimands which were directed at her.

Every day, Jenny L. arrived at the cafeteria back entrance before the first lunch period and returned with a cup of coffee and a Danish roll for another teacher. The cafeteria cashier and staff looked forward to her purchase every Monday through Friday.

After an intensive investigation by the school administration, it was determined that Jenny never reported to a scheduled study hall from the first day of school. Jenny had told the study hall teachers on duty that she had been transferred to work in the "cooking room" that scheduled period. The teachers were so busy the first day with getting everything settled-down in the mass study hall, so they accepted and trusted the child's statement as fact. For three whole months, Jenny was drinking savory coffee and eating delicious Danish rolls in one of the school's four girls' rooms.

Jenny L.'s body emitted a horrendous odor that could choke an elephant. It was difficult standing anywhere near the *student* while being engulfed with the terrible stench. My nostrils shriveled-up and my eyes formed tears from the putrid smell, which I suspected had something to do with her home's heating unit because the odor definitely was more nauseating in the wintertime.

I asked the girls' gym teacher if Jenny took showers after first period class. "No, and I can't force *students* to take showers if they refuse to," the woman coach disgustedly informed me. "Only about half of the girls in that first period class take showers."

This is the sad state of our "politically correct" public schools, which were ahead of their time because they were *politically correct* back in the early 1970s. School officials are afraid that some misguided, crazy parent is going to take them to court over making his or her *child* take a shower at the end of gym class. Fear of judicial decisions by liberal judges, fear of belligerent hostile parents, and fear of community scrutiny and criticism are the types of phobias plaguing contemporary school administrators. And school executives will bend to incredible postures to keep any hint of negative news out of the local tabloids.

Jenny L. wasn't the only *student* in need of soap, water and underarm deodorant. While squeezing my way through a throng of *students* down a crowded corridor on a sizzling September or June day, a variety of *student* body fumes and odors made an ordinary cattle-train boxcar smell like a French cologne factory.

As already mentioned, it was my misfortune to have the 8-6 symposium right after the *students* had first period gym. I soon learned that the *children* had very short attention spans, so I would divide each class session into three mini-lessons of fifteen minutes each. Three consecutive micro-lessons were essential, since the 8-6's had the concentration-focus ability characteristic of an average class of kindergarten *children*.

I tried relating to the *students'* interests, but the lessons would soon deteriorate into floundering and foundering. Once I tried writing sentences to diagram on the board about the topic of motorcycles, and the noisy impersonations that resulted from the boys in the class made me believe that my classroom had been converted into a testing laboratory inside the *Harley Davidson* factory.

The second daily fifteen-minute mini-lesson had to do with completing a worksheet, and the third fifteen-minute interval had to deal with either a quiz or a teacher-guided lesson summation. After January of that school year, I never felt guilty that the 8-6er's weren't accomplishing too much. Extensive self-evaluation of that type (blaming yourself) would bring the average teacher to the threshold of insanity.

The biggest swindle of all going on in American education is the disguising of *students* like those in the 8-6's in either homogeneous grouping or in heterogeneous grouping classroom designations. Despite the realness of 8-6 caliber *students* in middle schools and in junior-highs across the country, administrators condition the public into believing that there are few problems occurring in *their* respective buildings. When taxpayers motor past public schools in their communities, they presume that wonderful things are happening inside. And in some classes, they are, but in others situations like the 8-6's, it's just a lot of wishful thinking relating to teacher survival in an educational jungle!

One phenomenon fascinated me about the stars of the delirious, hilarious 8-6 sideshow. Tell the *students* in the 8-6 class a simple truth, and they instinctively reject its validity. Tell them an enormous fib, and they'll swallow the whole fabrication: hook, line and sinker. The gullibility factor of the 8-6ers amazed me. They will be the twenty-first century *parents* (yes, I know it's wrong to stereotype, especially when the stereotype is at least eighty percent correct) being scammed and fleeced by extravagant frauds at discount auctions and at cheap shopping marts. These nervous *individuals* are the future zealous fans at contrived roller derbies and at fake professional wrestling matches. And I don't consider myself cynical and presumptuous in stating those explicit predictions.

I had learned that I could do little to untangle the muddled home environment that had just about gangrened their personalities starting with Joe Dodge and then going on down the pecking order to Ted B. The 8-6 class had difficulty with temporal relationships, and with abstracting in general. Give them an assignment on Monday to be handed in by the end of the week, and no one would do it. Tell them that they would be quizzed at the end of the period, and most of the 8-6ers would make an attempt at paying attention. Their minds only seemed to value immediate rewards or events established in "real time"; weeklong projects to them seemed to be part of some obscure, distant fantasy.

On the other side of the coin, I have taught youth that have come from poor economic backgrounds that have valiantly struggled onward and earned valid high academic honors. Poverty is not the sole contributor to misbehavior and delinquency. Inadequate social experiences and maltreatment at home are the most active producers of what constitutes abnormal *student* behavior.

John Dewey's noble philosophy is least effective in urban school battlefields. The *students'* negative home environment (where seventy-percent of the *children* are raised in single-parent-homes) destroys more than the idealistic school environment constructs. And the urban ghettos' social sicknesses are rapidly invading America's pristine suburbs, and everyone is supposed to accept *that* threatening demographic pattern as the normal evolution of *democratic* education and of American *democracy*.

But in spite of the staggering 8-6 reality, educational alchemists consecrate new, loony theoretical formulas, and after fifty years of failure under the faulty John Dewey experimental "Learn by doing" model, the omnipotent Educational Aristocracy still aggressively peddles second-rate elixirs that have the remedial effect of Professor Trenoff's Cure-All Tonic.

If modern education was really working, then functional illiterates would not be graduating from high schools, then regular attendance would be evident in urban schools, and then *students* would be educating and rehabilitating their derelict, dysfunctional parents. American education desperately needs more practicality, more pragmatism, and less fantasizing with utopian idealism supported by anemic terminology like "cooperative learning" and "*democratic* education in the comprehensive high school".

Disciplining the 8-6ers was a terribly formidable chore. I felt that I had salvaged an excellent lesson if I had prevented widespread vandalism and pandemonium from occurring during a second period English seminar. Yelling at the 8-6ers had little or no impact. Most of the *students* in that inglorious section were brutally beaten, or emotionally abused, or completely ignored at home.

Eventually, each member of the 8-6's would search-out and discover his or her viable niche in adult life. From past experience with the 8-6-type of *students*, I knew that Ted B. couldn't add and subtract, but the restless perpetrator would eventually find a low-paying job as a clerk at a local convenience store. Maybe Jose R. couldn't speak English fluently, but the amorous Casanova would encounter little trouble working at a local pizzaria where the knowledge of only around two hundred essential words would be needed to get by.

American education walks all the way out to left field when its basic premise flirts with the notion that Ted B. should have the opportunity to become a brilliant mathematician, and Jose R. should have the right to become a nuclear scientist. If Ted B. or Jose R. ever decided to buckle-down and aim to achieve those particular goals, then *they* would finally apply themselves and work towards them.

Until the individual *student* becomes serious about his or her future, current educational theory is simply waiting for ludicrous miracles to materialize. The miracles won't happen because of pie-in-the-sky theory; they will only occur when the *student* decides to improve himself' or herself. And when *democratic* education is not out in left field, it is completely out of the stadium.

I found myself closing my eyes and envisioning the proud heritage of heralded teachers that had gloriously preceded my small contributions in history: Socrates, Plato, Aristotle, Thomas Aquinas, and Galileo. The catalogue of names clicked-off in a very pleasing mental newsreel. And then I would open my eyes and perceive the 8-6ers sitting and wiggling about before me. 'My God!' I would think. 'What would Socrates do if the great philosopher were exposed to this daily cruel tribulation? Swallow-down the poisonous hemlock a lot sooner than he did, I'll bet!'

Nothing is more fruitless or frustrating than asking a very serious question and then recognizing a *student* eagerly swinging his or her arm. The teacher calls on the hungry learner thirsting for knowledge only to hear, "Can I go to the bathroom?" "Can I sharpen my pencil?" "When's this stupid period over?"

Many of the 8-6ers were analogous to the Epsilons in Aldous Huxley's *Brave New World*. The unfortunate creatures knew little above the biological functions of eating, sleeping, going to the bathroom, and thinking about having sex. Sharpening a pencil or watching the clock became the great highlights of the pathetic 8-6ers' school day.

Educators should scrap the "self-fulfilling prophecy" theory and endorse the "home fulfilling reality" axiom, which regrettably is the biggest deterrent to normal *child* growth and contemporary development. When *children* are sociologically and psychologically dysfunctional, then the fault for failing to *academically* educate them should not be consigned to public school teachers.

Guidance counselors complain that *students* are taking Algebra I that couldn't pass refresher Math' the year before. *Students* that are deficient in English skills are taking Italian I, and Hispanic *students* are taking Spanish I even though many of them can't distinguish between a *si* and a *siesta*.

An obstinate parent can dictate the courses he or she wants his or her child to take, regardless of standardized test scores, teacher evaluations and grades that obviously contradict and oppose the parent's judgment and demand. The school officials know that the *student* and the course and/or curriculum are mismatched, but the school brass can do little about reversing the parent's wish.

Standardized tests should be given to pupils at the end of the eighth-grade year to determine each *student's* intelligence, skill level, and personal interests. Curriculum offerings should be synchronized to those specific criteria. Because that kind of "sorting-out" system is used in European schools, U.S. educators think that the weeding-out process is un-American. And so, high schools in this country worry that some unknown *child* will accidentally fall between the cracks and have his or her potential stifled because we have deprived the *student* and his influential parents of his or her freedom of choice.

Experts fear that a "late bloomer" aspiring to be in the academic curriculum might somehow be misplaced and doomed to toil in the wrong "vocational curriculum". Meanwhile, the entire system suffers because everyone's energies are focused on the unidentified few and not geared to caring one fragile iota about the needy majority. Schools and teachers should decide what is best for each *child* and not an obstinate lay parent who doesn't want his or her son or daughter stigmatized learning a skill in a vocational curriculum. More emphasis must be placed on the fact that blue-collar employment and trades' self-employment are honorable pursuits. A good plumber can make a lot more than a good teacher earns. Once bored *children* are removed from academic subjects and placed in vocational curriculums more attuned to their interests and aptitudes, then *academic* standards would improve, and grade-level norms could be maintained through free enterprise and promoting real competition among the best intellectually gifted *students*.

Instead of trying to unlock a *student's* social shell, let's provide less academically-inclined *children* with a *trade skill* that he or she can be proud of. If a self-employed contractor can make two hundred thousand dollars a year digging cesspools, his or her social acceptance will automatically follow his or her financial success.

An older English teacher back' in the '70s once told a *student*, "You'll never amount to anything; even if you attempt to go to college after high school!" That negative comment eventually motivated the *student* to start his own road paving business after working for an asphalt company for several years. That former *student* did not attend college, and is now one of the wealthiest people in the community, a great benefactor of the school district, and a past president of the local board of education. So, vocational education for forty-percent of the *student* population is a positive, viable alternative to academic education for everyone from the seventh grade on up.

American education must abandon its artificial goal of developing a society of future (unskilled) citizens possessing beautiful personalities. Plenty of students in the 8-6 class couldn't read or write but might be able to repair automobile engines or cut hair if given the opportunity to learn those trades at an earlier age. Forget trying to make Shakespeare, Washington Irving and Arthur Conan Doyle relevant to 8-6ers. If a child has a narrow skill level "reception window" to begin with, it is rather futile and absurd to be squeezing sophisticated literature stories and complex sentence structures through the 8-6ers tiny keyhole perspectives.

So, when an 8-6 *student* sputtered-out the monolithic phrase, "What does this crap have to do with me?" I had to defend *academics* by replying, "This is enrichment that I offer you. If I teach you what you already know (your interests), you'll never learn or study anything new!"

"But I want to study rap, or rock and roll lyrics!" the *student* might argue and exclaim. "That's what I really like!"

"O. Henry is not supposed to relate to what you already know," I would explain. "This story's meaning is designed to add to what little you do know! It is fundamental cultural knowledge that you presently lack! The plot will enhance your comprehension of the actual world that's out there!"

When confronted with a gallery of *students* like those in the 8-6 class, their every proclivity was directed toward stripping the teacher and his classroom of dignity and then establishing the negative home environment as the new norm in the classroom. No teacher should ever be exposed to a class like that one I've just described, but many are, and somehow, the purveyors of subject matter manage to persevere because the breadwinners must put food on the dinner table and pay their debts. Mischievous *students* are tolerable, but malicious, repulsive demons definitely are not.

The average anguished teacher given an assignment such as the 8-6 class will probably risk losing his or her job at least ten times during *that* year. If the teacher becomes intimidated, discouraged, defeated or disillusioned, then the *students* will sense victory and go for the kill. Teenagers are affected by conformity and by rebellion, but unfortunately, the devil-may-care 8-6er-type *students* are conforming to peer expectations and rebelling against adult and teacher authority. That's the plain simple truth of those troublesome teenage years.

But despite this valid conclusion based on thirty-four years of dedicated service, the Educational Aristocracy (consisting mostly of administrators that taught on the average of five to ten years and wanted out of the classroom to make more money) still preaches the impractical folly of its beliefs.

Looking back on my career, I prided myself' on refusing to surrender my heart and soul on the altar of popular educational theory simply to ascend the power staircase to the level of administrator, guidance director, or college professor. I never succumbed to the perpetual brainwashing given to teachers at college workshops and at county curriculum conclaves, even though many of my colleagues have endorsed the principles of contemporary school philosophy, psychology, and management.

But still, the educational mill grinds-on with more emphasis on quantity production than on quality control. New jargon is constantly being introduced to confuse critics and the general public, but the same inferior, dye-in-the-wool product is yielded. That's why our American educational system is basically "run of the mill".

At any rate, I did manage to make it through that crazy year of teaching, even with myriad daily conflicts with the second period 8-6 terrorists. One of the 8-6ers made it through a trade school after high school graduation and is currently my plumber earning a more than handsome self-employed salary. It was too bad that that former 8-6 *student* had to struggle through academic English rather than get background in working with his hands and doing what he liked.

The mildness of the summer winds had erased the negative memories of the 8-6 class, and a new bevy of seventh grade paragons was spiraling their way up to my jurisdiction. There would be another 8-6 class, but it could not compare to the one I had to teach during *that* unforgettable school year. On the last June day of school, I recall thinking, 'Thank God for aspirins and Alka-Seltzer'! I was never so happy to see the summer months arrive! In ten short weeks, another batch of a hundred and thirty *students* would be ascending into eighth-grade English class. I needed to be well-rested to be equal to the approaching September challenge.

Chapter 29
"The Teacher's Lowly Legacy"

Throughout my teaching career, I found that with each passing year, I was becoming more and more sympathetic with the "women's liberation movement". The earliest American public-school teachers were predominantly women, and today's teachers are often viewed and judged by the public from women teachers' stereotypes that had originated from the late 1800's and early 1900s. So, there are numerous connections between modern-day teacher serfdom and the exploitation of women (and women teachers) in pre-*World War I* American history.

Women had it really rough before the inventions of the *Industrial Revolution* provided machines to make kitchen and housework easier. A supper meal that required four hours to prepare after the *Civil War* era could be served in less than sixty-minutes in the early 1940s. Women were the custodians of the family children while their husbands, fathers and brothers ventured-out of the house to earn money for basic needs and to cover household expenses.

In the 1850s, women became active in the *Underground Railroad* and helped smuggle slaves through a network of secret stations and house cellars from the south into northern slave-free states. While considering the plight of the lowly "Negroes", many late 19th Century white women realized that *their* forsaken position in the American socio/economic/political power structure was in many ways comparable to that of the former black slaves. And because of childbearing complications, breast cancer, and the general drudgeries associated with women's daily travails, many enterprising male pioneers heading westward in their Conestoga wagons managed to outlive three different wives in *their* lifetimes.

American women's rather terrible post-*Civil War* depravation is epitomized in the fact that the suppressed male Negro obtained *his* civil rights and his right to vote with the passage of the *15th Amendment* in 1870. Women (white or otherwise) were not granted the right to vote until Congress put the *19th Amendment* into law in 1920, a full half-century after black men had been conferred the sacred franchise.

And so, the *Great Depression* generation of female teachers emerged from the monotonous and very difficult existence of early twentieth century women. The lady teachers were stern taskmasters that demanded excellence from their *students*. The schoolmarms were often spinsters providing for their own welfare. They loyally performed many different job responsibilities in one and two-room schoolhouses in rural American towns and villages. They often chopped firewood, stoked the fires in potbelly stoves, cleaned the desks and blackboards, mopped and swept the planked floors, and took home meager wages for their exhaustive labors. I remember three such two-room leftover schoolhouses in my community from my early childhood, and my maternal grandmother and my mother had attended two of them.

The first, second and *third (ranging from the Industrial Revolution* to *the Great Depression)* generations of predominantly women teachers were also janitors, cleaning women, mentors, and *principal teachers* in their schools. And from *that* origin, the idea of the chief school administrator emerged as being the *principal* person in the building. The adjective *principal* in time changed into the noun *Principal*. With the exception of Washington Irving's cowardly character Ichabod Crane, a modern male teacher can't really identify with too many masculine pedagogues involved in community schoolhouse education from 1787 to 1930.

Since most American teachers were women before and immediately after the *Great Depression of 1929,* there exists little doubt in my mind explaining why today's public values teachers about as much as it values dinosaur eggs or obsolete horse and buggies. The subordinate roles and tasks associated with women's exploitation (from the late 1700s up to 1940) are how the modern-day public inaccurately conceives and perceives school teaching and schoolteachers.

And I should pay homage to social crusaders Susan B. Anthony and to Elizabeth Cady Stanton, suffragettes of the post-*World War I* era as heroines of the women's liberation movement of the early 1920s, which is currently and belatedly triggering the teachers' liberation movement over eight decades later.

In addition to the rigors of childbearing and family raising, women were flagrantly encumbered to perform infinite household tedium: washing and ironing the clothes, baking the bread, grinding the cornmeal, sewing holes in shirts and pants, and churning the butter, just to name a few of the manifold chores. In the distant American past, women and wives definitely had a much harsher existence than men and husbands had.

If a woman was fortunate enough to find a man and get married, she was expected to be a faithful spouse who was especially loyal to her husband's whims and fancies. Women were virtually the dependent property of their husbands, more their squires, valets and chattels than being the man's marital partner. The word *partner* suggests "equality in rank", but in the early 1900s, women had not yet achieved that lofty station in societal or in family organization.

In the early 1900s, women were denied the *right* to vote, were often excluded from owning property, and were not permitted to divorce from *Holy Matrimony* obligations without the mutual consent of their *privileged* husbands. Essentially, the members of the fairer sex were completely subordinate to their husbands' success for *them* to be able to achieve any high degree of community status or national prominence.

Marriage was often a financial "work arrangement" for the female rather than a covenant based on mutual devotion and love. And if the lady of the house was not exploited by her husband's demands, she was probably efficiently used and exploited when employed in a clerical capacity or factory assembly line position by the male-dominated economic/industrial power structure of the time.

The only redeeming feature of such a male-oriented turn-of-the-century civilization was the fact that divorces were kept to a minimum, and children usually had a devoted mother in the house to bring stability to the family. As a result, greater family cohesiveness existed in the early 1900s than today, where nearly half of marriages end in separation or in divorce. A negative result of women's liberation has been its contribution to the high divorce rate, which in turn contributes greatly toward social disorganization and *student* dysfunction in today's *democratic* public schools.

Women (before, during, and after *WW I)* were compelled by Puritanical WASP morality to wear uncomfortable, cumbersome clothing ranging from dresses to bathing suits in order to sheath their alluring figures from men's wandering eyes. If a couple was without children, a wife might have supplemented her husband's income by obediently toiling long hours in unsanitary shop conditions in obscure garment and clothing factory basements. So, the legacy of the modern teacher is an outgrowth of the dismal history of women in the United States up until the post '50s *Korean War* period.

World War II contributed significantly to the women's growing independence movement. With American men in the military overseas fighting the Japanese along with battling Mussolini and Hitler's minions in Europe, women assisted in the war effort's cause by working in factories helping to assemble tanks and airplanes. Women soon realized that *they* could do the work of men if need be, and *that* particular liberating and revolutionary gender confidence has remained with us since the year 1942 up to the present modern atomic/computer age.

When the public thinks of a teacher, the image is one of an obedient-but-austere, scrawny, wrinkled, old shrew wearing a woolen shawl and sporting a cheap pair of bifocals on the bridge of her nose. The old dame rebukes ornery *children* who are very much afraid of her for her propensity to often use a ruler on an errant *student's* knuckles. The schoolmarms doing the scolding never thought twice about applying a birch switch across someone's hindquarters (this was before liberals and lawmakers thought-up the idea of corporal punishment as a wicked crime against *children*).

The predictable old dames hoarded every precious penny the parsimonious board of education was willing to dispense for their services. And if times were really tough like those during war or economic depression, the old spinsters would gratefully accept payment in script to sell or barter items at town businesses that gladly accepted board of education IOUs.

The plight of the modern-day teacher can be directly traced to the past exploitation of women and the schoolmarm's blind obedience to arbitrary community authority. Married women teachers have always merely supplemented their husbands' salaries. Because the lady instructors had throughout history shown intense fidelity to both their spouses and to the local board of education, female teachers were in effect "married to their jobs" as well as to their husbands. The village and town dames were too indoctrinated to *subordination,* both at home and at work, to openly campaign for teacher rights and teacher professionalism, and thus never dared to be *insubordinate.*

Salaries in high school districts are invariably higher today than those in kindergarten-to-twelve school systems because high school faculties generally have a greater percentage of men than elementary school faculties do. Men are still regarded as the main breadwinners in the household, so advances in salaries have been greatly generated from more males entering the *"noble profession".*

And so, when teachers negotiate to be compensated for after school curriculum revision, Office Detention remuneration, and stipends for parent conference nights, the redundant community reactionary-clichés are, "What's wrong with you teachers? How come you're not as *dedicated* as you used to be?" Even my brother-in-law has often teased me by laughingly saying, "John, you have a woman's job!"

When the American public speaks of teacher dedication, I think the word should be spelled *dead*ication. The taxpayers mean by *dedication* the legacy of women teachers subserviently conforming to and obeying traditional school board policy that actually might be exploitive and arbitrary in nature.

In American education, the word "dedication" means voluntarily doing something extra without getting paid for it. I have known scores of *dedicated* teachers that have spent hours at work before school and other hours after the dismissal bell tutoring *students*, preparing lessons, and running off worksheets. Some staff members even come in during the summer for a full week without pay to construct bulletin boards, to prepare classrooms, and to run-off worksheets without any additional remuneration.

But the public should not be too infatuated with that word *dedication*. A good teacher must first be effective, must second be efficient, and must third be dedicated in that particular order. Dedication in itself does not make a good teacher. The word is really a dusty anachronism carried over from the "Good Old Summertime" days around 1920 when women finally obtained the right to vote. I don't believe that too many "flappers" doing the *Charleston* in a speak-easy at night were also dedicated schoolmarms during the day.

The American public still maintains a very classic, defective interpretation of *dedication* that today amounts to robotically performing contemporary teacher serfdom. The two-century old perception of schoolmarms directly stems from colonial educational feudalism. Teachers were regarded as *public servants,* and the *vassals* were treated as if they were the domestic (old) maids of America's former colonial school systems. Sometimes, I think that three sacks of potatoes commanded more social recognition than a teacher did back in the 17', 18' and early 1900s.

I found it hard to comprehend how I (a member of the masculine gender) had been victimized by over two centuries of male chauvinism (against women) for thinking that a "woman's job" was "my profession". Like most of my male colleagues, I had deeply resented being viewed as a wrinkled-up, masochistic shrew being used as a community doormat and being labeled "unprofessional" when I objected to being assigned additional responsibilities without adequate compensation.

Today's American teachers possess the education of an aristocrat while receiving a proletarian's starting salary. The teachers happen to constitute the intellectual hub of the community. They know more about Machiavelli than members of town council do! Teachers know more about Colbert's theory of mercantilism than the town merchants do! They know all about Montessori methods and

Maslow's hierarchy of thinking just like the school board president ought to know, but probably doesn't! But teachers occupy the bottom of the school power pyramid and also the base of the town totem pole, principally because of tarnished images still haunting their existence still evolving from the nineteenth century.

Board of education members feel it incumbent upon themselves to emanate the reservoir of animosity that the taxpayers have toward lowly teachers. A good rule for teachers to remember is to vote for school board candidates that make more money than the lowly serfs situated at the top of the school district's salary guide do. Those newly-elected, successful businessmen and professionals will be more sympathetic with the advancement of teacher professionalism than a school board member that makes less than a beginning teacher and resentfully wants to limit spending and curtail vital school activities paid for by local taxes.

I have been told by school board members at local association contract negotiations (when I was representing my *professional* organization), "If you don't like it here, you can go teach somewhere else!" That kind of acrimonious sentiment belongs more to the age of nickelodeons, of silent films and of steam locomotives than to this technological age of computers, cell phones and *DVDs*, but *that* basic hostility toward teachers is still active and latently floating around "out there in the community". Pessimistic and degrading comments like that one from board members show little regard for the dignity of the *professional* person being admonished, and the speaker of those condescending words looks upon the teacher as a *subordinate employee* rather than as a professional person. 'No wonder why the district has a high turnover rate of classroom personnel!' I realized.

Board of education members are quick to tell the Rotary Club, the Exchange Club, the Kiwanis and the Lions that they believe in "quality education at the lowest possible cost". Talk about speaking out of both sides of the mouth at the same time! Quality anything has its attendant price. A luxurious *Cadillac* costs more than a mundane *Ford,* so the trademark *Cadillac* communicates the idea of better quality than the name *Ford* does. Boards of education want to provide a *Cadillac* education at a cheap model *Ford's* price. And a lot of the school board members' attitudes towards its *professional* staff have their basis in the turn-of-the-century stereotype of the "dedicated", obedient spinster schoolmarm.

And how many times have I heard in the community, "If you're so smart, then why aren't you rich!" The secret inference present in *that* pathetic statement is that "Only wealthy people are intelligent". I have known members of town council and of the board of education that envision teachers as pompous, unimportant windbags having microscopic bank and stock portfolio accounts. In America, one's status and intelligence are often tantamount to one's accumulation of sensational wealth.

I have been to numerous community charity events and hospital balls, and the loudmouthed town big shots are always surrounded by a horde of faithful and obliging disciples. When I was cordially introduced to several town bigwigs, the atmosphere of insensitivity was far too perceptible. But when the illustrious town tycoons discovered that I was also a businessman with boardwalk stores in Ocean City, Maryland and in Rehoboth Beach, Delaware, suddenly I seemed more interesting and worthy of acceptance than when I was simply attending the event as a mere, low-echelon, *academic* person.

At first (at the community's hospital charity ball), I had the impression that my parents must have been the Boston Strangler and Lucretia Borgia, but after I had been identified as a boardwalk businessman, I was held in much higher regard. I no longer was the 1900s spinster schoolmarm and dedicated serf working and slaving in a scholastic fiefdom.

Part of the community "image problem" is caused by teachers not doing anything about changing the erroneous public perception of *their* struggling profession. Teachers should daily strive to eradicate the false generalizations that people think the instructional *employees* should only work with children, and that the teacher's power is limited to the school building, and that a teacher's prowess only involves jurisdiction over *children*. I have been president of my town's Lions Club, a successful businessman, and an author of international repute. And on occasion, I write a monthly op/ed column in one of my town's newspapers. My activities outside education have changed the local community's perception of me as simply being a radical teacher trying to cost taxpayers more money.

Despite the general abuse that teachers experience from certain *students* and their distrustful parents, a cross-section of society still thinks and believes that teachers are grossly overpaid. The average person that is now a teacher devoted four years of arduous college preparation wrestling with the philosophical advances of Piaget, Bruner, and Thorndike while investing (or borrowing) around sixty thousand dollars to finally become fully certified. While working fulltime toward a teaching degree, the prospective educator could have been laboring somewhere else and thus making at least fifty thousand dollars a year doing menial work instead of experiencing the expensive college scene.

Simple arithmetic produces a unique sum:

- Five years of college to get a master's degree: $100,000

- Five years of menial work sacrificed to get an education: $100,000

Many states require teachers to have "Master's Degrees" before ever starting their careers. The total cost investment plus the loss in salary at doing other occupations while preparing to be an educator comes to around two-hundred-thousand-dollars, or around five times the average teacher's beginning salary *before* taxes.

Now I maintain that the prospective teacher had not made a very clever investment (either time-wise or money-wise) when one considers the overall *student* abuse, the financial hardships, the cost of raising a family, the community attitudes toward teachers as spinster schoolmarms, and the oodles of Joe Dodges just waiting for the next "kill" opportunity. Throw into the complex mix the concept of "Educational Socialism" rapidly contaminating all facets of "American Academic Democratic Education", and then seriously consider, weighing the prospect of achieving Quality Education being practiced in U.S. Public Schools from Grades K-12, a development has been quite diminished over the past half-century.

Chapter 30
"The Teacher and the Community"

Every school year, the junior-senior high school devoted two nights for "Open House" where teachers came into direct contact with parents. The first meeting (usually in September) was where the parents followed their *children's* daily schedule and attended each subject class for ten minutes. The instructors had to describe to the six classes of parents the curriculum, the textbooks used, the homework and testing policies, the *student* absentee procedures and the classroom rules all in six separate ten-minute intervals.

The second "Open House" was a little more trying and nerve-racking than the first one, and it usually occurred in November. The parents stood outside my English classroom in a long irregular line waiting to have a conference with the teacher about their son on daughter's first marking period report card grade. Five minutes were allotted for each conference, and I sometimes kept an already-set alarm clock placed on my desk to make certain that the conference didn't go overtime.

In that abbreviated five-minute time span, I had to relate the *child's* academic performance, test grades, social behavior and good and bad work habits. If a more comprehensive conference were necessary, I would advise the plaintiff parent to visit the guidance office and set one up during my *PPSA* (Planning, Preparation and Special Assignment period).

Now, here's where the second "Open House" conference night was absolutely unprofessional. First of all, it was done gratis without any teacher being paid. Secondly, fifty or so tedious conferences would take place back-to-back in one evening. At the end of the night, my fatigued brain didn't know whom I was speaking with or about whom I was speaking about, and I really didn't care.

Many impious moms and dads would eavesdrop (at the front door outside the classroom) on another parent's conference that was still in progress. And while I would be focused on a specific child and communicating to the parent his or her strengths and weaknesses, a raucous gossiping throng would be chattering-away out in the hallway, their conversations continually interrupting the teacher's concentration. The constant babble and the intense pressure were truly disturbing factors that did not promote the discussion of anything, let alone a *child's* progress. The din emanating from outside the room sounded more like a Noise Pollution Convention than like a collection of concerned parents.

It was interesting to note that out of the fifty stressful conferences on a normal "Open House" night, very few were with the parents or guardians of any 8-6 *student*. Some of the more assertive moms and dads waiting outside would deliberately grunt or audibly clear their throats to suggest to the teacher ending-up a conference that the allotted time had expired for the discussion-in-progress. What doctor, lawyer, accountant or other *professional* person would expose himself or herself to a farce like the one I am describing?

The teacher (according to the 19th Century schoolmarm tradition) rendered his or her service for free, while other professionals like doctors and lawyers are paid fantastic stipends for their consultation fees when the same parents happen to be patients or clients. Usually, only the parents having A and B average honor roll *students* show-up on conference night to hear the teachers loquaciously praise their special progenies.

A teacher seldom sees the parents of the *children* that are failing on the "Open House" night. Sometimes a parent holding a grudge will show-up and attempt to ruffle the instructor's feathers, so I would immediately direct that peeved mom or dad (or both) to the guidance office to schedule a (hostile) conference.

The teachers' manual (*Bible*) explicitly states that each *student* is a "public relations person" that goes home and reports to his or her parents everything ordinary and everything extraordinary that had happened during the school day. A most peculiar checks and balances' system exists where the *students* report to their attentive parents what they think of their teachers; next the interfering parents call the administration and the guidance counselors to report the alleged teacher malpractice, even if the alleged incident happened with another child other than theirs.

The mindful administrator arranges to have a meeting with the teacher and firmly reminds him or her that the entire school must reflect the attitudes and values of the community, which just happen to be the opinions, complaints and beefs of parents whose sole source of information had originated from the mouths of unreliable *children*. And the *child* might have inaccurately reported the information to the parent because he or she doesn't like the teacher, or perhaps he or she believes that one of *their* friends had been disciplined unfairly.

Many schools operate under the following premise: Forget about developing new supportive and constructive community attitudes about teachers, but instead, worry about the next distasteful phone conversation with an irate, incensed, incoherent parent who was not a witness to anything.

Conferences with parents at times can be amusing. Once on the November Open House Night I was discussing a *student's* grades and behavior with his jittery mother. "It seems that your son at times is absent-minded and loses track of what he's doing!" I diplomatically commented to the mother instead of telling her that her *child* was a confirmed space cadet.

After the conference finally terminated, the mother angrily got-up from her chair to leave the room. My classroom had two doors located to the right. The first one with the vertical glass panel led to the corridor, and the second portal opened into the room's closet. After listening to me talk about her son's lack of concentration, the perturbed mother opened the closet door while still speaking to me, exited inside the confined room, and then closed the door behind her.

Apparently, the mother was claustrophobic or frightened by darkness (or both), because she wildly pounded the door screaming to be released from her pitch-black confinement. When I opened the door and let the woman out of the closet and into the classroom's bright light, the crazed mother nastily blamed me for not showing her the exact door from which to exit the room.

One popular community criticism is that teachers only work a ten- month-year. Construction workers in northern climes also work a ten-month-year but are eligible to collect unemployment benefits when they are not on the job. Since teachers are *contract* employees, they can't collect unemployment, and they get no paid vacation or holiday time, and the employees are only paid for the hundred and eighty-three days that are stipulated in the master teacher contract.

Public school teaching is not the lark that the opinionated public thinks it is. The only thing greener on the teacher side of the fence is the slime that the instructors must contend with daily. Teaching is a *job* that is accompanied by unforeseen conflicts and situations that crop up out of nowhere. "The rightful definition of the word *job* is: J.O.B: Just Over Broke.

Children like the 8-6ers constantly tax a teacher's patience and emotional fortitude, and in addition, the profession will inevitably incarcerate its practitioner inside the plebeian economic bracket. Many beginning teachers with three children and a wife that is also a housekeeper would be better-off on welfare once free lunches and food stamps are factored into the equation.

I shudder every time my eyes see a distraught substitute teacher frantically seeking the nearest exit at the end of the school day. Her (or his) eyes are rotating like the spinning lemons and cherries on a slot machine's reels. The hard truth is that public school teaching is far-removed from the serenity of the mythical Elysian Fields.

Unlike many of my modest teaching comrades, I have had the opportunity to engage in other fields of endeavor besides education. I have driven trucks, farmed, operated retail fruit and vegetable farm markets, and owned and worked in boardwalk arcades and souvenir merchandise stores in three beach resorts. None of the above work situations could compare with the rigors of teaching a hundred and thirty *students* a day in an American public school.

In other lines of work, a person simply does his or her responsibility but doesn't have to worry about being buffeted about by nasty *children*, by WASPish livid parents, by conciliatory-to-parents administrators, and by narrow-minded, bullheaded boards of education members representing frugal taxpayers.

I have worked twelve-hour-days as a summer field manager on the largest cultivated blueberry farm in the world and have labored sixteen-hour-days on the Ocean City, Maryland boardwalk, but neither of those two responsibilities could compare to the pressure and aggravation a teacher feels most every day. Seven hours in a public school is plenty more frustration and anxiety than sixteen hours operating a boardwalk arcade, or twelve hours managing a thirteen-hundred-acre blueberry plantation.

In American education, the baffled teacher often feels as if he or she is an academic ping-pong ball with *students* and parents slamming him or her on one side of the small tennis table, and with administrators and boards of education pundits next swatting him or her onto the other side of the net.

Lawyers, doctors, pharmacists and accountants are *specialists,* but in contrast, the powerless teachers are *generalists*. When the public refers to a doctor or lawyer as being *professional,* the speakers are alluding to what the physician and the attorney are right *now.* When the public refers to teachers as *professionals,* the citizens are basically describing and thinking-about what lowly schoolmarms *were* doing a full century ago.

The public considers the doctor a professional person because people attribute to him or her a mystical-supernatural control over the mysteries of life and death. The public virtually deifies doctors to

Olympian status, and therefore, he or she wearing the stethoscope is entitled to all of the money he or she can grab while actively functioning in a private business practice.

The public views the attorney as a shrewd "word manipulator" that can cleverly represent plaintiffs and defendants, and who can ingeniously interpret laws and twist the outcome of justice by being articulate and convincing while eloquently speaking in court. By being knowledgeable and tricky, lawyers are entitled to all of the money the barristers can gather while profiting and owning their law firms. When the public assesses the value of teachers, they visualize second-class knaves that want higher taxes to easily better their subterranean station in life.

The only real professionalism I had observed in my three and a half-decade career was manifested in the pride a teacher took in the preparation and presentation of his or her lessons, and with me observing the admiration existing between teachers for each other's efforts. Professionalism in teaching is evident internally among the staff members and not externally coming from loyal community appreciation and recognition. The folks in the community equated teacher professionalism with nineteenth century schoolmarm bondage, and *that* hideous reality makes the teachers' social and economic predicament vastly incompatible with the all-too-expensive leisure time and costly luxuries of this exciting space age.

Even other professional people serving on the board of education advocated archaic discriminations against public school teachers. A medical doctor on the board of education might vote against teacher aides in the classroom and elsewhere in the school, even though he himself maintains a secretary for bookkeeping, a receptionist for greeting patients, and a technical assistant or attendant nurse to help with the dispensation of minor medical details. The professional doctor needs at least three assistants to deal with one patient at a time in his or her office. And the teacher is forbidden to have one aide to help him or her with a hundred and thirty *students,* and to assist him or her in running the cafeteria with as many as three hundred hyperactive *children* wailing away. Obviously, the medical doctor is specialized and the doomed teacher is to remain generalized.

"Never live in the community in which *you* teach" happens to constitute some very sound advice. A teacher's social activities and business in the community are constantly under public surveillance. Members of the public keep the teacher under scrutiny and gossip about how many martinis or beers he or she had consumed at civic club dinners or at private parties.

And if a parent that doesn't like what you've done to his or her *child* is present at said dinners or parties, mom or dad will seek-out allies and gossip incessantly with their comrades about *your* assumed negligence. They will chat about the teacher's lack of character or about insensitive discipline methods, and now the English or Science instructor has new enemies that are friends and acquaintances of people that can't stand him or her. The public is always quick to criticize and slow to praise.

On one particular day, I had received permission from the principal to leave school when the *students* were exiting the building to climb aboard their yellow buses. A vigilant parent noted my departure leaving early with the *students'* dismissal. I had a doctor's appointment out of town. The over-alert mother reported me as a renegade teacher to one of the school guidance counselors. When the subject came-up upon my next visit to the guidance department, I proceeded to lose my cool and aggressively chastised the dumbfounded counselor. "Look," I shouted. "I had permission from the principal to leave the building early."

"I just wanted to tell you that someone was watching you!" the concerned guidance counselor defensively-but-politely answered. "Your activity leaving the premises was under surveillance!"

"Well, I really don't care if that nosy mother knows members of the board of education or not!" I ranted. "And you can tell your friend, the scuttle-butting parent, to be on the lookout for obnoxious *student* behavior rather than doing unauthorized, military reconnaissance on teachers leaving the damned building. And make sure you explicitly tell the spy I told you that!" I hollered. "And if she doesn't like it, she can come in and see me, because I'm pretty damned mad about her unwarranted scrutiny right now! I resent being treated or talked about as if I'm a friggin' fugitive!"

Teachers must exhibit courtly decorum at community dinners, at social functions and at local smorgasbords and barbecues. If a male teacher is seen entering a town bar unaccompanied, he ought to be prepared explaining why he was out looking to tie-one-on or searching for a one-night Delilah when he should be home correcting papers, or selecting the words for tomorrow's big vocabulary test. And even if a beginning teacher's salary could only afford a *Salvation Army* type of wardrobe, the community expects him or her to dress like an *Esquire* or *Vogue* model.

I once had to leave school during my lunch period to make an important transaction at a local bank. After resting my left-arm upon the marble ledge in front of the teller's window, an inquisitive stranger came-up to me and initiated an odd conversation. The elderly man clandestinely whispered, "Aren't you supposed to be in school this afternoon?"

'My God! Doesn't this old fellow know that this is 1972?' I thought. I replied to my curious, anonymous interrogator, "My personal life is none of your damned business!" I criticized my public observer. "As far as you may know, I might be on my lunch break, I might have taken a personal day off from school, or I might be conducting official school business!"

The old man raised his eyebrows and then stammered, "You'll hear about your rudeness, young man!" the elderly gent answered in a very insulted tone of voice. "I don't know what's wrong with you teachers now-a-days!"

"Be sure to tell the superintendent in addition to reporting me to the principal!" I vehemently returned. "And after that, don't forget to call the governor and the president and tell them, too!"

The school administration is very uptight about what townspeople might be saying about a maverick member listed on their staff. The beginning of the school year faculty address usually always embodies the mandate, "If any teacher wants to leave the building, make sure you first *get permission* from the office." And then *that* edict is justified by further announcing, "In case you get an emergency phone call, we know where you are and when you'll be returning back!"

Professional people should just be expected to perform their professionalism and not be subjected to petty phobias about who had seen you in the corner drugstore, or sitting in the pizza fast food joint during lunchtime, or calculating how many *Southern Comforts* or *Jack Daniels* on the rocks the attending teacher had downed at the Veterans Ball.

Since teachers are the cognoscenti of any small community, their general roles should encompass more than simply delivering the upcoming generation's academic education. Teachers need to become proactive outside of their employment and run for town council seats, and if they should live outside the town where they teach, then instructors should be candidates for foreign board of education seats. If teachers can't improve education from inside a system, perhaps they can change school systems for the better by being board members in the system where they might reside.

Educators have anemic *professional* salaries, yet they are expected to set examples for *students* in dress, in character, and in behavior. A truck driver's wife can oftentimes dress more fashionably than a teacher's spouse can. In spite of the invention of flush toilets and electricity, many communities still insist that teachers wear conservative attire, and any sinister alteration of appearance such as a beard, a tie-less leisure suit, or a handlebar mustache might be regarded as emblematic of radicalism, or sporting revolutionary tendencies. Not only do the taxpayers' dollars procure less sophisticated clothing for teachers than the corporate dollars do for self-employed *professionals,* but also the loaves of bread are smaller and the slices of delicatessen meat tend to be cut thinner for teachers.

An educated classroom manager might know all about the *Peloponnesian War*, all about the literary merits of D.H. Lawrence and H.L. Mencken, and all about the veracity of the Malthusian Theory, and still have a checking account balance painted red and a financial future colored black. And most local badmouthing of teachers contains more baloney than the neighborhood delicatessen, but local gossipers will chew and then swallow every morsel of it.

The general public (being taxpayers) extends little empathy to the needs and problems of the average public-school teacher. When reminded of how challenging the art of teaching really is, a citizen is quick to switch the topic of conversation to a bad experience his or her sister-in-law's *child* had with a substitute teacher in Duluth, Minnesota. The public tends to become very inductive in always transferring or generalizing about negative episodes involving teachers, and as everyone knows, bad gossip travels at lightning speed when compared to snail-like good news.

Chapter 31
"Proud Parents"

Teachers serve more than an *academic* function in the community. They are also taxpayers, just like their major critics happen to be. Love doesn't always make the world go round; sometimes money does. The proprietor of the corner grocery store doesn't give a hoot about academics like the Pythagorean Theory, or the *Age of Enlightenment*. When a teacher buys a chicken pot-pie from the neighborhood grocery store owner, the appreciative businessman wants the teacher's greenbacks, and not his academic knowledge or his dedication.

Dedication is a wonderful attribute, but it cannot be chewed or swallowed. and it doesn't pay the rent, the mortgage or the electric bill. One never sees on *Action News* a teacher's *child* being shanghaied by kidnappers because most abductors are smart enough to know that the average teacher could never be able to pay the standard ransom. And so, teachers' *children* are usually safe from knowledgeable kidnappers.

Twentieth century *democracy* in education has been a dismal failure over the past fifty years. It has produced a society that features group socialism rather than a culture producing independent individuals who have attained Maslow's top-of-the-pyramid "self-actualization" level. Getting along with others in a sociological setting is emphasized much more in public schools than the idea of each *student* maturing into an *academically* oriented, autonomous human being. *Student* sociological adjustment must transcend academics in the modern American school.

The past five decades of John Dewey influenced "democratic education" has produced a batch of American citizens that have forfeited individual thinking for conformity to a group, company or civic organization's expectations. Most *students* that have graduated from public schools in the last fifty years have been "Pavlovianly" trained to acquiesce with their peers rather than educated to pursue self-realization by striving for life, liberty and happiness as prescribed by Thomas Jefferson, a great Founding Father that fully valued self-fulfillment and self-achievement.

And so, most of the non-thinking *students* of the past fifty years have now matured into the non-thinking adults of the present. These sociologically acclimated adults presently own businesses, serve on boards of education, complain of too much homework for their little

283

darlings, command officer positions in the *PTA,* and spend a good deal of time sitting in barber shops, in beauty parlors, and in taverns criticizing and demeaning teachers.

Schools today have to address gargantuan *student* social and psychological problems. Many classes like the aforementioned 8-6ers border on being maniacal and quasi-criminal. While schools are deluged with a cascade of unanswerable riddles, the *PTA* and/or the *Home-School Association* has its head buried in the sand. Instead of devoting its energies to *student* drug usage, *student* pregnancies, and *student* apathy, the *PTA* phlegmatically occupies itself with tureen suppers, with Founders' Day Dinners, and with banquets and hoagie sales to help send the marching band to San Diego, or the graduating senior class to *Disney World.*

The adults active in the *PTA* have been sociologically conditioned to value macaroni casseroles and Donald Duck over the real school problems that require immediate attention. Sociological behavior has been valued and emphasized over academic and intellectual development in our public schools, and most of this phenomenon can be directly attributed to *democratic* (socialistic) education in the comprehensive junior-senior high school.

A highlight of the school year for the *PTA* is the hallowed "teacher introduction night". The principal glibly reads-off the names of the faculty members in alphabetical order, and each instructor stands-up separately and is thoroughly and visually inspected by the parents seated in the audience. An undertone of chatter can be discerned as the anxious parents exchange cynical anecdotes and criticisms about each particular teacher.

The *PTA,* like the administration and the board of education, tries its best to avoid controversy because conflicting ideas cause the school system's image to have a bad public reputation. Instead of being concerned about the serious crises prevalent in public schools, most parents show-up on teacher-conference night to be praised and flattered about how *their* dynamic *child* is doing.

The parents of the discipline problem *student* or the slow-learner are seldom (if ever) seen by teachers on conference night. It is the parents of the well-behaved smarter *students* that mostly show their faces because those sociologically indoctrinated adults like to be delighted when hearing the teachers describe their *children* by utilizing streams of praising superlatives.

Most worthwhile innovations in education come from the bottom-up and not from the top-down. Teachers (at the base of the power pyramid) are the true innovators, the producers, the horsepower, and the real souls of the school system. As it is, American education is not improving but only artificially appearing to be doing so because of polished public relations' campaigns (propaganda) generated by administrators, by school board members, by positive-spin local newspaper articles, by state teachers' associations, and by *PTAs*.

The only way that teachers can ever become true professional people is for them to take over the management of schools and to disengage from parental influence over local school systems. Once the chains of antiquity are discarded, teachers will have finally been self-emancipated, and the true problems of American education can then be tackled and finally resolved.

As the present scenario dictates, parents, administrations, boards of education, educational philosophy, cloud-nine college professors, politicians, frugal taxpayers, teacher duties, and obnoxious *children* are the real hindrances impeding professional growth. A revolution in education is necessary to preserve the cherished American values of freedom and liberty balanced by personal responsibility. The entire hierarchal public education structure must be dismantled and then rebuilt with the new emphasis being placed on teachers instructing responsible *students* that really want to learn *academics*. Until that miracle happens, schools will remain *sociological holding platforms* and not authentic *academic institutions*.

As it is, teachers have a lengthy path to trek before they can achieve the community respect and honor that they so justly deserve. I heard once too many times fourteen-year-old *students* tell me, "Why should I listen to you? My father drives a dump truck and makes more money than you do. He must be smarter if he makes more than you!"

'Is your father literate enough to author fifty-five books?' I felt like retorting to each *student* but refrained from doing so. 'If it weren't for an *academic* education and a love for learning, I too would be a functional illiterate!' I should have replied each time.

If Allen Iverson could make a hundred times a teacher's salary dunking basketballs on fast breaks, then that's *his* business. But when *students* hypothesize that Allen Iverson must be a hundred times smarter than a teacher because of *his* fantastic basketball contract, then I feel that the individual teacher's worth has been unjustly maligned by our American materialistic civilization.

When John Q. Public finally realizes that "quality education" is an intelligent investment in the future, that smaller classes and teacher aides translate into better education, and that professional salaries and teacher recognition mean a better community, then teacher public prestige will finally parallel teacher self-esteem.

Many European countries invest a greater part of their gross national economy into their educational systems than America presently does. It's about time that Americans stopped complaining and started supporting the cost of "quality education", but first the system itself must be modified from *educational* to *academic* in order to function more effectively and efficiently.

Public schools today are now *"child*-centered" and not "teacher-centered" institutions as they had been up to the time of the *Korean War* in the early '50s. Families are now *"child*-centered" and not "parent oriented" as they should be. The underlying assumptions supporting all this societal madness can only lead to anarchy. Children are *not* adults, and the bulk of teenagers will never turn into responsible adults unless teachers and parents are respected as adult authority figures by the younger generation. We have to get back to "parent-centered families" and "teacher-centered classrooms" to save our American civilization.

The *child* must learn to fit-in and then identify his or her role inside the adult-centered home and in adult-centered school environments. *Children* that are raised to think that they are the entitled center of the universe have trouble later in life coping with the failure, with the rejection, and with the free enterprise and competition that the real world uses as measuring sticks of success.

In many households, parents are afraid of their teenagers because the kids had called the main shots ever since *they* had entered kindergarten. And now those same out-of-control *children* are intimidating peers and teachers in classrooms like the 8-6's, and when a teacher asserts his or her authority, an army of school personnel and vocal parents come to the spoiled *child's* defense.

This much-needed revolution in American education (and in society) can only be accomplished if teachers organized and exerted their intellectual muscle power. There are well-over two million teachers in the United States, and for the benefit of the nation, they could and should shut-down every school in the country in a mass concerted effort. The goals of the "educational revolution" would be to improve academics, to require *student* responsibility for learning, and to create an environment for teachers to finally become professional people by being recognized as *specialists* and not as generalists. The central focus of the "revolution" would be the promotion of "individual development", and not group conformity.

If parents want their *child's* teachers to be respectable and dignified role models worthy of pupil imitation, then they'll have to show more reverence for the respect and dignity of the teachers' image in the community. Every year American education loses thousands of very talented and competent instructors to industry, not only because of money issues, but also because of the non-professional aspects that teaching involves, along with a lack of community respect and support for mastering academics. Teachers are dedicated to their professions, but I honestly believe and maintain that in the final analysis, they are more dedicated to their families than to the *children* of other adults.

Despite the teachers' humble historical ancestry and his or her diminutive social rank in the community, they are expected to be charitable community leaders. If there is a hospital drive, the teachers will be called-upon to make large association donations and individual pledge contributions. When the *Red Cross Bloodmobile* cruises into town, teachers are expected to show that they're more red-blooded than the average citizen is.

And finally, most every proud parent is in his or her glory when eighth-grade graduation rolls around in June. Most schools don't honor the relic from the past and have dropped the archaic commencement exercise because just about every *student* now graduates high school. But even when my school system formed a junior-senior high (grades seven to twelve), it still kept the obsolete tradition of eighth-grade graduation because the parents wanted to see their little darlings dressed-up like adorable angels up on stage.

One full week of June school time is sacrificed while practicing and rehearsing for "the pageant extravaganza". During that challenging week, my consumption of aspirin and antacid tablets usually quadrupled. "Maybe some of the parents could assist in the graduation practice rehearsals," I suggested to the principal. "Then, the folks will see what the children are really like in real life rather than the little saints they view on graduation night!" Unfortunately, my noble recommendation fell upon deaf ears.

One full week of boring processional auditorium entrances and exits, a week of yanking rascally children out of line to be reprimanded, only to be placed back in line again, and soon even the more benevolent *students* became testy and irritable during the week-long ordeal.

The more scoundrel-type *students* actually enjoyed being kicked off the stage and leaving the sultry auditorium to visit the vice-principal in the air-conditioned Main Office. After a week of intensive rising and sitting, name list readings for receiving diplomas, and monotonous *student* speeches, the night of the annual gala finally arrived.

The *students* march into the auditorium to the venerable strains of "Pomp and Circumstance" to add a degree of majestic splendor to the ceremony. The already ninety-five-degree auditorium is roasting and brimming with proud parents, relatives and friends. As the *students* file-into the auditorium, they are systematically arranged from tallest to shortest order and are thus seated on the stage so that admiring family members can snap flash pictures with their cameras.

I chuckled each year when turning around from my front-row-seat and observing the parents fanning themselves incessantly with graduation programs. 'Now they're paying in terms of discomfort for not being willing to spend the money to air-condition the entire building!' I laughed. 'My classroom is abominable in September and in June, and I never received screens on my windows so that yellow jackets fly into the classroom and disturb my lessons every time I have to open the window!' I remember thinking. 'Air conditioning is a privilege enjoyed by the administrators, the guidance counselors, and their staffs'.

Surprisingly, even the Lucifers of the class look like they're celestial seraphim and cherubs at that special moment. As the program moves along through the *student* honor speeches and through the various awards' presentations, the event then culminates with the issuance of the coveted eighth-grade diplomas, the singular parchments available to anyone and everyone fourteen-years of age that happened to have attended the school that year.

The last row featuring the tallest *students* rises. The name of the *child* is read from the podium microphone, and the announcement is carried over loudspeakers to the delighted audience. A burst of spontaneous applause rises from the restless crowd when the principal reads off the first name. For all that the enthusiastic parents, relatives, and guests of *other students* know, the tallest kid in the class might have been a juvenile rapist or an avowed parent molester, but nevertheless, being called first elicits a tremendous ovation.

The parents indeed are proud of their *children's* achievement, which was really the teachers' survival achievement going unrecognized. I used to sit there thinking in the midst of the applause, 'I wonder what next year's 8-6 class is going to be like?'

Chapter 32
"Why Jimmy Brown Doesn't Write"

In 1972, I had read in local newspapers where the Federal Department of Education had blasted American public-school education for being responsible for declining standardized test scores. I had to chuckle when I read that one of the suggestions for improving the quality of education was to have the school year extended from a hundred and eighty to a whopping two hundred and ten days. As usual, quantity was the oversimplified solution where quality should have been the prime consideration.

Teachers know the real reasons for declining test scores while laboring inside the warped academic fishbowl and then looking-out. The present *democratic,* comprehensive, and infected American educational system (over the past fifty years) has generated massive waste and is grotesquely inefficient. For education to improve, certain simple basic steps need to be taken.

Students have to be sorted-out and then tracked into academic and into vocational curriculums after eighth-grade. Rigid academic standards must be maintained for the college preparation tracked *students*. Teacher duties must be eliminated so that the professional staff can have more direct interaction and more individual tutoring of faltering *students*. The fifty-to-seventy-five perpetual troublemakers that cause turmoil in the average-sized high school must be extracted out of the academic educational setting and placed either in the vocational curriculum at county high schools or in juvenile detention and custodial rehabilitation centers. Time consuming teacher duties should be handled by aides, and tough stints like the cafeteria (that require crowd control and the stoppage of fights) should be the responsibility of the local police department. And finally, teachers must become first and foremost respected *specialists*.

In 1972 I had driven to the town Pony League field to watch some of my fourteen-year-old *students* play baseball. I never really liked going to local public sporting events like organized baseball games because invariably, there would always be some parent that recognized my identity and then would give me a tin ear about how much expertise he or she had about schools and public education. Parents have always had the bad habit of trying to impress teachers when *they* automatically christen themselves official authorities on American public-school education.

I glanced-up at the home team bleachers and noticed four parents of *students* I had been teaching that particular year sitting up there masquerading as baseball fans. I discreetly decided to amble over to the visiting team's bleachers to quietly enjoy and view the game. No sooner had I parked my hindquarters on a wooden plank that Mrs. Brown, a very attractive and affable mom, climbed-up the bleacher steps and then occupied the space right next to me.

"Mr. Wiessner," Mrs. Brown began her introductory oration. "My son Jimmy has really learned a lot of literature, grammar and vocabulary in your English class!" she voluntarily complimented.

"Thank you very much!" I tersely answered while trying to suggest that I preferred to be an anonymous Pony League baseball fan rather than an itinerant English teacher at that specific time.

"But honestly, Mr. Wiessner," Mrs. Brown continued with a forced smile. "I do feel that you should have taught more writing lessons this year. As you certainly know, Jimmy is really weak in general composition writing."

"He's not in an Accelerated English class," I reminded Mrs. Brown. "Those *students* in my two Accelerated English sections write two dozen compositions every year. Jimmy's section writes two final drafts a marking period, and that comes to just eight every school year."

"Maybe Jimmy will have more writing in his ninth grade English class next year!" Mrs. Brown speculated while indirectly criticizing my writing teaching methods in my *general* English classes.

"You're right Mrs. Brown!" I hesitantly agreed. "Jimmy should have had more composition work this year." Then I thought, 'If Jimmy worked a degree harder and was in an accelerated class, he *would have had* sixteen more compositions to author,' but I smartly refrained and remained reticent to avoid antagonizing the overly concerned parent.

"Mrs. Brown, this school year I had almost burned myself out reading and correcting nearly three thousand compositions," I commented before clearing my throat. "And I already need reading glasses and have arthritis in both my hands!" That remark seemed to silence Mrs. Brown's attitude about my implied lazy work habits.

Mrs. Brown saw one of her lady friends ascending the visiting team's bleachers, so she very kindly excused herself to join her acquaintance, leaving me alone to ponder my most recent undesired, impromptu parent conference with a *grandstanding* mother.

'If only Mrs. Brown knew the entire truth rather than bits and pieces here and there!' I smiled and laughed to myself. 'Then her bogus opinion of the big picture might be a little more accurate than it is right now!'

Jimmy Brown's language problems begin, end, and revolve around two central facts. Jimmy was a well-behaved, above-average *student* who was well-liked and socially adjusted. Because of those sterling qualities, secondly Jimmy was an aspiring virtuoso who played saxophone in the school band. In my junior-senior high school where I was employed, band was the ultimate activity besides football. Influential people in the community valued band and athletics over *academics*. And so, the entire local value system was inverted where academics were treated as extra-curricular activities, and where band and football were handled as if they were core curricular school subjects. English, Science, Mathematics and Social Studies had been demoted in rank, and then band, football, soccer, chorus and other vital, cherished, extra-curricular activities had been elevated and glorified.

Jimmy left my General English class once a week to take saxophone lessons with the music instructor. The basic message Jimmy received from the sax practice was that music was primary and that English class was secondary because the lad never had to leave his music lesson to go to English class.

The band *student* missed thirty or so English classes that school year by simply taking once-a-week saxophone lessons. It then was *my* responsibility to make sure that Jimmy Brown completed all of the work assignments that the youth had missed while strenuously blowing into his saxophone. I had to provide Jimmy with worksheets and homework assignments, and then make sure that the young musician completed what he had missed when he should have been ambitiously working in my classroom. And please remember; little Jimmy was but one of a hundred and thirty hormone-driven *students* I had been designated to teach every single day.

I couldn't help but believing that Jimmy Brown was really missing-out on some serious literary insights when the class had to read stories by: Arthur Conan Doyle, O. Henry, Mark Twain, Washington Irving, Jack London, H.G. Wells, James Thurber, Herman Melville, Nathaniel Hawthorne, Hans Christian Andersen, Jonathan Swift, and Edgar Allan Poe. Because of his saxophone playing, Jimmy Brown had to read and study all of that literature work he had missed in class *on his own* for homework. The message Jimmy Brown received from *that* harmful time-substitution was that saxophone lessons were more essential than the masterpieces created by all-of-the-above distinguished authors.

And then, by virtue of his absence, Jimmy Brown missed-out on interesting vocabulary words like "prodigious, egregious, loquacious, surreptitious, assiduous, pernicious and avaricious". The kid also could have better mastered complex sentences with relative pronouns along with adjective subordinate clauses, and also those other complex sentences containing subordinating conjunctions beginning adverb subordinate clauses, not to mention the existence of noun clauses. So, because Jimmy's wonderful mother wanted him to play saxophone in the band and have individual lessons to improve his tooting and blowing, English class had now been mathematically reduced to a hundred-and-fifty-day activity for little Jimmy Brown.

Jimmy Brown, just like all the other eighth-grade *students,* had to take the school-mandated standardized tests to determine how his individual skill levels compared to national norms. Jimmy spent three English sessions taking the *California Achievement Test,* and two English classes were devoted to the *Differential Aptitude Test* for the Guidance Department's records. One additional English class period was used for the *Otis IQ Test,* the results of which were placed and kept in the *child's* "Confidential Guidance Folder". Now Jimmy's adjusted English class time was down to a hundred and forty-five sessions out of a possible hundred and eighty forty-five-minute periods.

Jimmy was absent from school the day the *Differential Aptitude Test* had been administered, so the lad then had to leave English class to take the Guidance Test he had missed. That same day, I had given an English test, which Jimmy had missed because he was making-up the heralded *DAT* he had missed because he was absent from school the day the Guidance Department had scheduled it. The message Jimmy Brown received from all of that *democratic* educational bureaucracy was that Guidance Office tests were more important than English class, than English tests, and also English teachers.

The classroom teacher was the one who really had suffered from all of Jimmy's absentee problems and from him completing school unfinished business outside of English class. I had to schedule a time slot after school later in the week so that Jimmy could make-up the English test that the boy had missed because naturally, *he* had to take the Guidance Department's *DAT.* The child had missed the *DAT* because he had been absent from school the day Jimmy's entire class had also missed English class.

Standardized tests the year before had identified Jimmy as a "gifted *child*" that had only average *academic* skills in reading and writing. So now, the eighth-grade *student* was also in the "Gifted and Talented" program and consequently, missed several English classes each month to participate in that special placement. Then also, Jimmy Brown had been selected to partake in the countywide "Olympics of the Mind" competition that required three more lost English periods in which to adequately prepare for the important interschool event. Jimmy's total English class days were now down to around a hundred and twenty-two.

Jimmy Brown and his eighth-grade peers were to be making a tremendous transition to their freshman high school year, and to accommodate that serious *social* adjustment, the guidance counselors met with each class section ten times. The purpose of the Guidance Department sessions was to ensure that the switch from eighth-grade to high school was not too traumatic for Jimmy Brown and his fellow eighth-graders. Of course, important matters like course descriptions, subject selections, available electives, and regular subject requirements for high school graduation (still over four years away for Jimmy) and college choices were all thoroughly discussed.

Even though the ten scheduled guidance meetings were distributed between regular English, Science, Social Studies and Math' core curriculum classes, Jimmy still wound-up missing four additional English sessions. Now it was important that Jimmy and his classmates knew where the cooking rooms, woodshops, family living rooms, and auto mechanics shops were located, so another English period was wasted so that Jimmy could tour the same building he had been attending school in since September. Jimmy's grand total was now down to a hundred and seventeen English sessions.

Notice how educational *academic* inefficiency was being generated because the school officials were so concerned about Jimmy Brown's sociological and psychological needs that academics had been coincidentally neglected and diminished. But already, sixty-three days of English class periods had been squandered for Jimmy Brown's delicate mental, sociological, and emotional needs.

Jimmy Brown was smart, gifted and talented, articulate. and sociable (but only average in *academic* skill proficiency), so the administration and the class advisor nominated the *student* to be a *School Guide* for the sixth-graders coming over from the elementary school to become familiarized with the junior-senior high school. So, little Jimmy Brown (who was developing *socially*) lost two additional English sessions guiding impressed sixth-graders around the same building where the young escort had lost five days being guided in and around by the Guidance Counselors, who were definitely experts on all kinds of guiding. His English class total was now down to a hundred and twenty sessions.

I am not being facetious, trite, cynical, exaggerating, or picayune here. I am stating exactly what had happened to little Jimmy Brown that school year, and I am demonstrating that it was quite remarkable that the *child* got to write and submit two compositions each of the four marking periods.

Now, I can do some more statistical tinkering. Jimmy Brown also missed three English classes because of scheduled school assemblies when the teacher had to bring the entire class to the auditorium. And then Jimmy missed three other English sessions where the class was reading the wonderful literature to Charles Dickens' "A Christmas Carol" because the band had to rehearse for the annual *Christmas* assembly show that had to be given twice to accommodate the entire *student* body.

Then also, English class had to be postponed twice that school year so that the *students* could view the *Christmas* movie and the spring *Easter* movie at other school assemblies. And Jimmy missed one other class because of a football pep assembly that had been held in the gymnasium. Jimmy's English class total has now been diminished to a hundred and eleven sessions.

And to top everything else, Jimmy Brown had missed eleven additional school days because of bouts with bronchitis, the common cold, high fevers and the flu. So, now we're down to a hundred school days where Jimmy Brown must master the intricacies of English grammar, composition, vocabulary and literature.

And don't forget that the teacher was also absent ten days that school year because of sickness, funerals and personal business. So actually, the total classroom teacher/*student* learning time Jimmy had *me* as his instructor was around a half a school year. Compound Jimmy Brown by a hundred and twenty-nine other s*tudents,* and you can amply appreciate why teachers often become frustrated, cynical and depressed.

Now here is the actual reason I had gone to the baseball park on that 1972 Saturday morning. I was still recuperating from a terrible Friday at school the day before. I figured I would watch a relaxing baseball game and then return home and mow my lawn.

That Friday morning, I was scheduled to have bus duty outside my school wing. It was a bleak, damp morning, but since it wasn't raining, I had to wait outside and supervise the *children* until it was time for them to enter the building. That regular fifteen-minute interval was normally spent getting my homeroom attendance cards ready in alphabetical order, filling-out lunch slips, and recording late homework assignments in my grade book from twenty-two *students* that had been absent the day before.

That morning, a pretty bad fight had erupted on the backside of the asphalt, and I had to run over and break-up the melee as three hundred *children* were hysterically screaming and shouting. Then, I had to admonish and warn other *students* that were throwing stones at each other to avoid a racial incident if the prospective violators should get involved in a second altercation.

When the entrance bell finally rang, I had to escort the first two combatants down to the Main Office for fighting outside. At the office, I had to pick-up Discipline Referral Cards to fill-out on both combatants during homeroom period while I also had to take attendance and perform cafeteria lunch counts.

The second period 8-6 class was nerve-racking, but I valiantly managed to make it to fifth period cafeteria duty. I had to admonish *children* and *students* that were bending spoons and flinging *Jell-o* at each other with their newly invented catapults. Toward the end of the forty-five-minute cafeteria period, the din sounded like an ancient chariot race crowd that had gone berserk in the *Roman Colosseum*.

"Wouldn't it be wonderful if teacher aides could do this job along with a few policemen!" I shouted to Tim Amoro (who later in life became a guidance counselor and then an elementary school principal). "Duties are what makes us unprofessional in the eyes of the public!"

"Yeah!" Tim agreed. "I already had my nose broken trying to break-up that big January fight we had in here. I want to retire from this job with two nostrils intact!"

"If we didn't have to be in here," I yelled to Tim, "then we could be assigned to either teach a class or tutor *students* in writing skills!"

"That will never happen!" Tim shouted above the *student* exodus din. "That's why I'm taking graduate courses to become a guidance counselor and evolve out of this crazy daily existence!"

At last, I made it to seventh period, my *PPSA* (teacher Preparation, Planning and Special Assignment). My eighth period general English class was almost as challenging as my second period

8-6ers, so I needed the free time to rejuvenate and catch my breath. 'I'll run-off some worksheets for Monday in the office and then take it easy!' I thought. 'Teaching is about the only job where you have to have the next school day's work done today!'

Six teachers were absent that day. The high school no longer had permanent substitutes, so I was notified over the intercom by one of the main office secretaries that I had to surrender my prep' period to teach "American Government" for the absent seventh-grade Social Studies teacher.

At *that* time, the daily substitute pay was only $35.00, so you could imagine how many times teachers were asked to sacrifice their *planning* time to have a *special assignment* (remember, *PPSA*) in another teacher's specialized subject area. And so, the school system had saved itself a rather remarkable $35.00 and had successfully inconvenienced six teachers that showed-up that Friday to cover the absent instructor's classes.

During my eighth-period class, the principal had me yanked-out because an irate parent had stormed into the office and wanted to see me right away. A Science teacher had to give up his *PPSA* to cover my last period class while I was confronting the livid parent about something of which I hadn't the slightest idea. The parent had misconstrued a comment I had made on Monday (remember it's now Friday), and then after listening to my plausible explanation, the agitated father left the school more peacefully than when he had angrily arrived.

I returned to my English class only to discover that the Science teacher covering for me had abandoned Edgar Allan Poe's "A Tell-Tale Heart" and was lecturing the *students* all about entomology and insects after a certain passage in the Poe story described noisy "night watches" in the wall. After the garrulous Science teacher excused himself for the last fifteen minutes of the period, I noticed some drawings and scribbling that had not been evident on five desks before I had been unexpectedly summoned by the principal out of my classroom to appease an irate parent.

Then that entire week after school, I had to serve Office Detention, the "Devil's Island Howdy Duty Show" (being assigned to teachers at no extra pay by the administration). I didn't know six of the twelve *students* in the detention and had trouble with three of the high school *children* that didn't like taking orders from an eighth-grade English teacher.

The shades to the side windows were closed, and several of the *student* friends of the defiant, *detained* high school *children* were outside banging their fists against the windows for the amusement of their *punished* pals.

When I finally made it home alive and still breathing, I had to work on the new computerized report cards. The new system required teachers to use a number two pencil to methodically circle-in grades instead of writing A, B, C, D or F on sheets of paper. Also, four comments for each *student* had to be shaded-in, requiring two circles for each comment. For example, "47" (two numbers) being shaded-in meant "talks too much in class" and "59" (two numbers) being shaded-in meant "more study needed at home".

It required three-and-a-half-hours to complete doing the new report cards instead of the customary hour, but on the plus side of the coin, the new system saved the office secretaries time that the clerks used to spend transcribing the written grades from the "Grade Sheets" onto the actual "Report Cards".

Because of all the stress and distress, I sometimes took "mental health days" when I wasn't actually physically sick. But the administration would call teachers on the carpet if they missed more than eight sick days of the twelve allotted by school/teacher contracts each year. A recent government report indicated that teaching is the third most pressurized job there is. An authoritarian administrator once told me, "Teachers that miss more than eight days a school year are *unprofessional* because they are disrupting the educational continuity and hurting *student* learning." Right!

If the public wants to improve standardized test scores, then the answer is quite simple. Keep kids inside their assigned classrooms where they're supposed to be learning core curriculum *academics*.

I hope that two things are now quite evident: why good teachers leave the profession or eventually evolve into guidance, college-professoring, or administration, *and* why little Jimmy Brown only wrote eight compositions in his *general* eighth-grade English class. And incidentally Jimmy Brown's team unfortunately lost the *Pony League* baseball game at the town park.

Chapter 33
"School Assemblies"

The Teachers Handbook prepared by the school administration explicitly states, "All school assemblies are scheduled by the main office and the meetings constitute an integral part of the total school program. Assemblies provide opportunities for the *cultural* and *intellectual* growth of *students,* and they contribute significantly to the development of school spirit and school morale."

I have attended in the neighborhood of three hundred school assembles in my thirty-four-year teaching career, ranging from pep' assemblies and science demonstrations to boring lectures, spelling bees and popular "G-Rated" movies shown before major holidays to "Keep the lid on".

Recently, the tone of assembly subjects has turned from *cultural* and *intellectual* to *bleak* and almost *macabre* subjects such as drugs, teen pregnancies, and improvised question and answer sessions with convicted prisoners with the convicts showing-up (with guards) in their official orange uniforms. However, several extraordinary assemblies that I had the misfortune of attending really stand-out in my mind.

Once, I had the displeasure of attending a junior-high school assembly in the high school auditorium. A circus clown wearing oversized shoes sauntered onto the front stage from behind the curtain and began doing magic tricks that were about as complicated as a basal reader. The *students* became quite restive and soon were hooting and shouting like a pack of vitriolic hyenas.

It is embarrassing to have to stand during the entire assembly and play Gestapo when the teacher himself' wished that he had an old Vaudeville cane to yank the idiot off the stage. 'A profit-minded huckster could amass a small fortune vending soft rotten tomatoes for the *children* to hurl at the zany entertainer,' I thought. 'That particular assembly definitely contributed to the cultural and intellectual growth of the *students'*, I cynically imagined.

The intellectually gifted *student* is often stifled spending thirteen years in a public school system that promoted *democracy in education* within the comprehensive high school. Ben Locanta was a gifted *child* whose public-school preparation was about as useful as a bamboo paperweight during a tornado. The gifted *student* possessed and exhibited admirable resourcefulness.

Whenever the school videotape machine went haywire, or whenever the intercom went amok, Ben was summoned to the office before any outside repairman was ever contacted. The young genius's knowledge of physics, electricity and chemistry was praiseworthy indeed. Regrettably, Ben Locanta was so advanced that his mental needs were sadly neglected by the school curriculum. In the early '70s, the high school had no modus operandi to effectively deal with the exceptionally talented *student*.

Usually in high school education, the intellectually precocious *child* gets the short end of the stick since the entire system is geared to raising the mentally downtrodden up to "academic mediocrity". When schools have *students* like Ben Locanta, that is when they need the "laboratory approach to learning," "independent study", and "the *student*-oriented curriculum".

As it is according to the mandates of *democratic education*, those three splendid programs apply to the masses and not exclusively to the gifted *student*. Ben was the type of *child* that really needed to explore, create, invent, discover, synthesize and push his intelligence to the max'. But in wasteful American education, *those* marvelous abstract terms were and still are harnessed mostly to *students* that didn't (and don't) know a Bunsen burner from a Franklin stove, and who in reality don't even care to know.

One afternoon, an opera company visited the school to give two assembly performances for the *student* body. Ben Locanta assisted the troupe with the stage arrangements, stationing the props', positioning and focusing the spotlights and the overheads, and operating the backstage electrical controls.

One of the more-cocky thespians, who was traveling with the opera production, bent-down to adjust a spotlight that would be shining on him during the first scene. The light had been turned on for only a minute and Ben cautioned the fellow, "You'd better not touch that right now or your hands will get scorched!"

The middle-aged fellow wearing a medieval costume with leotards felt more than slightly chagrined at being admonished by a young high school *student*. The actor snorted back to Ben: "I've been in show business all my life!" the fellow boasted. "Do you think I'm some kind of greenhorn when it comes to adjusting simple high school stage lighting!"

The enraged actor/baritone bent-down and grabbed the spotlight with both hands, and then an instant expression of agony beamed from his facial features. The fellow howled so loudly that I thought he was going to turn himself inside-out, and the heat from his sizzling hands almost triggered the school's fire alarm. Ben was gracious enough to escort the anguishing singer/actor down to the nurse's office where his seriously blistered fingers were quickly professionally treated and bandaged.

The assembly opera program did commence an hour later, and the distressed fellow with the gauze around his hands didn't even have to wear white gloves. "That guy was punished by fate for being so nasty to Ben," Bob Gordon confided to me. "He deserved to get roasted because the nurse told me he's about as sociable as the Abominable Snowman."

That same year I had been the advisor to the high school's chapter of the *National Honor Society*. Ben Locanta was president of the *NHS* and as usual, the week before the induction assembly, the entire ceremony program was rehearsed. This was in the early '70s during the *Vietnam War* era, and most of the male *students* in the school had long hair, sideburns, mustaches and wore bellbottom denim-jeans. I soon found-out that there was a degree of rebelliousness and anti-war sentiments, even among the school's most honorable *students*.

Towards the end of the *NHS* induction assembly, there was always a segment where the *students* broke away from formal decorum and did a "Have You Heard" routine where high school gossip was done between two *students* over two separate microphones. Of course, dauntless Ben and another *NHS* officer stepped over the line and announced that *students* with certain initials were having casual sex with *students* with certain other initials. Before the principal and the V.P. could scurry onto the stage and terminate the assembly, the *NHS* officers gave everyone the familiar '70s peace sign, and all of the *students* in attendance stood-up, cheered, and gave reciprocal peace signs to their honorary academic leaders standing on the stage.

"That assembly was a disgrace to this school!" the principal screamed at me in his office. "What kind of incompetent advisor are you, anyway?"

"Look, *we* rehearsed the whole program last week and none of that sex stuff at the end was in the practice session!" I defended myself by yelling back. "Those *students* inserted that dialogue at the end without my knowledge or permission!"

"You're through as *NHS* advisor!" the head honcho fanatically bellowed. "And this disgrace will definitely go into your personal folder!" the school executive petulantly added.

And so, that's the way it often goes in American education. Botch up unintentionally, and by a stroke of weird luck, the teacher is suddenly and fortuitously freed of an important, pressure-packed responsibility like being the *NHS* advisor.

At another strange school assembly, the faculty and *students* were honored to have an inspirational guest speaker whom John Rizzo had heard address the local Kiwanis Club. The Driver Education teacher had been very impressed with the hard life and tough approach of the self-made businessman, so Mr. Rizzo convinced the administration to schedule the fellow to be an assembly speaker.

The assembly was slated for eighth period, the final timeslot of the school day. John Rizzo introduced the self-made man, and a distinct hush followed by light applause filled the six-hundred-seat chamber. The fellow approached the podium and then began speaking didactically into the microphone. The man's "talking-down to his bored audience, and his style is completely turning-off his youthful listeners after only the first three minutes of his biographical presentation", I softly mentioned to a fellow teacher.

At first, I felt a degree of compassion for the silver-haired Pericles. I got-up from my auditorium seat like a dozen other teachers had done and patrolled the aisle chastising several snickering wise guys. But then, the speaker used an excessive amount of *selfish* personal pronouns like *I, me, my, myself* and *mine.*

The *students* were becoming more neurotic, impolite, obnoxious, and unruly as the man's rigid speech continued. Again, I rebuked several young, seated punks by saying, "This fellow is a self-made millionaire. He has gone from rags to riches!" I clearly lectured. "Maybe you can learn something important about success by paying this man the respect he deserves!"

But most of the *students* (who were used to being entertained at assemblies and not *lectured* to) were as interested in Horatio Alger stories as they were about studying quadratic equations. The elderly gent then sanctimoniously spoke with a heavy Polish accent about the need for patriotism, for nationalism, for free enterprise, and for loyalty to flag and country. By then, nine-tenths of the *children* in the jam-packed audience were becoming quite antsy and rebellious. The undercurrent of muffled *student* conversations could be heard throughout the auditorium when the entire assembly became less and less receptive to the self-made Polish immigrant millionaire's speech. Civil peace was rapidly reaching the danger level.

'This guy is completely turning these spoiled *students* off!' I thought. 'What was John Rizzo possibly thinking when he invited this man to speak? What works great at the Kiwanis Club might bomb when immature *students* are asked to sit still and listen for forty-five minutes!'

The end of the period arrived on the wall clocks, and the dismissal bell finally sounded. But the self-appointed Polish Demosthenes standing at the podium microphone disregarded the bell and kept on addressing the totally bored *students*. The guy just wouldn't shut-up!

The assistant principal and John Rizzo motioned and waved their hands for the man to finish his presentation, but the undaunted speaker simply waved back, responding to what he thought was a supportive salutation, and kept talking to his totally lost audience.

The old fellow then sensed the restlessness that existed in the packed auditorium, so he decided to demonstrate his physical dexterity. The former circus acrobat did three consecutive cartwheels on the stage for the benefit of his restless audience. The *students* then went crazy and gave the old gentleman a standing mock round-of-applause as the principal, the vice principal and John Rizzo first gesticulated with their hands, and then wildly and frantically signaled with both arms for the *students* to be seated so that an orderly dismissal could be initiated.

The hapless old gent started speaking again, since he interpreted the *students'* reaction as an appreciative relishing of *his* work-ethic philosophy. Ben Locanta came out onto the stage with a plaque to present to the guest speaker to finally terminate the bizarre assembly program. By then, the school day was over by a full ten minutes, and all of the bus routes to the elementary school were already messed-up and off schedule.

The now-enthusiastic *students* again stood-up after the brief plaque presentation, and the assembled *children* gave the oblivious speaker a second mock ovation. The old man left the school five minutes later, thinking that his inspirational talk had been well-received, and the proud speaker informed a red-faced John Rizzo on his way out of the building's front entrance that he "has renewed faith in the future of America based on the fine *students* in your high school".

At another daft assembly, just before the *Easter* holiday break, the *students* were slated to view an hour and a half Hollywood motion picture entitled *A Man Called Horse*. The *children* silently filed into the auditorium by homerooms, sat in their prearranged seating sections, the lights were dimmed, and the projector began flickering the film frames upon the stage's white screen.

One of the movie's opening scenes was a real eye-catcher. Actor Richard Harris had been stripped of his attire and was running naked through prairie grasslands while being chased by a virulent Indian tribe. Any teacher seated in the auditorium could hear a pin drop. The silent *students* were amazed that their high school (a bastion of Victorian middle-class morality) auditorium would suddenly be converted into a bawdy X-rated movie house.

The abashed school czars scurried to the back of the auditorium and had the head of the *student* audiovisual crew (now a prominent town councilman) place a flimsy piece of cardboard in front of the projector lens every time a bare pair of buttocks flashed onto the white screen. The unhappy *students* booed, jeered, and chanted every time their innocent eyes were denied the opportunity to view what they considered fantastic carnal pleasure.

A later scene in the film *A Man Called Horse* was one of the most gory and gruesome spectacles I had ever seen in a movie. The pursued cowpoke (Richard Harris) had been captured by the hostile Indians, and was about to be accepted as a leader in the tribe after winning the clan's approval by demonstrating extraordinary bravery. His acceptance as honorary chief was accompanied by a most bizarre and sadistic Indian initiation rite.

Two gaping incisions were made into the paleface's chest, one into each *breast* (if this were a woman being initiated, obviously the audiovisual crew would have had to swiftly cover the projector lens with the same piece of cardboard as had been commanded by the school principal standing nearby). Two meat hooks were tethered to ropes that had been suspended from a rafter, and then the hooks were inserted inside Richard Harris's chest.

The heroic white man (honorary chief) was then hoisted-up into the air, hanging and suspended in a vertical position from the ropes. The inserted meat hooks were intensely gleaming on both sides of his sternum. The actor's abused body was then spun around so fast that, as his rotating form assumed a horizontal plane, the honorary white chief resembled a laboratory gyroscope whirling around.

The scene was so hideous that even the most daring, pugnacious *students* had to turn their heads on lower their eyes. Not even the worst behaved *students* that were always *suspended* themselves' could watch the climax to the hideous Indian initiation exhibition.

But the entire *A Man Called Horse* movie assembly was quite indicative of our American Puritanical society. It's all right to show bloodshed, murder, death, suicide, homicide and shootings, so gore is generally regarded as acceptable, and almost commendable. But to show a man's buttocks, a woman's breast or a pubic hair required a rectangular piece of cardboard in front of the movie projector's lens. The elite *student* audiovisual crew, however, was able to focus the forbidden images onto their side of the piece of cardboard, and thus enjoyed a few visual treats, all to their own pleasure.

The week after *Easter (*now-called *Spring)* break, I conversed with Mr. Bill W., the assembly program advisor in the main corridor. "What happened with the administration after you showed that movie before the Easter break?" I asked. 'It was a real shocker!"

"I was really chewed-out!" the advisor confessed. "I guess they'll now get somebody else to order and show the films."

"Don't feel bad!" I empathized. "I was fired as *NHS* advisor after the honor *students* pulled a fast one on me and changed the ending of the assembly."

"Good, you can have my former job as assembly film organizer!" my colleague joked. "If the boss doesn't fire me, I'll quit!"

"No thanks," I replied with a grin. "I think I'd rather go into alligator mud-wrestling, or perhaps elephant training!"

Another interesting assembly was of the school spirit-pep' variety, and this one happened in the late 1990s. The middle school *football team* ran out onto the school gymnasium *basketball court.* The last *student* football player carried a manikin's faceless head with a woman's wig on top. He was enacting an imitation of a famous and popular *World Wrestling Federation* professional wrestler at the time, a grappler named Al Snow. Just like *WWF* fans had done on television many times in response to the appearance of the manikin's head, the energized *students* in the gallery wildly chanted, "We want head! We want head!"

The next morning, the beleaguered principal called the *student* that had held the manikin's head down to the office, and the *child* claimed that he was unaware that the chant "We want head!" involved any sexual connotation. "And besides, if it did," the *student* argued to the principal, "the kids in the stands were yelling the dirty words and not me! I was only holding the fake head up in the air!"

The clever *student* got away with murder after conducting his little "inappropriate" charade and received only two days of Office Detention for causing widespread chaos and instigating the ultimate in bad taste during a school spirit pep' assembly.

Of course, as expected, I had gotten the non-coveted Cafeteria Star next to my name upon reporting the following September on the first day of school. The non-desired Asterisk indicated that I was to be the head teacher responsible for all strange events, fight incidents *and student* discipline problems happening during fifth period Cafeteria Duty. Naturally, I was surprised to see the middle-school band director Joe Sacci showing-up and reporting for duty.

"Joe, what on earth are you doing in here?" I innocently inquired. "I don't believe you've ever had Cafeteria Duty!"

"As you know, John, all these years that I've been teaching I've had band practice scheduled for eighth period," Joe explained. "Then for four or five other periods, I would give individual music lessons to the motivated band *students.*"

"Well then, how come you're planted here in the cafeteria? Why the change?" I politely and curiously asked.

"The administration wanted me to teach five General Music classes and then keep the band eighth period," Joe sadly related. "I don't want to teach *music theory* to general *students*. I only want to teach *music lessons* to band *students* who like and can play music."

"So, why are you assigned Cafeteria Duty?"

"I strongly refused to teach the General Music classes, so the administration hired another music teacher, and as punishment, gave me three consecutive Cafeteria Duty sessions! Periods 5, 6 and 7."

"Joe, one cafeteria period is enough to make anyone transform into a daft funny farmer, but three in a row will easily get *you* admitted into the nearest State Mental Hospital! I gotta' respectfully tell you with a saddened heart; you have my deepest sympathy!"

Regularly, schools also have quasi-assemblies where films are shown on rainy days to fill the second half of a forty-five-minute lunch period. I usually stepped into the Main Office just before lunch duty and ask the principal what films might be available to show to the disenchanted eighth-graders in the auditorium after they had eaten their lunches in the cafeteria.

"Here, try this one!" the busy principal suggested. "It came from the county film library."

"*Code Blue!*" I exclaimed with surprise. "Have you screened or previewed it to make sure it's safe to show to eighth-graders?"

"I just told you it came from the county film library," the preoccupied school executive insisted. "So, it's probably something like *Blue Hawaii,* or something like that!"

"Okay, you're the boss!" I sarcastically complimented and then left the Main Office to set-up the film for viewing.

The *students* were expertly transferred from the cafeteria to the auditorium and after settling-down, I slowly dimmed the lights while the other teacher on duty started-up the projector. Neither music teacher Joe Sacci nor I had realized at the time that *Code Blue* was hospital terminology for "Emergency Operating Room".

The first bloody scene showed a gentleman with a bashed-up head being assiduously stitched-up by a very skilled surgeon. The second scene showed a huge Afro-American woman giving birth. The corpulent lady's legs were wide open, and all of her femininity was right there for the absolutely captivated audience of fourteen-year-olds to eagerly inspect and evaluate.

The other teacher on duty and I rushed to the projector to shut the questionable film off, when suddenly, the hospital scene shifted to two unconscious automobile accident victims in need of immediate surgery being wheeled on gurneys into the very busy emergency room/operating suite. The medical scene continued and showed the men being attended to and resuscitated by very qualified and competent hospital nurses and doctors.

Then suddenly, the hospital scene film shifted back to the beleaguered Afro-American woman giving painful birth to her second and third babies. Joe Sacci and I made a beeline to the film projector and awkwardly shut it off just as the second part of the bizarre lunch period came to an end. A deluge of boos generated from the disappointed *students,* and the loud auditory derision engulfed both my embarrassed music colleague and myself.

"I think I'll stay home after this fiasco," my good friend related. "I need a mental health day!"

"Me too Joe!" I concurred. "There's bound to be a ton of parent flak after this farce, that's for sure!"

The next day was Friday, and Joe Sacci and I both took a "mental health" (or "stay alive") day off from school. The following Monday, we both showed-up and were amazed to find out that not one irate parent phone call had been received in the office about multiple birth scenes shown in the second half of the previous Thursday's eighth-grade lunch period.

Being the main eighth-grade English teacher, I was assigned by the administration to conduct the annual middle school Spelling Bee. Next, I was appointed by the principal to preside over the area's three-school Spelling Bee. I did such a swell job in *that* second capacity that the area Knights of Columbus insisted that I become the official moderator of *their* County Spelling Bee.

Finally, in regard to the art of spelling, one other assembly program stands-out as being prominent in my current memory. In February of 1981, I had been selected to be the moderator of an area

8th Grade Spelling Bee between three competing schools: my school, another local public school, and the town Catholic School. Each school was allowed to have eight outstanding spelling contestants participating, and the highly-anticipated event had been scheduled to be conducted inside the Catholic School's auditorium/gymnasium, with around 250 biased *students* from all three schools in attendance.

The nerve-racking Spelling Bee went on for a full hour, and the advanced *students* from each of the three schools possessed tremendous command of English language words along with their associated definitions. Eventually, after twenty-three eliminations, an erudite winner had emerged victorious. The all-too-thrilled champion was a pretty, blonde-hair girl, a true scholar from the aforementioned Catholic School.

'Wow!' I remember thinking. 'This terrific *student* must've studied *Webster's Dictionary* her entire educational life. She knows every difficult word that had been presented along with its accurate spelling, right-down to the very last letter. I would love to have this precocious girl in one of my Accelerated English classes.'

The attractive, blonde-hair young lady apparently was very popular with her classmates. Immediately, after she had been declared the winner, around fifty exuberant girls euphorically rushed-up the stage steps in their Catholic school uniforms; the wild stampede nearly knocking both me and the speaker's podium over in the process. After all of the histrionics thankfully settled-down, over the microphone I asked the extremely intelligent girl her name.

"Kellyanne Fitzpatrick!" the winner boisterously shouted-out as her many classmates vociferously hooted and cheered. It should be mentioned that Kellyanne Fitzpatrick is today Kellyanne Conway, former political campaign manager, and later a key adviser to President Donald J. Trump.

Chapter 34

"The Educational Aristocracy"

The Educational Aristocracy is a loosely knit but very powerful confederation consisting of ethereal and quixotic college professors, plutocratic-but-altruistic school board members, New York textbook manufacturers, platonic public-relations-minded administrators, and lastly, alchemistic school specialists. Rank within the Educational Aristocracy is determined by how much money a member makes, and how much influence and authority that any member of the academic nobility wields.

The Educational Aristocracy has a sub' strata that includes office secretaries and the school truant officer. All of the members of the Educational Aristocracy share one common denominator: Each echelon at one time or another tells teachers what to do. The act of informing, commanding, ordering and controlling of faculty members (involving mostly role and procedural matters) is the main unifying factor of the shabby-but-all-powerful coalition.

If it were up to the Educational Aristocracy to educate *students*, then the true faults of this elite corps (and of American education) would stand-out and become glaringly obvious to the public. And yet, the zany crew of suspect bureaucrats perilously navigates the educational ark through *sociological dire straits* all the while mislabeling the treacherous environment as ordinary *"academic channels"*. Teachers are the designated shipmates that are the vital crewmembers assigned to keep the educational ark from becoming the *Wreck of the Hesperus*.

Politicians, legislators and the unwary general public blame teachers for the overall gross inefficiency of American education. Congressmen want to abolish teacher tenure, not realizing that such action would strengthen the administrators' stifling grip on education by making their instructors brownnosers and Super Teachers, always kissing-up to their bosses simply to keep *their* employment.

Politicians want to increase the power of local boards of education, not realizing that rank amateur board members (influenced by administrations that are influenced by fanciful college professors) would have control of the destiny of American education. And politicians want to see advanced ideas (generated by Ivory Tower university professors and outer-space educational psychologists) implemented to pretend improving the quality of education.

Crazy methods such as "the open classroom" and "cooperative learning" should be (according to politicians) the standards imposed on community schools. All of this insane posturing is done to disguise the true causes of educational inefficiency, and to keep the Educational Aristocracy in power throughout the United States.

Most of the perpetual, absurd tinkering is designed to make teachers more accountable and to make *students* more motivated to learn. But the teachers are not responsible for the grandiose failures of American education. The blundering and burgeoning Educational Aristocracy is calling the shots! Politicians listen to boards of education; boards of education listen to school administrators; school administrators listen to wifty college professors and also to airhead educational psychologists; but hardly anybody listens to the teachers.

Ethereal college professors and educational psychologists devise quixotic, suspect, and impractical classroom teaching methods and then entrust administrators to govern over teachers to ascertain that the (doomed to fail) philosophical nonsense is implemented. School board members usually know little more about teaching and learning than the average lay person does, so those wizards place implicit trust in the administrators' policies, goals and objectives, which are engineered by Marxist professors to be non-workable, and which will almost certainly reflect "teacher incompetence". That's the basic game plan. Administrators can stay in power, keep the status quo unproductive system going, and next blame the recipient teachers for not being able to get tangible results from a working model that is deliberately designed to fail.

Guidance counselors, school supervisors, curriculum purveyors, and space patrol college coordinators become middle management in the Educational Aristocracy and are commissioned as frontline defenders of the ineffective "democratic comprehensive school". The Educational Aristocracy and its "socialistic sociological education" (disguised as democratic *academic* education) are the real detriments and the real hindrances to teacher professionalism because the crafty sultans discourage *student* accountability by making teachers responsible for both teaching and for learning.

But the gullible, hoodwinked public points the finger of suspicion at the teachers and holds *them* culpable for being the cause of the incredible non-accomplishments of our failing *democratic* American educational system. The educational boyars overall management of our public schools is at best disappointing. The whole travesty is comparable to Ponce de Leon discovering diluted *Geritol* in the basin of the *Fountain of Youth*. The Educational

Aristocracy is bureaucratic, wasteful, parasitic, naïve, incomprehensible and irresponsible, yet the blundering corps of "leaders" decide the destiny of millions of *students* in American public schools.

The nimrod, cloud-nine college professors promoting "progressive education" champion the cause of the twin monstrosities commonly known as educational psychology and educational philosophy. Those Marxist romanticists are actually poisoning the mainstream of traditional American civilization. The bungling university sophists are forcing teachers to court disaster as if *we* were a rabble of imperceptible suitors. Our cultural identity along with our core values are in jeopardy because of the influence of these idealistic sophists (sophists were the phony, philosophical enemies of Socrates in ancient Athens) that have so much influence over American school philosophy.

The impractical "out-there" college professors' scheme-up certain spongy, porous, learning theories along with devising idealistic and rather dubious learning methods. Then the cunning charlatans entreat prospective teachers to "motivate and understand" *children* while providing textbook publishers, school supervisors, guidance counselors, and school administrators with a deluge of superfluous constructions that contradict the very real free enterprise economic competition system that's really out there.

I doubt very much that college professors and educational psychologists could last for thirty-four years as I had done implementing *their* pompous methods in American public schools. It all comes back to "It is easier to tell than it is to do." I would love to see any college professor come into a classroom of 8-6ers and motivate those twenty-five dysfunctional paragons to learn eighth-grade grammar, writing and literature from eighth-grade textbooks when the twenty-five *students* can only function on a third-grade level. Then, over the course of a hundred-and-eighty-day school year, the false teachings of the professors' magical theories would be glaringly revealed.

The college professors' Ivory Towers are so high up into the stratosphere that the occupants must be brain-dead from a lack of oxygen. College professors usually become distinguished eminent scholars by doing research on a remote obscure subject. Then, he or she writes a meaningless thesis that usually improves nothing whatsoever anywhere on the planet. Ultimately, by becoming an expert on nothing important, the college professor is now certified and qualified to tell the combat troops (the teachers) what "out there" fantasies that must be implemented.

People in education earn masters and doctorate degrees for authoring theses on such marvelous subjects as the various ways to heat and light classrooms, or the need for a second level industrial arts course at a certain high school. More serious research goes into the distillation of backwoods moonshine. When's the last time an educational doctorate was patented?

Since no absolute truths exist in American education, most everything, therefore, is relative junk that is floating around in the eighty-percent gray area "Twilight Zone" vacillating between right and wrong. For virtually every educational thesis that is written, valid research to the contrary could be mustered-up in no time. Nothing means anything! And because nothing means anything, the college professors' *democratic* innovative methods' models could float around in the gray area *Twilight Zone* for all eternity and never be recognized as garbage. And he or she never has to worry about their exotic theory (floating trash) being destroyed by sound educational research (that doesn't really exist). Sound research could accurately identify and assess bad classroom *democratic* methods (the space junk being perpetuated).

At large universities, professors of more exact and respected disciplines look-down on the professors of education because science professors and medical school professors know quite well that public school education is far from being a solid science. Those other university professors fully know that the graduates from *their* science, architectural, law and medical schools will make much more money and be much more successful in the American *free enterprise* society than the graduates of the universities' schools of education will be earning. A toy diploma prize out of a *Crackerjacks* box carries almost as much national prestige as a master's degree in education does.

Teachers on my school's faculty became demoralized when they entered the air-conditioned Main Office Suite and had to listen to the school psychologist complaining that she can't get the office temperature down to below seventy-seven degrees. After hearing the preposterous grievance, the teachers must return to their sultry, humble classrooms and then have to instruct twenty-nine or so *student* scoundrels in ninety-seven-degree sweltering heat.

The teachers might imagine that they are lost David Livingstones captured by twenty-nine savage cannibals, and five bothersome mosquitoes flitting around the classroom seem like a swarm of nasty tsetse flies. Such hallucinating is necessary to escape the horrid reality of teaching an 8-6-type class in ninety-seven-degree misery.

On hot, unbearable spring and late September summer days, teachers often journey and linger inside the Main Office Suite during their prep' and lunch periods. The air-conditioned offices are like welcomed oases amidst hot desert wastelands. Air-conditioning is definitely a status symbol enjoyed by the Educational Aristocracy and envied by the educational serfs (teachers).

School administrators, who once studied to become teachers, like to call themselves *educators,* but the big question is: "Who do they educate?" The answer is an emphatic "Nobody!" The description *educator* is a misnomer, a pseudo-title that embodies what school administrators ought to feel guilty about not being. Administrators are not educators; they are in actuality *former educators.* They are like caterpillars that have evolved into moths that still insist that they are caterpillars.

By abandoning the rigors associated with classroom teaching, school administrators have left the vast educational prairie in quest of greener ($) executive pastures. An aspiring person becomes a teacher because he or she wants to help humanity, but a teacher becomes an administrator because he or she wants to make more money. Most teachers will still admit *that* fundamental truth when they are still taking graduate courses, but after being absorbed and accepted into the Educational Aristocracy, administrators will deny *that* basic piece of reality.

It is an indictment of American education that a good teacher can't earn half as much as an ineffective school administrator can. Many teachers lose faith in their profession's ability to elevate itself above educational serfdom. The logical alternative is to acquire a master's degree in school management, and then marvelously, the teacher magically morphs from Gunga Din into maharaja in a mere thirty-six easily obtained college credits.

The teacher escapes serfdom and joins the Educational Aristocracy by taking a smattering of graduate courses and then writing a worthless thesis that gets stored away in college library archives only to be read by other prospective school administrators looking for a meaningless thesis idea to expound upon. Few educators ever regard their master's thesis as being any major contribution to their field of study. The thesis is a means to an end: that is, out of the classroom and making more money.

It doesn't require much imagination to conjure-up an impression as to what kind of paper an administrative thesis should be written on. *NATO* has a better chance of admitting and appointing North Korea to head its international operations than for any administrative master's degree making a significant impact anywhere *outside the inside* of a new principal or a new vice-principal's wallet.

In New Jersey back in the 1960s and early '70s, some school principals had never taught even a single year in a public school. The laws have changed since then, but I had worked for a high school principal that went straight from guidance counselor to principal. Now in 2003, guidance counselors and principals have to teach several years before ascending to their new positions in the Educational Aristocracy. But once *they* make the transition and cross over that lucrative bridge, they never want to teach in a public-school classroom again.

Educational aristocrats consider the act of teaching beneath their dignity, and then the same educational nobles suddenly view teaching *students* as being too demeaning for them. The school superintendent is the ultimate *educator* in the system because he doesn't want to have any direct contact with any *children,* especially any 8-6er existing in a volatile classroom situation.

Administrators in any area of endeavor are supposed to be financial gurus that are so sharp that they don't need erasers on the top end of their pencils. Real administrators in the business world can rival a computer for presenting accurate company records, statistics, or data on demand. However, in today's antiquated American education, floundering administrators are comparable to a guild of groggy-minded tailors that can't distinguish a miniskirt from a Freudian slip.

Much of the school principal's time is occupied with minute details (minutia). Line items on school budgets, school clubs, parent complaints, class treasuries, scribbled memos to teachers, and the general cleanliness of the school occupy most of their time. The vice-principal can't wait to become a principal somewhere somehow, because his daily responsibility is to deal with the same fifty to seventy-five disruptive *students* that cause turmoil in the building over and over again from September to June.

The principals and the superintendent are paid inflated salaries for spending large chunks of time on the telephone discussing trivial matters like the dress code, milk money, the prom, the new band or football team uniforms, and other secondary items with parents and with school board members. Adminis*trivia* is majestically elevated to the level of preeminence, and teachers and their important mission (education) are coincidentally relegated to the worshiping of administrative minutia.

Two main things justify the entire need for school administration: discipline problems and bad teachers. Administrators need *student* misbehavior and discipline problems for the same reason that the local police chief needs crime and criminals. If the principal had all respectable and courteous *students* in his school, and if the police chief had no crime committed in his community, then they both would be quickly put out of business. Why would we need a principal to have good kids sent to the office? Why would the police chief be needed to protect good citizens from moral and ethical citizens? The vice-principal and the police chief both must have chronic violators to justify their lofty positions!

School administrators need instances of teacher ineffectiveness and examples of dereliction of *duty* to justify their own need for employment to the board of education. Otherwise, if a principal has a wonderful terrific faculty that commits no mistakes, then the administrator's only alternative is to nit-pick and magnify trivia to constantly make *his* presence known and felt.

If all teachers in a large district were completely "thorough and efficient", then the school board would eventually realize that it doesn't need administrators to handle discipline problems that don't exist, or keep needless executives on the payroll to manage non-existent, incompetent teachers. But school administrators have a big ace trump card slickly hidden up their sleeves! The *democratic, sociological, comprehensive, school* system is inherently inefficient and ineffective, so therefore, no matter how efficient, effective and competent a faculty happens to be, there will always be problems with *students,* with learning, with parents and with teachers.

If a teacher is unhappy working in a school system, he or she is not that marketable when looking for a similar position in another school district. His or her finest move will be at best a horizontal one. But once a teacher becomes an administrator, he or she can bounce all over the state and country and with facility move vertically in terms of remuneration each time he or she transfers into another system.

And if an administrator really wants to be a ball-breaker, he or she can give a teacher a bad recommendation so that the instructor then will be blackballed from just about any district in the state. The closely-knit administrative fraternity will honor the submitted poor teacher evaluation, even though its basis might simply be a sharp personality conflict ongoing between the superior principal and the alleged inferior instructor.

Most school administrators could not hold administrative positions in industry. Take the experienced teachers out of the schools, and education would grind to a halt, and soon districts couldn't properly function; conversely, take the office guidance counselors, vice-principals, supervisors, principals, secretaries and superintendent out of the school building, and nothing major would be missed.

If a hospital administrator were to enter an operating room and start evaluating the way the surgeons were performing an operation, the hospital executive would probably be ejected for violating the doctors' professional ethics. But when school administrators enter classrooms and start negatively assessing and nit-picking a thirty-year teacher's job performance (when the administrator might have taught school for only three years), then the teacher is only an *employee* (not a professional) and is *not* being expertly evaluated by another professional educator.

The administrator is a former educator, and in actuality, not an educator at all. Administrators would have more credibility with teachers if they taught a minimum of two challenging classes like the 8-6ers every day. Then we would see how effective and what kind of educators the administrators really are!

Hospital administrators are quite proficient at interpreting financial data and at ordering medical equipment and materials. School administrators aren't competent businessmen who are worrying about turning a corporate profit and cutting expenses; and also, the building chieftains aren't skilled educators practicing their chosen profession. School administrators are the drones of the educational beehive that feast off of the teachers' labors, and then predator off of the failures of certain faculty members.

How could a principal that taught for only three years step into a Chemistry classroom or into a Trigonometry class setting and perform a meaningful evaluation? How could he or she criticize the teachers' methods when the administrator has a weak foundation in the subject matter, and the teacher being observed has thirty years of practical experience teaching the subject?

How does the classroom teacher feel after being evaluated by twenty different administrators and supervisors a hundred times over his or her thirty-four-year career? Is this pathetic pattern redundancy revisited, or what? Yet this sort of travesty happens thousands of times every school day all across the United States, and it is *principally* done to reinforce the idea that "I am the boss and you are the *employee"*. Classroom observations have more to do with re-establishing the school's vertical pecking order and less to do with improving the quality of education as school principals claim.

During school contract negotiations, many administrators ally with the board of education against the teachers' association. That's when negotiating teachers finally make the realization that the real battle in public schools is the serfs versus the feudal Educational Aristocracy. Many administrators have severed their membership in the *National Education Association*. The school executives know that the *NEA's* goals of improving education are inconsistent with *their* greedy goals of sustaining power over a status quo bureaucratic system that does not produce tangible results.

In the last forty years, the *NEA's* major thrust has been to establish teacher rights, privileges, and professionalism. The ambitious school executives have formed their own professional associations to represent *their* selfish interests that have little to do with education because administrators are not *educators* educating anyone. What doctor doesn't belong to the *AMA?* What lawyer refuses to join the bar association?

The school bureaucrats are smart enough to know that the acquisition of teacher rights translates into the surrendering of administrative "Divine Rights Power" and that teacher emancipation from educational serfdom means the eventual disintegration of executive absolutism in local fiefdoms (schools). And ultimately, the educational revolution will mean the final disintegration of the Educational Aristocracy's autocratic power structure.

And school administrators might just need a refresher course reviewing basic English grammar and spelling. When an English teacher would bring an executive's grammatical error to the principal's attention, he or she would invariably dismiss it as "A secretarial typographical mistake done in a rush". One particular administrative memo read, "I would like to use the upcoming assembly program to recognize student *accomplicements!"* Another gem had the creative use of homophones. "Teachers are to report *student* obscene *jesters* at once!" Tim Carley said to me, "Now John, did the principal mean obscene jesters or obscene gestures?"

"Tim," I answered. "I think the principal means obscene jesters making obscene gestures because obscene gestures making obscene jesters doesn't make too much sense when put in a logical context!"

When superintendents have been around too long, or when a board of education desires to replace one because of conflicting

317

points of view, the board might create a temporary new position like *assistant superintendent* to give a hint to the superintendent that he or she is on the way out. The school board could cut a slick deal with the superintendent such as a colluded contract buyout or a "plum incentive contract".

The superintendent's accumulative sick days could be bought out amounting to two to three years bonus salary. At one particular board meeting in my school district, the superintendent resigned, the assistant superintendent was elevated to be the new super', and then the assistant superintendent's position was eliminated.

At that same board of education meeting, the school board awarded a contract to Northern Brewster Educational Corporation. It just so happened that the suddenly retired superintendent lived on North Brewster Road in another community, and *he* was the new consulting firm being hired.

And so, in summary, the superintendent resigned as an individual and then was rehired as a contracted corporation at the same board of education meeting. It requires at least a month for an individual to become a corporation, so there had to be an element of collusion for a superintendent to resign, become a legal corporation, and then be rehired, all within an hour at a board of education public meeting.

The old superintendent's new corporation resulted in a new form of teacher harassment. The corporation would come into teachers' classrooms and observe them, write-up observations and have conferences to review the teachers' lessons.

The basic problem was that tenured teachers were already being observed twice a year by the building principals, and twice a year by department heads and supervisors, in addition to at least six spot observations a year where administrators would peek into a classroom. If something they didn't like was noticed, like scrap paper under a desk, a negative "spot observation" was written-up.

The present sociological, *democratic* philosophy of education that administrators are intensively advocating generates vast inefficiency and widespread academic mediocrity. State legislatures are currently mandating standardized tests with tough norms, and teachers are being told that they must make their *students* jump through those high hoops and pass the rigorous evaluations.

The chief causes of educational inferiority that the politicians should focus their attention upon are: democratic (socialistic) sociological education; *student* democracy (socialism) in education; the democratic comprehensive high school (one track fits all); and the Educational Aristocracy's exploitation of teachers using duties, subordination and adminis*trivia* as manipulative tools.

While the state and national governments should be devoting their energies to the real causes of educational inefficiency, instead, the distant politicians contemplate mandating irrelevant remote factors. State Senators and the Educational Aristocracy maintain that inter-school busing, teacher tenure, standardized tests at eighth-grade level (when some eighth-graders are reading on a third-grade level), direct parental involvement, along with "advanced teaching methods" are the truly important educational issues of our day. Legislatures are studying the symptoms of the disease and falsely calling the remote symptoms the causes of the colossal educational malady abounding in this country.

Now, this is what politicians ought to be focusing on and mandating about. Grade level norms must be established from first grade up to grade twelve. An eighth-grade teacher should only have to teach *students* that can read and write on a seventh-grade level prior to promotion to eighth-grade the following September. If a *student* cannot do eighth-grade *academic* work by freshman year, then that *student* must be transferred into the vocational track whether his or her parents like it or not. The responsibility for learning must be placed on the *student's* shoulders. If the *student* studies hard, and then desires to transfer back into the academic high school, he or she could switch back if the *child* can pass reading and writing entrance exams' geared to respective grades, nine to eleven.

Right now, teachers are responsible for both teaching and for learning. That's got to stop. The fifty to seventy-five *students* that cause havoc in each thousand-student public high school all across America must be taken-out and then put into vocational schools (or rehabilitation work camps) until *they* forget about bullying and intimidating others, can grow-up, and can get serious about preparing for their futures.

High schools must again become *academic* places and not *sociological* holding platforms where *academic* curriculum offerings are watered-down in order to accommodate underachieving *students*. Psychology has got to be demoted, and true intellectual *academic* pursuit needs to be promoted if our American civilization is to become stronger and be capable of surviving into the next century.

Remove the inefficiency factors (democratic sociological education) and the chaos (*student* discipline problems) from American high schools, and soon true *academic* progress would then finally be generated. But as long as the guardians of inefficiency and chaos (the Educational Aristocracy) are in command of the educational ship, then the vessel will always be perilously drifting and rocking between Scylla and Charybdis every school year. And in conclusion, the ranking officers guiding the passage of the educational ark next September will again be the powerful-and-privileged Educational Aristocracy.

Chapter 35
"Minor Duties"

The consecrated teachers' manual is distributed in early September to faculty members prior to the first day of school. The Teachers Handbook is over several hundred pages thick, and it is the *Koran* that outlines the district's rules for instructors, and it also contains duty rosters for Office Detention, In-School Suspension, cafeteria duty, bus duty, chaperone duty, hall duty, lavatory duty and study hall duty. According to the administrative manifesto, it was and is each teacher's *duty* to perform all those "Howdy duties" in addition to diligently engaging in both the art and the science of teaching *students*.

The thick document must have annually appeared quite impressive and regal to the proud school board members perusing it. But to the teaching staff that daily witnessed the enormous gulf between fantasy and reality, and between fact and fiction, the standard teachers' manual represented the code that justified and promoted teacher serfdom. Bob Gordon, Tim Carley, Tim Amoro and I viewed the hallowed Teachers Handbook as good furnace-ready material worthy of incinerator disposal.

The Teachers Handbook was and still is a peculiar blend of *Mein Kampf*, the *Communist Manifesto*, and *Mad Magazine*. But the manual was also the official administrative law that governed over the teaching staff with an iron fist. The all-powerful handbook outlined the code of ethics and the school policies and rules that effectively *subordinated* the teachers to administrative fiat.

The teachers' manual specified that each instructor on the junior-senior high staff was assigned to have Office Detention on a rotating basis, and the week-long event was to be held after school in a designated classroom. Sometimes, as many as twenty-five alien *students* were being disciplined inside the appointed Detention Room, along with the assigned teacher, who was also indirectly being punished by the administration by being given *that* horrible duty assignment.

The vice-principal or the principal had punished the *student* with Office Detention, but the teachers had to cover the *duty*. Instructors also assigned their own private after-school detentions to *students* that had given them a hard time in *their* own classes. But delegated teachers were not allowed to combine the administrative Office Detention *students* with *their* own private detention *students*.

One ugly feature of Office Detention was that the also punished teacher had to sit in the designated room enforcing a forced silence with many *students* whom he or she didn't even know. During one particular Office Detention, a *student* had placed his face on his assigned desk and then covered his head with his winter coat so that I couldn't see the *child's* eyes, nose or mouth. Three times I told the fourteen-year-old *child* to remove the coat from concealing his pimpled face, but the young viper pretended to be sleeping and not hearing my command. Then, I rose, walked over to the *student's* desk and ordered him a fourth time to hang the coat on the back of his seat. The *child* again ignored my clearly articulated instruction as the nineteen other punished *children* in the room thought that what *he* was doing to teacher authority was especially amusing.

I grabbed the coat from off the *child's* head, and the impudent violator lifted his noggin up from the desk slate, latched onto his coat, and soon a wild tug-of-war resulted over possession of the article of clothing. In the meantime, the *student's* desk flipped-over with him in it. The insolent-and-embarrassed *student* rose from the floor, uttered several derogatory expletives in my direction, and then briskly stepped-out of the room and left the building.

I reported the incident to the building principal via the intercom. The next day the *student* (that I didn't have in a regular English class) returned to school with his mother, who vehemently protested to the principal that I had molested her son in Office Detention and had committed "corporal punishment" for knocking him and his desk onto the floor. Nineteen *student* witnesses verified that they had observed the altercation, and that the teacher definitely was at fault.

I had to write (what amounted to) a four-page letter to the principal explaining exactly what had transpired during the incident. In addition, I had to spend four hours before and after school having conferences with the principal and with the irate parent, whose sister happened to be a former *student* of mine that had gotten pregnant in the sixth grade. All of this wasted time had been consumed because I had to type-up a descriptive letter, and then have a slew of meetings about how I had disciplined and abused the *student* that had covered his head with his winter coat in Office Detention.

More *irregularity* in logic exists in the Teachers Handbook than in a person afflicted with chronic constipation. Once, I had four fairly intelligent *students* serving in Office Detention for throwing food in the cafeteria. I felt a degree of human compassion for the convicted *children,* so I allowed the incarcerated sufferers to play chess and checkers if they remained quiet.

The principal stepped into the Office Detention room, and the administrator immediately observed that the *students* were quietly doing something and not just sitting there silently being 'punished' as he believed they ought to be doing. The following day, the school bureaucrat wrote-up a negative "spot observation" and later chewed me out in his office for violating the rules of Office Detention by having the *children* doing something constructive like quietly playing chess and checkers.

Bus duty before and after school was another hassle that teachers were assigned on a rotating or on a permanent basis. Any time *children* are allowed to congregate in large numbers, whether in the cafeteria, in the halls, or simply standing outside the building waiting to enter, potential trouble exists. Whenever teachers saw a group of more than four *students* huddled together, then *that* specific gathering was usually a sign that a fight was brewing, or it meant that the combatants' lieutenants were either officially negotiating the terms of a brawl or instigating an imminent conflict.

The almighty Teachers Handbook stipulated that staff members had to remain at assigned bus duty posts until the late bell rang in the morning, and also after the last yellow bus departed with its cargo of precious humanoids in the afternoon. "*Students* from other schools and *students* that are suspended (Out-of-School-Suspension and not In-School-Suspension) are not to be on the school grounds," one of the literary edicts commanded.

It didn't take the *students* too long to accurately size-up the situation. Teachers are *the fall guys* in winter, summer, and also in spring, too! They are major players in the daily educational comedy act, shivering out in the freezing cold, yelling at *children* to stay out of the flower beds, and obedient instructors are expected to be role-playing policemen while the local patrolmen are preoccupied at doughnut shops munching-away and drinking hot coffee.

Parents drove into the parking lot, dropped-off their *children,* observed the teachers standing there and thought, 'Look at those teachers just standing there! Teaching is really an easy job! Anybody could do what they are doing!' And those perceptive parents motoring in and out of the parking lot were absolutely correct. It did not require any professional skill to break-up a savage fistfight, to catch or stop *children* from defacing school property by the *students* writing vulgar words on the bricks, getting hit by errant snowballs, or having a tug-of-war over a winter coat in Office Detention. The ugly part of daily duties was that they were degrading, unprofessional, non-teaching assignments where instructors faced abuse from repulsive scamps, some of whom the teachers didn't even know or even have in *their* separate classes.

In the mid-80s, while I was assigned to after school B-Wing hall-duty, a certain Hispanic *student* would blurt-out the word "culo" (pronounced "coolo") to his amused friends (at least once a week) as the quartet passed by my presence as I was faithfully standing outside my classroom door. Now, I instinctively suspected that the reference "culo" was rather disrespectful and inappropriate in any language. So, I reported the incidents to one of the vice-principals, who happened to be bilingual.

"Does the word 'culo' mean something like the word 'asshole'?" I asked the slightly-embarrassed female school executive. "That's what I suspect it means in Spanish according to my gut instinct!"

The bilingual vice-principal confirmed my theory, and the next day personally interrogated the *student,* who then claimed to the disciplinarian that he liked and admired me so much as a terrific English teacher that the *child* was melodramatically emphasizing to his stellar Puerto Rican chums the obvious fact that "Mr. Wiessner was '*cool'!"*

"I also heard you use the term *jacketta* (local Spanish slang for masturbator) when you had walked by me in the hall with your three amigos. What does jacketta mean?"

"Mr. Wiessner, we were saying that you were wearing a really *cool jacket!"* the prevaricating future hood orally conveyed and lied.

I felt obligated to then address the school executive. "Mrs. R., if you naively believe *that* fabricated fib that we just heard," I lividly addressed the Hispanic vice-principal, "then you can also amply appreciate that I own the *El Morro Fortress* down in Old San Juan and that I'm willing to sell the historic location to you for a meager fifty cents!" But naturally, the extremely sly and conniving bilingual *student* violator had very cleverly gotten off the hook.

Every morning in the late '80s, a group of fourteen-year-old rogues would enter the building after the early bell rang, and as the potential delinquents passed by me, one of the more zealous *students* would yell "Hand job"! Being an English teacher, I was just as familiar with the usage of colloquialisms as I was with the communication of formal vernacular parlance. My main objective was to isolate and surprise the brazen offender some future morning and hopefully catch the *child* in the act.

A week later, the ensemble again marched into the building and paraded by my alert presence. One of the *students* scoffed, "I know an English teacher who is a hand job!" in a marvelously constructed exclamatory complex sentence with the relative pronoun "who" starting an adjective subordinate clause. Despite the grammatical correctness of the *child's* utterance, I did not find the connotative character of the toxic *student's* statement morally palatable.

I immediately separated the *child* from the other three luminaries, and then I conveyed the *student* to the Main Office. The three companions simultaneously entered the office suite and testified to the concerned principal that their savant friend had not uttered any profane language.

"What profane language?" I asked the *Three Musketeers*. "How do you three geniuses know that your friend is being accused of yelling profane language?"

"Yes, what profane language?" the principal inquired. "What is your friend being accused of saying?"

The assistant-principal eventually suspended the young orator for two days. But *students* will lie and creatively conspire against a teacher, and then it becomes the prosecutor's (the teacher's) word against *their* word (the defendants), and the affected teacher better have convicting evidence or be able to outsmart the shifty imbeciles in a hurry. The teacher could be fired, but the *students* can't be expelled. Those are the rules of engagement.

Four months later, the detestable *student* that had disrespectfully called the English teacher "Hand job" again crossed my path, but that momentous second time was off of school property. My mother-in-law had twenty-five cute little ducks that swam in the pond next to her home. The adorable chicks soon matured into relatively tame beautiful mallards and female ducks.

The same *student* that had been suspended for calling me a "Hand job" had ambled-out from a neighboring-woods with a shotgun, and the rogue quickly reduced the duck population to twenty-three with one pull of the trigger. I observed the incident from my mother-in-law's kitchen, recognized the trespassing violator, and immediately notified the local game warden. A heavy fine was imposed when a juvenile court judge found "the defendant" guilty as charged.

The boy's parents vigorously protested that the charge and penalty should be dropped, and they both questioned the judge's decision. "I don't want to see my son put in a juvenile detention home for just shooting two ducks!" the incensed father protested. "That teacher picked on my son at school, too!"

My in-laws refused to let the boy off the hook for killing the two ducks without some sort of punitive action being enacted. An alternate solution was finally agreed upon. The *child* had consented to pay having the ducks mounted by a taxidermist, and then was to present the trophies to my in-laws along with a verbal apology. Everyone was in accordance with those conditions, so the aberrant kid's parents consented and endorsed "the settlement".

Six weeks passed, but the agreed-upon compensation was not forthcoming. The doted-on *child,* used to having his own way at home with his parents, had been remiss and forgetful in fulfilling his verbal commitment. After my in-laws threatened the father over the telephone to have the charges reintroduced, the *child's* parents reluctantly had the ducks mounted, and they presented the trophies to my in-laws without the presence of their wonderful son.

Despite the *student's* propensity for abusing teachers and for shooting ducks, the *child* (according to educational psychologists) was still gallivanting around the town finding more mischief to add to his bad reputation. Several months later, the *child* smashed another *student* from behind into the hall lockers and loosened the other boy's front teeth during the brief scuffle. Two weeks after *that* incident, the *child* was arrested and temporarily detained for getting caught siphoning gasoline from an automobile. The *student's* burgeoning school record "Confidential Guidance Folder" revealed over the years a bundle of other in-school misdemeanors. That particular *student* had been found disruptive, disrespectful, belligerent, defiant, and destructive of school property, yet the little thug still remained "the *child*" according to the *Child* Study Team.

But still, other faculty members and I had to daily teach the *child.* I had to contend with the *student's* tawdry commentaries in the hallway, while lofty college professors were lecturing the next batch of teacher candidates, "Motivate and understand your *children,* and be sure that you conscientiously meet each *student's* individual needs!" What unmitigated absurdity!

A teacher never knows what might happen next when on bus duty. He or she can only suspect that something will come out of nowhere, and that the person on duty better be ready for it when the unforeseen event occurs. On one occasion, the Italian father of a new *student* from Sicily caused me some concern while on bus duty. Two Puerto Rican *students* were tormenting his son, so when the Puerto Rican *children* again accosted the new *student* from Italy in the parking lot, the father leaped-out of his car and then began pounding the two Hispanic boys something fierce. Another teacher and I slowly walked over to the scene of chaos because the vigilante immigrant father was only doing exactly what *we* had wished we could be doing to the detestable ruffians.

The police were notified of possible trouble resulting in future incidents stemming from the parental assault of two derelict *students* that suddenly needed protection from a hostile parent. Thirty members of the Puerto Rican boys' extended families were hanging around the school parking lot after dismissal for two solid weeks thereafter, and everyone feared a massive ethnic battle was going to happen between vigilante Italian immigrant parents and the Puerto Rican extended families. Thank goodness things finally settled-down to the same old routine of disorganized organization.

Bus and hall duties weren't exactly enlightening experiences, either. The son of a school board president approached me in the hall in the early '70s and cockily stated, "Mr. Wiessner, I think you should buy a telescope!"

Being curious about the *child's* wild comment, I asked him, "Why do you say that?"

"So that you can see Your-Anus!" the little fool smartly replied.

I was not-too-thrilled with the *student's* perverted sense of humor, and I was quite upset that the audacious youth lacked the discretion to distinguish what was acceptable and what was inappropriate to say to a teacher. I remembered that my college roommate had lost his high school teaching position for failing the son of a school board president in another district, so I had to be careful how I handled the situation with this son of a school board president.

"Your Uranus remark was in bad taste," I emphatically stated. "And I will see that it *mars* your day tomorrow because you have a detention with me after school for not showing good judgment when addressing a teacher!"

It doesn't pay to become too chummy with any *student*, because then, he or she thinks that you can be talked to as if you were one of the *student's* favorite peers. 'Always stay on the shelf above,' I mentally reprimanded myself.

Quite frankly, over the course of my career, I had heard *that* stupid Uranus joke being prefaced at least a dozen redundant times by the sons of *students* that had tried to implement it in the past, but each time I cautioned the young instigator, "Don't go there! I've heard that lewd joke a hundred times before, and I don't want to hear it again!" I would preemptively indicate.

A new wrinkle to hall duty was called "Sniff patrol", or better known as "Potty patrol"! Teachers were assigned to enter and stand in the boys' and girls' bathrooms between the changing of classes to make sure that no *students* were smoking when they were doing their thing. Such a degrading daily chore made me question what was professional about being a professional person. "Now we're going to be accused of voyeurism!" I told Tim Carley.

"I'm as thrilled about it as *Superman* finding kryptonite in his Christmas stocking!" Tim disgustedly replied.

The only school administrator that I ever felt any compassion for was the vice-principal, who held the most unrewarding job in the building. The assistant-principal was continually besieged with the same delegation of fifty to seventy-five *students* that repeatedly required discipline over and over again from September to June. The poor vice-principal never saw much progress in the deportment of the repeat offenders, and he seldom had any contact with the more productive *students* in the junior-senior high school.

Duties are damaging to the teacher's ego, spirit, sense of purpose and finally, to general faculty morale. While I was stationed in the hall on early morning duty, I observed an impulsive male *student* grabbing an unreceptive girl's arms and then wildly shaking her shoulders. I hustled over to the scene of molestation and yelled, "Stop harassing that girl!"

The aggressive thug looked me squarely in the eyes and instantly blurted back, using a common double negative: "I didn't do nothin' to *her ass!*"

Chaperone duty without pay was another headache prescribed in the administrative-mandated Teachers Handbook. "A teacher assigned to chaperone duty must be acquainted with the rules and regulations required for an activity or trip," the manual specifies. "The chaperone's attitude, actions and manners will set the tone for proper *student* deportment. Chaperones are required to check lavatories at frequent intervals. And the chaperones are to stay at the *school* until all *students* have safely left the *school* site."

The phraseology published in the Teachers' Handbook was written in an imperative command-mode tone, and the statements were usually worded to sound like something between the Code of Hammurabi and the Laws of Draco. I have known more teachers that have gotten into more trouble on "Duties" and while coaching teams, or when advising extra-curricular clubs than they had while instructing *students* in classrooms. Just recollect the *child* opening the bus window in the middle of the *Lincoln Tunnel*, the *child* with his coat over his head in Office Detention, and the *child* calling me a

"Hand job" while I was on bus/hall duty to fully comprehend the veracity of my claim.

Once while I was a chaperone on a splendid three-day and two-night Williamsburg Trip, a group of girls was loudly singing and bending the superintendent's ears with rock and roll lyrics with a few expletives imaginatively inserted here and there.

"Mr. Wiessner, can't *you* make those girls settle-down!" the oppressed superintendent complained as the traveling executive attempted to delegate responsibility for disciplining them to me. "I insist that you do something!"

"Just pretend that this field trip is to *Sing-Sing* and not to Williamsburg!" I indulgently laughed. "Girls will be girls!"

"Mr. Wiessner, I want you to quiet those young ladies down right now!" the humiliated superintendent sternly ordered. "Or else, I'll see you in my office next Monday!"

"Those girls are future pipe fitters and boiler room technicians just letting off a little steam!" I facetiously replied and laughed. "Okay girls, *settle-down,* or you'll have to *settle-up* with me!"

"Okay, Mr. Wiessner!" they all chanted.

On that same wonderful Williamsburg Trip, some anonymous *student* or *students* had placed a wad of chewing gum on the superintendent's seat while the bus was being boarded at a rest stop. The head school executive sat-down on the sticky mess, which adhered to the seat of his pants quite noticeably.

"Mr. Wiessner!" the superintendent exclaimed. "Didn't you see who had put the bubble gum on my seat?"

"No, I was too busy taking attendance!" I frankly confessed.

Then the superintendent asked the Science teacher chaperone if he could suggest a chemical or a compound that would effectively remove the bubble gum from his trousers.

"Go into a drugstore when we get to Williamsburg and buy some lady's fingernail polish remover!" the middle school Science teacher answered the livid superintendent with his tongue-in-cheek. "But just to be sure of that *solution,* I'll have to research the problem some more, and then I'll give you a more conclusive reply!"

"Your solution better work!" the superintendent threatened. "I still remember *you* ordering an extravagant, overpriced school bus for your Science Classes on last year's classroom requisition form for the school budget!"

"That school bus was to be used for scientific ecological experiments at the town park!" the Science teacher admirably stated, defending his school bus purchase request. "Maybe if I could get the new school bus lab' next year, I can figure-out a reliable formula for safe bubblegum removal!"

Chaperoning the high school dances was another headache supervisory duty. Most of the dances were seldom well-attended because the *students* preferred partying on their own in somebody's empty house with the parents being on vacation than to be supervised by chaperones in a semi-formal setting. When teenagers had access to alcohol, beer, tobacco, drugs and loose members of the opposite sex, the *children* found chaperoned high school dances rather boring and unexciting.

Even at the junior-senior prom, the *students* were like tigers trapped in a cage and couldn't wait to escape down the shore to freedom, and then stay up all night at rented motel rooms in Wildwood and Atlantic City. *Student* activities like proms, dances, cheerleading practice, and pep' assemblies that were big events back in the 1950s were now basically assessed as going-through-the-motions' anachronisms in the years 1970 to 2003.

In the early '70s, my wife and I had the pleasure to serve as chaperones for the junior-senior prom, which was held at a prestigious country club fifteen miles outside of the town. The *students* all looked suave and debonair, all decked out in tuxedoes and evening gowns. I told Bob Gordon that the boys must have all fallen into evergreen trees because they were "all *spruced* up"!

This was during the *Vietnam War student* protest era, so the junior-class officers wanted to show their independence of adult authority. The administration made a concession and permitted the *student* prom committee to select their own "acceptable orchestra" for the very formal occasion.

The band (orchestra) "The Infidels" did not show-up on time, and the administrators in attendance were becoming a trifle uneasy. Everyone seemed relieved when the attendees observed several shabbily dressed hillbillies carrying the equipment and the musical instruments inside for the hired, very expensive virtuosos. But then the senior prom' advisor and the school administrators were appalled to discover that the tawdry-looking hillbillies *were also* the illustrious virtuosos that had been hired to play for the *students* that were decked-out in their handsome tuxedoes and in their glamorous-looking evening gowns.

"At least the girls are still wearing gowns and not tuxedoes and the boys are not wearing gowns!" I related to fellow chaperone Bob Gordon. "This transgender thing is becoming the vogue," I jested.

"Even if they were," Bob answered, "the *orchestra* would still look like Hobos Incorporated!"

The minstrel yokels were really an "underground band" that played all unfamiliar, raunchy, rock and roll music. The oddball-looking musicians were dressed in ripped denim jeans, paint-spattered sweatshirts, tie-dye tee shirts, and tarnished tennis shoes and beach clogs. The musical hippie' bumpkins looked like shoddy derelicts and mendicants just returning from a *Bowery* "Hobos Incorporated" mission soup kitchen.

And after the introduction of the *orchestra* members, the six shabby-looking minstrels played their own anonymous songs, none of which were top '40s' chartbusters. "This is *democracy* in action!" I sarcastically told Bob Gordon.

"Let's move to Russia where things are safer!" Bob answered with a chuckle. "Then at least we could hear the *Beatles* sing a familiar song like 'Back in *the USSR*' on the radio!"

But the *student* committee had made *their democratic* decision for *their* prom, even if the adults in attendance had evaluated the fiasco as a disastrous affair. As the dissonant strains blasted away, I said to Bob Gordon, "When are music cycle fads going to bring back Guy Lombardo and Frank Sinatra?"

"J.W., you'll have to change your name to Guy Lumbago before that scenario ever happens and besides," Bob continued, "I sorta' like the psychedelic flashing strobe lights."

"They mustn't be working right," I indicated, "because those strobe lights are always on the blink!"

The almighty, imperial Teachers Handbook emphatically states, "The purpose of hall duty is to maintain order in all sectors of the building. Teachers must monitor the halls by standing outside their respective classrooms during the change of classes."

The hall duty administrative edict was about as foolish as Captain Ahab ordering Starbuck, Stubb and Flask to levitate *Moby Dick* twenty feet above the Indian Ocean to make the great white whale easier to harpoon. While the teacher was outside monitoring the hall, thirty *students* had already filed into the classroom. If a *child* shattered a window or broke another *student's* clavicle in the classroom while the dutiful teacher was busy in the hall monitoring the change of classes, then the instructor would be held responsible for the property damage, or for the personal *student* injury incurred. I rarely abided by the hall duty passage in the teachers' manual since the laws of physics have verified many times that a person can't be in two different places at one time. I always regarded the classroom as my cardinal *duty,* and the corridor as my secondary one.

If the teacher elects to supervise the corridor, then he or she is in for a special treat. Couples might be smooching next to their lockers, *students* might be bartering ecology patches for swastika metal-linked neck chains, other *children* might be shoving, smacking or deliberately or accidentally bumping into one another, and still other hyperactive angels might be tripping, kicking or grabbing their contemporaries. When I would witness the general ongoing chaos happening, I would then close my door and seal-off my individual responsibility from the external, un-intriguing mayhem.

"This is *democracy* in action in the comprehensive school!" I once declared to Bob Gordon while the aforementioned weird *student activities* in the hallway were transpiring.

"It's too bad these kids didn't have parents that eat their young!" Bob answered with a smile and a chuckle before we both entered our respective classrooms.

"Well Bob; it's too bad that youth is wasted on the young!" I regretfully replied. "Now Robert, when I was a commonplace teenager in high school, all I had to think and worry about was how to pass Algebra and Trigonometry!"

Chapter 36
"Degrading Grading"

The infallible Teachers Handbook instructions imperatively decreed, "Homework should be carefully planned to meet the ability levels and resources of the *students*." Quite obviously, I could never assign the 8-6ers eighth-grade level homework out of the eighth-grade grammar, vocabulary and literature textbooks because the "ability levels and resources" of the aforementioned eighth-grade 8-6ers ranged from third to fifth grade skill achievement.

I seldom gave homework to any of my six eighth-grade sections for various, strategic reasons. When I did prescribe homework, many parents complained that the exercises were too demanding on their *children* that had to go to dancing lessons, to sleepovers, or to night football practice. And when an English teacher has a hundred and thirty *students* scattered in six different classes every day, at least twenty of them are absent each day from mid-October to mid-April. And then during early December, a lot of the boys are not in school because of deer hunting week. One day, the first week of December, I counted nearly two hundred *students* absent out of eight hundred that were supposed to be in the building. And of course, in May and June, the *children* forget about school and head for the New Jersey boardwalks and beaches.

So, I quickly learned to compromise my academic values and rarely gave time-consuming homework assignments. There was also a valid educational reason for me not assigning homework other than required compositions that needed a full week to do going from outline, to rough drafts on notebook paper, to final drafts on composition or typing/computer paper. When grammar exercises were assigned, for example, the next day's class time was always spent *"reviewing* homework *reviews"* rather than concentrating on teaching new material. So, since I preferred propagating the curriculum rather than *reviewing* homework exercises all the time, I taught instead of reviewed.

A teacher can also risk getting into a big hassle with a hostile parent over something simple like homework. A parent called the guidance office in the early '70s and scheduled a conference. Any time that a parent initiated or requested the conference, a red flag went-up in my mind. When the teacher requested a conference, then the instructor always had the upper hand and could control the flow of the discussion because he or she knew exactly what the content of the conference would be all about.

I requested that the *child's* guidance counselor sit-in on the "potentially hostile" parent/teacher meeting and act as a neutral referee, if necessary. The father of the *student* and I got into it pretty hot and heavy. The debate billowed for thirty-five minutes (this happens sometimes when the parent believes he or she knows more about education than the teacher does). If Emily Post or Dear Abby were sitting-in on the debating, they would have had French conniptions listening to the wrangling that was going-on between the "hostile parent" and me. The parent was a former non-tenure teacher that had gotten canned by another school system because *he* had had trouble disciplining *students*.

The aggravated parent/father/former teacher was contending that I should not have given his son meaningless homework looking-up synonyms from an extensive vocabulary list and generally, he didn't find favor with my long-term "laborious and too-strenuous" homework project assignments. "My son likes animals!" the irate father ranted. "You should teach him more lessons about animals!" the school visitor loudly boomed.

I had had scads of college educational courses in which the father's type of weak logic had been preached. Ever since kindergarten, the *child* had teachers that diligently attempted meshing the curriculum to *his* personal needs, but the *student* still had difficulty in eighth-grade English in the areas of spelling, grammar, and organizing and presenting his ideas in writing. "Your son might be fond of animals," I told the enraged father. "But his writing skills are still deficient, whether he is writing about dogs and horses or writing about Jack London and Edgar Allan Poe!"

I mentioned to the crazed father that several weeks before the parent-requested conference, I had taught a literature lesson on dinosaurs, and two weeks before that, *we* had read and discussed a non-fiction story about camels, and still another one about ostriches. "Your son didn't have too much to contribute when we studied those three animal lessons!" I boldly challenged the fit-to-be-tied, axe-grinding father.

"You're acting unprofessionally, Mr. Wiessner!" the public-relations-minded guidance counselor intervened. "Please show more sensitivity to the *student* and to his father!"

I left the confrontational parent/teacher conference a little rattled, but I still had to maintain my composure and act as if nothing out of the ordinary had happened right through my next four teaching classes, and also through a nerve-racking cafeteria duty period.

The trend over the last fifty years in public school education has been to teach the "idea curriculum" to *students* that don't know how to read, spell, punctuate, write, add, subtract, multiply and divide at grade level. The *children* have been taught the "why" of theories and ideas while the "how and basic skills" have been relegated in status to be secondary in importance. And so, *students* sometimes understand the reasoning for multiplication, but don't know their multiplication tables (remember that *memorizing* is a dirty word in modern education).

Most *students* in eighth-grade were adept at identifying a story's main idea, but somehow, many were always weak in spelling, grammar and punctuation. Computers have compounded this problem with built-in grammar and spell check programs. In the late '80s, *students* began handing-in nearly flawless compositions for homework. But when the *children* had to write a paragraph in class to be handed in at the end of the period without mommy, daddy or the computer rendering valuable assistance, even the accelerated *students'* spontaneous writings were often rather atrocious in quality.

The elementary schools, which should be engaged in emphasizing *elementary* grade-level skills, are now havens for the fraudulent "idea curriculum". Math' can't be done effectively unless the *student* has mastery of multiplication tables and division rules, but now with every *student* having a calculator (a means to an end), *children* depend on the device to provide the skills they had never learned or mastered. So, the idea curriculum across the board from Math' to writing proficiency has detrimentally demoted and deferred basic skills to robotic calculators in Math' class and to robotic computers in Language Arts classes.

What good is a *student* that can think but can't read or write without a "servant machine" spelling and figuring-out information for him or her? Public schools are now full of *Harry Potter* young wizards that can't spell, write, or calculate on their own without the aid of *magical thinking skill machines*.

I found that fighting the wasteful "idea curriculum" was as futile as standing in a snow-covered valley and commanding an onrushing avalanche to get back on the top of the mountain. Only an alert and knowledgeable public will be capable of sobering-up the bureaucratic Educational Aristocracy and bringing both theory and practice down to earth where they rightly belong.

The porous trend to stress ideas over basic skills in elementary schools has hampered genuine educational progress from the early 1970s up to the present. Schools also wrongly emphasize group adjustment instead of emphasizing the development of individual academic autonomy. Machiavellian administrators allow educational psychology and community sentiments to combine to form the invincible Educational Aristocracy power structure. When all of these negative forces interact, teaching staffs across the country are put in tenable and unenviable positions. The harried instructors must teach *academics* to *students* that are lacking in basic grade-level skills development. Sociology then transcends academics as the dominant purpose of American public schools.

And when Jimmy Brown can't write well, and when Johnny Jones can't read up to par, the public is conditioned by the Educational Aristocracy (through the mass media) that more demanding teacher' standards are necessary to thwart and stop the decay. When the press releases statistics showing how standardized test scores are falling, the teachers are blamed, and not the quixotic theories of "Outer Limits" college professors and educational psychologists preaching their distorted gospel in the one-tracked, *Democratic,* comprehensive high school.

The teachers are both the villains and the victims caught in the philosophical/sociological/academic riptide. The pedagogues are trapped in a *sociological, student*-oriented maze that should really be a streamlined straight *academic* tunnel to success where *students* are held responsible for learning subjects. Each teacher must tote his or her cross while he or she atones each and every day for the bungling Educational Aristocracy's deficiencies and academic sins.

The almighty Teachers Handbook states, "Each teacher must send out warning letters and/or progress reports to all *students.* The warning letters to failing *students* and the progress reports to average and above average *students* are to be dispatched during the middle of each of the four marking periods".

Okay, the school year has four report card periods, and four mid-marking period warning letter intervals. That means that each of a teacher's hundred and thirty *students* must receive eight formal evaluations sent home to parents every single year. Every progress report and each warning letter must have four computerized comments for each *student,* and the same implementation goes for each report card distribution.

Figure it out. A hundred and thirty *students* times eight reports, times four comments per student, + marking period grades and comments = 4,680 circles that have to be colored-in each year with number two pencils upon the computerized warning letter/progress report tear sheets, and also recorded upon the computerized comment/report card spreadsheets.

I have more than once spent more time writing out a *student's* warning letter than the delinquent *student* who is receiving the bad recommendations had spent laboring in my English class. Midmarking period warning letters simply confirm the contention that *democracy in education* has synthesized *student* irresponsibility by making non-academic *students* take *academic* courses that must be watered-down to gracefully accommodate the weaker *students'* low skill levels.

When teachers must spend valuable time and energy completing warning letters, they are verifying that *students* are incapable of self-evaluation as prescribed by almost every *cooperative learning* teaching method. Also, the need for *student* warning letters confirms that many lackluster *students* don't go home and communicate to their parents the truth about how badly *they* are performing in school.

The school administrator will advise teachers not to fail too many *students* because then that will constitute an indictment of the instructor's inability to get the *academic* (sociologically adjusted and diluted) subject matter across to the *children* functioning in his or her care. And if a *student* becomes complacent and lazy after midmarking period warning letters are sent home, then the teacher must notify the parents of a significant drop in that *child's* grades.

The teachers must perform *that* additional service because the public-relations-minded administrators don't want to receive nasty phone calls from protesting parents that want to pin the tail on the teacher instead of on their own apathetic *children*. So again, the teacher's accountability is expanded to compensate for the corresponding decrease in *student* responsibility.

All along, the school administrators insist that teachers adhere to the increasing "professional obligations" (warning letters, phone calls to parents, parent conferences) that are really promoting *student* dereliction of personal liability while then coincidentally, also undermining *student* responsibility in a *democratic* comprehensive high school. This excessive delegation resulting in additional paperwork and liability makes the teacher even more of a *generalist* and removes him or her further away from becoming a professional *specialist*. When teachers have to do more record keeping and clerical work, they begin realizing how *futile* and *feudal* our

American educational system really is. More clerical work translates into *student* learning suffering from the instructor's wasted time constantly doing "keeping-up" secretarial bookkeeping.

The Teachers Handbook states in relation to *student* grades, "The minimum failing grade for any test or evaluation is to be the grade of 60. Grades below 60 are to be raised to 60 when factoring in the students' final marking period averages.

A	93-100	Superior
B	85-92	Above Average
C	77-84	Average
D	70-76	Below Average
F	60-69	Failure

The following shall be the scale for computing a student's marking period Grade:

A = 4
B = 3
C = 2
D = 1
F = 0

Note: The letter values for each marking period grade where the final average arrives at .5 or five-tenths will be rounded off to the next highest grade. For example, 84.5 average shall become a B (85).

Case	1st M.P.	2nd M.P.	3rd M.P.	4th M.P.	Final Average	Final Grade
(a)	F = 0	F = 0	D = 1	F = 0	0.25	F
(b)	F = 0	D = 1	F = 0	D = 1	0.50	D
(c)	D = 1	D = 1	C = 2	C = 2	1.50	C
(d)	D = 1	C = 2	B = 3	A = 4	2.50	B
(e)	C = 2	F = 0	F = 0	F = 0	0.50	D

First of all, the academic course is watered down to accommodate average and low ability *students*. Secondly, no test, quiz or homework grade could be less than a 60 in the teacher's grade book. If a *student* earns a 20 on a test, soon it magically becomes a numerical 60 failing grade. By rounding up a .5 to the final marking period grade, a *student* (*case e*) can fail three marking periods and get a C in one marking period and still pass the year. In *case b*, the *student* fails two marking periods and gets two D's in the other two marking periods, and the lucky (lazy) *child* still passes the course with a D average.

Now, let's examine the subtle changes in this grading system in even more detail by first looking at the old grading system for a particular 8-6 *student's* statistical marking period grades as had been recorded in the teacher's grade book:

20-30-75-85-95-100 = 400 points on tests
400 points divided by six grades = 66.7 Average (F)

The above 8-6 *student* in a watered-down curriculum would have failed English for that particular marking period. Now, I'll follow the same procedure under the new marking system, substituting 60's for all grades under 60.

60-60-75-85-95-100 = 470 points on tests
470 points divided by six grades = 78.3 Average (C)

The same 8-6 *student* in the diluted curriculum would have failed under the old grading system, but he or she now magically receives the marking period grade of C.

This new kind of grading is becoming popular all over the United States to further camouflage the severe inadequacies of *academic democratic education* (an obvious contradiction unto itself) in the comprehensive school. Fewer failures ensure better school-public relations, while the continuation of the issuance of letter grades projects the false illusion of "quality control" to the public.

The new sociologically engineered trend (that undermines true *academic* performance) is founded on two illogical premises. The *student* is graded as an individual according to his performance in a given subject, and the curriculum is then adjusted to the needs of each *student*. The grading system has been adjusted to each *student* and not the curriculum, and the 8-6 individual that should have failed is then rewarded with a C marking period average. And all of this inane charade was done *after* the teacher slowed-down an *academic* course, diluted it, made the tests easier, and graded each assignment more liberally than he or she would have done with an Accelerated English class.

The new type of grading system is *degrading* to teachers all over America. All standards are compromised in teaching the academic subject, and then again compromised in numerically evaluating the *student's* mediocre performance. English class suddenly becomes a well-oiled revolving door for even 8-6 *students* to pass through. Even with all of the concessions made for low-ability *students*, many of them would still fail if the final marking period grade was exclusively determined by performance on tests and quizzes. Teachers also give grades for class participation, for homework, for projects and for the completion of all compositions (class proficiencies) to balance-out documented low-test-grades.

Teacher-made tests are now being relegated in status in deference to homework grades, to attendance grades, and to class participation grades. Since about one-fourth of the eighth-grade *students* can't do grade-level work, eighth-grade teachers would be committing academic hari-kari if they "tell it like it is" and fail *that quarter* of the whole. And giving a final exam' to *students* could in itself be a veritable nightmare.

Once, I was administering the eighth-grade English Final Literature Examination to one of my six classes. A female *student* entered the classroom twenty-five minutes late while the test was in progress. Although the *student* knew all about the important exam', she had been in Home Economics class volunteering to clean-up a mess she had deliberately made to avoid coming directly to English class. The *student* then received an admission pass to my room from the Home Economics teacher, who was unaware of me giving a final exam'.

"You must take the exam!" I told the girl.

"But I had a pass from the Home Ec' teacher!" the *student* argued. "I'll never have time to finish it!"

"You're disturbing the class that is taking the exam' right now!" I insisted. "You were not absent from school and knew all about the fact that the final exam' was being given today. You were absent for half the period because *you* decided to spend the first half of it in the Home Economics room!"

"You're really a mean and insensitive teacher!" the *student* balked and squawked. "No wonder why the other kids hate you!"

The next morning, the principal received a nasty phone call from the girl's infuriated father. The school mogul summoned me to his office and editorialized, "I agree that the *student* must have been playing games and planned to miss your test," the school bureaucrat began, "but I can't support you making the girl take the whole test in only half a period. Your action would be hard to justify at a higher level. We're on shaky grounds here!"

"What should I do?" I requested knowing.

"Allow the *student* to take the test after school tomorrow so that everything becomes a wash!" the weak-hearted principal advised.

And so, I had to give up forty-five minutes of *my time* after school the following day to accommodate a *student* that had deliberately come to class late that wasn't prepared to take the exam' the day before. The *student* was guilty of being stealthy and deceptive. The teacher made a decision based on the known facts. The *child's* parent protested to the administrator. The school administrator admonished the teacher and rewarded the *student* for being irresponsible and ill-prepared for taking the exam' on the scheduled day. And finally, I had to eat humble pie and administer the exam' to the girl after school the following day on *my time*.

Whenever a teacher takes a stand that incurs a parent's wrath, the administration will normally side with the parent because the teacher is an *employee* (not a professional) that can be manipulated. The parent does not work for the principal. Just like the "customer is always right" in business, "The parent is usually always right in school matters when dealing with teachers"!

After a while, a teacher surrenders his ethical soul and plays the administrators' public relations game with parents. The core subject teacher then does not send too many negative warning letters home each mid-marking period, and he or she no longer fails too many non-performing, unmotivated *students*. The *academic* course is also significantly diluted to allow even the slowest of the slow and the dumbest of the dumb to pass with a D.

And amazingly, the teacher has suddenly made his or her job much easier! The teacher is now more into sociological education and has essentially exited the myriad troubles associated with academic education. Guidance counselors and administrators are no longer bugging the teacher about too many *student* failures, about too many warning letters, and about too many unpleasant parent phone calls.

The teacher of sociological education now has a lot fewer confrontational parent conferences to tie him or her up than when he or she was more into enforcing *academic* education. Furthermore, parents and *students* are no longer transferring the *child's* irresponsibility to the teacher and vociferously blaming the instructor for everything and anything. The teacher is now "a good sensitive person" because the kiddies (the true experts on education) actually like the benign, easy instructor. Even the teacher's pet dog seems to like him or her better than when he or she used to come home as a grumpy, *academic* education teacher.

Teachers soon learn that by playing the silly little administrators' game of "Simple Simon Says", everybody in the community now thinks and believes that those converted, sensitive, sociological educators are the greatest things going on two legs besides Britney Spears and Ozzie Osbourne.

Chapter 37

"The Williamsburg Field Trips"

Throughout my thirty-four-year teaching career, I had been on over a hundred field trips, mostly with seventh and eighth-grade *students*. Some of the more exotic destinations have been Philadelphia, Baltimore's *Inner Harbor,* Atlantic City, New York, *Hershey Park, Kings Dominion, Six Flags Great Adventure* in New Jersey, Luray Caverns, Washington DC, *Dorney Park* in Allentown, Pennsylvania, and over a dozen times on the emotionally traumatic Williamsburg/Washington DC field trip.

The three-day and two-night annual eighth-grade field trip to Washington/Williamsburg was definitely the most harrowing misadventure that could easily whittle away at a teacher's valued life expectancy. At certain times on the bus, the *children* would be screaming so loudly that I thought the juveniles were testing the malleability of my ears' tympanic membranes.

The *students* would kick each other across the bus aisle, slap and punch the *children* sitting behind them or in front of them, and quite mischievously put chewing gum (which was forbidden and against school rules) into girls' long tresses. Some of the more boisterous and aggressive *children* behaved as if they were rookies vying for starting positions in a professional football team's training camp. A traveling sideshow class of a hundred and fifty fourteen-year-old squealing demons could dramatically transform an ordinarily tranquil motel into a rather frenzied scene.

I recollect one particular excursion down to Williamsburg, Virginia very well. Four buses were commissioned to transport the pint-sized eighth-grade Philistines. I was assigned to Bus #1 along with another teacher Rob Renbeck and the superintendent of schools. "Where are you going to sit?" I asked the school system's chief executive before I boarded the bus.

"In the front," the superintendent replied. "I always like to sit in the front directly in back of the driver."

"Okay," I said, nodding my head. "I guess I'll be sitting in the back somewhere with Mr. Renbeck. First, I'll take attendance!"

I stepped onto the bus while the superintendent was gabbing with the other chaperones, with the principal, and with the school nurse. After surveying the caliber of *students* sitting aboard, I rearranged the *children*'s seats while I took the roll to make sure everyone on my Bus #1 roster list was safely accounted for. I made sure that all of the worse-behaved *children* were sitting up front with the superintendent with the better-behaved *students* moved in the rear with the other teacher and me.

After an hour of motoring southward (on the *Delaware Memorial Bridge* just before *I-95)*, the ornery tendencies of the more-naughty rascals surfaced in the anterior section of the bus. The *children* hooted, chanted and carried-on, testing the mettle of the school system's chief administrative official. And before a person could recite the Russian alphabet, the *children* seated toward the front of the vehicle then began singing popular television jingles with occasional dirty words imaginatively being substituted for the original rhyming ones.

Several of the boys up front started shouting and sounding like they were a covey of inebriated hoot owls as the energized rascals explored the boundaries of being free of parental control. Many of the less illustrious *students* had never been out of New Jersey before, and didn't know how to act civilized in public (or in private). In fact, the imps acted like little spoiled scamps, just the same way they had always been behaving in school.

While the back of the bus was rather calm, the front (where the superintendent had been sitting with *his* rigged audience) produced a racket sounding akin to an ancient Roman gladiatorial contest. The mystified school superintendent turned-around several times to get my attention, but I astutely ignored his eye contact, pretending to be taking in the blurred scenes flitting by my side window.

"The *super'* looks a trifle distressed!" I laughed to Rob Renbeck, my teaching comrade. 'It's good that he's getting a taste of reality!"

"The front of the bus sounds like a juvenile gang fight in a teenage cabaret," Rob chuckled and answered. "This is really great!"

"He must think we're fantastic disciplinarians," I jested. "Rob, let's step to the front of the bus and settle the little urchins down so that we don't have to quickly perform emergency *CPR* on the very rattled superintendent."

The flustered superintendent was a bald-headed, intellectual-philosophical type of character, and "Dr. Socrates" actually impressed me by showing a remarkable bit of disciplinary skill while at the booked Williamsburg motel. The *children* had just finished swimming that evening in the motel's pool. Next, the euphoric lads and lasses had dinner at the motel and at ten, everyone was supposed to be in their respective rooms. At ten-thirty, the superintendent was standing outside telling Rob Renbeck, Joe Sacci (the music teacher) and me how he had surprised several *students* that had tried sneaking out of a Washington motel room back in 1950.

"I was down by the pool at the Washington motel, just like we're standing out here right now," the superintendent explained to apathetic Rob, Joe and me. "Then I spotted two girls sneaking out of their motel room on the second floor and I yelled, 'Hey you, up there'!" the head honcho bellowed and then laughed as he turned and pointed-up to the motel's balcony without really looking up at it.

Well, it was a very unbelievable case of déjà vu. When the superintendent yelled-out "Hey *you* up there!" with his back to the motel's balcony and then turned, two girls sneaking out of their room had thought that the superintendent had caught them in the act of escaping while he was emphatically telling the three of us his mundane 1950 story. The startled young ladies re-entered their room thinking and worrying that they would be seriously reprimanded. The superintendent had caught and indirectly disciplined two girls at the Williamsburg motel violating the rules without his knowledge as the narrator was cheerfully describing in 1977 a similar incident in Washington that had occurred way back in 1950.

"What's so funny?" the Socratic-type superintendent asked when noticing that perceptive Rob Renbeck, Joe Sacci and I were holding our stomachs while laughing so hard.

"You tell the funniest stories!" I cleverly answered as Rob Renbeck nearly lost his balance and almost tumbled backward, nearly launching Joe and him into the motel's swimming pool.

On another trip down to Williamsburg from New Jersey, some nutcase sniper (on the passenger side of a passing left-hand-lane car) had an air rifle and took a shot at the driver's side window. The glass internally shattered while the bus was going sixty-five miles-per-hour down *I-95* between Wilmington, Delaware and Baltimore. All four chartered buses on the class trip heading south stopped, and we had to wait for the Maryland State Police to arrive so that a report of the incident could be filed.

That same beleaguered bus driver should have read *his* horoscope before re-embarking toward Washington. As the driver of Bus 1 made a wide right-hand turn heading onto Independence Avenue toward the *Capitol Building,* a taxi cab driver tried passing the bus on the right. The dual bus and auto' turned simultaneously, and the bus smashed the taxicab into a parked car.

The already stressed-out bus driver got into two heated arguments at the same time with the Iranian taxicab driver and an Iraqi that owned the stalled, parked automobile that had had its hood open. It was a unique dispute because neither the Iranian nor the Iraqi yelled and screamed in English, while the accursed bus driver was bellowing an assortment of expletives at the two foreigners using very understandable and graphic American language. The vehement yelling and cursing really entertained the *children* that had recently been evacuated from the bus after the collision.

The thought of the annual Williamsburg pilgrimage always made me shudder with apprehension. In 1978, the hundred and fifty screaming, neurotic demons were impatiently waiting for entrance into a *Smithsonian Institute* special exhibit area. A female teacher-chaperone brought it to my attention that the *students* were blocking the other tourists' access to the exhibit's single ticket booth, so I chivalrously commanded in a loud authoritarian voice for the eighth-grade *students* to "slowly shift to the right".

As I casually shuffled to the front of the *students'* irregular line, a young married couple began shouting a stream of criticisms directly toward me. The pair of "civilians" apparently had become unhappy campers mixed-up inside the legion of eighth-grade maniacs moving to the right, and the pair had been severely jostled around in the turbulent *student* migration. The young man yelled in my ear, "Look, Buddy. Your kids almost crushed my wife and me. We didn't appreciate being mauled and knocked about by your discourteous teenagers! Your kids are obnoxious!"

"Sir, I was only trying to show the other tourists some courtesy by making the ticket booth accessible to them!" I diplomatically replied. "I guess my maneuver backfired! But you're absolutely right about them being obnoxious!"

A crowd of bloodthirsty fourteen-year-old *children* crowded-around the stressed-out fellow, his protesting wife and me, and the throng of juveniles began shrieking, "Give him a shot in the nose Mr. Wiessner!" and "Teach him a little karate, Wheesey baby!"

I immediately felt like a frustrated toreador at a bullfight with my maneuvers geared to the emotional interests of aspiring adolescent delinquents. The *students* actually wanted to see their English teacher get into a wild fistfight with a simple, disgruntled tourist and his equally distressed wife.

"Sock it to him, Mr. Wiessner!" a young fight enthusiast boisterously hooted. "Hit him upside his head!"

"Listen Mister, do you see this mob of screaming young devils?" I told the shocked fellow as I pointed to the psyched-up crowd of idiotic youths. "How would *you* like to take my place and be in charge of these hormone-driven hellions?"

"No thank you!" the still-stunned husband instantly concluded and answered. "My wife and I have already felt their wrath!"

"God bless you!" the wife apologetically exclaimed as she and her spouse voluntarily moved away from the ticket window vicinity to the back of another exhibit line.

Events that suddenly emerge out of nowhere can make long-distance overnight field trips about as desirable as a chicken hawk colony flourishing on a poultry farm. As the buses rumbled through the federal government district of Washington, DC, I was amazed at the weird observations the more alert *students* were making while glancing outside their clean bus windows. None of the magnificent white marble monuments and obelisks that the young passengers had recently viewed at an eighth-grade *educational* assembly slide presentation had interested them in the least.

As the bus driver announced over the microphone, "There's the *White House* on your right!" several *students* looking in the opposite direction of revered 1600 Pennsylvania Avenue then yelled to their classmates, "Hey, look at that goofy guy selling balloons!" and "Check-out that drunk begging for booze money!" But that was not the rule for several of the more serious *students* that had asked when pointing at the magnificent *White House*, is that the *Capitol?* Or, is *that* the *Supreme Court Building?"*

The purpose of the Williamsburg/Washington trips was to cultivate an appreciation of American history and of our nation's cherished colonial heritage. But to the scads of nefarious-minded *students,* the highlights of the daily educational itineraries were staying-up all night, ambitiously pounding on walls, and having major wild pillow fights. The *children* also gladly reveled in playing strip poker with members of the same sex, sneaking out of rooms at four in the morning, and making the harried teacher-chaperones earn every cent of the money they weren't getting paid extra for.

If the social (sociological) experiences just mentioned were the culminating aspects of the *students'* field trip, then why did the teachers have to transport them three hundred miles away from home? We could have simply rented a motel five miles from the school and saved fourteen hours of needless transportation back and forth from Williamsburg. After all, the social experience should transcend the dull academic learning agenda, shouldn't it?

"It's a good thing we have the rule that girls sit with girls and boys sit with boys on the bus!" Rob Renbeck stated to Joe Sacci and me.

"Yes, and the girls are on the second floor of the motel and the boys all on the first floor!" Joe objectively added.

"Guys, the school field trip rules might actually be promoting homosexuality by keeping genders together without even realizing it!" I concluded, much to Rob and Joe's general amusement.

That night, we stayed at a motel on the Alexandria side of the *Potomac.* Several enterprising *students* somehow jimmied-open a soda machine's door, and the culprits committing the misdemeanor emptied-out the entire *Coke* dispenser (which had recently been filled) and generously distributed their booty among appreciative and already-hyperactive classmates. When the hotel manager discovered the grand theft, he really protested to the trip's coordinator, and the school was billed to compensate the motel for the juvenile larceny.

Rob Renbeck and I had unfortunately pulled the midnight to three-in-the- morning shift to check rooms and curtail male *students* from stealthily sneaking-out of their quarters and visiting members of the opposite sex on another floor of the enormous "No Vacancy" motel. I noticed across a side street that someone was performing a felony breaking and entering into a car, so I reported the crime-in-progress over my room phone to the motel's office. The night manager came running-up the concrete steps to the balcony overlooking the alleged crime scene.

"Look at that guy over there trying to start that car!" I told the night manager. "Mr. Renbeck here and I just saw the fellow break into the auto' three minutes ago!"

"Oh," the night manager calmly replied. "That's not happening on the motel's property, so I'm not going to worry about it! My advice is don't even get remotely involved!"

"But it's the stealing of an automobile!" I objected. "It's a major crime being committed!"

"Do *you* want to come back to Virginia and testify in court six months from now just to see obscure justice served?" the motel night manager asked me. "Look Mister. Do you really want to be inconvenienced like that?"

"No, I don't think so!" I replied in astonishment. "I live a hundred and fifty miles away!"

"Well then, if I was you, I would just forget that I had seen anything at all!" the night manager finished with a wink. "Now if you'll excuse me, I have some important paperwork to do!"

Rob Renbeck and I looked oddly at each other, and we both simultaneously shrugged our shoulders. We stood there and watched the entire theft transpire and then gave the anonymous criminal mock waves as the crook drove the stolen vehicle by the motel balcony.

While we were in Williamsburg on another class trip, a group of *students* was watching a colonial craft demonstration. A female Williamsburg employee dressed in 1700s garb was showing some of the *children* how pottery was made back in the time of George Washington. "Don't stick your hand near that spinning machine!" Rob Renbeck cautioned the *children*.

The last thing in the world a teacher can tell fourteen-year-olds is "Don't do that!" or "Don't try that!" An eighth-grade girl stuck her right index finger in the spinning pottery and got it caught in the rotating lathe. Blood was squirting all over the place. The rotating pottery wheel had to be stopped, and Rob Renbeck had to accompany the crying, injured *child* to the nearest infirmary and then call the parents and get permission for stitches to sew-up the wound. Renbeck had to spend five hours of *his* time making sure that all school procedures had been properly followed involving the peculiar case of "an unnecessary *student* emergency".

"Maybe that girl will grow-up and become a *spinster!*" I later told Rob that night in our motel room.

"I don't think so!" my beleaguered companion tersely returned with a forced smile. "Maybe she'll get a job in a casino operating the spinning roulette wheel!"

That night at the Williamsburg motel, I was rooming with music teacher Joe Sacci and with Rob. Joe heard some ecstatic *students* yelling into the air vents, and the chatty messengers were telling other *children* in neighboring motel suites that big parties were to be held in rooms 211 and 223. Joe stood on a chair, skillfully disguised his voice, and then announced into the air vent, "The biggest party is goin' to happen in room 217 at three in the morning!" Joe informed his anonymous air-vent audience. "We have two big bottles of whiskey and four bottles of wine!" Joe persuasively added.

At three a.m., there was a gentle rapping at our motel room's door. Joe triumphantly opened the portal and he, Rob and I yelled at the six astounded and petrified violators standing outside, "Busted! You're all busted!" in what was certainly the finest case of *student* entrapment I had ever been associated with on any challenging, overnight field trip.

On the way back from Williamsburg, the buses stopped at the distinguished and eminent *Kennedy Center* in Washington. After a brief tour of the famous cultural arts' facility, the *students* were conducted to the *Kennedy Center's* cafeteria. Some hungry *students* had beaten Rob Renbeck and me to the cafeteria, had mischievously opened-up the wall menu ledger, and then had deviously rearranged some of the word letters of foods available to diners. Servings of "Pussy Burgers" and "Dick Dogs" were suddenly imaginatively listed inside the *Kennedy Center's* cafeteria ledger. An incensed cafeteria manager ventured over, noticed the recently-created obscenities appearing inside the ledger, and soon boisterously screamed, "Who's in charge of these juvenile delinquents?"

Rob Renbeck and I looked frightfully at each other, quickly spun around, and soon deftly hid behind two tall and wide red pillars so that the columns completely obscured us from the distressed cafeteria woman's sight. The now-thoroughly appalled manager eventually got the raucous *children* to line-up and then assigned a Kennedy Center employee to change the ledger language back to the normal "Hamburgers" and "Hot Dogs" nomenclature.

The trip coordinators showed-up on the chaotic scene and had to listen to the cafeteria manager strenuously complain to Mrs. Finnian, to the school principal, and to the cloud-dwelling superintendent, "This is definitely the most embarrassing and humiliating thing that has ever happened in *my* cafeteria! It was absolutely mortifying and a horrible public disgrace!"

When the four buses headed-back north toward Baltimore, Bus #2 passed Bus #1, and the children got all excited about the little race the drivers were conducting. Rob Renbeck and I were on Bus #1 and watched in astonishment as a *student* on Bus #2 opened the roof-hatch and stuck his head out, giving the middle finger to the mesmerized *students* on Bus #1.

The buses were heading toward the tollbooths for the *Harbor Tunnel* just before traveling under the *Patapsco River*. The wise guy *student* on Bus #2 (giving the royal finger to the tunnel-vision *students* on Bus #1) was almost decapitated as Bus #2's raised hatch just made it under the *Harbor Tunnel* tollbooth's pavilion roof. Everyone held his and her breath until the bus's roof hatch was finally closed. The *student* suicide candidate received three days of Office Detention for nearly beheading himself and for using obscene gestures (not jesters as indicated in the Teachers Handbook) to his fellow classmates viewing the crazy spectacle unfold from Bus Number One.

The Williamsburg three-day-trip was eventually shortened in the 1980s to simply being the Washington DC two day and one motel night trip. That move was done for costly economic expense reasons. The high school seniors that used to go to Washington for their pregraduation trip now flew from Philadelphia to *Disney World* in Orlando, Florida, so the eighth-grade graduating class inherited Washington as its prime destination.

The first day of a 1990s eighth-grade class trip was rather grueling and exhaustive, since the tired students and chaperones had visited and toured the *White House*, the *Capitol*, the *Washington Monument*, and *Ford's Theater*, and then the entire entourage partook of a night dinner cruise upon an entertainment ship down the *Potomac River*.

That night, the wily chaperones deliberately kept the *students* touring historic sites and monuments to further fatigue the cherubs so that the *children* would sleep the whole night instead of bugging the heck out of us. After we had toured the *Lincoln* and *Jefferson Memorials*, the buses finally headed across the *Potomac* where that year the *children* were staying at an attractive Tyson's Corner motel.

Since the *young, historical experts* had been well-behaved on that particular Washington excursion, the chaperones rewarded them with a pizza party in the motel's exquisite Madison Room. When the pizzas and soda had been totally consumed, five chaperones escorted the first half of the *students* back to their rooms, which were strategically located in a remote section of the huge suburban motel. The four remaining chaperones (including myself) accompanied the second batch of seventy-five *students* from the Madison (mass dining) Room to *their* assigned room accommodations.

Mack Fascito and I made sure all of our *students* had evacuated the Madison Room, and we brought-up the rear guard of the second set of still-boisterous fourteen-year-old *children*.

Suddenly, a stocky male in his early twenties (chaperoning a Catholic high school sophomore class that was also staying overnight at the Tyson's Corner motel) came sprinting-up to Mack and me nearly screaming the larynx out of his throat.

"Are *you* in charge of those wild kids on the other side of the building?" the athletic-looking hollered, apparently not used to experiencing the deviant behavior of normal *public school* eighth-grade *students*.

"Yes, we are!" I rather politely answered. "There are five of our chaperones already over there getting the *students* settled in their respective rooms! We're bringing-up the remaining students!"

"Well, your kids are banging on the walls and setting a bad example for my kids!" the young, muscular fellow shouted with a crimson face.

351

"Look," I calmly replied. "I'm assigned to this group of seventy-five *students*. Our school already has five very capable chaperones over there to deal with *that* problem!"

Evidently, the muscular Catholic high school chaperone didn't savor my explanation, so the guy surprisingly took a huge swing at my face. I ducked-down just in the nick of time, and his blow glanced off the top of my head and knocked-off my red *Phillies* baseball cap. Then Mack Fascito latched onto the fellow's right arm, and I firmly gripped his left one, and the enraged junior chaperone finally realized that *we* weren't exactly wimps and that my friend and I could effectively restrain him and defend ourselves if necessary.

So, even while enjoying a pleasant field trip, a teacher's existence might be endangered by a chaperone from another school losing his temper from excessive stress, and then ultimately going ballistic. When Mack and I got back to our "Home sweet home!" motel quarters, we heard a major disturbance sounding like glass being shattered, the noise originating from the adjoining room.

Four of our eighth-grade *students* had indeed been pounding on the walls and had inadvertently antagonized a drunken tractor-trailer driver who had been occupying the neighboring room. The banging had aggravated the inebriated fellow to the point where the big-rig operator was *climbing the walls* from the *students' pounding on the walls*. The totally-upset fellow had aggressively entered the startled kids' room, had broken an empty bottle of *Southern Comfort,* and the infuriated tractor-trailer driver was in the process of threatening to slice-up the throats of the suddenly shocked *students* with the shattered weapon in his right hand.

Mack and I convinced the intoxicated motel guest that we were the *students'* unfortunate chaperones, and then out of sheer necessity, we humbly and respectfully apologized for any inconvenience the little terrors (presently being terrorized) had caused him. After Mack and I had promised that the "obnoxious *children*" would not bother the troubled gent again, the somewhat-appeased driver slowly staggered out of the boys' motel room, muttering under his breath how he indeed would inflict serious injury if the irascible rascals persisted in the continuation of their annoying high jinks. Remarkably, and much to *our* relief, the intimidated, wise-guy boys sensed that the fellow meant business and calmed-down their boisterous antics, and soon cooperatively went to sleep shortly after midnight.

The following morning, after enjoying a scrambled egg breakfast at the Madison Room, the buses were boarded to tour some sites in metropolitan downtown Washington. Mack and I had pulled the difficult midnight to three a.m. shift and were extremely tired the entire morning. After touring the *Vietnam Memorial,* Mack Fascito and I returned to our bus only to find four eighth-graders standing on the roof and being screamed at by at least twenty *Vietnam War* veterans (several of them were in wheelchairs) that the *children* had recently verbally antagonized. Police in the area arrived on the scene and adroitly broke-up the brief altercation, and the incident was then reported to the school principal for further disciplinary action.

At noon, the eighth-graders ate in a cafeteria in downtown Washington. Several *students* were making fun of an old man sitting alone while dining in the crowded facility. After noticing the old man reaching into his vest beneath his sport jacket and toying with an object that Mack and I believed was a handgun, my fellow teacher and I approached the boys' table and had them move into an adjacent dining room before any unnecessary tragedy might have happened.

While we were waiting for the buses to arrive, Mack and I casually strolled through a shopping mall browsing at window displays. Three of our *student*s raced by before I could yell-out "Stop!" Then suddenly, five motorcycle gang members in black leather jackets dashed by in hot pursuit of the three scampering *children.* Apparently, the *students* had made some irreverent remarks to the now-incensed gang members, who then hopped off their motorcycles and chased the young renegades through the busy shopping mall. Obviously, the offensive *children* must have been in better shape than the motorcycle enthusiasts because the pursuers eventually gave-up the hunt and disgustedly walked back past Mack and me in the direction of their parked *Harley Davidsons.*

At the *Smithsonian's Aerospace Museum,* Mack and I showed some bona fide *students* hanging planes that were similar in design to the *Spirit of St. Louis* that had been flown across the Atlantic from New York to Paris by Charles Lindbergh, and then we viewed several space-capsule models. We were really fatigued from a lack of sleep, so Mack and I did what we traditionally had done on all previous Washington trips. We entered the *Smithsonian Aerospace Museum's* planetarium to gladly rest our bloodshot eyes and our weary bones.

"Wake me up if I fall asleep," I told Mack. "I need a few toothpicks to keep my eyelids open!"

"And *you* wake me up if I fall asleep," my chaperone friend wearily requested.

Three fairly reliable *students* from our school were seated directly behind Mack and me, so I figured I would ask them for a small favor. "Guys! If Mr. Fascito and I both fall asleep," I stated, "please wake us up after the planetarium show!"

"Don't worry Mr. Wiessner!" the three dependable *students* assured me. "We know you both must be real tired!"

The lights went out, and fifteen minutes later, I heard Mack snoring, so I gave him a jolt to the ribs to bring him back to consciousness. Then ten minutes after that, Mack gave me an elbow poke to alert me that I too had been snoring.

Fifteen minutes later, I felt a hand upon my right shoulder. A planetarium usher was shaking both Mack Fascito and my shoulders, waking us up from deep slumbers. The three reliable *children* had abandoned us after the astronomy show had ended, so we had to suffer the mortification of being irresponsible chaperones falling asleep on the job and having to be awakened by a thoroughly amused planetarium program attendant.

Finally, on one memorable mid-1980s May Williamsburg Field Trip, my New Jersey school's four charter busloads of rambunctious, hormone-driven, eighth-grade *students* stayed overnight (while returning home) at a large Virginia motel, situated across the Potomac from Washington, DC. A female teacher had had a major discipline problem on her bus with an aberrant *student,* so the school principal asked a major favor of me.

"John; Mrs. X has developed a terrible headache this evening. I'm asking you to stay-up all night with a male *student* that had been acting obnoxious and disrespectful on her bus. I've arranged that you and he will be sitting outside in soft, comfortable chairs on the picturesque terrace. I realize that you don't teach or know this *student,* so that's why I'm requesting that *you* help *us* out! Remember," the principal imperatively resumed his instruction. "The kid's punishment is just like school Office Detention. You aren't allowed to speak or interact with this *student* until daybreak!"

'Thanks a lot!' I thought. 'I'm being severely punished along with this repulsive, impudent kid that I don't even know or even care to know!'

A certain variety of insects instinctively come alive and emerge out of the ground every seventeen years to both molt and mate. Everything went rather smoothly until around two o'clock in the morning. Hundreds of noisy Cicadas, a voracious species of hopping insects akin to grasshoppers and locusts, suddenly appeared in our midst and avariciously began madly leaping and jumping all around the two of us.

'This insane invasion is getting worse than an Old Testament Biblical plague!' I soon imagined and regretted as I brushed three, crazed, sex-driven creatures off of my lap. "There're dozens of these fanatical insects hopping all around this insolent kid and me! I can't stand this emotional torture any longer!"

"Look, Kemosabe!" I bluntly yelled at the alarmed fourteen-year-old chronic violator as if I were a maniacal Apache named Tonto from Toronto.

"What did you call me?" the toxic wise guy yelled-back as his arms were flailing-away and swatting at several dozen hopping, horny Cicadas. "What the hell did you say?"

"Look, *Friend!* I think I'm now going to send you right past high school and directly into college!" I smartly and loudly answered back amidst the ongoing insect mania.

"You called me *Chemo'* what!" the confused fourteen-year-old-brazen rogue being attacked shouted back. "What's the college?"

"Seat-in-Hall!" I screamed in his encumbered direction as I quickly pointed to the empty corridor space inside the motel's night manager's office. 'Yes, Pal!" I yelled as I emphatically pointed to our left at the glass door panel. "You'll just love the university. I'm sending you directly to Seat-in-Hall!"

Chapter 38
"The Guidance Game"

In September of 1976, the eighth-grade moved from the junior-senior high school to the two-story building where I had begun my teaching career in 1965. The new elementary school had been built in 1974. The original high school, which had become the elementary school in 1965 (after the second high school had been constructed), in 1976 became the middle school for grades six through eight. Despite the fact that the middle school was considered a separate entity from the former junior-senior high, it still retained the same office forms and the same procedures as the junior high (grades seven through nine) had maintained when it had been combined with the high school.

The middle school faculty was still governed by the same Teachers Handbook that stipulated, "The Guidance Department's philosophy is the view that the *student* is of central importance. By being *student*-centered, the following psychological concepts (Code Language statements) are endorsed by the Guidance Office:

1. *Student* behavior is caused. (Translation: Teachers must contend, cope and deal with *student* misbehavior).

2. Each *child* is unique. (Translation: Be prepared to deal with unexpected unique *child* misbehaviors and shenanigans).

3. No *child* is ever rejected as being *hopeless* or lost. (Translation: A teacher must cheerfully contend with anything, everything and everyone in the school including 8-6 type *hapless students* and other insidious *child* disruptors).

4. Teachers should understand the scientific facts that govern *student* behavior, maturation and motivation. (Translation: Teachers should not demand too much academically or else the nasty parents of nasty *students* will make their daily existence a virtual nightmare).

When the *Child* Study Team and the Guidance Counselors refer to Joe Dodge or to the kid that shot my in-laws' ducks (or to any other teenager with nihilistic intentions), he or she is called "the *child*" or "the *student*." Instead, the proper descriptive *labels* should be "young thug," "hellish hooligan" "wicked wiseass" or "insolent punk." And when the Guidance Department thinks that the *child's* rights are being jeopardized, the alluded-to violator is then referred to as "the *student* in a *democratic,* educational, learning environment".

As an exact science, psychology is only one shelf above phrenology. Exact sciences have cause and effect relationships that are predictable and that can be demonstrated over and over again in specific experiments, according to laws and formulas that work the same every time. This characteristic of true science is measurable in the natural laws that govern the flow of electricity, airplane dynamics (exhibited in taking-off and landing), or in energy being converted into power in a combustion engine. If psychology was an exact science, then murders, rapes, muggings, homicides and suicides could be prevented because those behavioral events would have been predictable every time.

It is true that educational psychology has identified *children's general* basic needs, but the *specific child's* emotional needs vary from *student* to *student,* or from let's say, Joe Dodge to Ben Locanta. Psychology is far less of a science than chemistry, biology and physics are. And as far as sociology is concerned, group dynamics is not quite as scientific as the mechanics of how the solar system operates, how the *Milky Way* galaxy behaves, or how the wonderful universe works.

Psychologists state that the human mind is like an iceberg, one-fifth (the known superego) floating above the surface, and four-fifths (the subconscious unknown) lurking and stagnating underneath. Enough sinister *student* icebergs exist in a class like the 8-6's and in *children* like Joe Dodge to sink an entire flotilla of *Titanics.* Putting faith in educational psychology is like betting on a long shot at the nearest racetrack. The obsessed gambler stands at best a five-to-one chance of winning.

Guidance counselors give *students* advice about college choices, about family problems, about sibling rivalry, about interpersonal relationships, about teenage sex, and about pregnancy and dating. Many guidance counselors aren't married, or are divorced or separated, yet they are certified school employees, and therefore qualified to guide *children* even though *the* adviser might be a failure in his or her own personal life regarding the issues he or she is giving a *student* advice about.

If a *student* is doing poorly in an *academic* subject, the Guidance Office counselor (specialist) will issue to him or to her a "Weekly Report Card", which ultimately results in more paperwork liability for teachers (generalists). As many as five *students* in a particular class may have these Weekly Report Cards, and the teacher must spend fifteen minutes of class time filling-out the weekly grades for those five *students,* and then make a weekly comment about each *student's* progress, or lack thereof. This is usually done on Fridays, so it's another reason why many teachers are not absent on *Good Friday* (payday) but then often miss coming to school on *Passover Friday* (the next non-pay Friday).

The Weekly Report Card is by no means a reliable index, for a weekly grade of A may be based only on one test or quiz grade, and a weekly grade of D might be based on four different evaluations (homework assignment, composition, *student* oral report, quiz, test, project). A parent might be misled into thinking that his or her *child* has a B- average when the *student* actually might be getting a D at the time all the analogous grades for all eight weeks in a marking period are tabulated.

Two other sources of teacher grief generated by the Guidance Office counselors are Guidance Referral Sheets and Homework Absentee Sheets. A teacher will go to his or her mailbox and see these sheets inserted in his or her slot compartment. Teachers (that might have a hundred and thirty or more *students* each day) are required by the Teachers Handbook and by the Guidance Department segment of the Educational Aristocracy to write-down confidential information about *student* academic, social and behavioral patterns. After the evaluation statements are jotted-down on the sheets, *the grades* recorded on the Guidance Referral Weekly Report Card sheets must then justify and correspond with those descriptive statements that the teacher had made.

The Homework Absentee Sheets are items also placed in teacher mailboxes when *students* are out of school for extended periods (two days or more). Instructors are required by the Teachers Handbook to fill-out class and homework assignments for a *student* that might be soon spending three weeks vacationing with his or her family in Honolulu or in Nassau in the Bahamas. Many parents demand to know what work the *child* will have to be doing two or three weeks in advance. I had been required to fill-out Homework Absentee Sheets for *students (children)* that have been suspended from school. This is another example of how *student* dereliction of responsibility means more paperwork accountability for teachers.

Here is a recent legal recommendation given by a local school board solicitor pertaining to *students* who are on suspension or that have been expelled:

"In view of the general requirement that the board of education grant free education to persons between the ages of five and eighteen years of age, it would seem evident that denying home instruction to a suspended or expelled *student* should be viewed as an extreme measure. Such cruel denial of service would be difficult to justify in a foundation of law."

So, in effect, no *student* is ever really expelled or completely divorced from the public school. In fact, *students* that are expelled are absolutely given special treatment. They must be privately tutored and have an individualized program (ISP-Individual *Student* Plan) tailored to their particular psychological needs as prescribed by the Educational Aristocracy on the suspect basis of guidance recommendations. That's the law in New Jersey.

Contemporary American education gleans mass mediocrity and inefficiency, and it capriciously rewards *student* delinquency in preference to demonstrating individual responsibility, while the system increases teacher accountability in the form of paper trails documenting *students'* lack of performance. This required anomaly all translates into the less work that *students* have to do, the more input that teachers must compensate in order to balance-out the educational equation.

After a few years laboring in the *academic* salt mines (classrooms), many teachers lose their idealism and become disenchanted with the bureaucratic system. The tenure teacher soon learns that if he or she plays the "guidance game" along with the administrative "*democracy* in the comprehensive school game" with the Educational Aristocracy and with the involved parents, then many problems associated with enforcing *academic* standards could be alleviated. If the teachers don't make waves, the educational ark smoothly glides through its daily course and won't capsize. Parents, the *children,* and administrators will then think and believe that you're a sensitive teacher doing an acceptable (mediocre) job.

A mini-cold war is usually going-on between the vice-principal's office and the Guidance Office. The assistant-principal is like a prosecutor, and the Guidance Office is like the *American Civil Liberties Union* defending the rights of the *students* and often incubating and promoting the qualms and grievances of impudent offenders (i.e., Joe Dodge).

Some more recent detrimental trends in education (supported by the Guidance Department) are "cooperative education" and "the open classroom" methodology. The new counterproductive "Vogue

Methods", or "Organizing Patterns", are based on the following spurious assumptions that result in doubletalk code language:

1. Youngsters must learn commensurate with ability. (Translation: Bend the system and compromise *academic* standards to each *student*).
2. *Children* must be allowed to learn according to their own interests. (Translation: Don't base grades exclusively on tests and quizzes or else too many *students* will fail).
3. *Children* must be allowed to use their best learning style. (Translation: Make the *children* the experts on education and allow them to evaluate each other for grades because the teacher's grades are often unreliable and invalid).
4. *Children* must be allowed to progress at their own pace. (Translation: Don't fail anyone (especially the *wrong student*) if you want to avoid problems and keep your teaching position).

Just about any allusion to "Individualized Instruction" is entertaining sheer folly. Teachers generally don't have classes with twelve or less academically-oriented *students* where individualized instruction could effectively occur. Individualized instruction might work with twelve or less *students*, a teacher aide in the classroom, a copious wealth of audio-visual aids, and a class of above-average, self-motivated *students*. Anything short of those factors will have the teacher spinning his or her wheels in quicksand on a daily basis.

Although sufficient money is probably not available to finance such fanciful practices as "cooperative learning" and "the open classroom", the Educational Aristocracy in many communities is advocating that those boondoggles as panaceas and effective educational reforms. A class of 8-6ers (if given their druthers) would create its own "open classroom" by knocking-down the walls with sledgehammers, mallets and bulldozers.

In its purist sense, the catch-phrase "individualized instruction" means a ratio of one teacher to one *student*. This new terminology is designed to make every teacher into a tutor while having thirty active *children* in the classroom. Educational psychology wants to transform the *children* into the evaluators of each other's work, and in the process, the practice would strip-away another symbol of teacher authority (the professional person that should be doing the actual evaluating of *students*). With ideas such as cooperative learning, the open classroom, and individualized instruction, the *students* are now-appointed by the frivolous Educational Aristocracy to be the true experts on grading, and the teacher is again relegated in importance by not giving most of the major grades.

First, the Educational Aristocracy gives a dedicated academic instructor twenty-five indignant cannibals like an 8-6 class. Next, the E.A. commands him or her to teach the *children* by using such techniques as cooperative learning and individualized instruction. This pattern amounts to nothing more than putting the patients in charge of the asylum, or assigning the prisoners in charge of conducting penitentiary discipline.

John Holt states in the summary of his book *How Children Fail* that the bright *child* is curious to learn. No wall or obstacle isolates the brighter *child* from wanting to find-out about his or her world. The dull *child* cares less about his or her environment and is more inclined to fantasize or be reluctant to try anything academic on his or her own. Popular panaceas such as the *open classroom* and *cooperative learning* are really detriments to the best interests of American society.

"*Student*-centered" methods are often doomed to failure because of inadequate funding to perform them effectively, because of large class sizes, and because of too many special needs *children* in our public schools that have been mainstreamed into regular classes to fully *democratize* education.

When teachers must have and instruct *students* with learning disabilities, with social problems, with emotional problems, and with low ability mixed in with average *students,* there is no way that grade-level norms or skills can be enforced. And so, the crafty Educational Aristocracy subjects the teacher to *that* harsh reality, and when the *children* cannot do well on standardized tests, the instructors become the convenient scapegoats that get blamed in a system that is designed to fail from the word "Go"!

Education (based on the pseudo-science of psychology) has no axioms or postulates that work all the time. The Educational Aristocracy and the "Guidance Game" demand that faculty teachers relate knowledge (*academics* in a subject area) to each *child's* interests and experiences.

If knowledge is like a medicine ball in size, and if the *students'* minds are like golf balls, how could the former be jammed into the latter when each *child* has limited interests and experiences? It's like attempting to squeeze an elephant through a keyhole! Physics accurately describes the reality as the law of density and mass.

Fanciful educational psychologists perceive that same artificial reality as a worthwhile illusion that must be implemented, and the Educational Aristocracy commissions the teachers to push elephants (subject matter) through keyholes (*students'* minds based on limited past cultural experiences) with the "Individualized Curriculum".

Dr. Benjamin Spock, toward the end of his life, recanted some of his philosophy regarding the "*child*-centered family". The *child*-centered family model had eventually led to the public schools' current "*child*-centered curriculum". These two "*child*-centered" systems have created two successive generations of bratty, self-centered, entitled *children* that have lost respect for parent and teacher authority, which had been present in the 1950s in "parent-centered homes" and in "teacher-centered classrooms".

Today's *students* generally desire instant gratification, and the kids don't know the meaning of the words sacrifice, labor, "No!" and perseverance. Teenagers have emotional and mental problems the same as adults, especially when stringent demands are placed on them by the American free enterprise system that emphasizes competition and *individual performance.*

The *child*-centered curriculum methods ignore one very important fact. *Children* want and need to be told what to do by responsible adults. Once that pattern is destroyed at home, and then again in first grade, it is difficult to re-institute in eighth or in tenth grade respect for adult authority. Children need adult examples to follow both at home and at school, and this necessary form of modeling should be starting in first-grade and ending at high school graduation.

Modern psychology has undermined *that* basic truth of the need for adult leadership, and it has created scenarios where parents are afraid to discipline their teenagers, and now, strongly want to be their friends. And when the *child* has problems with a teacher, the parent feels compelled to defend the *child* because true adult authority has been abdicated at home, and therefore, mom and dad believe that *teacher discipline* must also be opposed in the school. This borderline insanity is endorsed by the Educational Aristocracy, which includes the school's heralded Guidance Department.

Children cannot make adult decisions, since essentially, they are *not* adults. *Children* cannot easily mature into responsible adults, unless they have excellent, responsible adult role models both at home and at school. And I must reiterate that the human brain (especially the emotional and thinking areas) is not fully developed until a human being reaches twenty-one years of age.

The *child-centered family* has been an abysmal failure because the youngsters in the house cannot be the role models for their derelict parents; the *children* need *adult-centered parent-centered* family role models. The entire society is being convoluted because of what psychology has done in the home and by what the scourge is attempting to do in the schools in the name of educational *democracy* and the *child-centered* curriculum.

The time has come for the *Don Quixotes* that fabricate educational psychology to exhibit courage similar to that demonstrated by Dr. Spock. The *child*-centered curriculum must be renounced so that respect for *academics* and respect for teacher authority can be wisely reinstated and subsequently, grade level norms strictly enforced. Adults both at home and in school must be respected as role models for *children* to imitate.

Adult authority (parent and teacher) must become absolute and not relative factors in *children's* lives. Under the present system, teacher control is being demoted while *student* inclination is being praised and advanced. The *child's* whims and desires become primary while parents and teachers are relegated to secondary factors in the *child's* development. As parental and teacher authority continues to decay, educational and societal disorganization will continue to proliferate by leaps and bounds.

Failure should not be viewed in American education as a negative human experience. Humans learn from failure by modifying their methods and mistakes to eventually achieve success. In fact, failure is a better teacher than success is. But psychology is attempting to eradicate failure from *students'* lives to make the *children* happier.

According to educational psychology, success has to come without struggle or long-term determination. Classroom tasks must become easier to achieve so that negative *student* frustration can be avoided. And when *students* don't experience instant gratification, factors like drugs and teenage sex enter into the formula, and soon, self-esteem is surrendered within the new, flimsy educational equation. Educational psychologists neglect to understand that *student confidence* is a more solid emotional foundation than *self-esteem* is, and confidence results from overcoming failure, and contemporary self-esteem results from completing tasks that are definitely too easy.

Failure and disappointment are very real elements of adult life, so they ought to be vital parts of a *student's* experiences, too. Educators need to teach *children* how to adapt to failure rather than attempting to eradicate it from the *student's* educational existence. This author's desk drawers are full of publisher rejection slips, but failure has motivated him to dare to achieve success by modifying his writing style and voice so that he could eventually, in time, learn how to communicate more effectively. It was because of overcoming *failure* that the author learned to compete with millions of other skilled writers, and as a result, has attempted to excel in his new career.

Children are ushered through thirteen years of school by riding upward on the educational escalator from the kindergarten basement up to the twelfth-floor penthouse. By insulating *students* from failure and competition, schools are guaranteeing the psychiatry industry of unprecedented profits in decades to come. Today's spoiled and pampered generation (of *students*) exhibits little patience or coping mechanisms to address failure, to handle academic competition, or to deal with the rigorous, tough dedication necessary to achieve individual excellence in a free enterprise, performance-oriented, highly competitive society.

After high school graduation, *students* are often overwhelmed by the serious (and very real) challenges associated with hard work in college or in the industrial world. As long as educational psychology doesn't corrupt college academics like it has contaminated public schools and also the family core values, then there is still a glimmer of hope left for future generations of Americans. Until educators come to their senses and admit that success in life involves *hard work* and sacrifice, we will continue producing lackluster *students* for assimilation into an artificial, utopian society that doesn't exist.

Let's leave Russian roulette to the Russians. Historians know that great empires and civilizations in the past have collapsed, not because of being destroyed from external attack, but from being greedily eroded from within. Once a civilization's core moral values degenerate, its decline is imminent.

And as long as psychology is influential in the home, in the school and in the law, American civilization will be authoring its own destruction. The only hope for recovery is that right and wrong again be regarded as moral absolutes, and the *students'* homes being again blessed with parent-centered families, and of course, with the schools again supporting teacher-centered *academic* classrooms. Otherwise, this great country is speeding-down the path toward anarchy and toward spiritual disintegration. That eighty-percent gray area *Twilight Zone* (established by the Educational Aristocracy) between right and wrong must be immediately obliterated.

Chapter 39
"The Overprotective Parent"

As I begin this chapter, my wife (a third-grade teacher in another district) is having difficulty with a distrustful "too involved parent" that happens to be on her district's board of education. It seems that this father/board member is attempting to insulate his daughter from failure, but is going to great extremes in doing so. The overprotective parent has balked and protested to the school principal, and to other school board members, about his precious offspring receiving a B+ as a "Handwriting" report card grade.

I told my wife that school board members should only be school board members inside the boardroom and not act as a school board member/parent of a child in regard to a teacher's class. I said to my spouse, "He's only another parent and nothing more."

Parents not only get upset in the year 2003 when their *child* fails, but ome overprotective moms and dads even get upset and have confrontational conferences with teachers when *their* son or daughter in third grade gets a B+ in Handwriting.

In the mid-90s, the vice-principal called me to his office and informed me that a group of parents had requested that three *students* in my seventh period class, and two others in first period, not see excerpts from *Beetlejuice*, a creative movie I was showing to have my general classes analyze and write about the humorous film's imaginative elements.

"How come?" I asked the school executive. "That movie has plenty of incredible scenes in it that'll inspire the kids to identify plot development and continuity of ideas."

"The parents and their kids are Jehovah Witnesses that don't believe in ghosts," the school executive communicated, "and that movie is all about ghosts. I've had five complaints about it already!"

"But in October, we read a passage about Hamlet's father's ghost, and in December, we read the literature classic 'A Christmas Carol' that was about Ebenezer Scrooge being visited by four ghosts," I futilely argued. "And this year we also read Washington Irving's 'Legend of Sleepy Hollow' that featured another ghost, the Headless Horseman. Where were these vociferous parents then?"

"We have to be careful about this delicate area," the vice-principal diplomatically emphasized. "I advise you to send those five *students* to the library and give them an alternate assignment to write about while you're showing the film. Now here's a list of their names."

"Gee," I gasped and answered. "I thought that the only problem with Jehovah Witnesses was their kids not standing and refusing to say the *Pledge of Allegiance* during homeroom! I mean, the phrase 'One Nation Under God' shows that God exists on a higher plane than the nation," I argued in vain. "The next thing we'll encounter is parents protesting about reading the classic story 'A Christmas Carol' because it has the word *Christmas* in it!"

But I have noticed the emergence of the overprotective parent as far back as the mid-seventies. Overprotective parents come in all shapes, sizes and varieties. The breed doesn't usually arrive at a parent/teacher conference to hear about their son or daughter's weaknesses, progress, behavior or performance. The overprotective parent becomes a hostile protector that will savagely attack a teacher in a conference scenario over a trivial matter where the son or the daughter might have reported that he or she had been humiliated because a teacher had admonished ("picked on") him or her in class.

I have had several dozen "hostile parent conferences" in my career, and each one shared several pertinent characteristics. The parents are separated, are divorced or are constantly quarreling because either the dad or mom, or both, are involved in an extra-marital affair. The *child* feels neglected, has an incident with the teacher, and then blows it out of proportion, hoping to get mom and dad back onto the *child's* page and compatible with each other again. Waa-la! The teacher becomes the convenient target of this internal family venom, and the belligerent parents then transfer the blame for all their angst to the recipient teacher, with the *child's will* remaining intact and being fully gratified.

The big downside of hostile parent conferences is that the aggrieved adults keep appealing their complaints to school administrators and guidance counselors. The teacher must surrender hours of before and after school time having meetings with the irritated parents in school administrators' and in the guidance counselors' offices, too. And still, despite this constant pressure, the teacher has to later teach six classes having a hundred and thirty *students* and act as if nothing at all is happening (or had happened) outside the classroom.

The ongoing incident that I am about to describe occurred in October of 1984. I was administering a vocabulary/spelling test to an Accelerated English class. Melissa Bertuzzi was a good *student* in that advanced class who had carelessly numbered her answer-sheet from one to fifty in a rush, and had missed writing-down number twenty-one. Therefore, every answer after number twenty-one would be marked wrong because each response did not correspond to the proper test item numbers when the "answer sheet" would be corrected. Consequently, Melissa failed the test and had to write all of the incorrect words and definitions ten times each as was my class rule when dealing with advanced *students*.

The *student* had a 94.5 average at the time, and I had told her that if she wrote the words and definitions ten times each, I would erase the F in my record book since I knew she had made a careless mistake in numbering her paper.

The following Monday, I received a conference slip in my mailbox from the Guidance Office secretary. The form stated that Mrs. Bertuzzi wanted to come in and have a conference to discuss her daughter's F on the vocabulary/spelling test.

The next day in class, I told Melissa that there was no need for her mother to come into the building and have a conference because the F would be erased if the *student* simply wrote the vocabulary words and definitions that she had gotten wrong, ten times each. If not, I would have to give her another F for not completing and submitting the *"individualized* assignment", which was really a basic work-habit lesson emphasizing and reinforcing the fabled principle that "haste makes waste".

I never signed the conference form and never returned it to the Guidance Office. So, in effect I never agreed to have any conference with Melissa Bertuzzi's mother. Apparently, Melissa had withheld information about the F being eliminated if the girl had done the prescribed homework assignment, and the very axe-to-grind mother came unannounced into my classroom on Thursday during my forty-five minute preparation period.

The Guidance Office had scheduled Mrs. Bertuzzi's conference that I had never agreed to have at 10 a.m. on Thursday. I was busy correcting papers and recording grades in my roll book when the neurotic, aggressive mother made her unexpected entry.

Mrs. Bertuzzi sat-down in a *student* desk and addressed me in a quivering prosecutorial voice. "I want to know why you gave Melissa an F on her vocabulary test!" she began in a rather demanding, bellicose tone.

The purpose of a teacher requested conference is to discuss the *student's* grades and behavior, but when a parent initiates a conference, the teacher knows that the mother or father probably wants to indict the instructor and find fault with an incident, and then magnify *that* alleged event to protect the *child.*

"Mrs. Bertuzzi, I never agreed to having this conference with you. I never signed the conference form verifying that it was going to take place," I directly answered.

"I don't like your attitude!" the aggrieved mother rankled. "You're insensitive and uncooperative! Now, why did you fail my daughter on that vocabulary test when you knew all along that she had studied and was well-prepared with all the right answers!"

"Your daughter failed the test because she hurried while numbering her answer sheet and missed one of the items, number twenty-one I believe," I calmly replied. "Consequently, Melissa got all of the answers after twenty-one wrong and has to write the words and definitions ten times each, which is my classroom policy. By the way, she hasn't submitted that particular written work yet!"

"Do you think that's fair?" Mrs. Bertuzzi stubbornly challenged. "Do you think that failing my daughter over a minor technicality like that was fair?"

"I told your daughter that the F would be cancelled-out if she wrote the words and definitions ten times each like any other *student* that fails that kind of vocabulary test would do," I related. "I think that what I had done was quite fair!"

"But then you'd give her another F if she didn't do what you said about writing the words and definitions!" the mother yelled. "That certainly wasn't fair, either! Now, my daughter might get two unfair F's from you!"

"Look," I curtly countered. "I'm very busy right now correcting papers and recording grades. You have come in for a conference when none has been officially scheduled, since I haven't agreed to having any conference with you right now," I articulated. "Your daughter has a 94.5 average in the class, and if she writes the words and definitions ten times each to the items that she had gotten wrong, she still will have a 94.5 A' average in Accelerated English!"

The parent was not satisfied with my thorough explanation and said that she didn't like my "arrogant demeanor", so the woman proceeded with delivering her plaintiff' interrogation. "You still haven't explained why you had failed Melissa when you knew she was prepared and knew those test questions!"

"Mrs. Bertuzzi, I have already told your daughter that I reward *students* for doing the right things, and not for doing the wrong things," I affirmatively replied. "I've never praised a *student* for doing something incorrectly. Now I know you're a hospital nurse," I proceeded, "and if you made a small mistake, it could lead to a patient's increased pain or maybe even death. What I had done to your daughter will only benefit her in the long run!"

"Well," Mrs. Bertuzzi said in a quivering rage. "I don't appreciate *you* embarrassing my daughter in front of the whole class and saying that you didn't want to meet with me!"

"I merely quietly told Melissa that there was *no need* to meet with you because the F would be erased if she simply wrote the words and definitions! Did your daughter tell you that!"

"No, but it really doesn't matter, Mr. Wiessner!" the enraged mother ranted. "It's your disrespectful attitude that I'm now more concerned about! And also, that writing the definitions and words ten times each assignment is nothing but a wicked punishment!"

I explained to the distraught mother that the "embarrassing incident" she was alluding-to had taken place in less than thirty seconds. I also elaborated rather eloquently that the statement Mrs. Bertuzzi's fourteen-year-old *child* had interpreted' as "a reprimand" was just "an exaggerated perception in your daughter's mind". The remainder of the Accelerated Class had easily shifted into the next phase of the daily lesson without much regard or concern to what I had told Melissa!" I explained to the indignant mother.

Mrs. Bertuzzi was dissatisfied with my responses and persisted in launching a barrage of complaints and grievances in my direction. I interrupted the livid, trembling, sobbing mother several times, but all along, I felt a heated argument gradually developing.

"Mrs. Bertuzzi, I want you to know that I have done hundreds of constructive things in Melissa's class since school started in early September and yet," I resumed my narrative, "you persist in focusing on one certain event and are trying to engage in some sort of witch hunt prosecution here! Do you have anything constructive to say about the hundreds of positive classroom occurrences you are ignoring, or are you going to continue your contrived Fishing Expedition and dwell on the one alleged, negative event that you can't get out of your mind?"

"You're very unprofessional!" the mother accused while sobbing. "You're extremely inconsiderate and insensitive, do you know that!"

"Mrs. Bertuzzi, I strongly suggest that you judge me and my instructional methods in June and not in October," I countered. "You'll have much more information about my teaching style, methods and ability eight months from now," I indicated. "I hardly even know all the names of my hundred and thirty *students* yet!"

"You're impossible!" the incensed woman accused. "I trust my daughter's word before I'd ever trust yours!"

"Mrs. Bertuzzi, just look at this stack of warning letters on my desk!" I requested. "I need to meet and speak with the parents of these forty *students* that presently have D and F averages in English, and not the parent of a good *student* who has a 94.5 average that certainly is not in jeopardy, that is, if Melissa simply writes the words and definitions ten times each!" I exclaimed, a little out of character. "I think you're overreacting to circumstances that have been falsely reported to you by your daughter!"

I knew that the overzealous, upset mother was attempting to shield and shelter her already-overprotected daughter from both failure and criticism. Melissa was *perfect* in the mother's myopic vision, and the angry mom couldn't fathom why I had found fault with *perfection*.

"Mrs. Bertuzzi," I persisted. "I don't believe that parents are qualified or certified to evaluate teachers! You are trying to do the job of a school administrator!"

"You just gave me an idea," the livid woman retorted. "I'm going to report your unprofessional conduct right now to the principal!"

"Go right ahead!" I challenged. "Now just analyze for a moment how I feel about *that* threatening statement you just made. My father-in-law is on the board of directors at the hospital where *you* are employed. How would you like it if I reported your un-professionalism to him?" I questioned the nw-shocked mother. "I'll bet that wouldn't fly too well with you, would it? I would never do such a thing, but I want *you* to fully understand how I feel when you threaten to do such a *child*ish thing as reporting me to a higher authority! It's called adult tattle-tale-ing!"

"Why did you embarrass my daughter in front of her peers!" Mrs. Bertuzzi again quite adamantly demanded to know.

"Because I didn't think that a parent-teacher conference was necessary, since Melissa is not in any danger of failing English," I again explained. "Furthermore, your daughter has an A average if she simply writes the words and definitions ten times each, and Melissa is not getting a U in conduct at this time; nor is she receiving a caustic warning letter from me like these other forty *students* are!" I commented, raising my raspy voice as I pointed to the high stack of eighth-grade warning letters upon my desk.

"You're intentionally picking on my daughter, and I don't like it!" the mother accused. "You might not remember, but I was a former *student* of yours twenty-one years ago when you were a student teacher. You were an excellent teacher, but I knew way back then that *you* had a nasty temper!"

"Mrs. Bertuzzi, if you know I was and am an excellent teacher, what made you feel that I would do any injustice to your daughter?" I logically disputed. "If I was picking on Melissa, then there would have to be a whole series of incidents connected together by dots, and not just the two you have cherry-picked and described."

"Look Mister, if you continue to ride my daughter's ass, I'll march you across the hall to the administration!" Mrs. Bertuzzi warned.

I was appalled at the mother's acrimonious remark. I refused to be intimidated by any irate parent on the attack. I felt that Mrs. Bertuzzi was trying to make me back-off, and never admonish her daughter for anything Melissa might do in the future, in order to protect the perfect All-American girl from any further criticism, or from any further verbal punishment. I had listened to and heard enough of all I could tolerate of speculative, antagonistic recriminations being advanced by the emotionally distressed, whimpering mother.

"Adults usually handle their own disagreements without the need of appealing to a higher level," I volleyed-back in regard to her threat to plead her case to the school administration. I believed that instead of looking for a needle in a haystack, Mrs. Bertuzzi was stretching matters and searching for a haystack in the eye of a needle.

"I am not intimidated with your threats," I informed the over-aggressive, sulking, accusative parent. "And I will defend my principles or my classroom procedures if need be. And I hope *you* take this case all the way to the board of education so that then *we* can appear before them, and then the school board will see the kind of nonsense that teachers must contend with besides teaching a hundred and thirty *students* each and every day!"

"You are very crude and not treating me like a *lady!*" Mrs. Bertuzzi uttered during the parent-imposed conference that had never officially been scheduled.

"Look, *Lady!*" I angrily answered back. "I've put-up with enough of your insufferable abuse! I have a class coming in here in five minutes! I have to organize my thoughts after the stress of your unexpected and unnecessary visit!"

"Look, *Man!*" Mrs. Bertuzzi yelled-back while standing and pointing her rigid right index finger at my face. "I don't have to take any more guff from you. You're loud, you're mean, and you're also very unprofessional!"

I then reached into a desk drawer and produced and showed Mrs. Bertuzzi the original conference form with the vacant space where I had never signed my name, officially agreeing to the time and date. "The secretary in the Guidance Office had acted unilaterally in arranging the meeting without my expressed approval or confirmation!" I insisted. "In reality, this thirty-minute conference should have never occurred!"

Mrs. Bertuzzi then left my classroom in a huff, yelling a plethora of obscene comments as she hysterically exited in a rather animated frenzy. An alarmed Social Studies teacher that was sauntering by had witnessed Mrs. Bertuzzi's hasty departure and had heard the final remnants of her vehement oratory.

The male pedagogue entered my room. "What happened with that angry mother?" the curious teacher asked. "It must've been a hostile conference. I've had my share of those gems," he sympathetically added. "She was calling you a son-of-a-bitch and a bastard under her breath, which truthfully were several of the distraught woman's more complimentary descriptions!"

"Believe it or not," I defensively remarked, "that conference was never officially scheduled. I never agreed to having it today at this time and place by signing the official form and then returning it to the Guidance Office!"

Mrs. Bertuzzi's husband showed-up at my front door the next evening at suppertime and told me that I had verbally abused his wife (they were having marital problems at the time) and that he wanted an apology from me.

I told Mr. Bertuzzi that I had never apologized to any parent or to any *student* in my nineteen years of teaching and that I wasn't going to start with him, with his nutcase wife, or with his doted-on daughter. "And furthermore, I've never demanded an apology from a parent, either!"

"You have a terrible attitude for a teacher!" the father indicted. "My wife and I are definitely going to the administration and then to the board of education!"

"Be my guest!" I haughtily replied. "And the next time you step one foot onto my property, consider it trespassing, and the police will be instantly notified! Teachers have rights too, or do you just think we're all *your* humble public *servants!*"

Mr. Bertuzzi departed in a wrathful mood, and uttered several derogatory expletives during his abrupt exit from my property. The first of four administrative meetings had been scheduled with Mr. and Mrs. Bertuzzi inside the principal's office, with the new superintendent sitting in attendance. I later found-out that the new superintendent happened to be a fairly close friend of Mr. Bertuzzi.

I had requested that another teacher be present to sit-in on the conference and take accurate notes. The administration objected to my demand, but after I had contacted the *New Jersey Education Association* about the background leading to my meeting, the *NJEA* Uni-Serve Representative called the board of education's legal counsel. The school board solicitor advised the principal that it was my "civil employment right" to be able to have an alert, silent witness at the parent/administrative/teacher conference, if a potential teacher reprimand was involved.

I took the initiative at the conference's outset by insisting that I had not called the meeting, so it was up to Mr. and Mrs. Bertuzzi to explain why *we* were all present there in the principal's office. This ploy caught the parents by surprise because the seated plaintiffs had expected the administrators to be *their* prosecutorial hatchet men, taking the teacher for a spanking behind the old woodshed.

After the surprised pair nervously staggered through the matter's general background, trying to be as polite as possible, I had a few additional questions ready to ask. "What do you wish to be the outcome of this meeting?" I clearly asked. "What do you want the session to accomplish?"

"We want an apology for the way you treated me!" Mrs. Bertuzzi reflexively exclaimed. 'Yes, we want you to apologize!"

"And we want to see you punished for acting unprofessional!" Mr. Bertuzzi instinctively added.

"Well, I've never apologized to any parent in my entire career, so I don't believe I'll admit to any wrongdoing now!" I promptly asserted. "This is a classic case where a *student* doesn't like being corrected in class and goes home and complains about being held accountable to her mother," I maintained. "The mother is very protective and defensive of her daughter, and might actually be stifling the girl's emotional growth!"

"Mr. Wiessner, you have no credentials in psychology so please refrain from making statements of *that* nature!" the not-too-enamored, extremely *authoritarian* school district superintendent *(not authoritatively)* interrupted.

I ignored the superintendent's criticism and said to Mrs. Bertuzzi, "Isn't it true that when your first husband had died five years ago, that Melissa then became very talkative in her classes?"

"Mr. Wiessner," the building principal cautioned. "You are skating on thin ice here. You have no business discussing a parent's personal life like that!"

"I adroitly ignored the principal's entreaty. "I've read Melissa's folder and found some personal comments in there indicating that the *student* became talkative in class after Mrs. Bertuzzi's first husband Mr. DiGiovanni passed away? Is that not true, Mrs. Bertuzzi?"

The mother became so distressed that she stood-up crying, and yelling that I was a "mean, terrible person". She frenetically grabbed the knob to the principal's office door and tried hastily escaping the room, but her second husband latched onto her and dragged the distraught, tearful woman back to her seat.

"You called my wife, Lady!" Mr. Bertuzzi yelled at me in a vitriolic, harsh tone of voice. "That was completely unprofessional!"

"When you and your wife go to a show and the master of ceremonies comes out and says, '*Ladies* and gentlemen!' Are you insulted Mrs. Bertuzzi? Do you insist on walking-out of the theater?" I defensively asked. "Do you *not* enter a restaurant bathroom if a sign on the door reads '*Ladies* room'?"

"That example is irrelevant to why you had treated Mrs. Bertuzzi in an unprofessional manner!" the alarmed superintendent friend of Mr. Bertuzzi indicated. "I again caution you, Mr. Wiessner, to refrain from acting unprofessionally during this important conference!"

I was determined to make the mother pay for thinking that I could be crucified in one of my boss's offices just for her and her husband's edification. "Mrs. Bertuzzi, if I had acted unprofessionally as you and your husband have alleged," I replied, "would you call the remark *you* had made 'I'm going to march your ass across the hall to the administration' a professional comment?" I asked. "Would you consider the following expletives another teacher heard *you* calling me when you left my room a *professional* list of words?" I then pulled-out a list of words and phrases Mrs. Bertuzzi had nastily called me. "Here is the list Mrs. Bertuzzi," I proceeded. "I will now enumerate each word and spell it for everyone to hear that my colleague Mr. H. had heard you say. First we have…"

At that juncture, Mrs. Bertuzzi again stood, grabbed the doorknob and hurriedly rushed-out of the office as if she had been sitting with Frankenstein, the Wolfman, Godzilla and Count Dracula. Her supportive husband followed her out and then turned around and melodramatically threatened, "Look pal. this is not the last you'll hear from me!"

Mr. Soya, the woodshop teacher, had been assigned to cover my English class during the heated conference that had transpired in the principal's office. Upon my entering the room, the woodshop instructor immediately admitted to me that he was a "little rusty" in his English grammar skills but said that generally the class was cooperative and respectful.

"Did you have any particular problems of mention?" I asked as we stepped-out and then stood in the hall.

"Well, Melissa Bertuzzi opened her big mouth when I apologized to the class for not being too adept at English Grammar," the shop teacher related.

"What did she say?" I asked.

"She said to me," the shop teacher stated while shaking his head, "you had gone to college, didn't you? You should know this stuff!" Mr. Soya shared while still-shaking his head.

"The girl has unwarranted opinions about a lot of things," I told the disgusted woodshop teacher. "And I have a good idea exactly where she's acquired that bad habit!"

I again met with the on-the-warpath principal and the new superintendent, and both school executives agreed that I had been too crass in defending myself against two belligerent, hostile parents that were trying to ruin my reputation based on one suspect event in my Accelerated English classroom.

"Well," I responded. "I think that those determined parents were out headhunting. If there's a personality conflict arising here, I want that girl out of my Accelerated English class and put into another room with another teacher!"

"We had suggested exactly that prospect to the parents," the don't make waves principal informed me. "But they want her to stay in your class because they think you're a good teacher. They only wanted you to apologize, that's all!"

"Well, glaciers are gonna' have to form in *Hades* before *that* ever happens," I stubbornly communicated. "My pride is only exceeded by my integrity and by my dignity!" Then I told the administrators, "Abe Lincoln once said, 'You can't please all of the people all of the time'," I quoted our sixteenth President. "I have a hundred and thirty *students* with two hundred and sixty parents and guardians to satisfy," I pointed-out to the two high-ranking administrators that did not savor my audacity one iota. "It's hard to appease nearly four hundred potential critics every single day of every single year. I believe I'm doing a terrific job considering that less than one-half of one percent of my potential critics are finding any kind of fault with my teaching and discipline methods!"

"You're excused for now Mr. Wiessner," the principal uneasily told me. "You may return to your classroom!"

The following month Melissa Bertuzzi had to be corrected three times in my English class for talking out of turn and for arguing with the teacher. Each time she broke-down and cried, just like her mother had done during the conference that should have never happened.

The parents again complained that I was picking on their perfect angel, but I was not about to grant the girl a license to talk whenever she wanted and have a double-standard discipline situation existing in my classroom just because her parents thought that they could pull rank on the teacher.

Now here's the administration's report and conclusion about the blown-out-of-proportion matter in *Italics*:

The administration has made the following determinations in regard to the complaint against Mr. Wiessner given by Mr. and Mrs. Bertuzzi.

The written assignment to write the incorrect words and definitions ten times each (the original basis of the complaint) could be educationally defended in many ways, and therefore, was and is acceptable.

The teacher's announcing to Melissa Bertuzzi in front of the entire English class that he had no intention keeping an appointment with Mrs. Bertuzzi was totally out of order.

The teacher made the comment to the *student* so that an unnecessary parent/teacher conference need not be held. The girl had a 94.5 average and knew it would not be in jeopardy if she simply did the writing assignment, which would have erased the failing grade. Melissa withheld those key facts from her mother, and I still think it was because the girl saw the incident as an opportunity to get her parents approval with all three family members back on the same page again, all at the expense of the common enemy, the teacher.

There were instances during your conference with Mrs. Bertuzzi where you had acted unprofessionally, and your behavior cannot be tolerated by the administration. These include:

Your erroneous belief that you have a decision-making privilege regarding whether or not you will or will not meet with one of your student's parents or guardians.

Your expression "Look Lady!" when addressing Mrs. Bertuzzi was unprofessional, regardless of what she had said to you first. She is the parent and you are supposed to be the professional person.

Your unethical mentioning to Mrs. Bertuzzi that perhaps you should speak to your father-in-law, a member of the hospital board where the mother is currently employed as a professional nurse, was very inappropriate and done in exceedingly bad taste.

The administration finds your handling of this incident very unprofessional, and this is an official letter of reprimand that will be included in your personal folder. This is not the first time you have made a parent cry during a conference. You are hereby directed to conduct yourself in a manner befitting a professional teacher in our school system.

District Superintendent

I had mentioned to Mrs. Bertuzzi that going to the administration was like me complaining about her to my father-in-law, then in 1984 a prominent member on the local hospital board. My comment was stated in regard to the context that adults should be able to solve their own problems without appealing to higher authorities, and it was not a direct threat to the mother's employment at the hospital as interpreted by the Bertuzzis' and by the administration.

When I discovered that the new superintendent and Mr. Bertuzzi were close friends, I suspected that the administration might have just been chomping at the bit to get me into an uncomfortable disciplinary situation, since I had offended several school board members during recent local contract negotiations.

Teachers are not supposed to defend themselves while parents enjoy the liberty of finding fault with an event that had transpired in the classroom, as the plaintiffs ignore the hundreds of positive things that have happened in English class. Teachers are expected to remain serfs, and when a parent decides to verbally criticize an instructor, the teacher is just supposed to grin and bear it.

The parents were having a marital crisis, and the cropping-up of this incident was a convenient chance for the daughter and the bickering mom and dad to unite against a common enemy, that dastardly heartless English teacher villain, Mr. John Wiessner. The superintendent's letter's remark about other parents crying in my presence probably refers to the Guidance Department meeting I had had with Joe Dodge's mother thirteen years before the extraordinary Mrs. Bertuzzi conference. Is this evidence of teacher unprofessional behavior, or is it a classic case of teacher serfdom in America? I'll let the reader be the judge.

Chapter 40
"Democracy and Education"

Americans take pride in our claim that our coveted public school educational system is modeled after our *democratic* structure of *Constitutional* government. Our marvelous philosophy of democracy in the classroom, democracy in teaching methods, and democracy in our duly elected American school boards seems bubbling-over with Patrick Henry, Thomas Jefferson, John Adams, and the New England town meetings of colonial times.

But has the novelty of having laymen vicariously representing concerned taxpayers become obsolete in this era of technology, social mobility, and societal disorganization? Can a highly complicated function like American education be entrusted to the expertise of amateur school board members based on the presumption that the general will of the community should prevail? Should education be tailored after politics in an age where government teems with corruption, coercion, payoffs, kickbacks, pork barrel contracts, endorsements and political subterfuge? And don't forget that local and state educational politics also involve the influential *Chameleon Effect* from the State Commissioner and the County and local Superintendent on down.

First of all, education is modeled in the State of New Jersey after politics, and it mirrors the philosophical wrangling going on in Trenton. When a Republican governor is elected, education suddenly becomes conservative, and the emphasis is on *effective* education and standardized test scores like the *GEPA* (Grade Eight Proficiency Assessment) and the *HSPA* (High School Proficiency Assessment). When a Democrat is elected as governor, the focus shifts and is on *affective* education, and the school pendulum swings back towards the scary "*child*-centered curriculum".

So, in a sense, *democratic* education does reflect government, but it is more the *politics* that is going-on in the state capital than it is *democracy* being implemented in the public schools. However, even the state mandated tests advocated by the alluded-to Republican governor *democratically* concealed the reality of *student* lack of skill level while disingenuously projecting the false image of educational effectiveness to the public.

The *GEPA* results were and are skewed at the bottom in Reading, in Writing and in Math' to allow more *children* with very low-test scores to have passed the minimum skill level. Also, the twenty to twenty-five percent of the *special needs* fourteen-year-olds in the school (that would probably fail the *GEPA*) are exempted from taking the "State-Mandated Standardized Test". But the worst part of the *GEPA* preparation was and is the fact that teachers had and have to abandon many regular lessons to teach and practice the specific skills the *GEPA* and *HSPA* evaluated, and presently continues to evaluate. So, the instructors in eighth-and-eleventh-grades were and are "teaching the test" and not presenting to their classes what *they* would prefer to teach.

The ancient Greek philosophers, in the midst of their great polemics, heaped ample criticism on *democracy* as an honorable system of government (let alone as a viable form of education). In the Athens of Socrates, the Golden Age citadel of pure democracy, Plato described democracy as "in every way being weak, and also being unable to do neither great good nor great evil for civilization".

According to the wisdom of Plato, "The will of the people is the worst of all lawful governments, and the best of all lawless ones!" Plato believed that a Republic was the best form of government as stated in his work *The Republic*. A democracy would be doomed to mediocrity, and after examining what the deployment of *democracy* has been doing to our public schools, to the family unit, and to society in general, Plato was not far off the mark. The basic problem with costly American democracy (both in government and in the local schools) is that the society's problems and weaknesses are allowed to thrive and proliferate unabated at the taxpayers' expense.

Plato's argument seems credible even today when weighing into consideration issues like social welfare, unemployment, individual irresponsibility as *a human choice* (freedom to choose), and the weaknesses of local boards of education dispensing important and essential educational directives in every affected community in this presumably great *Republic*.

Plato wasn't the only brilliant mind that had doubts about the viability of *democracy* as an effective and efficient form of government. Other erudite Athenians such as Aeschylus, Sophocles, Aristophanes, Aristotle and Demosthenes distrusted the ugly problems that a democratic government (without a Republic's strong laws) might generate. *Freedom for everybody* usually means waste, expense, and widespread social disorganization, especially when the more industrious citizens must always do more to help, provide for, and assist the ever-existent slackers.

It has been the *American Republic's* idea of respect for law and order that has contributed to national stability throughout our country's history and not the democratic principle of pursuing absolute freedom (anarchy) for the masses. And when our schools pursue and mimic *democratic* freedoms guaranteed in the *Bill of Rights*, another wicked earthquake has shaken the foundation of our great American Republic.

Freedom without respect for authority (parents, teachers, judges, the law) eventually means chaos and turmoil, and as long as educational psychologists give more *democratic* freedom to *students* to misbehave, and in the process, then simultaneously transfer (steal) authority away from teachers, education will continue to decay, crumble and rot from the inside-out.

If the concept of *democracy* were distasteful to Plato as a form of suspect government, how would Plato have reacted to *democracy* being an ideal to pursue in the education of a great *Republic's* youth? Plato and his contemporaries knew quite well the differences that existed in human intellect. The greatest tragedy of American *democratic* education is that the Platos and Aristotles of today are hibernating in classrooms trying to help the less-gifted and more sluggish *students* with remedial level work.

Students with 140 *IQs* are naturally more inventive and creative than those *children* having *IQs* of 80 are. But it is the scheme of *democracy* in education to concoct a curricular recipe whereby the vast disparity in *student* mental talent on the intellectual spectrum is *democratically* indistinguishable. We swish the students around, blending them into a peculiar marble cake mixture, hoping that Joe Dodge will miraculously transform into another Ben Locanta.

But after high school graduation, in defiance of the system that groomed them, the brainy kids shine and finally show their repressed geniuses, while most of the slower *students* finally get (if they're lucky) those beneficial vocational jobs that the wasteful *democratic* comprehensive high school had systematically deprived them of, and detoured them from.

Leading educators emphasize trite *student* similarities (their general emotional and psychological needs) while the Merlins clandestinely minimize true specific individual differences (*IQs*, inventiveness, creativity). "All *students* residing in the district are quite capable of creating and inventing!" the wizards *democratically* and falsely preach and lecture.

But the truth is that current *democratic* American education is more fascinated with the learning process being a social method (sociological) available to the masses rather than an *academic* activity facilitating intellectual development of the best minds, and producing the current and future Platos, Socrates, Aristotles, Einsteins, Edisons and Hemingways.

The precocious *student,* the one that might someday cure cancer or write the best novel ever, is stifled while sitting alongside slackers in public school *democratic* classrooms. The brainiacs must *socialize* with *students* of Joe Dodge's caliber, learn respect for the group, do most of the group's work while the dawdlers get equal credit, and defer his or her affinity for true discovery until the college level.

It is the advanced *student* that is the true casualty of the American *democratic* comprehensive high school. Under the guise of *democratic* education, the individual needs of the gifted *student* are virtually ignored because the group identity is the most desirable objective. And if any teacher goes to bat for the *democratic* rights of the high-intellect *students,* he or she is *democratically* labeled an elitist and is judged as being prejudiced against the rights and needs of all the *students.* Everyone in authority must be "politically correct", so that more authority (a *Republic's* attribute) can be *democratically* transferred to the *students* (masses).

The only time the Educational Aristocracy speaks of "individual differences" is when the teacher must understand the enigmatic Joe Dodge personality that is trying to destroy the instructor's sanity, or when the teacher must encourage the bashful *child* to contribute to class discussions. Individual differences are also evident when the teacher must soothe the emotionally disturbed *child* or when the slow learner must be motivated. "Individual differences" in its popular context means negative or inferior *student* behavior or performance that the teacher must adapt to and adjust to.

Individual differences (in its popular context) do not pertain to the intelligence/cultural gap, or to the *academic* skill abyss evident between a Ben Locanta and a Joe Dodge. And if anyone on the teaching staff dares to refer to intelligence differences, automatically, the *democratic* principle of "don't be prejudiced" surfaces. According to modern theory, there should *not* be criticism of slower *students* (that practice would be prejudice), and there *should be* minimal praising of more gifted and talented *students* (praising smart kids for being intelligent would be assessed as being undemocratic).

The gifted and talented *students* (just like Plato predicted) will provide most of the leadership roles in the future. The one good feature of the intellectually gifted *students* surviving past high school graduation is that the cream will eventually surface to the top (in a capitalistic free enterprise society), no matter how hard psychologists and the rest of the Educational Aristocracy stir the coffee.

Democracy in education along with the comprehensive high school have made contemporary American public-school education vacillate between the bizarre and the appalling. Once, when I was teaching at the junior-senior high in the early '70s, an American Indian fresh off the reservation visited the school and addressed the *student* body (the masses) about the tribulations associated with being a member of the red minority in America. The junior class president (elected to office under the pretense of *democracy*) asked the Indian guest:

1. How come you are still an Indian and didn't move to the city?

2. Were you born an Indian?

That was the junior class president demonstrating his mental dynamics. This specific illustration typifies what a miscarriage of Jeffersonian *democratic* philosophy that the standard American high school actually is. The awkward shortcomings and liabilities are slickly concealed in psychological bureaucratic mumbo-jumbo, and only the glamour and the glittering aspects are filtered-out and transmitted in the newspapers to the undiscerning American public.

All that glitters is not gold, and *that* relevant maxim is very true of the typical American high school or average middle school. The goals of *democratic* sociological education are as frivolous and impractical as trying to fly a *767* through one of the *Holland Tunnel's* narrow tubes. If a teacher openly goes public and opposes the Educational Aristocracy and its many all-too-common sophist philosophical flaws, then that intrepid teacher is labeled a subversive, a dissident, a malcontent, a radical, or a narrow-minded, difficult, prejudiced person.

On one occasion, a cocky and disrespectful eighth-grade *student* received enough votes from his peers to merit the *American Legion's* "Good Citizenship Award" because the *student body* voted for all the nominees. The *child* respected teacher authority and school rules as much as a mongoose reveres a cobra. His antics throughout the year were quite disruptive, and the poor teacher in charge of the graduation ceremony regretted that the clownish fool had won enough *student* votes to gain the award.

"This is a disgrace!" the woman advisor criticized in the faculty room. "He's not deserving of the award!"

"The *student body* voted," I adamantly disagreed. "And this would be a rightful tribute to the ineffectiveness of *democracy* in education! It is a flawed system with too many loopholes!"

The baffled graduation ceremony advisor disgustedly replied, "Oh, we couldn't let that happen! It would be a scandal to let *him* receive the award! I'll talk with the principal and conduct the election again with *his* name removed from the ballot!"

Another time, the *students* elected one of the worst behaved *children* as their eighth-grade president as a cute-little joke, and the act done to rebelliously spite adult authority. "Maybe this will make *him* more responsible!" the class advisor said to me.

"It's an absolute travesty for you to say (or even suggest) something like that!" I angrily replied. "The buffoon was elected just to mock the school, and to spit in the face of tradition and decency. It's a form of teen rebellion, and *you* are tolerating it because you believe it is *democracy* in action," I objected and argued. "The most qualified *student* that is going to work hard for the class should have the honor of being its class president!" I maintained. "You don't allow someone to become class president, hoping that the new role is going to rehabilitate that *student* for the better! That assumption is absolute insanity!"

The *student* being described was not rehabilitated when serving in the role of class president, did hardly anything positive for the class all year long, and did not go to half the scheduled meetings (according to the class advisor). Then, at the end of the year, I refused to work on rehearsing, coaching and rewriting the class president's speech for the upcoming graduation ceremony. "I'm tired of making things look good for the sake of making things look good!" I told the disenchanted class advisor.

And so, educators often artistically cover-up the blemishes with thick, chalky makeup, and *we* liberally and *democratically* allow young barracudas a free reign to wander at will around the building and terrorize smaller fish in the great educational sea.

A more favorable feature of *democracy* has been the lowering of the voting age to eighteen. Some ungovernable senior *students* can now be taken to court and tried as adults. In being old enough to vote, the eighteen-year-olds have forfeited their *liberty* to disrupt school activities and to corrupt the values of freshmen by setting poor examples.

Since *democracy* as a form of government is a *planning* process and always changing and evolving, *democratic* education follows the same pattern by having a "planning" rather than a "planned" curriculum. In that way, schools can change costumes almost every year and effectively cover their tracks and slickly disguise their appearance. Inefficiency can better be concealed by not staying in one place long enough to make any deep imprints.

School administrators add to the zany sideshow by appointing public steering committees to get parents directly involved in the *democratic* educational process. Conscientious *PTA* mothers and band booster officers are now helping the amateur board of education determine what the long-range goals and philosophy that the community's schools should attain. The ongoing study will become circular file waste material before the goals and philosophies give way to newer goals and philosophies five years ahead. And, of course, the school district's administrators advise the steering committees on what they should *democratically* endorse.

Education is the only profession where rank amateurs sitting on steering committees along with other conjurers occupying elected seats on boards of education can have dominion and control over the philosophy, the goals, the ethics and the school system's anemic practices. In the final analysis of *democratic* education, everyone in the community is now an expert on education except the teachers that do the actual educating. Those *employees* are the lowly serfs actively and loyally serving in the Educational Aristocracy's public-school fiefdoms all across America.

Chapter 41
"Crazy Things Happen"

Crazy and unexpected things often happen to teachers laboring in middle, junior-high, and high schools. The teacher doesn't know when, how, why or where a strange event might happen. He or she simply knows that one inane, incredible incident will eventually occur. The unanticipated occurrence might suddenly materialize inside the classroom, in the hall, in the cafeteria, on the asphalt parking lot, in the office, in a lavatory, in the library, or on the cement pavement outside the building. And the teacher is expected to adjust to the situation and take it all in stride, even though he or she might have barely escaped being mutilated during the harrowing incident by the skin of his or her teeth.

I remember once I was on sixth-period cafeteria duty. The *children* had entered, the late bell rang, and the two other teachers on duty and I were about to send the seated *students* up to the serving line to be attended to by the gossiping lunchroom brunhildas.

The janitors had been painting the walls of the cafetorium (combination cafeteria and auditorium), but those employees had taken-off from that work detail to allow for *student* lunch periods five through seven. Suddenly, a loud crash was heard that scared all venial and mortal sins out of my heart and soul.

The metal scaffolding being used by the custodians to paint one of the walls had collapsed and plummeted to the cafetorium floor, crashing only five feet from where I had been standing. A minute later in *that* lunch period, fifty *students* would have been standing in the serving line directly under where the heavy metal scaffolding had fallen. A major disaster had been averted by blind fate.

In the early '80s, I was walking up and down the aisles between eighth-grade *student* desks inside my middle school classroom. The English teacher was diligently monitoring a silent reading literature activity. I casually looked-down and detected a suspicious bulge underneath a male *student's* blue lightweight jacket. As I scrutinized the bulge more intensely, I observed a vest underneath the blue-zip-jacket and a gun and holster underneath. 'I have to do something in a hurry!' I strategically and nervously thought.

I bent over and quietly whispered to the *student*, "One of the office secretaries wants to see you and give you a message from home!" I related. I deliberately avoided saying "Principal" or "Vice-Principal" because either of those two appellations might have *triggered* the *child* into a panic-state of mind. I then escorted the unsuspecting fourteen-year-old *student* from my back classroom door to the Main Office across the corridor.

Upon reaching the office, I surprised the *student* by hastily reaching my hand inside his blue jacket and quickly grabbing the concealed gun out of the holster, just like my mind had mentally rehearsed the act at least a dozen times while walking between the classroom and the office. I then roughly tossed the metal object onto the office counter, and the three astonished secretaries reactively gasped in shock and horror.

"Don't worry!" the *student* remarked to the petrified secretaries. "It's only a toy gun!"

Upon closer inspection, the gun indeed was a toy, but its barrel had been made out of metal, and its handle was wooden and looked rather authentic. The false pistol looked and felt like the real McCoy. 'If it was a real gun, I could have accidentally shot someone if it had gone-off when I threw the object onto the office counter,' I evaluated in a moment of wise hindsight.

The *student* was suspended for three days for bringing the item to school. The boy and his parents protested to the principal that I had "manhandled" the *child* while disarming the fake weapon from his possession. Fortunately, the school authorities placed little credence in the *student's* testimony and objections and did not honor his parents' grievance about "corporal punishment". However, in retrospect, I nearly had suffered a coronary during that very tense and very dramatic "false alarm".

An administrative investigation later revealed that the eighth-grader had brought the toy gun and holster to school to impress his peers that he could be a threat to larger *children* intimidating and bullying him around. The *student's* game plan was to scare the ruffians off with his fake weapon the next time the bullies would instigate their badgering and begin publicly humiliating the emotionally tortured *child* in front of their peers.

And whoever insists that schools don't need policemen patrolling the cafeteria and the halls has never had to disarm a *"student"* to prevent a potential hostage situation. 'Let the halls and the cafeteria become *police states,* and let the classrooms remain being safe *pretend democratic academic states!'* I concluded.

As an eighth-grade English teacher, I sometimes used films to inspire *students* to write compositions. Once, I was showing the Hollywood musical *Bye, Bye Birdie* starring Ann Margret, Dick Van Dyke, Janet Leigh and Bobby Rydell for the purpose of having the *students* describe the characters, settings and plots in organizing a lengthy eight paragraph composition.

One scene involved a situation where Janet Leigh (Rosie) had given a Russian orchestra conductor a glass of milk to drink containing a formula (*Speed-up*) that Dick Van Dyke (Albert) had ingeniously concocted. The *Speed-up* made the conductor move his baton faster so that the Russian ballet dancers moved around quicker on the stage to finish their performance, thus allowing enough time for Conrad Birdie to sing Albert's new song on national television.

It was my irresistible habit to get involved with a movie's scene to surprise and delight the *students* watching the film in the dark. As the Russian ballet dancers were jumping about at quadruple speed, I dashed to the back of the room where the television and *VCR* were located and began leaping all around, pretending to be one of the Russian dancers. The *students* all wildly laughed, thinking that my improvisation was rather comical for an old-fashioned English teacher to enact.

As I was thoroughly amusing my captive audience, a girl sitting in the dark near the *VCR* had not put her thick literature textbook under her desk. My right foot landed on the book's edge, and I immediately double sprained my right ankle. The teacher was jumping and howling around the back of the classroom in total excruciating pain, and the *students* were laughing hysterically, reacting to what they thought was my rather superlative *Keystone Kop* acting ability.

I managed to hop to the side heater frame where I parked my butt until the hilarious film and the wonderful class had ended. After most of the thoroughly entertained *students* left the room, I had the last girl leaving the area buzz the office by pressing the intercom button. The nurse arrived on the scene a minute later and had to cut off my shoe with huge sharp scissors (shears) because my right ankle had swollen-up to the size of a grapefruit.

A janitor drove me to the school doctor's office, and I was the first teacher in my district to collect "Workmen's Compensation" because I actually had been injured on the job. I was out for ten days with my uniquely acquired swollen ankle. 'Thank goodness I didn't injure myself in my classroom before 8 a.m., or I wouldn't be eligible for disability!' I recollected.

In the early '90s, I had assigned my Accelerated English Class classic novels for the *students* to read in order for them to deliver oral reports. Each *student* had to review the characters of his or her assigned book and then come-up to the lectern and tell the story and also identify the main plot and characters to his or her classmates.

One male *student* got five minutes into his ten-minute presentation when a combination of nerves, heat, and a poor lunch must have caught-up with him. The young man began wobbling back and forth at the lectern. At first, I just thought he was nervous at his initial attempt at formal public speaking, so I asked him a question to help alleviate the anxiety I believed the *student* was experiencing. But then, the boy suddenly slumped-over and went totally unconscious with his chest resting upon the lectern. Instantly, I dispatched a *student* in the first row to sprint-down to the nurse's office and to get her to my classroom "on the double".

I gingerly placed my hands under the boy's armpits and dragged the afflicted junior Demosthenes's limp body out into the corridor. 'Perhaps I should attempt reviving the boy by splashing some cold water onto his face from the water fountain!' I thought as I gently placed the unconscious speaker upon the floor and gently leaned his back against the hall lockers. 'I don't want to slap his face because his parents might sue me for corporal punishment after I have saved his life!' I remember thinking.

The school nurse dashed-down the hall to the emergency scene. She bent-down and proceeded to slap the lad's cheeks silly, rather robustly back and forth at least ten times, until the lad finally came out of his deep stupor. I carefully lifted the dazed *student* to his feet. And when his weak body rested against the hall lockers, the boy, with his eyes closed, continued giving his required oral book report out in the main hallway, and the groggy young man verbally proceeded from exactly the spot in the story where he had left-off at the lectern in front of my classroom.

In the mid-'90s, I was heading upstairs in the middle school building between third and fourth periods. My prep' period was fourth period, so I wanted to use the men's room, then run-off three worksheets in the office for the following day's lessons, and finally, relax and read a magazine in the school library. The bell had rung two minutes before, so the *students* had another minute to get to their fourth period classes.

As I approached the stairwell, I looked-up and a *student* (that I didn't teach or didn't know) leaped from the tenth step and soared right toward my forehead. I instinctively ducked-down and just avoided being decapitated by a flying dropkick. I turned around and amazingly, the agile *student* landed upright on his two feet after performing the very extraordinary and difficult acrobatic maneuver.

I accosted the young prankster and asked, "Okay wise guy; what's your name and what grade are you in?"

The interrogated *student* evaded direct confrontation and wouldn't even give me the courtesy of eye contact. I sensed that the *child* was about to bolt from my custody and also from my investigation. "What's your name?" I insisted as I got directly into his face.

"Get out of my face and let go of my arm!" the Hispanic *child* shouted. 'I don't know you, and you don't know me!"

"What's your name?" I again hollered, becoming more aggravated with each exchange of words.

"I don't have to tell you nothin'!" the wise-guy kid shrieked while effectively employing a double negative.

"Well then, young man, I'm going to have to escort you down to the vice-principal's office to finally find-out your true identity!" I emphatically indicated.

The *student* resisted my firm grasp and refused to voluntarily accompany me to visit the vice-principal. The hundred-and-twenty-pound *child* protested his capture and incessantly cursed and yelled while violently kicking me in the shins all the way down to the Main Office. I finally shoved him into a seat and guarded over the fledgling circus performer until one of the secretaries positively identified who he happened to be.

"Okay Jose, wait here while I write-out a Discipline Referral Card on you," I commanded. "You nearly kicked the kneecaps off my legs! Maybe you should think of becoming a champion soccer player?" I stated, as I realized that I was using my free time to collar and report the obstinate *student.*

From that day on, whenever I had free time to walk around the school building, I would wait until at least five minutes into my fourth period prep' time to venture-out into the hallways to avoid catching *students* I didn't even know who were misbehaving. Then, I wouldn't have to surrender my free time escorting someone like energized Jose to the office and getting brutally kicked and mugged all along the way.

I used to stay quite regularly after school to do additional work, to plan the following week's lessons, to construct bulletin boards in my homeroom (classroom), to correct compositions, and to *Xerox* daily class worksheets.

One afternoon, I was leaving the General Office and heading across the hall to my classroom at 2:50 (school had ended at 2:30). A *student* that I didn't know had been assigned Office Detention and had been given permission by the teacher on duty to leave the room and get a book out of his locker. The *student* was scampering down the hallway at full speed and heading right toward me in violation of the school rule "no running in the corridors".

"Stop running!" I shouted at the approaching hundred-and-thirty-pound *child*. The *student* ignored my directive and continued sprinting. I dropped my recently *Xeroxed* worksheets on the tile floor and held-up my hands signaling' "Halt!" I latched onto the *student's* arms to stop his forward progress. The *child* clowned-around by spinning himself' out of my clutches and then loudly slamming his body into the hall lockers outside my classroom. I then walked-over and started reprimanding him for his dangerously wild sprinting activity that had been enacted in the hall.

"Don't touch me!" the *student* shouted in my face. "You already hurt my arm! I'm gonna' call my mom and get you fired!"

"Who are you?" I demanded knowing. "What's your name?"

"I don't have to tell ya' nothin'!" came the familiar insolent *refrain* that should be *refrained* from all *students'* mouths. "You're gonna' be fired, jerk-off!" he yelled at me.

"We'll see about that!" I shouted. "If someone like you can make me lose my job, then my job isn't worth anything in the first place, now is it?" I angrily yelled. I then un-gently dragged the balking *student* into the office and wrote-out a Discipline Referral Card. 'It's a good thing this school's office orders a lot of pens!' I thought.

The following morning, the principal called me into his office before school and interrogated me about "the hall running assault". I want to hear your version of what happened!" the administrator imperatively stated. "The *student's* mother was quite hostile over the phone and wants to see you fired for attacking her son and slamming him into the lockers! Then she plans to sue the school!"

"There is no *my version* to the story," I angrily responded. "I'm the teacher, the authority person in the school, remember?" I testily answered. "I resent when *you* habitually put *students* on the same shelf as teachers!"

"Mrs. F. also called the Superintendent's Office and registered a very vocal complaint against your brutal actions against her son!" the principal confided. "The superintendent has enough aggravation without this incident suddenly cropping-up!"

"What should I do?" I impatiently inquired. "How can this new situation be addressed?"

"Write letters to the superintendent and to me describing in detail every aspect of the incident!" the principal recommended. "And don't use your fifty cent words, either!"

I spent two full hours drafting comprehensive letters to the principal and the superintendent explaining everything that had transpired. 'Sometimes doing less is better in education!' I concluded. 'If I hadn't been so dedicated and stayed after school running-off papers, then I would've never *run-into* that *student* in the hall during *his* Office Detention!' I decided. Ever since that day, I seldom stayed after school to work on anything. 'I'll correct all of my compositions in the quiet and safety of my home!' I thought.

In the mid-80s, a phoned-in bomb scare had all of the *students* and faculty quickly evacuating the middle school building. The principal approached and then informed me on the sidewalk that I would be assigned to search *student* lockers and classrooms in an effort to discover a possible bomb.

"Now just wait a minute!" I strenuously objected. "That type of dangerous work activity is not in my job description, nor is it in the negotiated teachers' contract, or in the school curriculum!"

"If you don't do as I direct during an emergency, you're then acting in an insubordinate manner," the school executive insisted.

"Did you ever hear of the idea that a criminal usually returns to the scene of a crime?" I replied in the form of a question.

"What's *that* comment supposed to mean in this situation? Stop being so vague and stubborn!" the school executive rankled.

"Well, in this particular case, the suspect has never left the scene of the crime," I alertly informed as if I was Sherlock Holmes. "Just direct your attention across the street to the telephone booth between the police station and the post office. If my eyes serve me correctly, that's one of our *less illustrious students* who's on today's absentee list. He's proudly watching the result of his bomb-scare-mischief from inside the phone booth."

School authorities soon apprehended the delinquent *student,* and his amazing punishment for brazenly committing a blatant felony and frightening and inconveniencing five-hundred-people was a mere five days suspension from school.

Then, in 1999, before cell phones became in vogue, a strange incident happened *before* school. An administrative rule in the *Students Handbook* specified that *students* were not permitted to use the hall payphone *before* school, but only *after* school to call parents to come and pick them up; another acceptable use was for private-but-important family business. If *students* believed they had to call home from school in the morning, they were supposed to go into the Main Office and ask a secretary for permission.

That morning, I stepped out of my classroom and noticed a talkative female eighth-grader speaking on the payphone. "You're not allowed to use this phone before school!" I informed the *student*. "Hang up and then go to the office and use the office phone!"

"I can't!" the *student* protested. "I'm talkin' *to* my mother!"

"You meant to say 'I'm speaking *with* my mother'!" I corrected, because I always preferred being grammatically correct as opposed to being politically correct. "Now hang up the phone and call your mom from the office!"

"Who's that?" the mother's voice echoed through the phone speaker. "Who's that telling you what you have to do!" the mother's all-too-penetrating voice screamed.

"Mom, it's *only* a teacher!" the chatty *child* reported. "He's always picking on me and tellin' me what to do!"

I reiterated to the *student* that I wanted her to hang-up the telephone, but the *child* again ignored and defied my *authority*. I then grabbed the receiver from her hand and told the mother at the other end of the line, "Your daughter will call you back in a minute from the General Office phone!"

"Who are you? Who the hell do you think you are?" the irate woman's voice squawked from the wall-telephone being held in my right-hand palm. I had had enough of listening to the mother's vicious incriminations, so I placed the payphone's receiver back into its slot and then conducted the girl into the General Office.

Fifteen minutes later, the crazed parent came storming into the building. "Where's that stupid asshole teacher!" she yelled like a female barbarian. "All the teachers in this fuckin' school are assholes! Where the fuck is he?" she again screamed as the *students* in the hall standing at their lockers all wondered what was going on.

The outraged mother then swiftly entered the Main Office, yelled discourteously at the appalled secretaries, and then told both the principal and the vice-principal to "Go to hell!" when they attempted to calm her down. "These teachers in this school are nothin' but a bunch of stupid assholes!" she kept repeating at the top of her lungs.

The irritated principal called me into his office during my preparation period. 'At least I won't get dropkicked in the head at the stairwell by a leaping *student!*' I imagined. 'I should be somewhat safe from physical injury in the principal's office!'

"Mr. Wiessner, next time you see a *student* talking on the phone before school, please use better judgment!" the very distressed administrator diplomatically criticized.

"But the *student* was blatantly breaking a school rule," I futilely argued, "and then she was insubordinate to my authority three times before I removed the payphone receiver from her hand and sent her to use the office phone!"

"You could've handled that situation much better than you did!" the apprehensive principal admonished. "Please use better discretion next time you decide to get physical with a *student!*"

"Look!" I strongly objected. "If a parent comes into a school acting violently and using foul, abusive language, then the administration should call the police and have her body dragged-out of the building in handcuffs!"

"We *are* pressing charges against the mother for causing a loud disturbance!" the principal reluctantly admitted. "We want to get a restraining order from her entering this building!"

"Yes, that's very nice and considerate of you," I suavely and sarcastically protested, "but the police should've been summoned and should have arrested her on the spot!" I insisted. "But *you* were afraid of having the cops solve a problem that *you* were obviously incapable of handling!" I forcefully yelled my objection in a most critical and angry tone of voice.

"You're dismissed. You can go to your next period class, Mr. Wiessner!" the aggravated executive commanded. "Everything that needed to be said has been said!"

I learned another valuable lesson that morning in the principal's office. Don't report anything wrong a *student* might do, and then the teacher won't get called on the carpet for doing his job. Hear no evil, see no evil, and most importantly, report no evil. As is sometimes the case, doing less is best. Doing more than a teacher has to do often leads to a career-threatening misadventure with a crazy *student,* or with the crazy *student's* crazy parent or parents.

Finally, one last episode made me realize that it was time to hang-up my diploma after thirty-four years of teaching in a public school system. I was in the office in mid-May of '99 at 7:15 a.m., busily *Xeroxing* copies of my final English exam'. 'Thank goodness no *students* are in and around the building at this early hour to cause me grief!' I thought and then prematurely chuckled.

Suddenly, I heard a loud bang outside, so I stepped to the window to investigate the source of the noise. The town street cleaner had been sweeping the teacher parking lot and had smashed directly into the rear of my year-old light blue *Buick LeSabre*. 'This is absolutely insane!' I mentally exclaimed to myself. 'My car's the only one in the whole damned parking lot and that street cleaner operator has accidentally collided into it!'

The damage to my *LeSabre* came to eight-hundred-and-fifty-dollars. The town clerk informed me that the municipality would pay my five-hundred-dollar deductible and that my insurance company would pay the rest.

I was without an automobile for an entire week; all because I had been a conscientious, dedicated teacher at work a full hour before I was supposed to be there. That's when I acknowledged the great degree of wisdom prevalent in the statement, "In American education, sometimes doing less is best!"

Chapter 42
"The Board of Education"

Imagine a giant corporation engaged in the process of selecting a new board of directors. The new *CEO* desires for the corporation to be thoroughly *democratic* and modeled after the internal functioning of the American government. The corporation appeals its needs to the communities in which the company has factories, plants and offices, and the *CEO* requests that the local citizenry elect local candidates to serve as policymakers for the giant conglomerate. The predictable outcome of such an American corporation would be certain bankruptcy within less than a decade. Yet, this is exactly how public-school education (a fantastically large national expenditure) functions in thousands of separate community units throughout the United States.

The school budget, the largest spending in most small-to-midsize communities, is managed and operated by men and women that are usually engaged in other fields of endeavor besides education. The folksy idea of local control of education by unqualified laymen sitting on boards of education is still adhered to as an American *democratic* institution in this age of mechanization and technology.

America doesn't need plumbers, landscapers, dentists, brew masters and farmers running its public schools. Having local citizens determine policy for indigenous school districts is perhaps the greatest detriment to educational efficiency besides the notion of *democratic* (sociological) education in a comprehensive middle, junior high, and high school. *Democratic* anything in American education means four very expensive adjectives: "wasteful, inefficient, impractical and ineffective."

Education in the United States is infatuated with the grassroots idea that each community is unique and autonomous. However, the provincial "unique and autonomous" theory is more myth than actuality. Kids in Sheboygan, Wisconsin and kids in Amarillo, Texas have more common traits than differences. Cable television, radio, computers, the Internet, and the press have virtually wiped-out regional and local distinctions, and now American culture is more similar all across the country than it ever has been.

Instead of leaving decision-making up to amateurs on local steering committees and up to other amateurs sitting on boards of education, a national panel of educational curriculum experts could best decide what is important for *students* to know, and what isn't.

By clinging to the theory that *democratic* education (sociological) is the best way to run our public schools, American education has successfully evaded reliable accountability, valid evaluation, and legitimate answerability.

Suspect community steering committees distribute unreliable questionnaires to *students* with arbitrary items printed on them to find-out what the *children* want to learn in school. When a person's pipes leak, that citizen doesn't call a shoemaker to fix the problem; he or she calls a plumber. If a person wants a room added onto his or her house, he or she contacts a qualified builder, and not an *Avon* lady or a *Fuller Brush* man. But when communities desire to renovate their decorative educational goals and objectives, the leaders assemble panels of well-intentioned novices to organize their local priorities, and then submit questionnaires to the school *children* asking for their *democratic* input.

Educational piloting committees are composed mostly of parents, school administrators, and local businessmen. This type of feeble *democratic* planning is indicative of the kind of *bum steers* that are guiding the destiny of today's American public schools. While rank amateurs are preoccupied designing elaborate and ethereal goals and objectives, other amateurs are permanent fixtures that have been planted in board of education seats for decades.

Former teachers that have evolved into school administrators usually have weak business acumens, but still, they're guiding community steering committees and boards of education. And the suspect administrators are also itemizing and manipulating school budgets. And then, the naïve community will blame the teachers for generating the colossal wasteful, expensive, and fantastically inefficient expenditures schools are causing the taxpayers.

Haphazardly entrusting the future of American education to the blundering (just enumerated) factions is analogous to having a dizzy throng of ancient Egyptians building the pyramids using blueprints designed for a Phoenician galley. The public control of American education is grossly unfeasible, impractical, ineffective, and also fundamentally ludicrous. The current fabric being woven throughout the USA is an amalgamation and manifestation of the inherent weaknesses associated with *democracy* as identified by Plato nearly two and a half' millennia ago. Schools are too complex and education is too complicated to be governed over by barbers, gas station owners, bowling alley proprietors and petunia growers voluntarily serving on district steering committees and on local boards of education.

In the local business community, commercial profitability is contingent-upon the owner having an amicable disposition along with a pinch of luck, good timing, and risk-taking success. Good business in small towns thrives on harmonious relationships with, as well as good service to, the public. But businessmen tend to be anti-intellectual because thinking leads to controversy, and controversy might breed ill will and potential hostility with customers.

Smart businessmen in small communities usually don't run for town council seats because if he or she is a Democrat, most of the Republicans will boycott his or her business, and vice-versa. The local board of education, therefore, is the safest haven for a businessman to wind-up at if he or she wants to safely and independently serve his or her community.

Successful town businessmen shy away from debate because thinking often leads to personality conflicts, to disagreement, and to confrontation, which translates into loss of business and profit. Forget about discussing hot topics like religion, politics, or education with clientele if one is a small business owner. Getting along with those that patronize his or her establishment is valued as being of paramount importance for economic success and survival anywhere on Main Street, or on Side Street USA.

But when those same businessmen occupy seats on the local board of education, they act as if the opinions in their educational repertoire had been passed on to them by Moses himself'. Board members want teachers to always make less money than they do because in many small communities, intelligence is often correlated more with affluence than it is with educational background or intellectual inquiry. Business success in the average suburban community depends more on an individual possessing a decent, sociable personality (along with a dab of good luck) than it relies on either high intelligence or higher education.

Older teachers on contract negotiating teams look across the table at school board members whom they had taught, and recollect that the individual sitting opposite him or her had required remedial reading or might have been "an 8-6er". But still, those new board members demonstrated noteworthy initiative and had managed to carve-out comfortable niches in the community because the sociable representatives knew how to smile and show their pearly whites when ringing-up the cash register.

Success to school board members has plenty to do with the maxim: "It's not what you know; it's who you know that really matters!" And so, in the various barbershops, beauty parlors, and

401

doughnut shops throughout the community, teachers are regarded as wallowing towards or in the bottom of the pecking order by the taxpayers, who argue that *they* subsidize high educational salaries.

Board of education members find it difficult and awkward dealing with delicate matters requiring deep thought such as academic freedom, teacher rights, and the arbitration of teacher grievances, and the sensitive "power brokers" don't like to be challenged when teachers (during contract negotiations) pepper them with Socratic, Platonic and Baconian logic. Complicated subjects demand deep meditation and not the suave, superficial, trite cordiality that businessmen/school board members practice daily in their quaint community shops and service offices.

In order to avoid intellectual conflict with the teachers' negotiating team, many school boards prefer to hire professional negotiators to represent the school's position on debatable issues. Since negotiating with teachers has little to do with keeping patrons as friends and with the art of making money, the business skills that the board member might exercise in his store or office are basically useless in the battle of ideas being waged at the negotiating table. Despite the disparity in brainpower, the teacher *Volkswagens* and Ford *Tauruses* can be seen sandwiched in between status-oriented *Lincolns, Cadillacs* and *Lexuses* aligned in the nearby parking lot outside the boardroom during contract negotiations.

Most candidates campaigning for school board seats run on pledges to safeguard the taxpayers' dollars and to limit spending. A few school board aspirants might allude to nebulous descriptions such as "quality education", and "equal opportunity to learn", and "*democratic* education," but most candidates don't have a clue as to what those blasé bourgeois descriptions really mean. The platitudes and terminology they use when running for office lack precise definition and clarity in the school board members' minds, which are more attuned to keeping customers happy and making a profit. Since teachers are school board employees and not revered business customers at the time of contract negotiations, school board members feel like they don't have to be overly cordial and pleasant to mere educational *employees*.

The school board defers the real issue of education up to the school administrators, including the chief executive, the superintendent, who likes to *super-intend* his (or her) will and whims on the subordinate teaching staff. And when a member of the *subordinate* teaching staff defends a debatable position, he or she is often regarded as being *insubordinate*.

In a major corporation, the board members are promoted from within on the basis of achievement and also in terms of total contributions to the company. But in public education, school board members are usually elected by the local citizens while promising to cut expenditures and overhead as the elected candidates make sure that the administration's inefficient and costly *democratic* education tradition is haphazardly implemented, practiced and continued.

Consider the flimsy qualifications needed for eligibility to be a school board member. The school board candidate must know how to read or write (to what skill proficiency or grade level is not specified), and he or she must be a U.S. citizen. Also, the prospective board member must have lived in the school district for two years. About the only people that have been excluded by the aforementioned, cursory qualifications are aliens, illegal aliens, illiterates, criminal fugitives, and international terrorists that are continually on the lam.

I once asked a school board member, "Do you know who John Dewey was?"

"Didn't he run against Harry Truman for President and was defeated?" the wondering fellow answered.

"No, I believe that was *Thomas* Dewey in 1948!" I replied while wanting to give the board member a Dewey Button. "John Dewey was the Socialist Father of Modern American Education!"

Over the course of the last hundred and fifty years, the *Pony Express* has become obsolete, the buckboard has been replaced by the automobile, colonial milliners have over time become garment workers, apothecaries have become pharmacists, but boards of education have remained boards of education. And additionally, teachers have remained serfs laboring in school district fiefdoms exclusively for the benefit of the Educational Aristocracy.

The composition of an average American school board might consist of the following: a baker, a produce broker, a salesman, an oil distributor, a dentist that is the oil distributor's brother, a construction executive who is the wealthy produce broker's cousin, an automotive parts tycoon, and a soybean farmer. A better, more diverse cross-section of American occupations could not be found if the board members had been randomly chosen from the *Want Ads* of the local newspaper.

This assemblage comprised of random educational amateurs is assigned the task of making big money decisions about curriculum, about employees, about capital outlay, about school philosophy, about goals and objectives, and about the elusive phantom known as "quality education" in the *democratic* comprehensive school district. Some more flamboyant boards of education would make the *Manhattan Project* look like the *Woodstock* rock festival.

Prudent board of education members are sworn to represent the frugal spending attitudes of the taxpayers, many of whom have deep-rooted, absolute contempt and distrust for the subordinate teaching profession. When millions of taxpayers' dollars are being wasted on inefficient and ineffective *democratic* education, the teachers have been commissioned to lead a losing crusade against illiteracy while championing the futile and wasteful cause of *democratic* education in the comprehensive school.

And most school board members claim that they are very much concerned about *academics,* not realizing that the *democratic* institutions *they* represent and govern over are essentially *sociological* bastions that are systematically de-emphasizing and dismantling curricular *academics.* If *students* were simply sorted-out into two bins (academic and vocational) after eighth-grade, billions and billions of dollars would be saved annually, and more societal stability would be ensured for future generations.

In many small towns, board of education elections are merely popularity polls, and the likeable candidate with the largest family (or the largest family that still likes him or her) is usually the successful nominee. If a local citizen has grandiose political ambitions and aspires to someday have his face carved on *Mt. Rushmore,* then a good place for the upward surge to national fame and recognition is at the pedestal of the governmental beanstalk. The local board of education represents a commodious steppingstone for anyone that desires to ascend to the lofty political palisades and be elected to the offices of Freeholder, Assemblyman, Congressman, U.S. Senator, or Governor.

Although many school board candidates are sincere in their motivations for running for local office, many others are in the hunt solely for the ego power trip. One board member was only interested in his special needs' son having an *ISP* (individualized *student* plan) created just for his shielded offspring. Other board members might want to see special school pork barrel contracts awarded to their business friends and associates, or just be in it for sports programs, or for school band or football team representation.

Many school boards do not represent the sentiments of the local population. In some school board elections, the apathetic public remains dormant, and board candidates may win seats with less than twenty percent of the plebiscite exercising its sacred franchise. Many school boards are no more representative of their constituents than Al Sharpton, Jesse Jackson or the Black Panthers are of the whole Afro-American community. School board members generally regard teacher salaries as just another item on the burgeoning expense budget. Teachers are given the same attention as school bus operations, general maintenance, textbook acquisitions, cafeteria supplies, and capital outlay. Few school board members will admit that good schools depend on good teachers, and that heating and lighting systems, storage sheds, school sidewalks, and pencil and paper supplies are secondary to the vital functions occurring in classrooms. Getting school board members to appreciate and support the teachers' desire to attain professional status is as futile as digging a parallel *Panama Canal* with a teaspoon in one hand and a tablespoon in the other.

The Educational Aristocracy enjoys its radiant prestige and views the teacher rights movement as a threat designed to dismantle, or even topple the bureaucratic local fiefdoms that champion the cause of mediocre *democratic* (sociological) education. Teachers have a definite advantage during negotiations because they tend to be more articulate and knowledgeable about what really goes on in schools than board members know, or even care to know.

Although teachers win most of the behind-closed-doors' battles, the cunning Educational Aristocracy holds all the trump cards and regularly wins the yearly negotiations' war. It was always quite discouraging for me to glance across the negotiating table and see school administrators in apparent alliance with the board of education, their entire mercenary allegiance invariably opposing constructive teacher initiatives.

During my first year at negotiations back in 1967, I used to feel guilty when the Educational Aristocracy cited specific instances of teacher negligence. But then around 1970, I realized that it was not the local teachers' association that had hired and had given tenure to the ineffective instructors. Teachers must gain the authority to police their own ranks so that the profession will not be blamed in the future for the gross inefficiencies that are supported and promoted by the Educational Aristocracy through promoting noxious *democratic* education in the comprehensive middle and high school.

As it presently stands, the supposedly overpaid teachers are labeled the academic felons that are responsible for higher taxes, for impractical public-school education, and for flagrant ineffectiveness reflected by low standardized test scores. All of this absurd buffoonery transpires while administrators draw *CEO* and corporate executive salaries as the Walter Mitty-types are managing school systems that they themselves have helped doom to failure.

College professors and educational psychologists grind-out whimsical teaching methods and proposals, and administrators annually sell the quixotic theories to amateur community steering committees and to amateur school board members. Most boards of education want to see teachers gain power about as much as they desire witnessing the ultimate destruction of the Educational Aristocracy, and with the medieval organizational arrangement being prudently replaced by genuine, revolutionary, achievement-oriented, teacher professionalism.

Chapter 43
"A Tale of Four Professionals"

It might sound like an educational contradiction, but in public school teaching, sometimes doing *less is better* for the instructor. The paradox of *less is better* can be better fathomed when examining the dedication exhibited by serious school coaches. The men and women gym personnel work hard enduring the challenge of instructing one or two health classes and four or five gym classes every school day. Many coaches direct school sports' team practices, oversee players engaging in inter-squad night basketball games, and still others supervise at inter-mural wrestling and field hockey tournaments, or are active at Saturday baseball, soccer, field hockey, and football competitions.

Most of these enthusiastic professionals are compensated extra pay for their extracurricular sports' endeavors, but when the money is broken-down to actual net pay per hour invested, the stipend often is at or just above federal and state minimum wage. But money is not what motivates coaches; the love of sports, the thrill of competition, and the desire to see *student* athletes excel under *their* leadership is what inspires people in American education to coach middle and high school sports teams. Ironically, *competition* in American education is usually between high school football teams and area marching bands, and rivalry between *students* is not normally advanced as an *academic* classroom pursuit.

Many coaches become burned-out over time, but it is not because of the rigorous and tedious work schedules they endure during and after school. Coaches feel excessive pressure from overbearing parents who think that their son is going to be the next Babe Ruth, Allen Iverson, or Joe Montana, or that their athletic daughter is going to start for the *Michigan State* women's basketball team, or for the *UCLA* ladies' soccer squad.

Fathers and mothers often live their lives in a vicarious way through the successes and triumphs of their *children.* Many parents actually embarrass their *children* at sports' events by boisterously yelling from the stands critical epithets at home and visiting coaches, at opposing players, and at neutral referees and umpires.

Statistics show that a very good high school athlete is probably not going to ever be playing for the *New York Yankees* or for the *Boston Celtics*. The high school football stadium does not read *Giants Stadium* on the outside, and the school gymnasium does not read *Wells Fargo Center*. High school competition is not on the quality level of the *NFL*, the *NBA,* or *Major League Baseball*.

A high school coach must often deal with an influential parent that has a *child* on his or her team, and that biased father or mother could sabotage even the best high school coach's career. A well-networked mom or dad might dislike the idea that their son is not the starting quarterback, or is sitting the bench playing second-string linebacker. And those influential parents might just happen to be hobnobbing friends with school administrators and/or board of education members. Possibly, one of the complaining parents might just be a board member all on his or her own initiative. Or maybe the influential parent or parents didn't approve of a particular disciplinary measure or punishment that their *child* had justly incurred. Bingo! The high school coach might be going on a magic carpet ride into sports' oblivion!

Forget the thousands of positive things that the coach had performed over a twenty-year-career. One questionable incident has alienated the wrong parent who won't quit pushing the envelope until that cruel coach is removed from his or her favorite passion. Local power brokers can swiftly form a cartel and make the coach a pawn on the feudal Educational Aristocracy's chessboard.

The coach might be demoted to junior varsity advisor just to show him or her who the boss is. The coach might become disenchanted and begin coaching at a rival high school, thus being perceived as a "traitor" by local fans and parents. Or the coach might just drop-out of sports altogether and quickly realize that he or she could make more extracurricular money by studying the stock market, by selling real estate, or by starting a viable lawn-care business after school.

After getting the axe from the power elite, the coach is now more relaxed, affable, rational and comfortable after discarding the heavy baggage that accompanies the travail of coaching school sports. Now, he or she simply has to prepare his or her daily teaching lessons just like any other instructor on the staff.

The coach has quickly mastered the idea that *less is best;* best for his or her physical health, best for his or her emotional stability, and best for his or her life expectancy. But then again, the coach that is now simply teaching gym and health classes and not coaching a high school extracurricular sports program might be expendable in the eyes of preying and vindictive administrative vultures.

The introduction I've just described has prefaced the educational life of Coach Jay L. I remembered Jay L. when he had been an All-

League basketball player for a neighboring high school back in the '70s. Jay L. was the most formidable forward in the entire league; a veritable scoring machine who exhibited dexterity, determination, skill, and tremendous basketball savvy. Opposing high school teams dreaded his appearance on the court. Jay L. was a scoring dynamo and an absolute defensive terror.

I had the privilege of working on the same faculty with Jay L. for twenty years. Jay was a gentleman, a very religious fellow, and a credit to the community in which he taught and coached. It was an honor and pleasure to be his friend and professional colleague.

Things abruptly changed for Coach Jay L. around 1984. The school board president's son was on both the high school varsity basketball team and in the varsity school band. The band journeyed south on a competition in Florida, and the two-hat basketball player missed an entire week of practices and games.

Jay L. had a rule that if a player missed a game while not being sick, then that player had to sit the bench for the next league contest. The board of education president thought that Jay L. had been insensitive by not bending his rule to accommodate her son. The next year Jay L. was no longer varsity basketball coach.

In June of 2002, I was at a local restaurant and had heard some terrible news that had been circulating around the town's gossip mill. Jay L. had been suspended from his teaching job on the basis that he had assaulted a *student* in an eighth-period gym class at the middle school. I have always been a staunch teacher/coach advocate and instinctively wanted to come to Jay L.'s defense. But I figured I would first garner some sober facts to fairly balance my instant emotionalism with reason. I gave the beleaguered gym teacher a call.

"What happened to you in eighth-period gym class?" I bluntly asked the besieged coach. "Even though I'm retired, I still try to keep-up with the school news!"

"It was two days before Easter Break," Coach Jay L. orally conveyed. "And the other middle-school coach and I did what we normally had done for the past twelve years."

"What's that?" I curiously interrupted.

"Coach B. brought his health class to the gym because the *students* get itchy and *ram*bunctious the last period before *Holy Thursday*, which would be a half-day session before the holiday vacation," Coach Jay L. revealed. "So, I did what we both ordinarily do just before every vacation break. I organized a basketball game for the eighth-period on Wednesday."

"You were trying to do *more* for the other teacher's health class kids!" I injected into the phone conversation. "Teachers and coaches usually get into trouble when they try to do more or extra for their *students!*" I maintained to Coach Jay L. over the telephone. "And right before any major holiday break is always a danger time when ya' have to be on red alert!"

"You're absolutely right there!" suspended Coach Jay L. agreed. "I came out of my gym office, picked-up a basketball, and was warming-up and about to take a practice layup. All of a sudden, a fanatical *student* from Coach B.'s team comes from behind and smashes me right into the wall when I was taking my practice layup! I've never experienced anything like that in my entire career!"

"Sounds like the *student* deliberately assaulted you!" I exclaimed. "You say the impromptu game didn't start yet?"

"That's right!" Coach Jay L. confirmed. "The kid just smashed into me without any warning. I mean, during a game you expect contact, but not when you begin warming up!"

"What happened next?" I asked. "Were you hurt?"

"That's it exactly," Coach Jay L. declared. "My shoulder and back really hurt pretty bad. I turned to the kid that I didn't know from Coach B.'s health class and yelled, 'What are you doing'?"

"What did the *student* say?" I questioned. "Was he remorseful?"

"He nastily screamed, 'Do you want some more of me!' and then made a threatening karate-like gesture," Coach Jay L. related. "I then instinctively raised my left foot to brush him out of the way, but instead, I mildly kicked him in the ribs. It all was a reflex action, and my instinctive leg movement took place in less than five seconds!"

"First, the kid assaults you and then threatens you," I replied, "and then you defend yourself with a leg sweep and are suspended. Don't *students* get suspended anymore?" I sympathized.

As it turned-out, the *student's* concerned mother called the principal and strenuously complained of Coach Jay L.'s physical attack on her *child,* and then after *Easter* break, the mom took her kid to the police station and filed assault charges. As soon as the school had been notified of the complaint to the police department, Coach Jay L. was told he could no longer teach his gym or health classes, pending a complete administrative investigation.

The lunatic *student* reported to school after the Easter holidays without any sign of injury. Jay L. had taught in the school system for twenty-two years, and had done thousands of wonderful things for *students*. But in American education, a teacher is just as good as the last thing he or she has done. Mess-up once (or allegedly mess-up once), and a teacher or coach's career could be radically terminated in a New Jersey second.

The worst part of the just-described scenario is that when a teacher gets into trouble as Jay L. had done, everyone in authority runs to cover their own rear ends. The principal, the vice-principal, the superintendent, and the board of education all abandon *their* professional *employee* as if Coach Jay L. had smallpox. Instead of taking a solid stand in defense of the teacher's twenty-two-year admirable record, craven administrators and the school board will let the lawyers and a judge in Trenton decide the case. But Jay L. is too good of a human being to be unceremoniously dumped-down the old educational laundry chute.

One thing's for sure. Jay L.'s reputation has been sullied by one unfortunate incident. Teachers like policemen are authority figures, but if a *student* hits a policeman from behind when *he* was not expecting it, would the assaulted cop have turned the other cheek? Some authority figures like policemen have authority, but other authority figures like teachers do not have the power to physically discipline a *student* that had just knocked him or her into a wall.

The mother pursuing the matter was having marital problems, and the kid's parents will soon file for separation. Sounds all-too-familiar, doesn't it? The local newspaper's Classified Ad Sheriff Sale Notice indicated that the *student's* parents' house was up for sale for back taxes and liens. Could the mother be thinking of making some easy money by suing the school system for Coach Jay L. attacking her son if my old friend could be convicted of a criminal act? Now, there is something major to think about.

The case is still in progress at the time of this writing, and Jay L. has been out of work for eight months, and out of work without pay for six months, all for a five second "blind moment". The *student's* family that was having internal problems found a convenient scapegoat in the form of the vulnerable gym coach. Jay. L. might just have been an unfortunate victim of the tried-and-true, old adage, "Misery loves company".

Frank P. was an elementary school fourth-grade teacher that started his educational career with me in 1965. Things had gone pretty smoothly for Frank until around 1985, when the administration decided it was time for Frank to be eliminated.

After twenty years of receiving good observations, suddenly the administration started finding every little flaw it could discover to bring the teacher into disfavor and purge him from his profession. Frank's bulletin boards were criticized for not being changed every month. Frank was caught carrying a cup of coffee from the teacher's lounge to his classroom, and that was recorded in a formal observation. The school principal kept focusing on Frank P. and was accumulating a folder of picayune things, deliberately building a case against the twenty-year veteran.

Then as further reprisal, Frank's salary increment was withheld a first year. If he did not follow the administration's recommendations for improvement, the man's salary would again be withheld a second year. And if Frank didn't show significant progress according to the administration's scrutiny and questionable "sage suggestions", then formal charges would be made to the state for Frank's removal from the school system, and also the loss of his teaching certification.

"What should I do?" Frank asked me over the telephone.

"Whatever you do, don't resign regardless of the circumstances!" I advised. "They're trying to make you question your own ability and doubt your worth. Your signature is worth something. They're initiating procedures against you, but to my knowledge, there has to be a settlement somewhere down the line as a resolution," I related. "Don't allow them to destroy your confidence!"

"They've promised me a good recommendation if I resigned," Frank told me. "Should I?"

"Don't do it!" I strongly replied." Get yourself an *NJEA* attorney and fight them all the way. They can't build a good case against you on the basis of bulletin boards and drinking coffee in the hall on the way to your classroom! That's preposterous!"

Frank's salary increment was then withheld the second year. He did not resign, much to the administration's chagrin. The fourth-grade teacher did get an *NJEA* lawyer and fought the charges in the state-established Administrative Legal Procedure. Frank could not go to a regular court of justice until after the Administrative Legal Procedure had been exhausted, right up to the New Jersey Commissioner of Education. So, in effect, the cards were neatly stacked against Frank P. since *former* school administrators (the educational magistrates) were *judging* the "inefficiency charges" that had been lodged against the fourth-grade teacher (being advanced by *present* school administrators).

I suspected that there was a smelly rat in the woodpile. Frank P. must have somewhere in his career antagonized an influential parent that had an axe to grind, and the administrators were now surrogate "hit men" out to get him fired. Based on the "inefficiency" evidence of mediocre bulletin boards and drinking coffee in the hall, I figured that some other ulterior motives were out there preying on Frank P.'s reputation. In my career, I have known three teachers that had committed suicide. And if the *students* and their parents were partially responsible for pushing the teachers to the edge, then the local Educational Aristocracy might have been another contributing factor in *their* demise, too.

Frank P. was a bit on the effeminate side, and that particular behavior might have been misconstrued back in the '70s and early '80s as being gay. It was my hunch that the administration couldn't fire Frank while coincidentally violating his civil rights, so the school brass chose the nit-picking harassment route to rupture his spirit and compel him to resign.

Frank's unexpected resistance to administrative pressure backfired on the school executives. They now had to assume the role of educational prosecutors trying to pin weak evidence on a teacher in the arcane Administrative Legal Procedure. The case advanced from the local level, to the county level, to the state level, and still Frank P. fought the establishment with his *NJEA* lawyer and didn't resign.

Finally, a settlement was arranged where Frank would be paid three years' salary if he voluntarily handed-in his resignation.

"Should I do it?" the teacher asked me in a telephone conversation.

"No!" I insisted. "You want your job back with the pay you've missed. That's what you want!"

"But John, the consequences if I lose will be that I will not only have my teaching certificate taken away, but also, I'll lose my pension!" Frank P. declared. "I can't fight them anymore and take those kinds of risks. I think I'll resign and take the money that's on the table. Thanks for your help!"

Frank P. had taught for twenty-two years in the school system. Three more years and he would have been eligible for a pension at age fifty-five, but since he hadn't taught for the required twenty-five years, the former fourth-grade instructor then had to wait until age sixty to collect his first pension check. So that's how educational justice often works.

Dan T. began teaching in the school system in 1969 and was with me on the junior-senior high faculty until 1976, when most of the junior-high teachers moved over to the middle school. I had always thought that Dan was one heck of a Driver Education instructor, and then later, a very effective middle school Social Studies teacher. In fact, Dan was the teacher-witness who had been taking notes in the

Principal's Office when I had had the confrontational conference showdown with Mr. and Mrs. Bertuzzi.

I believed that Dan T.'s employment problems with the school authorities had little to do with his stellar teaching ability. But Dan was dating a high school girl (age eighteen, I believe) whose father had some powerful contacts. The administration thought that Dan's personal life constituted unprofessional behavior, so the executive barons went after him through the back door in a similar manner as to what the same educational boyars had done with Frank P.

Dan T. had taken my place as a permanent substitute at the high school. After Bill Catello had passed away, the administration (several years later) eliminated the second of two permanent substitute high school positions (evidently, to get rid of Dan T.), but the brass kept the permanent sub' position at the elementary school where Dan T. was not certified to teach. So then, Dan T. saw the writing on the wall and went back to college at night to obtain another certification. He knew the school system had just invested in a Driver Ed. Vehicle, so "Mr. T." became the Driver Education instructor since no one else on the staff was qualified to fill that vacancy. Now, the high school had two driver education teachers; one for classroom instruction, and one for actual car instruction.

Dan and the school administrators had many differences of opinion, and the personable fellow was quite articulate and always defended himself and his positions on various issues quite well. The school executives still wanted to get rid of him, but Dan T. had acquired tenure and was willing to fight the school overlords to the hilt. The moguls at the top eliminated the half of the driver education program that involved *student* instruction inside the car. The other classroom instructor had seniority over Dan, so *he* could not be bumped-out of his Driver Ed. instructional position.

"What should I do?" Dan T. asked me. "I can't bump the other Driver Ed. Teacher, nor would I want to, even if I could!"

"Don't resign!" I insisted. "Whatever you do, don't resign! Your signature is worth something, whether you know it or not! What were you originally certified in?"

"Social-Studies!" the upset, soon-to-be-axed Driver Ed. teacher answered. "Social Studies in grades seven through twelve!"

"Okay," I said. "Don't resign like *they* want you to do. Bide your time and keep your eyes peeled. If a Social Studies position becomes open, you have a number of years in the system plus your tenure!"

Dan T. never resigned and then worked for several years in a Central Jersey chemical plant. Then in 1977, a Social Studies position became open and was awarded to another teacher already on the staff. Dan applied for the position, and with the help of *NJEA*, it was determined that *he* had seniority over the other teacher and could bump that instructor out of the Social Studies' job and into a recently opened mathematics slot. "Thank goodness I had all of those years working in the system!" Dan told me with a sigh of relief. "Sometimes it pays to *not* sign your name on the dotted line!"

The shrewd maneuver did not set too-well with the administration. In the mid-nineties, Dan T. was reprimanding a *student* on the middle school asphalt playground when the *student* gave him some insolent, verbal static. The excellent Social Studies teacher lost his cool, grabbed the *child* by the nape of the neck, and then escorted the defiant youngster into the building. Naturally, the alarmed parents protested the flagrant example of "corporal punishment". Dan T. eventually resigned after several salary-increment withholdings.

Doug C. has been the athletic trainer at the high school for the past eight years. He had worked for two years in a similar capacity at a central New Jersey high school prior to moving to the district where I had taught. In 1992, Doug had contracted Hodgkins Disease, an insidious form of cancer that attacks the lymph nodes. Doug C. courageously fought the usually fatal disease, and defeated it after a year of intensive hospital treatments. However, Doug's immune system has been severely weakened, and he does not need any more stress than his mind and spirit can presently handle.

Doug does have tenure as the school athletic trainer, but his tenure is meaningless. The trainer does not have a teaching certificate in any other area, so if his position were to be eliminated, his job would also be simultaneously terminated.

Doug C. and his wife had just purchased a beautiful home in a new section of the community, and he immensely loves working with the high school athletes and coaches, and he had admitted to me that he definitely enjoys living in the town. All of a sudden, Doug C.'s life is turned upside-down by classic, greedy, small-town politics.

Several members on the board of education are friends, in-laws and relatives of the physical therapists operating out of the local hospital. Now, the school system (with a twenty-million-dollar annual budget) is suddenly interested in a cost saving measure to contract the hospital for the district's physical therapy needs. I had contacted a school board member about the situation.

"You say you want to save the district money by possibly contracting the hospital therapists," I began the conversation. "So how much money does Doug C. earn?"

"Seventy-four thousand dollars a year!" the board member related. "The hospital could provide the same service that Mr. Doug C. is giving for twenty-five thousand dollars through *Blue Cross!*"

Doug C. lives across the street from my oldest son in the newest town housing development. I had a chance to meet and talk to the school athletic trainer at a party occurring in my son's backyard. I had known Doug's father and had attended high school with his dad back in 1960.

"Doug, if I may ask a personal question," I began after being officially introduced by my son. "What is your current physical therapist salary?"

"Forty-eight thousand dollars," he answered.

Right away I knew that something was amiss when the athletic trainer didn't say seventy-four thousand dollars. 'The twenty-five-thousand-dollar *Blue Cross* contract is like one of those 5% APR credit-card offers one receives as junk mail,' I hypothesized. After six months, the interest rates will go-up to twenty percent. No medical insurance company is going to award a twenty-five-thousand-dollar contract and then accumulate a hundred thousand dollars in service expenses for athletic rehabilitation without raising the initial fee.

"What the insurance company is trying to do is simply establish a foot-in-the-door proposal," I told Doug C. "Costs will escalate in a hurry during and after the initial twenty-five-thousand-dollar contract expires."

"I really want to continue working at the high school," Doug C. confided. "And the hospital physical therapists want me to work with and for them. If I do that, I lose my tenure, and I also lose my state pension."

"Just keep fighting them!" I suggested and answered. "You're well-liked in the community, and *that* fact could be a big plus, especially since athletics is often more important to parents in this town than academics are."

When the Doug C. controversy surfaced and soon circulated around the school population, six hundred irate *students*, parents and teachers showed-up at the next school board meeting to protest the possibility that Doug C.'s athletic trainer position was in jeopardy. The school board meeting had to be moved from the comfortable, plush boardroom to the high school auditorium.

Seeing the huge opposition to some internal politics that was going on, the school board president and vice-president told all in attendance that Doug C.'s job was presently secure and that the board was merely exploring another avenue where it could have saved the taxpayers' money. Okay class; let's now play *Truth or Consequences*.

Chapter 44
"Contract Negotiations"

Negotiating with a stubborn board of education can be comparable to swimming across Death Valley at high noon during a heat wave. Teachers involved in contract discussions with their employers can make a host of enemies in record time. One giant stumbling block has always been the establishment of a legitimate teacher grievance procedure. Administrators soft-soap the public into believing that the school system has no major problems, and now the teacher serfs want to declare that there is massive trouble in paradise and are conspiring to make *Valhalla* seem like *Hades* by insisting there is a need for an unneeded grievance procedure.

Many older teachers conditioned to be *employees* rather than professionals are reluctant to grieve any educational injustice as are expendable non-tenure teachers, who generally fear sudden and immediate loss of employment. Teachers don't like being publicly perceived as radical dissidents, so the majority begrudgingly play the total subordination and obedience game with the Educational Aristocracy rather than be publicly identified by board members as being either insubordinate or disobedient.

Boards of education basically prefer few language clauses in the teachers' association negotiated contract in order to stifle teacher grievances and to keep the power of the almighty administration indomitable. School boards and administrations prefer to run their schools by having their employees fear reprisals rather than to have them openly challenge policy and consequently weaken the iron grip that school executives enjoy wielding.

One area of contention (when I had been a teacher negotiator) was the sacrosanct school budget. The line-item titled *"Administration"* pertained exclusively to the superintendent and his office staff. The principal's salary, the vice-principal's expense and the supervisors and curriculum coordinator's wages were all included with the teachers' employment expenses on the proposed budget. The impression received by the public was that administrative expenses were being kept to a minimum, and that teacher expenses were completely 'out-of-control'. But the board of education maintained during negotiations that the budget was a "non-negotiable item".

When the intellectual establishment (teachers) collided with the community's elected economic establishment (town school board) at the negotiating table, it was no major Herculean task for the teaching gurus to vanquish the financial bosses at the noble art of forensics. Many school board members felt uncomfortable having their *employees* do battle with them on an equal, flat playing field.

Teacher proposals and teacher research were often regarded as threats and as intrusions into board and administrative prerogative. Many board members felt uneasy about subordinates making demands, and then audaciously challenging their policies and *their* assumed jurisdiction over the professional teaching staff.

Teacher rebuttals were often misconstrued as acts of defiance and as acts of rebellion against local authority. The board of education's trump card was always the privilege of saying "No!", and the rival members seated on the opposite side of the table resorted to that license whenever they felt imperiled, or whenever the opposing employers were on the ropes and about to make a concession that might diminish administrative power or discretion.

The teachers wanted "binding arbitration" as the terminal point of the highly debated grievance procedure. The board would not even consent to "mediation", but entrusted all decision-making power to the infallible school executives. Most grievance appeals were conducted by first notifying the principal in writing, and if the teacher's complaint was not satisfied, the complaint was then forwarded to the superintendent for examination. If the teacher still was unhappy with the disposition of the filed grievance, it was then submitted to the cosmopolitan board of education.

Now, if the grievance were protesting a school policy, or citing an alleged unfair administrative treatment, the *judges* in the matter (administrators, board of education) were also the *defendants* in the matter. Without binding arbitration as the next step after the board of education oversight of an issue, the initiator (teacher instigator) had about as much chance at receiving justice as a prisoner standing before a determined Pancho Villa firing squad. By not allowing binding arbitration as the end-point of the grievance procedure, the Educational Aristocracy effectively discouraged teacher filing formal complaints. The teachers fully understood that premise and got the background message that grieving was futile, and possibly a career-threatening death wish.

Arbitration is an American institution in labor union negotiating, and the practice should be honored as a fair and equitable resolution and conclusion to the teacher grievance procedure. A *Catch-22* situation exists where boards of education claim that teachers have no complaints, and that the school has no significant, observable problems. Teachers don't grieve their gripes for fear of losing their positions, or the *employees* stay mum because of the dread of having their careers tinkered with by crafty school administrators, and the public thinks and concludes that everything inside the schools is either a bed of roses or/and a fabulous Utopian Wonderland.

Teacher vassals dwelling in the Educational Aristocracy's feudal state have little chance of being vindicated during a grievance without the essential weapon of "binding arbitration", and the serfs stand a greater chance at being vilified by the absolute imperial sovereignty *employed* by their *employers*.

"Our teachers are happy!" board members proclaim to the public. "They never complain about anything!" the benevolent Solomons bluster. And one illustrious board member once related to everyone at the negotiating table about binding arbitration, "I don't want some outside yo-yo coming in here and telling us how to run things! That's why we have administrators!" Now *that* erroneous summary had to be one of the finest, non-Confucian-type statements ever.

That year the teachers had requested to be paid for curriculum development work done after school, and *that* was another area of contention where both sides came to loggerheads. The entrenched board of education insisted that curriculum development was a basic part of a teacher's *professional obligation* and that *dedicated* teachers should be content performing the service gratis. "Overtime pay" was a concept connected to industry workers, and not relevant to *professional* contract personnel on the teaching staff.

I was shocked to hear a school administrator say, "Teachers only work on the average of thirty-two hours a week, which is eight less than the average factory worker."

"That's not true!" I protested during the heated debate. "I know for a fact that I work thirty-two hours a week on the job in school, six hours a week before and after school, and ten hours at home correcting compositions, tests, doing report cards, warning letters and lesson plans! That comes to forty-eight hours, and not thirty-two hours like you're falsely claiming!"

I was appalled upon hearing a board member's response. "Figures don't lie, but liars do figure! Numbers can be twisted to prove or disprove anything!" the non-sagacious board member opined in argument refuting my testimony.

"Well," an administrator added, "we can always take the teachers' preparation period away and put them on *special assignment* to work forty-five minutes on curriculum development during the school day!" And so, worthy teacher proposals were counter-attacked and denounced by intimidating threats to enforce punitive measures specifically designed to stifle future teacher professional requests.

Sabbatical leave was another area of conflict during those first years of contract negotiations with the school board.

"If a teacher has worked for seven years in the district," I suggested, "then he or she should be able to have one year off at half-salary to tour the world and learn ideas to make himself or herself a more knowledgeable person and a better teacher."

"Are you kidding?" a school board member admonished and interrupted. "We aren't gonna' pay a teacher half salary to get a master's degree and then get a job somewhere else!"

'Who poisoned that man's mind?' I wondered. 'He really has less than a full thimble's respect for teachers!'

I soon realized that the entire thrust of the Educational Aristocracy was to avoid accountability for anything, while the school board and the administration wanted to have the teaching staff liable for everything and anything.

Teachers were and are expected to justify report card marks with test and quiz grades. Teachers were required to keep accurate attendance and grade records. Encumbered educators had to complete and submit warning letters, report cards, grade distribution sheets, weekly report cards, homework sheets, progress reports and lesson plans. And in addition, teachers have to correct papers, tests, compositions, perform duties, and have parent conferences besides teaching five or six classes each day, and then also monitoring trouble areas like the cafeteria and the halls.

Personal days constituted another delicate area of controversy while negotiating with the inflexible board of education, which was being advised by the illustrious school administration. Our contract stipulated the following language in regard to teacher personal days:

Personal Days

Personal business for the purpose of school policy is hereby defined as:

(a) Illness in the immediate family when the presence of an *employee* is required.

(b) Death of a relative or a close friend.

(c) Court summons or other legal process involving no moral turpitude on the part of the *employee*.

(d) Religious holiday.

(e) Other personal confidential matters.

(f) Any other valid reason, at the discretion of the superintendent.

Notice that teachers are referred to as *employees* and not as *professional* staff members. Our negotiating team's position maintained that (e) and (f) were separate and exclusive entities, according to standard Aristotelian classification. The school board interpreted that (f) was a clarification of (e), and that any reason for taking a personal day had to be given to the superintendent. Teachers were not qualified to decide what constituted a personal day other than requesting one for (a), (b), (c) and (d).

Avid public-relations-minded administrators didn't savor being put in the position of explaining why Mr. John Wiessner (on a personal day) had been seen in a drugstore, or inside a town bank during a school day. Inquisitive school board members or influential citizens ought not to be presumptuous about why a teacher would be anywhere outside the school building between 8 a.m. and 3 p.m. "Personal days" was another administrative autocratic control mechanism by which teachers could be kept in their cages, manipulated, and further subordinated.

When my father passed-away in September of '74, he had been buried on a Friday. That afternoon, I entered the school's Main Office and requested my bi-weekly paycheck. The principal's secretary said to me, "You haven't handed in next week's lesson plans yet! You can't get your check until you do!"

"But you know perfectly well that I was absent from school on *personal business!* I had other things on my mind this past week!" I angrily answered. "I'll hand in the sacred lesson plans on Monday!"

"Rules are rules!" the authoritarian secretary insisted, mimicking her administrative superior.

"Okay!" I exclaimed in frustration. "I'll turn the lesson plans in on Monday morning!" Then I left the building in total disgust.

The existing contract language in regard to items (e) and (f) compelled teachers to lie about reasons given for *personal days*. If a woman on the faculty had to have a test done for cancer of the uterus, she might not desire to discuss such a sensitive matter with the superintendent, or with anyone else in the building. If she checked (e), then the superintendent would enforce his (f) option. The lady teacher then risks losing a day's salary by not disclosing her private reason to the superintendent. So, instead of taking a personal day, she takes a sick day, and then, against her conscience, regretfully lies to escape revealing her reason to the superintendent, who is acting as if he is a nosy priest listening to a distraught parishioner inside a confessional.

One of the most expedient ways in which a school administrator can effectively thwart teacher professionalism is to treat his or her staff as if they were children. In that way, the predominance of the omnipotent Educational Aristocracy has been safeguarded.

My wife and I had taken a *Christmas* vacation to St. Thomas in the early '80s. Our return jet flight scheduled for January 2nd had been overbooked, so we couldn't fly home until January 3rd, a school day. I submitted a personal day form and explained in section' (f) why I had missed a day of work because of extraordinary circumstances involving the January 2nd flight cancellation in St. Thomas.

The school principal doubted my sincere testimony and called my travel agent on the telephone to verify whether-or-not I had been telling the truth. Upon getting confirmation from my travel representative, my personal day request was finally approved.

"What kind of place do you work in?" my travel agent asked me over the telephone. "Do you teach in Communist China?"

"A public school!" I honestly replied. "It's not the easiest place in the world to hold a job!"

"That's the first time a boss ever called me about something stupid like that," the travel agent admitted. "And quite frankly, I was a little angered in that *he* would think so suspiciously about your personal day claim and treat you so unprofessionally!"

"I'm glad to hear those words from a taxpayer!" I laughed.

"I'm sure glad I don't work in a public school!" my travel agent summarized. "It sounds like you're laboring in Purgatory!"

Chapter 45
"School Board Proposals"

The board of education submitted contract proposals to the teachers' negotiating team to thwart and offset our worthwhile demands. Some of the board's overtures were punitive in nature, and the already-distressed teachers on the negotiating panel desired debating the opposition's items as much as we desired receiving a series of after-midnight, anonymous phone calls from mischievous *children*. But nevertheless, the board's proposals had to be meticulously reviewed and discussed. Here is one of the gems.

"To better develop necessary cooperation, understanding and communications between our *professional* staff and parents, all members of the faculty will be required to attend all *PTA* meetings," one particular school board request recommended.

On the surface, requiring teachers to attend all *PTA* meetings might appear to be a constructive idea. But to the discerning teachers sitting on the association's negotiating panel, the suggestion had the sturdiness of a fifty-year-old cobweb. Board of education members rarely attended *PTA* meetings, yet the illustrious wizards wanted a total teacher presence at all scheduled meetings mandatory. *PTA* meetings are and were one step removed from colonial quilting bees, and the events are (and were) breeding grounds for the propagation of community gossip and inaccurate scuttlebutt.

The *PTA* issues statements and speaks for the vast silent majority of parents that don't belong (or don't care to belong) to the organization. The parents of the slow-learning *students*, of the behavior problem students, along with Joe Dodge's indulgent mom and dad, don't attend the *PTA* meetings, and they're the real adults that the teachers need most to see.

The moms and dads (mostly moms) that join the *PTA* ranks are more concerned with their *child's* extracurricular band and sports' activities than the active parents are with school problems, with teacher concerns, and with their *children's* scholastic progress (the *PTA* meetings are not conference nights). The moms and dads that belong to the *PTA* are the second generation of *students* graduating from the American *democratic* (sociological) comprehensive high school. And many of the gregarious parents and guardians that are active in the *PTA* are the same overprotective folks that bend the ears of accommodating administrators over the telephone about their *personal* concerns.

Teachers see little relationship between belonging to the *PTA* and escaping teacher serfdom in the Educational Aristocracy's imperial fiefdom. Trying to get chatty parents to support the realization of teachers' true academic freedom is similar to attempting to pin a diaper on an uncooperative, aggressive, adult gorilla.

Blood is thicker than water; truth is stranger than fiction, and the taxpayers' wallets are closer to home than either the lectern or the chalkboard is. The local teachers' association is the vehicle that will ultimately transport the instructors to obtaining the acquisition of professional dignity, and *that* attainment certainly won't result from listening to the prattle of perfumed. gossipy *PTA* mothers. Teachers' loyalty should be devoted to their local, county, state and national organizations, but until those associations identify and start fighting the true causes of teacher serfdom in America, along with the true sources of educational inefficiency, then regrettably, teachers are going to remain on a one-way trip to nowhere.

Another magnificent school board/administrative offering was as follows: "To help ensure that our school system's professional staff is keeping pace with the modern trends in the field of education, all faculty members will be required to successfully complete a minimum of three college credits a school year. The credits earned will be in the area of their teaching responsibility," the statement remarkably and almost-illogically advanced.

The declaration on the surface sounds pretty harmless, flawless and idealistic, doesn't it? The whole statement is a pathetic sound-byte that is laced with abundant hypocrisy. The board of education either doesn't know or doesn't believe that teachers have trouble keeping-up with their own grueling responsibilities of overwhelming night paperwork, let alone now having to take additional ethereal methods courses taught by Camelot-minded, nutty professors and wacky *child* psychologists.

And if anyone needs an introduction to *Education 101* and to *Academics 102*, it is the school board members that don't have a clue about the complexity and inherent weaknesses of American education as described throughout this work. But still, the hapless, clueless school board members liberally demand and then heap extra oppression upon the instructors' shoulders. This is like Jupiter telling Neptune that he needs to take swimming lessons when old Jove (by Jove) doesn't even know how to float all by himself'.

Another exquisite school board proposal was: "Due to the ever-increasing time necessary for teachers to adequately prepare for their teaching *duties*, no faculty member will be permitted to hold any other position or job which is not directly related to their teaching responsibility. Teaching should be a teacher's sole concern."

In other words, I would not be able to go down to Rehoboth Beach, Delaware and to Ocean City, Maryland to operate my boardwalk businesses on weekends in May, June and September. Board of education members resented the fact that I was an *independent* businessman in addition to being a school system *employee,* and that I was making more money in the summertime than I was making the other nine-and-a-half months teaching in their marvelous public school system. In America, *democracy* guarantees independence, yet the school board and the administration wanted to keep me from being *independent* of *their* mighty Educational Aristocracy.

If teachers were paid true *professional* wages, the board of education members would not have to worry about their staff "moonlighting" in the private sector of the U.S. economy. Many European countries value education more so than American towns and cities value *academics,* and a higher percentage of those countries' *Gross National Product* goes into financing *academics* than the USA' *GNP* does. Those European nations view education as an investment in the future (in civilization itself) and not as a costly taxpayers' expenditure for *sociological student activity.*

Most parents want their *children's* teachers to be model citizens worthy of imitation, but few beginning teachers with a family can subsist on the paltry starting salaries that the local board of education and the district taxpayers are willing to pay. The teachers' guide has thirteen steps (or years) to get to the top; however, the local policeman's more realistic and intelligently developed salary guide has five steps to get to the top of their pay scale.

And demanding that teachers not be able to hold another job (not that I approve of them doing so Monday through Friday) is really unconstitutional, and just like the hassle over personal days, such an insistence is an unwarranted encroachment into the teachers' personal lives. But who says that serfs working in an Educational Aristocracy's fiefdom are supposed to have any civil rights at all?

Many teachers (like myself) needed a supplemental income to make ends meet. Although starting teacher salaries are below sea level, boards of education want their faculty members to act like contented Alpine ski resort patrons. If a teacher's pig is lean, he or she can't live high on the hog.

I (like numerous teachers that have negotiated contracts across the country) have made many enemies among board members and among school administrators as a result of contentious contract negotiations. The relationship between board members and teachers during engagement in contract compromising is essentially an adverse one. Although I had always tried my best to be assertive and objective, it was a predictable consequence that somewhere along the line, I would inadvertently insult the fragile feelings of certain school board members who considered my quest for professionalism as being disobedient mutiny.

On one occasion, a disgruntled school board member nastily snorted in my direction, "There are too many ungrateful punks teaching in our school system!"

I tried to get the accuser to commit himself to a more specific insinuation. "Would you consider me to be one of those ungrateful punks?" I curiously asked.

A pregnant silence encompassed the school board chamber akin to the cold stillness of a dentist's waiting room. I solemnly waited for a sincere reply.

"You have given the school board and this school system a bad name!" the agitated fellow alleged in a stammering tone of voice. "Draw your own conclusion!"

I paused for a moment; somewhat staggered by his caustic remark. Then I laconically inquired, "Exactly, what did I say that has defamed this school?"

The befuddled proponent of the slanderous slur countered, "It's personal between you and me!"

I was alarmed at the vindictiveness of the school board member's assertion so I volleyed, "Well, if it's personal between you and me," I said rather testily, "and only *you* know about it, then I think you should say what you mean so that all present could bear witness!"

"You want to know something!" the B of E president yelled in my direction. "You're a nitpicker!"

"You're absolutely right!" I replied, pointing to my tightly woven sport jacket sleeve. "But I'm a lot better than being a nitpicker. I'm a double knit-picker!"

The board member lowered his eyes to the conference table and simply tapped his pencil against the slate. Nothing further in the way of interaction transpired between the two of us for the balance of the confrontational session.

Earlier in the meeting, the board of education committee desired discussing the seemingly important matter of "merit pay". But after *our* recent vitriolic exchange, I doubted very much whether I would ever be able to score highly on any administratively presented merit pay guide, or whether my teaching ability would have anything at all to do with my "merit ranking" on the subjective administrative scale. The negotiations reached the point where I could have proposed opening a window, and the board members would have said "no," just out of stubborn argumentative principle.

In 1977, I felt that I could no longer be of effective service as a negotiator for my faculty colleagues. So, I sadly retired myself out to the quiet educational pastures to begin arranging my thoughts for the organization of a truthful book about teaching and teachers.

I am aware that I possess an aggressive personality, and that I could get on certain people's nerves, especially those people that are supposed to be my superiors. On several occasions, I had made board members so hostile and livid that I believed that their tonsils and larynxes were going to leap right out of their throats.

But the fact that a school board member could openly perceive any *professional* teacher as a "punk" clearly indicated how low that businessman's esteem was for teachers in general, and for me in particular. Although my intent was to excavate the truth by digging below an issue's crust, my non-appreciative opponents viewed me as a swashbuckling pirate trying to sabotage the good name and image of *their* paradise school district.

The Educational Aristocracy must recognize that teachers are not automatons programed to execute the whims of amateur school board members, of amateur parent steering committees, of gossipy *PTAs*, of wifty, impractical college professors, of other-galaxy educational psychologists, or of fanciful, mildewed administrators. The blue-collar working class has also historically had a resentment for the white-collar, college-educated class. And even though many industrial workers earn more greenbacks than beginning teachers do, the reservoir of blue-collar class bias is often reflected by local school boards, with the employers supposedly *democratically* representing the sentiments of the local taxpayers.

While amateur school board community members are supposedly *democratically* operating the nation's public-school systems, local prejudices and biases, negative attitudes, area eccentricities, and national ignorance toward teachers' plights are being preserved, while general educational advancement (pertaining to teacher professionalism and to *academic* excellence) is being suppressed.

In many instances, the *function* of *democratic* education has become the antithesis of the *purpose* for having *democracy in education*. Teacher freedom of speech and freedom of academic pursuit in the classroom is hindered by sociological (*democratic*) education. Societal disorganization is rapidly expanding because of a national increase of *student democratic* freedom (shift toward misbehavior, rebellion and anarchy rule). *Democracy* translates into an increase in *student* rights, and a corresponding decrease in teacher authority. *Democracy* thriving in the school equates into dramatic increases in teacher responsibility, and conversely, in the process, *democracy* in the sociological, comprehensive high school is causing an attendant decrease in *student* accountability.

The *democratic* comprehensive school has effectively underwritten the need for autocratic imperial administrators and superintendents to reign supreme in the Educational Aristocracy power structure. Parents are *democratically* involved in formulating local goals and objectives while serving on steering committees that lack steering wheels. Whimsical college professors that *lecture* (but who can't teach) along with outer space educational psychologists are *democratically dictating* what the public schools must present, and how instructors should teach *socialism* labeled as *democracy*. And finally, the amateur school board members are *democratically* elected by small turnouts of apathetic voters that want to limit educational spending. The fact that teachers have obtained their coveted *sheepskins* from accredited colleges and universities is no reason for boards of education and school administrators to expect their *educators* to behave like timid and obedient lamb herds.

Democracy (freedom to act, think, and speak independently) in the public schools exists for virtually everyone except the teachers, who happen to be the victimized serfs trapped in a feudalistic governmental nightmare. The supreme Educational Aristocracy governs over all dominions in American education; it's a weird paradox, but it's as true as dead bodies buried inside a cemetery. Each public school system is an isolated educational fiefdom, and the overlord administrators and the allied school boards are the nobles, the dukes, and the barons, while the proletarian teachers are the lowly, subservient vassals and serfs. In reality, and in everyday school practice, employed American teacher-serfs are not thoroughly covered and protected by the first Ten *Amendments* to the *United States Constitution*.

Chapter 46

"Problem Students, Problem Parents"

Crazy *students* run rampant in public schools today because those crazy *students* usually have crazy parents, or crazy guardians, or crazy grandparents acting as crazy guardians. These crazy parents and crazy guardians are really crazy *children* that never grew-up and that are now residing in adult bodies. These crazy *adults* that are still rebelling against "adult authority" will do anything (lie, cheat or steal) to defend their alter-egos, their crazy *children*. The crazy parents' (or the crazy guardians') defense of their crazy offspring is done in an effort to drive the teacher crazy, and to go to any length to prove that their innocent *child* is not crazy like they are.

Crazy Parent V. showed-up for an after-school conference in the Guidance Office meeting room. The mother was upset that I had caught her fourteen-year-old *child* cheating, and the distressed woman came in for the session specifically to get her cherub off the hook by lying on his behalf.

"Mr. Wiessner, I want you to know that Bobby didn't cheat on his composition," crazy parent V. began. "It was all my fault!"

"Mrs. V., last week Bobby handed-in the exact same typewritten composition in first period English class as Tommy S. did in seventh period English class," I began and reviewed. "Each word of the five-hundred-word composition was exactly the same in the exact same sentences, in the exact same paragraphs in both Bobby V.'s and Tommy S.'s themes. The only things that were different were the *student* names and sections at the bottom of the second page!" I disclosed. "Even the computer fonts were identical, *Courier 12!*"

"Mr. Wiessner, I believe you're jumping to conclusions," Crazy Parent V. asserted. "I know it seems suspicious and that it appears that my son Bobby and Tommy S. had cheated, but let me explain what really had happened."

"Well Mrs. V., cheating is a very serious offense, and as you know, I have given both *students* F's on their compositions and probably will also have to give them U's (Unsatisfactory) in conduct," I indicated. "But tell me your story anyway. I'm a literature teacher and I enjoy good stories."

Mrs. V. neurotically explained that Tommy S.'s computer had broken-down and was being repaired. Tommy came over to his friend Bobby V.'s house and typed-up *his* final draft to his composition. The problem with the identical papers happened the following morning when Tommy came over to Bobby's house to get a printout of *his* composition. He signed and dated it, and then both innocuous boys walked over to school together.

"How come they both signed their names to different copies of the same composition?" I queried.

"I know this all sounds too crazy to be true," Crazy Parent V. declared, "but the boys were in a hurry, so I had volunteered to run off the compositions on my computer, which I was using for my own purposes at the time. I became distracted when the phone rang and accidentally ran-off the same compositions for both boys. They signed them in my kitchen without checking the titles before leaving for school. And that's the absolute truth! It was all *my* fault!"

"Well, it sounds better and more original than the dog eating the homework story I've heard several trillion times!" I admitted. "If that's the case, where is Bobby's or Tommy's missing paper? I can't tell which one is owed me because the two that had been handed-in were absolutely identical!"

"Here are copies of both compositions," Mrs. V. stated as she opened up an oak tag folder and handed me two separate two-paged writings. I hope that this evidence clarifies everything."

"Well Mrs. V., I must confess that I have never heard of this kind of special situation happening before," I revealed, even though I wasn't convinced of the veracity of the mother's explanation. "I'll tell you what I'll do! Both boys will receive the grade of C instead of F's and will not be given U's for misconduct!" I compromised.

"But that's not fair!" Crazy Parent V. insisted. "You should grade those papers as if they were freshly handed in today. I know Bobby's paper deserves at least an A-!"

"The problem is this," I replied. "You have showed-up with the two separate compositions a full week after the identical papers were handed-in!"

"That's because *you* didn't hand the corrected papers back until yesterday!" the parent yelled and accused, trying to transfer the blame to me. "You know; you're a very unfair teacher!"

"Mrs. V., I believe I've been more than fair in adjusting the grades from Fs to Cs. I did put the identical corrections and comments on both papers. And besides," I continued my explanation. "I had a hundred and thirty different eight-paragraph compositions to correct, and that's why it takes a full week for the papers to be finally returned to the *students!*"

"My son's right!" Mrs. V. accused. "You're a mean teacher! I'm taking this matter straight to the principal!"

"Be my guest," I answered. "This story will be a new one for him, too! But I remind you Mrs. V. I could've very easily given both *students* F's and also U's for misconduct!"

With computers and printers all over the school building, and also in almost every *student's* home, this sort of cheating had happened at least a dozen times each year from 1990-1999. Even though word gets out that the *students'* fraudulent enterprise had been caught, other audacious *students* still try beating the system. Usually, *students* will be a little sharper than Bobby V. and Tommy S. had been. The more-wily *students* also handed-in their papers in two separate class periods, but their submissions had different fonts and type sizes represented.

Xerox machines are another nightmare when parents photocopy work for their *children* and insist that the *child* is the original author of an encyclopedia or magazine article that the parent had retyped. And the *Internet* not only makes information readily available, but it also makes plagiarism a snap, and besides that, crazy parents can use their credit cards to buy term papers from various web sites for their crazy lazy *children* to submit to their English teacher.

Crazy Parent W. wanted the best for her daughter, but didn't desire to see Amanda W. work hard to achieve success on her own. The mother was unhappy that her daughter was getting a C in English. Mrs. W. thought that my grading methods were too harsh; the mom believed that I was too "insensitive", and the aggressive mother had accused me in the past of being too demanding in finding every tiny spelling and grammatical mistake Amanda had made on her writings. Crazy Parent W. came-in to initiate a confrontational conference, and the upset parent was not-too-thrilled or ecstatic about recent developments.

"Mr. Wiessner, I guess you know why I am here!" Crazy Parent W. began her complaints' litany.

"I presume you wish to discuss Amanda's report card C grade along with the fact that she talks too much in class and quarrels with several other girls she doesn't get along with," I returned.

The preplanned design of the overprotective and concerned mother was to successfully shield Amanda from criticism and from failure, and to then point the blame for all of the daughter's shortcomings on her English teacher. This parental method I call "Transfer of blame"!

"That's not why I'm here!" Crazy Parent W. harshly clarified. "I'm here because of the report you had filled-out for Stevens

Learning Center where Amanda is going to go to receive the English education she's not getting in your class!"

"Mrs. W., any time forms like the one you've just mentioned are filled-out, that information is supposed to be confidential in nature. It is unprofessional for any public-school teacher to share confidential information about *students* with their parents!"

"You've slandered my daughter's name!" the mother yelled as she pointed to a copy of the paper that I had believed was confidential information "for professional use only". "You state here that Amanda does not do her homework on time, has a 79 average, argues with three other girls in the class, and might be socially maladjusted!" Mrs. W. emotionally argued. "How could you say those horrible things about my daughter!"

"Those descriptions are the truth as I see them!" I insisted. "And furthermore, the purpose of a parent-teacher conference is to discuss the *student's* classroom performance and not to condemn the teacher. Unless you change the focus of this conference to Amanda's grades and conduct," I sternly pontificated, "then this conference has to be terminated. I have to teach five classes after this meeting and need to get into the right frame of mind so that I don't take anything out on one or more of my *students*!"

"I'm taking this matter right to the principal!" Crazy Parent W. hollered in an antagonistic tone of voice. "You're trying to wreck my daughter's reputation!"

"Okay, Mrs. W., have a nice day!" I finished. "Better yet; have a terrific day and a great week!"

A month later, a guidance counselor approached me in the hall. "Mr. Wiessner, I just received a call from Stevens Learning Center. It seems you've never returned the questionnaire they had sent you about Johnny Templeton!"

"And they aren't going to receive any further documentation from me about any of my *students!*" I loudly returned. I told the guidance counselor what had happened with Crazy Parent W. and her un-illustrious daughter. "I never want to go through *that* kind of mental torture again!" I definitively emphasized. "Tell Stevens Learning Center to get their background information from other teachers that happen to be more masochistic than I am!"

Crazy Parent X. was separated from his wife (a familiar story), and adamantly objected during a first parent conference in October that I had given his son Ted X. a U in conduct for not doing homework.

"Mr. X.," I said. "Ted has twenty-four zeroes in my grade record book this marking period for not doing homework and also for not having rough drafts and final drafts of compositions done on time."

"He does them eventually and hands them in, doesn't he?" the father angrily reminded me. "I think it's unfair that you give a U *conduct* grade for not doing *academic* work."

"Well Mr. X, if I add-up all of the zeroes and count them as an academic grade, then Ted fails English instead of getting a U in conduct," I politely stated. "Would you rather have him fail English, or get a D average with a U in conduct?"

"I'm taking this matter directly to your boss!" Crazy Parent X. viciously threatened. "He'll be a lot more understanding about it than you are!"

Several missing factors should be inserted here. Crazy Parent X. was separated from his wife, and he, his wife and their son were looking for a convenient scapegoat to blame for *their* own misery. Second, I had taught both parents when *they* were in junior-high school, and they might be getting even for something remote that had happened (involving me) to either or to both of them two full decades before. Third, the father had hit the million-dollar lottery and felt that his lethargic son didn't have to listen to any low-salaried English teacher's command directing *his* boy as to what to do. Fourth, Crazy Parent W. is a close friend of the school principal, and they often go hunting and fishing together.

The notified principal called me into his office to discuss Crazy Parent X.'s grievance about *his* uncooperative and defiant son receiving a U in conduct for not doing homework.

"Mr. Wiessner, why did Ted X. receive a U in conduct on his report card?"

"Because the *student* did not have homework and compositions turned-in on dates due twenty-four times last marking period," I justified. "This *student's* negligence is intolerable!"

"But Mr. Wiessner, aren't *you* confusing *academics* with *behavior*?" the principal seated in his comfortable, black-leather swivel chair questioned. "Homework is strictly an academic matter and has nothing to do with behavior or discipline!"

"Not doing homework is a sign of an *uncooperative attitude*, and in my book, a bad attitude is indicative of bad behavior!" I debated. "And we're not talking about *behavior* here! We are talking about *mis*behavior when a *student* deliberately refuses to get work done on time! I insist that this issue is primarily about discipline!"

"I believe you've treading on soft quicksand here!" the public-relations-minded principal warned me. "Giving a U in conduct for failing to do *academic* work cannot be justified educationally! I suggest Mr. Wiessner that you immediately erase the U!"

"I can't do anything about last marking period," I related, "but I won't give Ted X. a U in conduct *next* marking period if he doesn't do his homework!"

"Good. I'll call his father on the phone and tell him what you just said!" the school executive amenably declared with a broad smile, falsely believing that the problem had actually been resolved without Ted X. showing some motivation to do homework and compositions.

The following marking period, Ted X. again accumulated over twenty zeroes for not having homework and compositions submitted on due dates. The principal called me into his office after school.

"Mr. Wiessner, why did you fail Ted X. last marking period?" the head school official asked.

"Because Ted's in Accelerated English, and he's supposed to be a good motivated *student* in an advanced section. He failed to have homework and compositions done on time over twenty times during the marking period. According to *your* logic, I can't give him a U in conduct," I reminded the principal, "so Ted has failed the course for the marking period after I had converted all of the zeroes to 60s as indicated in the Teachers' Handbook!"

"Well, Mr. Wiessner, I don't know if you could fail a *student* just for not doing homework on time!" the chief school executive maintained. "I understand that Ted's test grades are all high!"

"Yes, but he also has poor attendance for being in an Accelerated English class that gets more assignments than a regular English class does," I impeccably answered. "I'm going to recommend that Ted be moved into a regular English class on the basis of poor attendance and not doing regular homework!"

"Well, I want *you* to know that both parents have called me and are deeply upset with what *you* had done to Ted, just for not doing homework! In *this* situation, A 'D' average would have sufficed!" the irate principal informed me. "Perhaps *you* could bend a little once in a while and not cause these kinds of problems for yourself and huge headaches for the vice-principal and me!"

"It seems that Mr. and Mrs. X. along with Ted and *you* are the ones having all the problems," I smartly responded. "I sleep well every night with a guiltless conscience!" I humbly insisted.

With the threat of being recommended to a "lower-ability section", and since other teachers had filled-out negative comments on *their* referral sheets to support Ted X.'s proposed shift into an average English class, the boy straightened-up and finally started getting his homework down on time.

Schools need academic disciplinarians in addition to behavioral disciplinarians. When a *student* like Ted X. has a bad attitude about school, is chronically absent, covertly defies teacher authority, and does not do class work or homework, then an alternative solution should be available to the teacher. As it presently stands, *students* must do overt things such as fighting, cursing, defacing school property, or getting caught with or while taking drugs in order to be properly disciplined. Not doing work in class and demonstrating a pattern of incomplete homework assignments are matters that also should require *student* punishment.

Even when I caught *children* cheating in class or discovered them handing-in identical compositions, I had written-out Discipline Referral Cards on those *children,* but the wary vice-principal's position was that such things as a "bad attitude" and "cheating" were not matters of "Discipline". If schools had academic disciplinarians to go along with regular behavioral disciplinarians, then maybe more academics would be done, and public-schools would be able to be run a little more efficiently than they presently are functioning.

Noreen Y. was a pretty good *student* in an Accelerated English class. The girl tended to be a little chatty at times, but overall, the *student* usually got her work done on time and was polite and receptive. However, Noreen had become a little lackadaisical fourth marking period. The *child* had not done homework on time on four occasions, and was probably mathematically figuring that she would be able to coast home. The girl had reckoned that she would get a B as a final grade average, even if she received a C or a D (or even an A) for the fourth marking period.

One Wednesday in early May, I was showing Noreen's class a film as a motivation for advanced *students* to write about comparing and contrasting the movie's main characters' personalities, including the protagonist and the antagonist. In the middle of the period, Noreen put her head on her desk and was talking with another female *student* that was seated erect in *her* desk. I stopped the *VCR,* hitting the "Pause" remote control button, and then softly admonished Noreen for having her head on the desk and talking to the other *student.*

Crazy Parent Y. had scheduled a parent/teacher session to take place in the Guidance Office conference room. I was a trifle leery because the parent had called for the conference and was not reacting to any warning letter, or to any teacher recommendation for a discussion. As already cited, whenever a father or mother initiates a conference, that action usually translates into "hostile parent", and probably an argumentative meeting.

"How could you give Noreen a lousy C?" Crazy Parent Y. began. "She's gotten three B's the first three marking periods!"

"Mrs. Y.," I said. "Noreen is getting a C so far this fourth marking period. I had indicated *that* information on her warning letter. But her average for the year will probably be a B when factoring in all four marking periods," I explained. "She has not had her homework done on time on four separate occasions according to my records."

The mother seemed disappointed by my answer, and she was expecting to take me to task over the C average *for the year* business. I had thrown her off-course when she had discovered that I was a fair teacher and that her daughter had misled her about the C being for the year, and not solely for the fourth marking period. Then the mother shifted gears and divulged her real reason for being there.

"I don't like the way you *yelled* at my daughter in class!" Crazy Parent Y *shouted* without ever being there when the admonishment had occurred. "Maybe you're getting too old to be teaching!"

"Your daughter was softly reprimanded in class because she had her head on her desk, and was disturbing the rest of the *students* by talking!" I answered. "Mrs. Y., it is now the month of May and not September. Your daughter knows by now what my classroom rules are, and one of them is that a *student* doesn't put his or her head down on a desk during a film!"

"You embarrassed and humiliated her in front of her friends!" Crazy Parent Y. boisterously objected and screamed. "You should've shown better discretion and asked her to go out into the hall if you needed to say something to her!"

"Well, Mrs. Y., based on past experience with other *students*," I stated, "I think that Noreen will think twice the next time she decides to not pay attention to the lesson and put her head-down on her desk in my classroom during a film."

"You're really a very mean teacher! Do you know that?" Mrs. Y. insinuated and boomed.

"No, I didn't know that!" I replied with a smile. "But if *you* want to discuss your daughter's academic work. or the fact that I might give her a U in conduct if her attitude doesn't improve, then you're welcome to stay. But if *you* want to slander the teacher, then let me remind you Mrs. Y. that this is not the *Jerry Springer Show!"*

"You make me so mad that I could slap you!" the mother ranted. "You're a very cruel man!"

"Look Mrs. Y., I don't really care if *you* become so angry that you turn into a giant termite and begin eating this wooden conference table situated between us!" I firmly replied. "But if you assault me in any way, I will most certainly report the incident to the police and definitely press charges!"

The indignant mother left in a huff, certain that I was indeed the most vile, brutal despicable English teacher in the whole-wide world. The following day the principal called me into his office.

"Mr. Wiessner," he commenced his preface. "I just received a negative phone call from Mrs. Y. She claimed that *you* made fun of her ethnic background at a parent-teacher conference yesterday!"

"How did I do that?" I wondered and curiously inquired.

"You said that she should be on the *Jerry Springer Show,* and the mother believes that your statement was making fun of her being a Hispanic-American!" the concerned principal shared with a frown upon his countenance.

"True, there are many Hispanics on the *Jerry Springer Show!*" I acknowledged. "But when I made *that* comment, I was referring to her confrontational nature. People yell at each other all the time on the *Jerry Springer Show* without making much sense," I attested. "That's why I made that *allusion!*"

"It wasn't any *illusion!*" the principal rankled. "Mrs. Y. said you were very nasty and acted unprofessionally."

"Well, good," I replied. "If I were you in *your* current situation," I firmly insisted, "I would be very insulted for allowing Mrs. Y. to be doing *my* job of evaluating teacher performance. The event you're citing did not occur in the classroom while I was teaching a lesson, but you're heavily relying on hearsay drivel coming from an angry parent about what had happened during a hostile parent-teacher conference inside the Guidance Office!"

"I see that I'm getting absolutely nowhere with you!" the perturbed principal testily declared. "Try being a little more sensitive with *students* and parents, and show more discretion when you say something!" the unhinged administrator suggested.

"Popeye said it all when he sang," I claimed, "I am what I am, and that's all that I am!" Then I got-up and left the school executive's luxurious, walnut-paneled office to go and hesitantly teach a rowdy General English class.

Crazy parent Z. had such a reputation for being so crazy that I made sure that the vice-principal was sitting-in on *our* conference that *she* had scheduled in the Guidance Office. As usual, whenever a parent requests a conference, the teacher can ordinarily expect (with relative certainty) that the mother or father wants the instructor to be the focus of the criticism, and not his or her son or daughter.

"Mr. Wiessner, why did you postpone this conference from Tuesday to today!" the woman started-off in a prosecutorial tone.

"Because if you really have to know, on Tuesday my mother had her heart pacemaker replaced at the hospital, and I felt it was more important for me to be there with *her* during the delicate operation," I calmly replied.

"I don't want to hear this fuckin' shit!" the enraged mother shrieked at me like a full-fledged maniac. "That's no fuckin' reason for puttin' me on hold like you did!"

"Look," I replied to the alarmed, shell-shocked vice-principal seated at the conference table. "If this lady makes another comment like that last one, I want *you* to call the police and have her put into handcuffs and yanked out of the building."

"Mrs. Z.," the still-stunned vice-principal stated in a placating tone of voice, "perhaps you can express yourself without cursing. We're all adults in this room, so why don't you tell Mr. Wiessner why you're here!"

"I wanna' know why you're always friggin' pickin' on my daughter!" Mrs. Z. hollered. "Who the hell do *you* think you are?"

"Mrs. Z., I correct most of the *students* I teach at one time or another," I emphasized, "but it just so happens that your daughter requires more correction than some other *students* do!"

"Barbara says you're always in her face!" Mrs. Z. wrangled and yelled. "Why are you always in her goddamned face?"

"The last three times I've corrected Barbara for talking, I was on the other side of the room and definitely was not directly in her face!" I corrected the mother's faulty accusation. "Now, do *you* Mrs. Z. want to talk about Barbara's academic grades and overall behavior, or don't you?"

"Listen jerk, who the hell do *you* think you're talking to? I'm not no damned eighth-grader!" Mrs. Z. intellectually reminded me.

"Do I have to sit here and listen to this perpetual abuse?" I suavely asked the worried assistant-principal. "To tell the truth, I really have other responsibilities to attend to!"

"Mrs. Z.," the vice-principal declared in a phony, soothing voice. "Perhaps you can tell Mr. Wiessner why you are here without using any further obscene language."

"I want to know why the hell do you show so many damned movies in class and don't teach my daughter anything!" the mother shrieked at about ten decibels above normal range.

"Mrs. Z., look at this stack of compositions in front of me. You should ask to see Barbara's writing folder!" I suggested. "If I assign a composition from the grammar textbook, I'm lucky if I get a one paragraph response from *students,* but when I use a movie to develop certain writing methods, I get eight paragraph compositions with about seven sentences in each paragraph. I call *this* type of academic experience that I'm now describing *'Edutainment'!* Now does *that* innovative teaching method answer your concern?"

"Barbara's right; you *are* a no-good bastard!" Mrs. Z. charged. "Now, the reason I'm really here is that I want *you* Wiessner to fuckin' tell me why you called my daughter a *pathological liar* in class! Try getting out of that one, asshole!"

"Your daughter was turned-around in her desk talking to another *student!"* I carefully recollected and stated. "I told Barbara to turn around and she said 'I am turned around' when she still wasn't turned around!"

"She was telling the damned truth!" the mother claimed while never being a witness to the event.

"Then, I told Barbara 'Turn around and stop talking!', and she loudly said 'I'm not talking'!"

"Why didn't you believe my daughter?" Mrs. Z. wanted to know. "My daughter never lies, yet you called her a goddamned liar!"

"Then I told Barbara to stop answering me back!" I continued. "And she spitefully said, 'I'm not answering you back!' when actually she was answering me back," I elucidated. "Your daughter Mrs. Z. was in a state of total denial. She denied that she was turning around, she denied that she was talking to the other *student,* and then she twice denied that she was answering me back when in effect, she actually was answering me back!"

"So, what the fuck does that have to do with her being a pathological liar?" the incensed mother rankled.

"Mrs. Z., please refrain from using inappropriate language!" the diplomatic vice-principal cautioned and advised without threatening or warning to take action.

"Mrs. Z.," I continued my explanation. "Any *student* that denies four consecutive times what he or she has been doing, that had been quite observable to the teacher, is not aware of her misbehavior, especially when he or she denies doing it," I indicated. "In psychology, that type of person is called a pathological liar!"

"You really think you're fuckin' smart, don't you!" Mrs. Z. shrieked. "I've never been so pissed-off in all my damned life!"

"Mrs. Z., I personally don't care if you explode at this table right now and disintegrate into a million pieces!" I unprofessionally volleyed-back. "Just don't get any of your chunks of flesh on me!"

"That will be all Mr. Wiessner!" the still in-shock vice-principal counseled. "I now want to have a few private words with Mrs. Z.!"

I thought about the hostile conference during my entire eighth-period class. That day I had after school bus duty, so I figured I would mention Mrs. Z. to Pete Santollis, another teacher assigned to after school bus duty with me.

"Pete, I just had one of the worst, hostile parent conferences ever!" I remarked. "It was beyond surreal!"

"Who was the parent?" my sympathetic colleague asked.

"It was Mrs. Z.!" I replied. "I know you've had a few loony parent conferences in your career, too!"

"Mrs. Z.! I know that name!" Pete informed me.

"You do?" I exclaimed, hoping that Mrs. Z. wasn't one of Pete's relatives for Pete's sake.

"Yes Mrs. Z.!" Pete recalled and continued. "When Barbara Z. was in my wife's elementary school class around four years ago, Mrs. Z. became hostile with her over the telephone."

"What did Mrs. Z. say?" I asked Pete.

"Mrs. Z told my wife, 'If you don't like what I'm sayin' about *you* pickin' on Barbara, then you can lick my cunt'!" Pete related while shaking his head in disbelief and wryly smiling, too.

"Then I'm glad it's not only me!" I confided and told my teacher friend with a wide grin. 'To tell you the truth Pete," I disclosed. "I'd rather be out here on this horrible after school bus duty that be in the Guidance Office interacting with mercurial Mrs. Z."

Chapter 47
"Inefficient Schools"

When the Educational Aristocracy and leading politicians speak about how they plan to make schools more efficient, their answers do not address the real causes of educational ineffectiveness. When the right winger conservatives state that *students* will have to pass standardized tests, or that teachers must take periodic exams' to remain certified, what they're really proclaiming is that teachers have to work harder and do more and *students* have to remain the same. And when the left-winger liberals discuss the *child*-centered curriculum and *affective* (as opposed to *effective*) education, those zany, other-planet pundits are actually calling for more *democratic* sociological education, and for less *academic* performance-efficient-oriented education.

I shudder whenever I hear and see commissioners of education, senators, congressmen and state governors criticizing American education and stating that teachers are primarily to blame for inefficient schools. Those critics want teachers to "raise the bar" as if education was some sort of *Olympic* pole-vaulting or high-jump contest. The government gurus claim that parents (Mrs. Bertuzzi, Mrs. Z. and Mrs. Dodge?) should have more *democratic* control over educational matters like curriculum, and also lord over the school district's goals and objectives. The underlying, subtle code message is that teachers must work harder and daily perform the impossible, while *students* just have to remain *students* and act like *children*.

The exercised impressive rhetoric sounds almost convincing to the average taxpayer, but teachers know that the hollow and shallow political prattle is little more than educational propaganda. I never enjoyed listening to those "authorities" that don't really educate anyone; the sophists pompous efforts mimicking Napoleon watching the battlefield from atop a hill, sitting upon a white charger. Forget the politicians' rhetorical solutions, and let's go back to square one.

I've heard the following statement many times. "The United States is eighteenth in *student* academic, educational performance out of the twenty leading industrial countries in the world," the often-heard quote goes. That poignant critique is designed to accomplish exactly what it had been formulated to achieve. Blame subject teachers for the mediocrity of *student* standardized test performance, and then in the process, send the instructors on non-adventurous guilt trips. I have always believed that a nation of

443

incompetent teachers is not the sole or main factor that is responsible for the *skewed,* statistical, international, standardized test data.

In most industrialized countries, *students* are *tracked* into different curriculums soon after becoming teenagers, that is, after taking a battery of standardized academic tests and also relative aptitude tests. Then the teens are either *efficiently* tracked into specific academic programs, or into highly-focused vocational curriculums.

The academic *students* in those other nineteen industrialized countries (besides the United States) then take the high-school equivalency standardized tests, and their total results are compared to the general American national *student* body enrolled in the *democratic* comprehensive high school. Most of the potential American "vocational *students"* are still factored into the fraudulent *academic* equation comparisons.

To compare American *students* to high school age *students* around the industrialized world is like comparing oxygen to arsenic, simply because both oxygen and arsenic are both chemical elements. If the vocational-type *students* that are presently attending academic *democratic* comprehensive high schools were factored-out, then the American teenagers would easily be ranked in the top three countries every single time. The European and Asian academic *students* are functioning in an exclusive *academic* scenario with vocational *students* being filtered-out, and *their* higher test scores are being compared to the American high school *student* scores, where most of the public-school *student* body has taken equivalent standardized tests, and the *general* USA *student* scores are recklessly being compared to the foreign *academic students'* test scores.

When I taught eighth-grade English, I usually had six classes on my daily schedule to instruct. Two classes consisted of Accelerated English *students,* and the other four sections (including the 8-6ers) were classified as General English classes. I would have been willing to put my two Accelerated English classes up against any of the same-age competition from the other nineteen industrialized countries, and *my* Accelerated English *students* would win, place or show every year. But when statistical results from a class of 8-6ers is inserted into the general *democratic* comprehensive school formula, then the data is slanted or tilted on an uneven playing field in the direction of *students* in the foreign countries that are essentially exclusively *academically* oriented.

And so, because American *students* all remain in one bin when they ought to have been sorted out into two educational containers (academic and vocational), the U.S. taxpayers' squander billions of dollars annually just because *democratic* education (sociological education) states that such a practice of sorting-out non-academic achievers from actual achievers would be highly *undemocratic*.

In the U.S., all the *children* up to age sixteen must remain in school. Even if a *student* is expelled from a *democratic* comprehensive high school, he or she must be treated to a costly individualized tutorial schooling under the law. Expulsion now means "excluded from the school", but the excluded *child* is still entitled to a formal education up to age sixteen. But the same *expelled student* would probably enjoy (without ever being excluded) a "hands-on" educational curriculum in an American vocational/trades school if he or she had attended one, instead.

The inefficiency dilemma expands and escalates when my six English classes graduate eighth-grade and then attend high school. Parents are afraid of having their *children* stigmatized as being "average or dumb", so they compel the guidance counselors to have their prodigies take "College Prep" courses. All of a sudden, there are now four College Prep' English classes (when there used to be only two Accelerated English classes), and only two General English classes (when there used to be four). Presto-change-o! *Democratic* education (parents having the right to decide) has significantly corrupted the academic talent pool at the ninth-grade level.

Lower ability *students* have been magically mixed-in with academic *students* in college preparatory classes. Those diluted classes, along with the remaining two General English classes, combine to form the American cluster that is then unfairly compared with the pure "academic *students*" from the nineteen other modern industrial nations.

So, that's why the international test results are erroneous, and it's also why politicians and the Educational Aristocracy are fallacious in their presumptions. The *democratic* comprehensive school (in the way it operates) is drastically inefficient, so if the system is inefficient, then so are the teachers trying to teach inefficient methods to many inefficient *students* that have been misplaced into the wrong classes because of parental *democratic* demands.

The United States schools' every *student* is then compared to Europe's and Asia's best academic *students,* so naturally, the deck has been stacked against American public-school teachers because we are working in an inefficient educational structure, and our *students* are being compared to academic *students* working in a more efficient educational model.

The lack of a simple sorting-out process into academic and vocational *students* then lays the detrimental groundwork for massive *democratic* inefficiency on a national level. Take the traditional middle school or high school, for example. A middle school might have six hundred *students*. A hundred and thirty of those *students* are special needs kids (about twenty to twenty-five percent). Another seventy-five to a hundred *students* aren't *students* at all. They are disrupters, educational saboteurs, instigators, vandals, abusers, bullies and anarchists in-the-making.

The seventy-five to a hundred disrupters are placed into regular classrooms (mainstreaming) along with most of the special needs *students,* and *democratic* education has given the chronic violators a license to behave any way that they want. Teachers must contend with these numerous "sassy" *students* daily, and the already-encumbered instructors are commanded (by administrators and college professors) to motivate unmotivated individuals.

And if one saunters-down to the Main Office, he or she will see elements of those same seventy-five to a hundred *students* sitting there waiting to be disciplined by the assistant-principal. And if the repulsive *students* sitting there don't get suspended, they return to class and do further terrorizing to other *students* and further corrupt the *academic* environment by belligerently answering back teachers. The unproductive cycle is repeated daily as the same twenty-percent of the *student* population explores its right to cause unrelenting havoc within the building.

The perpetual menaces each cost over ten-thousand-dollars a year to *democratically* educate every one of them. Those same hundred *students* often do not complete homework assignments, don't do homework, don't participate in classroom discussions, and generally exploit their capacity to fool around and harass others. These hooligans start fights, instigate other fights, steal personal property, and deface school property. The hundred *middle school students* (thugs) will cost a community at least a million dollars a year, and remember that the high school has an additional hundred hooligans of its own. So, every fairly large community is spending and wasting at least two million dollars on *students* that aren't *students* at all. Taxpayers might as well stuff several million dollars into a large suitcase and then simply burn the contents.

Each time that disruptive *students* interrupt classes and must be disciplined, teachers have to take the time to correct them. If each incident takes five-minutes of class time away from academics, and if there are thirty *students* in the class, then a hundred-and-fifty precious educational minutes have just been wasted on one five-minute-long disciplinary incident. That's a hundred and fifty minutes of total *student* learning time that can never be retrieved.

Now, compound that one incident by the thousands of major and minor disciplinary situations that occur in the average public middle and high school every year, and now one can begin to imagine the tremendous, inefficient money crisis that abounds across the nation. So, one must add at least another million dollars wasted in both the town's middle and high school to account for classroom disruption and squandered class time (a lowball figure). Quickly, the incredible total educational waste in a standard community having *democratic* comprehensive middle and high schools comes to between two and a half to three million dollars a year, a figure that is guaranteed to proliferate the following school year.

Teachers are expected to accept aggravating discipline problems and scenarios as if they are part of their daily *routine*. Many elect to pretend that the incidents aren't happening and don't risk "getting into disruptive *students'* faces". Those hundred disruptive middle and high school *students* (15-20%) justify the existence of (and the need for) school administration.

If all *children* were wholeheartedly honest, respectful, and basically courteous, then the various local communities throughout the country wouldn't need administrators to interview, to interrogate, to discipline, to suspend, and to expel (exclude) *students*. A weird symbiosis exists in American middle and high schools where an observable interdependency prevails between disruptive *students* and the requirement of principals and vice-principals. The two factions need each other to thrive in the *democratic* comprehensive school.

Most of the defiant and bellicose *students* later graduate high school without any real skills, and then enter the community and disrupt civil activities there, just like they had done in the public school. The dysfunctional, graduated, unskilled *students* have now evolved into dysfunctional adults who will perpetuate the ugly cycle into a new generation of irresponsible Americans.

Communities must then spend additional millions to subsidize an adequate number of policemen to protect its taxpaying citizens who continuously blame teachers for the entire mess that sociological *democratic* comprehensive schools and the inept Educational Aristocracy have created.

Now, if those hundred disruptive *students* in the high school could learn hands-on skills at a county vocational school, and then return to the high school for extra-curricular activities, the overriding problem could possibly be reversed. But first, *democracy* (socialism) must be taken-out of schools to avert anarchy from arising in the *student* population, to get (sort) *students* into the right curriculums, and to get parental opinion and influence out of course selection (College Prep' and Advanced Placement versus stigmatized General Education courses).

The vocationally-oriented *students* could then learn trades that could make them productive contributors to society, rather than the predators to civil life and property (as a definite pattern) that is being generated by the present American *democratic* educational structure.

If the vocational *students* become serious about wanting to learn in the new *academic high standards* high school, then they could transfer from the equally prestigious *county* vocational school into the local high school by passing a rigid grade-level entrance exam'. The transferring *students* must also sign a contract stating that if they are suspended more than once from the academic high-standards high school, that the vocational school is where they will remain for the balance of *their* high school life.

Upon graduation, the county vocational high schools would issue diplomas that would be equivalent to the ones conferred by high-standards academic high schools. Until a simple sage solution such as mandatory county vocational education for non-academic *students* is established, American diluted *academic* education (socialism) will continue operating wastefully and inefficiently.

The taxpayers' dollars, then being more practically invested, will be wisely utilized if non-academic *students* learn trades at county vocational schools. The synonym for *democracy* (*student* rights) should be balanced by *student* accountability, and not by teacher compensation for *student* irresponsibility. Until a *student* channeled into the vocational curriculum decides that he or she wants to learn in a high-standards academic school, and concludes that *that* classification is a good safe place to want to be, he or she first must develop and exhibit responsible character skills. He or she must first want to get-out of his or her "disruptor' mode" and evolve into having a more civilized contribution and participation mode. The *student* will not become a *student* until he or she decides it's time to become a truly genuine *student* and begin seriously *studying* and conscientiously preparing for the future. Remember, a *student* is supposed to be one who *studies*.

School board members and administrators tolerate the daily disruption accompanying *democratic* comprehensive schools as ordinary action that "comes with the territory". Defiant, belligerent and insolent *students* constitute a very serious discipline and safety problem. Other *students* are uncooperative in a more subtle way, and only exhibit indications of nastiness when challenged by teachers for not doing homework or class work.

When the disruptive *student* population reaches thirty percent of the national *student* body, then the crisis will have grown in magnitude to epidemic proportions, and the matter will finally have to be comprehensively addressed. And under the present system, schools that have behavioral disciplinarians also need academic disciplinarians to punish those covert *students* that refuse to do class work and homework, and to also satisfactorily prevent *them* from becoming additional overt disruptors.

Many other barriers besides the *democratic* comprehensive high school and disruptive *students* cause American education to be inefficient and ineffective. American public schools are modeled after the obsolete nineteenth century factory smokestack industry. Administrators and supervisors are the management, and the teachers are the lowly factory employees governed over by a board of directors (board of education). The *students* are the products of the thirteen-year educational manufacturing process, starting with kindergarten right up to twelfth grade, and the taxpayers are the investing stockholders.

This fixed factory pattern is supported and endorsed by vested interest groups such as the *NEA,* the *PTA,* the *National School Board Association,* and the *School Administrators Association.* Bureaucrats in all of those organizations don't want to see their security jeopardized by a grassroots teacher-led American Educational Revolution that ought to rival the *Industrial Revolution* in terms of impact and magnitude.

Another contributor to inefficient education is when irate parents bypass teachers and appeal alleged grievances against their *children* to (management) school administrators, who suddenly become parent surrogates aligned against the factory employee (teacher). Administrators pressure teachers to "get along with parents" and "don't make waves or push the envelope" inside their classrooms.

Teachers are not true professionals like medical doctors, lawyers, pharmacists, and accountants are. They are part of a system, and do not own their own private businesses. Accountants, too, don't have to answer to administrators, to parents, to taxpayers, and finally, to tone-deaf boards of education.

In summary, non-professional teacher duties further contribute to educational inefficiency. The tasks make teachers into generalists and not specialists in an age of specialization. Cafeteria duty, Office Detention, In-School Suspension, bus duty, lavatory duty, chaperone duty, and hall duty all contribute to educational inefficiency because the teacher could be doing something more educational working directly with *students* during those times of the day.

Teachers are kept in tow when they must agree to be *subordinated* to unprofessional non-teaching duties (adminis*trivia*), or else the frazzled instructors will be judged as being *insubordinate*. I could never understand how a *professional* teacher could ever be *insubordinate*. The two terms seem to be polarized at opposite ends of the respect and logic spectrums.

Teaching is the only job that I know of where educators must work in the present, in the past, and in the future. The middle or high school teacher works in the present by instructing a hundred-and-thirty *students* a day. He or she works *in the past* by correcting yesterday's homework assignments and last week's compositions. He or she works *in the future* by planning next week's lesson plans and classroom activities. I often found myself collecting September compositions in November. So, teachers also must be excellent bookkeepers having accurate grade records to defend positions that are often being challenged by *students* and parents *in the present.*

Once, as I recall, a parent showed-up with his son after school and insisted that I had not recorded a grade for a composition they purportedly had been handed-in a month before. I showed the parent and the conniving *student* the *child's* writing folder that had skipped the entry date for *that* particular composition. "If the composition had been completed, it would have been recorded and documented by your son in his writing folder! It wasn't, so therefore it had never been done!" I maintained. But teachers must always be prepared to justify everything and to defend anything.

I have always resented reading in the newspapers the glaring misperception that teachers are greatly overpaid and that they are essentially *inefficient*. On the contrary, the majority of teachers I have worked with from 1965-1999 were very dedicated people working in a *democratic* comprehensive school model that was doomed to fail because the model itself was grossly inefficient.

Chapter 48
"Fighting in Schools"

The sacred Teachers Handbook states in regard to *student* discipline: "Since the success of a *democratic* nation relies on the ability of its citizens to exercise self-discipline, it is the purpose of the school to teach *boys and girls* our main objective, which is the philosophy of self-control." Yes, everything looks good on paper where *democratic* education in the comprehensive school is concerned, but a tremendous *Grand Canyon* exists between educational theory and everyday public-school reality.

Seventy-five to a hundred nasty *students* are continuously disrupting the smooth operation of the average-sized middle or high school, and also suckering good kids into altercations, and committing uncivilized behavior through peer pressure, intimidation, extortion and other tactics. Those hundred young barbarians are as *self-disciplined* as a jungle colony of wild baboons. Educational psychology, the law and ultra-liberal *democracy* in a comprehensive school protect those seventy-five to a hundred terrorists from much-needed reprimand and police intervention.

The U.S. public schools are convenient dumping grounds for recalcitrant *students* that have been *expelled* from parochial schools and from private schools. The hands of school officials and teachers are tied when dealing with the riffraff, so the standard approach is to tolerate their antics and attempt to rehabilitate them by being especially nice to the young active thugs on a daily basis.

And then inequality in punishment when it is meted-out in small community schools is a daily practice. Given the same offense, the son of the village drunk is more likely to be suspended than the son of a prominent citizen is. The internal problems inside schools are often concealed, whitewashed, and squashed while only the good tidings filter-out into the newspapers. The only time bad news is published is when police reports are organized and available to journalists, so that is precisely why school public-relations-minded administrators are reluctant to call in the local cops and handcuff and arrest a *student*.

I remember one year when I was teaching at the high school that one of the boys' lavatories was virtually demolished. The crime scene looked almost as bad as San Francisco after the great earthquake of 1906. Ceiling panels were reduced to what looked like shredded wheat, sinks had been yanked out of the tiled wall, and cherry bombs had rocked the commodes from their anchoring. The story of the massive vandalism had circulated around the community, but since the police were not called-in to investigate, the immense destruction was only a gossip rumor to the common taxpayer. Administrators want only the superlatives leaking-out to the public, and the chance of the total school picture ever being accurately portrayed in the mass media is very slim indeed.

I want to reiterate that I had taught is what is regarded as a model school district, so I can't imagine what's going on in urban schools, or in schools with bad reputations for violence and vandalism. One thing is for sure, and that is fighting in any public high school with a *student* population of a thousand or more teenagers is as certain as death and taxes. But administrators regard student fighting as "business as usual", when in truth, the local police ought to be notified, come into the building, and arrest the brawlers with assault charges being issued against the main perpetrator.

I once had the pleasure of intervening in a juicy brawl in the C-Wing corridor while I was on my way to cafeteria duty. One fairly large *student* had another in a headlock with his left arm while the lad's right fist was riveting off the other *child's* head and face like a jackhammer destroying an ancient sidewalk. The recipient of the brutal blows' cheeks looked like crushed hamburger meat with a thick layer of ketchup being squirted on it.

I used the ice hockey official's approach and waited thirty more seconds until the *student* that was hammering-away finally became a degree fatigued. I sent the bloodstained victim to the nurse's office for medical attention, and then escorted the aggressor down to the Main Office where I had to write-out Discipline Referral Cards on two *students* I didn't even know.

That afternoon, I encountered the principal in the main corridor. "Just look at these bloodstains splattered all over my sport coat from breaking-up that vicious brawl this morning!" I frankly complained. "Do you think that the board of education would defray the cleaner's expenses if I submit a voucher?"

"That's perfectly okay, Mr. Wiessner," the amused principal jokingly responded. "The red stains almost blend right-in with the cranberry-colored jacket you're wearing."

At that particular moment, I vowed to my conscience that I would disappear into the woodwork the next time I would observe a wild student fracas erupting. "That's just great!" I answered the high school administrator. "Tomorrow I definitely will be wearing my green leisure suit with no tie!"

A teacher might suspect that a *student* involved in a bloody altercation might be on drugs or maybe on alcohol. One time back in the mid-'70s, three eighth-graders arrived at my homeroom hungover from a wedding reception they had attended the night before. I dispatched the trio down to the nurse's office for medical exams', and for verification of my intoxication theory. The nurse (under administrative suggestion) diplomatically had the boys sent home for "headaches" and for "feeling ill", thus averting adverse publicity in the newspapers and critical gossip among the local citizens.

If *students* are on drugs (illegal or prescription), it is more difficult to prove than when the *children* have imbibed alcohol. Hazy eyes might suggest narcotics usage, and then the teacher is reluctant to report evidence of drowsiness, hyperactivity, depression, or nervous twitching to the nurse, because many *students* show those same symptoms normally every day.

If a teacher is daring enough to send a *student* to the nurse on suspicion of drug usage, and if the instructor's observations prove to be false, then the possibility remains that a lethal libel lawsuit might result, claiming that the *child's* integrity had been maligned. The lawsuit might be filed against the teacher by the insulted parents, if the instructor had written a descriptive note to the nurse. That innocent teacher memo' could be used by the plaintiff's attorney as evidence against the accusing instructor.

Once, in the early '80s (after an intense high school home football game with a cross-town rival), one of the more eminent *students* was screaming a collection of assorted profanities at the opposing team's players. An assistant coach on the home team yelled-over to the *child* who was making the grotesque linguistics to stop in the interest of showing good sportsmanship.

The dastardly *student* resented being rebuked by the assistant coach in front of his equally obnoxious cohorts. The *student* then defied the bewildered coach by verbally bombarding *him* with a flurry of obscene idioms that are seldom heard in monasteries or convents. In seconds, the assistant coach and the vile instigator wound-up rolling around on the ground, hostilely flailing away at each other, and savagely thrashing about.

Coaches and players finally separated the two combatants. The *student's* eyes were spinning-around like cherries and lemons inside a slot machine's windows. The teachers on the faculty had long suspected for quite some time that the abusive *student* had been experimenting with drugs, but since his wealthy father was always quick to defend his son's bad deportment, no one was going to ever

453

accuse the "entitled teenager" of narcotics usage, and then have to defend their anemic position in court.

Daily cafeteria duty was without a doubt my greatest headache. Most high school teachers would prefer being trapped in an endless maze having a multitude of cul-de-sacs rather than being exposed to the cruel and unusual punishment known as cafeteria duty. Just imagine two hundred and fifty howling adolescents bending spoons into goose eggs, tossing macaroni at each other, and deliberately making messes to upset the disheartened teachers on duty. The poor head teacher's incantations over the microphone are ignored because the PA system is weak, the acoustics are bad, and the microphone only works every other time. Yet the teachers are responsible for maintaining an orderly dismissal.

I found that the best way to patrol the cafeteria was to revolve around the perimeter with my back to the walls while facing the *students* at all times. When I was courageous enough to bravely patrol the aisles between cloistered tables, then my moving anatomy constituted a convenient target for flying debris and miscellaneous (*missile*aneous) food chunks being launched from behind and then hurtling toward my head and my back.

Sometimes, my wife claimed she could tell the school menu that day by inspecting my sport jacket's fabric. My spouse was able to see and identify pea smears, string bean stains, and carrot splotches on different occasions that somehow had added a new exquisite design to my school attire.

The cafeteria is a mass situation where fights are most likely to flare-up in a hurry. In 1971, before John Rizzo and I could stave-off a *student* altercation, one teenaged anarchist had hit the *student* sitting across the table with a sticky meat particle. The victim then escalated the stakes by picking-up a pickle slice and a handful of lemon meringue pie, and next fiercely hurled the food into the first *student's* face. The crusaders that were supposed to be good friends then leaped-up onto the cafeteria table and started wickedly flailing away. That was a hard fight for John Rizzo, Tim Amoro, and myself to break-up because the brawlers were standing above us on top of the lunchroom table. Tim Amoro wound-up with his glasses being crushed and experienced a broken nose to boot.

Whenever a cafeteria fight is triggered, a sudden dichotomy of *student* loyalties develops, and if the teachers aren't quick to intervene, other *students* may intrepidly enter the ensuing battle. A distinct occupational hazard indeed exists. The teachers have to focus their energies on immediately separating the first two junior (or maybe even senior) gladiators, yanking them down to the vice-principal's office, and then dutifully returning right away to the rectum of the school building, its cafeteria.

In my younger days, I used to be more aggressive in stopping lunchroom brawls, but after being involved in over two hundred and fifty different *student* fisticuffs over a span of thirty-four years, I gradually became less assertive. And if the *student* that I despised more was getting the worse of it on the bottom while being mercilessly pummeled, then I would make sure I got to the scene a little slower than I ordinarily would have.

In my school district, an effective cafeteria disciplinarian was usually awarded an asterisk next to his or her name on the cafeteria duty roster. The un-coveted star signified that the teacher with the asterisk was in charge of the cafeteria and responsible for keeping order during the forty-five-minute lunch period.

The asterisk did not bring any additional monetary reward for being the official charge d' affaires. The only honor of being the possessor of the unenvied asterisk was having a defective microphone, of having a *student* audio-visual club (with the mechanical skills of the Marx Brothers) to repair the sound magnifier, and the undesirable distinction of being abused daily by the incessant adolescent mob. The asterisk certainly didn't qualify me to be a certified boxing referee.

Usually, the same teachers pulled cafeteria duty each year while the balance of the faculty members were assigned to easier study hall situations. Several cafeteria-assigned teachers learned that when they had performed a mediocre job in the lunch-room, they had been re-assigned to study hall duties the following school year.

Administrators and school board members contended that teachers can command respect from *students* in the cafeteria; whereas, cafeteria aides cannot. Teachers are saddled with the ugly duty because the public believes that certified instructors know how to manage *students* in mass situations.

The truth of the matter is that there is little transfer of *student* respect from the classroom to the school cafeteria. The same *students* that love a teacher in English might emulsify the instructor in the cafeteria. Teachers seldom have serious trouble with *children* in their classrooms, but in the cafeteria, sometimes even the good kids go sour or bonkers. Instructors are continually getting into hassles with *students* over who threw the napkin on the floor, who left the food tray on the table, or who threw his or her silverware into the half-full garbage can.

Daily cafeteria duty is one of the best ways to ensure acid indigestion. And then when the *students* finally return to their classrooms after lunch, oftentimes they must face a strung-out, exasperated teacher that had spent a very hectic forty-five-minute interval in the cafeteria dungeon. The emotions known as anger and frustration are not faucets that are easily turned-off. A teacher must be careful to not carry his or her petulance from the lunchroom into the next period classroom. Several times I had overly admonished *students* in the classroom immediately after cafeteria duty and had to then contend with parent-initiated hostile conferences.

In the early '70s, two brawny high school *students* were really hammering-away at each other inside the cafeteria. By the time John Rizzo and I hustled to the battle scene, boisterous *students* were shrieking and also scurrying to the altercation to add an additional dash of pandemonium to the mounting crisis. John and I tried tugging the brawlers apart, but the combatants were interlocked in a clinch like two magnetized mastodons. By that time, the cafeteria fight marathon sounded like a blend of the *Kentucky Derby's* homestretch and the climax to the Roman *Circus Maximus*. The teachers' inability to separate the grapplers added a dimension of slapstick comedy to the already exciting event.

The bigger *student* had the smaller one in a bear hug, while the more diminutive *child* had his arms locked around the huskier kid's head and neck. I leaped upon the bigger kid and managed to separate him from his opponent. The bigger *student* whirled around with the two-hundred-pound teacher attached to his back. I felt like I was a rodeo cowpuncher atop a berserk Brahma bull.

The larger *student* (with me on his back) re-entered the fight with the smaller *child,* who had wildly broken-away from John Rizzo's grasp. Siamese twins would have been easier to separate than those two battlers were. The other two hundred and fifty maniac spectators were raucously cheering the zany scene that was crazily transpiring before their eyes. Thank goodness a rescue squad of five male teachers zoomed into the cafeteria from the nearby teacher's lounge, or John and I would have lost what represented the *main event* of the day for the thoroughly delighted *students.*

In another cafeteria period scenario, several enterprising *students* thought that they would evoke certain behavioral responses from the female teachers on duty. Two boys stripped the husk from a healthy-looking banana, and in a gesture of inspiration, they ingeniously stretched a prophylactic over the fruit, which was then placed perpen*dic*ularly on the lunch table for other *students* to *rubber*neck and admire. Perversions of that nature are designed to rattle or unnerve the teachers on duty, so the worst thing an instructor should do is act appalled. But if the bad cafeteria behavior is not handled properly, a heated argument exchanged between the teacher and the mischievous *students* might ensue.

I took the wind out of the violators' sails by stating, "I didn't know that bananas were capable of contracting venereal diseases!" I had successfully stolen the boys' thunder and had reduced their queer impropriety to the level of "So what!" If one plans to last for thirty-four years in the educational field, minor occurrences like the banana/prophylactic incident should not ruffle a teacher's feathers.

Students cutting into the cafeteria line could constitute a major daily challenge for lunchroom duty teachers. Many of today's *students* belong to a peculiar breed. Besides thinking that *Hamlet* is some sort of new breakfast sensation (like an omelet), many *children* adhere to a unique, new *relative morality* where lying, cheating and stealing are acceptable modes of behavior. It might be easier to lasso a bucking bronco with a rubber band attached to a shoelace than to get the truth from an uncooperative *student*. Perhaps schools should teach more wisdom and less knowledge, along with more ethics and less irrelevant facts.

I remember noticing a husky lass slipping into an already-formed cafeteria line. I thought that her action had been unfair to the other *students*, so I told the young lady to have a seat and then later get-up to be served last. Although the girl heard my distinct directive, she acted as if I had been addressing her from a soundproof booth. I repeated my command more vigorously.

"Man, stop spittin' in my face!" she indignantly sneered at me.

"Sit-down and then get in the back of the line!" I repeated. "You know the rules! Honor them!"

"Fuck off bro'!" the incensed girl snarled back, much to the amusement of her appreciative peers.

In the midst of a temper tantrum, I told the cafeteria brunhildas not to serve the girl when she came through the line. The *student* next defied my authority by grabbing a platter and putting it on her serving tray, and she then promptly proceeded to the cashier. I immediately notified the office. The vice-principal was tied-up with another major discipline problem, so the available principal cruised into the cafeteria.

I explained the general situation, and the chief school executive told the bellicose girl, "Bring the tray back to the cashier because you didn't pay her!" the grim-faced principal diplomatically-but-imperatively commanded.

The hysterical girl arose from her cafeteria seat and sauntered back to the serving line, carrying her red tray. The perturbed principal followed the *student* into the serving area to ascertain that the girl would return her tray and then take a seat before moving to the back of the food line as I had directed.

A verbal exchange then resulted between the defiant *student* and the angry-at-being-ignored principal. The agitated girl threw food particles from her tray that instantly ornamented the school official's expensive haberdashery. The administrator reached to apprehend the disrespectful girl, and she took a wild swipe at his face. The female violator next zipped-out of the cafeteria and fled to a place of hiding.

The principal notified the police, and the girl was found seated in a telephone booth in the main corridor, holding the door shut while calling home for sympathy, advice and counsel. The principal and two policemen attempted wedging the door open as the young lady kept it shut with one hand while talking on the phone with the other.

I casually dismissed the craziness by thinking, 'Our great American *democratic* educational system is for all the *children,* and it is not just for the elite college-bound *students!'*

In the mid-'80s, a juicy fight broke-out in the middle school cafetorium. Two boys were really doing damage to each other's faces. I separated the boxers three times, but then they continued their furious donnybrook. I became angry from dealing with the continuous fighting, so I got the more aggressive *student,* flung him into the nearby ice cream freezer, quickly put the lid on the refrigeration unit, and then sat on top of the lid. The *student* inside was smashing the top from the frigid dark interior, but the *child* could not move the covering with my body weight holding it down.

"Chill out!" I yelled to the trapped instigator contained inside the closed ice cream box, much to the total delight of the surrounding student spectators.

A minute later, I opened the freezer. Several dozen ice cream sandwiches and chocolate pops had been damaged during the bizarre fiasco. Another teacher on cafeteria duty then escorted the cooled-off violator to the Main Office while I enjoyed eating one of the lesser-crushed chocolate ice cream pops. But sadly, I had to pay the cafeteria manager for the two-dozen destroyed ice cream desserts.

Strange things can often happen when a teacher is assigned by the administration to monitor Office Detention. A loudmouth girl was in *'O.D.'* for bullying another young female in the cafeteria and then punching her better-behaved enemy in the face.

"If you continue talking in Office Detention, I'm going to have to penalize you!" I threatened the belligerent young lady.

"Mr. Wiessner; I'm going to tell my mother what you just said. She'll call the principal and have you fired for saying *that* to me!"

"For your information," the pronounced word *penalize* (pee-nal-ize) means to give you additional punishment," I sternly corrected. "Please learn to speak and comprehend our wonderful English language a trifle better!"

Another time, I was in after-school Office Detention with a seventh-grade *student* that had told one of his teachers to "Fuck off"! The *student* had to write a sincere letter to the teacher apologizing for his irresponsible misdemeanor, so I was kind enough to depart from Office Detention policy (as prescribed by the administration) and allow the *child* to author the theme under my jurisdiction.

At the end of the Office Detention session, I commented to the *student*, "I'm glad you used your time constructively!"

"Blow me asshole!" the *child* nastily responded.

Sometimes it just doesn't pay to say anything at all (polite or otherwise) to a *student*. "What did you say?" I requested to know.

"I said 'Eat me raw asshole'!" the manner-less punk replied.

The recalcitrant *student* was given three additional days of Office Detention for using profanity directed toward a teacher. A week later, the *student* got into a nice bloody fight in the cafeteria while I was on duty. I broke the grapplers up twice, but the pair of combatants were still heavily exchanging punches. The *student* that had used the obscene references in Office Detention again began swinging at his adversary, gaining the advantage in the fight.

In a fit of anger, I un-gently grabbed the aggressor and pushed him through the cafeteria doors. The crazed *student* had already been broken-open from the fight, with blood soon cascading-down his face and cheeks, the crimson fluid originating from his forehead.

"Go to the nurse's office right now!" I bellowed to the *student* bleeding profusely upon the corridor floor.

"Fuck you!" the upset *child* yelled-back as the wise guy awkwardly got-up onto his feet. Before I could utter another word, the *child* darted out of the building, scurried across the avenue, and entered the police department to cite me for corporal assault just as Leonard Caro had done back in 1965. Luckily, the Police Chief returned the brawler to school jurisdiction, but I recently read in the newspapers of a similar episode that happened in a Pennsylvania school where the police came into the building and then arrested the teacher for assaulting a *student*.

In another cafeteria fistfight involving two huge eighth-graders, I forcefully pushed the main aggressor against the closed entrance doors in an effort to separate the fierce participants. The *child* hit his head against the wooden frame, and some blood was trickling-down from a small cut on his forehead. I quickly instructed the pugnacious *student* (who incidentally loathed me because he was failing my English class) to immediately go to the nurse's office, after which I soon wrote-out a pass and then directed a better-behaved student to deliver the message to the nurse. The vindictive instigator, instead of going to the nurse, intentionally entered the downstairs bathroom and proceeded to repeatedly slam his head against a toilet stall, thus making his head bleed excessively. The insolent *student* then stepped across the hall and told the nurse that I had caused the wide head wound incurred during the brawl. However, the time of the hall pass I had written compared to the lad's appearance in the nurse's office was a five-minute duration lapse. A half-hour later, the alert janitor discovered fresh blood that had been stained upon the bathroom stall wall, and thus, after the needed physical evidence had been presented, I was exonerated by the school administration from the frivolous accusation of unprofessionally beating-up the defiant *student* inside the school cafeteria.

Fighting is not only limited to the cafeteria. Brawls erupt in the halls and in study halls, too. A large study hall in the lunchroom can rival the treachery of cafeteria duty. On several occasions, fistfights had erupted in the cafeteria study hall before I could arrive there from my classroom, located on the other side of the building, over three-hundred lengthy feet away, and only accessible through crowded corridors.

I have had as many as a hundred-and-fifty *students* crammed into a cafeteria mass study hall, and out of that number, only about fifty of them are genuinely studying. Study halls in public schools are generally vast educational wastelands that operate on maybe a forty-percent efficiency level. Teachers are constantly taking attendance, moving talkative *students* to specially isolated seats, and correcting those infidels that are determined to violate the sanctity of the forced silence the teachers are trying to maintain. And one time during a *student* study hall fight, an anonymous, craven *child* spectator had punched me twice in the back while I was frantically attempting to separate two determined combatants.

A bloody fight may erupt in the halls while a teacher is casually en-route to his or her next class. In 1999, two eighth-grade girls (liking the same boy) got into a real fingernail, hair-pulling catfight. I was exiting the Main Office with a hundred and forty worksheets in my hand that I had just *Xeroxed.* A short substitute teacher was already on the scene trying to intervene in the fracas, but the poor fellow was taking as much of a beating as the two Amazons were.

I instantly dropped my papers onto the corridor floor and assisted the substitute teacher in his grave enterprise. I yanked one of the girls off, but she raised her feet and was savagely kicking-away at the other cat-fighter. The *student* in my clutches then kicked the fire extinguisher attached to the wall, and it tilted sideways, mixing its chemicals, and then giving-off a noxious spray. The corridor was filled and polluted with choking *students,* and the chemical vapors swirling in the air looked like a miniature atomic mushroom cloud. The alert vice-principal heard the commotion and exited the Main Office, lifted one of the combatants onto his right shoulder, and next carried the kicking female into the office, looking like Little Abner eloping with Daisy May on Sadie Hawkins Day.

I remember one instance where a school janitor attempted to break up a fistfight between two pretty big *students,* and the custodian wound-up in the hospital getting stitches and being treated for multiple lacerations.

Finally, I recollect a really terrible girls' fight that had erupted outside on the asphalt playground between an eighth-grade *child* bully and a new seventh grade transfer *student.* When I arrived on the scene, the two un-feminine warriors were really pummeling and mauling one another in what amounted to a vicious battle featuring wicked hair pulling and the vicious scratching of faces and arms.

Charlie Southard (an affable Math' teacher) and I separated the crazed felines three times, but the marathon battle ensued. It was one of the most difficult struggles I had ever dealt with, and it took Charlie and me five-full-minutes to restore some semblance of order among the shrieking *student* eyewitnesses.

A week after that horrible ordeal, Charlie Southard died from a massive heart attack. I have often wondered if there had been any connection between the stress and strain of separating the two female gladiators in that terrible fight and the passing-away of my good friend and colleague.

I really still consider it a minor miracle that I had managed to survive in public school teaching for thirty-four years. *Student* fighting comes with the total teaching package, and the duty has nothing at all to do with either teaching or with learning.

But today's school fights are not always one-on-one with fist against jaw combat being exhibited. The "wolf-pack mentality" is presently pervading many urban schools, and *students* are now employing the "herd attack" practice in rural high schools as well. Four *children* will now fight maybe six *students*. Sometimes, a *student* will be knocked to the ground outside the building, or to the floor inside the edifice, and five or six members of the assaulting wolf-pack will stomp and trounce the ribs and face of the unfortunate recipient of their collective hostility.

If a *student* fight happens first thing in the morning, it could set the tone for and ruin a teacher's entire day. Fortunately, for the already encumbered instructors, most days are more tranquil than those dates that are tainted with wall-to-wall *student* conflicts. On those chaotic, mind-boggling days (usually before extended holidays like *Thanksgiving, Christmas* and *Easter),* public school teaching could seem like the *Wild, Wild West.*

* * * * * * * * * * * *

I firmly believe that all *students* between the ages of thirteen and eighteen should be required to spend six weeks of each summer vacation involved in community service in order to develop a spirit of commitment and responsibility so that adolescents could realize from experience that there's more to life than the all-too-prevalent "me-first" attitude that most egocentric teenagers of today assume and practice. A strong sense of purpose among juveniles could drastically reduce the number of *student* fights that currently take place. And administrators and boards of education should treat school fighting as serious assaults and batteries worthy of police investigation, and not as business-as-usual events resulting in mere *student* detentions and suspensions.

Also, I think it would be beneficial to our great American society if each high school graduate be put on hold and have his and her college experience delayed for two years so that every eighteen-and-nineteen-year-old could fulfill a societal contribution by either serving in the military or by assisting in their communities as voluntary helpers given assigned humanitarian missions. Then perhaps our college dropout rates will be diminished when more mature, more disciplined and more ethically-minded twenty-year-old freshman *students* enter those hallowed university halls.

Chapter 49
"Teachers and Administrators"

Teachers are supposed to always behave like they're *dedicated professionals* devoted to the principles of self-sacrifice for the greater order, and to always give more than they receive. Teaching, like hospital nursing, exists as an "unsung occupation" where the practicing *professional* is expected to always go the extra-yard without hesitation, and without complaining.

I have gone on field trips, moderated assembly programs and countywide spelling bees, given writing workshops, and had always chaperoned, all for gratis. Twenty-eight times during my career, I accompanied eighth-graders on overnight field trips to Washington DC, to Williamsburg, and to Luray Caverns, Virginia, sometimes working three-consecutive grueling eighteen-hour-days without any additional compensation. These "come-with-the-territory" extras are "teacher expectations" that have their roots in the role of exploited women schoolmarms back in the mid-1800s.

Teachers must always go above and beyond the call of *duty*. That means beyond cafeteria duty, beyond Office beyond Detention Duty, beyond In-School Suspension duty, beyond hall duty, beyond lavatory duty, between class duty, beyond one-day field trip chaperone duty, and finally, beyond before and after school bus duty. Administrators always emphasize to teachers at faculty meetings, "Doing extra is part of your *professional* responsibility. Now we only need three more teachers to volunteer for the seventh grade *Great Adventure* trip next month, and incidentally, you'll be getting back to the school around eight-thirty p.m. on Friday the 13th. And," the principal might continue his remarks, "we need two more chaperones for the Eighth-Grade Graduation Dance. If no one volunteers, I'll have to assign people!"

One thing should be understood from all of this common administrative rhetoric. Teachers are *not* professional people. They are merely *school employees*. Administrators only tell teachers that *they* are *dedicated professionals* when extra things need to be done, and that it would be *unprofessional* to *not* do those extra duties. Classroom teachers follow administrative orders just like secretaries, janitors, cafeteria workers, school aides, and substitute teachers do.

Faculty members have little choice when their names are assigned on duty rosters to perform extra-non-paying, repetitious details, or random administratively-arranged professional expectations (Parent-Conference Nights, Open House Night, Teacher Introduction Night, after school faculty meetings, grade level department meetings, and also curriculum committee and textbook selection meetings). In terse summary, teachers are essentially school contract *employees* and nothing more than that.

Professional people are autonomous, and they work for themselves in the *free enterprise* marketplace. Doctors have their own clinics and practices, and lawyers have their own legal businesses. Pharmacists and accountants usually own their establishments. Those particular occupations are indeed *professional* because doctors, lawyers, pharmacists and accountants are independent of administrative fiat and answer only to their own consciences. Lawyers and accountants don't need supervisors and building principals telling them what to do, and what not to do.

True professional people are on their own to interpret their ethics, and are certainly above subordination to administrators. But when a teacher challenges an administrative edict, he or she becomes an uncooperative dissident for refusing to be subordinate, so he or she is then automatically labeled *insubordinate*.

Malleable administrators often reflect the community's taxpayers' sentiments and values, and every adult in the town or school district happens to believe that he or she is an expert in the field of education. The teachers that do education for a living are not regarded as authorities in what they actually have chosen for a life career. The taxpayers subsidize the freight, so teachers are just relegated and delegated *employees* enacting the will of the public.

According to the present educational system's power structure, teachers must be subordinate to administrators, to supervisors, to school board members, to parents, and most importantly, to the court of public opinion (the citizens, the *children* and the taxpayers).

The local taxpayers don't prescribe their own medicines, formulate their own pills, file their own legal briefs, defend each other against the *IRS,* or perform brain surgery on each other. The taxpayers rely on true, respected *professional* people like doctors and lawyers to perform those valued services for them.

Teachers are *employees* because they have no alternative other than to enact and perform what administrators say they must do. And the hardest part of being a public-school teacher is that the administration wants the Gumby-like instructor to please everyone out there populating the court of public opinion.

It is very difficult for a teacher to remain a strong *independent* individual and demonstrate a contrary point of view, or even minor convictions that oppose specific administrative directives. Either teachers on a faculty "kiss-up or leave the district". That's the rigid rules of the lop-sided administrative power game, and the didactic bosses have all of the trump cards.

A teacher that is tough on *students,* or who defends his or her positions, or who firmly answers parental grievances, is not playing the administrator's "concede, compromise and please-the-public game". And many irate parents have entered the building for a scheduled feisty conference with Mr. Wiessner, and then left in a more incensed frame of mind than when they had arrived. I never yielded to the complaints of any dissatisfied, prosecutorial, fault-finding, nit-picking parent. If the on-a-mission parent was respectful and supportive, then a conference generally went rather smoothly. But I always defended my convictions and my actions without blinking an eye when a "search-and-destroy" member of the general public questioned anything I might have done to his or her *child.*

The irate parent enters the conference and does not wish to constructively discuss his or her *child's* shortcomings. He or she wants to play the very popular "blame the teacher game" by transferring all responsibility for an incident to the targeted school *employee.* A true professional person would not have to contend with Mrs. Bertuzzi's', Mr. X.'s, or Mrs. Z.'s prolific guff and abuse.

And those vociferous, livid parents will magnify one alleged negative event (let's say reprimanding their *child* and supposedly embarrassing him or her in front of the class), and then attempt to vilify and indict the teacher that dared correct his or her perfect *child.* The hostile parent really doesn't want to hear about the thousands of wonderful things the teacher has done in the classroom. The angry mom or dad has tunnel vision, and only seeks satisfaction or an apology for something that the teacher might have said to their often-placated son or daughter.

Administrators are like water and always take the path of least resistance. Since parents are taxpayers and teachers are only mere *employees,* the school executives will generally advise the instructor to patronize the parent and suggest "don't make any waves". The principal and the superintendent know that teachers can be manipulated or coerced into surrendering to pressure, mostly out of fear of losing their *job security as an employee,* or also possibly out of fear of having a salary increment withheld as the first step in the removal of the teacher's tenure.

Teachers are indoctrinated from the time of their first *employment* that they must obey administrators and administrative edicts along with complying with administrative determinations. If a teacher boldly disagrees with an administrative decision, then that *employee* is being insubordinate to arbitrary executive mandates in the *democratic* comprehensive school. In other words, democracy is for everyone except for the school district's lower-level *employees*, which includes the teachers.

I really don't believe that too much true academic freedom exists in today's public schools. Until teachers become *professional* people and finally elevate themselves above serfdom in the medieval-style feudal fiefdoms that employ them, they are doomed to subordination to administrative prerogative and to executive mandate. The first thing to understand is that teachers must be liberated from the nineteenth century factory management (administrators and supervisors) overlords along with the remainder of the Educational Aristocracy System that governs over the entire instructional staff. When teachers understand that *employees* are *not professional* people, then the academic serfs can more readily develop a working model of what a genuine *professional person* ought to be.

One mechanism that administrators use to manipulate teachers is standardized test results that operate under the pretense that teachers are inefficient, when the actual fact is that the *democratic* sociological system teachers must work in is grossly inefficient. When I was given a hundred and thirty eighth-grade *students* in September, I always knew that at least forty-to-fifty of them could only do third-to-fifth grade work in reading and English. Then, the administrators tell the teachers (in a system that is rigged against the instructors to begin with) that they want ninety-five percent of the *students* to pass the new state *GEPA* (Grade Eight Proficiency Assessment) test given in March.

Now the *New Jersey State Department of Education* becomes part of the problem, too. Instead of giving the state's standardized tests to first-graders and then to second-graders, and so on, the state *first* gives the mandated *HSPA* tests to eleventh-graders (many can't do eighth-grade work). And concurrently, the suspect *GEPA* needed to be administered to eighth-graders in order to assess core curriculum standards. All of this bizarre craziness is done to place the blame for ineffective education on teachers, and not focus fault on the philosophy (*democratic* sociological methods) totally embraced by the shoddy U.S. education system.

And then on the writing part of the *GEPA* test, eighth-grade *students* are often asked to write on a subject they had never studied in school. English teachers all over the state have to abandon traditional curriculum to have *students* practice writing samples on *Cause and Effect*, *Controversial Issue* and *Problem Solving*, but the specific subject on the day of the test in any of those three writing areas is not known until *the test* is distributed.

Hours and hours of valuable class time are wasted on studying for a state standardized test that essentially lacks content validity. It's like me giving a vocabulary test on words that were never studied, or a literature test on stories that were never read, or a grammar test on chapters that were never covered. One thing I had learned from Dr. Trenoff in my college days was that such a test as the New Jersey *GEPA* lacked "reliability and validity".

Students are given a secret *Problem-Solving* question like, "How could you solve the homeless situation in your community?" The *children* are then expected to write a five-paragraph composition in thirty-five minutes on the random subject (Homeless People in Your Community) that the *students* probably had never thought of or cared about before. Steinbeck and Poe would probably have had trouble organizing their thoughts on such an arcane subject, and then writing five intelligent paragraphs in thirty-five minutes.

And the teachers are held accountable for the standardized test results! The *GEPA* preparation meant that a lot of Jack London, Mark Twain, and O. Henry had to be abandoned so that the *children* could practice writing samples in response to various practice writing prompts. And the worst part of the state writing test was that it was not a writing test, but actually first a *thinking* test. If a student became flustered and unable to think-out the secret *Problem-Solving* Solution, or to think-out the mysterious *Cause and Effect* scenario, or to think-out the remote *Controversial Issue*, then that *student* would be doomed to failure regardless of how well he or she could actually write on a more familiar topic.

It reached a point toward the end of my teaching career where I would have to spend sixty out of the hundred and eighty school days preparing for the *GEPA* writing question that was a secret known only to the state department of education.

One year only eighty-two percent of my eighth-graders passed the *GEPA* writing section, and the school administrators and my department supervisor were extremely upset at the low passing statistic, which I regarded as a minor miracle, considering the intellectual talent I had to work with that particular year.

"*Mr. Wiessner*, you'll have to spend additional time preparing for the *GEPA!*" I was told more than once.

The following year, ninety-six percent of the *students* passed the arcane *GEPA* writing section. "Great job *John!*" I was told and congratulated. "Next year, raise the bar to ninety-eight percent passing!" Right!

I neglected to tell the principal and my supervisor that the year ninety-six percent of my eighth-graders had passed the *GEPA,* I had spent only two class periods preparing for it. When only eighty-two percent had passed, I had devoted one-third of the English program to teaching the "secret state writing mystery test question scenario" that couldn't be taught.

State departments of education, college professors, educational psychologists and school administrators make teachers feel as if they are modern *Rumpelstiltskins* being commanded to change straw into gold. All of this state-generated madness is occurring nationwide, while at least twenty-five percent of the school population consists of identified "Special Needs *Students"*, with a second fifteen percent of the *students* hibernating within the building that are budding young terrorists, and a third fifteen percent of *students* that are generally lethargic and unmotivated.

Forty percent of the *students* in eighth-grade can't do eighth-grade work, and with the new state-mandated inclusion of all *students* in standard classrooms, all of the above are now in regular watered-down academic English classes. And the state and the district administrators still tell teachers that education must become more *thorough and efficient,* and the all-potent sultans insist that lazy and disinterested *students* need to be motivated.

While all of the bizarre insanity is prodigiously taking place, school administrators appear in local newspapers shaking hands with honor *students*, handing-out achievement certificates, and giving merit awards to deserving *children*. School officials make a teacher's responsibility more challenging by magnifying *the good* in the school, while the besieged classroom instructors must every day live with *the bad* and *the ugly*. All along the paper trail, the public gets the misconception that teaching is "a cake job" and that "teachers have it easy".

School administrators have a vested interest in maintaining the status quo. Everything in education, ranging from methods to curriculum, must change except school administration. Teachers must adjust to new state tests, new curriculums, new textbooks, new grade levels, and to new *students* and subjects each year.

First, the New Jersey school philosophy had evolved from "affective education" to "thorough and efficient education". Then

T&E switched into the "effective education". And despite all of those marvelous changes and titles that suggest improvement in quality, the schools and the society continue to deteriorate just like good old Plato had predicted would happen in an *inefficient democracy,* nearly twenty-five hundred years ago.

The whole administrative game plan is very simple: teachers are not supposed to feel too comfortable at any time and must always be changing subjects taught, grade levels taught, and commanded to loyally enforce *their* ever-evolving subject curriculums. But regardless of what colossal teacher changes and mandated adjustments that happen, school administration in 2021 must obsoletely function exactly as it had done in 1903.

Parental backdoor lobbying of school board members and associated administrators is another factor that undermines teacher professionalism, teacher authority and teacher respect in the local community. The code message teachers receive from everyday experience is that "You're on your own, especially when a crisis develops involving *you!* You're only as good as the last bad thing that happened in *your* classroom!"

Staff instructors quickly learn that they are making their lives more difficult, and placing their careers in jeopardy, by seriously trying to enforce true "efficiency standards" in an "inefficient system" that is engineered to fail. Don't be too academically demanding on *students* that are neglecting to do either homework or class work, or else, the nasty parents of the alluded-to nasty *children* will wear your shoes out "on the carpet" in the administrator's office. Most teachers learn to endorse the "lighten-up route", and just keep those eighth-graders with fourth-grade reading and writing skills riding upward on the legendary educational escalator.

The great American society needs to assess public school academic education as a *privilege* to be honored, and not as a *right* for everyone having malice or mischief in their hearts to attack and abuse. Until *that* distant day arrives, the rights of teachers along with the rights of good *students* will continue to be compromised by the *rights* and the destructive proclivities of disruptive *children.*

The state departments of education, the school administrators, and fanatical "education school college professors" will make sure that middle and high schools in the future will remain *inefficient.* That propensity will assure that the *democratic* comprehensive school maintains the present power position it occupies in American education. The Educational Aristocracy's game plan is to keep the blame on the teachers, while the entrenched educational bureaucratic elite gains more power and less responsibility for creating more of the messy quagmire the nation's public schools are in right now.

School administrators keep teachers subordinate to unprofessional manipulation be virtue of the Teachers Handbook, which contains several hundred pages of often-trivial school policies pertaining to mundane teacher responsibility (duties). A random passage from the Teachers Handbook is imperatively stated in the wording:

"No *student* will be summoned from a teacher's class by anyone except office personnel. The *student* will be called over the intercom by the office only in regard to *important matters*. In addition, *students* must not correct teacher papers or enter any grades in teacher record books. Delegating professional responsibilities to *students* is a breach of the teacher's chosen profession. All worksheets to be photocopied are to be done by the teacher and not by *students*."

Now here's how the administrative adminis*trivia* game works. *Subordinate* the entire faculty to a ton of minutia in the Teachers Handbook. Then violate the edicts in the handbooks because administrators have rank and privilege, and the faculty has the total school responsibilities and accountabilities.

Students are summoned to the office for a variety of petty reasons, and not for "important matters" as expressed in the Teachers Handbook. A forgetful *student* might be called over the intercom to the General Office to retrieve a lost book that had gotten found, to pay back lunch money borrowed from the office, or to learn that big brother or big sister will be picking him or her up after school. In effect, the office is actually rewarding irresponsible *students* for being negligent by having to constantly remind them of meeting their office obligations or their older brothers or sisters in the A-Wing parking lot.

Sometimes, the drone of *student* names being announced over the intercom is as lengthy as a boring Homeric catalogue in the *Iliad* or in the *Odyssey*. And although *students* can't do any work for teachers, many *student* office pages are nonchalantly assisting office secretaries dispense with many of their clerical chores.

The office secretaries have *student* office pages run-off papers on the duplicating machines, staple important confidential documents together, and also serve as inter-office couriers. One time, I observed one of my eighth-grade *students* (an office page) checking the names of teachers that had turned in their lesson plans for the following week. Many mornings, I had to wait my turn at the *Xerox* machine while conscientious office pages were running-off important documents for the office staff. It doesn't take beginning teachers long to realize that classroom academics and classroom teachers are *subordinate* to office discretion, no matter how trivial *it* may be.

So, in most schools, the mere act of teaching takes a back seat to adminis*trivia*. And teachers are constantly reminded to save the district money, while the school's office personnel squanders hundreds of reams of paper on trite memos' along with disposable, picayune announcement forms.

My school's *Xerox* machine had two starter keys for copy tallying. The first one was for the General Office use, and the second one was for all of the teachers on the faculty. If the office was so worried about saving money on paper products, the administrators should simply buy all its supplies from *Staples* instead of wasting hundreds of thousands of dollars annually making purchases from expensive educational catalog suppliers.

Teachers should not only reside in other communities than where they are employed, but also, their *children* should attend schools in other districts, too. I found that when my three sons passed through all twelve grades in the district where I had been employed, some teachers bent over backwards to give me daily reports on my sons' progress, while others treated them the same way they would handle any normal kids. But for some reason, the school administration came-down a little too harshly on two of my three sons.

Joey Wiessner was in eighth-grade in 1981. I had to chaperone a dance he was attending, so I dropped-off my son outside the school to wait for several of his friends. Then I entered the building. During the dance, a *student* informer told the principal that my oldest son had been drinking whiskey with three other boys behind a building across the street from the middle school.

While the dance was in progress, the determined principal separately interrogated the four accused boys, and my son confessed to taking a gulp under a dare, while the other three *students* denied any involvement in the incident, including the child that had brought the pint of whiskey. The on-a-mission principal suspended Joey for three days, while the other three boys got off the hook.

"But the boys were drinking off of school property!" I argued. "And all four of them were guilty of the same thing!"

"But your son confessed!" the principal insisted.

"So, you're gonna' lay the wood to my son because he was the only honest one!" I ranted. "A fine lesson you're teaching him here!

Lie and get off the hook! Tell the truth and be singled-out and ultimately punished!"

"That's the way I have to call it!" the chief school executive declared. 'I gotta' call them as I see them!"

'I just hope that this is not an indirect payback from the administration to me!' I thought. 'If the head honchos have something against me, don't take it out on my kid!'

In 2021 Joe Wiessner is now a successful real estate broker owning his own company, and having two prosperous business offices.

The most punishment that my second son John T. Wiessner ever received was a three-day detention for acting-up on one particular Washington DC trip. The class advisor had him and three of John's friends sit out on the motel's concrete steps from 1 a.m. to 3 a.m. for not going to sleep when the kids were supposed to be visiting dreamland. That penalty, I thought, was a case where the punishment was equal to the offense committed. J.T. Wiessner in 2021 is an actor, a model and a limo' chauffeur presently living in Woodbury, New Jersey.

However, with my youngest son Steve, my wife and I had a major disagreement with the high school administration. Steve was a superior high school basketball player, noted for his defensive prowess. The talented athlete was chosen for the league all-stars, and was given the honor of being selected to play in the all-league basketball tournament game. My wife and I were thrilled at our youngest son's basketball court achievement.

In Steve's last regular season basketball game, an opposing team's player's elbow slashed our son's scalp when Steve had driven to the hoop. Steve's head was bleeding profusely, so I immediately drove him to the local hospital to get stitches to sew-up his superficial scalp wound.

The following day, I was at the middle school teaching a late morning class when the curriculum coordinator rapped on my door and motioned for me to consult with him out in the hall. I told my *students* to finish doing the exercise on the grammar page we were working on, while I spoke with my unexpected visitor.

"John," the curriculum coordinator began. "I'll watch your class for you. You'd better go home right now!"

"What's up Ron?" I asked. "Why?"

"Because your son Steve has a bunch of seniors at your house right this moment," the informer related while whispering. "They call themselves the *Breakfast Club* after that popular movie!"

I thought about it for a long moment. "Look Ron, I don't want my son to have any special privileges to keep him out of trouble," I insisted. "If there are twenty or thirty high school kids at my house right now, then they all deserve equal punishment!"

"All right, if that's the way you want it!" the curriculum coordinator acknowledged. "The truant officer is going over to your place in about ten minutes. Are you sure that's what you want?"

"As long as everyone is punished the same, that's what I want!" I answered. "I appreciate you coming here and telling me, but no teacher's son should have preferential treatment!"

The truant officer did visit my house, but instead of rapping on the door, he trespassed inside. The thirty or so senior party-goers all fled the scene. The high school principal notified me over the telephone that afternoon of the disposition of the case.

"Mr. Wiessner, I spoke with the superintendent, and we have decided to suspend Steve from school!" the school executive imperatively informed me.

"What about the other thirty *students* that were there with him?" I asked. "Did they get suspended, too?"

"No, they didn't!" the principal related. "The other *students* had signed themselves out of school. Senior *students* have *that* special privilege, as you know!" the boss elaborated. "Steve was the guilty one because he had thrown the party at your home, and that's why the other seniors signed themselves out!"

"Now wait a minute!" I objected. "Steve was the only one at that party that had a bona fide, legitimate excuse for being absent from school. He had his head cut in the league basketball game last night, had stitches put in at the hospital, and then stayed home from school today to heal!" I argued to no avail.

"He's still suspended for three days!" the principal (that didn't like my leisure suits back in the early seventies) harshly reaffirmed.

In order for Steve to have the honor of playing in the league all-star game, the high school principal had to sign a release giving my son permission to participate. The approval paper that had to be signed was just a routine note stating that the *student* had not been involved in any current serious disciplinary action.

"The tournament game is a full week after my son's suspension expires!" I told the high school principal in his beautifully decorated office. "He should be off the hook!"

"I think this regrettable incident will teach your son a valuable lesson in responsibility!" the administrator austerely maintained. "I'm not going to sign the release!"

"But the tournament's event is happening at another high school!" I objected. "The suspension has expired! Steve has no other negative disciplinary incident anywhere in his entire school record! If the All-League-All-Star tournament were being held at *this* high school, I might have a little different slant on the matter!"

"I'm still not going to sign the release out of pure principle!" the principal adamantly reiterated.

"But Steve's the only player from this high school to be selected for that honor in the last five years!" I screamed like a maniac. "This is a once-in-a-lifetime opportunity for my son!"

"That will be all, *Mr. Wiessner!*" the closed-minded school executive remarked as he imperatively addressed me as a teacher *employee* and not as a taxpaying parent.

Steve Wiessner never did play in that once in a lifetime, all-league basketball game. Somehow my youngest son rose above that disciplinary adversity, graduated from Rutgers University, and is now employed in the city of Englewood, New Jersey as the Executive Director of a large environmental center.

Chapter 50
"Multicultural Education"

I had been named into "Who's Who Among American Teachers!" three times and two of those nominations have been by minority *students* (now Dean's List college achievers), one black and one Hispanic. Those *minority students* realized that *my* classroom standards were just as tough on them as they were on the majority Caucasian *students,* and that I gave them no special favoritism, slack or handicap for their minority-status ethnicity. I had always refused to "dumb down" the English curriculum (Grammar, Vocabulary, Literature, Writing Skills) to accommodate Accelerated English *students* that lacked motivation, desire, curiosity, cooperation, respect for teacher authority, and a willingness to learn.

A year before I retired in 1999, my Middle School's English Department had a special curriculum meeting, and the Administration and my Grade-Level Supervisor wanted to change and "modernize" the literature textbook program. The choice eventually narrowed-down to two distinct textbook series (grades six-to-eight), and my department's nine English teachers voted on which company's series to incorporate into the school's English curriculum. Obviously, administrative fiat (and pressure and trends from the State Department of Education) was more important than teacher *democratic* input, and the English Department's personnel overwhelmingly selected first choice was abruptly discarded because the other more "politically correct" literature textbook series from the administratively preferred company happened to have "more cultural diversity", and subsequently, was more "multicultural".

For thirty-four years, I had loved teaching imaginative literature featuring such accomplished authors including Edgar Allan Poe, Jack London, Nathaniel Hawthorne, Alexander Dumas, Charles Dickens, H.G. Wells, Washington Irving, Jules Verne, Mark Twain, S.E. Hinton, George Eliot, Sir Arthur Conan Doyle, Victor Hugo, William Shakespeare, George Orwell, Kurt Vonnegut, O. Henry, and James Thurber. Apparently, the fact that all of the aforementioned famous authors were "white" was a major problem because most of them had been effectively *excluded* in the newly-acquired middle school literature texts. The old literature texts and program were too "white-oriented", and were not consistent with New Jersey and USA politically-correct trends in "Multicultural Education".

The new eighth-grade literature textbook featured on its cover a painting of Sam Adoquei's *Portrait of Rockney C*. And a statement inside the text indicated that Sam Adoquei was born in the West African country of Ghana, and that Adoquei was a contemporary artist that loved painting landscapes. Older literature textbooks might have featured on their covers works by Michelangelo, Rembrandt, Vincent van Gogh, or Leonardo DaVinci, but in this day and age, those great contributing Renaissance artists of *Western Civilization* have been demoted (in public schools) in deference to people like Sam Adoquei of Ghana, West Africa.

I must honestly admit that the new eighth-grade administratively selected (and faculty overruled) literature textbook did have a token representation of established white authors. However, the bulk of the contributors had names like Gloria Gonzalez (Cuban American), Luci Tapahonso (Navajo Indian), Yoshiko Uchida (Oriental American), Gwendolyn Brooks (Black American), Gary Soto (son of California migrant workers), William Saroyan (Armenian American), Maya Angelou (Black American), Diane Mei Lin Mark (Hawaiian American), Julio Noboa Polanco (bilingual poet), Judith Ortiz Cofer (Puerto Rican), Langston Hughes (Black American), Julia Alvarez (Hispanic), Ophelia Rivas (Mexican), Nereida Roman (Hispanic), Rudolfo A. Anaya (Mexican American), Esmerela Santiago (Puerto Rican), Wing Tex Lum (Chinese poet), Naomi Shihab Nye (Palestinian), Ved Mehta (from India), Paul Yee (American Chinese) and Li-Young Lee (Chinese).

There is no doubt in my mind that Multicultural Education is contributing to *socialistically* "dumbing-down" American public schools. Many of the obscure "authors" being presented to American *students* in the name of "cultural diversity" have produced works that have weak vocabulary, shallow plots, lackluster characters, non-intellectual subject matter, and exhibit demonstrably unsophisticated writing skills. Yet these minority *writers* (I wouldn't call all of them "authors") are presented to naïve and impressionable eighth-graders as being valuable contributors to literature, when *their* works pale in comparison to those of more traditional great *Western Civilization authors* that are presently being systematically removed from literature textbooks, and gradually being replaced by (in most cases) obscure or lesser known "minority authors".

The same type of phenomenon is happening in middle and high school "History" classes' as is happening in Literature courses. When *Martin Luther King Day* was established as a National Holiday celebrated in January, George Washington and Abraham

Lincoln had to be diminished in stature to accommodate *MLK* on the school calendar. The traditional holidays of *Washington's Birthday* and *Lincoln's Birthday* were shrewdly consolidated into "*Presidents Day*", with "Washington and Lincoln's regular February birthdays being abandoned to allow room for *Martin Luther King Day* in January on the school calendar. And February (which used to almost exclusively belong to Washington and Lincoln) is now declared "Black American Month" in schools across the country. It is no wonder (or coincidence) that American *children* now know more about Harriet Tubman, Crispus Attucks, Malcolm X, Jesse Jackson and George Washington Carver than they do about George Washington, Abraham Lincoln, Thomas Jefferson, Franklin D. Roosevelt and Dwight David Eisenhower. History (and literature) is being re-written by contemporary *re-visionists* that are attempting to diminish and discredit the accomplishments of white people, and simultaneously magnify the deeds and works of lesser-known minority figures.

One unique irony of all this Multicultural and curricular craziness is that teachers are now being held accountable for higher standardized test scores and "higher academic performance", when *their* curriculums are being systematically watered-down and diluted to allow accommodation for the new-found priority implementation of "Multicultural Education".

Stories (by minority writers) in literature now have simple vocabulary and easy-to-understand (more simplistic) themes, characters and plots. Presently teachers are compelled to "teach-down" to the *students'* level of achievement instead of challenging the kids seated in the desks to raise *their* level of performance up to the plateau of superior subject matter content being read and studied in the works of Poe, Twain, Shakespeare and Orwell. And this sort of insane farce is happening in public schools all over America.

Teachers are being coerced into propagating a system of American public-school education that is both designed and destined to fail. Teachers are not only accountable for teaching "weaker subject matter content" with low-academic challenge; they are also now held accountable to the State for *students* acquiring sufficient subject matter skills for the learners to pass state sponsored "*academic* standardized tests". Whatever happened to the concept of individual (*student*) responsibility?

"Multicultural Education" should not be eliminated from the curriculum, but it should be diminished in influence to allow for a more accurate perspective of Literature and History to be presented to American school *children*. Crispus Attucks and Harriet Tubman should not supplant George Washington and Abraham Lincoln in February as historical equals sharing common textbook prominence. And furthermore, M.E. should be a part of regular traditional public-school History, Literature, Math' and Science courses, and not the entire curriculum in central core subject areas.

And there's no way that Sam Adoquei is in the same league as Picasso, or that Gloria Gonzalez and Yoshiko Uchida are the literary equivalents of Mark Twain and O. Henry. Our great American culture is being distorted and perverted enough by *MTV, VH-1* and by the *Comedy Channel,* without ineffective social engineering and an excess of Multicultural Education polluting our American public-school *students,* and also our public schools already ambivalent academic standards.

I have been scrutinizing and studying Multicultural Education for four decades now, and have heard too-many-times the lackluster educational jargon originating from college professors and from misguided advocates of M.E., and quite frankly, those "elitist arguments" have become rather redundant, hackneyed and monotonous. And to think that I once wholeheartedly espoused those ethereal Multicultural Education principles as an idealistic teacher beginning my career back in September of 1965.

Despite the "Happy Face" that supporters of Multicultural Education are attempting to promote and propagandize, one distinct adjective comes to mind whenever I think about Multicultural Education, and that particular dominant word is "insidious". To the unsuspecting layman or college student, "Diversity through M.E." is a nifty catch phrase that sounds awfully noble and pleasant to the ears upon hearing its utterance, but the process is actually quite detrimental to the implementation of effective American education. I deliberately describe the scourge as *insidious* because over the past forty years, M.E. has imperceptibly and very cunningly been introduced, advanced, and perpetuated by its militant proponents without the American public realizing exactly how harmful, how treacherous, and how detrimental the seemingly benign terminology appears to be.

Multicultural Education never clearly defines and identifies itself to the American public for what it really is. U.S. citizens automatically equate and associate M.E. with Bilingual Education and *ESL* (English as a Second Language), which the clever campaigners for M.E. never lucidly delineate and differentiate. Bilingual Education and *ESL* are indeed definite, positive, beneficial and necessary programs in our American public schools. Those two essential programs encourage and facilitate the cultural "Melting Pot" ideal, whereby immigrant and certain minority *students* learn English and *ESL,* and are hopefully successfully assimilated into regular grade-level classrooms after two-to-four years of exposure to a new language and a new culture.

But Multicultural Education is the complete opposite and inverse of Bilingual Education and *ESL.* Here's what Multicultural education really is: It is an attempt to manipulate History, English, Literature, Math' and Science to make those subjects appear to *all students* in *all classrooms* that blacks, Hispanics and other minorities have contributed as much (if not more) to *Western Civilization* than Einstein, Jefferson, Washington, Thoreau, Shakespeare, Cervantes, Hugo, Twain, Newton, Steinbeck, Hemingway, Poe, Socrates, Plato, Aristotle, H.G. Wells, Arthur Conan Doyle, Abraham Lincoln and other noteworthy Caucasians have.

Multicultural Education attempts to diminish in stature the great "White" benefactors of the *Western World,* while simultaneously elevating the works of obscure minorities to *their* plane. And the entire *student* body is exposed to and forced to suffer through this ruse in *their* various core curriculum textbooks, and it's not just *ESL students* and Bilingual Education *children* who are being exposed to the ongoing brainwashing. And once the American public fully recognizes *that* important concept separating M.E. from Bilingual Education and *ESL,* Multicultural Education will finally be satisfactorily challenged and ultimately rejected.

Although the Multicultural Education academic elitists claim to be "visionaries", they are in effect *critical race theory revisionists.* Their impractical goal is to create a Utopian *future* by first rewriting the *past,* and next changing the *present.* First, relegate icons like Shakespeare, Cervantes, Jefferson and Newton and then give equal or greater stature to James Baldwin, Langston Hughes, Jesse Jackson and George Washington Carver. It is true that George Washington Carver remarkably found over three hundred applied uses for the peanut, but the Multicultural Education activists want us to believe that the renowned black scientist is just as important to American culture, science, technology and history as is Thomas Edison, Albert Einstein, Franklin Delano Roosevelt, Bill Gates, Steve Jobs, and Thomas Edison. I don't think so!

This is not to say that minority inventors and authors are not to be studied in public schools. As a teacher, I remember enjoying reading terrific biographies of Louis Armstrong, Harriet Tubman and

Ralph Bunche with my literature classes, but if Multicultural Education advocates have their way, *that type* of minority-oriented reading should constitute the bulk of the Literature, History, Math' and Science curriculums being taught in our schools. And I truly admire the accomplishments of Colin Powell, Condie Rice, and Clarence Thomas because those African Americans didn't need any cause, any movement, or any national organization to inspire their' minds, hearts, and souls to pursue excellence. They (according to the American free enterprise tradition) reached-down inside and motivated themselves "as individuals" to strive for greatness, but many liberal socialistic Multiculturalists will call the three cited black achievers "Uncle Toms", since they have succeeded in the American competitive capitalistic culture on their own without a massive crusade or national "special interest agenda" advancing their *individual* attainments.

To get their stubborn way, the M.E. elitists must shrewdly label and demonize traditional curriculum by calling it "Eurocentric", which automatically connotes a bad, Anti-American moniker. The long-range objective of the M.E. masterminds is to first condemn "Eurocentric" History, Literature and Science, and then to systematically dismantle *"Western Civilization" and "Christianity"*, which in reality is what the stereotype "Eurocentic" means.

I have eight elementary questions that pertain to significant developments in the history of mankind to ask the Multicultural elitists:

1) Where did the concept of *Democracy* begin? (Clue: the city is the capital of Greece)

2) Where did the *Renaissance* happen? (Clue: a country that has   cities Florence, Rome and Venice)

3) Where did the *Age of Exploration and Discovery* begin? (Clue: cities like Genoa, Lisbon and London)

4) Where did the *Age of Enlightenment* have its roots? (Clue: Cities are found on rivers *Seine* and *Thames*)

5) Where did the *Protestant Reformation* take place? (Clue: Main players were Martin Luther of Germany and Henry the VIII of England)

6) Where did the *Industrial Revolution* get started? (Clue: a country that has cities named Manchester, Coventry, Sheffield, Leeds and New Castle)

7) Where did the *Atomic Age* happen? (Clue: the country has an eagle and an old chap named *Uncle Sam* as its symbols)

8) Where did the *Computer Age* have its origins? (Clue: corporations named *IBM, Microsoft, Intel,* and *Apple* inspired it to happen)

The phenomenal freedoms that Americans enjoy today are outgrowths from the eight Eurocentric eras just enumerated. The concept of *Democracy* had originated in Athens in ancient Greece. The *Renaissance* liberated the human spirit and gave birth to cultural creativity. The *Age of Discovery* and *Exploration* sent men on great adventures to distant continents. The *Age of Enlightenment* swiftly led to the development of modern-day political philosophy. The *Protestant Reformation* loosened church tyrannical authority and created an atmosphere where thinkers could contemplate and publish their works, where scientists could freely experiment, and established an atmosphere where inventors could create.

This new-found freedom of thought and expression eventually led to the development of Constitutional governments where the rights of citizens were protected under law. This fantastic, novel revolutionary *"Western Civilization"* liberty led to freedom of thought, which led to discovery, which led to technology, which led to progress and eventually, to our contemporary American (and European) way of life and high standards of living.

But if the determined Multicultural Education zealots had their druthers, the eight important eras of *Western Civilization* would be diminished and relegated because they are "Eurocentric", while in the process, the accomplishments of minorities will be elevated, given accolades, and praised in our public schools, thus dooming our *students* to perpetual mediocrity.

Now, knowing the above-mentioned salient facts, the majority of adult Americans would prefer having their *children* exposed to the same kind of "Eurocentric" education that *they* had received and understood in the past as *"Western Civilization."* Every mature U.S. citizen with any scruples wishes to have the culture and history of America expertly transmitted to the younger generation, for *that* particular function is one of the central purposes of schools besides teaching our *students* vital skills in reading, writing, speaking, mathematics, science and thinking. But if the adamant M.E. crusaders had their way, teachers would have to pretend that *Western Civilization* never happened, and be forced to preach that minorities were equally (if not more) responsible for the prosperity, economy and government that America presently maintains and enjoys.

The goal of Multiculturalists is to make every public-school *student* into a (tribal) member of a *UN* model "global village". This is why Multicultural Education is both un-American and unpatriotic. And those stubborn Multicultural Education advocates are very inflexible and quite obstinate in superimposing their convictions on the remainder of us, too. The M.E. proponents want you to believe that M.E. is a powerful new "science" and not a topic that should be comprehended as a "controversial issue" having an opposing, valid point of view.

I had submitted a critique of M.E. to a college professor that maintains an "Essays on Multicultural Education" *Internet* website. The academic elitist refused to post my article on the basis that my submission was a prejudiced and biased view of Multicultural Education based on popular "stereotypes". Well now, isn't that a wicked contradiction! The M.E. advocates suddenly take on a "ban-the-essay censorship Fascist mentality" when someone who values *Western Civilization* dares to present an alternative position on *their* suspect pet subject.

And this is perhaps the greatest danger that will materialize should intellectual democratic elitist educators get their way: intolerance to other people's points of view, and a blatant violation of *First Amendment* freedom of speech rights. And the irony of it all is that Multicultural Education is masked, marketed and sold as "democratic education". Such a canard is advertised as making American public-school *children* more aware of "diversity". I suppose *that* specific definition does not include *diversity* of opinions, or the allowance of contrary philosophical positions about Multicultural Education.

Once the general public fathoms the true nature of the Multicultural Education fanatics' motives, I am fully convinced that the adherents and their movement will subsequently be soundly defeated. Their radical agenda (and they do have an agenda) is disguised as (and masquerades as) a vital feature of "Educational Democracy (Socialism)," which conceals itself under the false mantle of "Educational Democratic Equality for All".

But if all *students* are *equal*, therefore no *student* could ever become more *academically* superior, more-wealthy, more outstanding, more achievement-oriented, or more creative, as long as he or she remains in a public school under the dominion of "Educational Socialism". In the Multicultural Education Universe, there can be no Valedictorians or Salutatorians because that type of *academic* honor *discriminates* against the masses, and makes the average *student* (minority or otherwise) feel inferior. "Just try and blend in with everyone else! Let's have a Melting Pot or giant mixing salad!" is the watchword of the M.E. enthusiasts.

Educational Socialism and Multicultural Education are conveniently bolstered in many classroom subjects with the implementation of a Neo-Industrial-Education-Factory-Oriented Classroom Model. As has been alluded to before, our American public schools are run like factories. Administrators and supervisors are the bosses, boards of education are the boards of directors, taxpayers are the stockholders, teachers are regarded as the employees within the system, and the *students* are the products of a twelve-year-long manufacturing process. This educational factory model has been in existence for over a hundred years now, and as long as it persists, and as long as administrators are influenced by state-supported mandates like Multicultural Education, then *mass mediocrity* will, in the final-analysis, be the end result. Schools are operated like factories, and Multicultural Education will still guarantee a very nondescript product (the homogenized "salad-Melting Pot *students*" constituting the entire *student* body).

Now here's where and why I believe that Multicultural Education will ultimately be vanquished. Multicultural Education proponents are generally also Educational Socialists. In addition to desiring to dismantle *Western Civilization* (calling it "Eurocentric"), the cultural saboteurs absolutely loathe capitalism, hating the indispensable economic engine of America. If it weren't for "free enterprise" (capitalism) and the economic security that the accumulation of personal (individual) wealth affords and provides, then our great American democracy would be vulnerable to eroding, eventually decaying into chronic civil unrest, and gradually heading in the direction of national anarchy.

Think about it! Our *free* enterprise economy is what makes Americans truly *free,* and the essential economic idea of "risk-reward" is hardly ever taught in our public schools, because it involves free enterprise and *individual* achievement.

But Ivory Tower Educational Socialists think that "capitalism" and "competition" cause *students* to become selfish, arrogant, and greedy without *sharing* with others. The loony university liberal arts professor frowns upon American Capitalism as being a negative influence, simply because the notion of *free enterprise* engenders *students* becoming too egocentric and independent, and therefore, capable of being distinguished as achievement-oriented *individuals* from the rest of the group (their *student comrades*).

In M.E. classrooms, *students* are discouraged from thinking outside the box, because then the independent-minded, future adults would be an obvious danger to the system, and would represent a threat to the dominance of Educational Socialism. Blend in and be exactly like everyone else inside the great *American Melting Pot*. Be an average pepper, a regular carrot, or a mediocre onion in the Giant American Salad. Don't aspire to accomplish more than your fellow *students,* and never be exposed to the evils of capitalism and free enterprise. "Now let's eliminate grades so that everyone can think and be on the same level at all times because we're all *equal*." That is another immediate goal of these educational, socialistic maniacs.

Capitalism (a wonderful concept of past Eurocentric *Western Civilization*) is the great hope and foundation of any free and democratic society. Capitalism (Wall Street and Main Street) is what gives the *United States of America* its stability and security. Heaven forbid that our entrepreneurs and risk takers are ever silenced! Those contributors employ people, and those same ambitious pioneers open new frontiers, thus establishing new dynamic *independent* businesses and corporations.

It's all quite simple and "Elementary, dear Watson!" as Sherlock Holmes would often state. Without capitalism, there would be no profits, no private-sector employees, fewer taxes being paid, no Wall Street companies, no Main Street businesses, fewer government programs, fewer public schools, fewer college endowments being financed and contributed to, and no personal wealth being created. Without capitalism, the *United States'* flourishing economy would soon deteriorate and go the way of the *Soviet Union*.

Thank Heaven that free enterprise is still the most vibrant and productive force in America! But please remember: college professors in general are liberal-minded, and many of the charlatans are elitists that despise free enterprise while simultaneously advancing the causes of Educational Socialism, of Karl Marx, of John Dewey, and of Multicultural Education.

Instead of endorsing a hypothesis that postulates that America is a great Melting Pot where all public-school students are *equal* (the same), American Education needs to get back on the right track and instruct its students, "If you want to achieve individual prosperity, become a capitalist and not a factory or office worker. You have the potential to become an employer, and not settle for just being an employee. Pursue excellence and work hard towards everything that you attempt or do, and never simply settle for being just like everyone else in a cultural salad! Dig deep-down inside yourself and produce more than your peers! Become viable, and be a true, productive *individual,* and don't be satisfied just being *socialistically* referred to as one!"

But *that* particular inspiration will never happen on a broad scale as long as elitist Educational Socialists (that hate American capitalism and past America) and Multicultural Educationists (that resent "Eurocentric" history and literature) are at the academic helm, wielding tremendous influence over the fate of millions of American public-school *students*. "Ambition" is now an absolute dirty word in American education! It suggests that an aggressive, self-motivated *child* will distinguish himself or herself from his or her fellow *students,* and that *student* will learn to grow, understand self-actualization, and excel as an individual.

The self-proclaimed critics of free enterprise again use labeling to endeavor smearing and debunking capitalism, accusing the greedy method of being "trickle-down economics"! But will someone please explain to me how gravity could be successfully defied by having "trickle-up economics"? And I boldly venture to state that most Multicultural Education elitists are also Educational Socialists.

In conclusion, only free enterprise (and our *students'* awareness of and their belief in its greatness), a continuation of the teachings of *Western Civilization,* and some sober realistic thinking will ensure the future of the *United States of America*. The public must first become aware that Multicultural Education is the problematic antithesis of this country's past glory. But as long as Multiculturalists are powerful players on the national stage performing their egregious harm inside American Educational Philosophy and Psychology, our public schools are destined and doomed to mediocrity.

Multicultural Education isn't even an irrelevant placebo, let alone a civilization-saving elixir. Our only hopes for a prosperous future are Free Enterprise (capitalism) and the preservation of *Western Civilization*, two extraordinary disciplines that the educational elite (in general) ignore, abhor and reject. Remember that the opposite of the phrase "Cultural Unity" is the phrase "Multicultural Diversity".

And it was principally because of *that* "politically correct and multicultural" new literature textbook series that had been administratively imposed upon my middle school's English Department that convinced me it would be quite expedient for John Wiessner to retire from the teaching profession after thirty-four years of dedicated classroom instruction.

Chapter 51
"The End of a Career"

Up until 1995, I had worked for administrators that were all older than I was. After 1995, my employment was under the dominion of less-experienced superiors that were somewhat intimidated by the veteran teachers on the middle school staff. I got the impression that the new generation of school executives wanted a faculty that was loyal to *them,* and the school administrators were a trifle defensive when dealing with instructors that were fixtures in the school system thirty years before the new power elite had made *their* appearances.

I knew that the end of my teaching career was near when instructional methods gradually changed to promoting sociological activity-oriented classrooms, as opposed to the traditional academic structured teacher-guided, teacher-centered approach. Hostile parent conferences increased in frequency from around four a year to eight. I had taught over four thousand *students* in thirty-four years, and I began thinking that I should go out with dignity while I was still on top of my game, and remarkably, still had most of my marbles.

I was not getting along too well with my supervisor, and also with the vice-principal, who both were my juniors by around two decades. The supervisor would always be putting *Mickey Mouse* memos into my mailbox, and I would correct all of the grammar and spelling errors (and there were many), and then rebelliously return them. The vice-principal was catering to hostile parents, and acting like *their* surrogate representative acting against teachers, rather than deflecting the overprotective meddlers into "complaint oblivion" where *they* rightfully belonged. I instinctively knew that the new school leadership wanted the old faculty to go, and in so doing, have teachers that *they* had hired and who were beholding to *them.*

And most of my old buddies had already retired from the *profession* including Bob Gordon, Tim Carley, Ron LeFey, Phil Tweston, Jim Kyle, Larry DeLancy and Rob Renbeck. Dean Miles had moved to another district in Pennsylvania, Tim Amoro had become a principal in another New Jersey town, Ron Carputis was now a curriculum coordinator in my district, Joe Sacci was now a school supervisor, and John Rizzo had gone into the oil business. Charlie Southard, John Magliari, Mrs. Finnian, Jack DeCicco and Bill Catello had over the years all died.

Mack Fascito had wanted me to retire with him in June of '99, but I was hesitant. As the school year progressed, I soon became more and more interested in the prospect of living to see retirement.

"Mack, I want to stay around for one more year and retire in 2000," I confided. "It's a nice round figure!"

"What difference does it make?" Mack maintained. "All the old guys are gone. The administration and your supervisor are gonna' make life miserable for you and besides, the board of education is offering a buyout for our amassed sick days. How many wonderful years have you accumulated?"

"Over two hundred and fifty!" I proudly answered.

"That means you're eligible for the maximum buyout!" Mack persuasively evaluated. "I think the time has come!"

"I think you're right!" I agreed. "The principal told me that the accumulated sick day buyout would be only a special one-year-deal. Take it or leave it! The window closes on September 1st!"

I was becoming quite fatigued from the rigors of teaching after my thirtieth year in the classroom. For several tolerable years in the early 1990s, I had been assigned to develop a special "Literature-Oriented Curriculum" for the 8th Grade Talented and Gifted Class. In May of the second year of my implementing the dynamic new program, the curriculum coordinator came into my classroom after school to hold a brief conference.

"John," the supervisor sanctimoniously began. "The administration has decided to alter the 'T and G' literature program you've put-together, and substitute it with the recent board-approved 'Great Books' teaching unit. You'll have to take three weeks off in July and attend a special workshop in Philly' at Temple University to study teaching the new course."

"I can't do that!" I maintained. "I have an important summer employment at Atlantic Blueberry Company. I'm the Field Manager in charge of 24 crew-leaders and 1,200 daily pickers."

"If you don't go to the Temple seminar, we'll have to take the Talented and Gifted program away from you, and give you another regular English class or cafeteria duty."

After losing the Talented and Gifted class and gaining another year of daily cafeteria duty, I quickly turned sour towards the omnipotent administration and its 'imperial fiat behavior'. I felt that I had labored rather extensively in organizing a terrific reading program that was far superior to the one that the administration wished for me to replace.

'I'm merely an expendable pawn on the principal's chessboard,' I sadly-but-realistically concluded. 'I believe I just got *rooked,*' I conjectured, remembering a joke that Bill Catello had once told me when we were both permanent subs' way back in the late 1960s.

I still kept my summer employment as a field manager at Atlantic Blueberry Company, the world's largest cultivated blueberry farm. I figured that since my wife was still teaching, that I would try substituting two or three days a week starting in September of '99 to keep my mind and spirit active.

Substitute teaching was not exactly a royal cup of tea. And local school districts were only paying substitutes seventy dollars a day. 'Gee, if I work for a hundred and eighty days as a sub',' I thought, 'I can make a whopping twelve-thousand-six-hundred-dollars! The average cleaning lady makes more than seventy-dollars-a-day cash, without deductions!' I mused. 'If it weren't for my pension and my sick day buy-out, I would be eligible for food stamps!'

Substitute teachers really have their hands full when taking on an assignment. *Students'* eyes light-up when they suddenly realize that the regular teacher is absent. The *children* have their own glossary of words to describe that festive realization: "Party!" "Kill!" and "Fun Time!" are some of the vernacular terms that naughty *students* use while their eyes widen as if they are a pride of lions spotting a fat, wounded water buffalo the very minute the sly instigators notice a vulnerable substitute ambling into the classroom.

Substitutes encounter interesting experiences such as chalk in eraser grooves, tacks or chewing gum wads on the teacher's desk chair, and *students* changing their seats to see if the sub' is smart enough to read a seating chart to relocate the *children* where they actually belong. *Students* will volunteer misinformation about where the regular teacher had left-off in the textbook, and often initially will try to leave the room at every possible opportunity to make a phone call, to visit the lavatory, or to take a stroll to the nurse's office. A hard day of substituting could wind-up being just about as rewarding as a full day touring the New York City sewer system.

"I would have to substitute one whole week to stay in a decent New York hotel for one night with meals included!" I told my wife.

"Grin and bear it!" Joanne answered. "A day of substituting at least pays the television cable bill!"

"Yes, but that's not including any premium channels or a digital box having many viewing options!" I elaborated.

One of my first substituting assignments was at a neighboring district's elementary school. The principal told me that I was to be in charge of only one male *student* that had In-School Suspension.
"How old is the boy?" I inquired.
"Five years old; a kindergarten kid!" the administrator informed.
"What did this *child* do to warrant In-School Suspension?" I inquisitively asked.
"He became angry and kicked a male teacher in the testicles during cafeteria period," the principal almost-guiltily replied. "I know you have plenty of experience with *students* and can easily handle the *child!*"
The volatile kid cried and protested for an hour and a half in the detention office, so I took him to the cafeteria and bought him plenty of snacks. After that "reward", I decided to bend the rules, became his friend and we played *Bingo*, checkers and card games until the 3:15 dismissal bell finally rang.
Any time a substitute comes into contact with a hundred and thirty *students* in an eight-period day, that instructor is bound to have conflict with at least one. I was subbing at the local high school in March of 2000. After taking attendance, I was ten minutes into the lesson when a *student* stood-up and started walking out of the room. "Where are you going?" I politely asked him. "I never filled-out a pass for you to exit."
"Oh, I'm not a *student* in this class!" the wandering nomad answered. "This is my lunch period, so I thought I'd just sit-in and see how *you* were doing!"
"Enjoy your lunch!" I responded with a smile. I registered in my mind what the anonymous sixteen-year-old junior-droll *child* looked like. Every time that same *student* was in a class where I was substituting, I would ask him, "Shouldn't you be in lunch now? The first time I had you in a Spanish II class, you were *out to lunch!*" The boy would always blush at my allusion, and then slouch-down in his desk in sheer admiration every time I mentioned those wonderful words as a reminder to him that I still possessed most of my scruples and had not yet entered senility.
Another time at the local high school, I had entered a remedial Mathematics classroom, and all the *children* were milling around. "Please sit-down so that I can take attendance and get the Math' lesson started!" I implored the twenty-six seemingly uncooperative and disenchanted *students*.
Everyone eventually abided by my request with the exception of one haughty junior girl. "Mrs. Warner lets us walk around and talk to

each other all the time!" the female arrogantly insisted. "Why do I have to listen to you?"

"Because Mrs. Warner isn't here today and I am!" I replied. "Now just sit-down, and enjoy my company, so that things can start in an orderly, organized manner!"

"You're mean! Do ya' know that?" the girl accused while still not sitting-down. "The principal or the guidance department should send you down to see the shrink!"

"Look!" I exclaimed. "I think you're being very uncooperative under the circumstances! I don't believe that asking you to sit-down is too much of a demand!" I added. "Why do you suppose these desks are in the classroom? Waiting for termites to devour them?"

"I've had about enough of your rude shit!" the girl yelled. "You're an asshole!" the distraught, judgmental girl screamed as she swiftly bolted out of the A-Wing classroom honoring *flight* in the notorious "fight or flight" mindset.

No smirking *student* in the class would tell me who the nasty girl was, so I quickly took roll and figured it out for myself. I buzzed the office and reported the girl as being *AWOL*.

"Oh, she's sitting in the office waiting to see either the principal or vice-principal right now!" the Main Office secretary related over the intercom. "I believe she's complaining about *you*! Send down a Discipline Referral Card on the *student* after *you* have time to write one up! The vice-principal will look into the matter."

I assigned the day's Math' lesson indicated in the absent teacher's lesson plan book, and then I wrote-up the aforementioned discipline card. A friend of the defiant young Miss (who was now seated in the office) raised her hand and requested to go to the lavatory.

"Okay, I'll write you out a pass as soon as I finish with authoring this Discipline Referral Card," I promised.

"I have to go right now because I'm having my period and I gotta' get a rag' from the nurse!" the girl snottily replied.

"Look, I promise you, you'll be out of here in just another minute!" I respectfully answered as I jotted-down the final information describing the first classroom incident with the other insolent girl. "Please try to have a little patience and extend to me some basic courtesy!"

"Fuck you!" the girl indignantly squealed as she defiantly walked-out of the classroom without possessing a hall pass. "Asshole!" she yelled-out into the otherwise quiet and empty corridor.

I had remembered the second girl's name because I had taught her when she used to be a respectful eight-grader three years before. I wrote-down the second incident on the back of the Discipline Card and reported the perturbed second girl as also being *AWOL* from the erratic Math' class.

The office secretary called the classroom over the intercom. "Mr. Wiessner, the new school policy is that two *students* can't be listed on the same Discipline Referral Card," the stern voice specified. "You'll have to present two separate cards to the office for each of the incidents involving the two different girls!"

I spent the balance of the period re-doing the first card, and then writing-up the second regrettable repulsive event. The class had become silent and cooperative once the remaining *students* realized that the substitute sitting in the front desk was not afraid to assert some authority and send *students* down to the vice-principal's office.

After the class was dismissed at the ringing of the bell, I had a teacher lunch period, so I had time to then drop-off the two discipline cards in the Main Office. As I was entering the sacred sanctuary, I observed two policemen dragging a hysterical girl (I had never seen before) out of the vice-principal's cubicle.

When I arrived at the teacher's lounge to consume my brown-bagged lunch and to enjoy a *Coke,* I asked the other faculty members seated at the table if anyone knew what had happened with the girl being taken into custody by the police.

"Oh," a social studies teacher said. "The *student* had called Mr. Jackson an *asshole* because she didn't like the way he had graded her essay question on a test!"

"So, regular teachers receive that kind of back-talk just like victimized substitutes do!" I laughed.

"Yes, Jackson wrote her up," the female Social Studies teacher continued, "and the vice-principal told the *student* to go to In-School Suspension because she had accumulated a whole series of violations, but the girl refused to budge from the chair in *his* office!"

"And then the vice-principal called the police?" I asked.

"Yes. I was in the Main Office at the time," another teacher seated at the lunch table politely interrupted. "The assistant-principal told the girl that if she didn't get up and go to In-School Suspension that then, she would be trespassing in his office! The girl was stubborn and refused to get-up, so the cops hustled her out of the building while she was screaming like a maniac!"

"You don't know how lucky you are being retired!" the first teacher added. "I wish I were *you* right now!" she honestly congratulated me on my thirty-four-year career.

I glanced around the crowded high school faculty room and noticed only one familiar face that I had known from the past. I felt like *Rip Van Winkle* must have when he had returned to his native village after sleeping for twenty years up in the *Catskill Mountains*. All of *his* old chums and cronies were sadly gone from the village.

I walked to the men's room and noticed that one thing hadn't changed in the last thirty years. The same *Coke* machine that Bob Gordon, Tim Carley and I had moved to trap John Magliari inside the teachers' lounge's men's room was still situated in the exact same spot it had occupied.

On my way to instruct the next class, I noticed a destructive-minded *student* walking down the crowded C-Wing corridor breaking four balloons in a row with his long fingernails. The decorations, along with accompanying crepe paper, were festooning the hallways because the high school football team was to play a major opponent later that week in an important league game.

'Let another teacher notice and report the balloon breakings!' I thought. 'I've already written-out two too many discipline cards today! Give me a break!' I pleaded as my eyes rolled-up to briefly view the C-corridor's ceiling panels.

Twenty feet ahead down the corridor, Mr. Joe Wilkins had deftly intercepted the *student* breaking the balloons and started escorting the young violator to the Main Office for a ride on the all-too-familiar discipline carousel.

Eighth period study hall was an absolute nightmare that afternoon. I was alone and in charge of fifty restive-but-lethargic *students* that just wanted to fool around and talk. I separated them into sets of two at various cafeteria tables, despite their group protesting. Two girls and a boy refused to break-up and move to another table. Finally, they did so, and the young ladies then tried grossing me out.

"Hey man, did you ever have sex on a washing machine when it was runnin'?" the first girl asked me.

"That's too personal of a question," I answered. "Now please move to another table or I'll have to write you up."

"Once I had sex with my boyfriend in the back of a church while a service was going on!" the second young Amazon disrespectfully informed me. "What do ya' think about that?"

"Look young lady, there are at least three ambitious *students* in this mass study hall that want to do some work!" I reprimanded. "Now please show more consideration for them. Not everyone wants to hear about your lackluster personal life. There's more to living than a mere biological existence!"

One of the girls and the aforementioned boy then slowly got-up and sauntered-over to another table. On my next rotation around the cafeteria mass study hall, I stopped at the table to where the two *students* had switched. "Say, Mr. Wiessner, did you know that Peggy and I like to have sex together with Greg here!" the girl named Jenn guiltlessly and shamelessly stated. "We like threesomes!"

"Maybe by the time all three of you mature into normal adults," I calmly replied, biting my tongue, "you'll finally realize that you all also have hearts, minds, and souls besides just simply having ordinary, mundane, physical bodies!"

My comment appeared to have an impact, because all three *students* actually opened books and began reading. I glanced-out the cafeteria's back windows and observed the board of education president, the principal, and the superintendent sitting at a picnic table eating barbecued meat. 'I wonder if any of them have any clue as to what has been going on for nearly forty-five minutes in this cafeteria mass study hall, only fifty feet away?' I wondered.

I was happy that no further incidents happened in that pathetic eighth-period cafeteria mass study hall. I thought about how cafeteria study hall *students* back in 1975 had mocked diminutive Jack DeCicco by calling him "Meatball!", and I quickly realized that things had not really changed that much in the past quarter-century. The only thing was that I was the new elderly Jack DeCicco being mercilessly tortured on patrol. When I checked out at the Main Office, the principal asked me in an affable tone of voice, "Did you have an exceptionally pleasant day, Mr. Wiessner?"

"The best!" I falsely replied. "It was without a doubt the absolute best! I wish I could do it all again!"

"Glad to hear that everything went smoothly for you!" the jolly administrator rather cutely enunciated.

As I left the building and proceeded to my car in the A-Wing parking lot, a red-haired *student* exited the high school and yelled, "Fuck this shit hole!" at the top of his lungs.

'I can relate to that!' I thought as I entered my automobile. 'This has been my worst day of subbing so far. Now where's the nearest bar? I think I need a double shot of *Southern Comfort* on the rocks right away! I'll dedicate my first one to the memory of venerable Jack DeCicco!'

In June of 2000, I received a phone call from the new middle school principal (my old middle school principal was now the new high school chief executive, and the old high school vice-principal was now the new middle school head honcho).

"Say *John*," the school executive enthusiastically prefaced. "How would you like your old English teaching job back from next September to *Thanksgiving*? Mrs. Grasi will be out on maternity leave, and I figured I would give you the nod."

"Okay," I replied. "I think I could handle that assignment. It sure beats regular subbing in certain subject areas, ones which I'm not that familiar with!"

When I had left my position as the major eighth-grade English teacher in June of '99, I had a hundred and ten *students* scattered over six class periods. Now, my attendance roster read a hundred and thirty-five *students* condensed into the same six classes. Special needs *students* requiring individualized attention had also been *mainstreamed* into the regular academic English classes.

Five of the classes had twenty-seven *students* each. The *children* generally were quite immature, and many of them were outright obnoxious. 'This is going to be a very challenging assignment!' I thought on the first day of school. 'It's a good thing this stint will be over in less than ninety days! I hope my heart holds out!'

I didn't win too much favor with the new school administrators when this substitute replacement English teacher criticized and slammed the basic unfairness of the *GEPA* writing test, my presentation being given to eighth-graders' parents during Open House Night.

And then the new middle school vice-principal was my old supervisor whose frequent handwritten memos used to receive my critical grammar and spelling corrections. Trouble was about to explode because the new Educational Aristocracy at the middle school embraced everything that *this manuscript* has been critically attacking from page one.

The vice-principal was acting like a surrogate representative of aggressive, overprotective, concerned parents that obviously thought I was being too stringent and severe with their *children*. Just about every day a memo' would be in my mailbox that Mr. or Mrs. so-and-so was complaining about something "insensitive and sarcastic" I had said to their son or daughter in class, or about me being too harsh in grading his or her *child's* compositions.

In mid-November, the vice-principal came-up to the second floor to briefly discuss a parental concern with me between seventh and eighth periods. I had just had a challenging session with the seventh period general English *students*, a class of twenty-seven *students* comparable in many ways to the old 8-6ers.

A seventh period *student* seated in the back of the first row next to the teacher's desk hadn't done homework or class work for the entire marking period. I was standing in front of the room at the lectern when the child stretched out his arms and loudly yawned as I was addressing the abominable seventh period class. The fatigued *student* had inadvertently knocked the set of metal bookends and the books inside off the teacher's desk onto the floor.

"Would you please pick-up the metal bookends from the floor and place them back and the books on the teacher's desk behind you?" I politely asked. "You should always correct mistakes that you do!"

"No!" the *student* adamantly replied and then put his head-down on the desk, feigning sleeping.

"Look, if *I* had accidentally knocked the bookends on the floor and then asked *you* to pick them up," I scolded, "I could then understand your refusal. But *you* have knocked them on the floor. Why don't *you* simply pick them up?"

"Stop buggin' me, man!" the *student* nastily replied. "Get off my damned case!"

When the new vice-principal (my former supervisor) accosted me out in the hallway, I told the school administrator that I would be writing-out a discipline card on the defiant *student* that had refused to put the metal bookends back on the teacher's desk.

"Okay Mr. Wiessner, but I'm really here to tell you that Mrs. Larson had called and thinks you shouldn't have embarrassed her son by reprimanding him so harshly in front of his peers!" the paranoid school administrator related.

"Well, I handled the situation just the way I always have in the past," I maintained. "I've never backed-down to any *student,* and I don't think I've going to start at this stage of the game!"

"Try being a little more sensitive!" the public-relations-minded vice-principal suggested. "The times are changing!"

"Look!" I firmly replied. "The classes *are changing* from seventh to eighth period, and right now I've got to get back to my primary responsibilities."

When I re-entered the upstairs classroom, I immediately noticed that the roll and grade book had been stolen from the lectern in the front of the room. While the garrulous vice-principal had been distracting me about a parental grievance, some nefarious *student* in the seventh period class had pilfered the vital teacher's records, and I had a good hunch that it was the same *student* that refused to pick-up the metal bookends off of the floor. I immediately buzzed the office and requested that the vice-principal come back up to the classroom. I explained what had happened, and the vice-principal said that the major suspects would be interviewed the next day.

"Interviewed?" I incredulously asked. "Valuable teacher records and school property have been taken, and *you* want to *interview* the suspects tomorrow? Get the police over here right now and have them *interrogate* the suspected *students,* and let's crack this mystery wide open today!"

"I'll *interview* the *students* first thing tomorrow morning," the politically-correct vice-principal related. "I can't keep them after school and have them miss their buses unless they've been given a full day's notice! It's school policy in the *Student* Handbook!"

On Thursday morning, I was on early morning bus duty when the on-a-mission vice-principal approached me. "*Mr. Wiessner*, it is the administration's position that if the grade book can't be found, that you'll have to prepare a new book with the grades in it for when Mrs. Grasi returns after *Thanksgiving!*"

"Well, I'm just a substitute teacher fill-in, and I'm not going to do it!" I bluntly answered. "The first marking period grades had already been submitted to the guidance office two days before the grade and roll book had been stolen from the lectern!"

"I think you're being quite difficult in regard to this matter!" the vice-principal admonished. "Didn't *you* take the time to make a copy of all the grades in the grade book?" the school executive verbally indicted.

"Look," I angrily responded. "In my thirty-four years of teaching, I have never had a grade book stolen! And I only remember it happening once to Mrs. Finnian back in the early 1970s at the high school when I was teaching there!" I emphasized. "A *student* has committed a punishable *crime, a felony,* by stealing school records, and *you* want to reward that *student* by having *me* spend time at home rewriting the entire grade book!"

The vice-principal realized that I couldn't be coerced into re-doing the roll and grade book, which was an impossible task because all of the first marking period individual test, homework, and writing grades for the hundred and thirty-five *students* were wholly missing. Later that day, I telephoned Mrs. Grasi about the theft, and she agreed to make-up a fresh roll and grade book starting with the second marking period.

On Friday morning, I was in the office during my *PPSA* picking-up my paycheck in my mailbox. I had just signed-out to temporarily leave the building to drive to the bank and deposit my hard-earned wages into my checking account.

"Mr. Wiessner," the vice-principal commenced her greeting. "I'd like to see you in my office immediately!"

"Well, I'm on my way to the bank right now, so why not make it later!" I answered while thinking that I never wanted to see or hear the vice-principal again, ever in this life or in the next one.

Two periods later happened to be my scheduled teacher lunch. The vice-principal entered the teacher's room and firmly hollered, "Mr. Wiessner. I want to see you in my office right now!"

"Does it involve the roll and grade book?" I asked.

"Yes!" the perturbed vice-principal testily replied.

"Has it been returned?" I queried.

"No!" was the terse response.

"Do you want to see me about a parent calling?" I questioned.

"Yes; now come to my office immediately!" the school official inflexibly demanded.

"Well then," I insisted. "The school has a definite procedure that the parent must follow. Have the parent call the Guidance Office and schedule a conference! Let the parent be inconvenienced by having to come in and complain about something instead of using the telephone and having *you* do his or her dirty work for him or her!" I suggested. "A parent has never to my knowledge called the school to arrange a conference to praise me! No, that has never happened in thirty-four years! This parent wants to have a hostile conference! And in two days, I'm officially outa' here!"

The aggrieved vice-principal felt that I was being *insubordinate,* and also showing a bad example in front of other younger teachers having lunch in the faculty room. One could easily hear a pin drop at the end of our heated disagreement. The school executive swiftly left the faculty room virtually in tears.

Five minutes later, I marched upstairs to set-up the *VCR* for a film I would be showing the following period. The principal entered the classroom and slammed shut the door behind him in anger.

"*Mr. Wiessner,* this is one of the hardest things I've ever had to do," the administrator anxiously-but-harshly stated, "but I'm going to have to ask you to leave the building because you have been *insubordinate* to the vice-principal."

"But I only have two more days until *Thanksgiving* break!" I replied. "Why don't you just let me finish my assignment *we* had agreed upon?"

"Sorry, but I can't tolerate teachers being *insubordinate* to administrators!" the principal emphatically declared. "You must leave the building immediately!"

"Well, I just want you to know that I told the vice-principal off because I don't think that school administrators should be the surrogates of overprotective parents!" I succinctly stated.

I knew that I had not signed a contract, but had only made a verbal agreement with the principal to teach until the *Thanksgiving* holidays. I sadly left the school building where I had taught for twenty-seven of my thirty-four years, departing with my mind in a stupor. I had been officially exiled for being *insubordinate* to administrative discretion, while the vice-principal had been acting as an undesired parent surrogate. 'Evicted from the school system I had worked with all my heart to *professionally* represent for thirty-four years!' I pondered and lamented.

I was happy that I had not surrendered my convictions and my principles right up to the very end. When I explained to my wife what had happened, she commented that she was not-at-all surprised at the outcome, and my supportive spouse sounded pleasantly optimistic about *our* future. "The new administration wanted you out because they believed you were influencing the younger teachers by setting a bad example!" my wife intelligently concluded. "You were a definite threat to their authority! You've always been sort of a rebel! Or should I say an untamed maverick!"

"Joanne," I said. "I'm just sick and tired of hearing bells ring all day long. The school bells ring seventeen times a day. Times that by a hundred and eighty days, and that comes to over three thousand times a year," I indicated. "Multiply three thousand times a year by thirty-four years, and I've listened to bells blast over a hundred and five thousand times in my exhaustive career. No wonder why *you* say I'm deaf!"

"And that's not counting the fifty-thousand-times you also heard bells ring between classes as a *student,* years before you ever became a teacher!" my wife impressively elaborated. "And don't forget the over seven hundred fire alarms you've impatiently listened to!" my wife reminded. "Look at the positive side," my better-half suggested. "You've taught over four thousand *students* in your educational career! And amazingly, you're still alive!"

The principal and the vice-principal taught the six eighth-grade classes the last two days before *Thanksgiving* break. My mother's cleaning woman's daughter was in one of the Accelerated English classes and related that the administrators had told the *students* that Mr. Wiessner had taken sick and could not teach them the last two days before the four-day-holiday vacation.

'They lied to the kids!' I considered and assessed. 'Education is not really about academics, or teaching, or learning, or knowing right from wrong. It is all just a big American power game where administrative might makes administrative right!' I sadly concluded.

"Well John, the principal is called *that* name because he's the *main person* in the building. Let's try to be a little more positive. Maybe *you* can begin that terrific writing career you've always dreamed of doing!" my wife recommended and consoled. "Writing has always been your forte!"

"You're right Joanne; my pension is safe and secure and now that I'm no longer a humble teacher," I added. "I can actually be an ordinary citizen with genuine freedom of expression and now enjoying other remarkable *Constitutional* rights! I might even produce several PG-13-type books with graphic content!"

I knew that I had written sixteen manuscripts from 1974-1999 while I had been an instructor, and this book *So Ya' Wanna' Be A Teacher* has become the sixteenth work.

"You're absolutely right!" I reiterated and agreed with my devoted wife. "Teaching is over in my life, and it's time for a new career! There *is* life after teaching!" I laughed. "Thanks to the principal and the paranoid vice-principal, now I finally have a good ending for book number sixteen! No more Teacher Serfdom!"

"At last, you've come to your senses!" Joanne answered with a smile. "Writing should be much more relaxing than substitute teaching was. Obviously, it's time for someone else to step-up and fill your big shoes!"

Addendum: A Historical Perspective
"Darwin, Einstein and John Dewey"

On the average, Democracies usually last for up to two-hundred-and-fifty years (Republics last much longer). That historical pattern gives the United States of America around three more decades until we're put on artificial life support, *our* systemic malady principally caused by moral decay, by legal and political corruption, by the cost of our expensive U.S. military defending the entire free world, and by widespread economic (educational and welfare) inefficiency. Yes, since WW I, we've created a grotesque-looking Ponzi pyramid.

Our only genuine hope for cultural survival is a return to what a *Republic* truly represents: respect for law and order, the practice of moral *absolute* values, and last but not least, the abandonment of deleterious public school "educational socialism".

At the acceleration rate the U.S. is presently going, in another thirty years government spending will drastically exceed GNP (Gross National Production), and three decades from now, an incredible seventy percent of the burgeoning American population will not be paying federal income taxes. And also, more money will be going out of Social Security and out of Medicare than entering into those specific government program safety nets.

The American *private sector* should always be eighty percent of all goods and services produced in this country. At the time of this writing, our U.S. total federal, state and local government expenditure is 39% of GNP, when 20% is the most desirable percentage ratio to fully assure national economic stability.

Our public schools, through the wasteful implementation of democracy in education (socialism), are vastly contributing to the establishment of an anemic "nanny state entitlement economy" where competition among individuals is discouraged, and where a "group welfare" *cooperation* system is conversely encouraged.

What other more obscure factors (besides excessive government waste, gross educational inefficiency, and federal and state over-regulation) will ultimately further accelerate the demise of the USA? It is this writer's contention that the decline of America will be attributable to an extension of the philosophies and teachings of three currently highly venerated, historical individuals: Charles Darwin, Albert Einstein and John Dewey.

Back in the early 1900s, Charles Darwin's controversial Theory of Evolution was not exclusively confined to the scientific realm. Instead, *Evolution's* basic premise of continuous change (along with an expanding spiral pattern progressively developing as geologic history advances) bled-over into such social disciplines as Political Science, Psychology, Art, the Law, History, Sociology, and most dramatically and unfortunately, fully into American education. Thanks to Charles Darwin, nothing in today's reality (not even God) is "absolute". As currently being taught in public schools, everything in man's environment constantly changes, and therefore, must eventually mutate or evolve into something else! Is not "change" the watchword of *our* present time in American history?

In regard to American public schools, the fundamental skills of reading, writing and basic arithmetic are now being diluted in the lower grades. According to this "ideas-oriented" credo, elementary schools now emphasize teaching advanced theories to the masses. Complicated principles such as Einstein's Theory of Relativity and Algebra are now being taught to six and seven-year-olds, the dominant prevailing thinking being that any child can learn higher level thinking skills at a very young age. This sort of crazy philosophy (idea-oriented elementary school curriculum) is actually defeating what it is supposedly designed to do. It's inadvertently "dumbing-down" academics by ignoring primary focus on basic skills (reading, writing, memorizing grammar rules and arithmetic times tables) by pretending that every *child* is going to *evolve* into the next William Shakespeare, Sir Isaac Newton, Galileo, John Steinbeck, Steve Jobs, or Charles Dickens.

For example, this writer did not produce his first fictional story for an English teacher until he was a junior in high school, but still, I have in my adult life managed to produce and publish fifty-five books in eight separate genres. I did all of this *creative* literary pursuit without any tremendous exposure as a *student* to the exotic "ideas curriculum", but I did have excellent influence in mastering fundamental spelling, grammar, punctuation, reading and sentence construction skills that had been repetitiously pounded into my head by strict Catholic school nuns in grades one through eight. So much for the ever-*evolving,* highly counterproductive public school "ideas' writing curriculum"!

Karl Marx and Vladimir Lenin were indeed highly affected by the notion of Darwin's *Evolution.* Those two pragmatic intellectuals reasoned that in ancient times mankind had Aristocracies (warlords, city-state rulers, and local despots). Eventually, the existence of *Aristocracy* melded into *Monarchy,* with one king controlling all activity within a certain region or country. And then in 1776, rebellion against King George III's tyranny resulted in the

Revolutionary War, and with great inspiration, a fantastic rebirth combining Greek Athenian *Democracy* and the concept of the Roman *Republic's* law and order gradually integrated into what is now the United States of America. The *Evolutionary Pattern* after 1776 was: Aristocracy-Monarchy-Democracy.

Marx and Lenin (being affected by Darwinian Theory) believed that Democracy would surely *evolve* into Socialism, and Lenin's successor, Joseph Stalin, theorized that Bolshevik Socialism should predictably *evolve* into another predestined disaster, Soviet Russian Communism. Just think of the millions of innocent victims that had (and have) died under the aegis of inflexible, iron-fisted Communist doctrine! But, according to Joseph Stalin, *that* exact progression was the new true political *Evolution*: Aristocracy-Monarchy-Democracy-Socialism-Communism.

Isn't it a marvelous miracle that the USA (along with its free enterprise and free market capitalist system) has, over the course of the last century, proven Marx, Lenin and Stalin to be total political frauds? And yet, with the obvious fact that Soviet Socialism and militant Communism have both miserably failed (as evidenced with the crumbling of the Berlin Wall), ironically, the USA today is rapidly moving in the direction of *Socialism* (especially in our schools) to attempt solving its proliferating domestic woes.

But please don't despair! There is still time for economic and educational salvation once Americans finally come to their senses and rediscover the importance of *individual competition*.

Certainly, if everyone in the U.S. took responsibility for their own lives and pulled their own weight in this land of abundant opportunity and free public-school education, then government could wisely shrink-down to twenty percent of GNP from its current 39% level, and our REPUBLIC (respect for history, culture, law and order) could be effectively preserved, and future financial disaster could be strategically averted.

But first things first: For *our* time-honored traditions (Christmas, Thanksgiving, Easter, the Fourth of July, etc.) and for our all-important historical heritage to adequately survive, the perils of political *evolution*, societal flux, along with class warfare must be removed from American culture. By *us* very foolishly eliminating Christmas, Thanksgiving, Columbus Day, Easter, Washington and Lincoln's birthdays, along with Halloween from our public-schools, American culture and history are selfishly being eroded (diluted) in the name of democratic education (socialism). Now try and tell me that this sort of detrimental educational cultural *evolution* (actually de-evolution) is good for the country?

Yes, Americans are truly living in the closest thing to a utopia that can be manifested by man on the surface of this wonderful Earth. When Judas Iscariot challenged Jesus, "Why do you spend *our* money on expensive oils when the money could be spent on the poor?" Jesus simply and succinctly answered, "Judas, there will be poor always!" Yes folks, social *welfare* is not the answer! But in truth, being poor in America is analogous to being upper-middle class most anywhere else on this blessed planet!

But unlike almost any other culture on this earth, the United States affords all its citizens the opportunity to take risks (to succeed or fail in a free-market *competition* environment). American citizens can engage in freedom of speech, freedom of the press, freedom of religion and finally, "individual opportunity" coupled with freedom of education to advance and to become upwardly mobile. All of those wonderful "liberties" are wisely based on individual initiative, on individual determination, on individual motivation, and on individual perseverance.

Let's carefully examine history. The only real success at *democracy* (following a revolution) had occurred after July Fourth, 1776 in Philadelphia's Independence Hall, and then over a decade of extremely difficult growing pains, regional rebellions and full-blown arguments over the tenets of the Articles of Confederation had ensued, and finally, the U.S. Constitution had been drafted and signed in 1787. The manuscript, containing the "democratic" Bill of Rights, had been completely ratified in 1795, nearly twenty years after the famous Declaration of Independence had been authored and proclaimed. All of *that* exhaustive and dangerous establishment of American democracy (the Republic) had required nearly two decades of great sacrifice to complete.

Now, look at what had happened in France after the French Revolution: Anarchy, Chaos, and a bloody Reign of Terror followed by the tyranny of Napoleon came into existence. What about the terrible Bolshevik Revolution of 1917? Socialism eventually *evolving* into Communism? Remember the film Dr. Zhivago? The good humanitarian doctor returns to Moscow after the "People's Revolution" and finds his house occupied by a rabble of belligerent dissidents that threaten to evict Zhivago from his own property if he doesn't abide by *their* (the *occupiers*) mob-rule control.

And what about the infamous Nazi Revolution in pre-WWII Germany, and the accompanying Fascist Revolt in Italy? Exactly how did Hitler and Mussolini ever improve their countries without thoroughly devastating Germany, Italy and most of Europe in the end? And how about the recent Iranian Revolution against the Shah? How did *that* historical phenomenon work-out for the still-dominated and greatly exploited natives of Iran? Was true *democracy* ever achieved?

And how could *we* be so naïve and gullible enough to assume that good things are now going to happen in Egypt, Libya, Algeria and Syria *after* their bloody "Arab Spring Revolutions"! More theocratic Mullahs sponsored by the radical Islamic/Muslim Brotherhoods, perhaps! How about a little Middle-East separation of "Mosque and State" like we have a fundamental division of "church and state" right here in America!

Yes, it is the popular thinking of the educational leadership in *this* great land that a hybrid American public school system must continue to *evolve* too, according to the present ongoing destructive, national counterproductive *academic evolution* trend. This is the world that political evolution and impractical educational evolution (inspired by Darwin's Theory of Evolution) has produced. Everything in both life and education must *evolve!*

And what about Albert Einstein's colossal impact on American culture? With the Theory of Relativity came the unique notion that everything in society is "relative": nothing anywhere in America (save death and taxes) is *absolute,* permanent, and fixed. And so now we have such things as the Bill of Rights to the Constitution coming into conflict with widely-recognized traditional American family values. The First Ten Amendments (under the guise of freedom of speech and freedom of expression) are now insidiously undermining the sacred Ten Commandments handed-down to Moses on Mt. Sinai, simply because now all truths must be *relative* and not *absolute*.

Take this rather disturbing gay rights marriage issue, for example, in regard to what Einstein's *relativity* has mutated into. Remember: today everything is *evolving* and must be "Relative" and not "Absolute" (for example, God's Ten Stone Tablet Laws). Two iconic Commandments are: "Honor Thy Father and Thy Mother" and "Thou Shall not covet thy neighbor's wife!"

Just think about *those* two simple-but-sage Commandments for a second. The principal purpose of heterosexual (man-woman) marriage is to biologically conceive children and then to nurture them through mature parenting skills. The very vocal gay and lesbian political activists want gays to get married, to adopt children, and then to have loving families.

Now someone please explain *this* paradoxical situation to me. How could an adopted child with gay "parents" know who the mother is if two males are his or her parents? If two lesbians are his or her parents, which one is the father according to the very explicit Commandment: "Honor Thy Father and Thy Mother?" And if two gay married men are living next door, according to the Ninth Commandment, which one is "thy neighbor's wife" to be greedily coveted, and the act being forbidden?

Under recent (*evolutionary* and politically correct *relative*) gay rights' laws, the idea of certain "sins" against God has been totally eradicated, and "sin" is now basically obsolete and simply a "relative" matter existing primarily in the past.

And needless to say, a woman's right to choose, or to have an "Abortion", also very obviously violates the Biblical Stone Tablets' ABSOLUTE Commandments, because a conceived child is sinfully *killed,* "Thou Shall Not Kill," and the fetus has no opportunity whatsoever to ever honor either a mother or a father. And indeed, if the very vocal in-your-face abortion rights activists had themselves been *aborted* before birth by "Right to Choose" mothers, we would not be having any verbal, legal, or moral wrangles with the whole lot of them at present.

Was Sodom and Gomorrah a Biblical myth, or could it all soon again be happening right here in America? I'll let *you* be the judge of that! But still, acceptance of gays, lesbians and tolerating a woman's right to choose are currently being taught in our all-too-liberal *socialistic* public-schools, thanks to the impact of Darwin's Evolution Theory and Albert Einstein's Theory of Relativity.

Finally, John Dewey is recognized as the "father of modern-day American public-school education". Dewey was a sociologist, and a psychologist in addition to being a radical *socialist* educator, and his "Revolutionary" classroom theories of *student cooperation* (as opposed to *student competition*) had been drastically influenced by (*his*) contemporaries) Charles Darwin (Theory of Evolution) and by Albert Einstein (Theory of Relativity).

John Dewey was undeniably a confirmed Socialist, and most of our contemporary public-school teaching methods and practices are based on the socialistic idea of "sharing" in a "community (commune) classroom" atmosphere. Isn't this entire "sharing" notion diametrically opposed to the American spirit of individual competition, and also totally contrary to the tenets of American exceptionalism? What about the all-important principle of American *individual* exceptionalism?

Dewey espoused the idea that "children learn by doing," and I often wonder if *this* particular theory of his pertains to the literal teaching of sex education inside the classroom, for without a doubt, the rampant implementation of sex education seems to be quite pervasive among brazen and indiscriminate young teenagers in numerous environments outside the classroom.

In the final analysis, Socialism in our public schools is stealthily taught under the harmful guise of *ever-evolving and ever-relative* "democratic education". American free enterprise in the form of student classroom *competition* is now being de-emphasized by modern educational psychology. *Individual* academic achievement is often discouraged in deference to group (class) accomplishment. Soon there will be no honored Valedictorians or Salutatorians at high school or college graduations because being "outstanding", or being "excellent", automatically makes the other lower-ability, less motivated *students* in attendance look publicly bad, and also makes *them* feel inferior in comparison.

In order for *democratic education (socialism)* to be successful, mediocrity must be both promoted and maintained in John Dewey's anemic academic performance system, so when public school teachers put *students* into classroom "groups" (Academic Socialism), the *children* that really want to succeed wind-up doing the bulk of the "group's work" so that *they* could get decent grades, while the less-motivated (and socially deprived) do-little freeloaders get-by with almost the same recognition given by the teacher. And if you further examine our current American economic "nanny state" welfare system, the productive members of society are greatly encumbered by carrying the weight of the un-motivated adult masses on *their* backs.

And so, classrooms all over the American landscape are slowly-but-surely *evolving* into miniature European-style socialistic "nanny states", both tolerating and promoting academic mediocrity to guarantee the continuation of John Dewey's counter-productive (and excessively expensive and inefficient) dumbing-down American Socialist Education System.

Dewey's egregious educational quagmire, combined with his associated quixotic child psychology enforcement has, over the decades, negatively led to child-centered families and to child-centered classrooms. Parents have been demoted in the home, and teachers have essentially been demoted in the classroom and are now labeled in academic jargon terms as "educational facilitators".

Free enterprise (student class/subject competition) has been conveniently junked to accommodate John Dewey's lunatic theories in regard to socialistic "class democratic" education *(students* working in cooperative group communes in order to minimize *student* individual exceptionalism).

Just as the jealous American economic Socialists desire the "redistribution of rich individuals' (and also corporate) wealth, the just-as-fanatical Educational Socialists are demanding scholastic "redistribution of achievement" by having the brighter, self-disciplined *students* doing the yeoman's portion of the "group sharing classwork" for those less zealous *children* that lack the strong desire, or the necessary wherewithal, to ever succeed on their own.

But please forget all of the *socialistic,* educational euphemisms! *Students* that aspire to academic excellence are wickedly stifled from doing so by Dewey-centered classroom mandates, and those ambitious, self-motivated kids are being falsely labeled as being "arrogant," "self-centered," "egocentric," "selfish", "greedy" and "uncaring" about the rest of the *collective* group.

As sure as the existence of oxygen, we do have plenty of really terrific *students* hibernating and vegetating in "group-dominated classrooms". They and their lesser-ability counterparts are being harmfully indoctrinated by present educational philosophy pretending to idealistically change the world for the better, but most of those sedentary, callow, well-intentioned, sorry socialistic souls lack the skill and the talent to successfully attain their "group dreams" of producing a better America. The *individual* must first improve himself or herself before ever having any significant impact on civilization.

It is only when *our* American *students* learn to pursue their own self-actualization and to introspectively explore their own singular individuality through dedication and through ambition that *those* presently victimized young people will learn to mature (not *evolve*) into responsible adults, capable of contributing to society and able to constructively distinguish themselves through community service, through charity, through compassion, and through a noteworthy career. Utopia can never be achieved on a society level, but it can be attained on an individual plane by hard work and personal sacrifice.

But some of the high school graduates of today will still manage to succeed in the American free enterprise economic system in spite of their socialistic public-school education, and not because of it. The truth of the matter is to first improve yourself (through competition, self-discipline and self-sacrifice), and after being successful on your own, then try to improve society. John Dewey's "group" methods have things working in reverse. We must get back to our nation's founders' grass roots' philosophy, have faith in the *individual*, and trust his or her academic potential.

But as a starter, American education must firmly reject John Dewey's detrimental "socialistic group-sharing" system, and in keeping with competitive free enterprise capitalistic democracy, everyone attending public school must drop this "group-sharing nonsense" and modify their behavior to confidently believe in themselves and in their own abilities and potential. Is there any wonder why many astute concerned parents elect to ignore lackluster public-school education and send their *children* to *faith*-based private and parochial schools?

While growing-up in New Jersey and Pennsylvania, my father had taught me several cherished principles that to this very day still govern my life. "Be self-reliant" and "Try helping others who are *temporarily* having bad luck;" and then there was Dad's favorite bit of advice, "The world doesn't owe you a living, so learn to distinguish and prove yourself! Show some passion about achieving *your own* personal dreams and goals!" Self-confidence trumps (classroom group therapy) superficial self-esteem every single time!

Americans must have both "the dream" and "the drive", but unfortunately, many of our citizens lack *that* second vital and more necessary quality: that is, a deliberate plan to apply yourself and to achieve "the American dream" through strong labor, sacrifice, and relentless desire.

John Dewey's *socialistic* "classroom group educational methods" deprive today's victimized self-motivated *students* of individually excelling. Competition in today's high schools is vastly limited to *group* band, *group* football (and other *group* extra-curricular sports), and not geared to individual *student* academic competition within the high school, or to individual *student* academic competition between various high schools. The truth is that Utopia cannot be achieved on a national collective basis.

Finally, the European nations along with the Japanese cannot afford a wasteful, expensive, educational *socialistic* system such as the American democratic (socialistic) comprehensive high school requires. Ironically, European countries are essentially socialistic in nature, but yet, they have abandoned John Dewey-centered *socialistic* ideology out of economic necessity. The American comprehensive high school is not cost-efficient, and it will eventually contribute to bankrupting the USA.

Having a more productive and cost-effective American model (like the European and Japanese systems advocate) where after eighth-grade, students branch-off into either an academic *or* a vocational curriculum program would be the best scenario for the USA to pursue. Teaching academics to *all* high school students causes myriad discipline problems, the excessive maintenance of expensive bureaucracy, and the unwise subsidizing of a plethora of rather mediocre academic results.

Why are American high school *student* test results the worst among the twenty industrialized countries of the world? It's not because American kids are more stupid! It's because *all* of the *students* that are involuntarily attending the average American comprehensive (democratic/socialistic) high schools are having their standardized test scores compared to just the *academic* students in the nineteen other *competing* industrialized countries, where forty-to-fifty percent of those foreign *students* are involved in vocational (and *not* academic) high school preparation; so therefore, in Europe and Japan, the vocational *students* are mostly exempt from taking the standardized academic tests.

And for those critics out-there that will insist that I am guilty of practicing discrimination, they are ABSOLUTELY right! I do possess discriminating tastes and values! Throughout history, right has always honorably *discriminated* against wrong, good has always *discriminated* against evil, and morality has always *discriminated* against immorality; otherwise, in stark contrast, there would be no distinct differences between the two polarized entities, namely, good and evil, with the two diametrically-opposed forces eventually blending into the same existence, and also into the same definition, just as radical left-wing *socialistic* rights' activists and litigious ACLU lawyers want to legitimize and finalize!

True productive, ambitious Americans (who firmly believe in the power of the individual) must vigorously fight the establishment of the nanny state womb-to-tomb, European-style government welfare system that's currently infecting and crippling *this* great nation, and which is now also grossly contaminating the majority of our public-school classrooms.

So, in conclusion, thanks to Charles Darwin and Albert Einstein's science theories as catastrophically interpreted by the disillusioned Socialist John Dewey, our present dysfunctional American public school educational system, our litigious-oriented legal system, and our corrupt political system (along with our ever-evolving and ever-*relative* changing morality) are entirely convoluted, and the sum of these negative social factors is presently without valid clarity or focus. Consequently, the United States of America is soon, because of excessive debt and declining morality, on the verge of entering a very dangerous self-destruct mode! If only George Washington, John Adams, Thomas Jefferson, Alexander Hamilton, James Madison and James Monroe could be resurrected from their graves to save the *American Republic* from an excess of *evolution, socialism* and *relativism,* all three toxic forces currently and falsely masquerading as vital elements of both societal and educational democracy.

Our present dilemma requires a past-but-noteworthy solution. The much-needed answer is not-too-difficult to implement. You don't have to be an avid rocket scientist, or a dynamic New-World prophet, to fully understand that the blessed United States of America desperately needs to rebirth itself into the same fantastic spirit that had inspired the creation of the U.S. Constitution, along with the miraculous freedom-bound Revolution of 1776.

In George Orwell's classic allegorical novel *Animal Farm,* Old Major was a wise, aged pig who, with his rhetorical and persuasive oratory, effectively inspired the other exploited Manor Farm pigs to have a political revolution against the absent owner, Mr. Jones, who was away conducting vital personal business.

The Orwell character Old Major is analogous to Karl Marx, the German philosopher who, along with Freidrich Engels, had authored the tenets and objectives of Socialism in the late 1800s, but the "Communist Manifesto" co-organizer had died in 1883, and Karl Marx never lived to participate in the historic Bolshevik Russian Revolution of 1917.

This book *So Ya' Wanna' Be A Teacher* outlines the elements of contemporary "Teacher Serfdom" that are quite prevalent in schools throughout the USA, but the manifesto's proposed "Academic Revolution" is specifically designed to promote true Democracy (and not malignant Socialism) to be implemented and practiced in American Public Schools. In *that* distinctive, noteworthy respect, the author's general treatise is diametrically opposite the *Socialist theses* that are advanced by both radical political architects, fictional Old Major, and non-fictional Karl Marx.

About the Author

Jay Dubya is author John Wiessner's initials (J.W.) and also his pen name. John is a retired New Jersey public school English teacher, having taught the subject for thirty-four years. John lives in southern New Jersey with wife Joanne, and the couple has three grown sons.

Jay Dubya has written other adult fiction besides *So Ya' Wanna' Be A Teacher*. *Black Leather and Blue Denim, A '50s Novel* and its sequel, *The Great Teen Fruit War, A 1960 Novel* are humorous adventure books. *Frat' Brats, A '60s Novel* completes the adult action/adventure trilogy. *Pieces of Eight, Pieces of Eight, Part II, Pieces of Eight Part III* and *Pieces of Eight, Part IV* are short story/novella collections featuring science fiction, paranormal and humorous plots and themes.

Ron Coyote, Man of La Mangia is adult humor and a satire/parody on Miguel Cervantes' *Don Quixote*, published in 1605. *The Wholly Book of Genesis* and *The Wholly Book of Exodus* are adult satirical humor. *Thirteen Sick Tasteless Classics, Thirteen Sick Tasteless Classics, Part II, Thirteen Sick Tasteless Classics, Part III* and *Thirteen Sick Tasteless Classics, Part IV* are adult satirical rewrites of famous literary short fiction. *Nine New Novellas, Nine New Novellas, Part II, Nine New Novellas, Part III* and *Nine New Novellas, Part IV* are sci-fi/paranormal collections written in the spirit of the four *Pieces of Eight* books.

Fractured Frazzled Folk Fables and Fairy Farces and *Fractured Frazzled Folk Fables and Fairy Farces, Part II* are adult satirical rewrites of popular children's tales. And *Mauled Maimed Mangled Mutilated Mythology* satirizes twenty-one famous ancient myths.

John has also authored a trilogy of young adult fantasy novels, *Enchanta*, *Pot of Gold* and *Space Bugs, Earth Invasion*. *The Eighteen' Story Gingerbread House* is a new collection of eighteen imaginative children's stories.

Jay Dubya likes '50s rock and roll music, and he also enjoys pop' songs by the Beach Boys, the Beatles, Fleetwood Mac, the Eagles, the Rolling Stones, *ELO*, John Mellencamp and by John Fogerty. When not writing stories or listening to music, Jay Dubya likes watching *76ers* basketball and *Phillies* and *Yankees* television baseball games.

Author Biography

Born in southern New Jersey in 1942, John Wiessner had attended St. Joseph School up to and including Grade 5. After his family moved from New Jersey to Levittown, Pa in 1954, John had attended St. Mark School in Bristol, Pa. for Grade 6, St. Michael the Archangel School in Levittown for Grades 7 and 8 and then Immaculate Conception School, Levittown, Pa. for Grade 9. Bishop Egan High School, Levittown Pa was John's educational base for Grades 10 and 11, and later in 1960, the aspiring author graduated from Edgewood Regional High, Tansboro, NJ. John then next attended Glassboro State College, where he was an announcer for the school's baseball games and also read the nightly news and sports over WGLS, GSC's radio station.

John Wiessner had been primarily an English teacher for 34 years, specializing in the instruction of middle school language arts. Mr. Wiessner was quite active in his school district's Teachers Association, serving in the capacities of Vice-President, building representative and finally, teachers' head negotiator for 7 years. During his lengthy teaching career, John had been nominated into "Who's Who Among American Teachers" three times. He also was quite active giving professional workshops at various schools around South Jersey on the subjects of creative writing and the use of movie videos to motivate students to organize their classroom theme compositions.

John Wiessner was very active in community service, being a past President of his town's Lions Club, where he also functioned for many years as the club's Tail-Twister, Vice-President and Liontamer. John had been named Town Lion of the Year in 1979 and in 2009 received the prestigious Melvin Jones Fellow Award, the highest honor a Lion can receive from Lions International.

John also was a successful businessman, starting with being a Philadelphia Bulletin newspaper delivery boy for two years in the late 1950s in Levittown, Pennsylvania. After his family had moved back to New Jersey in 1959, John worked at his grandparents' and at his parents' respective farm markets, Square Deal Farm and Pete's Farm Market. After marrying, he later managed his wife's parents' farm market, White Horse Farms for three summers.

Also, in a business capacity, for 16 summers starting in 1967, John Wiessner had co-owned Dealers Choice Amusement Arcade on the Ocean City, Maryland boardwalk, and also co-owned the New

Horizon Tee-Shirt Store for eight summers (1973-'81) on the Rehoboth Beach, Delaware boardwalk. In addition, "Jay Dubya" was a co-owner of Wheel and Deal Amusement Arcade, Missouri Avenue and Boardwalk, Atlantic City. And then, for 18 consecutive summers beginning in 1986, John had been the Field Manager in charge of crew-leaders for Atlantic Blueberry Company (the world's largest cultivated blueberry farm), both the Weymouth and Mays Landing Divisions.

After retiring from teaching in 1999, writing under the pen name Jay Dubya (his initials), John Wiessner became the author of 55 books in the genre Action/Adventure Novels, Sci-Fi/Paranormal Story Collections, Adult Satire, Young Adult Fantasy Novels and Non-Fiction Books. His books exist in hardcover, in paperback and in popular Kindle and Nook e-book formats.

Google: Jay Dubya books